WORLD ANTIQUES

Introduction by Roy Strong
Director of the Victoria and Albert Museum

HAMLYN
London · New York · Sydney · Toronto

CONTENTS

Published by
The Hamlyn Publishing Group Limited
London · New York · Sydney · Toronto
Astronaut House, Feltham, Middlesex, England
© Copyright The Hamlyn Publishing Group Limited 1978

ISBN 0 600 39354 2

Phototypeset by Tradespools Ltd, Frome, Somerset
Printed in Hong Kong

WORLD
ANTIQUES

Editor: Hazel Harrison
Design Editor: Ian Muggeridge
assisted by Karel Feuerstein

Half title page: Blue and white ewer of the Persian Safavid dynasty,
early 17th century

Frontispiece: ewer of Meissen porcelain, one of a pair, decorated with
ormolu mounts attributed to Jacques Caffieri, late 1740s

Title page: gold and enamel lever watch with matching fob, English,
hallmark 1835

Following page: Indian prayer rug, late 17th century

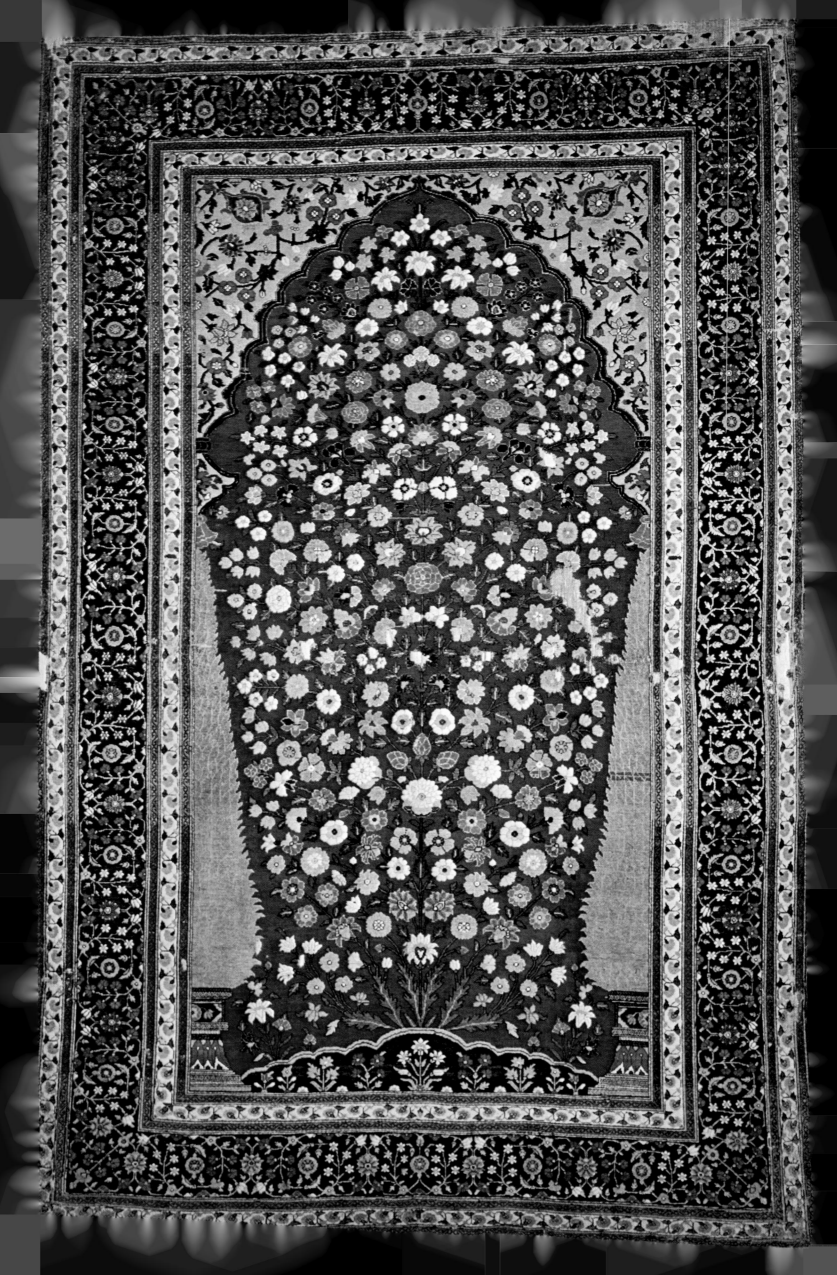

INTRODUCTION

The world of antiques as we know it was largely the creation of the late Victorian period. We can trace its coming of age rather sharply at the turn of the century in the advent of collectors' magazines: *The Connoisseur* (1901), *The Burlington Magazine* (1903), *Antiques* (1922) and *Apollo* (1925). With their arrival the type of research, scholarship and attitudes which had hitherto been almost exclusively reserved for painting or sculpture began to be extended to include furniture, tapestries, ceramics and the whole gamut of the domestic artefacts of past ages. Simultaneously this development was mirrored by the fashionable furniture emporia of the day, such as Gillow's and Maples, who opened sections of their shops carrying stocks of 17th- and 18th-century furniture and domestic fittings. That the American journal *Antiques* included throughout the 1920s a regular feature entitled 'Living with Antiques' reflects the fact that this was still something of a novelty which its readers needed to learn about. Since then, and more particularly since 1945, the cult of antiques has reached an apogee reflected in a wide range of movements: the professionalisation of the trade in such bodies as the British Antique Dealers Association; the multiplication of sale rooms and the extension of the sale seasons; the arrival of antiques fairs as regular features up and down the country; the weekly antique street markets in London and in Paris; the glut of collector's books evidenced in the art book explosion of the 1960s; the popularity of antiques programmes on both radio and television; and the proliferation of societies dedicated to their study. In Britain alone there are The Ceramic Circle, the Glass Circle, the Silver Collectors, the Costume Society, the Furniture History Society and the National Association of Decorative and Fine Art Societies, while many similar societies exist in Europe and America. Perhaps even more significant is the acceptance of antiques as an important and fundamental ingredient of modern interior decoration.

The growth of the cult of antiques is one of the most puzzling phenomena of our age. Not only have we witnessed the spread of collecting throughout every sector of the society, but in addition we have seen an incredible extension of what comes within the bracket of the term 'antique'. A glance at the closing chapters of this book reveal much about this transformation – the term now embraces areas virtually unheard of in this context a generation ago, for example chess sets, toys and pastimes, Victorian papier mâché, costumes, needlework, the accoutrements of war and scientific instruments. And, as for period, 'antiques' now stretch with certainty into the 1950s. As quickly as a style becomes obsolete and definable in retrospect it becomes the province of the collector, entering the magic category of the antique.

All this can only be described as bewildering, both to an older generation of collectors for whom antique was old oak or gracious Georgian with 1830 the safe watershed, and equally to a younger, because of the sheer range, both in terms of time span and of the artefacts themselves. The concept of this book springs from this very dilemma, and is an attempt to give the collector some comprehensive guidelines. The options, of course, are essentially personal ones – some may choose to collect vertically within a given media or horizontally within a period, or indeed to be, something much less compulsive, a magpie. But whichever path the reader may take, a knowledge of past styles and artefacts is essential to any would-be collector; indeed to be visually illiterate is no longer acceptable to any educated person.

Such ignorance is also, of course, financially short-sighted. In an era when money has become almost meaningless, the purchase of antiques and works of art has combined safe investment with personal discrimination and knowledge. This is no new phenomenon; possessions have always been seen as financial assets in times of crisis, as well as being treasured for their beauty and workmanship. In earlier times it was mostly personal jewellery and plate which went into pawn, was sold off or melted down for the gold or silver content, while in our own age such crises are met by the sending of things to the sale room. Thus the triple role of antiques – as furnishings, as investment and as an expression of personal taste – remains remarkably consistent. To the discerning it will always, however, be the last of these aspects which remains the most fascinating and challenging of all.

ROY STRONG
Director of the Victoria and Albert Museum, London

DECORATIVE STYLES

EUROPE FROM THE GOTHIC TO *c.* 1900

Edward Lucie-Smith

The evolution of European decorative styles, from the 14th century onwards, can be considered from at least three different points of view. First, there is the apparently autonomous dynamic of change which leads the visual arts from one phase of their development to another. Second, there is the impact of social and economic progress, which brings new necessities and prompts the invention of new forms. Third, there is the influence of ideas and techniques imported from non-European cultures.

The Gothic age

In the Gothic period, little distinction was made between the craftsman and the fine artist. This means that Gothic art is a continuum, and that there is always a connection between the humblest artefacts and the most ambitious and elaborate ones. In the 14th century, architecture was the major form of artistic expression, and all decoration tended to derive from ideas first put forward by the master-builders. Thus, when we look at surviving pieces of Gothic furniture, and at things such as the then popular ivory or metalwork caskets, we tend to find in them what is really architecture writ small. The elaborate canopy of Edward II's tomb in Gloucester cathedral, which dates from *c.* 1341, represents a kind of intermediary stage between the craft of the architect and that of the furniture maker. It indicates, too, the pride in the virtuoso handling of materials which typifies the High Gothic.

Occasionally, the current runs the other way, and it is something small which provides the inspiration for something big. Thus the south transept door of Rouen cathedral shows the use of motifs which seem to derive from secular ivory carvings, and the tapestries of the great Apocalypse series now in Angers derive from illustrations in slightly earlier manuscripts.

The unity of Gothic art is exemplified by another characteristic as well—the difficulty we find at this period in drawing a distinction between the religious and the secular. The Apocalypse tapestries, despite their subject matter, seem to have been commissioned for largely secular use; it was only later that they fell into ecclesiastical hands. Emblems connected with the patron, Louis I, Duke of Anjou, brother of Charles V of France, are woven into the background of the designs.

In terms of the domestic environment, the Gothic age shows a very slow progression towards anything resembling domestic comfort. The life of the great was still largely nomadic. They moved from castle to castle, taking most of their possessions with them. Only a few bulky pieces of furniture—massive tables and chairs of state—were left behind. In stylistic terms this meant that there was an emphasis on the portable, and also on the colourful, since colour helped to mitigate the bleakness of the permanent environment. Tapestries (see p. 228) fulfilled these particular criteria, and so too did the elaborate pieces of goldsmiths' work which delighted royal and noble patrons (see p. 122). These had the additional advantage of providing a reserve of cash, since they could easily be pledged, thanks to the intrinsic value of the materials, or even melted down.

One must not, however, be tempted to think of Gothic stylistic attitudes as naive. Indeed, one of the things about Gothic art which is largely wasted on a modern audience is the immense amount of information it conveys by symbolic means. Where this symbolism was not religious, it was largely heraldic. In the 15th century, in particular, great men had a passion for allegorical devices, and it was these which provided a large part of the decorative stock-in-trade used by designers. If we see, in one of his portraits, that Duke John the Fearless of Burgundy wears a robe which is embroidered with carpenter's planes, this is because the duke adopted the device in response to that chosen by his nephew and rival Louis of Orleans. The Duke of Orleans had chosen a wooden cudgel as his personal emblem—the cudgel with which he threatened to break the heads of the Burgundians.

The court of Burgundy—the richest and most extravagant in the West at that time—provides examples, not only of complex symbolic and allegorical thinking, but of the pervasive European nostalgia for a chivalric past which was already rapidly receding. Burgundian wealth was based not so much on agriculture as on primitive forms of industrialisation, and especially upon the Flemish cloth-weaving industry which supplied the whole of Europe. Ducal power was continually challenged, not only by other potentates, but also by the restless corporations which governed the cities and towns of the Low Countries. One would never guess any of this when looking at surviving specimens of Burgundian court art, which is obsessed with the chivalric myth. 15th-century Gothic, with its yearning for a heroic age which perhaps never existed, demonstrates yet another way in which style evolves. Artists, and particularly decorative artists, are asked to supply, from their own reservoir of fantasy, whatever seems to be missing from the society that surrounds them. Stylistic change can be due to deliberate innovation; it is also, and perhaps more frequently, motivated by the desire to recreate, rather than to create something afresh. Revivalism, or attempted revivalism, was not the sole prerogative of the 19th century.

Leading artists in the Low Countries, foremost among them the Van Eycks, often worked for two very different sets of patrons—the court on the one hand, and the rich merchants on the other. Jan van Eyck's *The Marriage of Giovanni Arnolfini and Giovanna Cenami* gives us one of the best-known representations of a European interior of the first half of the 15th century. It was painted for a member of a well-known Lucchese merchant family, resident in Bruges. While certain Gothic details are noticeable—in the carving of the furniture, and in the forms given to the arms of the candelabrum—one of the impressions which the spectator takes away from this strikingly true-to-life picture is that of comparative indifference to the idea of decorative style. The objects shown are there because they are useful to those who inhabit the room, and would have been treated by these inhabitants with the same fond indifferent familiarity as the pet dog in the foreground. We must be careful not to put greater emphasis on a given style than it would have received from those contemporary with it.

This is also the impression conveyed by a very different painting, which comes from a very different artistic milieu. Vittore Carpaccio's *Dream of St Ursula* is an enchanting vision of the bedroom of a rich young Venetian girl. The date is 1495—about 60 years later than the 'Arnolfini Wedding'—and there are occasional details which speak of the early Renaissance as eloquently as

1 Tomb of Edward II, Gloucester Cathedral, *c.* 1431. The canopy is an outstanding example of medieval carving.

2 Jan van Eyck: *The Arnolfini Wedding*, signed and dated 1434. A brilliantly detailed depiction of a 15th-century interior.

1

2

similar details in Van Eyck speak of the late Gothic. But there is an identical lack of visual self-consciousness, joined to an absence of all superfluity. People had not yet begun to fill their houses with objects, or to treat the decoration of the spaces they inhabited as an end in itself. The simple furniture attempts, sometimes clumsily, to fulfil certain ideas about basic convenience.

Renaissance and Mannerism

One effect, as yet too little discussed, of the coming of the Renaissance was the way in which the new secularism changed the thrust of collecting. The impulse to collect, to accumulate objects which are not necessarily useful but which give great pleasure and comfort to the possessor, is something deeply rooted in human psychology, and has been known since the earliest times. In the Middle Ages, the energy of great collectors was directed mostly towards devotional objects, and particularly to relics. Extravagant sums were often spent to obtain these. One little-known cause of the downfall of Gilles de Rais, the black magician and mass-murderer of children who was a companion in arms of Joan of Arc, was the ardour with which he pursued this kind of material for his Chapel of the Holy Innocents in his castle at Machecoul. His family objected strenuously to the inroads which this made into an enormous fortune which they regarded as being theirs as much as it was his.

5 In the new epoch, artistic and scientific interests took the place of these devotional pursuits. Hans Holbein's *Ambassadors*, signed and dated 1533, shows the two figures standing one on either side of a plain wooden whatnot, upon which a variety of objects are displayed. On the upper shelf are a celestial globe, a portable cylindrical sundial, a table-quadrant, a polyhedral sundial, and an instrument called a torquetum, which was used to determine the position of celestial bodies. On the lower shelf there are, amongst other objects, a terrestrial globe, a lute and dividers.

The significance of these objects may well be allegorical, and personal to the sitters, but they also indicate one of the directions in which the decorative arts were moving–towards a more rational, scientific attitude to design, under the impact of the new humanism. We can pick up other clues from the painting as well. For example, the top shelf of the whatnot is covered with a small table-carpet, evidently imported as part of the flourishing English-Levantine trade (the picture was, of course, painted during Holbein's period of service as Henry VIII's court-painter). Such imports were to have a significant influence on the development of European textiles.

It may seem perverse to emphasise the rationality of Renaissance design when so many of the decorative products of the 16th century are deliberately fantastic and perverse. This tendency developed rapidly after the first quarter of the century as a result of the stylistic trend we now call Mannerism. But such possibilities were latent even before Mannerism took root. Illustrated here is a bronze table candlestick by the Paduan sculptor Riccio, or by a member of 4 his workshop. This demonstrates another and very important facet of humanist taste–a nostalgia for the antique world of Greece and Rome which rivalled the nostalgia of the Burgundian court for a lost era of chivalry. Small bronzes of this kind were first made to satisfy those patrons who could not find the antique originals which it was now becoming fashionable to collect. Gradually these small sculptures acquired an identity of their own, and they can now be thought of as being amongst the more typical decorative products of the High Renaissance. The satyr, though impeccably Classical in ancestry, also carries with him the suggestion of the medieval wodwo, or wild man.

The way in which a medieval residue lingers even here, in the most clearly humanist of objects, helps to explain how Mannerism established itself so rapidly and completely as a decorative style. The High Renaissance, with a very few exceptions–scattered, and exotic in any other context but an Italian one–was an extremely short-lived phenomenon. The purity of forms that was typical of it

9

3 Tapestry from the Apocalypse series, woven for Louis, Duke of Anjou, in Paris, c. 1380.

4 Satyr candlestick by the 16th-century Paduan sculptor Andrea Briosco (Il Riccio), or from his workshop, which turned out many small bronzes inspired by the humanist taste for the antique.

5 Hans Holbein: *The Ambassadors* (detail), dated 1533. The still life symbolises the intellectual interests of the sitters.

6 Design for a cup by Fantuzzi after Rosso. Such engravings spread the gospel of Mannerist design throughout Europe.

3

4

5

6

proved too difficult for any but the most sophisticated architects and designers to achieve. In most of Europe, therefore, the High Renaissance style did not flourish, and the transition was almost directly from the Late Gothic to some version of Mannerism. Gothic forms were first overlaid with vaguely Classical ornament; then, later, the structure of the building or object itself became classicised. But the spirit of Mannerism was never Classical: it relied on effects of shock and surprise, achieved through incongruity and disproportion, which were the very opposite of the Classical ideal.

One thing which Mannerism did take from the new humanism was the fact that it regarded the audience for the visual arts as an élite. Gothic art, because of its commitment to the Christian faith, had always been forced to consider the needs of all Christian spectators; Mannerism addressed itself chiefly to the princely patron, and its aim was to create an artificial paradise. The decorative schemes undertaken by the School of Fontainebleau for Francis I and subsequent French kings, and the work done for the Emperor Rudolph in Prague supply obvious examples of this. Hermetic and

esoteric allusions, far more complex than the Gothic allegories which they succeeded, are mingled with an eroticism which was in itself a gesture of defiance directed towards the prejudices of the common herd.

Yet despite this deliberate élitism, there was a sense in which Mannerism was international, just as the Gothic had been before it. The style achieved an extraordinarily widespread dissemination, and was astonishingly uniform within the boundaries that it made for itself. It is only rarely that we can speak of a 'provincial' Mannerist style, or even of one with a marked national accent of its own, though there was a distinction between art in the south – in Italy chiefly – and art in the north – in France, Flanders and Germany. The chief exception to the rule was Tudor England, which did develop both a kind of architecture and a kind of art which were visibly different from what was being produced in the rest of Europe – different chiefly because of a characteristic linearity, a lack of plastic articulation, and a lack of sophistication in using the basic vocabulary which Mannerist artists had evolved.

Another thing which set England apart in the 16th century was

7 Vittore Carpaccio: *The Dream of St Ursula, c.* 1495. A detailed depiction of a Venetian girl's bedroom in the 15th century.

7

the fact that she was a Protestant power. This made no difference to the ostentation displayed by her rulers, but it did mean a certain puritan resistance to the nude, and the nude played a very important part in Mannerism's decorative vocabulary. Also, England, separated as she was from the mainland, could find few leading foreign artists to visit her, Holbein and Pietro Torrigiani being exceptions to the rule.

The idea of a European community of artists was already well established in the 16th century. Leading painters travelled widely. in search of patronage. Rosso Fiorentino and Francesco Primaticcio followed Leonardo da Vinci into the service of the Valois kings of France, and it was they who gave the School of Fontainebleau its character (see p. 50). The Emperor Rudolph's court attracted artists and craftsmen of all kinds to Central Europe. The most effective factor in creating a uniform art style, however, was not the artist's own willingness to travel, but the wide currency gained by the ornamental prints which were now being produced in great quantities.

As a means of conveying stylistic information, the print first

began to make its influence felt at the very end of the 15th century. Perhaps the first major creative genius to benefit from the widespread trade in printed images was Albrecht Dürer. His engravings and woodcuts had an effect in Italy as well as in the north, and were used by leading Italian Mannerists such as Jacopo Pontormo. But a print did not need to be a complete composition in the conventional sense. It was an ideal way of conveying information about ornamental detail, and soon pattern books began to be put out in which leading jewellers, silversmiths and other craftsmen recorded their ideas. Often, too, designers who had no direct experience of the craft in question would supply ideas for others to execute. 6,16 This was done by leading Italian artists such as Rosso Fiorentino and Giulio Romano.

The widespread use of prints as a source of information about styles had important effects upon the decorative arts taken as a whole. In the first place, it tended to encourage the passion for intricacy and elaboration, which in any case lay at the very heart of Mannerism. A print anatomised a complex of decorative motifs and made their relationships clear in a way which was often missing

8 This etching, *The Wise Virgins*, by Abraham Bosse, shows the sobriety of many 17th-century interiors.

9 The queen's bedchamber, Ham House. The almost untouched interior of Ham illustrates English plutocratic taste at the time of the Restoration.

10 Detail from the Oxburgh Hangings, embroideries worked *c.* 1570 by the captive Mary, Queen of Scots, and her hostess, Bess of Hardwick.

11 François Boucher after Antoine Watteau: *La Coquette*, an engraving dated 1727, and exemplifying the then new Rococo style.

8

9

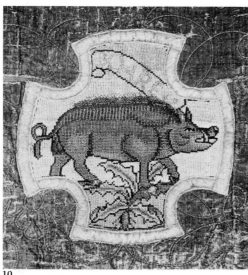

10

11

from the completed object. In the second place, it tended to divorce the creative and executive aspects of craftsmanship. In the earlier period, it was the head of the workshop who had been responsible for evolving the form of the object which was to be made, even if the bulk of the physical labour was done by assistants and apprentices. Now, he was often asked to copy, though perhaps with slight variations, a design produced by someone who had no real acquaintanceship with the craft processes involved.

One must not, however, take too vigorous a view. Many of the decorative crafts remained in the hands, not of paid professionals but of amateurs, and work such as embroidery was largely done within the household where it was to be used. The Oxburgh Hangings, worked by the captive Mary, Queen of Scots, and her hostess Bess of Hardwick, are a good example of this kind of ambitious amateur enterprise. Such work is frequently more wayward and idiosyncratic than that produced in the professional craft workshops.

Baroque and Rococo

The keynotes of Mannerism were hermeticism, disproportion and the wish to surprise. To some extent every form of decoration conformed to the same rules, which prescribed the pursuit of novelty at all costs. Yet this pursuit became wearisome, and at the same time the temper of the world had begun to change. One great influence in bringing about this change was the Catholic church, which from the 1560s onwards had been mounting a vigorous counter-attack to the challenge of Protestantism. What the Church needed for its mission was an art which was directly emotional and easily understood. Mannerist artists were usually ill-equipped to supply this, though in North Italy, from the High Renaissance onwards, there had been a rebellious attachment to an ecstatic but realistic religious art which is seen at its most typical in pilgrimage churches, such as those on the Sacro Monte at Varallo.

Now, however, not merely the Church but the secular public was becoming weary of the restlessness and barren complication of the predominant style. The result was the reaction we now label the Baroque, which was first felt in the 1590s.

Baroque art was at first a matter for painters rather than for the inventors of decorative ensembles, and it was pioneered by two groups of painters—Caravaggio and his followers; and the three members of the Carracci family. Caravaggio was born in North Italy, and he brought with him to Florence, and subsequently to Rome, a passionate realism: a tactile, illusionistic realism created by the action of light. By its very nature, the art he practised was opposed to the notion of style, though it is possible to say that his earliest paintings—often genre-pieces with ambiguous emotional overtones—are the last gasp of the Mannerist impulse to shock. Illusionism was the one weapon left to the painter who had exhausted all the other means of tickling the jaded palates of his audience.

The Carracci family, and more especially Annibale Carracci, the most gifted of them, also began with a kind of realism that flouted the idea of style. But Annibale's talent was more flexible than Caravaggio's, and when he too came to Rome from his native Bologna he was awarded the most challenging decorative commission of the time—that of creating a series of frescoes for two rooms in the Palazzo Farnese.

The frescoes in the Farnese are seminal for the Baroque decorative style as a whole. Carracci took over from Mannerism many of its favourite effects—for example, the idea of large figures supporting various scenes, which was a stock-in-trade with the decorators at Fontainebleau—but he completely changed the spirit in which they were used. Illusionism now became the means of creating an environment which was directly and sensually exciting because of the plasticity and tactility which the painter was able to suggest. All the minor arts responded to the new sensibility—furniture acquired swelling curves, and was often illusionistically carved; metalwork, too, showed a swelling three-dimensionality.

12 Chinese Pavilion, Potsdam, a Chinoiserie addition to the Palace of Sanssouci, built in 1741-47 for Frederick the Great.

13 William Hogarth: *Early Morning*, dated 1743, from the *Marriage à la Mode* series. A Rococo composition in a Palladian setting.

14 François Desportes: *Peaches and Silver Platters*, *c.* 1730. The silver represents the best in French Régence design.

15 Interior of the Court Theatre, Munich Residenz (1751-53) by François Cuvilliés, who brought the French Rococo style to Germany.

12

13

14

15

But we must not try to force the whole of 17th-century decorative art into a single mould. If we look at illustrations of the interiors of the time, and especially at those which date from the first half of the century, we are often struck, not by their exuberance, but, on the contrary, by their severity and quietism. This is true, for instance of the work of the engraver Abraham Bosse. His print, *The Wise Virgins*, which dates from about 1635, gives a good impression of a very typical kind of 17th-century interior, still equipped with very little furniture, and that of the plainest kind. The only details we can call Baroque are the design of the hanging candelabrum and of the chimneypiece, and even these are very subdued.

In fact, from the standpoint of the decorative arts, this is the most various epoch we have yet encountered. The 17th century, far more than the Renaissance, laid the foundations of modern society. The seriousness of its cast of mind was often reflected in the sobriety of its domestic decoration. This was true of England under the Commonwealth, and to some extent of Protestant Holland. Paradoxically, it was also true of Holland's defeated opponent, Spain. In the Europe of the period, Italian exuberance often seems the exception rather than the rule. Yet there was, too, a great flow of wealth from the trading stations which had now been established in the Far East by the European maritime powers. Holland, as the premier trading nation, received a particularly rich variety of exotic products; and the abundant Dutch still-life paintings of the period lovingly record the Chinese and Japanese porcelains and the rare shells which the Dutch Indiamen brought back to home ports. The sources of inspiration open to designers thus became increasingly various, and European technology was challenged by what had been achieved far away across the oceans. The search for the hidden formula which would produce true porcelain had of course already begun, and the experimenters were to persist until they achieved success in the early 18th century.

The rise of the bourgeoisie in Holland and in England was accompanied, elsewhere, by an increasing awareness, on the part of absolutist rulers, of the need to preserve and emphasise their absolutism. One of the functions which the High Baroque willingly undertook was that of glorifying not only God, but the temporal monarch. The decorations executed for Louis XIV at Versailles, under the direction of Charles Le Brun, where a deliberate attempt to turn the king into a kind of demi-god – the Sun King of popular legend.

One of the characteristics of the Baroque decorative style was an integration rather different from the type we find in Gothic art. The illusionism so fundamental to the Baroque was only one element among many, but it stresses a constant theatricality of effect. The Baroque designer thought in terms of a totality which enveloped the spectator, and which provided an immediate and overwhelming experience, moving both mind and heart through an overpowering excitation of the senses. It is significant that many elaborate interior schemes in this style are meant to be looked at from a single fixed viewpoint; and that it is only when the spectator reaches the exact spot chosen by the artist that the imagery takes on its correct proportions and falls into its proper place.

Yet the Baroque, even when it eschewed puritanism, could be much less ambitious than this. As it evolved into a commonly accepted decorative convention, it also became simply a means of displaying energy and wealth. The elaborate interiors and equally elaborate furnishings of Ham House, created for the Duke of Lauderdale in the reign of Charles II, speak eloquently of the vulgar passion for display which had succeeded the austerities of the Commonwealth.

The Rococo, which succeeded the Baroque, is at first sight a mere extension of an already established style, making use of the same curvilinear forms, though in a lighter and more capricious way. However, though many of the forms are the same, the spirit

13

16 Peter Paul Rubens: *The Birth of Venus*, design for a silver dish. Several leading painters and sculptors in the 17th century supplied designs for craftsmen to follow.

17 'Gothick' design from Chippendale's *Director*, first published in 1754.

18 An engraving of 1823 showing the 'Gothick' interior of Fonthill Abbey, built for William Beckford, 1796-1813.

19 Print by Nicolas Delaunay after N. Lavrience, *c.* 1785. A good example of a Louis XVI interior, containing Classical elements, but not consistently Neo-classical.

16

17

18

19

is very different. The Rococo is a reaction against Baroque flaccidity and pomposity, and it also speaks of a desire for a very different manner of life. Bored with the endless public parades of church and court, the men of the early 18th century sought something more intimate and more informal. The spirit of their search was 11 expressed in the *fêtes galantes* painted by Antoine Watteau, who in his apprentice days also had a hand in pioneering a new manner of decoration, well suited to the small rooms and charming trifles to which it was usually applied.

Rococo takes its name from the French word *rocaille*. This was given to the use of shells and rockwork as decorative motifs. This became common at the beginning of the 18th century, and showed the Baroque moving into a more abstract phase, in which the energetic movement of forms tended to replace outright illusionism. The silver platters, and especially the small cream-jug 14 which appear in a still life by François Desportes, now in the Nationalmuseum in Stockholm, are good examples of this new phase of decoration, while the tall ewer on the right, with its triton spout and dragon handle, is faithful to an older convention.

Just as the leading Mannerists had done, Rococo designers spread their message throughout Europe by means of decorative engravings, often collected into pattern books. They also revived many conventions which were originally invented by Mannerism. The 'auricular' forms (so called because they resemble the struc-

ture of the human ear) which are lavishly employed by leading masters of the Rococo such as François Cuvilliés, were first em- 15 ployed by German 16th-century goldsmiths, among them the celebrated Wenzel Jamnitzer.

One important element in the Rococo was its love of the theatre, in a rather different sense from the theatricality of the full Baroque. The improvised Italian comedy provided much of the subject matter for Watteau's paintings, and after him for the modellers in the various porcelain factories which were now starting to spring up all over Europe. Meissen and Nymphenburg in particular produced notable groups of Italian comedy figures.

In a more general way, the idea of the masquerade attracted designers and even architects. Chinoiserie was a Rococo invention, and few structures are more typical of the style than Frederick the Great's Chinese Pavilion at Potsdam. Related to Chinoiserie was 12 a frivolous revival of Gothic. This flourished particularly in England, where it provided a more capricious alternative to the prevalent Palladian taste. 'Gothick', as it was called, enjoyed a 17,18 surprisingly widespread, if also rather shame-faced, popularity, and made a particular impact on English furniture design, as can be seen from Thomas Chippendale's *Director* (see p. 63), which 17 proposes designs in both the Gothic and the Chinese manners.

Palladianism was peculiar to England itself, and served to express some of the differences between English social institutions

20 Interior of the hall at Syon House, designed by Robert Adam. The work was carried out in 1762-63.

20

and those to be found in the rest of Europe. As its name suggests, Palladianism derived from the work of the 16th-century north Italian architect Andrea Palladio, who, in turn, modelled his work very closely on the recommendations of the Roman architectural theorist Vitruvius. Palladio's work was seen and admired by English noblemen undertaking the customary Grand Tour to complete their education. His particular admirer was Lord Burlington, who seems to have found in Palladio a perfect reflection of the Roman spirit of the English oligarchy.

Continental Rococo was an expression of the boredom and restlessness of the European élite; Palladianism, on the other hand, spoke of growing English self-confidence. It is, for example, significant that the various scenes of Hogarth's famous *Marriage à la Mode* series, a satire on the worthlessness of fashionable life, take place for the most part in recognisably Palladian settings, though the compositions themselves are arranged according to what Hogarth called 'the line of beauty'—the typical S-curve of the Rococo. In *Early Morning*, for instance, the sober magnificence of the setting seems to rebuke the activities going on within it.

Neo-classicism and revival styles
Palladianism can also be regarded as a kind of precursor of the Neo-classicism which was to dominate taste in the second half of the 18th century. England predictably took it up with greater

enthusiasm than her neighbour across the channel. Robert Adam's magnificent interiors, based on his study of the remains of the Emperor Diocletian's palace at Spalato (Split), are far closer to the Classical world than French ones of the same period. Yet, as can be seen from contemporary prints, such interiors showed not only many would-be Classical details, but a concern for comfortable living which was the product of a far more rational attitude towards design. Significantly, the leading French cabinet-makers of the period showed unsurpassed ingenuity in devising small pieces of furniture to serve a particular purpose—a case in point is the tea-table/work-table in the foreground of the illustration.

Neo-classicism did not always grow more practical as it grew more stringent. The interiors designed by Thomas Hope for his own house in London, and illustrated in detail in his book *Household Furniture and Interior Decoration*, published in 1807, are clearly much less comfortable than those provided by the fashionable decorators of the Louis XVI period, or even by Adam himself.

In fact, Neo-classical design occupies an ambiguous position in the history of European taste. On the one hand it represents an impatient reaction against the irrationality of the Rococo, and on the other it is the spearhead of the stylistic revivals which were to dominate the history of design throughout the 19th century. The decorative arts were a prey to conflicting impulses. On the one hand there was the desire to exploit the new industrial technology

15

21 The Flaxman or Star Room, Duchess Street, London, shows the fully developed Neo-classical style. It was designed by Thomas Hope for his own use, and illustrated in his book *Household Furniture and Interior Decoration*, 1807.

22 Johann Zoffany: *Charles Towneley and his*

Friends, 1781-83. The room is unrealistically crowded with items from Towneley's celebrated collection of antiquities.

23 The Portland Vase, by Josiah Wedgwood, an exact imitation of the ancient cameo-glass original now in the British Museum.

24 Textile designed by A. W. N. Pugin for

F. Crace & Son, *c.* 1850. Pugin pioneered a more serious attitude to the Gothic than had previously been found.

25 Interior view of the Mediaeval Court at the Great Exhibition of 1851. The exotic products displayed in other courts gave an immense stimulus to designers.

21

22

23

24

25

to the full, and on the other there was a revulsion against the dishonesty of using mechanical processes to imitate handwork, and against the horrors of the industrial society itself.

In England, the Gothic style was taken increasingly seriously, and all kinds of moral virtues were attributed to it. It was the Gothic which attracted the most intellectual artists and designers. A. W. Pugin, who designed most of the furnishings and decorative details for Barry's new Houses of Parliament, was one of the first of a long line of committed men who tried to reform design through their theoretical writings as much as through the example of what they themselves produced.

Victorian wealth and Victorian ambition prompted work whose idiosyncratic splendour is now widely recognised. The interiors designed by William Burges for the Marquess of Bute at Cardiff Castle are a good example of 19th-century Gothic design at its most integrated and uncompromising. On the other hand, the sheer quantity of information available to the designer often led to an overloaded eclecticism.

A great influence was exercised by the international exhibitions which were typical of the second half of the century. Starting with the Great Exhibition of 1851, they made a wealth of exotic products available, and introduced Europeans to aesthetic conventions (such as those employed in Japanese art) which had hitherto been either unfamiliar, or known only in diluted form. These exhibitions also encouraged designers to make deliberately competitive 'exhibition pieces'. These often borrow from many sources to create a stylistic amalgam we now recognise as being characteristic.

New directions

The attempt to reform design eventually took two different forms. The one which attracted the most publicity at the time, and

which still benefits from a greater degree of attention today, was the Arts and Crafts Movement inspired by William Morris, and also, though rather more distantly, by Ruskin. Morris, who was associated with the Pre-Raphaelite Movement, preached a return to simple forms and to honest hand craftsmanship. The firm which he founded, Morris & Co., did indeed succeed in evolving a recognisable alternative to the gimcrack clutter which satisfied most middle-class Victorians. The superb wallpaper and fabric patterns designed by Morris and some of his associates are still on the market today. But, while Morris later came to recognise that the machine had its own possibilities and its own merits, he never succeeded in catering to more than a minority, and an affluent minority at that. The products made under his aegis were always luxuries, to be bought by the discerning few, and this was still truer of such things as the superb pottery produced by middle-class craftsmen such as William de Morgan.

The late 19th century, however, also saw the appearance of the first men who really deserve to be called 'industrial designers' – men who thought about the machine and its possibilities, and allowed this to govern their work. One man whose work has again begun to attract attention in recent years is Christopher Dresser. As a theorist he was much less influential and less widely read than Morris, but his designs for metalwork have a radical simplicity which was otherwise achieved only under special conditions – for example, by the Shaker furniture makers in America in response to their own strict religious tenets. Objects designed by Dresser, dating from *c.* 1880, foreshadow the so-called Modern Design of the 1920s, and do so because they obey the same rules of utility and rational construction, and have the same absence of superfluous ornament. They herald an age in which the notion of 'style' was to take on a very different nuance.

26 The Inventions Vase, designed by Léonard Morel-Ladeuil for Elkington & Co., and hallmarked 1863.

27 William Morris' bedroom at Kelmscott Manor.

28 'The Owl', woollen cloth tissue designed by C. F. A. Voysey and dated 1897.

29 Panel of 16th-century Iznik tilework. Oriental pattern making had great if intermittent influence in Europe.

30 Scrolling border patterns, such as that on this early Ming dish, were adapted by European artists for use in other media.

31 Dish by William de Morgan, painted in ruby

and pink lustre, *c.* 1900.

32 The Shaker sect in America, untouched by outside trends in design, produced strictly functional furniture.

33 Glass claret jug designed *c.* 1879 by Christopher Dresser, a pioneer of functional design.

26

27

28

29

30

31

32

33

34 The Summer Smoking Room, Cardiff Castle. The interiors were designed for the Marquess of Bute by William Burges in 1861 in the Gothic, Arab and Classical styles.

34

THE NEAR AND FAR EAST

THE CERAMICS OF CHINA AND JAPAN

Gillian Darby

In AD 960 the Sung came to power in China, and there followed an era during which the arts in general flourished, and the manufacture of ceramics reached one of its highest peaks. The preceding T'ang dynasty (618-906) had been a prosperous time, a period of expanding trade and stable government, but also one of some intellectual turmoil, which matured during the more introspective period following the Mongol invasion and the rise of the Sung dynasty (960-1279). As technical expertise increased, so the hearty and robust pottery of the T'ang, with its colourful but limited decoration, gave way to more elegant, subdued wares with strong emphasis on subtlety of form and glaze colour. Court patronage and a general increase in production have meant that many more Sung wares survive than from the preceding Han and T'ang dynasties, from which times much of our ceramic knowledge is based on objects manufactured for placement in tombs.

Amongst the first Sung products were Ting wares, which took their name, like so many Chinese ceramics, from the area in which they were made. Descendants of the porcelain first discovered during the mid T'ang period, they were covered with a lovely
35 ivory-cream glaze and decorated with incised or carved, and later moulded, designs. Bands of copper disguised the ground-down rims of many pieces which, unlike most other wares, were placed in the kiln face down, thus picking up sand and grit during the firing process. Wares similar to Ting, but made from a high-fired stone-
37 ware, were the Northern Celadons, which utilised the same carved and moulded decorative schemes of flowers, animals—and more rarely humans—but which were covered with a thick, lustrous, olive-green glaze. Both types were made in a wide range of useful shapes, including bowls, dishes, vases, ewers and pillows.

One short-lived factory produced, specifically for court use, an extremely high-quality pale blue-glazed stoneware known as Ju
36 ware, but more common is its relation, Chün ware. These stonewares with thickly applied opalescent glazes ranging from almost green to a strong blue were sometimes brightened by the addition of purple or crimson splashes. Shapes were mainly mundane, usually bowls, jars, flower pots and incense burners.

On the borders of Hopei and Honan provinces were the kilns
38 making Tz'ŭ-chou stonewares, the production of which continued over many centuries, although regarded by the Chinese until recently as rather commonplace articles. The body was usually covered with a creamy-white slip and overpainted, skilfully and freely, with dark brown designs of plants or animals. It is odd that while the art of painting was held in such high esteem this, the only Sung ware to display painted motifs, was so largely ignored by so cultivated a court. Other Tz'ŭ-chou pieces were covered in slip or glaze, which when hardened was incised or stamped, exposing the body beneath. During the succeeding Yüan and Ming dynasties, some Tz'ŭ-chou was painted in a limited palette of green, yellow, red and brown on the cream ground.

Brown-glazed wares were made at kilns both in the north and south of the country, the common tea-bowl form being much admired by the Japanese, who adapted it for their own Tea Ceremony wares.

Of all Sung ceramics those probably best known and admired are the celadons of the Southern Sung period, made after the court had fled from the north in 1127, after the taking of the capital, Kaifeng, by Chin Tartars. The court was re-established at Hangchow, and southern kilns were soon catering for its needs. The Lung-ch'üan kilns of Chekiang province made a wide range of whitish- 50 bodied porcelains with rich glazes in shades of light bluish-greens. Decoration was minimal until the late Sung, Yüan and Ming periods, when incised and applied ornament was employed, and potting became clumsier and sizes generally larger. *Kuan* (official) celadons were made for court use, the dark grey body being covered with layers of glaze, each layer often displaying a deliberately induced, differently sized, crackle, producing an antique appearance which complied with current court interest in the art forms of earlier times.

A last type, again regarded by the Sung only as an everyday and export ware, was the porcelain called *ch'ing-pai* (bluish-white) which was similar to the northern Ting ware, but had instead a beautiful pale bluish-green tinted glaze. At best they are delicate in form and colour, although by the Yüan period they became slightly coarser and over decorated.

The Ching-tê-chên region of Kiangsi province, where *ch'ing-pai* was made, was soon to become the most important porcelain-producing area of China, and has remained so until the present day. Conveniently located near natural deposits of kaolin (china clay) and *petuntse* (china stone), the vital ingredients for porcelain manufacture; Ching-tê-chên was well placed for the easy transportation of its products to the rest of the country. Under the Mongol Yüan (1260–1368) and early in the Ming dynasty (1368-1644), porcelain making became highly organised and, precipitated by the introduction from Persia of cobalt pigment, a new style of ceramic art appeared. The by then highly refined porcelain body was painted with patterns in an infinite variety of subjects in cobalt blue, and the whole was covered with a transparent glaze and then fired. Porcelain painted in underglaze-blue, and more rarely 39 and less satisfactorily in underglaze copper-red, soon became 42 extremely popular, and formed a major and enduring product. This shows no significant changes throughout the Ming era, but rather a long and gradual evolution of painting styles, glaze colour and texture, and slight variations in the colour of blue employed. The painted reign marks of emperors appeared on porcelain early 52 in the 15th century and have continued in use ever since, but as they have been regularly imitated, they provide no accurate guide to dating.

As well as producing blue and white, the early Ming potters made an excellent range of monochrome-glazed wares of high quality, usually in blue, copper-red or plain white, these last often having delicate moulded relief decoration beneath the glaze. During the reign of the Emperor Ch'êng Hua (1465-87) overglaze enamels were discovered, which enabled the potter to enliven with red, green and yellow enamel the outlined design executed in blue under the glaze. This *tou-ts'ai* (contrasted colour) palette was succeeded by a wider range of enamels used in combination with underglaze-blue, known as *wu-ts'ai* (five colour).

Contemporary cloisonné enamels inspired another class utilising the large range of medium-temperature glazes. The porcelain or stoneware body was covered with glazes which were prevented

35 Porcelain plate with a mould-impressed design under an ivory glaze. The plate is rimmed with a copper band. China, Ting ware, 12th-13th century.

36 Stoneware dish, the blue glaze splashed with purple. China, Chün ware, 12th century.

37 Porcellanous stoneware ewer with incised peony design under a celadon glaze. China, Northern Celadon ware, 11th-12th century.

38 Stoneware bottle painted in dark brown over a cream ground. China, Tz'ŭ-chou type, 13th century.

39 Porcelain flask painted with dragons in underglaze cobalt blue. China, early 15th century.

35

36

37

38

39

from running into one another by raised strips or *cloisons* of clay. These richly coloured glazes, often aubergine-purple, turquoise-blue, yellow or green, were also used in the making of roof-tiles and other architectural detailing, adding a sumptuous note to the Ming environment.

By the end of the Ming era trade with the West was well established through the various East India Companies, but it was not until the 18th century that the vast bulk of porcelain reached Europe. The Ming dynasty had fallen, to be replaced by the Manchu Ch'ing dynasty (1644-1912), and after a period of re-building and re-organisation the Ching-tê-chên kilns started quality production on an unprecedented scale. The reign of the Emperor K'ang Hsi (1662-1722) witnessed the revitilisation of blue and white porcelain manufacture, which had somewhat declined in the latter years of the Ming. A new, strong, clear cobalt was used, with the designs first outlined and the infill achieved with thin washes of blue. Decoration included the already familiar ranges of animal and plant form and mythological subjects, as well as many types of religious and auspicious symbols, often placed in ornamental panels

and borders; while the vigorous Ming forms were refined to ones more taut and elegant.

A new enamel palette, known as *famille verte* (green family), was introduced; based on that of the Ming, but with the addition of an overglaze violet-blue which replaced the underglaze cobalt. *Famille verte* was made in two styles: in one, all the enamels were applied to the surface of the glazed pot; in the other, the enamels were used as glazes put directly on to the biscuit (fired but unglazed) porcelain. On this latter type the coloured enamels usually cover the entire surface, giving a rich effect.

Another revival of interest in antiquities in the K'ang Hsi period which continued into the subsequent reigns of Yung Chêng (1723-35) and Ch'ien Lung (1736-95) prompted the manufacture once more of monochrome-glazed ceramics. The colour range was enormous, but particularly popular were the *sang-de-boeuf* (ox-blood) and the softer, mottled, pinkish 'peach-bloom' reds. All shades of celadon were reproduced, but with glassier, less trans-luscent glazes than their Sung predecessors. Although not intended as export wares, many monochrome pieces found their way to

40 Porcelain vase with the flowers of the four seasons painted in *famille verte* enamels on the biscuit, with a yellow ground. China, K'ang Hsi period (1662-1722).

41 Porcelain jar, lotus design with slip relief and coloured glazes. China, *c.* 1500.

42 Porcelain stem cup with a bright copper-red glaze. China, early 15th century.

43 Porcelain dish painted in *famille rose* enamels with a bird on a magnolia branch. China, period of Yung-chêng (1723-35).

44 Porcelain dish painted with the arms of Lee quartering Astley and views of London and Canton in enamel colours and gilding. China, *c.* 1730.

45 Porcelain jardinière painted in underglaze cobalt blue with a fisherman casting his net. China, K'ang Hsi period (1662-1722).

40

41

42

43

44

45

46 Europe, where they were frequently mounted in ormolu (see p. 158).

The introduction to China, from Europe, during the reign of Yung Chêng, of a pink enamel, brought about the use of a new **43** group of colours known as the *famille rose* (pink family), in which some of the colours were mixed with white to produce a light, bright range. With the sweetness of the colour scheme came an added delicacy of painting style and the bold, all-over designs of the *famille verte* gave way to the more asymmetrical *famille rose* with more than a hint of European Rococo influence.

Throughout the 18th century, following the re-opening of Canton, shiploads of porcelain were unloaded on European shores, providing ample inspiration to the newly formed porcelain factories of that continent. Much export porcelain was similar to that made for Chinese taste; but large quantities were produced to specific, purely Western designs. Into this category falls so-**44** called armorial porcelain, with its decoration of the coats-of-arms of the families who ordered it, while other pieces display finely painted copies of European prints and paintings. Western silver

shapes, such as sauce-boats and handled mugs, which provided prototypes for European potters, were also faithfully reproduced in China. Later in Ch'ien Lung's reign and into the 19th century, some blue and white or undecorated wares were exported, and enamels were added in the West.

There were two wares not made at Ching-tê-chên, which were imported into Europe since the late Ming, and were very influential there: the red-brown stonewares of Yi-hsing in Kiangsu, frequently made in the form of teapots, and the tea-bowls and models of the white *blanc-de-chine* porcelain from Tê-hua in Fukien province.

The growth of the European ceramic industry brought about a gradual decline in trade with China, and apart from some well but fussily painted wares, the products of the 19th century tended to be weak copies of those made during previous eras.

The ceramic art of the Japanese, an island race, have been influenced from early times by China and Korea. Stonewares enjoyed a long period of production, porcelain not being made with success until the early 17th century, when the necessary clays were found at Arita. Sung ceramics influenced the stonewares of **47**

46 Pair of fishes, porcelain painted in enamel colours, with French ormolu mounts of about 1745-49. China, 18th century.

47 Porcelain plate in underglaze cobalt blue. Marks on the base: *fuku* (happiness), and the incised inventory mark of the Dresden Palace Collection. Japan, Arita porcelain, late 17th to early 18th century.

48 Tea bowl, coarse brown *raku* ware with an olive-brown glaze, possibly by Koetsu. Japan.

49 Square earthenware dish painted with a bridge over an iris pool, made by Kenzan and painted by his brother Korin. Japan, Edo period, first quarter of the 18th century.

46

47

48

49

50 Porcelain jar and cover with a celadon glaze. On the base under the glaze is the incised character *ti* (earth). China, Lung-ch'üan ware, 12th-13th century.

51 Porcelain vase in double gourd form, painted in Kakiemon-style coloured enamels. Japan, Arita porcelain, late 17th century.

52 Porcelain jar and cover painted in underglaze cobalt blue and enamel colours. Mark and period of the Chinese emperor Chia-ching (1522-66).

50

51

52

53 Group of moulded hexagonal tiles from Takht-i-Suleyman, Iran, with dragons and phoenixes in turquoise and *lajvardina*.

54 Bowl of Sultanabad type, with three phoenixes. White on grey background, and green outline. Iran, late 13th century.

the late Kamakura (1185-1333) and early Muromachi (1333-1573) periods, made in the area known as the 'Six Old Kilns', with Chinese-style incised or stamped decoration. The glazes, greenish-yellow to brown, were produced from wood-ash.

Brown-glazed Chien wares provided inspiration for the utensils used in the rituals of the newly developed Zen Buddhist Tea Ceremony. Best known is the low-fired Raku pottery, made in deliberately irregular, unaffected forms with plain black, rust-red or yellowish glazes; while the Karatsu tea-wares, made by immigrant Korean potters, display slight, spontaneously painted designs. Other kilns, such as those of Bizen, Iga, Seto and Satsuma, produced strongly formed pots of deceptively artless appearance.

The first blue and white porcelains to be made were almost identical to Korean ones, and when political troubles in China following the Ming downfall prompted the Dutch East India Company to turn to Japan for porcelain, there was a rapid development of the new industry. Use of over-glaze enamels soon began and notable among the late 17th- and early 18th-century products were

Kakiemon porcelains with their milky-white body and soft, yellow, green, blue, red and black palette. Decoration was naturalistic, sparse and often charmingly asymmetrical. A more vivid family were Kutani wares with overall patterns in thick, striking green, blue, ochre and aubergine enamels. Another contemporary was 'Imari', a popular export ware painted in an underglaze violet-blue, with added iron-red and gilding. 51

Possibly the finest porcelain of the early 18th century was made originally for the Nabeshima family, and took their name. These pieces had flawless glazes and a small but delicate range of colours which were used to great effect with a glowing underglaze-blue.

The 17th century onwards saw the rise of the great artist-potters with their highly individual styles: men such as Ninsei, whose works were frequently based on lacquer forms, and Ogata Kenzan (1664-1743) with his distinctive calligraphic painting style. By the late 19th century industrial productions were of a generally poor quality, and it has been the artist-potters who have preserved the earlier and valuable ceramic traditions. 48,49

ISLAMIC POTTERY

Yolande Crowe

The geographical position of the Islamic countries, placed as they are between Europe and the greater part of Asia, makes influences from both East and West possible, the former dominating until the 17th century, when the East India companies gradually introduced new ideas from Europe. However, a tradition of purely Islamic decoration, with the emphasis on geometric and abstract designs, continued through the centuries, and by as early as the 13th century new techniques, such as tin glazing, lustre, slip painting, *sgraffiato*, *minai* (overglaze colours) and soft-paste had been thoroughly assimilated.

During the late 13th and 14th centuries the Eurasian continent was open to Eastern influences, and these are noticeable in manuscript paintings, textiles and pottery. The new trends in ceramics first appear at Takht-i Suleyman in north-west Iran, on the tile decorations of the summer palace of Abaga Khan (1265-82). Dragons, phoenixes in flight and lotuses, mainly in the traditional lustre and turquoise, bring a refreshing note to the earlier vocabulary of scrolls, geometry, calligraphy and stylised figures. *Lajvardina*, which means lapis lazuli in Persian, is the name given to the new rich dark-blue background of cobalt on to which was applied a geometric decor of small gold-leaf lozenges with added white and red touches. This appears on both bowls and tiles even as late as the 14th century in the tomb decorations of Samarqand. It is most often found on bowls, however, some of which have the new

emphatic T-shaped rim and a rather small base ring. They are characterised by a grey slip background and decoration based, it appears, on textile designs, outlined in dark green with a thick white slip to emphasise the main pattern—birds, does or figures in a loose foliate setting. Although these wares are known by the name of the Iranian town of Sultanabad, they are also found north of the Caspian and in Egypt. 54

Ultimately all the iconography stems from China, but in early times, such motifs had become incorporated into the Buddhist repertoire, and found their way to Iran when Buddhism was forcefully introduced by two Buddhist Mongol rulers in the 13th century. Some of the less obviously Buddhist motifs survived, after the elimination of the alien religion, and combined with a new wave of influence from China starting early in the 14th century, when Western Asia was flooded with Yüan and early Ming blue and white porcelain and celadon. These large bowls and dishes were in fact specially made for the Islamic market, and although the decorative vocabulary was specifically Chinese—lotus ponds, dragons, peonies, chrysanthemums, spiky lotus-leaf scrolls and wavy borders—the distribution of the motifs followed an Islamic visual order.

Potters from Egypt to Transoxania were soon unconsciously picking up these new ideas, and by the first half of the 15th century, Chinese blossoms had become harmonised into the regular patterns

53

54

55 'Miletus ware' bowl, grey earthenware, painted in dark blue and green on white slip under clear glaze. Iznik, early 15th century.

56 Mosque lamp in Iznik style, with formal stylised scrolls, handles in the shape of dragons, and cartouches with calligraphy. First half of the 16th century.

57 Dish in Iznik style with typical central *saz*, blossoms with branches on a sealing-wax background, and an 'ammonite' border. Second half of the 16th century.

58 Dish painted in red, blue and green with a sailing boat on waves. Iznik, second half of the 16th century.

55

56

57

58

of blue and white tiles in the Muradiyeh mosque of Edirne. Even as late as the first part of the 16th century Yüan and Ming porcelains were still favoured as models by the court designers of the Ottoman sultans, now well established in Constantinople and surrounded by Chinese porcelain brought back from campaigns in Egypt and Iran. Faithful copies of the vine design or the kylin amidst plants were added to the courtly style, with a preference for the Yüan wave pattern as a border. But by the middle of the 16th century the wave and spray had been transformed into an 'ammonite' scroll, the standard border motif of later Iznik wares, and after that time Ottoman pottery betrays little Chinese influence.

57

The radical transformation of the decoration which began at this time illustrates clearly the development of true Ottoman ceramics: on bowls, dishes, bottles and tankards of European inspiration the rather formal Chinese-influenced themes in sober colours were replaced by the use of textile-inspired designs and the representation of realistic flowers from the Anatolian plateau in striking

polychrome. Hyacinths, tulips, pinks and thistles with their large leaves, known as *saz*, became great favourites with the Iznik potters; later, ships, buildings and sailors appeared to satisfy a more popular demand around the Mediterranean. The best of this pottery, in the second half of the 16th century, is distinguished by radiant colours, especially a sealing-wax red, from an iron clay available in the vicinity of Iznik, close to the main kilns. Other kilns producing these wares include Kutayha, which backed up the Iznik production of tiles when orders were at their peak, and later, in the 18th century, developed a charming style of its own, mostly in polychrome.

57
58

Syria, Egypt and Tunisia all had their ceramic workshops, producing tile panels inspired by Constantinople but developed along local lines. Ganakkale, in the Dardanelles, was the centre for more rustic wares in the 18th and 19th centuries, and a short-lived attempt at porcelain manufacture was made at Constaninople (Istanbul) under the sultan's patronage in the late 19th century.

59 Zodiac dish with the traditional motifs in blue and white. Iran, 1563.

60 Dish covered with brown glaze and painted in white. Probably Kirhan, Persia, 17th century.

61 'Kubachi ware' dish, painted in blue and brown with the portrait of a man. North Persia, early 17th century.

62 'Gombrun ware' bowl, with the typical hard, thin, white body and pierced decoration. Persia, 16th or early 17th century.

59

60

61

62

In Iran, the potters at first worked along the same lines as their Ottoman counterparts, though often in a more original manner. In the 17th and 18th centuries, they fell under the direct influence of Wan-li and later Chinese blue and white porcelain (the only ones in the Islamic world to do so), as the ships of the Dutch East India Company sailed regularly into Gombrun with loads of Chinese export wares for the Safavid court. When the supplies were cut off 60 from 1661 to 1682, the bazaars of Kirman were called upon to produce substitute wares to satisfy the company's demands.

It is difficult to pinpoint exactly the manufacturing centres of these and other sophisticated types of soft-paste wares, despite travellers' journals and the occasional potter's signature, but they can be grouped roughly by the trading centres: Samarqand, Bukhara, Mashad, Yazd, Kirman and Qandahar in the east; Tabriz, Isfahan and Shiraz in the west. Often Chinese decorative themes were misinterpreted, as in the case of Taoist symbols, or simplified, as with the Chinese dragon, and they could become almost comic, for instance, when garden scenes were transposed from Chinese blue and white without any understanding of the particular anecdote. However, the brush work was often truly remarkable

on some of the better imitations of *Kraak* wares or on some of the large bowls with flower sprays and birds. Occasionally the cobalt blue was replaced by a very effective almost black colour. Ewers, bottles, posset pots, bath rasps and *kalyans*, large dishes and smaller ones with four, six or eight sides, were often decorated in a composite manner, partly with Chinese detail and partly with a floral composition often recalling local textiles. Pale green, red and yellow were sometimes added to the basic blue and white colour scheme.

Besides the production of blue and white, the Iranian potters followed a creative path of their own, though at a slightly later date than the Ottomans. After two changes of capital in the 16th century, Shah Abbas the Great settled in Isfahan in 1598. He established a large merchant community of Armenians south of the town in New Julfa, and the prosperity which marked his reign attracted numerous foreign traders.

Isfahan is best known for the impressive tile decorations of its many religious buildings of the 17th and 18th centuries, but Iran is also noted for its so-called Kubachi wares, named after the town in 61 which they were found. The best of these are freely decorated with polychrome stylised flower sprays and figures of youths, courtesans

63 Fragment of tile panel outside the mosque of Rustem Pasha,
Istanbul, 1561. The touches of red enhance the composition of stylised
flowers and *saz*.

64 Plate of Sultanabad type with underglaze painted decoration. Iran,
14th century.

63

64

65 Ornamental dragon ring of translucent
green jade (nephrite) with brown on one side,
Yüan or Ming dynasty (14th-16th century).

66 Belt plaque of pale grey-green jade
(nephrite) largely calcified to fawn and brown.
Yüan or early Ming dynasty (c. 14th century).

and foreigners; a crackled glaze and weak colours characterise the less attractive tiles and dishes. Another group of ceramics consists of moulded bottles with hunting and shooting scenes in green and yellow; those decorated in lustre show more textile patterns or vague landscapes with a stream. At the same time, an extremely fine white body was developed in imitation of *blanc-de-chine*, which enabled the walls of bowls and dishes to be pierced or carved in geometric or floral patterns under a transparent blue or colourless glaze. The pierced technique survived into the 19th century, but was far less attractive, with underlining in over-emphatic blue lines.

The pink colour of the *famille rose* also appeared in Iran, as in every other country, and was used to its best advantage on large tile panels, such as those at Shiraz and Kirman. In the 19th century, European porcelain invaded the market at the expense of the local ceramic production, which came to concentrate more on these large tile panel schemes—in Tehran, the new capital of the Qajar dynasty, and in provincial towns such as Qazvin and Kirman. Of the small tiles, the best-known subject is that of the hunting falconer on horseback, in the Neo-classical style.

Although Eastern influences pervade Islamic pottery through most of its later period, the main Islamic themes of decoration remained constant. One of the most traditional of these consists of radial panels filled with abstract devices on the *cavetto* of dishes and bowls: this goes through a series of variations, from the *lajvardina* examples to those in black on turquoise, or blue and white on turquoise, often with stylised petal panels on the outside. The Ottoman dishes of the 15th century, known as 'Miletus wares',

which have geometric designs on a white slip over a red body, fall within this category, as do some of the large Hispano-Moresque dishes and bowls, usually painted in ruby-red lustre with the occasional use of blue.

Arabic calligraphy remained the major form of decoration, and is best seen when used on tile panels, either in the later cursive style or in the early Kufic, an angular and dignified script. On 14th- and 15th-century mosques in Iran or Transoxania this was often built into the shape of a monumental square, with glazed and unglazed bricks on vast panels. The versatility of calligraphy provided the ideal linking element in any type of decoration, whether on tiles around the portal of a building or on the *cavetto* of a bowl. Like all other motifs of Islamic art, writing can suit any shape or size–it may run round a rim, occupy vertical panels of a bottle, or fit into the cartouche of a mosque lamp. On the large bowls and goblets of the Mamluk period in Egypt, which have an unusual (and short-lived) colour scheme of dark brown and amber, bold if coarse *sgraffiato* decoration records names of owners, together with various blessings.

Islamic glazing techniques had much influence on European pottery, and some of the shapes, too, were adopted in the West, for instance, the drug jar was taken over by the Italian tin-glaze potters (see p. 93) as the *albarello*. This vessel, often decorated in blue and white, and strong enough to withstand transport, became the ideal container for spices and other exotic goods. Its practical features consist of an elongated body with a slightly constricted middle for better handling, and an everted lip which holds down the tie of the parchment cover.

CHINESE JADE

Judith Moorhouse

Jade and jade carving are pre-eminently associated with China, since in no other region of the world has the material been worked with such skill and with such an unbroken tradition. The Chinese word *yü* covers a variety of precious and semi-precious stones, of which it most commonly denotes two, nephrite and jadeite, each having a different physical composition but both known in the West as jade. Nephrite–the most commonly used in Chinese jade carving–contains calcium, magnesium and aluminium, while jadeite contains sodium and aluminium with additional elements such as chromium or iron. Varying elements can give distinctive colourings, the most notable of which in jadeite is the bright green 'kingfisher' jade. Both nephrite and jadeite have an interlocking crystalline structure which makes them extremely hard-wearing. For this reason, although jade is usually said to be carved, it is in fact ground by the use of rotary tools and abrasives.

Nephrite is found in the region of Khotan and Yarkand in Central Asia and near Lake Baikal in Siberia as well as in parts of Europe, North America, Africa, Australia, New Zealand and Taiwan. The main source of supply for the Chinese appears to have been Central Asia. The jadeite which first reached China in quantity in the late 18th century was imported from Burma, but it is also found in Central and North America, Japan and the East Indies.

Although jade carving has been practised in other cultures, it is a peculiarly Chinese art. There is evidence for its use from Neolithic times, and it has continued in an unbroken chain of development until the present day. For the Chinese it has traditionally embodied both material value and magical significance. Its association with immortality is no better illustrated than in the discovery of the jade burial suits fashioned to cover the bodies of Prince Liu Sheng and his consort Princess Tou Wan in the 2nd century BC. Confucius

is said to have seen in jade the essential human virtues, and generations of scholars and statesmen have sought to emulate the qualities it symbolises, though in art, because of its early use in ritual, it is a medium through which archaic shapes and patterns have been transmitted over a period of some 3,000 years.

By the beginning of the period covered by this volume these shapes and patterns had become stock items in the craftsman's repertoire, despite having lost their original significance. Most notable are those derived not from ancient jades but from early bronze work. The ancient ritual vessels of the Shang and Chou periods (c. 1600 to the 5th century BC) provided a wealth of subject matter, the most prominent decorative motif being the *t'ao-t'ieh*. This is a monster mask, usually of bovine form and originally without the lower jaw, which also has the peculiarity of dividing into two animals, each half of the mask with its own body. From these separate halves of the mask grew the 'k'uei', a small dragon-like animal seen in profile with open jaws and used by itself for much supporting bronze ornament. By the end of the first millennium BC the term 'dragon' more closely defined the lithe and sinuous beast with horns and rudimentary claws whose progeny are seen throughout Chinese art, either in lizard form or as the more imposing scaly monster which became the imperial insignia itself. Ancient jade shapes, for example the mystical tube known as the *tsung* with its squared outer and circular inner perimeters and the equally enigmatic pierced disc, *pi*, are reproduced throughout the history of jade carving, as are the coiling dragons and other sinuous beasts which are a feature of the complex openwork girdle pendants of the Eastern Chou and early Han periods (7th-3rd century BC). Nevertheless the constraints experienced by the earliest jade craftsmen still prevailed in later periods, the most ineluctable being the

67 *Tsung* of white jade (nephrite) with brown striations and markings. 13th-15th century. The ancient jade form is faithfully reproduced nearly 3,000 years after it first appeared.

68 Pair of hairpins in the form of a dragonfly and a butterfly. Bright emerald green jadeite with pearls and kingfisher feathers set in gilt metal. Ch'ing dynasty (1644-1911).

69 Horse in grey jade (nephrite) with black areas and lighter markings. Late Ming or early Ch'ing (17th-18th century). The carvers of these large animals achieved a balance of design despite the limitations on shape imposed by the material.

70 Rhyton cup, pale greenish white jade (nephrite) with rust markings. Ch'ien-lung period. The cup is incised with a eulogy by the Emperor Ch'ien-lung and with a date corresponding to 1787.

65

67

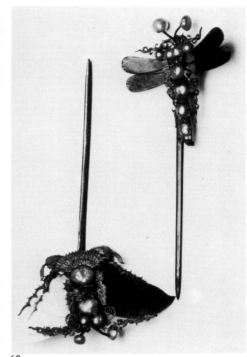

68

66

69

70

availability and limited size of jade boulders. The hardness of the stone itself also tended to be restricting, although increasing intricacy of carving suggests greater sophistication of tools and use of abrasives.

The period dealt with here covers two phases in the later history of jade carving. Firstly, the period between the 14th and 17th centuries largely covered by the Ming dynasty (1368-1644) and, secondly, the period between the 17th and early 20th centuries, largely covered by the Ch'ing dynasty (1644-1912). Both had long periods of peaceful rule under strong central governments. The Ming emperors were of native stock, unlike the Mongol rulers of the previous Yüan dynasty. They rebuilt the capital at Peking on the site of that of the great Mongol leader Kublai Khan and continued an imperial patronage of the arts, begun by the Mongol emperors. Certain styles and a degree of excellence demanded at court were disseminated through official conscription of artisan labour from all over China. The Ch'ing dynasty rulers, though of Manchu origin, brought little of their native steppe culture to bear on the arts of China. Having risen to power on the fringe of Chinese administration, they had by the time of their conquest in 1644 absorbed much of Chinese culture, and even re-emphasised the spirit of conservatism which had imbued the arts since Sung times. **70** Under the Ch'ien-lung emperor (1736-95) this conservatism was expressed in a previously unseen elaboration of shapes and

decoration based on traditional themes, and when regular contact with Europeans began in the 18th century, this ornate palace style was considered to be the essential Chinese style.

Two broad influences prevail in jade carving of the Ming and Ch'ing dynasties, the first being an archaising tendency which was first given full expression in the Sung dynasty (960-1279), when a serious reappraisal of Confucian values was sought as a basis for moral order. With this came a concern for the methods and paraphernalia of ritual ceremony; an imperial collection of ancient bronze ritual vessels was formed, and it became the responsibility of officials in charge of ceremonial arrangements to organise reproductions of these. The invention of printing during the Sung dynasty facilitated the archaising process, as illustrated compendiums of the ancient bronzes became more generally available, and craftsmen settled on conventional versions of the antique based on the woodcut illustrations. This antiquarian interest resulted in a range of quasi-antique ornament which found expression in many mediums. The ancient monster mask, *t'ao-t'ieh*, became a dominant theme, as did the dragon, though both had lost much of their original **65** ferocity.

The second broad influence in jade carving was the move towards more naturalistic representation, not only in small three-dimensional pebble-shaped animal carvings, but also in larger vessel forms and their embellishment. The act of grinding jade in the production of

71 Vase and cover, pale greenish white jade (nephrite). 18th century. The elegance of form and perfection of finish testifies to the high degree of craftsmanship attained during the 18th century.

72 Lotus vase in pale greenish white jade (nephrite). 18th century. The culmination of the naturalistic style in fruit or flower-shaped vessels which began in the Ming dynasty is seen here in a more complex arrangement of stems and the self-conscious positioning of the flower head.

73 Mountain in greenish jade (nephrite) with darker markings. 18th century. Carved from a boulder, the mountain harbours a cave where Taoist scholars pore over a scroll bearing the cosmological *yin-yang* symbol.

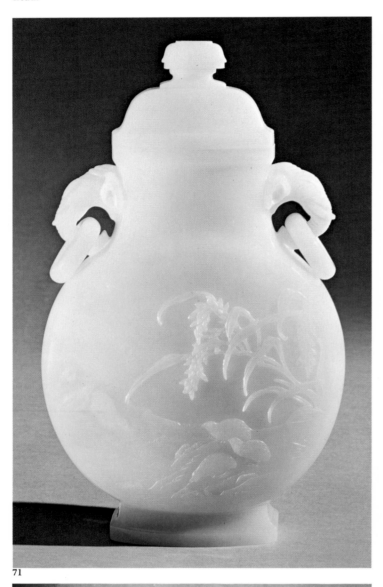

71

72

73

shapes or patterns lends itself easily to the traditional Chinese preference for curving or circular movements in design. During the Ming dynasty even the archaic shapes and patterns show this penchant for more rounded form. Ornamental objects such as items of jewellery employ strange archaic motifs or exhibit a variety of floral and foliate patterns freely arranged and executed with skilful undercutting in complex openwork designs. Flowers or continuous scrollery are the most typical ornament, but even where the motifs have lost all visible connection with their natural origins, the movement of the lines is reminiscent of curling stems or undulating bodies. Vessels in the natural forms of fruits entwined with leaves and tendrils date from this period, as do figure carvings, usually of animals or birds carved in compact rounded forms showing both economy and ingenious use of the stone. Horses and buffaloes are represented in supine pose with legs tucked underneath and often with heads lowered or turned back. These suggest the original shape of the stone – whether pebble or boulder, from which the craftsman has ground away as little as possible of the precious substance. Some of these animals are massively carved: a reclining buffalo in the Fitzwilliam Museum at Cambridge measures 17 inches (43.2 centimetres) in length.

The practice of commandeering the services of artists and craftsmen for palace work became more organised in the Ch'ing dynasty, and by 1680 some 30 palace workshops were in operation producing objects in enamel, glass, bronze, gold, lacquer, ivory and jade. It was the collecting zeal of the Ch'ien-lung emperor (1736-95) which promoted the greatest activity in the arts, and above all in jade production. During his reign, Khotan was designated an area for direct central government, and this had the effect of securing a large proportion of its jade export for the palace workshops. Several thousand men were employed to quarry the stone, and

74 Three *inro*. Top right: two-case *kinji* (literally 'gold ground') with metal appliqué, depicting the poetess Ono Komachi washing her book of poems, early 19th century. Top left: four-case *kinji* with fan-shaped panels of birds, flowers and foliage in Shibayama style, early 19th century. Below: four-case *ro-iro* (black lacquer ground) with waterfall and rocks in *aogai* (blue-green seashell) and gold *takamaki-e*, signed Soetsu in his 82nd year. Early 18th century.

75 Crane dancer, with his arm raised and holding a fan to give the silhouette of the bird. Wood, signed Shugetsu on the hem of the robe. 18th century.

illicit trade in jade became a capital offence. While jade carvers devoted much of their skills towards archaistic work, this did not exhaust their resources of imagination and technique. Large size was much admired, indeed the jade vessels made for Ch'ien-lung's numerous palaces had no equal in earlier times. Quality was judged by the excellence of the material, the freshness and originality of carving and the skill in choice and presentation of the subject. Certain jade colours became highly prized, notably the dark 'spinach' green and the pale greenish white called 'mutton fat'. The archaic vessel shapes took on new embellishments of loose ring handles or long chains attached to lids, each a *tour de force* of craftsmanship, and each creation fashioned from one piece of stone. In contrast, vessels were made in plain rounded forms where the accent was on perfection of finish, highlighting the purity

71

of the stone. Imitations of jade workmanship from Moghul India extended the craftsman's repertoire to include tiny, closely worked floral designs and floral knops. The scholar's traditional appreciation of the stone now found new scope in a wealth of objects fashioned for his table: seals: table screens carved in low relief with mountainous scenes peopled with poets and recluses as well as auspicious Taoist emblems; brush-washers, brush-pots and writing brushes. Boulders left largely in natural form and representing a mythical mountain paradise were carved with hidden pathways, wandering scholars, pines and pavilions. Later, in the 19th century, a profusion of personal jade ornaments in the form of pendants, earrings, bracelets and hairpins appeared, often in bright green jadeite and embellished with gold, pearls and precious stones.

73

68

NETSUKE AND INRO

Judith Moorhouse

The *netsuke* (end attachment) and *inro* (seal case) are two of the miniature art forms for which the Japanese are justly famed. Together they comprise a carrying arrangement for objects suspended from the belt of the kimono, the traditional dress of the Japanese, which lacked pockets. The *netsuke*, shaped as a small toggle, provided an anchor at the waist for twin cords which passed under the sash and suspended in front several *sagemono* (hanging things), among which might be an *inro*. The *inro* is a box of vertically arranged fitted trays threaded down each side by the cord, the manipulation of which at a bead above (*ojime*) allows the trays to be opened and closed. The origin of the convention of wearing these accessories is obscure, but they appear to have gained popularity in the early Edo period (1615-1868), and the skill of the craftsmen who made them flourished until the kimono was

supplanted by Western dress in the late 19th century.

During the 200 to 300 years of their manufacture *netsuke* developed from simple wood toggles to miniature works of sculpture. Measuring between 1 and 2½ inches (2.5 and 6.35 centimetres), they have four main shapes: the *katabori*, or representational carving of animal or human figures, including dolls, puppets and dancers; the *manju*, a flat round form like a rice cake; masks based on characters from drama; and the *kagamibuta* (mirror lid) where a decorated metal plate is inserted into the *manju* form. *Netsuke* could also be utilitarian objects such as seals, abacus or sundials, or even diversions such as self-righting figures, beehives with loose but unremovable larvae or lotus pods whose loose seeds cannot fall out. The only constraint on their form was their need to be rounded, without protuberances which might snag the

76

77

74

75

76 *Manju* with applied figures of the popular gods Daikoku and Ebisu (two of the seven gods of good fortune) as Manzai dancers. Ivory with applied stained ivory, mother-of-pearl and lacquer. Signed Shibayama in an ornate mother-of-pearl cartouche on the back. 19th century.

77 Head of a Buddhist guardian king in the form of a mask. Wood, the eyes inlaid and ringed in gold lacquer, signed Koseki. Late 19th –early 20th century.

78 Badger with distended belly using a lotus leaf as a cloak. Ivory, signed Kogyokusai on the back. 19th century.

79 Four-case *inro* with *rogin* (silver lacquer) ground, decorated in *sumie togidashi* (*sumie* is 'ink-painting') with the foxes' wedding procession. Signed Toyo. 18th century.

76   77   78

79   80   81   82

clothing, and to incorporate two holes through which the cords might pass to suspend the *sagemono*.

Their necessary qualities of strength and durability ideally required them to be fashioned from a single block of material, and for this reason woods, particularly boxwood, ebony or cherry, were popular, most frequently carved with a natural wood finish, but sometimes painted or lacquered or inlaid with hardstones or shell. Ivory was also a favourite medium; this, like wood, improves both in colour and texture with age and usage. Other materials include horn (usually stag horn), porcelain, carved red lacquer and a variety of gourds and shells used in their natural state. For subject matter, the *netsuke* craftsmen drew upon almost every aspect of nature as well as a wide repertoire of native folklore stocked with such characters as deities, wizards, priests and devils, figures representing virtues (such as filial piety), mermaids, samurai and figures with more mundane occupations such as ratcatchers, all depicted with the craftsman's delight in provoking horror or amusement. Subjects from the natural world were provided by studies of domestic or wild animals, singly or in tumbling groups and represented with the cartoonist's eye for exaggeration and attention to detail. Similarly treated are insects and a variety of different forms of marine life as well as flowers, fruits and vegetables.

Particular subjects were associated with certain craftsmen, and ultimately with schools of craftsmen who operated under a single name. The names of many individual specialists are known: Tomotada of Kyoto for his extraordinarily skilful carvings of oxen in ivory or wood; Masanao of Kyoto for animals also in ivory and wood; and Toyomasa of Tamba (1773-1856), a carver of seals by profession, but also famous for his *netsuke* of legendary animals with tortoiseshell inlay. Other craftsmen gave their names to distinctive styles, for instance the name of Shibayama became a generic term applied to the technique of encrusting a carving with various materials in a mosaic pattern. Over 1,000 signatures and

seals of *netsuke* craftsmen who worked between the end of the 18th century and the beginning of the 20th century are known, and hundreds of others worked anonymously on original pieces or in imitation of the famous schools or artists.

The *inro* was originally designed to carry personal seals and ink pad, necessary equipment for a man of business, and during the Edo period they were used to carry any kind of small loose object. They measure approximately $3\frac{1}{2} \times 2 \times 1$ inches ($88.9 \times 50.8 \times 2.5$ centimetres), have between one and five compartments and are normally composed of a decorative lacquer coating over a light wood core, though examples exist of leather, paper, metal, silk and cloth. Every surface is finished, including the inside, which often shows a fine use of red, black or gold lacquer. The appeal of the *inro* lies in the decorative uses to which the lacquerwork is put, and the Japanese lacquer techniques displayed on these small boxes draw upon a history of craftsmanship of almost 1,000 years. It is the *maki-e* technique, or sprinkling of gold and silver dust into the lacquer, which became an essential part of this art, and indeed forms the basis of much of the decoration on *inro*. The technique is one of building up a design by repeated applications of lacquer alternated with the sprinkling of metal dust on the surface which is rubbed down after each application. The finished surface design is achieved by this constant sprinkling, which produces a convincing sense of depth and can vividly evoke an atmosphere – such as a moon appearing through a veil of cloud, sunlight on rippled water or mist around a mountain top. Different names are associated with the different processes which produce these effects, for instance, *hiramaki* ('flat sprinkled picture'); *takamaki-e* ('raised sprinkled picture'); *togidashi* ('appearing by rubbing'). There are others for different background effects, all of which may use varying sizes of metallic dust fragments. Natural woods also play a part in the design where graining can be enhanced by coatings of clear lacquer, and conversely lacquer can be made to simulate wood or even metal or pottery. Much use was made of decorative inlays or

Margin references (left column): 75,77 / 76,78 / 76,77 / 78 / 76

Margin references (right column): 74,81 / 79

80 Two-case *inro* with *ro-iro* ground decorated in high relief, and depicting a samurai with servant kneeling before him. Signed Jitokusai Gyokuzan; in scratched characters Toshiyuki; inlaid metal seal Baibun or Bairyu, the latter being one of the seals used by Tokoku. 19th century.

81 Two-case *inro* with *fundame* (matt gold lacquer) ground. Two broacade balls are shown in *takamaki-e* with *kirikane* (gold foil cut to form decoration) and *somada* (shell inlaid with thin iridescent haliotis shell on black lacquer ground) detail. Signed in scratched characters Zeshin. 19th century.

82 Four-case *inro* with *kinji* ground shaded with *yasuriko* (lacquer ground of fine gold or silver powder), decorated in silver and gold *takamaki-e* with touches of shell. Signed Shigehide. Early 19th century.

encrustation with mother-of-pearl, tortoiseshell, ivory, coral, wood, porcelain, malachite and soapstone.

74 Like *netsuke*, decorative themes in *inro* reflect a keen observation of nature, often in its more subtle forms–the haphazard tracery of leaves against the sky, clustering of stars or scattering of petals; an insect on a leaf or tracks through snow. Such studies in miniature delighted the wearers of *inro*, which could be matched with the *ojime* and *netsuke*. Other pictorial compositions derived

79 from the rich source of folklore, and the identification of the stories

depicted could produce some intellectual diversion.

The names of some families of lacquer artists are well known, and many *inro* are signed. Some names associated with a particular technique are Masanari (late 17th century) for his *togidashi*; Zeshin (1807-91) for his finely engraved detail; Toyo (mid-18th 79,81 century) for his *togidashi*; Korin (1658-1716), a famous painter, much admired for his lacquer work in which he excelled in the interplay of textures; and Ritsuo (1663-1747) for his use of ceramic inlay.

CHINESE FURNITURE

Margaret Medley

Chinese furniture falls into three main categories, the first and most important being hardwood furniture. The second is lacquered furniture, usually on a softwood carcase, and more common to south China than to the north; and the third is bamboo and rattan furniture. This was intended for summer and out-of-door use, and was always regarded as expendable. The actual furniture consists of several types of table, such as those on which to unroll painting and calligraphy scrolls, altar tables for family offerings, and those for dining; a number of different kinds of cupboards; beds; an unfamiliar kind of couch; and at a later date, chairs. The traditional

83,85 couch, called a *k'ang* in the north and a *ch'uang* in the south, was provided with its own type of table.

A great deal of the hardwood came from the west and south-west of China, but the best was imported mainly from South-east Asia and Indonesia. The timbers include the rosewoods, or *Pterocarpus* series, the *Dalbergias*, called by the Chinese *huang-li mu*, 'yellow flowering pear tree', and the *Cassia siamosa* or *Ormosias*, called by the Chinese *chi-chih mu*, 'chicken wing wood'. The Chinese names, however, are conceived on the basis of the grain and colour of the wood when cut, and generally have nothing to do with a species. These hardwoods are highly resistant to insect attack, and lacquer, similarly impervious, was adequate to protect the more vulnerable softwood on which it was normally used.

The most interesting feature of the hardwood furniture is that it is always constructed in such a way that it can be taken to pieces and packed flat for transport. The joinery is of a highly

90 sophisticated mortice and tenon type, with limited use of dovetailing and pegs–glue is only used for repair work. Another reason for mortice and tenon construction is that it allows for expansion and contraction in accordance with the fluctuating temperatures and humidity, which can be considerable, not only from season to season, but also from one region of China to another.

A peculiarity of the hardwood furniture is that except for the top surfaces of tables, stools and *ch'uang*, the outward facing members are either slightly concave, the concavity usually being approximately a thumb width, or very slightly convex. Legs of tables, too, which look as though they would be round in cross-section, are in fact slightly oval; this is probably due to the fact that the hardwood was worked with a spokeshave. Leading edges are also very often made with a narrow beading. These three refinements in the finishing of Chinese hardwood furniture do much to give it the special quality that distingusihes it from the furniture of other parts of the world.

Nearly all the furniture is built on the box-frame principle, the

85 earliest being the *k'ang* and *k'ang*-table, furniture unique to China. The *k'ang*, which derives from the raised brick platform used for both sleeping and living in north China, was heated from under-

83 neath in the cold winter months. The southern version, the *ch'uang*, is free-standing, with a raised back and sides and a woven mat seating area which was usually provided with flat cushions. Because the raised back and sides had to be detachable and yet

strong and firm enough to sustain a leaning body, a special system of joining these parts to the box frame was devised, known as the slide lock mortice and tenon, so that the upright parts which were tenoned at the bottom could be slotted into specially shaped tapering mortices in the top of the box frame, and then tapped firmly sideways to lock the tenon into the thickness of the top member of the frame. The sides and back were often decorated with low-relief carving or, if they were openwork, the numerous parts were locked together with mitred mortice and tenon joints.

Tables were of two types of construction, either the box frame type, like the *ch'uang*, or of tressle construction, in which the legs are splayed and held in place with strengthening members called braces. Both types of construction have aprons running round below the flat top, and these were often inset into the under side of the top and might pass through the tops of the legs. The top may be a single board or be composed of a central panel in a mitred frame. In early pieces of the second type, little attempt is made to conceal the construction, and tenons are frequently taken right through the mortice of the mitred corner to be finished on the outside. This type also frequently has stretchers fixed on the underside of the frame using mortice and tenon joints, and in a few rare cases the stretchers are mitred as well, which involves cutting triangular segments out of the frame.

The table legs are locked into place using a very complicated system to ensure strength and rigidity even when the apron passes through the top of the leg. Sometimes there were mitred, morticed and tenoned stretchers. The legs, however elaborately curved or modelled, were always cut from a single piece of timber, making the best use of the grain; the *k'ang* or *ch'uang* table legs often have a very pronounced curvature. A particularly interesting feature of the *k'ang* table is that there are extension grip pads on the legs to allow the table to settle on the upholstery and remain firm, at the same time allowing the decorative treatment of the legs to be fully visible. In the 15th century some of these tables have a cabriole leg, and the proof of the European adoption of this feature of the claw and ball foot is seen in the acceptance of the same type of grip pads.

The *k'ang* and *ch'uang* table and the various other types, such as the square dining table, are traditional, having a long history that in later centuries was to run parallel to furniture of a different character. In early centuries in China life was lived at floor level, and this was not to change until the introduction of the chair, which not only raised the level but altered everything else as well. The chair seems to have appeared first in about the 2nd century AD, but did not gain general acceptance until the T'ang dynasty in about the 8th or 9th century.

The Chinese chair is either of a rigid box-frame construction, with high straight or rounded back, or it is a collapsible type with 84,87 a round back, usually called a horseshoe chair. It is worth noting that even the folding chair is entirely of wooden construction; there are no metal parts. The long rounded back sweeping down

83 *Ch'uang*, rosewood and chestnut couch, with heavy horsehoof feet mitred into the apron. Late 18th or early 19th century.

84 Round-backed chair of *huang-hua li* wood worked to resemble bamboo. Late 16th to early 17th century.

85 Rosewood *k'ang* table of the late 15th century.

86 Trestle table of *huang-hua li* wood, 17th to 18th century.

87 Straight-backed chair with curved splat, made of *huang-hua li* wood. 16th century.

88 Carved red lacquer table with dragons, phoenixes and floral scrolls. Early 15th century.

83

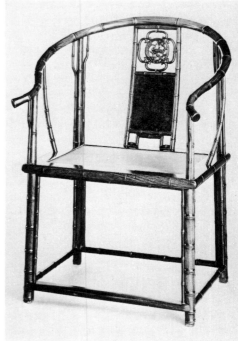

84

85

86

87

88

89 Detail of a red-lacquered, painted and gilt cupboard of the late 16th century.

90 Exploded view of the mortice-and-tenon system of joining, much used by the Chinese to give their furniture rigidity and strength.

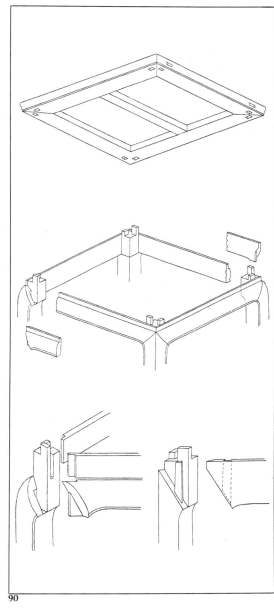

89   90

to make the arms is made up of three or five parts joined with double tongue-and-groove, half lapped and pressure pegged. Some of the collapsible chairs incorporated a foot-rest.

The rigid box-frame chair may have a straight back with a 87 carefully curved central splat, or it may have an elegant yoke back with a similarly curved central splat. The splat is modelled to suit the individual for whom the chair is made, as is the height of the seat from the foot rest. Chinese chairs were for the most part very personal 'tailor-made' pieces of furniture. The armchairs used to be made only for men; women, until up to as late as the 13th century, were expected to sit on stools, chairs being seats of honour. The seats were usually made of woven rattan matting, and it was normal to add a rather flat cushion. It was also not unusual to have a long cover which could be draped over the whole chair.

The introduction and final adoption of the chair as a normal piece of everyday furniture involved not only a change in posture, but a raising of levels all round. The chests previously used for storing clothes were now unsuitably low, so cupboards were introduced, often with a double cubic hat cupboard on top. These were generally made in pairs to stand alongside each other and were designed so that their proportions were appropriate not only to each other but to their architectural setting. Such cupboards were strictly rectangular and vertical at the sides, but other cupboards intended for books or scrolls were designed with battered sides. This meant that the doors were wider at the bottom than at the top so that they had to be carefully balanced to ensure that they did not become self-closing. There were two ways of doing this; either the hinge was a wooden pivot fitting into slots in the

lintel, or they were brassy alloy, two to each door of the ring and post type. The former was more difficult to take to pieces if it had to be transported to a new house, while the latter, found on most early cupboards, was more practical because by opening the door at right angles it could be lifted off the posts to lay flat for packing, the rest being easily taken apart and similarly laid flat. The hardware, such as hinges and handles, was generally countersunk and always designed for a specific piece of furniture.

Drawers, which in principle made their appearance in the 8th century, were given brail handles. These were countersunk with pins for attachment bent back at right angles on the inside and also countersunk. This type of fitting, like many of the Chinese shapes, was copied in Europe after the introduction of cabinets with drawers, which at the moment cannot be dated earlier than the middle of the 16th century. This date accords well with the opening of the Portuguese trade in the decade following 1514, when the Portuguese first arrived in Canton.

Lacquered furniture is broadly similar to hardwood furniture in design, but since lacquer lends itself to a variety of decorative techniques there is often much more decoration and a wide variety of colours. Painting and gilding are both extensively used, and on a dark ground are very effective. In later pieces, especially in cupboards, the practice of inlaying coloured stones, mother-of- 89 pearl and coloured glass, became an added elaboration. The most richly decorated pieces are undoubtedly the carved red imperial furniture, of which the 15th-century table with dragons and 88 phoenix is the earliest surviving example. The basic design is simple, closely resembling the best of the Ming hardwood furniture,

91 Mamluk Turk rug, Egypt, 15th-16th century. The origin of this strictly panelled design with subtle interlacing foilage can be traced from tiled fountain courtyards, garden designs or derived octagonal Turnoman *guls* (see plate 114).

92 Ushak rug, Turkish, 16th-17th century. Interlacing panels form unusual circles not unlike the contemporary Spanish 'wreath' design, surrounded by a border in which the pattern of leaves suggests animal shapes.

93 Turkish Bergama rug, about 1800. The simplified octagons of this colourful village rug represent a development of the Holbein design (see plate 99).

94 Turkish Ushak rug, 16th-17th century. The fine tightly drawn repeated design is only limited by the border. The arabesque drawing

but the gorgeous decoration with its panels and spandrels filled with marvellously well-carved dragons, phoenixes and floral scrolls make this an outstanding example of furniture design, though it is not perhaps to everyone's taste. A later example, of an imperial throne, with somewhat similar decoration, is heavy in form and fussy in detail by comparison.

Although Europeans have adopted certain elements of Chinese furniture without always being aware of it, we have not adopted the formal arrangement preferred in China. The carefully calculated

disorder of the European room would have been regarded with acute distaste, if not horror, by the Chinese, who preferred to place the pieces in carefully spaced groups against the wall, often in pairs on each side of a door, or facing across a room so that a balanced and harmonious unity was maintained. This was especially important in formal reception rooms. The furniture was normally designed for a specific room, so that perfection of proportion was established, unlike Europe where it was not unknown for a whole house to be constructed round one or two pieces.

ORIENTAL CARPETS

Robert Chenciner

The carpets of the East rank with the paintings and sculpture of the West as true works of art; their variations of pattern and design are vital expressions of the history, religion and culture of the people who made them. But they also fulfil the most practical of functions: for rich and poor alike they are the main item of furniture, serving not only as floor coverings, but as beds, cushions and wall-hangings.

Carpet making is a very ancient tradition in the East, probably going back to Assyrian times. Floor coverings are frequently mentioned by historians and poets though, as woven fabrics are perishable, none has survived from such early times. The earliest known knotted pile carpet, which was preserved in a tomb at Pazyryk in the Altai mountains of Central Asia, dates from the 3rd century BC, and the skill and sophistication with which it was woven suggests that the art of carpet making had reached a very high standard. Nothing remains from the next few centuries, but knotted carpet fragments have been found at Turfan on the old silk route, dating probably from the 5th century AD, and there are pieces of cut-looped Coptic carpets in Egypt, dating from the 6th to 9th centuries.

There is no further documentary evidence until the time of Marco Polo (*c*. 1254-1324), who mentions textile covers which could have been knotted carpets, and implies that on his travels in Asia he found well-established textile industries. Judging from earlier Sassanian woven fabrics, there certainly should have been a carpet industry, and miniature paintings from the times of the Mongol invasions in the 13th century bear this out to some extent, though

it is difficult to be sure whether floor- and tent-coverings illustrated are carpets, tiles or other fabrics.

But whatever the uncertainty about early carpets, the industry was definitely established by the 14th century, when the Mongol ruler Tamerlane set up court carpet workshops in Persia, probably following Sassanian and Arab custom. So too did the Mamluks in Egypt and the Moors in Spain, and in the 15th century the Ottomans in Turkey followed suit. The large court and town manufactories produced masterpieces of design, building on the original motifs of the nomadic peoples.

There is a confusing variety of types of Oriental carpet, but they can be divided into three broad categories, the differences between them lying in the different conditions of manufactures. Rugs were made by wandering nomads, by stationary villagers and by the court and city workshops.

The nomads, who roamed old Kurdistan in Eastern Turkey, the Caucasus and Western Persia, from the more northern areas of Siberia, Mongolia and Turkestan, used vivid primary colours and unconnected patterns, the use of colours being determined by the dyes available. Each tribe had its own particular preference in the juxta-positioning of certain colours. The motifs also tend to be simple and traditional: the nomads made symbols from the animals, people and plants that they saw around them. These rugs were not usually made for resale.

When the tribes settled to form villages, they continued to make brightly coloured rugs, but their stylistic traditions became modified because they were now trading rugs, and the buyers often

91

92

was probably influenced by Persian draughtsmen captured after the battle of Caldiran in 1514, or those transported later.

95 Turkish Ottoman court table carpet, 17th century. Precisely drawn tulips, carnations and roses, similar to those found on Iznik pottery, decorate this cruciform carpet.

96 Spanish rug, Cuenca, 16th century. The artistic influence of the Moors outlasted their presence in Spain, producing hybrid art forms, as in this carpet, where the powerful octagonal Islamic design holds together Renaissance wreaths, dragons and wyverns.

97 Turkish double *mihrab* rug, Kiz-Ghiordes, 18th-19th century. This finely woven rug may

have been part of a dowry. The design is unusual; the original nomadic design being subdued by the influence of a pedantic French style.

98 Turkish Ushak prayer rug, 17th century, a type usually found in Transylvania. These brightly coloured rugs have patterns derived from a magnified Ushak star motif.

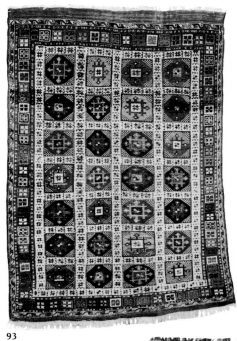

93

94

95

96

97

98

99 Ushak rug, Turkish, 16th century. This type of small-patterned rug in which each design motif shows slight variations was painted by Hans Holbein, and was imitated in Europe.

100 Persian floral rug, 16th century. Under the patronage of Shah Tahmasp such classic rugs were made with silk weft and warp, areas of silver brocade and dense knotting.

101 Persian Senneh, 19th century. This saddle-cover follows an ancient artistic tradition surrounding horsemanship. In this example the field is black-blue, the drawing precise and the weave very fine.

102 Safavid so-called animal carpet of the 'Sanguszco' group, Tabriz, late 16th century. These carpets are designed with animals in

symbolic perpetual combat, observed by ministering angels in the corners and seen through heaven-bound ducks in the centre.

103 Caucasian dragon Kuba, 16th-17th century, the bold layour including fabulous beast such as dragons and kylins. Although these rugs appear to have been designed from a cartoon, it is not known where or for whom they were made.

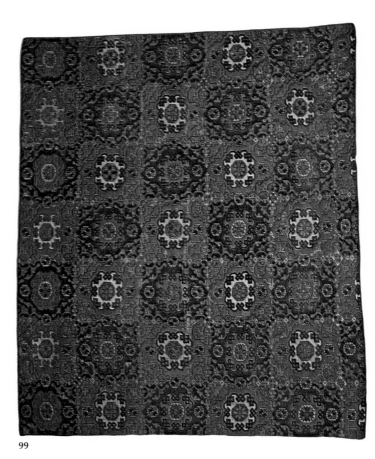

99

100

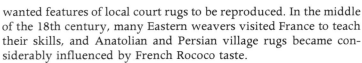

101

102

103

wanted features of local court rugs to be reproduced. In the middle of the 18th century, many Eastern weavers visited France to teach their skills, and Anatolian and Persian village rugs became considerably influenced by French Rococo taste.

The design of court rugs was derived from miniature paintings and leather book covers. The borders of a court carpet are designed to flow smoothly around the corners, unlike the discontinuous borders of nomad and village rugs. The colours used in these finer carpets tend to be subtle blends of primary colours, giving a mellower appearance, and the motifs most often seen are arabesques, hunting scenes, flowers and cloud bands. The patterns are continuous, often representing up to three lattices superimposed.

95,105,106, 109

Court carpets tend to be more curvilinear than nomad or village rugs, and there is greater unity in the design, both in the balance of various motifs and the sympathetic relationship between the border and the field, or centre, of the carpet.

Since the days of Muhammad, carpets and the Muslim religion have always been intertwined, and many rugs were woven for specifically religious use. These prayer rugs usually represent the central prayer niche in the mosque (the *mihrab*) as a pointed pattern, often with a symbolic representation of a prayer lamp in the middle. The worshipper kneels on the *mihrab* to pray, in the mosque, at home or out of doors, but always facing towards Mecca. A more unusual form is the multiple-niche rug, called a *saph*, made so that a

93,11
97,11

104 Persian nomad *qasq'ai* (saddlebag), mid-19th century. The design is woven from memory in tapestry and brocade set out in a varying mosaic.

105 Persian court vase carpet, possibly Kerman, end of the 16th century. In this flamboyant design huge flowers and vases seem to intertwine at random, concealing a balanced composition contained by a border of opulent arabesque tendrils.

106 Persian court medallion carpet, Tabriz, early 16th century. The austere rectangularity of lines in the three planes created by the grand arabesques has given rise to much debate over the dating of these carpets.

104

105

106

family can pray together. The largest number of prayer rugs was produced in Turkey, but they were also made in Persia, the Caucasas and Turkestan.

But the self-contained design of prayer rugs is unlike that of most Oriental carpets, which normally show part of an infinite pattern which is cut off and framed by the borders. Broadly speaking, there are three main layouts of field: the medallion, the tile design and the lattice.

The first shows a large central medallion surrounded by other medallions which can be similar or complementary, and which are usually cut off by the border. The scale of the medallions can range from a large central one dominating the whole field to many

small ones, and they can be curvilinear to octagonal—all shapes between these two extremes can be found in Ushak carpets. There is a continuing debate as to whether medallions are derived from Persian ogival forms or from Turkoman octagonal *guls*.

The tile design, which divides the field into a chequered board pattern, is found in the ancient Pazyryk carpet, Coptic carpets of AD 600, Kurdish garden carpets up to the 19th century and Turkish 'Chequer Board' carpets of the 16th and 17th centuries.

The lattice design is made of regular crossing diagonals. In Persian carpets from the Safavid dynasty (16th to 17th centuries), the lattice design formed the grid which symbolically divided God and man.

106

111

39

107 Garden carpet, North-west Persian, 18th century. The design, an enclosed garden with four rivers flowing away from it, is probably derived from representations of Paradise.

108 Silk 'Polonaise' carpet, Isfahan, 17th century. This type of carpet is so named because it first appeared at a public exhibition from the collection of a Polish prince. Such carpets, made in court workshops, were often given to visitors to the Persian court or to foreign rulers.

109 Mughal dynasty court carpet, North Indian, 17th century. A varied profusion of flowers, drawn in the crisp Mughal formal style, is set out simply on a claret field.

110 Carpet from North-west China, early 18th century. The simple colours of this rare carpet, made for refined domestic use, reflect the recurrent Chinese tendency to look to the art of the past.

107

108

109

110

111 Anatolian or Syrian (?), 16th century. The so-called Chequer Board rug contains eight-pointed stars, cut off at one end by the border, which is a series of stylised foliate cartouches.

112 Caucasian Kazak, 18th century. This type of village rug is descended from the Kuba dragon carpet (see plate 103), the evolution of

style through a remembered design producing an original and dynamic variation.

113 Eastern Turkish prayer rug, 18th-19th century. At first sight the design of this nomad rug appears chaotic, but a balance emerges on closer inspection. The wool is shaggy and glossy.

114 Turkoman carpet, Tekke tribe, early 19th century. Each nomadic tribe made and cherished rugs with traditional designs of round shapes called *guls*.

111

112

113

114

To understand the evolution of style in Oriental carpets, it is necessary to look first at the Turkish rug tradition because of its pervading influence. The earliest known Turkish carpets were found in the Alaeddin mosque in Konya, and were probably made for the Seljuk rulers in the 13th century. They have all-over abstract or fomalised plant lattices, reminiscent of the Chinese Han dynasty silks which exist from the 2nd century AD.

Many 14th-century Turkish carpets with encircled animals, derived from Sassanian textiles, appear in European paintings, and Hans Holbein and Lorenzo Lotto both painted Anatolian medallion
99 carpets with stiff arabesque designs, often incorporating octagons. These, which came to be known as 'Holbein rugs', were made at Bergama or Ushak, and all have the brick madder red typical of this area. During the early Ottoman court period, exquisite floral
95 medallion carpets were made which matched the Isnik pottery produced from the 16th century. Ushak continued as a carpet centre up to the 18th century, and similar carpets were produced over the whole period. Many Ushak carpets were found in
98 Transylvanian churches, which have the same red, but brighter colours, while the designs are spacious tendril flowers and vase patterns.

From the early 18th and 19th centuries carpets in the French taste were made for export, and production was centred at Ghiordes, where many prayer rugs were made. But tribal rugs also continued to be made during the 19th century, and these showed a direct resemblance to the octagonal-motif carpets painted by Holbein. Of course, Turkoman tribes in present-day Russia and Afghanistan are the descendants of the Seljuk Turks and the Ottoman Turks, so
114 it is not surprising that they still produce octagonal (or *gul*) design rugs in many distinct shades of red. In fact it is possible to see, in 19th-century Turkoman rugs, almost every motif which appears in Turkish rugs. Broadly, each Turkoman tribe has its own *gul*- and colour juxta-positioning and weaving technique.

Another branch of the Turkish people became the Mamluk rulers of Egypt from the 14th century until they were defeated

by the Ottoman Turks, and they set up court manufactories producing deeply coloured red, green, blue and brown octagonal 91 medallion rugs in very elaborate designs.

In Persia in the late part of the 14th century the traditional Turkic nomad rug was imposed over the Sassanian tradition by Tamerlane, and the new style was developed by the Turkman dynasties which followed until 1500—elaborate arabesque floral lattice rugs can be seen in Timurid paintings. The Safavid rulers then brought in a new court style which was directly influenced by a more naturalistic approach to painting. Court medallion carpets 106 showing more naturalism were produced in Tabriz in the early 16th century, and possibly towards the end of the century a family of naturally drawn floral, vase and palmette carpets made their appearance.

Vase carpets show an enormous variety of flowers linked in 105 traditional lattice forms, often with the Chinese Ω shaped cloud bands being included in the designs. The Persian love of flowers is also demonstrated by garden carpets, which symbolise Paradise, 107 and have vertical and horizontal rivulets dividing spaces filled with flowers, shrubs and trees. The design is probably based on symbols derived from the Garden of Paradise myth.

Floral carpets were also made in Lahore in Northern India under the Mughal rulers from the 16th century, but the Indian court carpets were more formally laid out, with greater naturalistic 109 detail in the flowers and animals. There is one amazing carpet in which the arabesque lattice is formed by many animals' heads out of whose mouths sprout tendrils which in their turn terminate in further animals' heads.

In Persia under Shah Abbas (1571-1629) huge floral rugs were made, which include angels, beasts of the chase and animals in combat, and from the early 17th century silk floral carpets in pastel colours were produced, often as gifts—these are known as Polonaise 108 carpets.

Some of the vase-technique carpets have serrated leaf patterns as well as vases and flowers, and these, through north-west Persia,

115 Turkestan *saph*, or double prayer rug, Khotan region, 19th century. Khotan rugs contain a mixture of Chinese, Tibetan, Mongolian and Turkish designs from the Tarim basin, a 'melting pot' where trade passed from Han times, if not earlier.

116 Storage bag, Turkoman, 19th century. This would originally have formed part of the furnishings of a nomadic tent. The tribe is uncertain because of conflicting technical and design features.

115

influenced the court carpet makers of the Khans in Armenia and the Caucasus. From the late 16th century this region produced bold geometric rugs with serrated leaf lattice designs and stunning 103 colours. One group had the lattice centres filled with dragons and chilins, while others were derived from vase designs, but became more broadly drawn, rectangular and flamboyant. From the end of the 18th century unusual rugs are found where men and monsters are treated with humour.

Carpets were brought to Spain by the Arab invasions and occupation from the early days of Islam, and continued to be made after the expulsion of the Arabs in 1492. The main production centres for the court carpets which survive from the 15th to the 17th 96 centuries were Alcaraz and Cuenca. There are octagonal strapwork tile carpets of the 15th century which, like Mamluk rugs, show the early Arab abstract geometric interlacing designs combined with Turkic *gul* patterns, as in the Holbein carpets. The Spaniards also produced Lotto pattern rugs, using the Chinese colour range of yellow, beige and shades of blue.

The Spanish carpets show a Western Turkic influence which was also felt in the 16th and 17th centuries in England, where copies of Turkish carpets were made (see p. 237). This influence spread eastward as well: in Turkestan and China, trade as well as repeated invasions of Steppe nomad tribes since Han times has produced a village carpet tradition. The rugs from Samarkand and Khotan from the 18th and 19th centuries show a mixture of Turkic and Chinese designs as rich as the mixture of peoples who inhabited the Tarim basin, for instance the pomegranate design rugs combined a stiffened Chinese lotus-and-tendril design with bold Turkic reds and blues. Chinese carpets do not seem to have been made before

the Kang-Hsi period (early 17th century), and it appears that they were considered less important than other Chinese artefacts, such as jades, silks and bronzes. Nevertheless, the delicate blues, yellows and beiges and the very subtle overall design of Chinese carpets 110 and Mongolian saddle rugs have always been treasured in the West.

It is often difficult to date carpets, because there was a strong conservative tradition in the carpet centres, carried on for centuries. If the materials and dyes used remain the same, it is only possible to date a carpet with precision by comparing it to another dated piece (and these are rare), though to some extent the motifs can be linked to other Islamic arts.

Identification also poses problems. With experience it is usually possible to identify carpets by a detailed comparison of the many variations of size, field and border designs, patterns and colours, but this is not always sufficient, as trade on the silk route from China to Persia, as well as tribal wars and invasions, led to much cross-influence in the carpets of Persia, Turkey and the Arab world. If a design was popular it was often copied by weavers in another area.

The most certain way of identifying rugs is by examining their structure, such as the twist and composition of the various materials used in weaving—lambs' and goats' wool, silk and cotton—and the chemical analysis of the colours used in dyeing. Thus it is necessary to understand how rugs are made.

The method is to tie knots into a flat-weave matrix or net composed of warp threads (those running from top to bottom) and weft threads (those running from side to side). The warp and weft knots are usually made of twisted wool, though sometimes they are of cotton, or silk, which is finer.

There are two main types of knot: the symmetrical Ghiordes knot and the asymmetrical Sehna knot, but the type of knot is not a sure indication of origin, nor is the density a measure of the quality. Knot density ranges from about 16 to the square inch in Atlas mountain rugs to over 1,000 in Persian silk carpets. Turkish and Caucasian rugs vary between 40 and 150 knots to the square inch, with Chinese rugs lower than average and Persian and Turkoman higher.

A rectangular loom is used to draw the warp thread tight while the weft is passed from side to side, inside and outside alternate warp threads. Row by row the knots are tied and the new weft is combed down tight. The edges are bound strongly with the weft looping around one or more large warp threads—this is called the selvage. The ends are finished with wefts alone, and the warps are left as a fringe. Ends, selvages and centres usually show wear first.

There are also flat-weave rugs which have no knots, kilims being the most common. These are made of a tapestry weave, which completely hides the warps. Another flat-weave is the Soumak

116

117 A woven woollen Kashmir shawl of the type that became so much sought after in Europe.

118 Fragment of painted and dyed cotton, probably part of a bed cover. Made in India, on the Coromandel coast, for the European market. Early 18th century.

carpet, made with a herring-bone looped-over weave, which also hides the warps. The so-called Polonaise carpets from 16th- and 17th-century Isfahan used metallic gold and silver threads. The knots are tied around the warps and pressed together by the weft, which is combed down hard.

Only rarely does a carpet have a known pedigree, and inscriptions are equally unusual. The most useful guides to identification are the density and type of the knot, and the warp and weft material—twisting and position, such as the number of wefts between each knot, and whether the alternate warps are depressed. The length and texture of the pile are also indicators.

Natural dyes were used up to 1865, when there were progressively replaced by chemical dyes which look superficially the same but age badly. They tend to fade into unpleasant colours bearing little relation to the original, or in the case of some modern dyes, not at all, while the natural dyes merely mellow with age. Happily, the Persians are now encouraging the use of natural dyes again.

Natural colours come from three primary dyes: madder—lac or cochineal—produces all reds, browns and purples; indigo blue produces colours from light blue to almost black; various plant dyes produce yellow or mix with the other two to make greens and oranges. White and brown are natural colours, but the latter can be darkened by using the other dyes. Most carpets use between 6 and 12 colours, the main one being red, except for Chinese carpets which are usually in shades of gold, blue, brown and white.

The patterns at first sight appear too complicated to understand, but there is a universal visual principle which can make them easier to grasp: that is that all patterns can be looked at in several ways, for instance, you can look at the spaces in between the main motifs or at the motifs themselves. The continual changes when looking at the background or the foreground, or at one set of shapes to their complement gives Oriental carpets their special power. Natural objects are often formalised into nearly symmetrical patterns filling a central field which is framed by a series of enclosing borders filled with repeating designs. Border and field are tied together with visible and invisible echoes of shapes.

In general, most Oriental carpets began to decline in excellence from the 17th century, a process which accelerated in the last 100 years. Exceptions are the energetic Anatolian tribal rugs and the Turkoman nomad rugs of traditional design. Nomad rugs are still being made in Kazakstan, Kurdistan, Quasgai, Shirvan and Anatolia, and it is possible to find 19th- and 20th-century examples which all show influence from earlier rugs. Also there are modern Persian copies of small court rugs from Tabriz, Nain, Qum and Kirman.

EASTERN AND MIDDLE-EASTERN TEXTILES

Susan Mayor and Christopher Lennox-Boyd

The varied types of textiles found in the East depend upon the natural resources of each country: for instance, the Chinese, and later the Japanese, bred silkworms, and exported their silk throughout the world; the Turkomen and Greeks both used linen made from flax; the Kashmiris' fine wool came from the mountain sheep, while other Indians wove cotton. Textile styles have been formed by many different cultural influences, the great migrations and conquests often creating large but localised industries.

The weavers of the city of Srinagar in Kashmir developed one of the most spectacular of these industries, using the finest wool, which was not shorn or even combed off the animals, but collected from the bushes against which the sheep rubbed themselves. From this incredibly soft cloth, they made shawls decorated with simple formal floral borders, the finest of them taking three years to complete.

By the end of the 18th century, these shawls had reached the European merchants of Calcutta and Khadenagur, who exported them to Europe, where they sold at a vast profit. The original simple shawls suited the severe Classical dress style of the Regency and Empire periods, but as fashions changed, so did the Indian shawls—to please the European market, the weavers altered their designs from long and rectangular to small and square. Unfortunately for the weavers, the shawl quickly became a symbol of opulence, like the mink coat in the present century, and cheaper imitations were made in Europe, using Indian patterns but cheaper wool. To compete with these, made at Paisley, Norwich and other centres, the Kashmiri debased their own goods, introducing first embroidery, and later, designs supplied by French merchants working for the Paris market.

With the fall of Paris in 1871, the Kashmir industry collapsed, and shawls ceased to be luxury goods at 200 guineas each and became symbols of working-class success at £1 a time—or even a few shillings if the shawl was printed. The effect on Kashmir was disastrous. As is the case with most luxury articles, the profit had

117

118

119 A 17th-century coat of blue and yellow brocade from Persia.

120 Detail of a linen bedspread from Skyros, embroidered in coloured silks with seven caiques.

121 Half a linen pillow case, probably from Naxos, embroidered in red, green and blue silk.

122 Part of an embroidered skirt from Crete. 18th century.

123 A cotton curtain from Bokhara embroidered in coloured silks. Early 19th century.

119

120

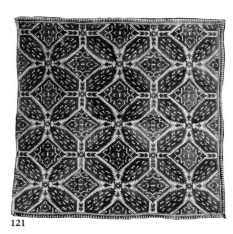

121

122

123

been made by innumerable middlemen, the weaver himself being the lowest paid of all those involved. The middlemen, faced with a drastically reduced profit margin, turned to other goods, and Kashmiri weaving became once again a purely local industry.

Elsewhere in India, cotton was the staple cloth, and women in almost every village produced vast quantities of embroidery. In the large trading cities of the coast, where the Indians had seen the fine English embroideries brought by the East India Company with the intention of exporting to China, an industry sprung up producing indigo-dyed patterned hangings in imitation of the embroidered hangings. These were made by painting or printing the clothes or chintz with wax to divide areas not to be dyed – these areas constituting the pattern – and then steeping them in very hot water to allow the dye to take. The hangings, known as Indienne or Pintado, were exported to Europe as summer curtains.

In Persia and in the Persian-dominated states of North India, other decorative textile industries grew up, where silk was brocaded and cottons printed, often with regular repeating patterns of flowers and trees. These were made up into hangings and prayer mats, which were later sometimes cut up and re-used as table-mats – it is not unusual to find small pieces of 17th- and 18th-century brocades or cottons remounted with later pieces.

In the 17th century, Kashan, Isfahan and Yezd were the major weaving centres, producing superb velvet brocades with pictorial patterns, sometimes small scenes, and often with birds or human figures.

The inhabitants of some of the wealthier Aegean islands produced extremely fine embroidery, both on skirts and on bed hangings. The patterns vary from island to island, and appear to derive principally from the styles fashionable among the Italians at the time that each island fell to the Turks. The materials and

methods also varied: some islands embroidered, usually on imported materials such as linen, and using silks which were only made in a few of the islands, while others knitted.

In the Dodecanese, the 12 islands ruled by the Knights of St John until 1532, there is no outside influence, as the knights were monastic. The embroidery of these islands is characterised by large isolated formalised motifs, often seemingly based on leaves or conifers. In the Cyclades, many islands embroidered hangings and dresses to their own patterns, the most famous being those produced on Naxos. These red embroideries are covered almost entirely in darning stitch, the pattern occurring where the background shows through.

The embroideries of the Sporades (Northern Islands), such as Skyros, show strong Turkish influences, and include more naturalistic but isolated motifs, sometimes depicting elegant Turks, vases of flowers or ships. In Crete, the hems of skirts were elaborately embroidered with formalised vases of flowers with, hidden among them, birds and palmette-like flowers. The Ionian islanders embroidered in cross-stitch, decorating the borders or, in the case of smaller items such as cushion covers, the whole surface, with angular patterns of peacocks, deer and trees, often accompanied by drawn work.

The embroideries found further west in the Mediterranean, in most parts of North Africa, are cruder, with rather garish colours, though in Morocco the standard was higher, and each city had its own distinctive formal patterns in red and blue silk. In Tetuan on the north coast particularly fine hangings were made, the borders and bases embroidered in multicoloured thread in double-darning, double-running and satin stitches. Their floral borders were surmounted by large formal flowers and a border of rose sprays. In Algiers, curtains were embroidered with diagonal brick,

124 A long smock, embroidered in red cross stitch trimmed with sequins. Rumanian, probably from Vilcea or Southern Craiova.

125 A Chinese *k'ossu* robe of the late 19th century.

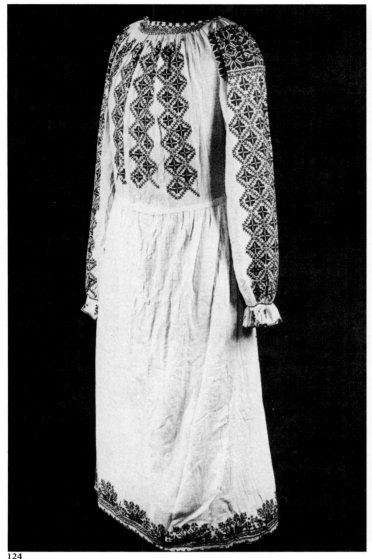

124

125

double running and satin stitches, the pattern consisting of vertical rows of an oval device made up of a conventionalised floral medallion with eight similar but smaller devices around it.

Throughout the Balkans, similar Islamic-style patterns were used, mainly on regional costume. However, the Balkan peasant 124 used smocking and ruching, unlike the North Africans, whose costume has little or no tailoring, so the embroideries cannot really be compared. Of Balkan embroidery, only the towels have any genuine similarity to the North African work, and these, in which many colours of silk as well as silver and gold threads were used, are much grander.

In the Caucasus, in Dagestan, cushion covers—a necessity not a luxury—were embroidered on cotton with cross-stitch, their formal patterns of elaborate crosses, stars and octagons deriving from Persian and Caucasian carpets. The Uzbecks and other nomadic 123 Turkomen tribes also embroidered on linen, mainly making hangings for their tents, but also sometimes ornamenting their robes. In the 18th century, the large tent hangings were covered in brightly coloured flowers, and by the 19th century, these had become large and formalised, with predominating colours of purple and crimson.

The centre of the silk trade had always been China, and here the silk was brocaded, embroidered, woven as tapestry or *k'ossu*, or made up into velvet. During the Ming dynasty, in the 16th and early 17th centuries, *k'ossu* was the predominant material, and was 125 used for both robes and hangings. In the late 17th century, under the succeeding Manchu Ching dynasty, velvet, damask and brocade came into fashion, while in the declining years of the 19th century, embroidery became popular, followed by harsh analine dyes.

In Japan too, silk was the most favoured material, and was printed, brocaded and sometimes embroidered. In the outlying islands, however, cottons were used, and dyed with indigo by the wax-resist method, as in India. The national dress, the kimono, was made either of thin silk or cotton, while the *obis*, or sash worn with it, was of heavy brocade. Another silk garment was the *kesa*, or priest's robe, a square rectangular over-garment. This was originally made up of patches to symbolise poverty, but later it degenerated, and pieces of expensive brocade were specially cut up for the purpose. The robes are usually ornamented, with a broad floral or animal pattern, and often with the imperial chrysanthemum against a gold background. Sometimes they are set with small patches of an older and even finer brocade.

Further south, the Malays of Java developed resist dyeing to a fine art, Tjanting batiks being made with extremely elaborate patterns. Both sides of the cloth are covered with wax from a small funnelled vessel, and the cloth is steeped in indigo and then plunged into cold water to crack the wax. This produces a network of fine blue lines, one of the features of Javanese batiks. The cloth is then cleaned, rewaxed with a different pattern, dipped in sago bark, which goes brown and red-brown, and even sometimes dipped again in a red dye. The patterns, which are traditional, are mainly intricate floral designs, sometimes with the addition of Hindu gods and peacocks, or Islamic symbols, such as wings.

It is believed that this art developed in the royal courts during the 18th century as an occupation for the ladies, just as embroidery was the civilised occupation in European households. Batiks require very finely woven cotton, which was originally imported from India, and later from Europe and Japan. They were used for sarongs, head-cloths and shoulder-cloths, and are still made in small quantities in Java. However, they are a great luxury, as a batik sarong may take as much as two weeks to complete, while up to 20 printed cotton sarongs can be produced in one day.

FURNITURE

GOTHIC AND RENAISSANCE STYLES

Penelope Eames

The character and use of furnishings in the later Middle Ages were governed by the habits of life, the habits themselves belonging to a feudal structure in which the interdependence of men and the relative power of individuals was expressed symbolically through the everyday things they used. The maintenance of an individual's position in society depended upon following set rules which were regulated by precedence. If an individual wished to extend his influence, as did the Valois dukes of Burgundy in the 14th and 15th centuries, it was necessary to increase household expenditure and create an extravagant display of power through the deployment of precious objects and symbolic forms in furnishings, attracted men of talent to the lord's service, and created a favourable climate for the formation of political alliances.

The household, as a potent instrument in the aggrandisement of individual lords, was considered second only to the exploits of war, and obviously in such circumstances there was little room for idiosyncratic choice in furnishings, for at all levels of society value, form and decoration expressed social realities rather than quirks of individual taste. A puissant lord influenced men and events by being approachable to persons of all pursuits, and thus a great household was often thronged with the unruly and ill-mannered, as well as with those of educated behaviour. This public nature of the lord's household had more influence upon the appearance of furniture than any other single factor, because significant display had to be achieved largely through the manipulation of movable and adaptable valuables, such as textiles and plate, rather than through arrangements of elaborately ornamented fixtures, such as furniture. Textiles could be speedily hung upon walls, and plate could be temporarily assembled on buffets, and removed and locked away after use, but elaborate furniture was ill suited for survival in such restless circumstances.

The needs of the itinerant household further confirmed the relative importance of textiles and plate, which were an essential part of the household equipment, stowed in baggage carts and on the backs of sumpter horses. They were brought out at each journey's end, and placed on the massively strong wooden furniture, which itself remained *in situ* (it was often, for convenience, legally held with property, passing with it from heir to heir). Since no man was judged by his furniture, quantity responded to need, and halls and chambers were sparsely furnished, to be the more readily re-arranged to suit a variety of pursuits. The hall, so often the scene of communal meals, became an open space for dancing, target practice or even jousting, with the stacking of forms, boards for tables and their separate trestles around the perimeter.

Yet, despite the general priorities in furnishings, there were significant exceptions, and a few individual pieces of furniture were important in their own right, rather than acting merely as hidden frames supporting freely draped textiles and furs. This group of specially significant pieces, which important artists were commissioned to create, is most accurately described as 'furniture of estate', and we can follow its development clearly in the special chairs supplied with protective cases, and in cradles, such as the 126 example made for one of the children of Marie of Burgundy and Maximilian of Austria in 1478-9, preserved at Brussels. The impulse to refine and elaborate had its beginnings in furniture of estate, and this tendency to embellish furniture made significant advances during the 16th century, until furniture finally became the equal in value, and therefore in importance, to its earlier rivals, textiles and plate.

Although the great seigneurial households favoured textiles and plate for display purposes, the wealthy burghers enjoyed comparatively private households and lived in circumstances which did not inhibit the use of elaborate furniture. The comfortable and intimate domestic surroundings of 15th-century merchants are familiar to us in the works of such Flemish masters as Jan van Eyck, and some carved furniture which closely corresponds to 127

126   127   128

126 The silver throne of King Martin of Aragon, given to Barcelona cathedral in 1410. The chair would have been accompanied by a matching footstool, or raised upon a draped dais.

127 Portuguese chair of 1470, with finely carved flamboyant Gothic back.

128 Oak buffet from the Netherlands, *c.* 1620. The intarsia perspectives contrasting with

carved work are typical of the mid-16th to early 17th-century style.

129 *The Marriage of Alexander and Roxana,* 1512, by Giovanni Antonio Bazzi. Note the bed, with its carved posts and canopies, contrasting with the hung beds of earlier times.

130 Plate from Hans Vredeman de Vries's *Differents Pourtraicts de Menuisere, c.* 1580,

showing the fashion which first appeared in the late 15th century of post beds with canopies of massive, exposed wood.

131 Bavarian bed with delicate strapwork outlines executed in ebony, and ivory arabesques, demonstrating the advanced refinement and aristocratic feeling of German 16th-century work.

129

130

131

132 Oak buffet, c. 1540, Westphalia. Carved Renaissance arabesques and acanthus columns replace the linenfold or flamboyant Gothic tracery which would have been used in the 15th century, but in other respects this is a medieval piece.

133 Cabinet-on-stand, veneered in tortoiseshell and ivory, typical of the Antwerp workshops of c. 1630.

134 Woodcut dated 1533 by Peter Flötner, who worked in Nuremberg as a carver and designer. This panel was inspired by stucco decoration in the Villa Madama in Rome.

135 Armoire of oak and ash, dated 1541, from a design by Peter Flötner for the Nuremberg patrician family of Holzschuher.

136 Late 15th-century German armoire made of various woods. The stressed horizontals are carved with high relief contrasting with areas of plain wood; such pieces were often painted.

132

133

134

135

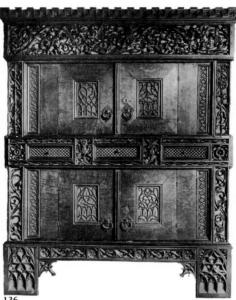

136

137

138

pieces in their paintings has survived. However, in spite of the quality of much of this furniture, inventories show that it was of far less value than the cloth which hung upon the beds and covered the seating, and the greater emphasis upon textiles and plate remained unchallenged for as long as feudal concepts survived.

In the 16th century, because of the disintegration of feudal society and the consequent development of privacy, stability and security within doors, commissions for elaborate woodwork became more widespread, and it is particularly interesting that elaboration grew from such objects as beds and buffets, the very areas where textiles and plate had made such a significant contribution to the display of power and wealth. Important 14th- and 15th-century beds were totally draped, with integral canopy and heading, and this style was superseded by lavishly carved structures with exposed woodwork in which heavy posts supported massive canopies (though the fully draped model returned to favour in the 17th century). The buffet or dressoir, originally draped from top to bottom, became the finely worked, composite piece known in England as the court cupboard (or board for cups, as used at court).

129,130,131

These items were extremely prestigious, and were used in the 15th century to denote degrees of privilege – the bed by the presence and size of its canopy and by the quality, decoration and form of its hangings, and the buffet by the number of steps or stages it displayed, as well as by the form, quantity and quality of its precious burden. Such attitudes to particular pieces of furniture were remarkably persistent, and highlight the importance of the

Middle Ages in terms of the history of furniture as a whole; for instance, canopies on state beds (such as Robert Adam's design for Osterley Park) demonstrate the way in which symbolism could outlive the reality which created it. The buffet altered its shape as the display of plate was reduced, and more of its open spaces were enclosed as it merged with the armoire (keeping, in English, the misleading name cupboard), but it retained its position as an object worthy of a place in the reception, or display, areas of a house.

128,1

In the 16th century, a new creation, the cabinet-on-stand, made its appearance, and this may be seen as the vehicle through which the Renaissance attributes of learning and taste were expressed in furniture. The creation of a study and library, set apart from other activities within the household, is first noticed in 1367-8, when such a room was especially equipped for Charles V in the Louvre, and it seems likely that the Renaissance idea of a study grew from the intimate private libraries of the rich men and princes of the 14th and 15th centuries. In Renaissance times, the cabinet was actually needed as a repository for the much-collected curiosities such as coins, shells, cameos and hardstones; yet a glance at these ornate and technically brilliant pieces of furniture shows that they were, first and foremost, furniture of estate, symbolic of a new age of enquiry, rather than practical solutions to particular storage problems.

133

148,1

The significant social, economic, intellectual and spiritual changes taking place in Europe in the late 15th and 16th centuries produced a highly favourable climate for artistic change, and Gothic art, symbolic of many outmoded concepts, was weakened and finally submerged by the vital aesthetics of the Italian Renais-

137 Oak chest from the North Netherlands, c. 1530. Except for the carved motifs, this retains a medieval form and character. The panels are filled with portrait medallions amid grotesque work.

138, 139 Italian walnut *cassone*, c. 1550, one of a group of four. The strongly delineated

borders form a perfect foil to the frieze of figures, with its central coat of arms.

140 Italian bench, or *cassapanca*, with storage compartment beneath the seat. The perfect proportions of this piece, derived from antique art, are enhanced by restrained ornament.

141 Spanish *vargueño* on stand, c. 1550, with rich Plateresque inlay.

142 Spanish *vargueño* on stand, c. 1530-40, decorated with pierced boxwood carving on a velvet ground, and portrait medallions set within a Classical framework.

139

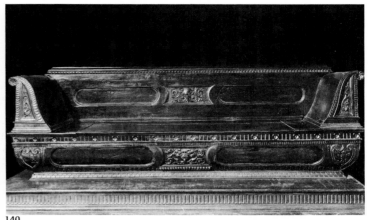

140

141

142

sance. In Italy, furniture design reflected the logical development of Renaissance art, but the calm and measured forms of Italian 15th-century work have few parallels north of the Alps. Although historically important exceptions exist, it is true to say that the rest of Europe did not experience the full influence of the Renaissance until Mannerism had sharpened and distorted the earlier harmonies.

The process of change is first seen as providing a gloss upon old traditions; for instance, we find Renaissance medallions and Italianate arabesques displacing Gothic arcading upon furniture which still retains its medieval form. The surprising speed with which Renaissance ornament, if not Renaissance form, dominated furniture decoration in northern Europe from the second quarter of the 16th century was largely due to the arrival of the printed pattern book, a new phenomenon which became the standard instrument of change for succeeding centuries. It follows that pattern books also engendered uniformity, and instances of extreme eccentricity in both design and technique, which had been common in furniture throughout the Middle Ages, were a casualty of progress. The influence of pattern books was enhanced by the development of shop-working practices for all skills involved in furniture making, and the highly mobile nature of craftsmen in medieval times became less pronounced as towns increased in size and number and guilds proliferated, often through a division of responsibilities.

The most influential Renaissance-inspired designs to appear in the 16th century concentrated upon the fundamental science of architecture and its ornaments. This was a natural as well as an

economic priority, since it provided basic instruction in the elements of a new form of art which was of equal utility to architects, goldsmiths, carvers and the makers of every kind of artefact. Specific designs for furniture, though rarer and less important, became common after the earliest work of Daniel Hopfer during the 1520s.

There are many national features which enable Renaissance furniture from different countries to be placed in context. Italian work stands apart from the rest of Europe in a number of ways, for although Renaissance art profoundly affected furniture design outside Italy, example was primarily derived from architecture and its embellishments rather than from furniture itself. The strong classicism in Italian work was never fully grasped elsewhere at the same time, and the intellectual rigour which linked decoration and form has no parallels outside Italy until later periods. The evidence of surviving rooms, paintings and contemporary descriptions suggests that furniture in Italy was kept to a minimum, the ideal interior allowing the eye to concentrate upon patterned floors, bold architectural details and the richness of large frescoes or individual paintings in gilded frames. Chests, seat furniture and tables often achieved Roman monumentality, and the Classical X chair, associated with lordship from ancient times and used throughout the Middle Ages, was still much favoured. Intarsia decoration, a form of inlay often incorporating trick perspective, was used on walls and furniture alike, and was to prove an enduring influence on other countries.

Next to Italy in importance stands Spain who, as a strong political force in northern Europe in the 16th century, was in a

143 Armoire showing the influence of the printed designs of du Cerceau and Hugues Sambin, made in the second half of the 16th century, possibly at Dijon.

144 Woodcut by Lorenz Stöer from his *Geometria et Perspectiva*, 1567, showing the type of design which was available to the unknown maker of the *Wrangelschrank* (plate 148).

145 Netherlandish buffet of oak and ebony, *c.* 1640, with bold geometric mouldings derived from the Spanish *Mudéjar* style, separated by pilasters of Mannerist inspiration.

143

144

145

position to disseminate her own, unique vision in three particularly important fields–materials, design and decoration. In the area of materials, the Spaniards developed their medieval tradition **126** of making silver furniture (in 1399 Henry IV of England owned a Spanish table plated with silver), which later suggested the silvered, wooden surfaces so admired in the late 17th century. In design, Spain produced an invention of major significance called the **141,142,146** *vargueño* which, with the various mutations of the buffet or cupboard, was the forerunner of the cabinet-on-stand and the direct ancestor of the scriptor. And in the field of decoration, the **146,149** Spanish *Mudéjar* style gave Europe the arresting geometric outlines which produced such an interesting contrapuntal element in Renaissance linear ornament, adding a staccato rhythm which seems so eminently suited to the thrusting, dynamic spirit of the **131** age. The *Mudéjar* style joined arabesque work as a Spanish contribution to European Renaissance ornament, but whereas arabesques were first assimilated in Italy and transmitted by her, **145** the *Mudéjar* influence entered European consciousness in its pure form, directly from the Spanish example.

In France, the most influential expression of the spirit of the Renaissance was the work which the Italian artists, Rosso Fiorentino and Francesco Primaticcio, carried out at Fontainebleau for Francis I. Here, panelled walls with individual designs of symbols and trophies were surmounted by plaster *amorini* and strapwork framing allegorical frescoes, the whole being held together by ceilings of geometric ornament. The School of Fontainebleau provided long-term guidance for innumerable craftsmen and designers throughout Europe, and the style was freely used by the

French architect, Jacques Androuet du Cerceau, who published his first designs in 1549, after himself visiting Italy. Du Cerceau produced flamboyant and extravagant furniture designs which, **143** in common with examples in other pattern books, tended to be used as a source of ideas, rather than as a blue-print, by other furniture makers. Direct use of his motifs is found in remote Derbyshire in the sea-dog supports of a walnut table at Hardwick Hall, which was recorded there in 1601, and still survives. Burgundian furniture, famous for many notable examples of 15th-century Gothic work, was advertised in the 16th century through the printed designs of Hugues Sambin, whose terms combined **143** easily with du Cerceau's work to form a common source for copyists.

The furniture of the Netherlands was widely known through a publication of ornamental motifs and furniture designs of about 1580 by Hans Vredeman de Vries. His son, Paul Vredeman de **130** Vries, published two books in 1630, reprinting some of his father's designs and adding his own sense of refinement and balance. On the whole, the Netherlands produced and inspired somewhat **128** ponderous furniture, taking ideas from several sources and welding them into a recognisably homogeneous style much favoured in England. This furniture featured carved narrative scenes continuing a strong medieval tradition; bold, geometric work of Moorish derivation, and the use of intarsia borrowed from Italy **145** and skilfully manipulated by craftsmen in Antwerp. The high- **133** backed chairs, upholstered in velvet or leather, with turned supports and low stretchers, were based on Spanish prototypes.

The 16th- and early 17-century furniture of the German states

146 Detail of an early 16th-century Spanish *vargueño*, decorated in the *Mudéjar* style with marquetry of coloured woods and ivory on the drawer fronts and drop-front secretaire.

147 German walnut chest dated 1551 by the Master HS, showing a skilful if conservative design implemented by fine workmanship.

148 German cabinet known as the *Wrangelschrank*, dated 1566, made in Augsburg, and so named because it was taken as war booty by the Swedish commander, Count Wrangel, in the Thirty Years' War.

149 Spanish 16th-century armoire of pine, ornamented with an eye-catching geometric pattern derived from the *Mudéjar* style.

150 Detail of the *Wrangelschrank* showing the right-hand side elevation with its elaborate and intringuing intarsia design.

146

147

148

149

150

151 Armchair and light stand, Italian, made *c.* 1690 by Andrea Brustolon. They form part of a suite of furniture he carved for the Venier family soon after he settled in Venice.

152 Ornately carved and gilded side-table, made in Rome about 1690.

is characterised by an extraordinary facility of technique which proclaims its craftsmen as the masters of Europe. This virtuosity developed naturally from 15th-century work – many examples of 136 armoires carved with splendid, sinuous Gothic details survive to demonstrate this earlier excellence. In the 16th century, a fashion for elaborate carving and intarsia work featuring exaggerated perspectives overshadowed painted decoration, and the first half of the century saw many printed designs for furniture and ornaments, 147 including the conservative designs of the Master HS and the 135 attractive grotesques of Peter Flötner. Whatever the current opinion of the aesthetic merits of the intarsia designs produced in such centres as Augsburg and Nuremburg, it cannot be denied that with such works grand furniture of estate had arrived, setting a pattern 148,150 for development elsewhere. The creation of such breathtaking works as the *'Wrangelschrank'*, leave no doubt as to the ability of furniture to convey ideas of privilege and power as forcefully as tapestries, brocades and silver and gold plate had done in the past.

As the Gothic world gave place to the influence of the Italian Renaissance, more general developments in European furniture began to emerge. Upholstery, though known in the 15th century, became commoner throughout the 16th, though it was still applied to seating with rigid contours. Armoires, storage receptacles from early times, lost none of their old importance, though they were probably less frequently built into fabric, in the medieval manner. The importance of the chest gradually diminished – except for travelling types, where the use of drawers increased – and the medieval tradition of leather and velvet coverings continued. Storage arrangements in all case furniture became more complex, with a multiplicity of drawers, pigeon holes, and cupboards combined with shelves, often given visual interest by the use of receding planes, overhanging cornices, panelled divisions and columnar supports (the use of Classical pilasters at vertical divisions was an easy transition from Gothic arcading). Turned furniture, common in the Middle Ages, continued to be popular and often reached an absurd and uncomfortable exuberance, while solid 15th-century panelled work developed a new insubstantiality.

Oak was the most fashionable and admired wood for furniture throughout the Middle Ages, but during the 16th century walnut gained in importance, and oak gradually declined in favour and eventually lost its metropolitan associations. The use of inlay became widespread and the combination of unusual woods with materials such as ivory, pewter and tortoiseshell introduced new levels of sophistication in furniture. Harmonious effects began to be created by suites of seat furniture, though the wider concept of integrating furniture with architecture lay in the future.

THE BAROQUE AGE

Julia Raynsford

Italy c. 1650-c. 1730

The furniture that stood in the great Italian palaces in the latter half of the 17th century was designed as an integral part of the whole magnificent interior scheme of decoration, and the bold curving forms perfectly reflected the essential character of Italian Baroque architecture and sculpture. Sculpture, particularly, had a vital influence on furniture design, and certain pieces of the period, especially the tables, are entirely sculptural in conception. Typical of the forms of such tables are human figures twisting and turning; *putti* frolicking among abundant foliage; swirling scrolls; eagles; acanthus leaves and ornamental shells, usually supporting heavy marble slabs. Console tables were designed to stand between windows with richly carved looking-glasses hanging above.

One of the most talented of the Italian sculptors who turned his attention to furniture was Andrea Brustolon, who spent much of his career in Venice. Some excellent examples of his work survive there, such as the suite of furniture carved for the Venier family now 152 in the Palazzo Rezzonico, which displays his bold and original approach to furniture design to perfection.

The splendid cabinets made during the Baroque period were probably the pieces upon which the most skilled craftsmen were employed and the rarest and most expensive materials lavished. These cabinets had evolved from the earlier relatively small caskets into grand architectural pieces with cornices and columns, sometimes supported on stands in the form of human figures. They were often used as a vehicle for the display of ivory carvings, exotic woods or panels of *comesso di pietra dura*, the name given to the technique of making patterns or pictorial designs with inlay of semi-precious stones such as lapis lazuli, porphyry, agate and jasper. Florence was the centre of *pietra dura* production, and many 161 remarkable examples of the technique were produced there, primarily for the Medici family.

Smaller pieces of furniture made in Italy at the time were sometimes decorated in imitation of oriental lacquer; this was particularly favoured in Venice, a city that had for centuries been one of Europe's closest points of contact with the East.

151

152

153 Ebony coffer, painted and inlaid, made at the Opificio delle Pietre Dure, Florence.

154 Table top made of *scagliola* in imitation of *pietra dura*. Anglo-Dutch, *c.* 1675.

155, 156 Cabinet-on-stand, Dutch, made *c.* 1690 by the Amsterdam cabinet maker Jan van Mekeren.

157 Cabinet, French, veneered with marquetry of ebony, brass and tortoiseshell. Attributed to André-Charles Boulle.

153

154

155

156

157

The Low Countries c. 1650-c. 1730

The general prosperity in the Low Countries during this period is clearly illustrated by the many surviving 17th-century Dutch genre paintings showing the everyday activities of ordinary people taking place in comfortable and well-furnished houses. It is also reflected in the individual pieces of furniture produced there: cabinet-makers had greatly improved their technical skills, and were now capable of matching veneers and applying marquetry decoration with a remarkable competence. Pierre Golle, who became ébéniste to Louis XIV, and Jan van Mekeren, who had a highly successful workshop in Amsterdam, were both exceptionally skilled marqueteurs and produced cabinets that displayed panels of floral marquetry of extraordinary complexity and brilliance. Antwerp was famous as the centre of production of the distinctive ebony and tortoiseshell cabinets which were made in large numbers and widely exported.

By the end of the 17th century, however, cabinets were becoming much plainer, and Dutch practicality is seen in the popular arched cupboards, solidly built and very functional, made in the Province of Holland. These were usually decorated with applied mouldings of ebony and oak. Another common type of cupboard was that constructed in two stages, standing on round bun feet.

Of quite a different nature to either vivid marquetry or the plain oak furniture were the pieces carved in the fleshy auricular style, which was first employed in Holland by the silversmith Paul van Vianen (see p. 134), and thus described because of its resemblance to the human ear.

Some furniture, such as the tables with bases composed of *putti* and floral swags, sometimes with caryatid legs, showed a more Italianate tradition, but by the end of the 17th century French fashions were the most obvious foreign influence. This became dominant after the Revocation of the Edict of Nantes in 1685, when so many Huguenot craftsmen sought refuge from religious persecution in Holland. Among them was Daniel Marot who, having received his training in Paris, joined the service of William of Orange (with whom he later went to England). His work was influential in spreading knowledge of the French approach to style and ornament and, because he was concerned with every aspect of the decoration of a room, introduced a new concept of unity to interior design. His engraved designs, published in 1702, cover an astonishingly wide range of objects from textiles and garden furniture to sedan chairs.

France c. 1650-c. 1720

For French craftsmen, the first half of the 17th century had been mainly a period of apprenticeship served under foreign artists and craftsmen whose skills in the decorative arts were at that time superior and more sophisticated than their own. Flemish and Italian craftsmen had been drawn to France by powerful and discerning patrons, among them Henry IV, Marie de'Médici, Cardinal Richelieu and the young Louis XIV's ministers, Mazarin and Fouquet.

When Louis XIV assumed power in 1661 he initiated policies that were intended to glorify the monarch and to make France supreme in Europe, not only as a military and political power but also as leader in cultural and artistic fields. This ambition was realised, largely thanks to the energy of his minister of finance, J. B. Colbert, who in 1663 founded the Gobelins workshops. The magnificent furnishings and works of art produced there under the brilliant direction of Charles Le Brun were created solely for the enrichment of the royal palaces, and the indisputable grandeur of Versailles provided a model which kings, princes and the European

158 Side-table, made in the Netherlands *c*. 1670, and carved in the auricular style.

159, 160 Cabinet, French, *c*. 1670, known in France as the 'toilette of Mme de Maintenon'. The panels are of *pietra dura* and the carved figures represent the four seasons.

158

159

160

aristocracy tried to emulate for the next 100 years.

Cabinet makers were by now known as ébénistes, a name that had been in use since the Regency of Marie de'Médici, when Jean Macé had introduced from Holland the art of veneering cheap woods with ebony. The most famous of the ébénistes working for 157 Louis XIV was André-Charles Boulle, who veneered his furniture with a combination of tortoiseshell and brass, sometimes combined with pewter, lapis lazuli or exotic woods. The term 'boulle work' has subsequently been applied to all examples of furniture decorated in this manner, regardless of date or country of origin.

In France, as in other European countries, Eastern art excited great interest, and the foundation of the *Compagnie des Indes* in 1664 gave an added impetus to the taste. Lacquer pieces of every kind were in demand, but lacquer cabinets were particularly popular. Special stands were made to support them, and Oriental pots placed on top and on the stretchers contributed to the exotic effect.

Towards the end of the 17th century, the cabinet began to lose some of its former importance and was being replaced by the chest-of-drawers, which in France was described first as a bureau and later as a commode. The term bureau came to mean a writing table, while a bureau-Mazarin was one which stood on eight legs with a 163 kneehole flanked by drawers. Large centre tables with leather tops were described as bureaux-plats, and were also used for writing 180 purposes. Tables, bureaux and cabinets were all embellished with 178 ormolu, or gilt bronze, mounts (see p. 158) in the form of acanthus leaves, sunbursts, female heads, grotesque masks or figures taken from Classical mythology. The carving on furniture of this period, although of rich and complex character, tends to be more restrained and disciplined than the carving seen on contemporary Italian furniture.

Beds, which were among the most magnificent creations of the period, were the work of the upholsterer rather than the ébéniste, 162 the wooden canopy and framework being entirely hidden by costly hangings, gathered and hung in swags, loops and festoons and enriched with fringes and tassels. Chairs were also upholstered

161 Table top of *pietra dura* made in Florence between 1633 and 1649 for Ferdinando II de'Medici.

161

in a splendid manner, the backs characteristically tall and rectangular, the arms curving and the legs which were joined by stretchers, carved into a baluster or scroll shape.

In the last years of Louis XIV's reign the rigid grandeur of the French Baroque began to be superseded by a lighter and more flexible style. One of the designers responsible for this new direction was Jean Bérain, who developed a decorative style composed of light-hearted motifs such as monkeys and tight-rope walkers combined with arabesques. The style was derived from the Classical 'grotesque', a type of ornament seen on the walls of ancient Roman villas, which had been re-discovered by Italian artists in the 16th century. Bérain's designs are seen in the marquetry of some of the later pieces made by A.-C. Boulle.

During the period known as Régence, from the Regency of Philippe d'Orleans (1715-23), furniture became steadily lighter in form and decoration. This is most clearly demonstrated by the work of the best-known ébéniste of the period, Charles Cressent, 177 whose finely veneered furniture is further distinguished by its

superb ormolu mounts. He chose to cast these himself although this led to constant trouble with the guilds—it was strictly against their rules for one craftsman to practice the skill of another.

England c. 1660-c. 1730

After the gloomy years of the Commonwealth, the restoration of Charles II initiated a feeling of national optimism which was clearly expressed in the art and decoration of the time. In contrast to the plain furniture used by the previous generation, the rich and fashionable now filled their houses with gilded or ebonised furniture, usually highly carved and upholstered with the most expensive velvets, brocades and silks. Colourful lacquer and marquetry cabinets stood against the walls, and elaborate plaster-work and carvings adorned to fireplaces, walls and ceilings. Foreign craftsmen, particularly the Dutch, were responsible for introducing these new opulent schemes of interior decoration, as they were for bringing to England the latest cabinet-making techniques.

55

162 This illustration shows the complexity and richness of late 17th-century bed hangings.

163 Writing-table, French, *c.* 1700, veneered with marquetry of red tortoiseshell and brass. This is known in France as a *bureau Mazarin*.

164 State bed, English, *c.* 1695, made for the first Earl Melville, a minister of William III. It is very close to designs published by Daniel Marot in 1702.

165 Bookcase, English, *c.* 1675. One of a set of bookcases made for Samuel Pepys.

166 Set of silver furniture bearing the cypher of Charles II and presented to the king by the City of London in 1670.

162

163

164

165

166

167 One of the most important of these new techniques from Holland was the art of veneering. A distinctive veneer known as 'oyster-work' became popular, a term describing small round pieces of veneer that display their annual ring marks, obtained by cutting across the smaller branches of walnut or laburnum trees. Oyster veneers were often used in conjunction with marquetry, which was also introduced into England at this time, primarily from Holland, and a number of different woods, such as box, holly, tulip and sycamore were used in bold floral designs. A wide range of furniture including tables, longcase clocks, boxes and particularly cabinets-on-stands, was decorated in this way.

Towards the end of the 17th century, seaweed or endive marquetry, consisting of finely cut, sinuous scrolls and arabesques, became fashionable, but in the first decade of the following century the taste for marquetry began to wane, and craftsmen preferred to use plain walnut veneers carefully cut and matched to gain maximum effect from the natural figure of the wood.

Lacquer cabinets were very highly prized, indeed such was the demand for lacquer at this period that the East India Company's trade could not possibly satisfy the market. It was impossible to produce real lacquer in Europe because the essential ingredient, the sap of the shrubby tree the *Rhus vericifera*, was not obtainable in the West and could not survive the long voyage to Europe. It thus became necessary to find a substitute, which would achieve the same exotic effect, but which could be produced in England.

In 1688 John Stalker and George Parker published *A Treatise on Japanning . . . and Varnishing . . .*, in which they set out to describe all that the potential japanner should know about the art, both 170 supplying recipes for mixing the necessary varnishes and providing suitable Chinoiserie designs.

Common during this period were sets of furniture consisting of a mirror and rectangular table flanked by two candlestands. Such sets were frequently decorated with marquetry or plain veneer, but sometimes they were covered with plates of heavily embossed silver. Unfortunately little of this lavish silver furniture has 166 survived, as in times of economic crisis it was all too often fated for the melting pot.

Sometimes a rich effect was obtained by applying silver plaques to ebony furniture. A table decorated in this way can be seen at Ham House in London, which received a complete face-lift in the 1670s under the auspices of the Duchess of Lauderdale. Fortunately much of the original furniture and textiles survive, and the importance attached to textiles at this time is clearly illustrated by chairs magnificently upholstered with brilliant damasks, silks and velvets, and hung with fringes and tassels.

Less grand, but nevertheless popular with all classes of society, were cane chairs. These were made in vast numbers, and no doubt 169 their popularity was to some extent due to the demand for decorative but relatively cheap furniture after the Great Fire of London in 1666. The early examples of the 1660s had low backs and simple

167 Table, English, *c.* 1675. The oyster veneer is of walnut, and surrounds panels of marquetry of various woods.

168 Carving of limewood in the form of a cravat by Grinling Gibbons, late 17th century. It belonged to the diarist Horace Walpole.

169 Cane chair, English, *c.* 1670. These were very popular between about 1660 and 1690.

170 Cabinet-on-stand, English, *c.* 1675. The cabinet is japanned in imitation of Oriental lacquer; the stand is carved and silvered.

171 One of a pair of walnut chairs, English, *c.* 1725. A shell motif is to be seen on the back-rail and on the knees of the front legs, which terminate in claw and ball feet.

167

168

169

170

171

twist-turned supports, but the backs gradually became taller, and the carved stretchers and frames more elaborate.

The florid carving to be seen on so much English furniture of this period was strongly influenced by the contemporary Dutch school, and scrolls, foliage and pot-bellied *putti* are among the most familiar motifs. The outstanding carver of the time was Grinling Gibbons, who produced naturalistic ornaments designed to hang in panelled rooms, and composed of fruit, flowers, musical instruments and dead game in limewood or pear-wood.

A completely new piece of furniture which appeared in the latter half of the 17th century was the glazed bookcase. Samuel Pepys, troubled by his books that were 'growing numerous and lying one upon another' on his chairs, commissioned 'Simpson the Joiner' to make a series of glazed bookcases in 1666. These, now in the Library of Magdalene College, Cambridge, constitute the earliest known English examples. It is interesting that this request was made of a joiner, which was unusual because by this date the functions of the joiner and cabinet maker had diverged, the joiner being more frequently employed on the interior fittings of a house, while the making of fine case furniture was reserved for the cabinet maker.

The influence of continental craftsmen was greatly strengthened after the Revocation of the Edict of Nantes in 1685 (which meant that Huguenots could no longer live in France without fear of persecution) and the accession of 'Dutch' William to the English

throne in 1689. The influence of the Huguenots was particularly valuable, as many of them were exceptional craftsmen who had received their training in the Gobelins workshops; the designs of Daniel Marot, the Huguenot designer who came to England in the wake of William III, made a particularly deep impact on English furniture produced at the turn of the 17th century. The English state beds influenced by his designs – the Melville bed in the Victoria and Albert Museum is a fine example – were among the most splendid creations of the period. The headboards were carved into complex Baroque designs and covered with damask or silk, while the sumptuous hangings, which fell into heavy loops and swags, were enriched with fringes and tassels. Chairs lined up against the walls and upholstered *en suite* with the bed contributed to the opulence of the bedroom which, in the most ambitious houses, such as Dyrham and Belvoir, formed the climax to a series of superb state rooms intended to reflect the rich and splendid lives of their owners and occupants.

By the early years of the 18th century English craftsmen had largely assimilated the new skills and styles introduced from Europe and were producing furniture of high quality, which was for the most part veneered with walnut. Cabriole legs were now commonly to be seen on tables and chairs, and stretchers became redundant. Early examples of the cabriole leg terminated in the scroll or hoof, but these were replaced by the club foot and the claw and ball. This simple but pleasingly designed furniture was to exert a con-

172 Chest, English, *c.* 1720, a good example of Palladian furniture. Carved and gilded gesso on wood.

173 Hadley chest, American, *c.* 1710. The flat carving is characteristic of these chests, which were made primarily in the Massachusetts towns of Hadley and Hatfield.

174 Chair, Portuguese, *c.* 1680. The back and seat are made of embossed and incised leather.

175 Butterfly table, American, first quarter of the 18th century. This piece is of maple, and was made in New England.

176 Highboy, American (Massachusetts), *c.* 1730. Made of white walnut, or butternut, with inlaid decoration of birch and sycamore.

siderable influence on that made in many other countries.

172 In striking contrast to the relatively plain walnut furniture were the pieces made to the designs of architects working within the Palladian school. They emerged as a group in the 1720s under the leadership of Lord Burlington, who had been so impressed by the buildings of the Italian Renaissance architect, Andrea Palladio, that he determined to revive the Classical principles of architecture that had first been expressed in England a century earlier by Inigo Jones. Obviously the great country houses built by the Palladians, such as William Kent's Holkham, had to be suitably furnished, but here architects were confronted with a problem, for there was no original Classical furniture on which they could base their designs. Moreover the plain 16th-century Italian furniture still to be seen in Palladian villas was hardly appropriate to the splendid English Palladian interiors with their coffered ceilings, columns and pediments. Consequently it was to contemporary Italian furniture that the Palladians were forced to turn for inspiration, in spite of their protestations against the iniquities of the Baroque style. Tables and case furniture were usually gilded and formed of consoles, heavy scrolls, cornices and columns, embellished with ornament taken from the Classical repertoire, including key patterns, female masks and shells. The design of candlestands and furniture clearly showed the influence of Daniel Marot. Even if their sources were not as pure as they would have wished, the Palladian architects succeeded in creating furniture that was entirely suited to the opulent Baroque interiors which present such a remarkable contrast to the strictly Classical exteriors.

Germany c. 1650-c. 1730

The Thirty Years War had a stulifying effect on artistic output in Germany, but by 1648 it had at last been brought to an end, and the latter half of the 17th century proved a time of exceptional creativity. In Southern Germany, the Baroque style, introduced from northern Italy, made a deep impact on architecture and the decorative arts, being particularly influential in Munich, capital city of Bavaria, where palaces were furnished with cabinets, tables and chairs which were designed to complement the profusion of plasterwork, *boiseries* and painted decoration of the rooms in which they stood. Augsburg and Nuremberg maintained the reputation they had established early in the century for the production of magnificent pieces involving craftsmen skilled in many different media.

As in the rest of Europe, both Oriental and imitation lacquer were much in demand, and Gerard Dagly, appointed Director of Ornament to Wilhelm, Elector of Brandenberg, developed a particularly beautiful style of japanning, frequently using a white ground, that earned him an international reputation. Fine inlay decoration had for long been a speciality of German craftsmen, and in Eger, a small town in Bohemia, a method was developed of decorating cabinets and boxes with panels of inlay carved in relief, usually depicting religious or mythological subjects. Carved furniture, for instance the massive two-doored cupboards which generally stood in the hall, displayed the influence of the Dutch auricular style, which was to some extent popularised by the designs of Friedrich Unteutsch, who handled this strange fleshy ornament with considerable skill.

Germany, like most of Europe, fell under the sway of French influence at the end of the 17th century, and perhaps the most skilled of a number of German cabinet makers working in the French manner was H. D. Sommer. At his workshops in Kunzelsau, Swabia, Sommer produced furniture decorated with marquetry of mother-of-pearl, horn and pewter that can be compared not unfavourably with the work of A.-C. Boulle.

The Baroque style was taken to its greatest extremes in the

177 Commode, French, attributed to Charles Cressent, and perhaps
after a design by Nicolas Pineau.

178 Carved and gilt table in the style of Louis XIV, made *c.* 1680, and
designed to harmonise with the panelling of the room in which it stood.

177

178

179 Cabinet-on-stand, Spanish, 17th century, known in Spain as a *vargueño*. The interior contains a number of small drawers.

179

German states, and this is demonstrated by many of the designs published by Paul Decker and J. J. Schubler in Augsburg and Nuremberg between 1711 and 1724, which display astonishing imagination and elaboration. Thus it is perhaps not surprising to find that in Germany the Baroque was slower to give way to the Rococo than in most other parts of Europe.

Spain and Portugal c. 1650-c. 1730
Although Spain was not the great and wealthy power that she had been a century earlier, she nevertheless continued to provide a flourishing market for fine and expensive furniture. One notable characteristic of Spanish furniture of the period is the elaborate turned decoration seen, for instance, on beds, chairs and on the
179 stands of *vargueños*. The last-mentioned is the name given to a distinctive type of writing cabinet consisting of a chest with a falling front which, when open, reveals a set of drawers. Another type of cabinet without the falling front was the *papeleira*, which was veneered with ebony, ivory and tortoiseshell and usually surmounted by a pierced gallery. Chairs were produced in a variety of designs and, from the middle of the century, a number display marked French influence. Another type, introduced from Portugal, had a tall, shaped back, brass finials and a wide scrolling stretcher.

In 1640 Portugal regained her independence from Spain, and her new nationalism is clearly reflected in the highly original furniture made during this time, much of which made use of rare woods such as jacaranda and pausanto, imported from Brazil. A common type of Portuguese chair was that designed with arched back, turned supports and ball feet and covered with the heavily embossed
174 leather for which the country is famous. The Portuguese *contador*, a cabinet similar to the *papeleira*, was often decorated with geo-

metrically shaped panels that indicate Dutch influence. Some splendid lacquer pieces of the period also survive, a result of Portugal's long-established trade with the East.

America c. 1650-c. 1750
Early American furniture was above all practical, and in form and decoration was closely based on English pieces produced half a century earlier. Indeed, until the end of the 18th century, America continued to lag behind the latest English fashions by at least several decades.

By the 1650s Europeans had settled along most of the east coast of America, but nearly all of the surviving furniture made at this date comes from Massachusetts and Connecticut. Pieces such as cupboards, writing boxes and chests were simply made, but often vigorously carved with strapwork and foliated scrolls. Such motifs are of obvious Anglo-Dutch origin, but the oddly flat way in which the ornament was treated is entirely American.

The chest, which could fulfil such a variety of functions, was perhaps the most common 17th-century piece, and a number of distinctive types were produced. The Hadley chest, named after a 173 town in Massachusetts, was raised on short legs with one or two drawers forming the lower section, and was carved in low relief with flowers and foliage, and painted black, red, brown or green. Among those associated with its production are Samuel Belding, John Hawkes, John Allis and his son Ichabod. The Hartford chest was of a similar type, but characteristically decorated with a tulip and sunflower motif, oval bosses and applied spindles. From such pieces developed the chest-of-drawers; an early example dated 1678 displays both painted and turned decoration.

Turning is frequently to be seen on 17th-century American furniture, and turned spindles are the most notable decorative feature of the rush-seated Brewster and Carver chairs, thus named after two leaders of the early Massachusetts settlers. Also popular were wainscot chairs, clearly derived from English examples made in the early part of the century. Joined stools and 'stretcher' tables were of simple rectangular form with turned supports and thick stretchers. A few beds with high posts and canopies were produced, but these must have been in the nature of status symbols, for in general beds were very plain. Court cupboards and presses were considered to be the grandest and most important pieces, and were ornamented with geometric panels and the usual spindles.

In the last decade of the 17th century some of the new cabinet-making techniques practised in England 20 years earlier began to reach America, and high-quality furniture began to be made in Philadelphia, Newport, New York and Charleston as well as Boston.

The highboy—a 19th-century term—is one of the most impressive 176 pieces produced during these years, and consists of a veneered chest supported on a stand. This contains drawers flanking a central opening, and has turned legs joined by curving stretchers. The term lowboy indicates a similar stand, but one used as a dressing-table. Another piece of storage furniture was a large two-doored cupboard known as a *kas*, a legacy of the Dutch immigrants, based on 17th-century Netherlands prototypes. The American version was generally painted with *grisaille* still-life paintings.

At the turn of the 17th century, a number of new types of chair appeared, the most splendid of these being an upholstered armchair with a high back and 'wings'. Bannister-back chairs were less elaborate versions of the English cane-seats, and ladderback chairs designed with horizontal splats were also popular. John Gaines, one of the few furniture makers whose name has survived from this period, was responsible for some fine chairs with vase-shaped splats.

Tables were also much more varied by the early 18th century, and a distinctive American variation on the gateleg theme was the so-called butterfly table, oval in shape, with two folding wings and 175 standing on exaggerated splayed legs.

The best English furniture was nearly all made in London, but America had a number of equally important cabinet-making centres, with the result that 18th-century American furniture displays marked regional characteristics. Furthermore, certain

180 Writing-table, French, *c.* 1740, known in France as a *bureau-plat.* The ormolu mounts are in the fully developed Rococo style.

181 Settee, German, *c.* 1755, made by the Spindler brothers for the Neues Schloss in Bayreuth.

timbers became associated with certain areas, for instance, maple was used extensively in New England and Pennsylvania, while cherry was popular in Connecticut and New York. Black walnut was employed all along the eastern seaboard, but white walnut (butternut) was much rarer and to be seen mainly in country pieces.

Rich dark mahogany is one of the distinguishing features of furniture made in Newport, Rhode Island, where the Goddard/Townsend family of cabinet makers earned a particularly high reputation. In Boston, and in Massachusetts generally, furniture was notable for its fine lines and proportion, but in New York,

pieces tended to be squarer and sturdier in appearance in spite of the fact that the traditional Dutch influence became gradually less obvious. Philadelphia, which had developed into a city of great wealth, was possibly the most important cabinet-making centre in America.

Although English styles remained the prime source of inspiration for American cabinet makers, a more native tradition can often be seen in the country pieces. For instance, windsor chairs, which became popular in the middle of the 18th century, were made to a variety of original designs, among them being the hoop-back, fan-back and comb-back.

THE ROCOCO AGE

Julia Raynsford

France c. 1730–c. 1760

During the reign of Louis XIV the grand French Baroque style had begun to give way to a lighter and more flexible approach, and with the reign of Louis XV came the full flowering of the Rococo, characterised by flowing curves, abutting C-scrolls, undisciplined foliage, human masks, asymmetrical cartouches, animals and birds, to name but a few motifs in the new decorative repertoire. Two of the earliest and most successful exponents of the style were the designers Nicolas Pineau and Juste-Aurèle Meissonier.

Louis XV's personal preference for living in the intimate surroundings of the *petits appartements* in Versailles as opposed to the great rooms of state did much to encourage the development of more comfortable and informal furniture. A new departure, for instance, was the *bergère,* a deep wide armchair fully upholstered and with a thick cushion, and a relaxion of strict etiquette is clearly indicated by some of the names given to seat furniture, such as the *canapé à confidante* (a type of settee with a corner seat at each end) or the *tête à tête* (a seat designed for two people).

Chairs were often designed to stand in a specific position within a room so that the shape of their backs and their carved decoration could reflect that of the panelling behind. Beds were made to a number of different designs, among them the traditional *lit à la française* crowned with a canopy, and the more secluded *lit à la polonaise,* which was contained in its own special alcove. Tables were as varied in design as the seat furniture, each one being made for a special purpose, and they were consequently produced in an astonishing range of shapes and sizes. An innovation of the period was the *encoignure,* or corner cupboard, which was usually surmounted with shelves, although these rarely appear to have survived.

188 Oriental lacquer continued to be immensely popular throughout the Rococo period. The most successful imitation lacquer was first patented in 1730 by the Martin brothers, and subsequently

became known as *vernis martin.* The varnish could be produced in many different colours, and as well as being used to decorate furniture, was often applied to coaches and sedan-chairs.

Perhaps the most familiar piece of Rococo furniture is the *bombé* commode, sometimes made of lacquer but more often veneered in a rich variety of woods in floral and geometric marquetry and overlaid with sinuous ormolu mounts. The consistently high quality of the ormolu decoration (see p. 158) is one of the distinctive features of French furniture, and the most accomplished exponent of the art in the Rococo period was Jacques Caffieri, who frequently worked with A. R. Gaudreau, one of the outstanding ébénistes active during these years. But there was a host of distinguished ébénistes working in the middle years of the century, among them J. F. Oeben, his brother-in-law, Roger Vandercruse (also called Lacroix), Bernard van Risamburgh (B.V.R.B.) and Jacques Dubois. Fortunately it is possible to attribute many pieces of French furniture to their makers with some degree of certainty, because of the insistence of the guilds after 1741 that the ébénistes stamp their work.

England c. 1730–c. 1760

The Rococo style, with its emphasis on natural form and asymmetry, could not have been more contrary to the Palladian ideal. Yet as the style became more widely known and appreciated in England, many Palladians began to let the new idiom creep into their predominately Classical designs. Classicism was never entirely abandoned even when the Rococo reached the height of its popularity; often the basic form of a piece of furniture remained essentially Classical, the only obviously Rococo element being the carved decoration. Familiar Classical motifs such as the acanthus leaf and the shell still frequently appeared, but tended to be used in a more elastic and flexible manner.

From about 1730 mahogany was the timber chiefly used in

180

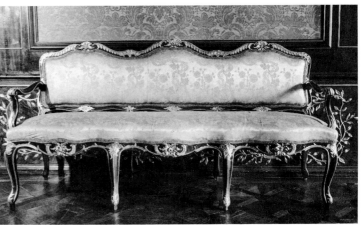

181

182 Bedstead, English, *c.* 1755, from the Fourth Duke of Beaufort's 'Chinese bedroom' at Badminton House, Gloucestershire.

183 Armchair, English, *c.* 1760, made after a design by Matthew Lock for the portrait painter Richard Cosway.

184 Cabinet-on-stand in the 'Gothick' style. English, *c.* 1760.

185 Commode, German, *c.* 1765, made by Johann Melchior Kambli in Potsdam. Kambli worked as a sculptor and cabinet maker at the court of Frederick the Great in Berlin.

186 Combined toilet- and writing-table, French, *c.* 1750, known in France as a *toilette à transformations*. Attributed to J. F. Oeben, it is fitted with elaborate mechanical devices.

187 Japanned writing-cabinet, German, *c.* 1735, made by Martin Schnell in Dresden.

182

183

184

185

186

187

188 Commode, French, made by N. J. Marchand. The central lacquer
panel is framed by Rococo ormolu mounts.

188

cabinet-making. Apart from its strength, rich dark colour and
greater immunity to woodworm, it was found to shrink and warp
less than other woods. The so-called Spanish mahogany from San
Domingo, Cuba and Jamaica was the first to be imported to England,
but later Honduras or 'Baywood' mahogany from Central America,
with its lighter, softer colour, was found to be particularly suitable
for veneering curved surfaces.

Matthew Lock, a carver and designer, was perhaps the first
183 English craftsman to grasp fully the essence of the Rococo. His
designs for mirrors and tables published in the 1740s show how
well he could handle the style, while the surviving pieces carved
by him illustrate that he could also successfully translate his
designs into furniture.

The most famous English cabinet maker of the mid-18th century
202 is undoubtedly Thomas Chippendale. While the furniture made
in his workshop was certainly among the very best to be produced
at that time, his fame rests largely on a book of furniture designs
published in 1754 (later editions 1755 and 1762) called the Gentleman and Cabinet-maker's Director. The book, full of new and
imaginative ideas, was important in disseminating the Rococo style
in England, for while other Rococo designs had appeared in earlier
pattern books, no one had yet produced such an original and
comprehensive collection of designs as those included in the
Director. It contains designs for all conceivable types of furniture
from 'Lanthorns for Halls or Staircases', 'Library Tables' and
'French commodes' to 'Picture frames', 'Bed Pillars' and 'Chamber

Organs'. Chippendale was an astute business man and he made
certain that copies went to the right people, in other words
potential patrons, architects and his fellow cabinet makers.
Because the designs in the Director received such wide circulation
and have been so often copied, Chippendale's name has been
attached erroneously to a vast number of pieces, when in fact the
amount of furniture known to have come out of his workshop is
relatively small.

It was not long before other publications modelled on the
Director and produced by cabinet makers and designers began to
appear. Among these were the firm of Ince & Mayhew, Thomas
Johnson and Matthew Darly, and numbered among the leading
cabinet makers who had their workshops in St Martin's Lane were
Vile & Cobb (Vile was cabinet maker to King George III), William
Hallet, Samuel Normon and Thomas Chippendale. St Martin's
Lane was also the street in which Slaughter's Coffee House was
situated, the meeting place of many of the most enthusiastic
supporters and exponents of the Rococo style.

The French Taste, however, was only one aspect of furniture
design in the middle years of the 18th century, for these years also
marked a new upsurge of interest in the East, and Chinoiserie, the
name given to the European imitation of Oriental art, was much in
evidence. Beds and cabinets were sometimes made with pagoda 182
tops, tables embellished with Chinese fretwork and chairs given
Chinese legs and splats, while many pieces were japanned in a
variety of colours. Chippendale produced some fine japanned

189 Commode, German, made in 1761 by Johann Adam Pilcher of Munich for the Kurfurstenzimmer in the Residenz.

190 Cabinet, German, c. 1750, decorated with intarsia panels carved in relief. This technique was developed in Eger, a town in Bohemia.

191 The queen's dressing room in the Palazzo Reale, Turin, with intarsia furniture by Pietro Pifetti.

189

190

191

furniture for Badminton House, and a bed was made for the same house to one of his designs for a 'Chinese' bed with pagoda canopy, red dragons and latticework headboard. Latticework was applied to all kinds of furniture—in the splats of chairs, around table tops and on doors of cabinets. Thomas Johnson, one of the most imaginative designers and carvers of the period, often included riotous collections of Chinoiserie motifs in such pieces as mirror frames and candlestands.

While the Chinoiserie taste was international, the mid-18th-century 'Gothick' style was peculiar to England for, in spite of the Renaissance, medieval traditions had never been entirely forgotten by English designers. Chippendale produced some designs for 'Gothick' furniture, but in these Gothic ornament is usually applied to well-established 18th-century forms, such as the library desk or canopied bed which might equally well have been decorated with Rococo, Classical or Chinoiserie ornament. Although at first sight it would seem that these styles have little in common, it is not rare to see all the traditions mingled together on one piece of furniture.

Italy c. 1730–c. 1770

The marked regional differences so obvious in 18th-century Italian furniture are a reminder that the peninsula was at that time made up of independent states. The Rococo was most immediately apparent in the north, particularly in Turin, where rooms of buildings such as the Palazzo Reale and the Castello di Stupinigi

are among the most remarkable essays in the Rococo style to be found anywhere. The architect Juvarra and the cabinet maker Pietro Pifetti collaborated to produce for these interiors furniture of extraordinary complexity, much of it decorated with intricate marquetry and overlaid with ormolu.

In Venice many pieces were lacquered, and a cheap method called *lacca contrafatta* was devised to give an impression of lacquer decoration. This process entailed varnishing painted furniture which had been decorated with specially printed coloured paper cut-outs of Chinoiserie design. The Rococo curves of chairs and commodes made in Venice were sometimes exaggerated to the point of unintentional caracature, but although such pieces may have lacked sophistication and technical skill, these faults were amply compensated for by their colourful exuberance. The traditional sculptural influence on furniture continued to be upheld, and some splendid pieces were designed by the Venetian sculptor Antonio Corradini, which can be seen in the Palazzo Rezzonico in Venice.

In Rome it was less easy to distinguish between the Baroque and Rococo, for here the prime concern of the nobility was with dignity and ceremony, and the massive sculptural furniture on display in the state rooms since the 17th century remained little changed. The influence of the Rococo is much more evident in the furniture made for the smaller living rooms of palaces and for the house of the prosperous bourgeoisie.

Pietra dura continued to be produced in Florence, but was

192 Commode, Italian, c. 1760. Painted in green with design picked out in gold.

193 One of a pair of chairs attributed to the Venetian sculptor and furniture maker A. Corradini.

194 Part of a set of seat furniture designed by M. Gasparini about 1770 for the Royal Palace in Madrid, where it still stands.

192

193

194

154 prohibitively expensive. *Scagliola,* an imitation marble made of a composition of plaster and glue to which ground marble was added, was much less costly and, as a result of improved methods of painting the material, developed by Enrico Hugford, *scagliola* panels and table tops of great beauty were produced. From this time *scagliola* became more widely appreciated, spreading to other countries–the many fine examples still to be seen in the great English country houses testify to its popularity there.

In general, foreign influences were reflected in much of the seat furniture made all over the Italian peninsula, but a purely Italian invention was the exceptionally long sofa designed for ballrooms known as a *portegha.* Dutch and English influences are also evident on some of the case furniture, perhaps most clearly seen in the bureau cabinet.

Germany c. 1730-c. 1760
At this time Germany was divided into many separate courts, each ruled by Electors, Bishops and Princes, and thus it is hardly surprising that the contemporary furniture should display a remarkable diversity both in style and decoration. In the great palaces, such as Pommersfelden, the Zwinger, Wurzburg and Nymphenburg, furniture frequently based on French prototypes but of unmistakable German character was made to impress and astound all who beheld it. In the north, however, furniture tended to be of a more practical and less flamboyant nature, suited to the wealthy bourgeois patrons for whom it was made, and Dutch and

English influences are to be seen.

During the 1740s, Frederick the Great, King of Prussia, set about redecorating his palaces of Charlottenberg, Potsdam and Sanssouci, placing G. W. Knoblesdorf in charge of the operation. Knoblesdorf, who proved an able administrator, gathered together a talented team of craftsmen, among them J. A. Nahl, whose seat furniture with its bold curving lines and vigorous carving represents some of the best of the early German Rococo. Nahl was followed at the post of *Directeur des Ornements* by a succession of distinguished designers and craftsmen; the Hoppenhaupt brothers, the Swiss J. M. Kambli (particularly remembered for the superb ormolu 185 mounts that embellish his furniture) and the Spindler brothers, 181 who had been previously established in Bayreuth, and whose furniture was both beautifully designed and superbly executed.

The furniture of Saxony shows marked French influence, especially in the commodes which, although of rectangular form at the beginning of the 18th century, had by the 1740s adopted undulating curves. An exception to the predominantly French influence were the chairs based on English models made by the court chairmaker, J. P. Schotte. English originals also provided the basis for the design of Dresden cabinets. Martin Schnell, a pupil of the famous 187 japanner Gerard Dagly, made a number of these cabinets, which were formed of two stages with a writing bureau below and two doors with panels of mirror glass above.

Mainz was famous for the production of cupboards and writing-cabinets of curving form, decorated with elaborate marquetry

195 Philadelphia highboy of mahogany, *c.* 1765-67.

196 Chair, Portuguese, *c.* 1740. Although based on English prototypes, the carving and flamboyant curves are typically Portuguese.

197 Chair, American, made in Philadelphia by William Savery, *c.* 1765.

198 Chest-of-drawers, Danish, *c.* 1730. Although typically Danish in form, the painted decoration on this piece is of unusually high quality.

195

196   197

198

and carved volutes, while not far away in Aachen and Cologne, sensitively carved oak furniture was produced which is close to French examples.

In Franconia the most courtly furniture was made for the great Residenz in Wurzburg, where initially French craftsmen were employed. They were later replaced by distinguished native cabinet makers, among them K. M. Mattern and J. G. Nestfell, both high skilled marqueteurs. The Wurzburg court sculptor Johann Wolfgang der Auvera was also involved in furniture design and was responsible for some excellent Rococo console-tables. Another court close to Wurzburg was established at Bayreuth, where in the Schloss Fantasie the Spindler brothers produced a remarkable marquetry room. Ansbach and Bamberg were two other notable Franconian centres of furniture making.

In Munich, capital of Bavaria, the Rococo found two of its fullest and most successful expressions in the decoration of the Residenz and in the Palace of Nymphenburg. Here François Cuvilliés and Joseph Effner, both of whom had received their training in Paris, were responsible for much of the daring, sophisticated, and often wildly asymmetrical, interior decoration. The tradition they established was continued into the 1760s by the carvers J. M. **189** Schmidt and J. A. Pilcher.

Other European countries c. 1730-c. 1775
By contemporary European standards, much of the furniture produced in Spain during these years was old fashioned, the Rococo being in many cases merely grafted on to traditional forms.

Chairs, for instance, continued to be covered in leather, although the stamped design itself was now likely to be of French origin. Cabriole legs were joined by outmoded stretchers, and chair backs were made too tall for the latest fashion. The strongest foreign influence came from England rather than France, and furniture **196** clearly derived from English early 18th-century pieces was to some extent brought up to date with Rococo embellishments.

The Rococo was perhaps most successfully expressed in the carved and gilded looking-glasses and the console-tables made to stand below them. Mirrors were a notable feature of the Spanish interior, indeed in 1736 Philip V founded a royal factory at San Ildefonso especially for their manufacture. More extensive royal workshops, similar in principle to the Gobelins, were later established by Charles III, and in 1768 they were placed under the direction of a Neopolitan, Matteo Gasparini, whose influence led to **194** the production of more ambitious furniture.

Portuguese furniture makers of this period also mainly drew their inspiration from English sources. The good relations between the two countries had been firmly established by the Treaty of Methuen in 1703, and a sizeable English colony had grown up in Portugal in connection with the wine trade. French and Dutch influence is also apparent on many tables and chairs and in the case furniture, but beds, with their highly carved head-boards and bold cabriole legs, remained distinctly Portuguese in character.

In the 17th century the Dutch cabinet makers had made an appreciable contribution to the evolution of English and French furniture, but in the following century this position was reversed,

199 Blockfront desk, American, *c.* 1770, made by John Goddard of Newport, Rhode Island.

indeed, by the mid-18th century the guilds required cabinet makers working in the Hague to produce an 'English cabinet' for their masterpiece. But although chairs with cabriole legs and pierced splats, bureau cabinets with glass panelled doors, and slender tea-tables are of a strongly English character, French influence is discernible in *bombé* commodes with floral marquetry, and carved oak cupboards from Liège are closely related to French examples.

Scandinavian furniture of the 18th century is largely an amalgam **198** of English and Dutch styles, although French influence was predominant in the higher-quality court furniture. Early 18th-century forms would often be 'modernised' with a fancy piece of Rococo carving, for instance a number of chairs made in Norway and Denmark, based on English prototypes of about 1730, have curious lopsided Rococo ornaments. In these countries German styles generally remained the strongest influence; but in Sweden the impact of the French Rococo was far more significant, and Swedish architects and craftsmen were sometimes sent to Paris to complete their training.

America c. 1750-c. 1790
In spite of the political differences between England and her American colonies which were to culminate in the Declaration of Independence in 1776, English pattern-books continued to be in demand in America throughout the 18th century. Of all the design books to reach America, Chippendale's *Gentleman and Cabinet-maker's Director* was undoubtedly the most influential, and the splats of chair backs were now invariably pierced with designs based on those published in the book.

Philadelphia continued to flourish, and a galaxy of talented furniture makers emerged there, among whom were Thomas **197** Affleck, Benjamin Randolph, William Savery, Jonathan Gostelow and Jonathan Shoemaker. The most splendid piece produced in **195** Philadelphia at this time was the highboy, standing about 8 feet (2.43 metres) high, and built of richly coloured mahogany with bold scrolling swan-necked pediments.

Massachusetts furniture was still characterised by its delicate and slender proportions. Indeed, the cabriole legs of chairs tended to be so refined that stretchers were retained in order to provide additional structural strength, although elsewhere in America they were by this time unfashionable.

Block-front cabinets and desks were made in a number of towns, but some of the best examples were of Newport origin and made **199** by the Townsend/Goddard family. These pieces, generally made of solid wood, have alternate concave and convex sections and display elaborately carved motifs. Block fronts were also produced in Connecticut, but tended to be less sophisticated than those made in Newport, and characteristically have fluted and chamfered corners and carved sunbursts.

In New York a hint of the Rococo can be seen in the serpentine lines of tables and in the design of chair splats, but in general it made little impact on the cabinet makers, who continued to produce furniture of somewhat heavy and square proportions.

In Charleston high-quality furniture was produced on a large

199

scale. Probably the most distinguished cabinet maker working there during this period was Thomas Elfe, who had an extensive workshop. Much of his furniture was ornamented with applied fretwork.

Outside the mainstream of English-based fashions was the furniture made by German-Swiss immigrants, who had settled in Pennsylvania late in the 17th century. Known as Pennsylvania Dutch, these pieces are notable for their lively and colourful decoration. Christian Selzer of Jonestown, Dauphin County, was responsible for a number of long rectangular chests painted with tulips, hearts and horsemen and such severely moralistic mottoes as 'Better be Dead than Faithless'.

NEO-CLASSICISM
Julia Raynsford

France c. 1760-c. 1825
In the course of the 1750s it became clear that, in academic circles at least, a strong reaction to the Rococo was developing. A number of artists and scholars, among them Lalive de Jully, the engraver Nicholas Cochin and the Comte de Caylus urged the abandonment of Rococo superficiality and the adoption of Classical ideals. Interest

in antiquity had been greatly stimulated by the excavations of the recently discovered cities of Pompei and Herculaneum and, although Louis XV himself continued to patronise Rococo artists, the Neo-classical movement was fully established by the end of his reign in 1774.

The decade from 1760 to 1770 was a period of transition between

200 Writing-bureau (secretaire), French, *c.* 1780, made by J. H. Riesener. The high quality of the marquetry is typical of Riesener's work.

201 Table, French, *c.* 1785, with ormolu mounts in the manner of Pierre Gouthière. Attributed to Adam Weisweiler.

202 Beechwood armchair with gilt gesso carved in relief with Neo-classical motifs. English, 1764. From a set of eight armchairs and four sofas made by Chippendale to designs by Robert Adam.

203 Pier-table designed by Thomas Hope for the Flaxman room at his house in Duchess Street. English, about 1805.

204 *Causeuse* (small settee), French, with a beech frame carved with Neo-classical motifs, and upholstered with Beauvais tapestry. Late 18th century, made by Georges Jacob.

200

201

202

203

204

Rococo and Neo-classical taste, during which time furniture forms became more rectilinear while decorative motifs were increasingly taken from the Classical repertoire. The outstanding *ébéniste* active in the middle of the century was J. F. Oeben, whose furniture is renowned for the excellence of its marquetry. Oeben made great use of geometrical patterns such as cubes and lozenges which were used in conjunction with floral marquetry, but in the latter part of his career he developed a more pictorial style. The fashion for pictorial marquetry was greatly encouraged by the number of German craftsmen, highly skilled marqueteurs, established in Paris at this time. David Roentgen, in particular, achieved astonishing results in this medium, and introduced a more fluid and painterly style of marquetry decoration.

Oeben's furniture is also distinguished by complex mechanical devices which operate secret drawers and compartments, enabling a single piece of furniture to combine several functions. The second half of the 18th century saw the development of many new types of multi-purpose furniture, such as the *bonheur-du-jour*, which combined a dressing- and writing-table, and the *table à pupitre*, which served both as work table and reading desk.

After Oeben's death in 1763 his workshop was taken over by J. H. Riesener, probably the most famous of all the ébénistes working in the latter half of the century. His early pieces reflect Oeben's pictorial style, but by about 1775 his marquetry designs became more geometric and were often composed of a lozenge or trellis pattern, while in the 1780s he was using less marquetry, more often decorating his furniture with a plain mahogany veneer in

the English manner. Riesener was a prolific maker, and in the course of his career produced the whole range of contemporary furniture, including cabinets and commodes with straight sides and projecting central sections, writing tables, jewel boxes and roll-top desks. The ormolu mounts which embellish his pieces are of exceptional quality; and it has been suggested that they are the work of Pierre Gouthière, who was one of the foremost *fondeurs-ciseleurs* (workers of ormolu and bronze) of this period.

During the reign of Louis XVI it became fashionable to decorate furniture with plaques of Sèvres porcelain, although the Sèvres manufactory appears to have supplied suitable plaques to only a few dealers, notably Poirier, and later, Daguerre and Lignereux. One of the most successful makers of Sèvres-mounted furniture was Martin Carlin, who also incorporated lacquer panels into a number of his pieces. A. Weisweiler, one of the German ébénistes who enjoyed the patronage of Queen Marie Antoinette, decorated much of his furniture with the imitation lacquer, *vernis martin*. His veneered pieces are notable for their finely figured wood, and the ormolu mounts are also of exceptional quality.

Georges Jacob, one of the few non-German craftsmen to be patronised by Marie Antoinette, was the most accomplished *menuisier* (joiner) of the period, and his originality and imagination is seen in the wide variety of chairs he produced between 1770 and the Revolution in 1789. Some were made with round, square and medallion backs, others were of mahogany with carved and pierced splats, while a number, such as those made for Marie Antoinette's 'Diary' at Rambouillet, were in the Etruscan style – a

68

205 Chair closely related to a design published by Thomas Sheraton in the *Encyclopaedia*. English, *c*. 1805.

206 Shield-back chair similar to designs published in G. Hepplewhite's *Cabinet-maker and Upholsterer's Guide*. English, *c*. 1790.

207 Chair of beechwood in the Greek Klismos style, painted in terracotta on black. English, *c*. 1800.

208 Bed-side table made in Florence, probably by Giovanni Socchi, *c*. 1805.

209 Hanging-cupboard of mahogany inlaid with brass, ebonised metal and various woods. The crocodile is a manifestation of the Egyptian taste prevalent at this time. English, *c*. 1800.

210 Writing desk inlaid with ivory and various woods, made by Rosario Palermo for Pope Pius in Rome, *c*. 1780.

205

206

207

208

209

210

style which appeared shortly before the Revolution and combined Etruscan and Classical decorative motifs. In the course of the 1770s A. J. Roubo and J. C. Delafosse published some new designs for chairs which are typical of French Neo-classical taste, with straight tapering legs and curving frames decorated with swags and garlands.

This rich creative period in the decorative arts came to an abrupt end with the Revolution, and it was not until the comparatively peaceful climate of the Directoire that cabinet makers began once more to find patronage. However, there was now much less money to lavish on expensive pieces, and furniture consequently took on a more severe appearance, which also reflected the more academic approach to Classical art prevalent in the early 19th century. The paintings of the most famous artist of the period, J. L. David, show furniture with unadorned surfaces and strong clear outlines, and chairs with sabre legs modelled on the ancient Greek chairs depicted on Classical vases.

Some craftsmen who had served under the *Ancien Régime*, among them Georges Jacob, managed to survive the revolutionary years. As a result of the suppression of the guilds, Jacob could now legally practice as both a menuisier and an ébéniste. In 1796 his sons took over his business, operating under the name of Jacob Frères, and by the Empire their workshop had become the most distinguished in Paris. Jacob's second son Jacob-Desmalter produced many fine pieces, a good proportion of which were made to furnish Napoleon's imperial palaces. Superb ormolu mounts are a distinctive feature of Empire furniture, and some of the best mounts

were produced by P. P. Thomire, who had been a pupil of Gouthière.

Desmalter's furniture is closely related to the designs of the architects Percier and Fontaine, whose book *Recueil de Décorations Intérieures,* published in 1801, was of such immense importance in the formation of the Empire style. In such palaces as Malmaison and the Louvre they created rooms and galleries that, while displaying grandeur sufficient to indulge Napoleon's imperial tastes, remain elegant and restrained. Another book which had a considerable influence on the development of Empire furniture was *Voyage dans la Basse et Haute-Egypte*, published by Vivant Denon in 1802 on his return from Napoleon's Egyptian campaigns. This book, which was also very influential in England, was the source of inspiration for many of the Egyptian motifs which were such a feature of the Empire style.

Some delightful designs for more ordinary domestic furniture were provided by Pierre de La Mésangère in 'Collection de Meubles et Objets de Gout', which appeared between 1802 and 1835 in a magazine called *Journal des Dames et des Modes.*

England c. 1760-c. 1825
Even when the Rococo was at the height of its popularity many English architects and craftsmen continued to work in a predominantly Classical style. The more scholarly appreciation of Classical art had developed later in England than in other parts of Europe, and was not to be abandoned lightly. The English aristocracy considered the Grand Tour to be a vital part of their education, and consequently many young noblemen spent some months in

211 Combined work-, writing- and reading-table, known in France as a *table à pupitre*. French, *c.* 1780. The use of porcelain plaques is a feature typical of the work of the maker, Martin Carlin.

212 Commode made by David Roentgen, *c.* 1785. The front is decorated with a scene from the *Commedia dell'arte* from a design by Januarius Zick.

213 Writing-table, Spanish, *c.* 1795. This type of rich marquetry decoration was popular in Spain during the reign of Charles IV.

212

211

213

Rome, where they would earnestly study the Classical ruins and possibly form a collection of antique vases or sculpture. The passion for Classical learning had led to the foundation of the Society of the Dilettanti in 1732, whose aim was to 'encourage at home a taste for those objects which had contributed so much to their enjoyment abroad'. Through their patronage of architects and designers, the members of the Society, who included Lord Spencer, Francis Dashwood and Lord Rockingham, were enormously influential in the development of English Neo-classicism. One of the most successful of their protegés was James 'Athenian' Stuart, who, after studying Classical remains in Greece, returned to England and between 1756 and 1765 carried out a commission to redecorate and furnish a series of rooms at Spencer House, London. These have been described as the earliest Neo-classical interiors in England.

It was still relatively unusual for architects to study in Greece, and Italy remained the training ground for most of the leading architects of the day, including Sir William Chambers and Robert Adam. Adam spent four years based in Rome, and on his return to England in 1758 initiated a new approach to Classicism. In the great country houses where he worked, such as Osterley Park House, Kedleston Hall and Saltram Park, his intention was to create a totally unified interior, with each element, however insignificant it might appear, subordinate to a ruling design. He used many of the same sources as the Palladian architects, but instead of the massive scrolls, columns and entablatures employed by Kent and his school, Adam introduced refined mouldings, panels of light grotesque ornament and low-relief plasterwork. He conceived of furniture as an extension of his interior architecture, and not only designed each piece individually but also planned its exact position in a specific room. Thus the state rooms of a house such as Osterley Park, where most of the original furniture survives in its original positions round the walls of the room, have a strictly formal appearance; it was not until the 19th century that furniture began to be moved into the centre of the room.

Stuart, Adam and Chambers all published architectural and furniture designs and drawings of Classical ornament that were closely studied by the principal cabinet makers of the day, including Chippendale – who produced some of his best pieces in the Neo-classical style – Vile & Cobb, John Linnell and the firm of Ince & Mayhew. By the third quarter of the 18th century they were producing furniture with fluted borders, swags, *paterae*, tripods, vases, sphinxes and grotesques, which were painted, carved or inlaid. Marquetry decoration came back into vogue, but was less colourful and more two-dimensional than the late 17th-century fashion. At first Classical ornament was merely applied to the curving forms typical of the Rococo, but soon the forms themselves began to change: semi-circular shapes became rectangular, the legs of chairs and tables straight and tapering, and the frames of pictures and looking-glasses often oval or square.

Among the cabinet makers to absorb Adam's ideas was George Hepplewhite. No piece of furniture has ever been identified with his workshop, and his fame rests entirely on the design book *The*

214 Cabinet designed by Robert Adam for Elizabeth, Duchess of Manchester, in 1771 to display 11 *scagliola* panels. Made by the firm of Ince & Mayhew.

215 Chair, Spanish, *c.* 1760. The carved ornament is typical of Spanish work.

216 Commode, Portuguese, *c.* 1785, with marquetry of exotic woods.

214

215

216

217 Lady's cabinet and writing table, Baltimore, 1795-1810.

218 Commode, Swedish, made c. 1780 by Georg Haupt, who had worked in Paris, probably with J. H. Riesener.

219 Chest-on-chest, attributed to William Lemon. Design and carving attributed to McIntire. Salem, 1796.

217   218   219

Cabinet-maker and Upholsterer's Guide, published by his widow in 1788. This book, which was immensely successful both in England and abroad, includes designs for shield- and oval-back chairs, dressing-tables, secretaire-cabinets and pembroke tables, all of which illustrate his facility for adapting the Neo-classical style to ordinary domestic furniture.

Hepplewhite may have served his apprenticeship with the firm of Gillow which, with workshops in both Lancaster and London, was one of the most prosperous cabinet-making concerns in the country – it was described by a German visitor in 1807 as producing good solid work 'though not of the first class in inventiveness and style'. Seddon & Sons was another thriving firm of cabinet makers, where at one time 400 craftsmen were employed, including joiners, carvers, upholsterers, gilders, workers in ormolu, locksmiths and makers of mirror glass.

By the 1770s Adam's style of decoration had become well established, and was carried into the following century by the architects James Wyatt and Henry Holland. But side by side with this in the early 19th century existed a *mélange* of decorative styles: the Greek, Roman, Etruscan, Egyptian, Gothic, French and Oriental tastes all found expression in the furniture made in England during the Regency. Much furniture, however, was plainly formed, with marquetry decoration and carved ornament becoming less fashionable, and cabinet makers relying for their effects on the striking colours and figures of such woods as amboyna, zebra-wood, maple and particularly rosewood, often combined with brass inlay.

Thomas Sheraton, like Hepplewhite, has been credited with some of the finest late-18th-century furniture, although there is no evidence to suggest he ever practised as a cabinet maker. His fame is a result of a series of design books that he published between 1791 and his death in 1806: *The Cabinet-maker and Upholsterer's Drawing Book* (1791-94), *the Cabinet Dictionary* (1803) and the uncompleted *Cabinet-maker, Upholsterer and General Artists Encyclopaedia* (1804-06). His designs are often more original than those of Hepplewhite, but many are highly eccentric and could never have been executed. Sheraton was responsible for introducing such features as reeded supports, Egyptian figures, Grecian couches, monopodia (one-foot) and lion-paw feet that were to be so much employed by cabinet makers in the Regency period.

In the early years of the 19th century it became apparent that many architects and connoisseurs were adopting a more scholarly and archaeological approach to antiquity. The most determined in this pursuit was Thomas Hope, a wealthy collector and discerning patron whose book *Household Furniture and Interior Decoration*, published in 1807, is a record of the decoration and furnishing of his house at Duchess Street, London. Here every element had been carefully chosen and copied from a Classical or Egyptian source and related to a central theme. The furniture made after his designs

is often of austere appearance, with the plain surfaces inlaid with small motifs of brass or ebony. He designed such pieces as stands in the shape of tripods, tables supported on monopodia, X-frame stools and klismos chairs. His ideas were much too scholarly to be accepted by the general public, but were popularised by the cabinet maker George Smith, who in 1808 published *A Collection of Designs for Household Furniture and Interior Decoration*.

The Prince Regent, who became King George IV in 1820, was deeply concerned with the arts, and his patronage and influence were of very great importance. His chief interest was in French art, and he chose the architect Henry Holland, who had evolved a style of decoration that had much in common with that of Percier and Fontaine, to organise the re-decoration and re-furnishing of his London residence, Carlton House. A more general interest in French furniture had probably been stimulated by the large amount that had reached England after the Revolution, and one way in which this found expression was in the production of 'boulle-work' furniture. Appreciation of French art became even more widespread when after the Battle of Waterloo in 1815 France was once more open to English visitors.

Carlton House was unfortunately destroyed, but the Prince Regent's summer residence, the Brighton Pavilion, has survived as a testament to the exoticism of the period. The firm of Frederick Crace made a number of suitably Oriental pieces of furniture for the Pavilion, characterised by spiky outlines, applied fretwork and decoration of brightly coloured Chinoiseries. It is with some justification that the Brighton Pavilion has been described as the greatest monument to Chinoiserie in the Western world.

Italy and Germany c. 1760-c. 1825

Despite the spreading tide of Neo-classicism, much of the furniture produced in Italy during these years retained a sculptural almost Baroque appearance, one of the finest pieces in this idom being a table made in 1789 (now in the Vatican), which is formed by eight bronze statues of Hercules that support a huge slab of ancient Egyptian granite.

Tables are included among the designs for furniture by G. B. Piranesi, the most famous and influential Italian artist working in the Neo-classical period. The ornament to be seen on his furniture designs is derived not only from Classical Rome but also from Etruscan and Egyptian sources. Piranesi's passionate and romantic visions of Roman antiquity inspired the construction of some 'ruin rooms' in the 1750s, but unfortunately none appear to have survived.

One of the most accomplished cabinet makers active in the late 18th century was Guiseppe Maggiolini, who established his workshops in Milan and worked for powerful patrons, including the Archduke Ferdinand, Governor-General of Milan. Maggiolini's

220 Sideboard, American, c. 1800. Attributed to Nehemiah Adams of Salem, Massachusetts.

221 Armchair, American, c. 1807. Made by Duncan Phyfe of New York for William Bayard.

222 Room from a Danish manor house, Lille Haesbjerg. The furniture displays both French and English influence.

220

221

222

furniture, rectilinear in form, is distinguished by its brilliant marquetry decoration. Another north Italian furniture maker was G. M. Bonzanigo, who achieved a wide reputation, particularly for the high quality of the carving which embellishes his work.

The lack of furniture designs produced by native artists meant that many Italian cabinet makers turned to English publications for inspiration but, after the invasion of Napoleon in 1796, French influence not surprisingly became predominant. With French craftsmen practising in Italy and passing their skills on to Italian craftsmen, it often becomes difficult to distinguish between their respective work, and the problem is accentuated by the fact that in many cases French ormolu mounts were applied to furniture of Italian construction.

Even after the fall of Napoleon and his family, the Empire style, with its severe profiles and mixture of Classical and Egyptian ornament, continued to be fashionable, but gradually furniture became heavier in form, and was increasingly overlaid with carved and gilt decoration.

German cabinet makers were in general slow to adopt Neo-classicism, and even the most fashionable of them were producing Rococo pieces as late as 1775. The outstanding exception was David
212 Roentgen, whose Neo-classical furniture became famous throughout Europe, and who numbered among his patrons Catherine

the Great and Louis XVI. In 1772 he took over the direction of the workshops at Neuweid which had been established by his father Abraham Roentgen in 1750, and in 1780 he was registered as a master ébéniste by the Paris guild. His pieces were built with complex mechanical devices that operate secret drawers and make doors unexpectedly spring open, but his furniture is chiefly renowned for the remarkable quality of the panels of pictorial marquetry. These were frequently derived from paintings by Januarius Zick, and are among the finest creations ever produced in this medium.

During the 1770s the use of Classical ornament became increasingly common on German furniture, and in about 1780 a number of Neo-classical designs for furniture were published by Franz Hessig in Augsburg. The influence of the French Empire can be best seen in the great German palaces, many of which were extensively re-decorated in the early 19th century.

When the Napoleonic wars were finally concluded, there was a noticeable reaction against grand and costly pieces, and in response to the demand for furniture that was both functional and comfortable, the Biedermeier style developed, distinguished by its unadorned surfaces and pleasing lines. This remained fashionable with the prosperous bourgeoisie until the middle of the 19th century.

Some of the more original furniture of the early 19th century was made to the designs of the architect F. F. Schinkel, who was working in Berlin, while in 1804 in Vienna, Josef Danhauser founded a highly successful cabinet making firm.

Other European countries c. 1760-c. 1825

French and English furniture had become so popular in the Netherlands during the latter half of the 18th century that in 1771 the guilds insisted on an import ban. But in spite of this, native craftsmen, among them Andries Bongen, were able to satisfy the demand by making furniture in the French style, and consequently marquetry decoration and lacquer panels are to be seen on many pieces of Dutch furniture made during this period. They are distinguished from their French prototypes, however, by the minor part played by ormolu mounts.

In 1808 King Louis Napoleon converted the Amsterdam town hall into a royal palace, and it was redecorated in the Empire style. This is one of the finest expressions of the later Neo-classical taste to be found in the Netherlands. After Napoleon's final defeat in 1815 the Empire style continued to flourish, but in due course gave way to the Biedermeier style, which persisted until the middle of the 19th century.

Furniture made in the Iberian peninsula in the latter part of the 216 18th century clearly shows the influence of the Hepplewhite and Sheraton designs, but the clearest lead in fashion came from France and, in the case of Spain, also from Bourbon Italy. Many of the pieces produced at this time display exaggerated proportions, for 215 instance, chairs often have seats that are too large for their delicately carved backs. Chairs were frequently painted white or cream with gilt embellishments, but examples based on 16th-century prototypes were also produced, and sometimes decorated with different coloured japans.

There is little to distinguish Spanish furniture of the early 19th century from that of the preceding two decades, but after the restoration of Ferdinand VII in 1814 a style known as 'Fernandino' developed, the designs being derived from the Empire style. The forms, however, are heavier, and the decoration less restrained than in the French originals.

No national style of furniture was evolved in Portugal during the first quarter of the 19th century, which is not surprising in view of the foreign occupation, wars and political upheavals which troubled the country at the time. But Empire and Regency styles were copied with varying degrees of skill by Lisbon furniture makers, and after the accession of Maria II and her German husband in 1826, the influence of the Biedermeier style became apparent, particularly in the production of chairs.

In Scandinavia the influence of Neo-classicism on furniture became apparent as early as the 1750s. The French sculptor J. F. J. Saly, who was appointed Director of the Academy in Copenhagen about 1753, was instrumental in spreading knowledge of Neo-classical principles to many Scandinavian architects, artists and craftsmen, and the official line adopted by the Academy was an influential one, not only on fine art but also on the decorative arts. Cabinet makers were required to have the designs for their masterpieces vetted by the Academy, and having passed this initial test, the completed piece was then judged by the guilds.

The best-known cabinet makers of the period were the Swedish 218 craftsmen Christopher Fürloh and Georg Haupt, both of whom worked for a time in Paris, possibly in the workshops of Riesener, before travelling on to London. Fürloh decided to remain in England, but Haupt returned to Sweden in 1769, and there he produced some superb pieces in the French Neo-classical style. It was the French taste that appealed most to the Swedish market, although English influence is often to be seen in the design of chair backs.

In 1777 a Royal Emporium of Furniture was founded in Copenhagen, with the intention of boosting the work of Danish cabinet 222 makers who, succumbing more to the influence of English fashions than their Swedish contemporaries, made many fine-quality mahogany pieces after designs by Hepplewhite and Sheraton.

Norwegian cabinet makers generally took a lead from the Danes,

and consequently much of their furniture is also based on English prototypes, though in the 19th century the close contact between Scandinavia and England was disrupted by the Napoleonic wars. The 'Danish Empire' style is a mixture of English, French and German ideas, while the 'Late Empire' style was largely the creation of one man, the Danish designer G. F. Hetsch. He had studied under the French architect Percier, and his personal conception of Neo-classicism influenced furniture until the middle of the 19th century. The 'Hetsch' style was also prevalent in Sweden, but about 1820 a reaction to Neo-classicism cleared the way for the various Romantic revivals which characterised furniture design for the remainder of the 19th century.

America c. 1780-c. 1825

In spite of the War of Independence, English fashions remained the principal patterns for American furniture, and English pieces were still imported in substantial numbers. American cabinet makers responded with particular enthusiasm to the designs published by Hepplewhite and Sheraton, and the influence of Robert Adam 217,2 was also clearly in evidence.

Much of the furniture produced in the Federal period was inlaid or painted with Classical motifs, and in this way the eagle, being the official emblem of the new republic, achieved a widespread popularity. A number of exotic woods were introduced at this time, including satinwood, which was used very extensively. Chests-of-drawers and side-tables now outnumbered highboys 219 and lowboys, while semi-circular commodes and pembroke tables were made in increasing numbers. The sideboard based on designs 220 by Hepplewhite and Sheraton made its first appearance in the late 18th century. The roll-top desk largely replaced the fall-front type, and a breakfast cabinet combined with a desk, known as a Salem Secretary, came into vogue.

Although communications had greatly improved along the eastern seaboard since the days of the early settlers, regional differences remained a feature of American furniture made during these years. Some of the better-known furniture-producing towns, such as Newport, declined, while others, notably Salem, New York and Baltimore, became prominent. Salem had in the course of the 1780s developed into a flourishing port, and consequently furniture made there was exported to places as far apart as South Africa and the East Indies. The most famous of the Salem cabinet makers was Samuel McIntire, who is thought to have begun 219 his career as a carver of ships' figureheads. The carved decoration on his furniture is of a particularly high standard, and the motifs most frequently used by him include flowers, vines, baskets, books and cornucopiae overflowing with fruit.

Among the distinguished cabinet makers working in Boston, which maintained its reputation for the production of fine furniture, were John Seymour and his son Thomas, who are especially remembered for their veneered roll-top desks. New York began a period of great activity and prosperity when George Washington began his first term as President there in 1789. Of all the accomplished cabinet makers working there at this time—among them Michael Allison, and the French emigré Honoré Lanuier—none is more renowned than Duncan Phyfe, whose reputation justifiably 221 spread well beyond New York (one of his more exotic commissions was to provide a bed for Henri Christoph, King of Haiti). As his career covered some 50 years, a wide range of styles is reflected in his work, from the English Neo-classicism embodied in the style of Hepplewhite and Sheraton to the French Directoire and Empire styles.

Philadelphia remained throughout these years one of the foremost centres of cabinet making in America. Carving was less conspicuous a feature on the case furniture made there than in other parts of the country, but large areas of contrasting veneers were used to great effect. Baltimore now also became established 217 as an important furniture-producing town, and is associated with motifs such as bell-flowers, shells, floral and leaf designs and oval or lozenge-shaped glass panels decorated with gold and black allegorical figures painted on the reverse side.

223 Rococo fly-chair designed in 1834 by Philip Hardwick for the court drawing room at the Goldsmith's Hall, Foster Lane. Made by W. & C. Wilkinson.

224 'Elizabethan' mahogany four-poster bed at Scotney Castle, Kent, designed by the architect of the house, Anthony Salvin, c. 1843.

225 Design for a Rococo sideboard from the *Cabinet-maker's Assistant*, 1853.

THE 19th CENTURY: *c.* 1830 TO 1900

Gillian Walkling

Great Britain

Stylistic development was as diverse in the 19th century as it had been ordered in the 18th. The factors which contributed to its extraordinarily versatile and experimental course are both numerous and various. The inevitable results of the Industrial Revolution –a growth in population and hence demand for material goods, improvements in transport and communication both at home and abroad, the greater distribution and accessibility of printed material and the establishment of recognised industrial centres–all contributed to the general atmosphere of prosperity and inventiveness which characterised the period.

Contrary to general belief, although machinery for cutting veneers was used early in the century, mechanical advances had surprisingly little effect on the furniture industry until about 1870. The alteration in the structure of the industry was based more on social change than on technical advances. The rise of the bourgeois middle class, attempting to emulate the tastes and standards of the aristocracy, presented new opportunities for commercial exploitation. The resulting dichotomy between commercialism and aestheticism was to occur throughout the century, and the splendid and individual furniture of leading architects and designers such as William Burges, Ernest Gimson, Philip Webb and A. H. Mackmurdo, names so immediately associated with 19th-century furniture design, in fact reached a very small public. By the end of the century the search for comfort, novelty and an indication of material wealth had for the greater part superseded demand for true craftsmanship and principles of design. This did not, however, reduce the influence of such men, for although in terms of numbers their work was minimal, in terms of effect it was far-reaching, and their designs were widely imitated by many commercial manufacturers.

The Great Exhibition at the Crystal Palace in 1851 and the many International and Trades Exhibitions that followed were also important factors in disseminating designs and ideas. Although many pieces made for these exhibitions were even at the time considered museum material, their importance lay in their influence on commercial production and the role they played in upholding of standards of cabinet work.

Revival styles

Furniture design during the first half of the century has been both characterised by and criticised for its revival of historical styles and their eclectic combinations. Neither phenomena, however, were new, but it is perhaps their close chronological occurrence and the freer and richer interpretation of such styles that make their integrity questionable. The period 1830-50 saw a rapid succession of fashions for Greek and Egyptian, Rococo, Elizabethan and then Gothic design. It is significant that J. C. Loudon in his *Encyclopaedia of Cottage, Farm and Villa Architecture*, published first in 1833 and in a third edition in 1857, entirely accepted the simultaneous occurrence of all these styles over a long period of time. 'The principal styles of design as at present executed in Britain may be reduced to four, viz., the Grecian or modern style which is by far the most prevalent; the Gothic or Perpendicular style, which imitates the lines and angles of the Tudor Gothic architecture; the Elizabethan style, which combines the Gothic with the Roman and Italian manner; and the style of the age of Louis XIV, or the florid Italian, which is characterised by curved lines and an excess of curvilinear ornaments.'

At the turn of the 18th century a movement away from the refined Neo-classicism of Robert Adam had produced a more compromising Classical style with the addition of Egyptian and Assyrian motifs such as sphinx heads and animal legs. Furniture tended to become structurally heavier and carving coarser, while gilded surfaces gave way to plain mahogany. A distinctly masculine and solid domestic style evolved which was considered to be particularly well suited to dining rooms or public buildings. In 1844 Henry Whitaker designed the furniture for the Conservative Club in the Grecian or 'Modern' style.

Whitaker was a prolific designer and produced several furnishing publications; *Designs of Cabinet Upholstery Furniture in the Most Modern Style* (1825), and in 1847 the *Practical Cabinet Maker and Upholsterer's Treasury of Designs* and the *Practical Furnishing, Decorating and Embellishing Assistant*. His intention was to encourage improvements in manufacturers' designs, and the latter work consisted of 'original designs in the Grecian, Italian, Renaissance, Louis XIV, Gothic, Tudor, and Elizabethan styles', covering

237

223

224

225

226 Papier mâché balloon-back chair, English, *c.* 1850, japanned black with painted mother-of-pearl inlay. The back has a painted panel portraying Warwick Castle.

227 Carved and inlaid table designed by A. W. N. Pugin in the Gothic style. An engraving of the Mediaeval Court in the Official Catalogue of the 1851 Great Exhibition shows a table similar to this one.

228 William Morris 'Sussex' armchair with rush seat.

229 Cabinet designed by the British firm Jackson & Graham and exhibited at the Paris Exhibition of 1855, where it was awarded a Medal of Honour.

230 Top of the Pugin table (**227**), showing the fine grain and the inlaid border and central medallion.

226

227

228

229

230

not only furniture but also architectural details, chimneypieces, curtains etc.

The acceptance of so many and varied styles produced a close alliance between an individual style and the function of particular rooms. While Grecian or 'Modern' furniture had sober and masculine associations, so Rococo became acceptable for drawing-rooms and ladies' boudoirs. The furniture designed by Philip Hardwick and made by W. & C. Wilkinson for the Goldsmith's Hall in 1834 followed just this pattern.

The Rococo, or Louis XIV, revival had begun in 1824 with Benjamin Dean Wyatt's designs for a salon at Belvoir Castle, Leicestershire, for the Duchess of Rutland. In the same year Wyatt began work on the building of Crockford's Gaming House in St James' Street, London, a project which incited much criticism at the time. The furniture was composed of elaborate gilded and carved scrolls and embellished with excessive curved ornament. These and other Rococo pieces were condemned for both their structural inadequacy and their historical associations with the affluence of the Court of Louis XIV – in Loudon's words, 'unsuitable to the present advancing state of public taste'.

Despite disdain from contemporary architects and designers the

Rococo revival sustained its popularity until the middle of the century, when established firms such as Jackson and Graham and Gillows of Lancaster exhibited Rococo furniture at the Crystal Palace in 1851. Although Rococo designs were abundant on that occasion, they were totally omitted from the 1862 exhibition, which indicates a rapid fall from favour. Its largest contribution to 19th-century furniture was perhaps the creation of the essentially Victorian balloon-back chair and the popularly named upholstered 'grandfather' or 'grandmother' chair with squat cabriole legs and sweeping curved back.

During the first four decades of the century various antiquarian studies and publications laid the foundations for a more studied and intellectual approach to historical revivals. The Elizabethan and Tudor architecture and interiors illustrated in such works as Thomas Hunt's *Tudor Architecture* (1830), Joseph Nash's *Mansions of England in the Old Time* (1839-49) and C. J. Richardson's *Architectural Remains of the Reigns of Elizabeth and James I* (1840) helped create a demand for both antique 16th- and 17th-century furniture and wall panelling, and the new production of such items. The romantic and literary associations of the novels of Walter Scott in the 1820s and the furnishing of his own home,

223,225

226

231 Satinwood settle supplied by the Century Guild to Henry Boddington for Pownall Hall, Cheshire. Probably designed by A. H. Mackmurdo. The brass panels designed by Bernard Creswick.

232 Cradle designed by the architect Richard Norman Shaw for the second son of the artist Alfred Waterhouse in 1868.

233 Ebonised sideboard with panels of 'embossed leather' paper. Designed by E. W. Godwin and made by William Watt, *c.* 1867.

231   232   233

Abbotsford in Scotland, with antiquarian relics of the Tudor, Jacobean and Stuart periods paved the way for the refurbishing in a similar manner of important houses such as Hardwick Hall, Derbyshire; Knebworth Park, Hertfordshire; and Charlecote Park, Warwickshire, and to the building of new Elizabethan houses such as Mamhead in Devon and Scotney Castle in Kent, both designed by Anthony Salvin. Inevitably an 'Elizabethan' interior became common in the homes of the fashion-conscious middle class.

Although the Elizabethan style was most strongly felt in architecture, publications such as Henry Shaw's *Specimens of Ancient Furniture* (1836) and Robert Bridgens' *Furniture with Candelabra and Interior Decoration* (1838) were influential among furniture designers. Since antiques were generally in short supply, furniture makers began to produce buffets, cupboards, sideboards and four-poster beds from old oak fragments. This economic practice was described by Loudon: 'it is seldom necessary to manufacture objects in this manner farther than by putting together ancient fragments which may be purchased at the sale of old buildings'. Less discerning makers produced such furniture with a variety of carving, both in origin and quality, often lacking overall cohesion. Pure reproduction pieces were also made.

The Elizabethan style found its strongest competition in the Gothic Revival, where again antiquarian studies and romantic literature had substantial influence. Thomas Rickman's *An Attempt to Discriminate the Styles of English Architecture* (1817), A. C. Pugin's and E. J. Willson's *Specimens of Gothic Architecture* (1821-23) and John Britton's the *Cathedral Antiquities of Great Britain* (1814-35) did much to promote an appreciation of true Gothic architectural principles. Even so, Gothic furniture suffered greatly in the hands of commercial designers whose pieces were generally characterised by the application of Gothic ornament only, in the form of tracery, crockets, pinnacles and buttresses. Loudon significantly stated that 'what passes for Gothic furniture among cabinet makers and upholsterers is, generally, a very different thing from the correct Gothic designs supplied by Architects who have imbued their minds with this style of art'.

The most notable, if not the only exception to this rule during the early stages of the Gothic Revival, was Augustus Welby Northmore Pugin, who published *Gothic Furniture*, a study based on late medieval prototypes, in 1835. Although some of his furniture shows a compromise between true medieval principles and a broader approach to decoration, he at least adhered to simple Gothic construction. Perhaps his largest contribution to 19th-century design was his organisation of the Mediaeval Court at the Great Exhibition of 1851, which provided a basis for later Gothic reformers such as Burges, Eastlake and Talbert. Certainly the high point in his career came with his work on the New Palace of Westminster, the Houses of Parliament, where he designed every detail of the interior—furniture, carpets, wallpapers and metalwork. Although the competition, which had specified that designs must be in either the Gothic or Elizabethan style, was won by the architect Sir Charles Barry, it is to Pugin that the greater credit for this Gothic masterpiece must be given.

The Great Exhibition at the Crystal Palace in 1851 marked the beginning of a period of change. The large variety of styles of the pieces contributed, as described in the official catalogue—'Elizabethan, Tudor, Gothic, Louis XIV, Renaissance, Italian, Arabic and Old English Illuminated'—emphasised the dangers of eclecticism and the tendency to allow ornament to over-rule utility and construction. In many pieces, particularly those contributed by provincial cabinet makers, a variety of conflicting and often inappropriate ornament was present.

The various reviews and editorial comments on the exhibition illustrated clearly the recognition of the problems, but few suggestions for improvement. Richard Redgrave, artist and authority of industrial design, made several criticisms of the exhibits in his *Supplementary Report on the Exhibition of 1851*. 'The hunger after novelty is quite insatiable; heaven and earth are racked for novel intentions, and happy is the man who lights upon something, however outré, that shall strike the vulgar mind, and obtain the run of the season . . . Ours is certainly a chaotic period. The Exhibition shows that we are most skilful mimics, that we know how to reproduce the classics—that we can restore everything. But what do we create?'

It also became obvious at the exhibition that the few French cabinet makers who made contributions had a greater understanding of, and taste in, their use of ornament, although they tended to use it more excessively than their English counterparts. The International Exhibition in Paris in 1855 showed a marked improvement in English exhibits, mostly in the Louis XV and Louis XVI styles, to a large extent due to the employment of immigrant French craftsmen and designs by leading firms such as Jackson and Graham. The splendid cabinet which won them a Medal of Honour at the 1855 Paris exhibition, although designed by a Frenchman, M. Eugene Prignot, was superbly executed by English craftsmen. This piece was also notable for its large expanse of mirror glass, the use of which became common at this date as British makers finally mastered the art of mirror production.

By the time of the 1862 Exhibition in London French influence had become more apparent, and cabinet furniture showed a return to the refined Neo-classicism of Robert Adam combined with the French use of tortoiseshell and metal decoration, ormolu mounts, porcelain plaques and inlay of ebony and ivory. At the 1867 Paris exhibition the firm Wright and Mansfield gained the only gold medal awarded to a British contributor for their satinwood cabinet in this 18th-century style, decorated with fine marquetry, gilt mouldings and Wedgwood plaques. Their intention to produce an entirely British designed and made piece was internationally recognised and appreciated, and they gained credit not only for its high quality but for the successful use of a light wood as a background at a time when ebony, rosewood and darkly stained woods were so popular.

Although the exhibitions can be criticised for showing too many such 'exhibition' pieces and too few examples of mass-produced

234 Carved table made by Henry Eyles of Bath and exhibited at the Great Exhibition at the Crystal Palace in 1851.

234

commercial furniture, they did set an example in taste and provide a pattern for general manufacturers to follow.

During the first half of the 19th century the rising popularity of sculpture led to a return to naturalistic woodcarving. A clear distinction was made in the furniture trade between the carver of ornament for decorative purposes and the artistic woodcarver, whose elaborate schemes sometimes entirely concealed the basic structural form. This type of excessive carved furniture was on the whole limited to isolated groups, and is primarily associated with the firm of Arthur J. Jones in Dublin, the Rogers family in London and the Warwickshire School of Carving, where the Cookes (later Collier and Plucknett) and the Kendalls of Chapel Street in Warwick were the best-known firms. Two Tyneside carvers, Thomas Tweedy and Gerrard Robinson, are also well known in this connection: the former for the extraordinary Robinson Crusoe sideboard which won him an Honourable Mention at the 1862 exhibition, and the latter for the Chevy Chase sideboard, made for the Duke of Northumberland. The activities of G. A. Rogers, who provided drawings for amateur carvers and organised an Exhibition of Ancient and Modern Carving at the Albert Hall, helped contribute to a general vogue for home woodcarving, a practice which reached even members of the royal family. Although superb individual pieces of carved furniture were made, the standard of decorative carved ornament on the whole fell when several patents for woodcarving machinery were registered in the 1840s.

New forms and materials

239 The period 1830-70 saw the emergence not only of new styles, but of new materials and new forms of furniture. Davenports, music canterburies, loo tables, chiffoniers, heavy sideboards, large simple wardrobes and solid wood half-tester beds became the vogue in most middle-class homes, and seem to have evolved on the whole independently of prevailing definable styles. If any, some show Rococo influence, but in a reduced form. Ornament

tended to be confined to restricted naturalistic carving, and woods were usually plain mahogany or walnut. This independence also characterised upholstered furniture, where a desire for comfort and 236 improvements in upholstery techniques produced a wealth of sofas, ottomans, love seats, *priedieu*, elaborate footstools and that peculiar Victorian invention, the 'cosy corner'. The rich effects of deeply buttoned velvet were enhanced by excessive ponderous drapery and heavy fringes.

A material which in itself was not new, but which was exploited by furniture makers during the 19th century, was cast iron. Iron furniture of all types was produced from about 1830 onwards in ever-increasing quantities and in all manner of styles. Production was centred in the industrial Midlands, and Birmingham manufacturers soon gained the highest reputation amongst the trade in in this field. The best known Birmingham firm was R. W. Winfield, who also experimented with brass, both tubular and strap, and various other metals. Winfield exhibited some fine pieces at the 1851 Exhibition. Metal furniture was particularly recommended for use in bedrooms on the grounds of hygiene – hence the ubiquitous brass or iron bedstead – and for public buildings and open spaces. Metal seat furniture was often painted and grained in imitation of wood. The first actual patent for a metal bed was registered in 1849, but by this date they had already become commonplace items, and by 1875 some 6,000 metal beds are claimed to have been made in Birmingham alone in one week.

Although cast-iron furniture followed prevailing fashions, and hence provides interesting documentation for studying 19th-century design, the industry was highly criticised at the time for not employing trained designers and therefore failing to attain high design standards.

Another branch of the furniture industry which has received little attention is the production of marble furniture. Situated primarily in Derbyshire, the industry flourished during the first half of the century, producing mostly inlaid table tops and chimney

235 Bedstead and washstand designed by William Burges for the Guest Chamber of Tower house, Melbury Road, London, in 1879.

235

ornaments. S. Birley of Ashford won a medal in both the furniture and mining classes at the 1862 exhibition for a black circular pedestal table inlaid with coloured foliage, flowers and birds. It was subsequently bought by the South Kensington Museums for the then large sum of £240. Such high prices, necessitated by labour and material costs, soon rendered production uneconomic, and the industry was severely diminished by lack of demand during the 1860s. Other materials, such as slate and coal, were also utilised, but such pieces must now be considered curiosities.

A material for which the Victorians are always given credit, but which in fact had originated in Persia and the East and was used for decorative purposes in Europe during the 18th century, was papier mâché. However, its use for furniture, and its often rather gaudy japanned decoration in the forms of gilded patterns and painted mother-of-pearl inlay was essentially 19th century.

Two manufacturing methods were employed, firstly that of pasting strips of paper on to moulds, and secondly that of pressing paper pulp between dies. Papier mâché was obviously best suited to the production of small decorative articles—trays, pen cases, workboxes etc. (see p. 288), but chairs, tables, music canterburies and other small items of furniture were common. It became obvious before long that the material was not really suitable for structural use, so premoulded decoration was applied to basic wood or metal forms. Undoubtedly the most famous producers were Jennens and Bettridge of Birmingham, and it was they who introduced the use of pearl inlay in 1825. Sometimes coloured prints and painted panels were incorporated in papier mâché wares.

Reforms in design

The initial reaction against the excesses of commercialism and impetus for reform came during the 1860s with the theories of William Morris and his associates and the establishment of their firm Morris, Marshall, Faulkner & Co. in 1861. Ironically, it seems that Morris did not design furniture himself, and it is well known that the Sussex chairs and upholstered adjustable-back armchairs 228 that bear his name were in fact based on traditional country chair designs. It is also surprising that he did not publish his influential theories on furniture design until as late as 1877. However, his statement 'have nothing in your house that you do not know to be useful or believe to be beautiful' (1880) had been exemplified in the firm's production from the very beginning, and many early pieces could be criticised for being merely vehicles for the paintings of Morris' fellow artists. Their approach to basic design and construction—respect for materials, solid and straightforward joinery, functional simplicity and total lack of false decoration and embellishment—soon began to influence other artist and architect-designers, but initially found little favour with the general trade.

Most of the firm's early furniture was designed by Philip Webb, but contributions were also made by his other Pre-Raphaelite colleagues, Ford Madox Brown, Edward Burne-Jones, Dante Gabriel Rosetti and Holman Hunt. One of the most splendid pieces shown by them at the 1862 exhibition was a cabinet or desk designed by J. P. Seddon and painted by the pre-Raphaelites (with the exception of Hunt) and Morris himself. In 1865 the firm was re-organised and re-named Morris & Co. Despite lack of acceptance from the trade the business continued to grow, and in 1890 they acquired the premises of Messrs Holland in Pimlico. At this date they began to produce a different type of furniture, closer in feel to commercial cabinet work of the period, but generally of superior quality. The three designers employed during this period, George Jack, an architect trained under Philip Webb, Mervyn Macartney and W. A. S. Benson, were chiefly responsible for this change of direction. Benson, famous for his metalwork, became company chairman after Morris' death.

While Morris & Co. were producing superbly individual pieces of furniture, some of their contemporaries, equally concerned over the plight of the furniture industry, were making sterner attempts to ally art to commerical production and to revitalise, rather than

236 Design for an upholstered settee from *Designs of Furniture,* a catalogue of furniture produced by James Shoolbred & Company, Tottenham Court Road, 1874.

237 The 'Thebes' stool patented by Liberty's in 1884, and based on an ancient Egyptian model. The Egyptian Revival during the 1880s was short-lived.

238 Writing cabinet designed by Ernest Gimson for Kenton & Co. Ltd, *c.* 1890. Executed by A. H. Mason and C. Smith with marquetry by J. Beaner. This piece was shown at the Arts and Crafts Exhibition of 1890.

239 Walnut davenport, *c.* 1860.

240 Renaissance cabinet designed by Stephen Webb for the firm Collinson and Lock, 1890. The ivory inlaid in rosewood was executed by Webb himself.

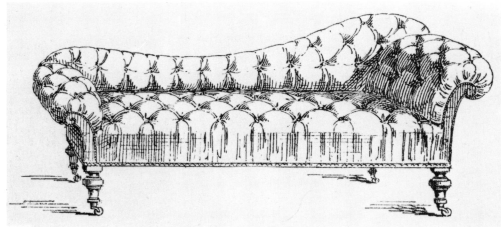

236

237

238

239

240

divorce themselves from, the industry. During the 1870s, Art Furniture, originating in the work of Burges, Godwin, Talbert and Eastlake, soon acquired positive characteristics, and by about 1875 Art Manufacturers were listed separately in trade directories from other furniture producers. While the work of Burges and Eastlake showed strong affinities with the Gothic style of Pugin, and Godwin's inspiration remained patently Japanese, Art Furniture became characterised by the use of ebonised wood with lightly incised decoration and shallow carving picked out in gold. Turned legs and balusters were common; curves were totally eliminated and even small decorative details tended to be square or rectilinear. Many pieces of Art Furniture were based on historical revivals, but the quality of workmanship and a greater understanding of such styles was more evident than in the previous half century. Well respected firms such as Collinson & Lock, Jackson and Graham, and Holland & Sons, became associated with the style. In 1871 even the renowned firm of Gillows began to produce ebonised furniture.

Charles Lock Eastlake's contribution to Art Furniture lay in his *Hints on Household Taste* (1868), in which he advocated simple rectangular forms with a minimum of decoration, and simple medieval construction. His influence was more strongly felt in the United States, where a positive 'Eastlake' style evolved. Another exponent of medieval principles of construction was William Burges who, as a writer, artist, furniture designer and one of the first collectors of Japanese prints, is to be remembered not only for his practical design work but also for his theories linking the qualities of medieval work to those of Japanese design. Reviewing the 1862 exhibition of the *Gentleman's Magazine* Burges wrote: 'if the visitor wishes to see the real Middle Ages he must visit the Japanese Court for at the present day the arts of the middle ages have deserted Europe and are only to be found in the East. Here in England we can only get Mediaeval objects manufactured for us

with pain and difficulty, but in Egypt, Syria and Japan, you can buy them in the bazaars'. His furniture, however, shows few traces of Japanese design and is Gothic in construction, painted entirely in gold and bright colours with scenes from the middle ages and Gothic ornament.

Burges' furniture was designed for individual clients, but E. W. Godwin supplied designs to many commercial firms – Gillows, Collinson & Lock, W. & A. Smee and William Watt. Although trained as a Gothic architect, Godwin produced ebonised furniture based on Japanese forms, and his Anglo-Japanese style was extensively imitated. His early work was made by the Art Furniture Company, and a comprehensive study of his designs appeared in a catalogue of *Art Furniture* issued by William Watt.

Other advocates of the Japanese style who contributed to the general fashion were the artists and designers Christopher Dresser and James McNeill Whistler. Other important Art Furniture designers were Thomas Jekyll, who actually designed Whistler's famous Peacock Room; T. E. Collcutt, who designed for Gillows, Maples and Collinson & Lock; and B. J. Talbert, another Gothic proponent. Although trained as a woodcarver, Talbert was employed as a furniture designer by Doveston, Bird & Hull in Manchester and Holland & Sons in London. In 1867 he published his influential *Gothic Forms of Ornament Applied to Furniture.*

The work and ideas of William Morris lay at the root of perhaps the most famous 19th-century art style, the Arts and Crafts Movement. During the 1880s and 1890s small groups of artists, architects and designers · gathered together to work towards social reform and the re-establishment of the guild system where craftsmen were apprenticed to a designer and produced entirely craft-made goods, in the old tradition. If the movement can be claimed to have failed in the long run it was due to the inability of its members to recognise that craftsmanship was uneconomic,

235,241
233

235
233

241 Sideboard designed by C. L. Eastlake in about 1868. Its simple 'Gothic' design is close to a sideboard illustrated in his *Hints on Household Taste*.

242 Gothic mahogany dining table, probably made in New York, c. 1840.

243 Advertisement for the New York firm of Joseph Meeks & Sons. Lithograph by Endicott & Swett, New York, 1833.

241

242

243

and that the buying public could not afford to patronise such a time-consuming enterprise. However, the enthusiasm for 'craft' furniture which the movement inspired was reflected in the commercial production of craft imitations.

The first group to be formed was the Century Guild, established by the architect A. H. Mackmurdo in 1882, with the aim to 'render all branches of art the sphere no longer of the tradesman but of the 231 artist'. Although a single piece of furniture may have been designed co-operatively, the attribution was always to the Guild as a whole. Mackmurdo probably designed most of the furniture himself, and strangely, the early work was executed by the commercial firms of Wilkinson's of Bond Street and Goodall & Co. in Manchester. Century Guild designs are generally characterised by balanced rectilinear forms, Classical cornices and very little ornamental decoration.

The Century Guild was closely followed in 1884 by the non-commercial Art Workers Guild, formed by a group of artists and designers who met together to hold discussions and exhibitions for their own enlightenment in an attempt to ally designers and craftsmen, and to terminate the distinction between the applied and fine arts. Their meetings led to the formation of the Arts and Crafts Exhibition Society from which the movement gained its name. Under the chairmanship of Walter Crane, principally a designer of wallpapers and textiles, the society held its first exhibition in 1888 and further exhibitions in 1889, 1890, 1893, 1896 and 1899. The aims of the exhibitions were to show articles under the designers' names rather than that of the actual producer. This practice found little favour with the trade, and although in 1890 several leading firms—Collinson & Lock, Gillows, Liberty's and others—were invited to exhibit, it seems that no agreement was reached, and further invitations were not proffered. Members of the 238 society included George Jack, Ernest Gimson, W. R. Lethaby, C. R.

Ashbee, Reginald Blomfield, Lewis Day and Sidney Barnsley.

Another guild arising out of the society's work was C. R. Ashbee's Guild School of Handicraft, 1888, where individual craftsmen were given credit for their work and were not linked to a particular master or firm. This co-operative enterprise began in East London and later moved to Chipping Camden, Gloucestershire. The Guild executed mostly Ashbee's designs, but also made for other designers, notably H. M. Baillie Scott.

Another short-lived organisation was Kenton & Co., formed in 238 1890 by a group of architects—Blomfield, Lethaby, Gimson, Macartney and Barnsley—which produced work both made and designed by individuals. Lethaby and Gimson produced furniture only in oak. Kenton & Co. soon dissolved from lack of funds, and Barnsley and Gimson combined to set up workshops in the Cotswolds, near Cirencester, where the English rural craft tradition was continued. Gimson had served an apprenticeship with a rural chair-maker while an architectural student, which stood him in good stead for guiding the work of the Cotswold School. Their furniture is characterised by the predominant use of oak and simple methods of joinery.

Despite the work of such individuals and divorced from the West End cabinet trade, the last quarter of the century saw the solid establishment of the East End furniture trade in London and its counterparts in other cities. Such firms were supplying goods to satisfy the demand of the middle and lower sections of society, and their furniture was generally badly made with poorly executed designs and poor-quality woods. This type of commercial furniture was widely illustrated in a wealth of trade journals and catalogues such as the *Furniture Gazette, Furniture & Decoration* and the *Cabinet Maker*. Such firms vied with each other for custom and novelty at the various trade exhibitions held regularly after 1881. Most journals employed a resident designer to supply hints and

244 'Fancy' chair by Lambert Hitchcock of Hitchcocksville, Connecticut, c. 1825-30.

245 Rococo chair made in laminated rosewood by John Henry Belter of New York, c. 1855-60.

246 Ebonised mahogany armchair in the Louis XVI style. Made in New York in the 1870s.

247 Cast-iron garden seat stamped 'E. T. Barnum, Detroit, Michigan', and made c. 1885.

248 Part of a Renaissance Revival walnut bedroom suite made by the Berkey & Gay Company of Grand Rapids, Michigan, and exhibited at the Centennial Exposition in Philadelphia in 1876.

249 Bedstead in the 'Eastlake' style, made by the Herter Brothers of New York.

244
245
246
247

248

249

ideas for the trade, and some of these are so lacking in taste that it seems unlikely they were ever adopted.

This type of firm also introduced the use of bamboo for Japanese furniture incorporating Japanese lacquer panels, leather paper and woven matting, and re-introduced the fashion for cane and wicker furniture. At the same time large quantities of bentwood furniture was imported from Austria, and all three forms of furniture became popular for use in halls, conservatories, restaurants and smoking rooms.

An independent section of the furniture industry was based in High Wycombe, and this has remained the centre of country chair-making until today. The largest early 19th-century producer was Benjamin North who, like many others, made all types of windsor and spindle-back chairs.

The 19th century then saw a revolution in the furniture field. The move from craft to industry, despite the vain attempts of a few individuals to return to the old system, paved the way for the mass-production of the 20th century, a now seemingly irreversible trend.

Europe

The history of 19th-century furniture in France is dominated by a love of pastiche and by technical supremacy in the field of cabinet making. The political upheavals of the late 18th century had substantial repercussions on the furniture trade, and as early as 1797 a series of industrial exhibitions at the Louvre were initiated to encourage the application of advanced mechanical processes

in all areas of design. The growth of the middle class and the decline of aristocratic patronage under the Bourbon Restoration and the July Monarchy created new demands and less well-defined tastes, giving further encouragment to commercialism.

The Empire style prevailing under Napoleon lingered well into the century, but gradually concessions to comfort led to less architectural forms, while a new inventiveness produced a wider variety of decorative embellishments. Architect/furniture designers were replaced by ornamentalists, and a large number of publications on ornament provided pattern books for commercial manufacturers. The works of La Mésangère, published between 1802 and 1835, as well as those of M. Santi in 1828, Michael Jamsen in 1835, Alphonse Giroux in 1840, and Edouard Lémarchand and Aimé Chevenard in 1836, all contributed to the continuation of historical styles in furniture, but at the same time encouraged concessions to mechanical processes of manufacture. The ability to machine-cut veneers led to a fashion for *bois clairs*, the use of figured woods such as birds-eye maple and burr walnut, until about 1840, when this was superseded by the use of darker woods, ebony, stained pear or oak, offset with porcelain plaques, panels of *verre églomisé* and painted decoration. The use of elaborate ormolu mounts became minimal.

The decade 1830-40 saw the growth of Romanticism marked by a return to naturalism in the form of carved flowers and fruit, and ornament inspired by the Orient. At the same time a widespread interest in the middle ages gave rise to the Gothic or *troubadour* style. Gothic architectural motifs were applied to both furniture

250 'Moorish' smoking room from John D. Rockefeller's House on West 53rd Street, New York, designed *c.* 1880.

251 Cherry dining table by the Tobey Furniture Company, Chicago, *c.* 1888.

252 Oak buffet designed by H. P. Berlage, Amsterdam, *c.* 1900.

251

250

252

and interior decoration, which naturally led to new interpretations of the French Renaissance of the late 16th century.

The period of the Second Empire, 1848 onwards, saw further eclectic revivals of historical styles: the boulle work of Louis XIV, 3,254 the Rococo of Louis XV, and the more architectural and highly decorative styles prevalent under Louis XVI. Although of historical inspiration, all these styles suffered from a distinctly 19th century, and often insensitive, interpretation, aimed at a bourgeois market. Individual styles soon became associated with particular rooms—ebony and rosewood for libraries and smoking rooms, Rococo or boulle for salons, and elaborate drapery and upholstery for boudoirs.

During the first half of the century great advances occurred in upholstery, and various new pieces of furniture such as *confidantes à deux places, indiscrets à trois places, canapés de l'amitié, pouffes* and *crapauds,* became universally popular. Such renowned cabinet 257 makers as Fourdinois and Jeanselme exhibited upholstered furniture at the Paris Universal Exhibition in 1867.

The International Exhibitions of 1867, 1878, 1884 and 1889 demonstrated clearly the need for improvements in design and an escape from eclecticism. The loudest voice for reform was that of Comte Léon de Laborde, who had published in 1856 *De L'Union des Arts et de L'Industrie* to encourage the alignment of good design with mechanisation. His pleas for a return to true craftsmanship bore fruit in the establishment of the Union Centrale des Beaux Arts Appliqués a L'Industrie in 1865 which became the Union Centrale des Arts Décoratifs in 1877. The work of this organisation,

combined with the teachings of the architect Viollet-le-Duc, who advocated a return to Nature and the use of floral ornament, contributed to the final break away from historicism, and produced the entirely new and exciting universal style of Art Nouveau (see p. 295). The first exhibition of work in this style, the 'Salon de l'Art Nouveau', was organised in Paris by Samuel Bing in 1895, and was instrumental not only in creating an international style, but in laying the foundations for the Modern Movement.

Although Danish furniture was strongly influenced by the French Empire style both from France and Germany, the low state of the economy following a long series of hostile encounters with other nations produced a simple national style making good use of indigenous cheaper woods such as maple, ash, alder and birch. This 'Danish Empire' style infiltrated into both Norway and Sweden and was translated in the second quarter of the century into the 'Late Empire' style. This again originated in Denmark from the work of Gustav Friedrich Hetsch, who had studied in Paris under Percier. He introduced more severely Classical forms relieved by carved mahogany ornament to replace the more expensive ormolu, rather than the marquetry decoration of the former style.

The remainder of the century followed a similar pattern to that of England, France and America, with eclectic revivals of past styles following an identical sequence. In Sweden, however, the reaction to Classicism occurred earlier than elsewhere and a Neo-Gothic room was designed for the Stockholm Palace as early as 1828.

253 Gilded settee in the Louis XV style. French, c. 1860.

254 Rococo armchair with the original upholstery, made by the Horrix Brothers' Factory in The Hague in about 1870.

255 Laminated rosewood chair made by Messrs. Thonet Bentwood Furniture Manufactory, Vienna, c. 1836.

256 'Renaissance' portfolio stand signed Luigi Frullini, Florence, 1873.

257 Renaissance cabinet by Henri Fourdinois, c. 1855. Shown at the 1867 Paris Exhibition from which it was purchased by the Victoria and Albert Museum for £2,750.

258 'Old Norse' table and chair designed by Gerard Munthe in 1895 for a hotel near Oslo.

253

254

255

256

257

258

Scandinavia was also exceptional in that the standard of craftsmanship on the whole remained extremely high, and greatly facilitated the return to integrity of workmanship urged by international reformers towards the turn of the century. The 1870s saw the emergence of the 'Old Norse' or Viking style, which drew upon medieval Nordic ornament, and from which the Art Nouveau designer Gerard Munthe drew so much inspiration in the 1890s.

In the Netherlands the Empire style was still in evidence throughout the second quarter of the century, although various adapted forms of Biedermeier furniture were also produced. After the middle of century stylistic development was hampered by the growth of furniture factories, mass-producing goods of all types and tending to disregard many important design features. The first of these successful manufacturers were the Horrix Brothers in the Hague, established in 1853, and their range of designs included both Gothic and French revival examples. The quality of machine-made furniture rapidly declined, and the reforming voices of H. P. Berlage and K. P. C. Bazel in Amsterdam at the end of the century greatly improved matters by advocating logical construction and honest craftsmanship. At the same time in Belgium Victor Horta and Henry Van de Velde were struggling to gain recognition for their radical Art Nouveau designs.

The presence of Napoleon's Imperial delegates in Italy had firmly established the French Empire style, and its popularity was reinforced by large numbers of immigrant French craftsmen who had accompanied them. Ultimately the Italian sculptural tradition affected design, and interpretations of French styles produced elaborate, heavy and curvaceous forms with florid carving and large expanses of gilded wood.

The Gothic Revival found little favour among Italian patrons, and it was natural that Renaissance forms and ornament were widely adopted. Throughout the century middle-class demand upheld the commercial production of X-frame chairs, heavy carved tables, *cassoni*, and grandiose cabinets, with ornament drawn from

medieval and Renaissance paintings and 15th- and 16th-century Italian furniture.

Germany's largest contribution to 19th-century furniture history was the creation of the Biedermeier style. The influence of French Empire furniture was little felt after 1815, when social and political circumstances had radically reduced the spending power of both the courts and the middle classes. Demand for function rather than decoration produced bare, simple forms with little, if any, ornament. The severity of Biedermeier furniture was slightly relieved by the use of more decorative woods, mostly maple or fruitwoods, sometimes with inlaid lines of ebony. Emphasis lay largely on seat furniture, and interiors tended to be sparsely furnished.

As elsewhere, the decline in design quality occurred with the revival of interest in the Middle Ages. An unusually competent example of the application of Gothic architectural motifs to furniture was exhibited at the 1851 Great Exhibition in London by the firm of Carl Leistler & Son of Vienna.

The simultaneous revival of the Rococo style was most strongly felt in more conservative Vienna, where various 18th-century styles had prevailed despite Empire influence. Leistler was employed to decorate the interior of the Liechtenstein Palace in the Rococo manner between 1842 and 1847.

Soon commercial manufacturers turned to revivals of Renaissance and Baroque forms and eclectic interpretations of varying qualities inevitably became the norm.

Reaction against the historical approach to design did not occur until the 1890s, when a small group of artists in Munich, influenced by Belgium, France and England, began to produce work in the Art Nouveau style. The chief exponents of Art Nouveau in Germany were August Endell and Henri Van de Velde who, although Belgian, exhibited his work in Dresden in 1897 and settled in Germany in 1899.

Vienna also became the centre of a completely new part of the

259 Watercolour by Johann Erdmann Hummel of an interior showing Biedermeier furniture, c. 1820-25.

259

furniture industry, with the establishment of Messrs. Thonet's bentwood furniture manufactory in the 1830s. The Thonet Brothers perfected the process of steam-bending various woods, and hence were able to mass-produce furniture of an entirely original form and design. They held a virtual monopoly in bentwood furniture throughout the 19th century and by 1891 are said to have produced over seven million chairs with wholesale outlets throughout the Western world

America

As in the previous century, 19th-century American furniture styles closely followed European examples. By 1830 the improvement in transatlantic communications had considerably speeded up the process of dissemination of European technical knowledge and ideas and made prevailing tastes more accessible to a wider American public. The Neo-classical styles which had dominated English furniture design until the 1820s remained in favour in America in various forms until after 1850. The final phase of the Classical style, now referred to as the Greek Revival or American Empire, reflects the simplicity of French Restoration design as exemplified in George Smith's *Cabinet-maker and Upholsterer's Guide* (1826). Designs taken from Smith were first published in America in 1833 in an advertisement for a leading firm of New York cabinet makers, Joseph Meeks and Sons, and again in 1840 in the country's first published furniture design book, *The Cabinet-maker's Assistant* by John Hall of Baltimore. Characteristic of this style are simple forms, smooth surfaces and a lack of applied ornament.

The furniture industry during this period was still based in East Coast towns, and regional styles developed in accordance with local preferences for particular sources of Classical ornament. From the beginning New York was considered to be the centre of trade, attracting both immigrant and native cabinet makers, and the names Duncan Phyfe, Charles Honoré Lannuier, Michael Allison

and Joseph Meeks are synonymous with superior quality in both design and execution. Meeks established an American and Foreign Agency, and dispersed his goods throughout the United States.

Leading makers in provincial towns became universally associated with particular design features; Samuel McIntire in Salem, for instance, was well known for high-quality carved decoration, as were the Hancock Brothers in Boston. Also in Boston were Thomas Seymour, who worked in the style of Sheraton, and Lemuel Churchill, who produced Regency furniture emulating the style of Gillows of Lancaster. In Philadelphia Henry Connelly and Ephraim Haines favoured Sheraton designs, Joseph Barry produced Egyptian, and Antoine-Gabriel Quervelle Greek revival furniture. Baltimore provided some of the most accomplished interpretations of European styles and also produced a form of 'fancy' furniture, allied to Sheraton designs, but with the added features of painted or highly inlaid decoration, and cane or rush seating. Lambert Hitchcock of Hitchcockville, Connecticut, was also well known for fancy furniture of this type.

Another development which occurred at this time, but totally independently of outside influence, was furniture produced by the Shakers, a religious sect who believed in absolute purity of form, based on function. Its 'country' appearance belies its fine quality and perfect construction.

Although the Classical fashion sustained its popularity for almost 50 years, other styles intervened and were simultaneously exploited. The Gothic Revival, which had made such an impact on English design, was less acceptable in America, where romantic and literary connotations were absent. It did however find some favour, more with architects than furniture designers, and was acknowledged as suitable for the furnishings of particular rooms— libraries, smoking parlours and entrance halls, for example. Various English periodicals and publications were available for consultation: George Smith's *Household Furniture* (1808), Augustus Charles Pugin's designs in Ackermann's *Repository of Arts* (in book form in 1827), his son A. W. N. Pugin's *Gothic Furniture in the Style of the 15th Century*, Henry Wood's *Furniture Decoration* (1845) and J. C. Loudon's *Encyclopaedia of Cottage, Farm and Villa Architecture* (1833). George Smith's pupil Robert Conner, who emigrated from England and settled in New York, published America's first book of Gothic designs, *The Cabinet-maker's Assistant* in 1842. As late as 1868 an anonymous author in Philadelphia published a *Gothic Album for Cabinet-makers*.

Undoubtedly the chief exponents of the Gothic style were the architect Alexander Jackson Davis and his associate Andrew Jackson Downing, a landscapist. Davis' first major commission executed in the Gothic style was Glen Allen, built in 1832 for the Gilmores of Baltimore, and at Lyndhurst, built for William Paulding, the mayor of New York, he also designed Gothic furniture for the interior, and Downing collaborated in the design of the gardens. In 1850 Downing included Gothic designs in his *Architecture of Country Houses*. It is interesting to note that, as in England, the more accomplished designers in the Gothic style tended to be architects, while commercial furniture designers on the whole only applied Gothic ornament in the form of pointed arches, tracery, heraldic devices and crockets to incongruously basic forms of furniture.

Far less successful than its Gothic counterpart was the Elizabethan Revival. It too suffered from a lack of history and romance, and Elizabethan forms gradually merged into a general 'Renaissance' style in which eclecticism was the dominant feature – 16th- and early 17th-century French architectural ornament was erroneously combined with Carolean spirals and Flemish strapwork. A Renais-
248 sance bedroom was designed for the Philadelphia Centennial Exhibition as late as 1876.

The dominant mid-19th-century style of furniture was undoubt-
245 edly Rococo. Following on from the preceding French Empire style and supported by the large number of French craftsmen working in the furniture industry, the Rococo style soon acquired the names of 'French Modern', being the prevailing fashion, or 'French Antique', being still a revival of past forms. The 'S' scroll and the cabriole leg of the Louis XV style were combined with heavy, naturalistic carving, carved ornament which could, incidentally, be mass-produced by machine. One of the most famous 19th-century American cabinet makers producing Rococo furniture was John Henry Belter, who was born and trained in Wurtemberg, Germany, and emigrated to America and set up business in New York in about 1844. Although German, he concentrated on producing furniture in the French style, as did many others, and he applied his perfected use of laminated wood, usually rosewood, oak or ebonised hardwood, to the production of lacy, naturalistic Rococo carving.

246 After about 1865 Louis XV gave way to Louis XVI, but again, although following 18th-century precedents, the style became heavier and squatter than the original. Many of the firms producing Louis XVI furniture were founded by French cabinet makers. The renowned Paris firm of Ringuet LePrince and Marcotte established a workshop in New York, while Alexander Roux & Co., Julius Dressoir, and Bembe & Kimbel, all in New York, exhibited high-quality French furniture at the 1853 Crystal Palace Exhibition. Another successful German craftsman, Gustav Herter, sent his brother Christian to Paris before the business passed to him in 1870, to study with the decorative artist Pierre Victor Galland. French and German cabinet makers became pre-eminent in other areas: in New Orleans there were François Seignouret and Prudent Mallard, while the Stein Brothers in Muscatine, Iowa, became the principal providers of furniture for the Upper Mississippi Valley and the Great Plains.

Out of the fashion for Louis XVI emerged the 'Victorian Renaissance' style, with Classical architectural features, plaques of bronze, terracotta and porcelain, and fine marquetry panels. Surfaces became flatter, and carving was almost completely eliminated. The eclectic combinations of various historical elements again became dominant.

At this time also antiquarian interest in America's history stimulated a vogue for reproduction of Old Colonial or Old World

Furniture in traditional 18th-century American styles.

Furniture during the period 1830-70 suffered not only from an eclectic application of revived ornament, but from a general verbal confusion. Hence the term Renaissance came to be used not only to refer to heavy Elizabethan forms but to refined French Neoclassical elements of design. It was not until the Philadelphia International Centennial Exhibition in 1876 that any attempts to break away from conventional styles became apparent. The majority of decorative arts exhibits were condemned as being 'vulgar renditions of the French Renaissance', and only a small minority of objects showed any evidence of infiltration of the Arts and Crafts Movement from Europe and a fresh approach to art and design.

The most influential voice in America in the movement away from large-scale manufactured furniture was that of Charles Lock Eastlake, whose *Hints on Household Taste* (1868) was published in America in eight separate editions between 1872 and 1890. In it he advocated a return to simple medieval methods of construction and rectangular forms. In his own words, 'the best and the most picturesque furniture of all ages has been simple in general form. It may have been enriched by complex details of carved work or inlay but its main outline was always chaste and sober in design, never running into extravagant contour of unnecessary curves'. Eastlake's name rapidly became associated with Art Furniture and, although some manufacturers assumed the title 'Eastlake furniture' for their products, the majority of pieces bore very little resemblance to Eastlake's own furniture designs. Methods of construction may have adhered to his 'medieval principles', but the various forms of applied ornament, which he had in fact stated were permissible, were perhaps executed with a greater freedom than he himself might have found acceptable.

The most popular form of Art Furniture was of ebonised wood with inlaid or painted surfaces and gilt incised decoration. The Herter Brothers produced furniture of this type with exceptional 249 skill and they, like many others, began to introduce into their work more exotic design elements, Japanese, Moorish and Egyptian, which were enjoying so much favour in Britain in the 1870s. The Japanese contribution to the Philadelphia Centennial Exhibition excited great interest, as had the Japanese Court at the International Exhibition in London in 1862. The principal source of Japanese design for American makers was a catalogue of E. W. Godwin's *Art Furniture* issued by William Watt in 1877. No attempts appear to have been made to study true principles of Japanese design, but isolated Japanese motifs were successfully combined with features from other sources.

Initially related to the Japanese style, but soon independently fashionable, was bamboo furniture. A large amount was imported from England, but a few makers are known to have established production – Nimara & Sato and J. Lovezzo & Bros. in New York, and J. E. Wall in Boston. In the late 1870s Clarence Cook in the *House Beautiful* recommended bamboo as 'capital stuff' for furnishing country houses and referred potential purchasers to Vantine's New York Emporium. More in demand apparently was imitation bamboo, usually of maple with turned frames. C. A. Aimone, the Kilian Brothers and George Hunzinger in New York were the principal producers.

Sometimes associated with bamboo, but in fact totally unconnected, was wicker or rattan furniture, which was commercially produced as early as 1850. Mr Topf from New York was the sole contributor of wicker furniture to the Great Exhibition at the Crystal Palace in 1851. Little credit has so far been given to the ingenious designs and surprisingly sturdy methods of construction of such pieces. Demand for wicker furniture stretched well into the 20th century.

Another exotic phenomenon of the last quarter of the 19th century was a vogue for Moorish interiors, a fashion which relied mostly on imported accessories, heavy drapery and elaborately upholstered furniture. The invention of the coiled spring had enabled upholsterers to expand their repertoire, and deep buttoning, heavy fringes and rich tassels soon became the vogue. How-

260 Engraving of a Gothic cabinet made by Carl Leistler & Son of
Vienna and shown at the Great Exhibition, London, in 1851.

260

ever, Eastern motifs were also applied to commercially produced
furniture: particularly common are rows of small spindles and
fretwork decoration, as seen on imported Moorish screens. The
Tiffany Glass and Decorating Company and Tiffany Studios were
producing furniture exhibiting Eastern influence during the 1890s,
and Tiffany's associate Lockwood de Forest, recognising the
potential of Eastern products for the furnishing market, established
a business in Ahmadabad in India to supply his New York store.
The Brooklyn Museum possesses perhaps the most splendid
rendering of the Moorish style, the smoking room supplied by the
firm Pottier & Stymus for John D. Rockerfeller's house in the early
1880s.

An individual type of furniture entirely outside the mainstream
of international design was furniture made from animal's horns.
Such pieces, hideously constructed, must be considered as mere
curios. The movement towards the West and consequent new
settlement areas must have invoked an interest in America's
geography and natural history among more sophisticated East
Coast society, and animal-horn furniture evoked the wild life
that the early settlers had to endure. Presidents Lincoln and
Roosevelt were both presented with horn chair 'trophies' by
admiring citizens.

A material which really came into its own during the 19th
century in many fields was cast iron. Improved mechanical processes meant that iron could be used to produce the first form of
standardised furniture, with interchangeable parts. The centres of
the iron industry were Baltimore, Boston and New York, and a wide
ranges of furniture reflecting all styles were produced in vast
quantities after the middle of the century. It was considered
particularly suitable for gardens, and rustic chairs and seats
commanded the greatest demand. Many pieces were painted and
grained in imitation of wood. Bent wire furniture was simultaneously produced, but in lesser quantities; it lacked the obvious
strength and durability of cast iron.

Another popular material throughout the 19th century was
papier mâché, but furniture made of this material (see p. 79) seems
to have been mostly imported from England.

During the last two decades of the century the foundations of a
national style were laid. The first sign of a break from tradition
appeared in the work of the architect Henry Hobson Richardson.
After visiting Europe in 1882, he created an individual Romanesque
style with the use of Byzantine ornament and architectural forms.
His use of spindles and spirally turned legs is best exemplified in
the furniture designed by him for the Chamber of the Albany
Court of Appeals. Much of his work was executed by the Boston
firm of Irving and Casson and Davenport.

It is ironic that while the World's Columbian Exposition at
Chicago in 1893 was displaying the very worst aspects of commercial furniture design, epitomising the eclectic application of
historical styles, a small group of individuals in the same city were
initiating a radical movement away from the past and an entirely
fresh approach to art and architecture. The architectural reforms
of Louis Sullivan and Frank Lloyd Wright made a far-reaching
impact on the furnishing industry, which foreshadowed the
Modernist style of the 20th century (see p. 308). Wright had joined
the firm of Adler & Sullivan in 1887 on his arrival in Chicago, and
set up in independent business in 1893. His Oak Park style, which
began at this date, advocated the use of organic forms where both
architecture and interior design would merge into their natural
surroundings. His influence is strongly felt in the straight lines
and simple finishes of furniture produced by the Tobey Furniture
Company, one of Chicago's best-known makers.

Wright's innovatory ideas were also to influence the Craftsman
style promulgated by Charles and Henry Greene in Pasadena,
California, and Gustave Stickley in Eastwood, New York.

Although commercial production in traditional styles continued
until after the turn of the century, the progressive ideas of this
small group of men had set an indisputable precedent for the future.
Clarence Cook's review of Stickley's Exhibition of Craftsman
furniture at Grand Rapids in 1900 had significantly stated that 'the
day of cheap veneer, of jig-saw ornament, or poor imitations of
French periods, is happily over'.

CERAMICS

EUROPEAN LEAD-GLAZE AND STONEWARE

Paul Atterbury

When the Romans withdrew from Europe, they left behind a legacy of style and technique that continued to influence pottery production for several hundred years. A feature of Roman pottery, as with other art forms, was its internationalism—broadly, the Romans were able to impose a universal standard of style and production throughout Europe, so that the wares showed only limited regional variations.

After the withdrawal, Roman technology survived to a varied extent in different countries. In Britain, there was a gradual return to Iron Age styles and techniques, a move encouraged by the unstable social and political nature of the country during the various Nordic invasions. This pattern continued until the Norman conquest, although pottery from the Eastern counties of England show a greater level of sophistication because of the direct influence of Northern Europe.

In France and Italy the survival of the Roman tradition was more direct. In Italy particularly, direct descendants of the coarser type of Roman pottery were produced side by side with a new range of lead-glaze wares of some quality, designed primarily for table and pharmaceutical use. These wares prepared the way for the high-quality pottery produced during the medieval period.

Lead-glazing, the ability to make pottery non-porous with a coating of coloured glaze based on powdered lead in solution, was a technique known to the Romans, although it was not widely practised. After the collapse of the Roman Empire it died out, to be revived later in Italy and France. The technique then spread throughout Europe, giving potters a new stylistic freedom.

Decoration and modelling became more adventurous, although the tradition of internationalism established during the Roman period still continued. Although quite distinct regional forms appeared, medieval lead-glazed or slip-decorated pottery was broadly speaking international in style, a development encouraged by the considerable export trade that existed from one country to another. For example, the close stylistic links between English and French medieval pottery were created by the extensive export trade between northern France and Britain.

The first real break with the international medieval style came in Italy with the development of the so-called *mezza maiolica* slip-decorated pottery of the 14th and mid-15th centuries. These wares, decorated by scratching a design with a sharp point through the layer of white slip that covered the red earthenware body, gave the potter a new freedom in design based on the bold red-white contrast. Secondary colour could also be introduced by a clear or tinted glaze laid over the ware. These wares, decorated with motifs drawn usually from heraldry, legend or religion, were produced from the 14th century onwards in a number of Italian centres, including Venetia and Lombardy in the north, Tuscany and Umbria in the centre, and Calabria and Apulia in the south. In these centres, production was based on the workshop tradition that was an important part of the Renaissance philosophy, and so there were inevitable links with the styles of maiolica decoration that were being developed in Italy at the same time.

The technique and styles of Italian slipped wares varied from centre to centre, but the general pattern of development was from the heavy, bold style of the 15th century to the more delicate and free sketchy styles of the 16th. The northern and southern workshops tended to use varied colours and styles, while the central-Italian potters preferred the stark red and white *sgraffiato*.

261

262

261 Basin, coated with slip, with incised decoration. Italy, Faenza, 14th century.

262 Salt-cellar, lead-glazed earthenware with decoration in brown clay. France, St Porchaire, *c.* 1540.

263 Oval earthenware dish with green, yellow and brown lead glazes, decorated in high relief.

France, second half of 16th century.

264 White stoneware tankard with relief decorations, showing scenes from the life of Christ. Germany, Siegburg, dated 1559.

265 Dish in green-glazed earthenware decorated in low relief with emblems of the Passion and royal coats-of-arms. France, Beauvais, 1511.

266 Spouted jug of white stoneware. Germany, Siegburg, dated 1590.

267 Stoneware jug with a brown salt glaze, decorated with a relief of centaurs. Germany, Raeren, dated 1576.

268 Stoneware bellarmine with light brown salt glaze. Germany, Cologne, *c.* 1530.

263

264

265

266

267

268

These stylistic variations in Italy were both equally influential in France, where a range of pottery of remarkable quality and originality was produced during the Renaissance. The most remarkable is the type of cream-coloured pottery with inlaid and applied decoration in darker-coloured clay produced at Saint-Porchaire in Poitou between about 1530 and 1570. Also known as 'Henri Deux' ware, these pieces have aroused the interests of collectors and scholars for many years, partly because of the intricacy of the technique, and partly because no one has yet been able to identify satisfactorily the potter who made them. The decoration, usually a combination of arabesques and Renaissance motifs, were applied with a delicacy and a sense of pattern that suggests links with contemporary typography and book bindings. This technique was revived during the 19th century in France and England.

A few examples of Saint-Porchaire ware were traditionally decorated with reptiles modelled in high relief, linking them with Bernard Palissy, the one great personality known from this period. Despite his reputation and his enormous influence on pottery, Palissy is still a rather shadowy figure. His life and activities are still clouded by legend and half-truth, but certain basic details are known. Born in Agen in about 1510, he practised first as a maker of stained glass before becoming a potter and moving to Paris in 1566. He developed a range of coloured glazes which, combined with his great skill in modelling, produced a style of pottery that was

influential throughout Europe until the 19th century. His techniques were also new. He made casts from actual reptiles to ornament his pieces, and he also related ceramics to other art forms, drawing many of his ideas from contemporary sculptors such as Jean Goujon.

The other great French pottery centre at this period was Beauvais, which produced a great range of wares, usually with a green or yellow glaze. These include domestic and tablewares, as well as religious plaques and models of animals and humans. These Beauvais wares had a direct influence on other countries, in particular England and Germany.

In Germany, lead-glazed earthenware underwent the same pattern of development as in other parts of Europe, although by the beginning of the 16th century German potters had started to concentrate on the production of tiles or plaques for stoves. The links between the potter and the stove maker are partly geographical and partly practical. The colder climate of northern Europe had prompted the development of more sustained and controlled forms of heating, and clay had long been used for insulation and for even distribution of heat. By the 14th century it had become a common practice to glaze the clay panels surrounding the stoves, and so characteristic styles of decoration slowly evolved. The stove itself had in the meantime become an important part of the interior design of the building, relating closely to wall and floor tiling.

Because of their dependence upon architecture, the stoves inevit-

269 Stove tile with figure in relief, probably representing Isabella of Portugal. Germany, probably Nuremberg, c. 1540.

270 Earthenware 'face-jug', modelled and incised. England, Laverstock, 13th century.

271 Lead-glazed earthenware 'tyg' with slip-trailed decoration and pads of stamped white clay. England, Wrotham, stamped for John Livermore and dated 1649.

272 Lead-glazed earthenware dish with slip-trailed decoration, by Thomas Toft. England, Staffordshire, c. 1675.

273 Lead-glazed earthenware dish with slip decoration in different colours. England, probably Staffordshire, c. 1700.

269

270

272

271

273

ably reflected contemporary styles, particularly the Gothic. The stove itself became a typically Gothic structure, surmounted by a tower decorated with niches and arcades, some of which contained relief-modelled figures, crowned by complex tracery. The dominance of the Gothic style meant that Renaissance techniques had less impact in Germany than elsewhere in Europe. The early German potters used the familiar green and yellow lead glazes, and although a polychrome palette spread north from Italy in about 1500, it did not greatly affect the overall styles. The colours of Italian maiolica were quickly absorbed by the makers of tiled stoves, but they were still applied primarily to relief decoration. This pattern did not change until the mid-16th century, when the Mannerist style gradually replaced the Gothic. Because of their basic architectural qualities, there are links between the products of the Della Robbia family and the German stove makers.

Many other wares besides stove tiles were made by the German potters, but they all show the stylistic influence of the tiles. Banded relief decoration was common, linked often with formal tracery and arcading, and the scenes depicted were generally of religious and mythological inspiration. Nuremberg was the centre of German earthenware production until the 17th century, by which time the emphasis had switched to stoneware and faience production. Lead-glazed wares continued to be produced, but largely on a peasant level which, although lively, lacked the fine quality of the earlier wares.

The development of salt-glazed stoneware in Germany towards the end of the 14th century revolutionised pottery production in Europe, its effect being similar to that caused by the development of porcelain in the early 18th century. Stoneware is a highly fired

vitrified material, with hard, resonant and non-porous qualities that gave considerable freedom to the potter. The ware was usually glazed with salt, a process achieved by throwing a certain amount of salt into the kiln during firing. The salt vaporises, and combines with the silica and alumina in the clay, producing a thin, colourless smear glaze on the surface of the ware, lightly pitted like the skin of an orange.

The origins of stoneware production in Germany are uncertain, with several areas claiming the development of the process. Siegburg and Hessen were both early centres of production, but the most significant development took place along the Rhine. The combination of rich clay deposits and the transport facilities offered by the river Rhine ensured a rapid growth of the stoneware industry. Centres developed at Grenzenhausen, at Siegburg, at Frechen and at Raeren to the south. Extensive potteries also developed at Cologne, which became the trading centre for the industry. From Cologne German stonewares were shipped to the Netherlands, to France and to England. Another centre grew up at Kreussen, in Franconia, using a dark brown salt glaze.

Early stonewares were a dull grey colour, relieved later by a coloured wash which ranged from dark brown to pale yellow, and mottled effects were also common. However, the clay used at Siegburg had good white firing qualities, and so was generally uncoloured. In the late 16th century, the grey Westerwald stonewares were first decorated with cobalt blue, a style that became characteristic of German stonewares, and survives to the present day.

The styles of German stoneware follow the same pattern of development as other types of European pottery. Early wares were

264,266,267

267
268

90

274 Dish of white earthenware with moulded decoration. Bernard
Palissy or his school.

274

wheel-thrown in medieval style, with simple incised or banded
decoration, and the shapes frequently had high necks and a waisted
foot. During the 15th century stamped and cast relief decoration
was applied to the surface of the wares, in the style of contemporary
metalwork, a technique that became increasingly popular. The
decorations included medallions, arabesques, rosettes, scrolls,
animal, human and foliate panels or friezes, heraldry and inscriptions and overall geometric patterns. Many wares were also wholly
cast, with a proportion of the surface decoration included in the
mould. During the early 16th century the traditional Gothic imagery
was replaced by a rather heavy interpretation of Renaissance
motifs; these affected particularly the shapes, which became more
adventurous and Italianate, relating closely to contemporary metalwork, especially in precious materials. Designers also were influenced by the graphic artists of the Nuremberg School. These
wares paved the way for the general introduction of Mannerist
styles later in the century.

Raeren, Siegburg and Cologne dominated the manufacture until
the early 17th century, when the Thirty Years War brought about
the decline or closure of the workshops. The emphasis then
switched to the Westerwald area, with many potters emigrating
there from the Rhine and taking their techniques and moulds with
them. By about 1630, the typical Westerwald type had emerged,
with its ovoid body, simple stamped floral patterns and cobalt-blue
decoration.

Stoneware was also produced in France, particularly in the
Beauvais area. Here, however, the designs and decorative styles
were adapted freely from the earthenwares, and so were more
closely linked to the Renaissance.

The styles and techniques of German stoneware were particularly
influential in England, helped greatly by the thriving export trade.
Vast quantities of fairly basic stonewares came into England via the
Netherlands, including bottles, flasks, cooking pots and other
domestic items. Perhaps the best-known example is the Bellarmine,
a fat-bellied jug decorated with a bearded face in relief. These jugs
were said to lampoon Cardinal Bellarmine, the persecutor of the
Protestants, but in fact the tradition of face decoration can be traced 270
back to the Romans.

Through the 17th century there were many attempts by English
potters to produce an adequate local replacement for the imported
German stoneware jugs, but no one seems to have been successful
until the Fulham potter, John Dwight, took out his famous patent
in 1671, which granted him the rights to produce 'The Mistery of
Transparent Earthenware, commonly knowne by the Names of
Porcelain or China and Persian Ware, as alsoe the Misterie of Stone
Ware vulgarly called Cologne Ware'. Recent excavations at the site
of Dwight's pottery have produced no traces of his porcelain, but
vast quantities of stonewares of largely Germanic form. These
indicate that his products were able to replace a proportion of the
German trade.

Dwight also developed a range of fine stonewares, which he used
for both tablewares and ornaments. He was able to make a very thin
stoneware that, while not actually a porcelain, could be made to be
almost transparent. He used both white and grey-firing clays, which
were sometimes blended with black clay to produce a marbled 275
effect. Many of his wares also have applied cast reliefs, a simplified
version of the German decorative style which anticipates both the
18th- and 19th-century domestic stonewares decorated with hunt-

275 Brown salt-glazed stoneware bottle with marbling and applied reliefs. England, probably from John Dwight's Fulham pottery, c. 1690.

276 Grey salt-glazed stoneware figure of Lydia Dwight, dead daughter of the potter. England, John Dwight's Fulham pottery, c. 1673-74.

277 Unglazed red stoneware mug with applied moulded decoration. England, probably the Staffordshire pottery of John and David Elers, end of the 17th century.

278 Teapot in the form of a camel, white salt-glazed stoneware. England, c. 1745.

275   276   277   278

ing reliefs and, perhaps less directly, Wedgwood's jasper ware (see p. 109).

However, Dwight's greatest contribution to ceramics was a range of finely modelled figures, including both mythological characters and life-size portrait busts. The quality of the modelling is emphasised by the smear glazing achieved by the salt, and these models represent a standard of ceramic sculpture not to be seen again until Kändler started working at Meissen (see p. 98).

The technology that Dwight had developed inevitably spread to other parts of England, despite his attempts to retain control of the process by court action. Among the potters mentioned in his petitions were James Morley of Nottingham, and John and David Elers of Fulham. Morley made a range of brown stonewares at the end of the 17th century; the quality and style of these can be seen in the surviving trade card, which shows examples with the pierced outer wall typical of Nottingham wares. Similar brown stonewares have also been excavated in Staffordshire, Derbyshire and Yorkshire, and so it is apparent that stonewares were in general production in Britain by the end of the 17th century.

The Elers brothers also made brown stonewares, but their fame rests largely on their red stonewares which they produced in quantity after moving to Bradwell Wood, then in the wilds of Staffordshire. These fine pieces, based on the Yi-hsing Chinese wares imported extensively at this period, are notable for the delicacy and thinness of their potting, and for their cast and stamped decoration. The quality of finish shows an understanding of both slip-casting and lathe turning, techniques vital to the later development of the industry in Staffordshire and elsewhere.

By the 1730s salt-glazed stoneware had become the standard English substitute for Chinese porcelain, the body made white by the addition of ground flint and white clay from the West Country. It was produced in quantity for table and domestic use, and many techniques were involved in its production, including slip-casting, press moulding, carving, piercing and engine turning. There was a dependence on cast relief modelled decoration, a surviving link with the stonewares of Germany.

Coloured decoration was rare, but cobalt blue was sometimes applied to the surface or filled into a design scratched into the un-fired surface—a technique known as scratch-blue. Later in the century enamelling and transfer-printing techniques were also used, by which time white salt-glazed stoneware was in large-scale production throughout England.

But the salt-glaze potters in England, unlike those in Germany, did not dominate the market, but had to exist side by side with the makers of earthenware, who continued to thrive. By the end of the medieval period, English potters had become thoroughly familiar with the techniques of lead-glazed earthenware production. Elaborate modelling and coloured glazes characterised wares produced at centres such as Nottingham, but the most significant developments took place in the West Country and Kent. Here, the slipware technique evolved, a method of decoration using different coloured clays trailed on to the surface of the ware in a liquid state. The tygs produced at Wrotham, with their dark ground and raised

decoration in lighter slip, are typical and show the general influence of Tudor styles of decoration. There are decorative links with furniture, tapestry, metalwork, and even with imported German stonewares. In the West Country slipware was decorated by the *sgraffiato* technique, similar to the 15th-century Italian wares, with the design carved through a layer of applied slip. Slipwares made in Devon were exported in great quantities during the 17th century to the new colonies in North America, from ports such as Bideford and Barnstaple.

However, the greatest development in slipware took place in Staffordshire. Here the process was reversed, and slip-trailed decoration in brown and orange clays was applied to a cream background. In this emergent industrial area, with its rich deposits of clay and coal, the skills of the slipware decorator were developed to the utmost. The families of potters usually associated with this technique, the Tofts, the Simpsons, the Woods and the Taylors, relied on a variety of decorative techniques and imagery which included Royalist portraits, mythological and religious themes, and abstract pattern-making drawn partly from the Renaissance and partly from contemporary work in other materials. Another technique was combing, where different coloured slips were merged together in a haphazard manner, to produce patterns similar to those on marbled end-papers.

Staffordshire was the centre of slipware production, but there were many other areas where similar work was produced. By the early 18th century slipware had been replaced by other styles and techniques, but it survived on a low level until the 20th century as a method of decorating cheap, country-produced table and domestic wares.

Many of the techniques developed by the English slipware potters, such as marbling, combing and *sgraffiato* decoration were adopted by stoneware and earthenware potters working in the early years of the 18th century. Similar techniques closely associated with stoneware, such as stamping, sprigging and casting, were rapidly adopted by makers of earthenware, and so there was a very fertile exchange of ideas and styles from one technique to another. In Staffordshire agate ware was developed, a technique whereby coloured clays are blended together to produce marbled effects that continue throughout the body of the ware, and there was increasing use of mechanised processes such as engine turning. New coloured glazes were developed from metal oxides to give the decorator a greater freedom, and there was an expansion of figure modelling, which ranged from small press-moulded toys and simple animals to elaborate groups made from rolled clay with a remarkable concern for intricate detail. Many of these figures and models were produced in both salt-glazed stoneware and in earthenware, the latter crudely decorated with splashed colours that relate them to the earthenware figures produced at Beauvais during the 16th century. Perhaps the most important development, however, was that the great names who were to mastermind the expansion of the industry during the 18th century, the Whieldons, the Astburys, and the Wedgwoods, were already at work in Staffordshire and elsewhere in England.

EUROPEAN TIN-GLAZED POTTERY

Paul Atterbury

The technique of decorating pottery with an opaque white glaze formed from tin oxide is perhaps the best known one in the history of Western ceramics. No other technique has crossed both geographical and cultural frontiers with such ease, to produce a style universally applied throughout Europe. Tin glazing probably developed in Mesopotamia in the 9th century, and is one of the few ceramic processes not to have evolved through the Far East. Ironically, later manufacturers of tin-glazed wares used the whiteness of the glaze to imitate Chinese porcelain, but the roots of the material and the style are essentially Islamic. The technique changed little as it passed from Islamic potters to Spain and thence to Italy in the 14th and 15th centuries, and then spread rapidly throughout Europe. Centres of tin-glaze production were established in the far corners of Europe, in Denmark, in Sicily, in Bohemia and in Ireland, and yet the wares produced differed only in degree and sophistication. The universality of the technique is underlined by the many names used to describe it—faience, maiolica, delftware, fayence—most of which mean exactly the same. The names were generally taken from centres of production, for example the French and German 'faience' and 'fayence' come from Faenza in Italy, while the English 'delftware' clearly comes from Holland. The Italian word 'maiolica' comes from Majorca, thought then to be where the process originated.

The technique itself is relatively simple, with a clearly defined end product. Unfired pottery is covered with liquid glaze, leaving an even deposit on the surface. This is then painted in a number of oxide colours, the palette being limited by the high temperature of the firing. The tin-glazed surface is absorbent, and so all painting has to be direct and free, and without mistakes. The decorated ware is then fired, fixing the colours into the opaque white glaze. Many pieces also underwent a second lustre firing.

The secrets of the Islamic potter were introduced into Europe via Spain during the period of Moorish dominance. Tin-glazed wares decorated with a lustre glaze in the style of Kashan pottery were first produced in Malaga in the 13th century. These wares were widely admired and were exported as far as England and Sicily. From Malaga the technique spread to Cordoba, Aragon, Valencia, Lisbon, Catalonia and Manises, and as it spread the style changed. At first the wares were close copies of the Islamic originals, but gradually European imagery and themes were intermingled. Heraldic designs with Kufic inscriptions were mixed with elements borrowed from Gothic, Romanesque and Renaissance styles, while foliate ornamentation acted as a link between the two cultures. At 279 Manises, representational subjects were produced, including sailing ships and human figures in a recognisably European context. Most of the pieces produced were ornamental plaques, painted on both sides, but by the end of the 15th century, the Spanish potters had started to make more functional items, including architectural, domestic and tablewares. Toledo and Seville became the centres of this type of production, the most important aspect of which was architectural tile panels for floors and walls, a direct legacy of the Islamic potters.

From Spain the tin-glazed technique spread first to Italy, helped by the popularity of imported wares from Manises. The first examples of Italian maiolica date from the late 11th century, but the significant development of the style took place in the 13th and 14th centuries in centres as far apart as Sicily, Orvieto, Ravenna, Faenza and Padua. There were a great number of centres of maiolica production in Italy, and differences tend to be regional rather than local; it is thus quite hard to define the characteristics of particular centres, for there is a considerable stylistic overlap. Early maiolica tends to be simple in design, with decorative elements drawn from heraldry, foliage, animals and geometry, freely painted without the precision and formality of the Hispano-Moresque wares. The greater variety of shapes reflected the more domestic quality of the industry in Italy. Freed from the restraints imposed by Islamic ritual and iconography, the Italian potters were able to concentrate more on function and form.

During the 15th century there was a development of both technique and of the range of colours available, and so for the first time maiolica became a part of the mainstream of Renaissance style. The 282,283 greater control and skills available to potters allowed them to introduce both portraiture and Gothic details, and there was an increasing concern to paint the whole surface of the wares—with tight, well-developed patterns, based frequently on Gothic foliate or Persian palmette designs.

From this greater confidence developed the *istoriato* style of painting, first at Faenza, and later at other centres, such as Deruta 283 and Cafaggiolo. This style, with its dependence on imagery drawn from religion, mythology and history via prints and drawings, represents the high point of Italian maiolica. The wares are linked not only with contemporary painting, but also with parallel developments in other countries. The painters of the *istoriato* style inevitably worked mainly on large plaques, but other shapes were also used, including pilgrim bottles and the familiar *albarello*, or drug jar.

Another aspect of this phase of maiolica production is the emergence of individual potters' personalities. Within the Renaissance workshop tradition there was a considerable tolerance of individuality, and so the first master potters and painters appear during this period, identifiable either by name or by the characteristics of their style. Also easily identified are works by the family of ceramic sculptors working during this period, the Della Robbias. Although 284 three-dimensional wares had been produced at Faenza and elsewhere, the Della Robbias—Luca, Andrea and Giovanni—developed a quite distinct style of ceramic sculpture. They relied on scale, adapting their ideas from marble and bronze, and on a range of bright, opaque colours which made them unique among maiolica potters.

In the 16th century the range of maiolica style increased further. 281 An awareness of Chinese porcelain introduced both new decorative imagery and the use of a blue and white palette. The painters looked increasingly to prints and to literature for their ideas, and, at the same time adopted a free and sketchy approach to drawing. Techniques developed as well, including the iridescent lustres particular to Gubbio, while others, such as piercing, were borrowed from other fields of ceramic production. However, despite this awareness of other techniques and materials, maiolica continued to thrive and develop in Italy until the 18th century. New centres of production grew up, some to produce new styles, such as the fantasies and grotesques of Castelli and Liguria, while others continued to use the older styles which gradually became more simplified, debased and repetitive. New artistic styles, such as Rococo, were reflected in maiolica and, at the same time, the maiolica potters were forced to compete directly with other ceramic materials. Finally it was this competition, with porcelain and with English and European creamwares, that greatly reduced the industry in Italy, as in other centres of the tin-glaze production.

By the end of the 16th century the centre of tin-glaze production had shifted from Italy to Holland and Britain. The first recorded

279 Hispano-Moresque bowl with lustre glaze depicting a sailing ship. Manises, early 15th century.

280 Maiolica jug painted in brown and green. Italy, Siena, 14th century.

281 Maiolica dish painted in delicate colours and with a border of foliage in relief. Italy, Angarano, late 17th century.

282 Polychrome figures representing the Nativity decorate this object, probably an inkstand. Italy, Faenza, c. 1509.

283 Italian maiolica plate in the High Renaissance style, painted by Master Jacopo, c. 1510.

279

280

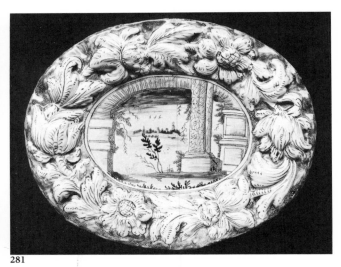

281

282

283

tin-glaze pottery in Holland was established in 1564, by the son of a maiolica potter from Casteldurante. Another descendant of the same potter moved to England, establishing tin-glaze potteries at Norwich and later in Lambeth. The other early tin-glaze centre in the Netherlands was Antwerp, which developed an early reputation for tile production. The styles of 16th-century Dutch tin-glaze, or delftware as it later became known, were primarily north Italian, with an emphasis on grotesques and ornamental designs taken from engravings, cut leather and wrought iron work. A number of colours were used, but there was already a concentration on blue painting, the essential characteristic of delftware. Antwerp potters spread northwards to Dordrecht, Haarlem and thence to Delft and Rotterdam, thus launching the highly productive Dutch tin-glaze industry which dominated European ceramics from the mid-17th to the mid-18th century.

In Holland, and particularly at Delft, there occurred the first significant break with the tin-glaze traditions of Spain and Italy, affecting both technique and style. Changes in technique included the blue and white palette, the use of outlines drawn directly on to the unglazed pottery and the application of a lead-glaze over the tin to give an added surface sheen. The stylistic changes were more significant, for the Renaissance was replaced by China as the source of inspiration. The import of Chinese porcelain in large quantities by the Dutch East India Company had started early in the 16th century, and from this trade there developed all the characteristic

styles of Dutch delftwares. At first the Chinese styles influenced both shape and surface decoration, and many mid-17th-century productions were close copies of Ming porcelain. Later the European Baroque style was also influential, and so by the end of the century the Dutch potters had compromised on a strange but harmonious blend of Eastern and Western cultures. A vast range of wares was produced from the domestic to the ornamental; the latter included huge display vases and cisterns, decorative plaques and, of course, the tiles, the most significant productions of the Dutch tin-glaze potters.

Although large tile panels for wall decoration were an established part of the tin-glaze tradition, the Dutch contribution was quite new. The designs were no longer ritualistic or geometric, but were an important part of the Baroque scheme of decoration. The emphasis was on the mass, not on individual tiles, and so huge decorative schemes were produced, based on flower and fruit sprays, allegorical, religious and historical scenes, landscapes, seascapes and domestic and heraldic details. In these tile panels the Chinese influence was generally minimal. On a more limited scale, tiles were also produced to fill niches, to surround fireplaces, and for use in dairies and kitchens.

In the early 18th century the same pattern of production continued in Holland, although many designs had become stylised through constant repetition, losing much of their original liveliness. One important development was the introduction of a red colour

285

286,2

284 Circular relief of terracotta by Luca della Robbia showing the Lamb of God.

284

which allowed the tin-glaze potters to copy the 'Imari' styles of Japanese porcelain made as Arita. Faced by increasing competition from both Chinese and European wares, the Dutch potteries gradually declined, and very few Delft potteries survived into the 19th century.

The origins of the tin-glaze in England were closely related to Holland. The first potters probably arrived from Holland during the 1570s, and by the end of the century the industry was well established in Lambeth. Styles and techniques at first followed maiolica closely, with the designs taken mostly from contemporary engravings. Only occasionally were pieces produced which related directly to England and Holland. However, by the mid-17th century characteristic English styles had appeared; some were developed from Palissy's modelled earthenware, but more important was the range of blue-dash chargers, so named because of the pattern of blue dashes around the rim. These were painted with effigy portraits of English kings and queens, scenes of horsemen, **289** Adam and Eve or sprays of local flowers. This style first appeared after the restoration of Charles II, and its bold, colourful and stylised type of decoration has close links with contemporary slipware.

Delftware was made in Lambeth continuously until the early 19th century, and from there potters moved to other parts of Britain. Centres were established at Bristol and Liverpool, and tin-glaze was also produced in the West Country, Ireland and Scotland. Most British tin-glaze potteries were either in seaports or in areas with

direct links to the sea, which partly explains the close stylistic links between British and Dutch production. At first, the English potters followed closely the Chinese styles popular in Holland, but their results were far less skilful. English techniques were less refined, and there was less understanding of the Chinese styles being copied. Oriental designs on English tin-glaze tended to be decorative in the Chinoiserie sense, rather than purely Chinese, and this pattern did **291** not alter until the mid-18th century, when English potters began to suffer more from the direct competition of imported Chinese porcelains. Attempts were made then to make English delftware look like Chinese porcelain, but such moves were too late to save the industry.

Generally English delftware was a simple, unsophisticated product, made in large quantities for a domestic market. Although tiles and tile panels were produced, they lacked the splendour and scale of the earlier Dutch pieces. English styles as a whole tended to be drawn from European sources, and so were generally derivative and low key. However, some of the English versions of Dutch designs were effective, especially the landscapes. Painters also made use of engravings after artists such as Teniers and Gravelot to develop genre scenes. The landscape-decorated wares reflect the developing English interest in landscape, and relate closely in style to paintings by Gainsborough and Watteau. This style is particularly associated with Bristol, as is the *bianco-sopra-bianco* technique of **291** decoration introduced to England from Sweden, in which decora-

285 Delft wall-tile, tin-glazed earthenware painted in blue and displaying portraits of William and Mary in medallions. Factory of Adrianus Kocks, c. 1694.

286 Delft tulip vase, c. 1700, tin-glazed earthenware painted in blue, with manganese-purple outlines.

287 Tin-glazed earthenware jug painted in polychrome with gold. Delft, c. 1690.

288 Double gourd vase painted in over-glaze enamel colours. Germany, Fulda, 1741-44.

289 Dish painted in yellow, manganese, grey, green and blue, depicting Adam and Eve. London, c. 1660-75.

290 Ship-bowl made for a captain, painted mainly in blue. Liverpool, c. 1750-60.

291 Dish with Chinoiserie central design and a border in the *bianco-sopra-bianco* technique. Lambeth, c. 1747-55.

285

286

287

288

289

290

291

tion in white slip is added on top of the already painted tin-glaze ground. One particularly English development was the range of finely painted ship bowls, made primarily at Liverpool to commemorate particular vessels. The painting of many of these is as fine as anything achieved in Holland, and they represent the high point of English tin-glaze in terms of both technique and originality of subject matter. Apart from pieces of this quality, which all the main centres certainly produced, English tin-glaze remained a derivative and often crude style which lacked the vitality of contemporary earthenwares and could not compete with other materials. It was developed too late to have any impact on international styles, and so remained largely a localised product. It is significant that tin-glaze does not seem to have been produced in Staffordshire, where other superior materials and techniques already controlled the market.

Because of the truly international quality of tin-glaze, it is important to consider some other centres of production. Development in France followed a similar pattern to Italy, and the first tin-glazed wares were probably produced in the 14th century. Styles at first came fairly directly from Moorish Spain, but gradually Italian influences began to predominate. Italian potters were working in Lyon early in the 16th century, and they developed a centre producing *istoriato*-style decoration. From Lyons the technique spread to other centres, introducing new Italianate styles of decoration in the process. The most important of these centres was Nevers, where a number of Italian potters were established by 1600. Gradually maiolica styles were replaced by decoration based on contemporary ornamental engravings, and later by country scenes and pastorals. Another characteristic Nevers 17th-century style was to reverse the technique, and paint in white on a solid blue ground. Tin-glaze then spread to Rouen, where the first licence to manufacture the ware was granted in 1644. The Rouen potters followed closely the styles of maiolica, and then of Holland before developing their own techniques early in the 18th century. The most important of these was the *style rayonnant*, a regular geometric form of decoration derived from drapery. Further south, centres also developed at Moustiers and Marseilles, where there was an emphasis on landscape, 'genre' and pastoral scenes.

Unlike many other countries, France developed its tin-glaze production to new levels of sophistication during the 18th century, in terms of both scale and richness of decoration. The French potters managed to come to terms with the challenge posed by Oriental porcelain, and used Oriental styles to enrich their own productions. This move was led by Rouen potters, but the other centres rapidly followed. Tin-glaze was produced in vast quantities to suit all levels of the market, and this concentration and refinement enabled the potters to hold their own against competition. New centres developed, among which was Strasbourg, whose potters introduced new colours, new realism of modelling and painting, and the making of figures, inspired largely by contemporary German porcelain (see p. 98). Faience in France in the mid-18th century achieved qualities of finish, technique and style quite above the general pattern of development of tin-glaze in Europe. On all levels the material was able to compete with porcelain, and it was not until the widespread introduction of English creamware into France in the 1780s that the tin-glaze potters began to lose ground.

In Germany, tin-glaze development followed a different pattern, because its origins were related to the manufacture of stove tiles. German potters were familiar with relief modelling, and so adapted this style to suit the technique of tin-glaze. There was also less dependence on Italy, for styles derived more from Mannerism and wood engravers such as Dürer. In northern Germany there was also a direct Dutch influence, especially in centres such as Hamburg and Hanau. The most distinctive German tin-glaze was produced at Frankfurt, a centre started in the 17th century, whose products were characteristically exuberant in scale, ornamentation and colour. Their decoration was generally based on a mixture of Chinese and Dutch styles. Another feature of German production were the *Hausmaler*, or outside decorators, who were able to break the regular pattern of factory production and impose decorative styles borrowed from other fields, such as glass decoration. In the 18th century German tin-glaze production followed a similar pat-

292 Vase in double gourd shape, painted in blue. Germany, Hanau, *c.* 1680.

293 Polychrome-painted dish depicting the Rape of Europa. France, Nevers, *c.* 1675.

294 Faience tureen with polychrome decoration. Sweden, Rörstrand, 1768.

295 Gadrooned oval basin, painted in blue with touches of red. France, Rouen, *c.* 1710-20.

296 Hunting group in faience with polychrome enamel *petit feu* decoration. France, Strasbourg, *c.* 1750-55.

292

293

294

295

296

tern to France, with the potters becoming more sophisticated as the competition from porcelain and other materials increased. As in France, their adaptability enabled them to survive until the end of the century.

Tin-glaze pottery was produced in many other parts of Europe, the most important of which was Scandinavia. Development was later, but followed a similar pattern to France and Germany. There were some localised influences, for example the large-scale production of stove tiles, but generally styles followed the 18th-century sophistication of other European potters. There were centres in Sweden, Denmark and Norway, the most important of which were **296** at Stralsund, Rörstrand, Marieburg and Copenhagen. Scandinavian production was generally very similar, partly because there was a

considerable migration of potters from one centre to another, and partly because the wares were for a broadly local market. This localisation resulted in a number of typically Scandinavian styles which included shapes derived from contemporary metalwork, and large plaques to be mounted as table tops or trays.

There were many other centres of tin-glaze pottery in Europe, all broadly reflecting the international quality of the material. In terms of both scale and length of production, tin-glaze can claim to be one of the most important and long lasting of European ceramic developments. Styles were able to cross frontiers very freely because the potters were able to adapt the materials to suit all levels of the market. No other ceramic style could express so well both peasant charm and court sophistication.

THE GOLDEN AGE OF PORCELAIN

John Cushion

From at least AD 850 potters in the Far East had been using china-clay and china-stone to produce what we refer to today as hard-paste porcelain, but the manufacture of a comparable material did not begin in Europe until the first quarter of the 18th century, when the now famous porcelain factory of Augustus II, Elector of Saxony, was established at Meissen in 1710. Before this time, however, there had been some production of artificial porcelains, now referred to as soft-paste, first in Italy and later in France.

The early so-called Medici porcelain began to be manufactured about 1575, at the Florentine court of Francesco I de' Medici and, although Francesco died in 1587, production appears to have continued in very limited quantities up until about 1613. The finished ware was composed of about 80 per cent white clay and 20 per cent the materials of glass. Records show that at least some of these early wares were fired by Flaminio Fontana, a maiolica potter from Urbino, who was at Florence from 1573. There are about 60 examples of this manufacture recorded today; they are nearly all of European form, with painted decoration in underglaze-blue (cobalt), sometimes with the addition of purple outlines acquired by the use of manganese. These two colours are among those few known as 'high-temperature' colours, a term describing those that can be fired at the same temperature as that of the glaze. Cobalt was used to produce underglaze-blue decoration in China from about AD 1300, whereas manganese can only be used as an underglaze colour on the lower-fired soft-paste.

Whilst the decoration of these early porcelains was obviously inspired by the Oriental imports, the forms were mostly those of contemporary earthenware vases, jugs, basins, dishes and bottles. Records indicate that a few similar wares were made at Pisa in about 1620 and at Padua during the second quarter of the 17th century.

No further attempts to manufacture a ware resembling the hard-paste porcelain of China appears to have been made in Europe until 1673, when Louis Poterat, a French earthenware potter from Rouen, was granted a patent for the manufacture of porcelain. However, Poterat seemingly made little use of his licence to manufacture 'porcelains and pottery in the fashion of Holland', and there still remains a great deal of doubt as to the authenticity of the few minor tablewares of soft-paste porcelain attributed to his hand. He died in 1696.

Knowledge about the porcelains made at Saint-Cloud by the family of Pierre Chicaneau is based on much surer evidence. This family produced an attractive creamy coloured soft-paste porcelain from about 1693 until 1766, and Saint-Cloud managed to survive the monopolies later given to the factories of Vincennes and Sèvres, being under the protection of 'Monsieur', the Duke of Orleans and brother of Louis XIV. Saint-Cloud porcelain was often decorated in under-glaze blue in the designs favoured by the decorators of Rouen

faience (tin-glazed earthenware), and polychrome enamel colours **298** were also frequently used, often in imitation of the Japanese 'Kakiemon' style.

Germany and Austria
When Augustus II, King of Poland, succeeded to the title of Elector of Saxony in 1694, he requested his economic adviser, Count von Tschirnhaus (d. 1708), to conduct a survey into the mineral wealth of the country, with the aim of locating the materials necessary for the manufacture of a porcelain akin to that of the Far East. Most of the credit for discovering how to make a true porcelain from materials found in the State of Saxony is given to Johann Friedrich Böttger, a capable young alchemist, who had formerly been concerned with the attempt to produce gold from base metals. Before a white porcelain was produced, the joint experiments of Tschirnhaus and Böttger resulted in the manufacture of a fine hard-red stoneware, capable of being engraved and polished as a semi-precious hardstone.

In 1710, two years after the death of Tschirnhaus, enough success in the manufacture of a hard white porcelain had been achieved to warrant the establishment of the Royal Saxon Porcelain Manufactory. It has recently been acknowledged that the earliest Meissen porcelain did not include the material of china-stone, and alabaster was used as an alternative until about 1718, after which a higher percentage of china-clay made the Meissen porcelain even whiter than that of the Chinese potter. Böttger died in 1719, and before this time the Meissen porcelains were decorated almost entirely in gold together with copper lustre – they apparently had difficulty in successfully applying enamel colours to the hard feldspathic glaze.

In 1720 the Meissen factory acquired the services of the talented enameller and designer Johann Gregor Höroldt, who had formerly worked for the rival factory of Du Paquier in Vienna. Höroldt's first designs were inspired by the engravings illustrating books on travels in the Far East, but soon after he introduced his renowned and highly original Chinoiseries, sometimes again inspired by the work of 17th- and 18th-century engravers. These paintings were followed by stylised Oriental flower paintings, erroneously referred to as 'India flowers' (*indianische blumen*) because of the association of the East India companies with the China export trade. During these same years many tablewares were decorated with mercantile and harbour scenes, silver-miners, heraldic devices, parkland scenes or groups inspired by the French painter Watteau.

From 1731 Höroldt was faced with real competition by the arrival at the factory of the modeller, Johann Joachim Kändler, a **299,3** young pupil of the court sculptor, Benjamin Thomae. Before producing the small figures which won him such fame, Kändler worked on the modelling of some of the large figures of animals and

297 Tureen in the form of a rabbit, soft-paste porcelain, painted in enamel colours. Marked with an anchor in red enamel. Chelsea, *c.* 1755.

298 Sugar-bowl and cover, soft-paste porcelain, painted in underglaze-blue. Saint-Cloud, first half of the 18th century.

299 Figure of a goat, hard-paste porcelain, glazed but undecorated, modelled by J. J. Kändler. Meissen, *c.* 1732.

300 Vase and cover, hard-paste porcelain decorated with enamel colours, probably by Johann Ehrenfried Stadler. Marked 'A.R.' in underglaze-blue. Meissen, 1727-30.

297

298

299

300

birds demanded by Augustus for the furnishing of his Japanese Palace, and his earliest designs also include those for large ewers, vases, candelabra, clock cases and soup tureens. Among the early table services modelled by Kändler was the well-known Swan Service, made in 1737 for Count Brühl, who had been appointed as Director of the factory following the death of Augustus II in 1733, and another made for Count Sulkowski. The Swan Service consisted of over 2,000 items, all based on an aquatic theme, with the swan predominating. From about 1738 Kändler modelled a profusion of miniature figures averaging about 6 inches (15 centimetres) in height, made primarily to replace the sugar and ice confections which had formerly been used to decorate the lavish banquets of the Court of Dresden. Today the most valuable of these miniature figures are those characters and groups of lovers based on the *Commedia dell'arte*, such as Harlequin, Columbine, Scaramouche, Mezzetino, the Capitano, Pantaloon, the Doctor and so on.

By the mid-18th century the Meissen factory was employing over 500 hands and exporting large quantities of fine wares to Russia, Turkey, France and England. This period of prosperity, however, was brought quickly to a close at the start of The Seven Years War (1756-63), when the factory was occupied by the troops of Frederick the Great of Prussia, and it never really recovered from this disaster. This same period also saw the end of the Baroque styles and the introduction of the lighter and prettier style of Rococo, a style which did so much to 'arrest' the naturalistic and animated postures of the earlier figures.

The Meissen figures modelled in the Neo-classical manner which followed the Rococo were left in the unglazed 'biscuit' porcelain condition. The idea was to imitate antique sculpture, but in fact they bore little resemblance to sculpture, and were a cold hard white, very different to the soft-paste porcelain figures made at Sèvres from the models of Falconet.

In 1864 the factory was moved from the original site at the Albrechsburg Castle to a new factory erected by the state, at

300,301,305

301 Punch-bowl and cover on ormolu base, hard-paste porcelain painted in enamel colours. Marked with crossed swords in underglaze-blue. Meissen, *c.* 1755.

302 Cup and saucer, soft-paste porcelain, decorated in underglaze-blue (*bleu lapis*) and gilt. Marked with crossed 'L's enclosing letter 'A' for the year 1753.

303 Coffee-pot, hard-paste porcelain, painted in enamel colours and gilt. Marked with an anchor in red enamel. Venice, Cozzi's factory, *c.* 1770.

304 Bowl, soft-paste porcelain with enamel decoration painted on to a tin-glaze in the Japanese Kakiemon manner. Marked with a hunting-horn in red enamel.

305 Teapot and cover, hard-paste porcelain, Meissen, *c.* 1715. Painted in enamel colours, probably by J. F. Metzch at Bayreuth in about 1740.

301

302

303

304

305

Triebischtal, near Meissen, and production of many of their early models is still continued to this day. Their modern wares are still marked with the underglaze-blue crossed-swords factory-mark, originally adopted in 1723, but by comparison the material is very grey.

The factory at Vienna was first established by Du Paquier in 1717, but achieved very little until 1719 when C. K. Hunger, a gilder, and Samuel Stölzel, the kiln-master, deserted from Meissen to help produce some very fine hard-paste porcelain. The Vienna wares made during the Du Paquier ownership of the factory (1717-44), were mainly decorated in Chinoiserie styles which often included some attractive *Laub-und-bandelwerk* (leaf-and-strapwork) designs, inspired from earlier prints by such people as Paul Decker, Caspar Gottlieb Eisler and Jean Bérain.

In 1744 the factory was sold to the Empress Maria Theresa, who expanded it considerably, employing several new modellers who produced many attractive figures, often inspired by those of Meissen. The figures, modelled by Anton Grassi, mainly in the Neo-classical style, showed more originality.

From 1784 the factory was under the direction of Konrad von Sorgenthal, under whom it prospered well into the 19th century. It was during the early decades of the 19th century that so many of the highly decorated wares with a profusion of well applied gilding on coloured grounds were made. These wares, marked with the 'two-bar shield' in underglaze-blue, are among the most imitated porcelains made in many minor factories today.

By the middle years of the 18th century, more and more workmen who had acquired knowledge of the manufacture of hard-paste porcelain were becoming prepared to sell their secrets to the highest bidder, with the result that during the second half of the century

there were no less than 23 factories producing wares from a porcelain based on the original Meissen formula.

Johann Josef Ringler, who had been a kiln-hand at Vienna, left the factory in 1750 and went to Strasbourg, where he passed on the secret to Paul Anton Hannong. Ringler was also responsible for imparting the knowledge to the factory at Höchst, where Simon Feilner (1751-53), and later Johann Peter Melchior, produced some very attractive figures. The work of Melchior was highly original; his best and most easily identified models date from the 1770s, when the painting of the flesh, clothing and grassy bases are all in pale enamel tones, and clearly show the influence of the French painter François Boucher. The colours used on his models after his departure in 1779 for the factory of Frankenthal are much less pleasing. The Höchst factory, which used a six-spoked wheel as a maker's mark, eventually closed in 1796.

Porcelain was made at Fürstenberg from about 1753 and Simon Feilner was employed as a modeller until 1768, during which time he produced many Italian Comedy figures—he is credited with nearly 100 original figures and groups made while working at Höchst and Fürstenberg. From about 1770 the extreme Rococo style, which had dominated the Fürstenberg tablewares to that time, gave way to early forms of the Neo-classical style, probably as the result of influence from the contemporary fashions of the Berlin factory, all much inspired by the wares excavated in the ruined city of Pompeii. From the last decade of the 18th century many plaques were produced in biscuit porcelain, made in imitation of the blue-and-white jasper-ware cameos of the English factory of Josiah Wedgwood. C. G. Schubert also produced some well-modelled portrait busts.

In 1763, after The Seven Years War, King Frederick the Great

306 Temple of Bacchus, hard-paste porcelain, painted in enamel colours and gilt. Marked with a sceptre in underglaze-blue. Berlin, late 18th century.

307 Figure of Columbine, painted in enamel colours and gilt, modelled by Franz Anton Bustelli. Marked with the shield of the arms of Bavaria, impressed. Nymphenburg, 1755-60.

306

307

purchased a factory which had been established in Berlin two years earlier by J. E. Gotzkowski; this was to become the Royal Factory, with a monopoly of porcelain sales throughout the entire state of Prussia. The factory was exempt from normal tariffs and taxes and in consequence enjoyed great prosperity.

J. J. Ringler was again responsible for the introduction of the fine porcelain made at the Nymphenburg factory in Bavaria from about 1753 (experiments had been taking place from 1747 under the patronage of Elector Maximilian III, Joseph of Bavaria, but with little success). In 1756 Franz Anton Bustelli was employed as the Director of Modelling, remaining until at least 1763. Whilst Kändler must be regarded as the master porcelain modeller during the Baroque period, he was surpassed during the Rococo years by Bustelli, whose early figures have much in common with the work of the Munich sculptor and wood-carver, Franz Ignaz Gunther. Bustelli used the wave-like scrolls of Rococo as an attractive alternative to the customary tree-stumps or pedestals to support his figures. He was succeeded as *Modellmeister* by the sculptor Dominikus Auliczek, who is best known for his realistic groups of fighting animals.

In 1755 Paul Hannong, from Strasbourg, started to manufacture a hard-paste porcelain at Frankenthal under the patronage of Carl Theodor, Elector of the Palatinate, who purchased the concern in 1762. The outstanding modellers of the Frankenthal figures are Wilhelm Lanz, Konrad Linck and the brothers Johann Friedrich and Karl Gottlieb Lück. The work of the Lück brothers has a 'doll like' simplicity, whereas the Neo-classical styles of Linck show a far greater talent.

The porcelain of Ludwigsburg can often be recognised by the distinct rather drab 'broken-white' tone. The factory was first

established in 1758 under the patronage of Duke Carl Eugen of Württemberg. Their chief modeller, J. J. Louis, engaged from 1762-72, was responsible for the delightful miniature groups, sometimes of a satirical nature. It is fortunate for the collector that the majority of the 18th-century German porcelain factories adopted, and generally used, an approved factory-mark, applied in underglaze-blue.

Italy and Spain

The first true Italian porcelain was that made in Venice by Francesco Vezzi, whose wares had much in common with those of Meissen. His concern was in operation from 1720-27, during which time production was dominated by silver-shaped tablewares, decorated with raised ornament and bright enamel colours including strong reds, greens and yellow. The factory was almost certainly forced to close by the prohibition on the export of the clays from Meissen.

Another Venetian factory was established in 1764, founded by Geminiano Cozzi, and remained in production until 1812. The porcelain, considerably inferior to Vezzi's, was usually of a grey tone decorated in a wide variety of styles with bright enamel colours and a superior-quality gilding procured from gold coins.

The rather coarse greyish ware, with a smeary glaze, produced at Doccia, near Florence, was often disguised by using an opaque white tin-glaze. This factory was founded about 1735 by the Marchese Carlo Ginori, and it was here that plaques, boxes and other useful wares were first introduced, 'with figure subjects in low relief'. This form of decoration has for many years been wrongly associated with the porcelains of Capodimonte, probably because the Doccia factory used the mark of a crowned 'N' on wares of this type in the second half of the 19th century. It was of course

303

308 Cup and saucer, soft-paste porcelain, painted in enamel colours and gilt. Marked (on saucer) with the date-letter 'L' within double 'L' cypher in blue. Sèvres, 1764.

309 Cup and saucer in hard-paste porcelain made for Marie Antoinette. Marked with interlaced 'L's enclosing letters 'KK' for 1788, and the mark of the painter Fumez. Sèvres.

310 *Veilleuse* (tea-warmer), hard-paste porcelain, painted in enamel colours and gilt. Marked 'Flamen Fleury A. Paris' in red enamel. Paris, early 19th century.

311 Cream-jug known as the 'Goat and Bee Jug', soft-paste porcelain, painted in enamel colours. Marked with an incised triangle. Chelsea, 1745-49.

312 Jug, soapstone porcelain, with moulded and painted enamel decoration. Worcester, *c.* 1760.

308

309

310

311

312

the Royal Factory of Naples which used such a mark from 1771, and not the earlier factory of Capodimonte.

Today the figures made at the Capodimonte factory between 1743 and 1759 are among the most sought after, and consequently the most expensive, of all European porcelain figures. The soft-paste porcelain of Capodimonte is a beautiful material, very white and highly translucent, with a well-fitting glaze which sometimes takes on a rather matt appearance. In 1759 the factory was moved by Charles of Bourbon to the Buen Retiro Palace, near Madrid, and later in the century the clay began to be obtained from a different source, which resulted in the wares becoming decidedly inferior, and decorated with loud garish colours. The Buen Retiro factory, which in common with Capodimonte used a mark of a fleur-de-lys, was destroyed by the British military forces in 1812.

France

In 1725 an important soft-paste porcelain factory was established in France at Chantilly under the patronage of the Prince de Condé. Their earliest and most desirable wares are those decorated in the Japanese Kakiemon style on a white tin-glaze, a style used until about 1740. The factory is probably better known for the many wares made during the last quarter of the 18th century, often decorated in underglaze-blue with such patterns as the 'Chantilly sprig', a style copied by the English factory at Caughley, Shropshire.

Perhaps one of the most beautiful of all soft-paste porcelains was that of Mennecy, produced between 1734 and 1806. This concern

started in Paris and later moved to Bourg-la-Reine. The material was a milky-white, with a 'wet' and brilliant glaze, which absorbed the decoration – versions of naturalistic German flower painting – in an unmatched manner.

The greatest of all the French porcelain factories, Sèvres, had its beginnings as early as 1738, when two brothers, Gilles and Robert Dubois, arrived at Vincennes from Chantilly claiming to have the necessary knowledge for the manufacture of a fine porcelain. Orry de Fulvi, the French Superintendent of Finances, arranged subsidies and premises for them, but their claims proved false and they were succeeded by François Gravant. The result was that in 1745 a company in the name of Charles Adam received official recognition; it was also probably at this time that the Vincennes factory was granted the privilege of using the fleur-de-lys or king's monogram as their mark. In 1756 the production was moved to new buildings at Sèvres, and the factory was purchased by the king in 1759, as a further royal factory. Production of a soft-paste porcelain continued until about 1772, when newly discovered ingredients necessary for the manufacture of hard-paste were also put to use.

Porcelain figures as decoration for the banqueting table now gave way to lavishly decorated but useful wares. It is recorded that something like four-fifths of the production of Vincennes was devoted to the manufacture of porcelain flowers mounted on metal stems, to be placed in vases or used to decorate chandeliers or candelabras. A wide range of tablewares including plates, bowls, ewers, trays, and ice-pails were beautifully decorated with natural-

304

302

313 Figure of Pantalon, made at Fürstenberg c. 1755 from a model by Simon Feilner.

314 Pot-pourri in the form of a hare, soft-paste porcelain, painted in enamel colours on gilt-bronze base. Saint-Cloud, c. 1750.

315 Pair of hounds, hard-paste porcelain painted in enamel colours, modelled by J. J. Kändler c. 1740. Meissen, marked with crossed swords in underglaze-blue.

313

314

315

316 Group of *putti* with goat, symbolic of Spring. Hard-paste porcelain painted in enamel colours. Plymouth, *c.* 1768-70.

317 Toy tea-service, soft-paste porcelain, painted in enamel colours. Bow, *c.* 1760.

318 Figure of a gallant with dog, soft-paste porcelain, painted in enamel colours and gilt. Derby, *c.* 1757-58.

316

317

istic flowers, birds or landscapes; in many cases the work can be clearly identified from the mark of the painter or gilder, usually accompanied with a letter to denote the year of manufacture—no such guidance was given by the Meissen factory. The soft-paste porcelain was an ideal material for the application of some outstanding coloured grounds, sometimes broken down with gilt decoration.

308,309   Following the move to Sèvres and the purchase by the king, the factory enjoyed a new prosperity, helped no doubt by the patronage of courtiers, who wished to seek royal favours from the new owner and Madame de Pompadour, who died in 1764. During this period the light fantasy of Rococo became overshadowed by a much heavier and grander style of decoration, which at times left little of the white porcelain to be seen, and the fine tablewares seemed to find less favour than the large ornamental vases used to decorate interiors. It was also at this time that porcelain plaques began to be included in the work of some of the most outstanding cabinet makers. Genuine work of this period can often be clearly recognised by the superior quality of the gilt decoration. Bad management caused the factory gradually to decline, until in 1793, with the fall of the monarchy, the concern was taken over by the French Republic. Very few wares worthy of mention were made at this time, with the exception of large documentary table services, but with the establishment of the Consulate and the Empire, Sèvres was restored to prosperity under the direction of Alexandre Brongniart, the manufacture now consisting entirely of hard-paste porcelains. It was during this period that many large orders were received from the Emperor, both for his personal use and as diplomatic gifts.

Several new factories were established in France when the ingredients of china-clay and china-stone were discovered near Limoges in 1769. The earliest of the Limoges factories was that patronised by the Comte d'Artois, which was sold by the owners to the King in 1784, but the relationship between the two factories was far from successful and ceased at the Revolution. Numerous factories soon opened in and around Paris, usually safeguarded from the monopolies of Sèvres by the protection of a member of the

310   royal family. Although these so-called 'Paris porcelains' are usually of a good quality, in nearly all instances they slavishly followed the fashions of the Sèvres concern during the Louis XVI period.

England

Unlike so many of the Continental factories, the smaller English undertakings did not enjoy any royal or princely patronage, and thus they stood or fell by the popularity and sale of their wares. There seems little doubt that the first commercially successful concern in England was that established by Nicholas Sprimont, the Huguenot silversmith, at Chelsea in 1745. Evidence has recently

318

been found suggesting that the secretary to the Duke of Cumberland, Sir Everard Fawkener, was financially involved with the venture. The soft-paste porcelain made at Chelsea is usually referred to by the type of mark often used during recognised periods: the incised triangle from about 1745-49; the 'raised-anchor' 1749-52; the red-anchor from 1752 to about 1758; and the gold-anchor about 1758 until 1770. Then the factory was taken over by William Duesbury, the proprietor of Derby, who continued to run the Chelsea works until 1784, giving the term 'Chelsea-Derby' to this period.

Many of the early tablewares produced by Sprimont were fashioned in the same styles as his earlier silver, but the factory did not produce much original work–during the Baroque period it tended to imitate Meissen, and from about 1755 to seek inspiration from Sèvres. Their finest wares and figures were those made during the red-anchor period. From about 1749 until 1766 many Chelsea figures show the skill of the modeller Joseph Willems, who not only cleverly imitated the wares of Meissen, but also produced more original pieces from engravings.

It was during the Chelsea-Derby years that some of the more practical tablewares were produced in the Neo-classical styles; these wares were really made to serve a useful purpose, whereas so many of the earlier Chelsea examples simply relied on visual appeal.

The factory at Bow on the outskirts of London produced far more useful wares, due partly to the quality of their porcelain which, for the first time to our knowledge, included the ingredient of calcined animal bone (bone-ash). Their early patent, taken out by Frye and Heylyn in 1744, referred merely to the manufacture of the materials for the making of porcelain, and it was not until 1749 that a further patent concerned with the actual porcelain was applied for. Unlike Chelsea, Bow aimed at producing modestly priced wares in great

quantity, many of which were decorated in the Chinese manner with underglaze-blue decoration. Very similar porcelain was made at the smaller factory at Lowestoft in Suffolk, where from about 1757 until 1799 a wide range of charming tablewares and other useful items was produced for sale at holiday resorts and local fairs.

In 1748 a factory was established at Bristol by Lund and Miller, using for the first time in England the material of soaprock, which enabled them to claim that their wares were tested with boiling water. The concern was taken over by Dr John Wall of the Worcester Porcelain Company and his 14 original partners in 1752, and it is now very difficult to say which wares were made at Bristol and which during the early years of Worcester. The finest Worcester wares were made before about 1770, after which they had a tendency to overdecorate their productions in the gold-anchor fashion of Chelsea. Many of the pieces made during the 1750s and 1760s were decorated in fine underglaze-blue painting, and others show the skills of the talented engraver, Robert Hancock.

It was not until 1768 that William Cookworthy, the chemist from Plymouth, established a factory for the manufacture of a hard-paste porcelain in England. In 1770 the concern was moved to Bristol, and was later under the direction of Richard Champion, who finally sold the unexpired years of the exclusive patent for the manufacture to a group of Staffordshire potters, who formed the New Hall factory. Here the manufacture of a hard-paste porcelain was continued until about 1812, after which, in common with most contemporary china potters, the factory went over to the production of the popular English body of 'bone-china', introduced by Josiah Spode c. 1796. It was unfortunate for the Plymouth and Bristol ventures that they were started so late, because by that time the good quality and low prices of the mass of Chinese export blue-and-white porcelain being brought to England by the East India Company were extremely hard to compete with.

INDUSTRIAL PRODUCTION IN THE 18th CENTURY

Reginald Haggar

The 18th century can be seen in many contrasting lights, but it was certainly an age of elegance and taste, and just as certainly an age of fine craftsmanship. Nowhere is this more apparent than in the field of English pottery and porcelain, which reached unparalleled heights of achievement in this period. In the actual manufacture of pottery, the 18th century was also a revolutionary age, when what had once been a localised country or urban craft was transformed into a full-scale industry concentrated in the large manufacturing regions of England, particularly North Staffordshire.

The coarse red earthenwares of the country potter, which were easily chipped and broken, gave way to the far more colourful and attractive tin-enamelled pottery made at Lambeth, Bristol and Liverpool, the fine brown stonewares made in Nottingham and the white salt-glazed stonewares of Staffordshire. As the century moved on, these in turn were replaced by the improved cream-coloured earthenware made by Josiah Wedgwood and his contemporaries in Leeds, Liverpool and Bristol.

While these plain wares catered for the everyday needs of the middle classes and nobility, they did not satisfy the rich, who looked to China or to Europe for the finer types of pottery and porcelain. To meet this demand, English factories in the later 1740s began to provide admirable porcelains decorated with Chinoiseries in colour or in blue and white. Bow and Worcester soon became large and important manufactories, efficiently organised and run on a commercial basis similar to many of the later earthenware potworks in the Staffordshire Potteries. The Bow factory was certainly producing fine-quality porcelain in bulk by as early as the 1750s.

These changes were brought about by a number of factors: the discovery and use of better raw materials for pastes, glazes and

colours; the application of new manufacturing processes; the building of rationally planned factories; improvements in machinery and tools; and the creation of an effective and disciplined use of labour.

Although John Dwight of Fulham, in the latter part of the 17th century, had been aware of the clay resources of the Isle of Purbeck, it was the potters of North Staffordshire in the 18th century who were to make commercially effective use of the white-firing plastic ball-clays of Dorset and Devonshire. These were later supplemented by china-clay and china-stone from Cornwall. John Astbury of Shelton is said to have become aware of the ceramic possibilities of ground flints following an accident to his horse during a journey to London.

Mr. Astbury being on a journey to London, on Horseback, had arrived at Dunstable, when he was compelled to seek a remedy for the eyes of his horse, which seemed to be rapidly going blind. The hostler of the tavern at which he stayed, burned a flint stone till quite red, then pulverized it very fine, and by blowing a little of the dust into each eye, occasioned both to discharge much matter and be greatly benefitted. Mr. Astbury, having noticed the white colour of the calcined flint . . . and its clayey nature when discharged in the moisture from the horses eyes,–immediately conjectured that it might be usefully employed to render of a different colour the Pottery he made.

The story may be apocryphal, but it is certainly true that the introduction of ground calcined flints into the earthenware and stoneware bodies, however it was brought about, greatly increased both their strength and their whiteness. The flints were brought to the Potteries from Gravesend and the coast of Sussex.

319 Glazed red earthenware teapot with applied stamped reliefs. Probably Staffordshire, *c.* 1745.

320 White salt-glazed stoneware coffee-pot with the deep blue glaze usually associated with William Littler, and decorated with white enamel painting. Possibly Staffordshire, *c.* 1755.

321 Teapot in salt-glazed stoneware, painted in black with a pattern of stripes and chequer. The handle and spout are pink. *c.* 1755.

322 Josiah Wedgwood's 'Apotheosis of Homer' vase in jasper ware. The model was prepared by the sculptor John Flaxman, and the subject owes its inspiration to a vase in the British Museum. Staffordshire, late 18th century.

319

320

321

322

Country potters traditionally glazed their coarse wares with powdered galena or lead ore, and they continued to do so in isolated places, such as Farnborough, until the time of Queen Victoria. The result was neither very even nor particularly attractive, and by about 1730 Staffordshire potters were abandoning the use of powdered galena applied to the unfired clay, and were dipping their wares after they had been fired to the biscuit state in a liquid glaze solution, and refiring them for the second time in a glost kiln. Enoch Booth is stated to have been the first potter to do this, but it soon became the general practice of the trade.

Mould making is one of the more complicated processes in pottery and porcelain manufacture, and has a long history. Metal moulds were undoubtedly used by David Elers for the sprigs with which he adorned his little red 'porcelain' teapots, and pitcher moulds were used for the production of hollow-wares during the first half of the century. However, it was not until the introduction of absorbent plaster-of-Paris moulds that bulk production of embossed and irregular-shaped articles became a possibility. The idea is believed to have come from France, where Ralph Daniel saw such

moulds being used in about 1735. Flat- and hollow-wares were subsequently made by pressing bats of prepared clay into or on to suitably formed moulds, and complicated relief-decorated vessels and figures were produced by pouring liquid clay (slip) into plaster moulds which absorbed surplus moisture and formed a shell conforming to their shape. Slip-casting has remained in general use ever since.

The number of machine tools used by potters in the 18th century was small. The potter's wheel underwent some improvements at the instigation of a man named Alsager, which gave the thrower greater control of speed and rhythm, and the wood-turner's lathe was brought into use to impart smoothness and finish to wheel-made articles. The use of an eccentric engine-turning lathe made it possible for the manufacturer to impart abstract repeating patterns to the surface of otherwise undecorated wares. Steam power was not introduced until the 1770s, when it was used to raise or pump water, as at Bow. Later, it was applied to the grinding of raw materials and colours, and for turning the wheels.

Before the time of Josiah Wedgwood, master potters were crafts-

323 Teapot in the form of an apple with leaves, probably modelled for Thomas Whieldon by William Greatbach when Whieldon and Wedgwood were still partners, *c.* 1757.

324 Figures of the Four Seasons in enamelled cream-coloured earthenware. James Neale, Hanley, *c.* 1780.

323

324

325 Teapot in the form of a cauliflower, earthenware covered with a clear and brilliant green glaze. Josiah Wedgwood, Burslem, *c.* 1760.

326 Colour-glazed coffee-pot by Thomas Whieldon.

327 Tea caddy in the form of a pineapple. Josiah Wedgwood, Burslem, *c.* 1760.

328 Colour-glazed figure of a man on a buffalo, Whieldon type, *c.* 1750.

329 Pierced oval dish, cream-coloured earthenware, transfer printed with a landscape and Classical ruin in black. Josiah Wedgwood, Etruria, *c.* 1780. Marked 'WEDGWOOD'.

325

326

327

328

329

men producing the kind of pottery which met the current demand, and usually selling their wares by hawking them round the towns and villages. Some followed the practice of Thomas Whieldon, who took his knife handles and snuff boxes to the cutlers of Sheffield and the hardware-men of Birmingham to get them mounted. Adventurous and successful potters looked to the developing retail trade in fashionable cities like Bath, Norwich and York, and some even established overseas agencies, as John Baddeley did in Amsterdam. The advertisement that William Hassells, Staffordshire pot-maker, inserted in the *Ipswich Journal* in 1759 gives an indication of the types of ware then in demand and of the sales methods of the potters.

322,326

WILLIAM HASSELLS, POT-MAKER, *Begs Leave to inform his friends and customers, that he is just returned from his Pot-House in Staffordshire, and has brought a large assortment of all sorts of Stone and Earthen-Ware of the newest patterns, viz. white stone, blue and white ditto, Agate, Tortoise-shell, Cream Colour and Black, both gilt, painted and enamelled . . . He will attend at the old-accustom'd Pot-Warehouse . . . near the New Wool-Hall,* BURY ST. EDMUNDS, *on* WEDNESDAYS *and* THURSDAYS *only; and at his Warehouse in* WYER-STREET, COLCHESTER, *on* SATURDAYS *and* MONDAYS *only . . .*

This was the pattern of industry and trade when Josiah Wedgwood first set up in business, and these were the kinds of wares he began by making. They did not, however satisfy him for long.

Wedgwood was born in 1730 and served an apprenticeship to his brother at the Churchyard Works in Burslem. A serious illness diverted his attention from process to material, and as a consequence he set about a course of experiments to improve current bodies and glazes and to invent new ones. A series of brief partnerships with two minor potters and one major one, Thomas Whieldon, gave him

an insight into the problems of handling men and the requirements of trade. In 1759 he was ready to start up on his own, and did so at the Ivy House Works in Burslem. His industry and enterprise were well rewarded, and he was soon forced to move to a more spacious factory, known as the Brick House Works. Wedgwood's cauliflower wares, with brilliant copper green glazes, are associated with the Ivy House Works, while at the Brick House Works he began to make improvements to the popular cream-coloured earthenwares, which soon commanded a ready sale because of their good functional shapes, their neatness of appearance and their durability. The cream-coloured wares found favour with the Queen, and became known, as did all English cream-coloured pottery thereafter, as Queensware. It was this that formed the basis of Wedgwood's success as a master potter.

But he was a good business-man as well as a potter, and knew that the manufacture of good utility earthenware was not enough. At that time the Potteries district of England was relatively isolated, and means of transport were essential for the import of raw materials and the export of finished goods. Wedgwood pioneered new roads and sponsored the construction of the Trent and Mersey Canal—of which he cut the first sod. When trade began to exceed manufacturing potential he decided on a further move. Buying the Ridge House estate, between Newcastle and Hanley, he built a fine house for himself, a modern architect-planned factory on the banks of the new canal (the much earlier New Canton factory at Bow must have been similar in scale and appearance) and a model village for his workers. He called the factory and village Etruria because he hoped to revive there the lost art of the Etruscans.

A planned factory was not much use without a disciplined labour force, and Wedgwood set about achieving this by a system of rules, timing, fines and cost accounting. He established agencies for home and overseas trade, established rules of conduct for his travellers,

330 Vase, cover and stand in green, blue and white jasper ware, decorated with a portrait medallion of George, Prince of Wales. Josiah Wedgwood, Etruria, c. 1785.

331 Tureen and stand in cream-coloured earthenware painted with a pattern in black. Josiah Wedgwood, Etruria, c. 1785.

332 Pierced chestnut basket and stand in cream-coloured earthenware, c. 1800. Marked 'LEEDS POTTERY', twice.

330

331

332

sought every means available for advertising his manufactures, and produced costly prestige pieces to focus public attention upon them. Such a piece was the Portland Vase, in black and white jasper, copied faithfully from the famous Hellenistic cameo glass vase now in the British Museum. The large cream-coloured earthenware dinner service which he made to the order of the Empress Catherine of Russia was exhibited, and served the same purpose.

Although supreme as a potter, Wedgwood knew he could not stand alone in the expanding competitive world of the 18th century. He knew also that many of his contemporaries and rivals were producing similar excellent wares in great quantities. He set about organising the trade, bringing together a number of these other firms in a research association. This was short-lived, but more successful was the Chamber of Trade he then formed from the group, to influence government on such matters as trade treaties, taxes and freight charges.

Wedgwood produced one distinctive and original body, a fine porcellaneous white stoneware that could be stained throughout its entire substance with colouring oxides. This he called jasper ware. It is best known in a delicate shade of blue, although it was made in many other shades of blue as well as pastel tints of yellow, green, lilac and pink. In this new body, which was as fine as porcelain, Wedgwood made hundreds of cameos, portrait medallions – of both the illustrious dead and the inglorious living – beads and ceramic jewellery, mounts for sword hilts, insets for mantelpieces, bell-pulls, and numerous Classical vases. Many of the best portraits were modelled by a local artist named Hackwood, but the eminent sculptor John Flaxman modelled the splendid 'Apotheosis of Homer' vase with Winged Pegasus surmounting its cover. Wedgwood always employed the best available artists, although he did not always know how to handle them.

Many other types of pottery were made by Wedgwood, although

none of these were new inventions; for instance, blackware, named 'basaltes' was a new and improved form of the old Staffordshire black Egyptian. Try as he would, he never succeeded in bettering the red porcelain made by John Philip Elers, although he gave it a fine-sounding name, 'rosso antico', while caneware and other so-called 'dry' bodies were made by all the best potters of the day. When the demand for creamware slackened and there was an evident desire for something whiter, Wedgwood was able to satisfy it by modifying the body and glaze, but in this he was only following market trends, rather than setting them. And the carefully kept secret of jasper ware soon leaked out.

Meanwhile his rivals were flourishing, and some of them were turning their attention to the manufacture of porcelain. Continental porcelain manufactories in the 18th century generally enjoyed royal or princely patronage, and so might well be regarded as art manufactures. The English porcelain ventures, with the possible exception of Chelsea, were not financed in the same way. Most of the successful firms were commercial enterprises, Bow, for instance, was a purpose-built factory employing a large number of skilled workmen, which managed to build up a large overseas trade. Worcester, too, was a considerable undertaking; the Dyson Perrins Museum in Worcester provides ample visual evidence of the quantity, quality and types of ware that it supplied to the market. Indeed, all the early English porcelain manufactories were essentially industrial undertakings, and it was inevitable that general earthenware potters should turn to porcelain production as soon as the difficulties of its manufacture were better understood. Thus, by the end of the century well-known porcelain factories like those of Derby, Caughley, and Coalport were joined by James Neale, Enoch Wood, the New Hall joint stock venture, Josiah Spode, 324,334 Thomas Minton, Miles Mason and others.

The changes in manufacturing processes which came about in

333 Earthenware plate transfer printed with the message, 'Keep within Compass', and signed 'J. Aynsley, Lane End'. John Aynsley, c. 1790.

334 Earthenware dish transfer printed in blue with the 'Two Figures' pattern, and impressed 'SPODE'. Josiah Spode, Stoke-on-Trent, c. 1790.

333

334

the course of the century were matched by changes in decorative techniques, which brought into play brighter and more pleasing colours and a greater variety of patterns. The staining of the lead glaze with colouring oxides seems very attractive in retrospect, but it must have become rather monotonous to many contemporaries, who wanted something fresh. The impetus for change probably came from the porcelain houses, and the earliest was the introduction of on-glaze enamel colours. These could be used either for the working out of repeated patterns or for painting flowers, birds, landscapes or figure subjects on either pottery or porcelain. The second and most important development was the technique of transfer printing from engraved copperplates. The process was first used at the Worcester porcelain factory, where a great deal of engraving was done by Robert Hancock, and then at Liverpool, where Liverpool tiles and Wedgwood earthenware was transfer printed by the independent decorating establishment of Sadler and Green. At first the transfers were applied in black over-glaze (jet-enamelled), but soon potters began to exploit the possibilities of

cobalt, and to apply transfers to the biscuit ware before glazing and firing in the glost kiln. The earliest results, with designs based on imported blue and white Chinese porcelain, were rather dark and heavy, but from about 1780 the earthenware potters became interested in the process, and a greater variety of patterns appeared. The great period of blue and white had begun.

Throughout the century English potters aimed more and more at the production of fine-quality tablewares, and these were made in uniform sizes and an immense variety of shapes, decorated in colour and gold with patterns which could be matched whenever required. To meet the demand, manufacturers issued illustrated catalogues of shapes with descriptive text in several languages. Many such catalogues survive, notably those of Wedgwood, the Leeds Pottery, Castleford and the Hanley firm of James and Charles Whitehead. That which had been, at the beginning of the century, little more than a country craft, had now been transformed into a major industry with a great export trade to Europe and the rest of the world.

19th-CENTURY CERAMICS

Barbara Morris

The period from 1830 to the end of the 19th century saw an incredible variety of styles and technical innovations, and it is therefore only possible to indicate the main trends both in Great Britain and in Europe. From the middle of the century the international exhibitions, from the Great Exhibition of 1851 to the Paris Exhibition of 1900, provided an additional stimulus to manufacturers both to produce impressive pieces and to compare their wares with those of their native and foreign competitors. The eclecticism and revival of historical styles which affected all the arts was nowhere more apparent than in the field of ceramics, but these influences were more noticeable in ornamental and decorative pieces than in domestic wares and table services, which tended to develop on more traditional lines.

In Great Britain, the popular underglaze-blue transfer-printed earthenware continued in favour throughout the first half of the 19th century both for home consumption and for export, but by the 1830s the Chinoiserie and Classical designs, rural scenes and botanical patterns had given way to more romantic designs which reflected the literary and artistic tastes of the times. Some of these

designs were copied from published engravings, such as Finden's *Landscape and Portrait Illustrations to the Life and Work of Lord Byron* (1833), but the majority were purely imaginary, with fanciful castles, pagodas and ruins, often set by a lake, with figures, statues and urns in the foreground.

Although blue, paler than in the early years of the century, remained popular, particularly for standard designs such as the 'Willow' pattern and 'Asiatic Pheasants', other colours began to be introduced from 1836. Green was much used by Copeland and Garrett, notably for the 'Aesop's Fables' series (introduced by Spode about 1836) and for a series of Italian views with an elaborate Rococo border. Brameld at Rockingham also used green for the 'Don Quixote' series based on the Stothard illustrations. Red, pink and purple were used as well as black, which became increasingly popular in the 1850s and 1860s, particularly for designs made for export to Greece, the Balkans and Russia. Brown, which had been used since the 1830s, became the predominant colour for the Japanese-style patterns with bamboo sprays, fans and birds and asymmetrically arranged ornament in the 1870s and '80s.

335 Coalport porcelain vase in the Rococo revival style, painted and with applied flowers. About 1830.

336 Earthenware soup plate, transfer printed in underglaze-blue from a design by James Cutts. Impressed mark 'Rogers' and 'Z'; backstamped 'Chinese Porcelain'. John Rogers & Sons, Burslem, c. 1835.

337 Colour-printed plate, the scene engraved by Jesse Austin after a painting by Thomas Webster. F. & R. Pratt, Fenton, c. 1850.

335

336

337

338 The 'Minster' jug, white stoneware with figures in Gothic niches. Made by Charles Meigh and registered in 1842.

339 Salt-glazed stoneware jug with applied decoration and handle in the form of a dragon. Made *c.* 1845 at Voisinlieu, near Beauvais, probably to the design of J-C. Ziégler.

340 Porcelain *vaisseau à mât* after an 18th-century Sèvres model decorated by Antonin Boullemier *c.* 1890 and made by Minton.

341 Earthenware plate designed and painted in the Japanese style by Eléonore Escallier for Théodore Deck. Shown at the Paris exhibition of 1867.

342 *Tazza* and cover, painted by Stephen Lawton in imitation of Limoges enamel. Minton, *c.* 1855.

338

339

340

341

342

Successful experiments were also made into multicoloured transfer printing in the late 1840s, notably by F. & R. Pratt of Fenton, T. J. & J. Mayer, John Ridgway and William Smith of Stockton-on-Tees. This method was especially popular for the pictorial pot-lids and polychrome transfer printing featured prominently at the 1851 Exhibition. Later in the century, although monochrome designs continued, transfer printing was more generally used for outlining designs which were tinted by hand.

Most European countries also produced transfer-printed wares, although few firms achieved the success of the English factories. In France, the factories of Montereau and Creil (which had English connections), De Boulen at Gien, Utzschneider at Sarreguemines and Fouque Arnoux at Valentine, all produced scenic designs in the 1830s and 1840s, while in Belgium similar wares were produced by Boch Frères at Keramis. English designs were closely imitated by Rörstrand and Gustavsberg in Sweden, and a number of designs emanated from factories in Germany and Russia.

A process invented by Lafon de Camarsac in 1854 enabled photographs to be printed on enamel and porcelain. Examples of his work were shown at the London Exhibition of 1862, where he received a gold medal. From the early 1860s several other firms experimented with the process, and during the last quarter of the century Wedgwood used a photographic process for reproducing drawings on ceramics.

A characteristic, essentially English, product of the period from 1830 to the 1860s was the moulded jug with relief decorations. The material was usually stoneware, either off-white or coloured buff, blue or grey-green, with a smear glaze, but parian porcelain and brown salt-glazed stoneware were also used. The designs ranged from the narrative, such as the John Ridgway 'John Gilpin' and 'Tam-o-Shanter' jugs of the 1830s, to the Neo-Gothic in the 1840s, together with rustic scenes of gypsies and deer, naturalistic designs

of flowers, tree-forms and ears of maize in the mid-century. By the mid-1850s and 1860s the designs had become more formalised, with Renaissance and Classical motifs predominating. The Japanese influence was apparent in the 1870s, with relief decorations of prunus blossom, flying cranes, sparrows and fans. In the 1880s there was a revival of imitative jasper ware, with applied patterns in white of Classical figures, wheat and grapes, ferns and lilies-of-the-valley, usually on a straight-sided tankard-shaped jug in brown, blue or green stoneware. 'Aesthetic' style designs of sunflowers or Japanese motifs are also found.

Relief-decorated moulded jugs of this type were not produced to the same extent in Europe, although a number of examples came from the Montereau factory, and a parallel development in salt-glazed stoneware took place when the painter Jules-Claude Ziegler joined the works at Voisinlieu near Beauvais, producing running patterns of floral decoration on jugs and vases.

During the earlier years of the 19th century, the Classical influence affected the shape rather than the decoration of pottery and porcelain, but the 1840s saw a revival of interest in imitations of ancient Greek figure vases, normally called 'Etruscan' at the time, and examples were produced by Dillwyn of Swansea and by Samuel Alcock at the Hill Pottery, Burslem. Similar vases were shown by Copeland in 1851 and later, in the 1870s and 1880s, black-ground vases were made by Davenport Beck & Co. Terracotta Classical vases were produced by the short-lived Bishops Waltham Clay Co. in Hampshire in 1866 and 1867 with transfer-printed Classical figures, and also by the Watcombe and Torquay potteries in the 1870s and 1880s. A number of continental firms produced similar imitations, and a fine pair of Classical urns, in biscuit porcelain, designed by Jean Louis Hamon and painted with polychrome Classical figures, was shown by Sèvres at the 1851 Exhibition.

The revival of Classical wares was logically followed by a revival

337

338

339

343 Porcelain sugar pot decorated in *pâte-sur-pâte* by Léonard Gély and shown in the Paris Exhibition of 1855. Sèvres.

344 Parian porcelain vase with *pâte-sur-pâte* decoration by Marc Louis Solon. One of a pair made by Minton, 1875.

345 Ivory-tinted porcelain vase in the Japanese style, made by the Worcester Royal Porcelain Factory about 1872 and designed by James Hadley. One of a pair.

346 Parian porcelain figure of Herbert Minton, modelled by H. Protat and made by Minton, *c.* 1855.

347 Biscuit porcelain figure of a dancer, from the table setting known as *Le jeu de l'écharpe* modelled by Agathon Léonard for the Sèvres factory. Shown at the Paris exhibition of 1900.

348 Painted biscuit-porcelain figure of a Russian woman in local dress. Made by the firm of M. S. Kuznetsoff, *c.* 1880.

343

344

345

346

347

348

349 Stoneware vase with green-streaked red glaze, produced by Adrien Dalpayrat at his Paris pottery in 1896.

350 Porcelain vase with underglaze painting by Arnold Krog. Royal Porcelain Factory, Copenhagen, 1888.

351 Stonevase with mottled purple glaze made by Auguste Delaherche c. 1891.

350

349

351

352 Dish and plate from a faience service with decoration designed by Félix Bracquemond and commissioned by Eugène Rousseau. Shown at the Paris exhibition of 1867.

352

of Renaissance forms. The work of the 16th-century potter Bernard Palissy (see p. 89), in high relief with coloured glazes, including the well-known designs with snakes, snails and ferns, were first imitated in the 1840s by Charles Avisseau of Tours, and other French potteries followed suit. In England many examples were produced by the Minton factory, and more or less exact copies of Palissy ware were made by Mafra & Son in Portugal, founded in 1853. The sophisticated Saint-Porchaire ware (see p. 115), inlaid in coloured clays on a cream body, was imitated under the title of 'Henri-Deux' ware. This was sometimes made by the original technique, but sometimes merely by painting, as at Choisi-le-Roi. Minton made many pieces in imitation of Saint-Porchaire ware—one of the earliest was a *tazza* decorated by Leon Arnoux in 1859—and examples were shown at the 1862 London Exhibition. Later, in the 1870s, a number of Minton pieces in this style were decorated by Charles Toft, and similar pieces were made by Wedgwood. Palissy and Saint-Porchaire ware was also imitated at Sèvres in the 1860s.

The painted Limoges enamels of the 16th century also provided inspiration for a number of factories. At Sèvres a studio for enamelling functioned from 1845 to 1872 under the direction of Jacob Meyer Heine, the principal artist being A. T. Gobert, and the technique was imitated on porcelain. Minton produced a number of pieces in the so-called Limoges technique, but perhaps the most successful were those painted by Thomas Bott at Worcester from the early 1850s until his death in 1872. These, painted in white enamel on a deep blue ground, were in a variety of styles ranging from ancient Greek to Renaissance-inspired examples.

The imitation of Italian Renaissance painted maiolica was practised in several countries from the 1850s onwards. In England this was a speciality of Minton, which produced some fine examples designed by the artist Alfred Stevens as well as more derivative examples. Many of the painted scenes by Emile Lessore for Wedgwood in the 1860s were clearly inspired by Renaissance maiolica, although his designs were original and not copies. His later work is more pastoral. The Berlin State Porcelain factory also produced this ware, as did the Gien factory and Ulysse of Blois in France. Many

factories in Italy were naturally inspired by their earlier native product, including the Ginori factory at Doccia, the Castellani factory at Rome and the Cantigalli factory in Florence, established in 1878.

In England particularly the term 'majolica' as it was then spelt, was used to describe wares with relief decoration under coloured glazes. This was introduced by Léon Arnoux when he came to Minton from Toulouse in 1849, and the Minton majolica pieces were first shown at the 1851 Exhibition. The technique was used not only for tablewares and ornaments but also for large sculptural pieces, including a fountain with a life-size figure of St George which formed a central feature of the 1862 London Exhibition. Majolica was also used for life-sized models of animals and birds, for garden furniture and jardinères and for architectural schemes such as the Royal Dairy at Frogmore and the Old Refreshment Room at the Victoria and Albert Museum (1867). Impressive negro caryatids were made from the designs of Carrier-de-Belleuse, and the pair of elephants made for the Paris Exhibition of 1889 have graced the premises of Thomas Goode of South Audley Street since that date.

The success of the Minton majolica inspired Sèvres to set up a majolica workshop in 1852, an enterprise that lasted for 20 years; a number of large majolica urns were shown in the exhibition. The chief designer was the sculptor Jean-Denis Larue. Majolica was produced throughout the later part of the 19th century by Wedgwood, George Jones, Thomas Forrester and other Staffordshire firms, and by many European firms including Rörstrand and Gustavsberg. The later examples tend to be rather crude.

Islamic pottery—Persian and Turkish, particularly 'Rhodian' styles—provided another important influence during the latter half of the 19th century, and the theme was taken up by many firms, including Collinot of Paris, Cantagalli of Florence, Zsolnay of Pècs in Hungary and Marie Drews of Berlin. Theodore Deck, who embarked on serious research into Persian and Turkish pottery, produced many Islamic-inspired pieces in the 1860s and 1870s, including some based on glass mosque lamps. Somewhat akin were the pieces made with 'Byzantine' or 'Alhambresque' ornament, often

342

with openwork pierced decoration, such as those shown by E. D. Honoré at the Industrial Art Exhibition at Paris in 1844, and by Tito Ristori of Marzy, near Nevers, at the 1855 Paris exhibition. A more exotic influence was that of Javanese batiks, which inspired the work of Theodorus Colenbrander at the Rozenberg factory at the Hague in the 1880s, and was to contribute to the Art Nouveau style later in the century, culminating at Rozenburg in the delicate porcelain vases made under J. Jurriaan Kok's directorship from 1894–1913.

For the future development of ceramics, however, the most important exotic influence was undoubtedly that of Japan, which affected not only shapes and decoration, but was eventually to lead to the emergence of the studio, or artist, potter. Among the earliest examples of the Japanese influence was the faience table service commissioned from Félix Braquemond by Eugène Rousseau, made by Leboeuf & Millet at Montereau, and shown at the Paris Exhibition of 1867. This ware, with its decoration of cocks, fish, insects, butterflies, flowers and plants, based on Japanese prints (particularly those of Hokusai) and haphazardly arranged with no differentiation between the border and centre of the plate, was clearly the inspiration for the 'Naturalist' service designed by the painter W. S. Coleman for Mintons in 1869. Pieces in imitation of Oriental cloisonné enamel were also made by Minton in the late 1870s and 1880s, and Worcester too produced a range of wares in the Japanese style, notably some designed by James Hadley in 1871 with relief panels of Oriental figures in imitation of lacquer inlaid with ivory. The Japanese tradition was continued at Sèvres in the 1880s by Albert Dammouse, who painted many pieces, while some services were actually painted in Japan. Other impressive Japanese-style pieces shown at Paris in 1878 were decorated by Eléonore Escallier for Theodore Deck.

Porcelain, particularly tableware, tended to develop on more traditional lines, mostly in revived 18th-century styles. At Sèvres, which was under the management of Alexandre Brongniart from 1800 until his death in 1847, the influence of easel-painting and goldsmiths' work dominated, and the pieces in the Empire or Neo-classical style, whether monumental vases or table services, were regarded as a field for pictorial decoration integrated with rich gilded ornament. The paintings of Raphael, Watteau and other masters, as well as contemporary paintings, images of the successive rulers and their families, flowers, landscape and genre subjects were all executed with consummate skill on Sèvres wares. In a time of changing political régimes, much of the production consisted of commissions for services and toilet sets to adorn the palaces and for trophies and presentation pieces, but after Brongniart's death, and stimulated by the international exhibitions, the factory entered on a more experimental period, under the directorships of Ebelman (1848-52), Victor Régnault (1852-71) and Louis Robert (1871-79). All three were assisted by the same chemist, Alphonse Louis Salvetat. They were followed by Charles Lauth (1879-87), Theodore Deck (1887-91) and finally Emile Baumgart, assisted by the chemist Georges Vogt. Much of the research was concerned with developing a satisfactory soft-paste porcelain close to the Chinese, known as *porcelaine siliceuse*, and a product called *grosse porcelain*, which permitted the artists to model their pieces directly. During the period 1850 to 1870 new shapes based on Italian Renaissance and French 17th-century models were introduced, and the same period saw the production of the delicate pierced porcelain, usually left undecorated, which was also successfully made by Worcester in the 1860s, sometimes with Oriental fret patterns. Further new shapes, some of which were almost Baroque in conception, were introduced by the sculptor Albert Carrier-de Belleuse, who had worked at Mintons from 1850-55.

In 1831 the ownership of the Meissen factory was transferred from the crown to the state, and the appointment of Kuehn two years later brought a number of technical changes but little artistic development. Most of the production was in revived Rococo styles, with some impressive pieces painted in Limoges style in the 1860s, and some *pâte-sur-pâte* from 1878.

By 1830 the revived Rococo style was fully developed at the English factories of Rockingham, Derby, Davenport and Coalport, and it remained the dominant style until the mid-1840s. Many of the pieces are unmarked, and it is often difficult to differentiate between the productions of the various factories except by reference to extant shape and pattern books. The Minton productions, in bone china rather than true porcelain, ranged from copies of 18th-century Sèvres, Meissen and Chelsea, with figures based on Meissen and French models, and pieces with Gothic ornamentation appearing to derive from Paris porcelain. From about 1840 most of the Minton tablewares and ornaments were French inspired, and from 1865 the process of acid gilding was used for richly painted services in the style of 18th-century Sèvres with scenes after Watteau, Lancret, Boucher and Angelica Kauffman. These were at first designed by Emile Jeannest and painted by Thomas Kirkby and others, and in 1872 Antonin Boullemier, who had previously worked at Sèvres, took over the design. Among the more original pieces were a service painted with heather made for Queen Victoria in 1879, and another of the same year, painted with wild flowers and ferns. The cups of these had delicate butterfly handles, a fashion revived by firms such as Shelley in the 1920s and 1930s. Most of the Minton vases were in Sèvres style, but from 1860-90 more original productions based on Chinese cloisonné, Chinese monochrome wares, Japanese lacquer and ivories, and Oriental bronzes and jades were produced, together with some rather eccentric pieces designed by Christopher Dresser.

Pâte-sur-pâte decoration, which was to become a Minton speciality, was first introduced at Sèvres. In this form of decoration the design was built up by the application of a porcelain slip, usually in white on a dark ground, giving the effect of a carved cameo. A number of *pâte-sur-pâte* pieces, decorated by Léonard Gély for Sèvres, were shown at the Paris Exhibition of 1855, and the technique was further developed by Marc Louis Solon, A. T. Gobert and Eléonore Escallier. Draped figures, cherubs, 'cameo' heads in Classical style, and winged fish and birds were much favoured for this style, as the varying thicknesses of the slip application, ranging from a thin transluscent veil to opaque relief modelling, was satisfactorily exploited by such motifs. The technique also gave ample opportunities for the subtle rendering of light and shade.

After the Franco-Prussian war, Solon emigrated to England, joining Minton in 1870. He brought with him the technique of *pâte-sur-pâte*, which was to become Minton's most esteemed and characteristic production throughout the late 19th century—it continued in production to a limited extent up to 1937. Many of Solon's designs for Minton show a strange mixture of fantasy and eroticism, based on Classical and Renaissance styles, with an occasional design showing a Japanese influence. Solon trained a number of apprentices, including Alboine Birks, H. Sanders, T. Mellor and Frederick Rhead, but he continued to paint the figures himself until his retirement in 1904, and thereafter worked on a freelance basis until his death. High-quality *pâte-sur-pâte* decoration, on earthenware instead of porcelain, was produced by George Jones & Sons of the Crescent Pottery between 1876 and 1886, mostly carried out by a Bohemian artist, F. Schenk. The technique was also used by C. H. Pillivuyt of Mehun-sur-Yèvre for some impressive vases and jardinières decorated in Persian style and shown at the Paris exhibition of 1878.

Another important innovation was the development of 'parian' ware, a fine-grained porcellaneous body deriving its name from its resemblance to marble, and first perfected by Copeland in the 1840s in the course of experiments aimed at reviving the old Derby biscuit porcelain. The material was immediately seen as ideal for statuettes and portrait busts, and examples were shown by Copeland at the Manchester Exhibition of 1845-6. Minton and other factories quickly followed suit with models after well-known pieces, such as Dannecker's *Ariadne* (also made by Meissen in biscuit porcelain) and Hiram Power's *Greek Slave*, as well as some from original models by the sculptor John Bell. The parian body, which was sometimes covered with a smear glaze, was generally preferred in white, but by the 1850s a method of tinting parian was

335

340

345

341

343

344

344

346

353 Two plates from the 'Naturalist Service' designed by W. S. Coleman for Mintons in 1869 and registered by them in 1870.

354 Grotesque stoneware bird with moveable head made by Wallace Martin, 1887.

355 Dish designed by William de Morgan and painted in ruby lustre on Staffordshire earthenware. Merton Abbey period (1882-88).

356 Vase in Florian ware with a poppy design in blue, by William Moorcroft, 1898.

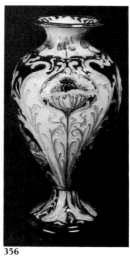

353   354   355   356

developed, and some pieces were made in a combination of colours. Parian was also used for ornaments and tablewares and in combination with painted bone china and porcelain, as with the centre-pieces and candelabra made by Minton, and glazed parian was used as the basis for some *pâte-sur-pâte* wares. Fine-quality parian was also made by Samuel Alcock, William Brownfield, W. H. Goss and Robinson & Leadbetter.

The pottery established at Belleek in County Fermanagh in Ireland in 1863 also produced parian, but the factory's speciality was a very light porcelain body with an iridescent nacreous glaze. This was used for table services and openwork baskets adorned with flowers, and for centrepieces, salts and ornaments imitating, or decorated with, marine forms such as shells and corals.

From the 1860s Gustavsberg used parian porcelain for high-quality figures and other wares, but some of the continental figures and vases are considerably below the standard of the British. Parian, indeed, was essentially an English product, most continental firms preferring biscuit porcelain for their figures. The Sèvres factory produced a number of biscuit figures, which culminated in the superb dancing-figure table setting known as *Le jeu de l'écharpe*, modelled by Agathon Léonard and shown at the Paris Exhibition of 1900. Biscuit-porcelain figures derived from Thorvaldsen's sculptures were made by the Royal Copenhagen Porcelain Factory, and the Gardner factory near Moscow produced attractive painted biscuit figures of Russian peasants. Fine biscuit figures were also made by the Royal Porcelain Factory, Berlin, often of contemporary personalities, and similar figures and busts of royal personages, composers and writers, were made by Meissen.

The sale of the Royal Copenhagen Porcelain Factory to the Alumina Earthenware Company in 1883 led to a period of experiment, and Arnold Krog, an architect and painter, who joined the company in 1885, introduced the characteristic underglaze painting in muted blues and greys, a style that has persisted until the present day. Generally the decoration was derived from Danish sources—landscapes, birds and animals—but a Japanese influence was also apparent. In 1886 crystalline glazes were developed there, a feature which was also to appear at Rörstrand and Gustavsberg, as well as in France. The Royal Copenhagen figures modelled by Krog and others, particularly those of birds and animals, with their smooth rounded forms and subtly shaded colouring, were to set a new style for porcelain figures.

The emergence of the Art Nouveau style (see p. 295) in the 1890s brought a fashion for taller, slenderer forms, emphasised by floral and plant decoration and sinuous elongated motifs. At Rörstrand this style took the form of floral decoration in slight relief, delicately painted in underglaze colours, with the petals cut out at the top of the vase. From 1897 Sèvres produced porcelain vases with floral decoration in Art Nouveau style, sometimes in low relief, but the more thoroughgoing Art Nouveau pieces, with three-dimensional figures and swirling decoration, such as those designed by Hector Guimard, were more often made in stoneware, and date from 1900 or later.

The concept of the artist potter, and with it the gradual emergence of the modern studio potter, arose first in France when Theodore Deck set himself up in Paris in 1856 to make domestic earthenware, at first painted individually by artist friends. The idea was echoed to some extent by the Minton Art Pottery Studio (c. 1870-90), where biscuit pottery was decorated by artists such as W. S. Coleman, William Wise and students from the South Kensington School of Art. Deck was also much concerned with research into glazes, and in the 1880s he embarked on the making of porcelain, developing some fine *flambé* glazes before becoming art director at Sèvres in 1887. Glaze techniques were more fully developed by Ernest Chaplet, who pioneered the 'barbotine' method of decoration—a technique which involved painting in coloured slips—at the Laurin factory at Bourg-la-Reine, and later at the Haviland factory at Limoges. In the 1880s Chaplet began to make stoneware and porcelain with *flambé* glazes, which equalled in quality those of the Far East.

Other important French artist potters included Edmond Lachenal, who entered Deck's studio in 1870 and set up on his own in 1880, producing painted earthenware as well as elaborately glazed stoneware and porcelain, and Auguste Delaherche, who worked for a time with Chaplet, and whose work is remarkable for its strength and elegance of form. Adrien Dalpayrat, who set up a workshop at Bourg-la-Reine in 1889, and Albert Dammouse, who had worked at Sèvres, were both concerned with the elaboration of glaze effects on stoneware and porcelain, while Clement Massier, the son of a Vallauris potter, produced attractive pottery with crystalline and other glaze effects at his workshop at Golfe-Juan. In Germany the artist-potter movement was not fully under way until after the turn of the century, but Max Läuger (1864-1952) produced some remarkable Art Nouveau style earthenware with raised slip decoration and majolica glazes at the Kandern factory near Karlsrühe from 1896 onwards. In Finland some attractive earthenware with *sgraffiato* designs was produced by the English-born artist A. W. Finch at the 'Iris' factory at Porvoo for a few years from 1897. Finch came to Finland from Brussels, where he had worked with Henri van de Velde, and his work shows a distinct affinity with the artist's style.

In England, the Aesthetic movement, and above all the Arts and Crafts Movement of which William Morris (1834-96) was the guiding light, contributed to the development of the artist potter. Morris's firms had sold the Rhenish stoneware known as *Grès de Flandres* from its earliest days—one of the few products not made expressly for them. The salt-glazed stoneware produced by Doulton's of Lambeth and decorated by students from the Lambeth School of Art from the 1870s may perhaps be considered the first English artist pottery. Among the artists were Hannah Barlow, famous for her incised animal designs, her sister Florence and brother Arthur, and George Tinworth, who also produced monumental sculptural reliefs in terracotta. Much of the production was inspired by German examples, and decorated with beading and moulded bosses in shades of blue and brown. A 'silicon' ware in hard unglazed brown stoneware was developed in the early 1880s,

347

348

350

351

349

and a dense white stoneware known as 'Carrara' appeared a little later.

The first studio potters in England are generally considered the Martin Brothers who, after working by arrangement with C. J. C. Bailey at Fulham, established their own workshops at Southall in 1877. The eldest brother, Robert Wallace Martin, who had earlier worked at Doulton's, was the guiding light: he was responsible both for the mixing of clays and glazes and the firing, and was also the 354 most experienced modeller. Most of the grotesques – the character jugs, birds, miniature bandsmen and chessmen – were his creation. Edwin, the youngest brother, excelled in the finely drawn ornament of flowers and grasses, birds and fishes, which showed a strong Japanese influence, while Walter was the principal thrower. Charles, the second brother, was particularly concerned with the business arrangements. The Martin Brothers' earliest work was somewhat 'medieval' in style, and this was followed by designs based on Italian Renaissance ornament, with formalised leaf and flower motifs, masks and grotesques. Their later and most effective style, characterised by organic vegetable forms with a marked Art Nouveau feeling, was developed after a visit to the Paris Exhibition of 1900. All their pieces were of stoneware.

William De Morgan, who was closely associated with William Morris, is usually considered as an artist potter, but most of the actual production was carried out by others, albeit almost exclusively from his designs, which were inspired by Near-Eastern and Hispano-Moresque pottery. Some of his earliest wares were painted on Staffordshire blanks, and on tiles made by Carter at Poole. Many of his designs, which included huge dishes and vases painted with ships, fishes, peacocks and Persian and Turkish-inspired floral decorations, were painted in 'Persian' colours, predominantly blues and greens, and these colours were also used for his large pictorial tile panels. His most important contribution, however, was the 355 revival of lustre painting, and some of his finest works, designs of

grotesque beasts, deer, serpents, fish and peacocks, were in this technique. The earliest examples were mostly in a strong ruby-red lustre, derived from copper, on a white ground, but later examples, including his triple lustre, were more often on a blue ground.

Apart from the imitative Hispano-Moresque wares, lustre painting was also used extensively in Europe in the late 19th century by Maximilian von Heider and his three sons in Shöngau, Bavaria; by Herman Kähler at Naestvas, Denmark; and by Vilmos Zsolnay, in conjunction with the chemist Vince Wartha, at Pècs in Hungary.

The late 19th century in England was noted for its 'art pottery' as well as for its artist potters. From the 1880s Sir Edmund Elton produced pottery at Clevedon Court in Somerset under almost studio conditions, his pieces being characterised by relief patterns of flowers and foliage built up in slip with incised outlines, mainly in mottled shades of blue and green. Later, from about 1900, he produced wares with a crackled metallic surface. Other west-country art pottery included that of C. H. Brannam, established at Barnstaple in 1879, and the Aller Vale ware made near Newton Abbot from 1881. At Birkenhead in the North, the Della Robbia Pottery, founded by Harold Rathbone, produced individual pieces decorated with *sgraffiato* and painted decoration by recently qualified local art students from 1894 to 1906. Christopher Dresser designed for art pottery made by Henry Tooth at Linthorpe from 1879 to 1892, and later for William Ault (who had at one time been in partnership with Tooth) at Swadlincote.

One of the prime exponents of the Art Nouveau style in England was William Moorcroft, who joined the firm of James Macintyre & Co. of Burslem in 1897. A year later he was given facilities for developing a range of art pottery, known as Florian ware, in which 356 the characteristic floral designs, combining the influence of William Morris with Art Nouveau, was outlined by fine slip trailing. Florian ware was sold extensively by both Liberty of London and Tiffany of New York.

POTTERY AND PORCELAIN IN AMERICA
Ian Bennett

Of all the applied arts of the New World, American ceramics are perhaps the least individual. This is not to say that fine pieces were not produced, both commercially and in the art pottery movement which began in the 1870s. It is simply that the naive crudity of European folk art tended to dominate American production – not in itself a sin – and this crudity, while acceptable in the products of, for instance, the German settlers of Pennsylvania, was ill-suited to the factory products of the mid-19th century. Again, when an American factory made a significant contribution to the development of ceramic design, it was copied, with monotonous adherence to the original designs and colours, by other factories all over the United States.

One of the strangest phenomena of American ceramic history, however, was the apparently inexplicable lack of porcelain production, despite a wealth of natural resources, including rich deposits of kaolin. In Europe, Böttger at Meissen had discovered the method of producing hard-paste porcelain in the Chinese manner in 1710, and thereafter, much hard-paste porcelain was produced in Germany, some in France, and soft-paste porcelain throughout Europe. In the United States, however, no porcelain is known to have been made much before the late 18th century, and production in any quantity only began in the 1820s.

The earliest production of porcelain is associated with a Huguenot immigrant called André Duché, who was also one of the first to make stoneware in the United States. Duché is first recorded as a manufacturer of stoneware in Philadelphia in the 1720s, and it is interesting to note that the first piece of dated American stoneware

was made in 1722 by Joseph Thiekson of New Jersey. In the 1730s, during a stay in Savannah, Georgia, Duché, who was something of a ceramic chemist, discovered deposits of a fine white material of great plasticity suitable for the production of soft-paste porcelain. According to his later testimony, he did in fact experiment successfully, producing two cups. It is also known that he was instrumental in exporting the material to the Bow factory in England. Certainly no commercial production began in the United States at this time.

The earliest example of a factory seriously attempting to produce porcelain on a commercially viable scale comes in 1770, when Bonnins and Morris of Philadelphia began making soft-paste porcelain of a surprisingly high quality, in a style reminiscent of Bow. The process, however, was obviously costly and time consuming, with a high breakage factor. Less than 25 examples of Bonnins and Morris porcelain survive today.

The next commercial porcelain ventures come in the 1820s with the establishment of a number of small factories in Philadelphia. 359 The most famous of these was that of William Tucker, later Tucker and Hemphill, which was founded in 1825 and lasted 13 years. Stylistically, Tucker's pieces are undistinguished, tending to copy 363 French Neo-classic porcelain with little of the latter's sophistication. The more simple of the American pieces are often painted with 364 sprays of flowers and embellished with gilding. The factory was particularly well known for its large jugs or pitchers. Tucker subsequently moved into the more lucrative business of importing ceramics from Europe and the Far East, and thereafter, porcelain played a minor and undistinguished role in the development of

357 Redware bowl with dark brown glaze and stylised bird decoration, 18th century.

358 Part of a Leeds dinner service made for the American market *c.* 1790-1820, and painted with the Arms of the United States.

359 Painted porcelain dish by John Vickers of Philadelphia. Dated August 1824.

360 Three-piece pottery teaset with brown glaze, from the model by Daniel Greatbach, American Pottery Company, Jersey City, New Jersey, *c.* 1833-45.

361 Rookwood pottery vase in the Standard Rookwood Mahogany glaze. Painted by Matthew R. Daly and dated 1890.

357

358

359

360

361

362 Pennsylvania Dutch deep dish with *sgraffiato* decoration. Dated January 29, 1772.

363 Pair of large porcelain vases in French Neo-classic taste by Tucker & Hemphill of Philadelphia, *c*. 1835.

364 Tuckerware porcelain pitcher with painted decoration and gilding. Dated 1828.

362

363

364

American ceramics until the work of Adelaide Alsop Robineau in the early 20th century.

Not surprisingly, the earliest surviving examples of American ceramics are earthenware, and in a style derived from European 362 folk art – the slip-ware and *sgraffiato*-ware so popular in England, Germany, the Low Countries and Scandinavia. The earliest documented potters, Philip Drinker of Charlestown, Mass. and William Vincent and John Pride of Salem, Mass., all arrived in the New World in 1635. In the 18th century, German immigrants settled principally in Pennsylvania, becoming known as Pennsylvania Dutch, the latter word a corruption of *Deutsch*. These Germans were prolific craftsmen, self-sufficiency being not so much an ideal as a necessity. They produced domestic earthenwares in great quantity, specialising particularly in the best-known forms of early 357, 362 American pottery, redware and slip-painted *sgraffiato*-ware, both covered in a clear lead glaze.

Apart from the individual potters, whose small workshops supplied the essential needs of the surrounding small towns and villages, there were also journeymen potters who produced what was requested of them by the inhabitants of the places they visited. 18th-century America witnessed, in addition, the establishment of a number of religious communities of various shades of Presbyterianism, which had come to America to escape persecution and intolerance in their native European countries. Certain Swiss and German communities were well known for the production of pottery, while the Shakers from England became internationally famous for their superb furniture (as well as for inventing the circular saw, the washing machine and condensed milk).

The two religious communities associated principally with ceramics are the Swiss Moravians of Bethabara, North Carolina, and the German Pietists of Zoar, Ohio. A third worthy of mention was the Harmony Society of Economy, Pennsylvania. The Moravian factory was the earliest of the three; it is known that by 1756, production was under the management of Gottfried Aust, one of the most significant figures in the history of early American ceramics. Aust worked at Bethabara until 1771, and then moved to another Moravian community at Salem, which had an active pottery factory from 1768 to 1830 (Aust himself died in 1788).

Moravian ceramics were made strictly for use within the community itself, and therefore their style reflects the religious austerity of their makers and users. The majority are covered with a plain black glaze. However, at Salem, Aust produced not only fine stoneware but also creamware, the technique of which he had learned from an English immigrant, William Ellis. The latter had worked at Wedgwood's Etruria Factory on the production of Queensware, arguably the most successful and influential English pottery of the 18th century.

The Pietist Community's pottery was under the supervision of Solomon Purdy; like the Moravians, the Pietists were self-sufficient, and were more extreme in their isolationism than the Swiss brotherhood. Their pottery is redware of the utmost simplicity, yet extremely refined. The Harmonists, in contrast, did trade with the

outside world, with the result that their pottery is often painted.

Stoneware, a more durable and less porous material than earthenware, began to be produced in the United States at the beginning of the 18th century. Natural deposits of clay and their closeness to available modes of transport caused the centres of the industry to be established in New York, New Jersey and Philadelphia, with New York the most important of the three. The most significant, and longest surviving, factory was that of William Crolius, a native of Coblenz, Germany, who had emigrated to the United States in 1718. His factory was established in 1730 and lasted for 157 years. The establishment of the stoneware factories was one of the prime causes of the disappearance of the semi-itinerant folk earthenware potters, added to which the development of salt-glazing from the mid-18th century gave a welcome relief from the lead-glazing of earthenware which, even at that date, was known to constitute a health risk.

The style of American stoneware remained remarkably consistent. Being produced largely by potters of German descent, its most obvious characteristic was its indebtedness to Rhenish stoneware, sometimes called *Grès de Flandres*. The grey-brown salt-glazed body was usually decorated with a combination of incising and cobalt painting. All the pieces were made for domestic use, and dishes, storage crocks, jars, jugs and pitchers have survived in great quantities. There are very few decorative items such as vases, and the quality of the decoration itself is rarely equal to the Pennsylvania earthenware dishes and jars.

However, throughout the 18th century, pottery and porcelain was imported from Europe and the Far East in quantities which exceeded domestic production. Not only were there sophisticated porcelain services for the rich, often painted with appropriate American themes, but also a variety of less fine decorative wares 358 from Staffordshire. It was inevitable that American factories, especially in the fervour of their Independence, would seek to produce items of a similar type, and a number of factories were founded in the first half of the 19th century. The most important were the American Pottery Company of Jersey City, New Jersey (1828-45), Charles Cartlidge and Company of Greenpoint, Long Island (1848-56), and William Boch and Brother, later the Union Porcelain Works, also of Greenpoint (1850-1910). 368

The best known, however, was John Norton's Bennington Factory, founded at Bennington, Vermont, in 1795. This was re-styled the United States Pottery Company in 1853, under which name it continued production until the factory closed in about 1900. The factory's main claim to fame was a mottled treacly glaze which had been developed by Christopher Webber Fenton, who had joined the factory in 1843. Patented in 1849, this glaze was in fact a copy of that used on wares produced by the Rockingham Factory in England, after which its American counterpart was named. The Bennington Factory's success with their Rockingham 366 glaze caused it to be imitated by many other factories throughout the United States.

During the 1870s, many of the countries of Europe began to

365 Moulded jug with a Rockingham glaze by Harker, Taylor & Co. of East Liverpool, Ohio. Made *c.* 1847-51.

366 One of a pair of Bennington Rockingham glazed figures of poodles. Unmarked, *c.* 1849-58.

367 Stag group with a Rockingham glaze, probably designed by Charles Coxon at the Swan Hill Pottery, South Amboy, New Jersey, *c.* 1858-60.

368 The Century Vase, designed by Karl Mueller for the Union Porcelain Works of Greenpoint, Long Island, *c.* 1876.

365

366

367

368

experience the first stirrings of an aesthetic revolution as a young generation of critics, painters, sculptors, architects and designers revolted against the stale eclecticism of High Victorian art which, in combination with new methods of mass production, began to churn out objects of the utmost hideousness. It was at this time also that the artefacts of hitherto little-known cultures began to reach Europe, none having a more dramatic impact than those of Japan.

In Europe, and especially France and England, the effect of these new ideas and sources of stylistic inspiration on the applied arts, including ceramics, was remarkable. In France, many individual studio potters—Chaplet, Carriès, Delaherche, Dalpayrat etc.—set up workshops, while men such as Théodore Deck, director of Sèvres, breathed fresh life into the commercial factories. In England, the studio potter was a phenomenon which, with the exception of the Martin brothers and Sir Edmund Elton, did not appear until the 20th century; the emphasis was on the establishment of art potteries, in which philanthropy often played as great a part as art. This new movement soon spread to the United States.

The years between 1880 and 1910 saw the establishment of well over 150 art potteries in the United States. While many produced interesting work, only three have any real claim to greatness, Rookwood, Chelsea (and its later offshoot Dedham) and University City, the last named primarily for its association with Adelaide Alsop Robineau and the French potter Taxile Doat. To this list we should add the Losanti porcelain of Louise McLaughlin and the porcelain made independently by Mrs Robineau; both of these ladies may be considered among the first American studio potters. American collectors would certainly wish to add Grueby Faience, and Tiffany pottery to this list, and possibly also the Artus van Briggle and Weller potteries. It has to be said, however, that the products of these factories, compared to the finest European art ceramics, have no great merit.

The Chelsea Keramic Art Works, founded in 1872 by the Robertson family at Chelsea, Mass., was the first of these new American factories. Initially its products consisted of beautifully painted red-ware in the styles of ancient Chinese and Greek pottery, similar to the work produced at Watcombe and the Torquay Terracotta Company in England. The factory's greatest work, however, was the result of individual experiments carried out by the finest 19th-century American potter, Hugh Robertson who, in the 1880s, was attempting to produce high-fired metallic oxide glazes, particularly copper red; the same search was also to occupy two of the greatest European ceramists, Hermann Seger and Ernest Chaplet. Robertson perfected the technique in 1888, roughly contemporaneously with Chaplet; he produced some 200 perfect examples, the finest of which, such as the famous 'Twin Stars of Chelsea' now in the Museum of Fine Arts, Boston, must be considered among the supreme achievements of American ceramic art.

The name of Ernest Chaplet is also linked with the products of Rookwood, which was founded in Cincinnati, Ohio in 1880 by Maria Longworth Nichols, later Storer. In 1871, while working at the Laurin factory in Limoges, Chaplet had finally perfected a

method of slip painting on earthenware in a loose, almost Impressionist manner, which technique he called 'barbotine'. It was this technique and style which was to be the principal influence on the Rookwood Pottery, although it is arguable that the first and best practitioner of it in the United States was Louise McLaughlin, an independently minded Cincinnati potter. Rookwood developed a commercialised version of barbotine, the most popular colour scheme having a brown-yellow ground called Mahogany, one of a range of glazes called 'Standard Rookwood'. The measure of its popularity can be gauged from the fact that few of the factories which opened in the wake of Rookwood's success failed to produce their own version of Standard Rookwood. This is particularly true of the 40 or so factories established in Ohio. In name at least, the Rookwood factory lasted until 1971.

METALWORK

THE ART OF THE GOLDSMITH

Anne Somers Cocks

Luxury objects of a primarily decorative function, superbly made by goldsmiths and other skilled craftsmen, have been produced through the ages to delight kings, princes and other wealthy patrons of the arts. The medieval period in Europe is no exception, though there are far fewer surviving examples of the goldsmith's art from this period than from later epochs, and thus they are less representative of their time.

Our view of medieval goldsmithing is more elevated and serious than it should be, simply because most of the striking pieces which remain are of a religious nature, and have been preserved in the treasuries of churches and cathedrals for that reason rather than because of any aesthetic merit. All three medieval works illustrated here come from treasuries, but they are included firstly because they are examples of outstanding craftsmanship, and secondly because they demonstrate the aesthetic standards, techniques and type of designs which would have been favoured for other more secular pieces. The reliquary known as the Golden Rossl (little golden horse), for example, makes extensive use of *émail en ronde bosse*, or enamel, overlaying the gold itself, which is in high or complete relief. Thus the Virgin's gold robe is totally covered with white enamel and her face is flesh-coloured. This technique is frequently mentioned in the late 14th- and early 15th-century inventories of the French princes, and indicates a marked tendency in the goldsmithing of that time – to make gold appear other than it was, very much like a polychromed sculpture. It is also a sign of great sophistication to take a precious metal and work it so that it appears to be a much simpler one, as one sees again in the 17th century, and even later in the work of Fabergé, who turned gold into branches, flowers and leaves.

It is known from contemporary inventories that Charles V of France possessed a number of rare and beautiful objects, kept in his study of the castle of the Bois de Vincennes. These were similar to the Golden Rossl, but secular in nature, and demonstrated a definite tendency towards the figurative and naturalistic. There were many cameos, both ancient and new, as well as splendid jewelled and enamelled items. These often had humorous subjects, for instance one was a statuette of a man riding a cock and holding a trefoil mirror, while another was a camel on a terrace, decorated with pearls, balas rubies and sapphires, the hump of the camel being made of a shell.

Many of these treasures represented the great wealth of the sovereign, which raised him above the ordinary people, converted into suitable items for display. The manner of their display was established and ritualised during the late 14th and 15th centuries, when large buffets began to be built at the great feasts and banquets. These huge, temporary structures of wood were hung with the arms of the host and furnished on the lower levels with his silver plate, on the middle with his silver-gilt, and on the top with the most precious of all, the solid gold and the gem-studded objects. This remained an essential part of court ceremonial right into the early 19th century, and by the 16th century famous architects were being called in to design these massive exhibitions of wealth.

Some of the smaller precious objects, such as the camel on his terrace, were made as part of the courtly etiquette of presenting gifts. Sometimes they were given to preserve good relations between members of the family, or between noblemen and foreign princes, and sometimes to reward loyal subjects. Such present-givings usually took place on certain specific occasions, for instance on New Year or to celebrate the birth of a child, and in many cases conferring gifts was the equivalent of the payment of a salary or a feudal due, but gave the appearance of greater formality and delicacy.

A number of mounted crystal and semi-precious stone vessels which survive from the late 14th and early 15th centuries clearly demonstrate that the technical ability to grind and polish hard stones, well known in Classical times, had been rediscovered. Some of these late medieval vessels found their way into the treasury of that great Renaissance patron and collector, Lorenzo de'Medici. The crucial difference, however, between the status of Lorenzo's collection and those of the dukes and kings of France was that the former was primarily the expression of an antiquarian and aesthetic urge to possess, while the latter were part of their owners' monetary assets, certainly more beautiful to look at than mere coinage, but to be just as readily disposed of when heavy bills had to be paid. Lorenzo de'Medici, as an inventory dated 1492 tells us, had a study in the Palazzo Riccardi which was filled with vases and cups of semi-precious stone with gold mounts brilliant with gems and enamels, as well as numerous cameos and intaglios, both Classical and contemporary.

Some of these hardstone vases have bodies in the Classical style, but it is clear that Lorenzo had no aversion to the Gothic, because in a few of the surviving instances he made no effort to change the Gothic mounts. The covered cup illustrated has a splendid body of semi-precious stones, and was probably made around 1400, but has 15th-century Italian mounts, and the rather Gothic embossed lobes on the foot are combined with Classical volutes supporting the angular knop. The enamel on the foot is translucent, in the brilliant shades popular in 15th-century Italy, while the enamels on the lid show the gold-painted details on a solid enamelled ground, a technique which was particularly popular in Venice. Like many pieces from Lorenzo's collection, even the tiniest cameo, the cup bears his name engraved on the side – a token of his pride of possession. This tradition of collecting was kept up by Lorenzo's successors, and also spread rapidly to the courts of Germany, France and even England.

Very few of the rich jewelled objects produced in France in the 16th century survive, but it is known that the crucial figure behind their commissioning was Francis I, who appreciated the Italian Renaissance sufficiently to invite countless craftsmen to decorate his palace of Fontainebleau, employed Benvenuto Cellini, the great sculptor, goldsmith and medallist, and commissioned Cellini's only surviving piece of goldsmith's work, the gold and enamelled salt now in the Kunsthistorisches Museum, Vienna. Another one of the few surviving pieces of plate made for Francis I is the crystal ciborium or reliquary made about 1530-40. This is in the tradition of the 15th-century mounted and jewelled crystal and hardstone cups, but is designed in the new Classical idiom. The growing enthusiasm for those miniature relics of Classical art, cameos and intaglios, led the unknown goldsmith who made it to set them into the vessel. The gadroons on the upper part of the foot, the acanthus leaves on

369 Rock-crystal reliquary mounted in silver-gilt and set with cameos, gemstones and pearls. This is one of the six surviving objects made for Francis I of France by the Paris court workshops atound 1530-40.

370 The reliquary known as the Golden Rössl (little golden horse), listed in the inventory of Charles VI of France, and made in 1405.

371 Sardonyx cameo of Jupiter with his eagle. Soldered on the base is the royal coat-of-arms of France surmounted by the crown, and on this is an inscription stating that Charles, King of France, son of King John, gave this jewel in the year 1367, the fourth of his reign.

372 One of a pair of Hungarian coats-of-arms in frames, made of silver parcel-gilt decorated with enamel. These were evidently made before 1367, because in that year they were given to the Hungarian chapel in Aachen Cathedral by Ludwig the Great of Hungary.

373 Vase of semi-precious stone mounted in silver-gilt, from the collection of Lorenzo de' Medici. The stone is 14th century; the mount 15th century.

369

370

371

372

373

374 Satuette of St George in jewelled and enamelled gold. Made around 1585, perhaps by Hans Schleich, pupil of Hans Reimer.

375 Agate standing cup mounted in enamelled gold and set with jewels. It is unmarked and attributed to Melchior Baier of Nuremberg, dated 1536.

376 Onyx ewer mounted in enamelled gold and set with jewels, presented by King Charles IX of France to Archduke Ferdinand of Tirol in 1570. Unmarked, possibly made in Paris.

377 Jewel casket of silver-gilt with plaques of mother-of-pearl, set with semi-precious stones, a Christmas present from the Elector Christian I

to his wife. The overall design is the work of the great Nuremberg goldsmith Wenzel Jamnitzer, though the maker's mark is that of a goldsmith in his employ, Nikolaus Schmidt.

378 Covered bowl of silver-gilt with painted and translucent enamels and set with cameos, made in the second quarter of the 16th century.

374

375

376

377

378

the lid, the ball-and-claw feet, the S-curve volutes supporting the knop, are all commonplaces of the Classical vocabulary. The strap-work (so called because of its resemblance to leather straps) mounts down the side of the crystal bowl are especially typical of northern 16th-century design, and had their immediate origin in the plaster-work cartouches in the rooms at Fontainebleau.

The Dukes of Bavaria were the first to declare some of the precious objects in their collection as inalienable heirlooms of their line. This collection, which has survived remarkably unscathed, includes a remarkable descendant of the type of jewelled and enamelled statuette listed in the inventory of Charles V of France's treasury, **374** the statuette of St George, made around 1585 for Duke Wilhelm V. Its descendants, in turn, are the jewelled toys of the Dresden court and the Edwardian Fabergé bibelots of St Petersburg. The figure of St George is made of gold, and his horse is carved from chalcedony. Every detail is perfectly observed: the armour, for example, is blued like real armour – but executed in enamel or jewels. The horse trappings are covered with the finest champlevé enamelling with delicate scrollwork in reverse; the whole is studded and hung with jewels, the reins with diamonds and rubies, the dragon's spots with cabochon emeralds. The base is silver-gilt, set with pearls and gems and decorated with more enamel, this time of the *ronde-bosse* variety. Even at the time, this piece aroused amazed admiration, and in 1619 the sophisticated Augsburg art dealer, Philip Hainhofer, valued it at 300,000 guilders.

Another rare and remarkable creation in the treasury dating **375** from this period is the agate cup, carved to resemble a nautilus shell

and mounted with chased, enamelled and jewelled gold. It was made to exalt the family and legal authority of the man who commissioned it, the Margrave Georg von Brandenburg-Kulmbach: the foot bears six embossed portrait medallions of members of his family and their wives. The cover is chased in low relief with four scenes illustrating Justice: first, the corpse of the father being used as a target by the sons disputing his testament; second, the skin of the unjust judge draped over his chair as a warning; third, the blinding of King Zalenkos; and lastly the judgment of Solomon.

The choice of objects collected in Northern Europe grew con-tinually more complex: a representative collection, it was felt, must reflect a wide range of interests – the fruits of the sea, the animals of the land, the minerals from the depths of the earth, the planes and angles of geometry, and the triumph of man's ingenuity. The finest work of a goldsmith might be shown next to a stuffed bird of paradise, because both would be seen as the product of the Divine creative force behind the universe, the distinction between the man-made and natural, fundamental to modern ways of thinking, being of little consequence. This distinction, however, does seem to have been clearer to the Italian collectors, who tended slightly less to *wunderkammer* (cabinets of curiosities) and more to straight-forward art collections.

A true collection has to be organised and categorised, and in this respect one of the finest of the *wunderkammers* was that of Archduke Ferdinand of Tirol in Schloss Ambras. An inventory dated 1596 describes the way in which his objects were arranged, in different-coloured cupboards. The first, which was blue, contained the

379 House altar of ebony decorated with figures and ornamental plaques of enamelled gold and set with jewels. It was probably made by Abraham Lotter the Elder in Augsburg in 1573-74.

380 Relief in *pietra dura* of Cosimo II of Tuscany in prayer, made between 1617 and 1624. The frame is late 18th century.

381 Nineteen-part tea service of silver-gilt and agate made by Tobias Baur of Augsburg between 1696 and 1700.

382 Small casket with figures of the great Elector and his wife, Louise Henrietta of Orange, in many-coloured amber. Probably by Jacob Heise, Königsberg, *c.* 1650.

379

380

381

382

Italian rock-crystal vessels with gold and enamelled mounts, mostly in the shapes of fantastic animals; other semi-precious stone vessels; and the presents from Charles IX of France, given in 1570, including an onyx ewer with bands of gold enamelled on a mauresque pattern and inset with jewels.

In Germany, the rising demand for high-quality goldsmiths' work was satisfied largely by the great goldsmithing centres, Augsburg and Nuremberg, and by goldsmiths working directly for the princely households. Certain families of goldsmiths rose to particular distinction, such as the Jamnitzer family of Nuremberg. Many of the pieces bearing the Jamnitzer mark in fact have been the product of collaboration in the workshop, with Wenzel Jamnitzer, the doyen of the family, providing designs for the guidance of the other goldsmiths. This was obviously true in the case of the silver-gilt casket with mother-of-pearl and set with semi-precious stones which Elector Christian I of Saxony gave to his wife. The maker's mark is that of Nikolaus Schmidt, a goldsmith in Wenzel Jamnitzer's workshop, and the details owe a great deal to Jamnitzer, for instance, the beetles and small reptiles on the lid are cast from life, a technique which Jamnitzer is supposed to have perfected. He is also said to have invented a machine for stamping out the pierced mounts of the type which decorated the lower edge of the casket.

These fine pierced mounts, whether fretted or stamped, became very popular during the last quarter of the 16th and early 17th centuries. They were usually applied to a contrasting ground, especially ebony; many of these decorated caskets and cabinets come from Augsburg, which specialised in the production of ebony

furniture. One particularly fine example in the Munich Schatzkammer demonstrates a host of different techniques, combining architecture, sculpture, and painting in the miniature medium of goldsmithing. It is a portable house altar mounted in gold with brilliant *ronde bosse* and *champlevé* enamelling, numerous lacy pierced mounts and a mass of gems. The remarkable thing is that it is not an isolated instance; a series of such altars, most of which survive, were made for the Duke of Bavaria around this time.

In the early 17th century, the ebony furniture produced by the Augsburg cabinet makers grew larger and more adventurous: they began to make cabinets which were complete *wunderkammers* in their own right, with hundreds of drawers in which to sort and conceal precious objects. These were major—and immensely expensive—commissions from the princes, indeed the Duke of Pommern-Stettin's cabinet was regarded as so important that a painting was done of him receiving the completed work. The duke of Tuscany had one, and so did the king of Sweden; the latter has its function made explicit by being crowned with shells, a mounted coconut cup and minerals. It was made by the goldsmith Ulrich Baumgartner and the joiner, Martin Biller, between 1625 and 1631.

Enamel had been used extensively during the 16th century to provide contrast and colour for the metals, but in the 17th century painted enamel became extremely fashionable. Clock cases, miniature cases, and whole vessels were first coated with an overall background of opaque enamel, and figurative scenes, landscapes, and flowers were painted on to them, after which they were fired. The covered bowl of the Landgraves of Hess and Kassel in the 378

125

383 Silver-gilt and enamelled clock known as the Hubertus clock because of the scene of St Hubert and the stag on top. The movement is by Johann Gottlieb Grampner (after 1716), and the case by the Dresden court jeweller Johann Heinrich Köhler, 1718.

384 Nautilus cup mounted in gold and set with intaglios, made for the Polish King Stanislas in August 1770 by Jean Martin, who worked at his court from 1769 to 1791.

383

384

Kunstkammer is a splendid example of this, with the serpents enamelled in translucent green by way of contrast. The cameos thickly studded all over this piece reflect the large numbers of craftsmen now involved in this very popular branch of artistic production. Most if not all of them are 16th or 17th century, although some are in the Classical manner. A number of vessels in the Hapsburg collections (Vienna, Kunsthistorisches Museum) are similarly decorated.

The skill required for cutting semi-precious stone vessels and gems led to the invention of a new art form in late 16th-century Florence—the picture made of semi-precious stones and marbles. This is equivalent to marquetry in woodwork, but is obviously more difficult because of the intractability of the material involved. Parts of the design were sometimes sculpted in low relief, as in the case of one of the most famous *pietra dura* panels, the portrait of Cosimo II of Tuscany in prayer (1617-24). This is a triumph of the sophisticated jewellers' and goldsmiths' desire to transcend their materials, making things appear what they are not; for example every detail of the marble sky behind the Duomo is painstakingly represented.

This *pietra dura* technique is the ancestor of the many hardstone boxes and seals made in Germany during the 18th century—the main centres of box production being Berlin and Dresden—and it survived into the 19th century in the form of the hardstone mosaics used to make the brooches, boxes and bracelets which tourists brought back from their visits to Italy.

The blackness of ebony, the whiteness of ivory, and the multi-coloured splendours of enamel and gems were exploited to the full

in the 16th and 17th centuries; indeed, the desire for new textures, colours and effects sometimes led to the use of rather rough, rude substances, like the horns of the mouflon. The dull glow of amber was particularly appreciated in Northern Europe during the 17th century, and statues, house altars, caskets, chandeliers and sometimes whole rooms, were constructed of this material.

During the later part of the same century, the new ritual of tea drinking provided opportunities for some extraordinarily fine fusions of the enamellers' and stone cutters' art with the best goldsmithing of the day. Most goldsmiths' work now came from Augsburg, which had totally eclipsed Nuremberg and become a centre which exported in large quantities, mostly to Central Europe, Scandinavia and Northern Italy.

The *kunstkammer*, or art collection, of the Kings of Saxony, now known as the Green Vaults in the Palace of Dresden, was greatly enlarged in the 18th century by Augustus the Strong (1670-1733), whose taste ran to what in many cases can only be described as toys of gold with jewel and enamel. One of the most splendid of these is the famous cabinet piece by the great goldsmith Johann Melchior Dinglinger called 'The Princely Household at Delhi or the Birthday Gift of the great Mogul', which consists of 132 small figures of gold, enamelled and jewelled, on a vast silver-gilt stage. This was the ultimate in the tradition of figurative goldsmiths' work, which began in the middle ages, the aim of which was to arouse wonder, amazement and admiration in the viewer. Even the more functional objects made for Augustus were technical *tours de force*, such as the gold and silver-gilt enamelled and bejewelled clock with huntsmen in every corner and St Hubert and the stag on top.

385 One of the earliest recorded examples of Renaissance silver in England: the silver-gilt Boleyn Cup belonging to Cirencester Church. The foliate chased foot, the fluting trumpet-shaped bowl, the engraving and the queen's personal falcon badge surmounting the cover are all typical ingredients of Renaissance form.

386 The Burghley Nef, made in Paris by Pierre le Flamand, probably in 1505. The silver-gilt mermaid supports the nautilus-shell ship, on which tiny figures playing chess probably represent Tristram and Iseult. The rigging is modern.

387 Hour-glass salt in purely Gothic form with alternate panels decorated with scrolling flowers and foliage on a punchwork ground. It was made in London in 1516; the maker's mark is a crescent enclosing a mullet.

RENAISSANCE SILVER

From the 12th century until the end of the 15th century, Europe gloried in the ingenious, pinnacled style known as Gothic. It was a style that could be called an ecclesiastical one accepted by the Courts of Europe. Its successor, the Renaissance, was primarily a courtly one that came to dominate ecclesiastical and secular design alike. Its birth was wholly Italian – a product all the more marvellous in view of the tormented, fragmented history of Italy during the later Middle Ages. Within a mere half-century, that re-ordering of Classical design themes which was to inspire the arts for centuries to come was born, and during the next 50 years was disseminated throughout France, Germany, the Low Countries, to England and to Spain and Portugal, until all Europe eventually came under its spell.

The first impetus of the new learning came with a revived awareness of the past: first of all from the literature of Greece and Rome, and soon after from Rome's ruins and antiquities. The frescoes that had somehow survived the centuries in the grottoes and tombs of the capital, the ruined masonry and the marble statuary and urns captured the vision of the goldsmith-painters and the architect-sculptors who worked so assiduously to beautify the houses dedicated to God and the palaces dedicated to the temporal princes of Europe.

It is significant for the minor art of gold- and silversmithing that the court painters of Italy were usually trained first as goldsmiths, who studied the 'behaviour' of metals just as scholars pondered the behaviour of men. With no metal artefacts from Classical times so far discovered, however, they had to transfer the shapes and ornaments from stone vases and urns, pillars and sections of moulding to their gold, silver and bronze, and transform the painted 'grotesques' into three-dimensional virtuosity.

Although the leading Italian goldsmith-painters included such illustrious names as Antonio Pollaiuolo, Andrea del Verrochio, Sandro Botticelli and Domenico Ghirlandaio, assessment of their goldsmithing skills can only be made from the cups and other treasures shown in their paintings. It is not until the early years of the 16th century that rare examples of plate by known masters can be identified – by Valerio Belli of Vicenza, for example, soon to be followed by the redoubtable Benvenuto Cellini.

The innovators of the new style did not wholly discard the themes of the Gothic, but rather at first reinterpreted them against a Classical background. The scrolls, festoons, pilasters and fluting, caryatid figures and heroic finials, shells, strapwork, scrolling foliage and paw feet were arranged with an almost measured balance that inevitably discarded the squatter Gothic forms, the tall pointed arches and the crocketed details of Gothic design, and introduced grace as well as dignity. Such could not fail to find admirers in courtly circles, and as the knowledge of the Renaissance designs spread, no prince or potentate could afford to neglect the high fashion. Engravers began to reproduce the Classical shapes and ornaments, artists made bronze, pewter, boxwood and other models from which the goldsmith could work, and travelling craftsmen carried them across the Alps into southern Germany and France and on to the north and west.

The copying of antique forms and their adaptation to metal-working did not for long satisfy the creative skills of the 16th-century silversmiths. However aesthetically satisfying were the ingredients of Renaissance designs, the craftsmen were soon seeking to express their own creativity. They were nothing if not inventive. Invention, in Renaissance terms, meant assimilation and adaptation, not innovation for its own sake. On the whole, the patron who wanted 'an antique vase' to display his knowledge and appreciation of what Cellini called 'the beautiful art of the past' was prepared to

385

386

387

388 Clock-salt, in the high Renaissance style, probably made about 1540 in Paris. The use of cameos is notably French, but the rest of the ornament is international.

389 This silver-gilt salt, made in London in 1569, is one of the most famous of the English architectural standing salts made during the 16th century. The female figure finial holds a

shield of the Arms of the Vintners' Company, to whom the salt was presented in 1702.

390 A rare form of covered beaker, known as a Magdalen cup. This example, with the maker's mark 'M', was made in London in 1573.

391 Rosewater ewer and basin, made in London in 1545, and given to Corpus Christi College,

Cambridge, by Archbishop Matthew Parker in 1570.

392 This small standing salt, only 2 in. (5 cm.) high, made in London in 1578, may have been a wealthy merchant's own miniature 'standing salt', less ostentatious than the grand ones placed before the queen or other high nobles.

388

389

accept the spirit of a plausible invention—or at worst was deluded by the ploys of the artist or entrepreneur. During the 16th century, a good many imitations and even forgeries gained considerable currency, not only in Italy but in Germany and farther afield.

The taste for splendour coincided, fortunately, with new sources of precious materials from the Americas, not only gold and silver **386,406,** but precious stones and organic materials such as nautilus shells **405** and mother-of-pearl, coral and coconuts, brought home in treasure-laden argosies which eventually found their way into European treasuries.

The strange shapes and materials from exotic places, the scientific and quasi-scientific investigations of scholars and the keen interest of collectors in natural phenomena and the unusual all inspired artists, and especially goldsmiths, to use the elements of Renaissance design and twist and turn them into the imaginative style called Mannerism. Between about 1540 and 1620, Mannerism spread through Europe, in much the same order that the pure Renaissance design it succeeded had spread: first to France, then to southern Germany, the Low Countries, and, lastly, to the periphery of the

richer princedoms and kingdoms, to England, Spain, Portugal, Northern Germany, Scandinavia, Poland and Russia.

When Cellini went to Paris as court goldsmith to Francis I in 1540, he recorded the consummate skills of his rivals there at casting and chasing. By then French craftsmen were already well versed in the new Classical style, though little of their work survives. One of the most notable is the Burghley House nef, now in the Victoria and **386** Albert Museum. The superb nautilus shell on the back of a silver-gilt mermaid is rigged as a ship, and probably served the same function at table as the standing salt in England—as a symbol of dignity and precedence. It possibly dates from 1505, though an earlier date has been argued, or it may be rather later. In more elaborate style and recorded by 1550, when it was in the English royal collection, where it remained until sold after the execution of Charles I in 1649, is the Paris-made clock-salt, now in the collection **388** of the London Goldsmiths' Company. An interesting feature is the inlaying of carved cameos, a taste that spread from France to southern Germany where, south of Trier, the twin towns of Idar-Oberstein had long excelled at gem cutting. Cellini's work for the

393 Tankard of parcel-gilt with repoussé foot and cover chased with fruit, and strapwork. Made in London in 1579, maker's mark an eagle's head between 'IC'.

394 The double cup, with the cover a mirror image of the lower cup and fitting tightly together at the rim, was a German conceit. Nüremberg, end of 16th century.

395 Mannerism constituted many varied styles of drinking cup, each more exotic than the last. This silver-gilt gourd-shaped cup was made in London.

396 This fork, from a set of knife, fork and spoon, was made after a drawing attributed to Antonio Gentile, probably in Rome towards the end of the 16th century.

397 The bowl of this complex Mannerist cup and cover made in Augsburg about 1550 is supported by seated satyrs, a theme repeated on the cover which is surmounted by a vase and bacchanal – drinking above the eight Latin couplets engraved on the rim which eulogise sobriety.

390

391

392

393

394

395

396

397

398 Figure of a *Buttenmann* carrying, in one hand, a tub with barley husks and berry, and in the other a spade. By Christopher Zorer, Augsburg, *c.* 1580.

399 The Lambard cup, made in England in 1578, probably by John Bird. It bears the arms of England, of the Drapers Company, and of Sir William Cordell, Master of the Rolls.

400 Cups in the form of birds or animals were popular on the Continent from the middle ages onwards. This finely tooled Falcon Cup (the head is removable) was made in Antwerp in 1561. The Renaissance-style oblong pedestal is finely engraved and forms a casket, perhaps for sweetmeats.

401 *Jungfrauenbecher* (sometimes called a

milkmaid cup, or wager cup) in late 16th-century dress. It bears an early 17th-century Rotterdam control mark, but is otherwise unmarked.

402 This superb Mannerist *tazza* and cover, with the addorsed arms of Sir Walter Mildmay, who gave it as the Founder's Cup to Emmanuel

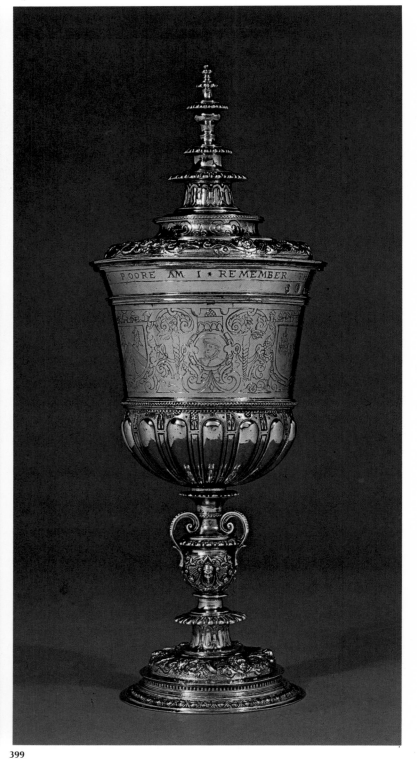

398   399

French king apart, represented today by his superb gold salt, French craftsmanship of the mid-16th century shows a fine appreciation and ready assimilation of the Classical repertoire–elegant caryatids, finely executed scrollwork, intricate mauresques and the skilful use of enamels and hardstones, of which the few survivors offer tantalising glimpses of the splendours consigned to the melting-pot a century later to pay for Louis XIV's incessant and extravagant wars.

Two great centres dominate silver during the 16th century–the German cities of Augsburg and Nuremberg. There were, of course, thriving guilds of goldsmiths all over Germany–at Lubeck and Hamburg, Franco-German Strassbourg and even in smaller towns such as Luneburg, which produced for the civic treasury a huge collection of plate between 1472 and about 1600, of which 29 pieces of plate survive, 27 of them in the Kunstgewerbemuseum in Berlin.

The powerful trade guilds maintained a high standard for the hundreds of standing cups, goblets, tankards, beakers, dishes and ewers, figure-groups, caskets and other plate for secular use.

Almost all was on a grand scale, even ostentatious, intended to display the wealth–and therefore the importance–of the owner. In every castle and palace of Europe, princely patrons strove to outdo their neighbours with more splendid and more intricately conceived designs. Foliate patterns, especially the trailing scroll-work and interlaced motifs known as arabesques and mauresques, strapwork, cartouches, figure-work and the exuberant and mannered grotesques of the mid-16th century changed Renaissance formality into the aptly named Mannerism. The crafts of the caster and the chaser became supreme, made richer with the aid of the modeller, the enameller and the lapidary, many of whom established themselves as court goldsmiths far from the lands of their birth. Hans Holbein, for example, was born in Basel in 1497, but worked and died in London. Wenzel Jamnitzer was born in Vienna but worked in Nuremberg. Many others, of course, excelled in their native countries, such as François Briot, the renowned French model-maker, while Hans Sebald Beham, Albrecht Dürer and Virgil Solis made Germany and design synonymous, as did the Collaerts

395,

unidentified Antwerp silversmith. Dated 1541.

403 This silver-gilt dish, chased in high relief with fabulous creatures, men and horses, shows the Portuguese transition from Gothic to Renaissance. The dish bears the rare Lisbon ship mark, dating from *c.* 1525.

404 In England quantities of the brownish-red

stoneware from the Rhineland, known as tigerware, was mounted to make jugs and tankards. This jug, mounted in Exeter about 1575, has an unusual lion sejant finial, very like those used on spoons of the period.

405 The pitted yellowish shell of the ostrich egg was another popular exotic material. This rare silver-gilt-mounted egg (the egg itself is

modern) was mounted in London in 1584 with straps holding the eggs formed as male and female caryatids.

406 The lustrous nautilus shell was one of the exotic materials often mounted in richly worked silver-gilt throughout Europe in the 16th century. This example was made in Augsburg *c.* 1580.

400

401

402

403

404

405

406

407 One of the service of 'Emperor' *tazzas* made for the Aldobrandini family, probably in Augsburg in the late 16th century. Each footed dish is chased with scenes from the life of one of the twelve Emperors of Rome, this example showing the Emperor Domitian, with scenes of his life in the dish.

408 From left to right: a gilt beaker made in Basle, Switzerland, engraved with Salome and the beheading of John the Baptist on one side, the Sermon on the Mount on the other. A Nuremberg beaker of about 1585 by Hans Keller with an applied band of cast strapwork contrasting with the delicate engraved designs below; and a slightly earlier Nuremberg beaker

by Hans Multerer, Sr., *c.* 1560, engraved with hatched strapwork and arabesques.

409 Drinking-horn with silver-gilt mounts made in Bergen, Norway, *c.* 1610 in the Gothic style on 'griffin-claw' supports, but with typical Renaissance engraved foliate and strapwork ornament.

408

407

409

in Antwerp and Theodor de Bry in Liège. Throughout Europe the art of sheer extravagance in silver and gold flourished as never before nor since.

Certain items of domestic plate were fashionable to a greater or lesser extent in different parts of Europe. Covered tankards, for instance, were not made in the Latin countries, but were of considerable importance in the beer-drinking lands of Germany, Holland, Scandinavia and Britain. In Russia the favourite drinking vessel was the *bratina*, a deep bowl, or 'brotherly' cup. Most coconut cups were made for northern patrons, and so were buffalo and other drinking horns. Standing mazers, successors of medieval wooden bowls 'tipped with silver' were still made in Scotland, but in southern Germany, northern Italy and France rock crystal and other hardstones were cut and mounted most lavishly—and were, of course, much esteemed elsewhere. Antwerp craftsmen were particularly noted for their nautilus shells, some of which were finely carved. Venetian *latticino* glass with its milky white patterning, Near Eastern pottery, oriental porcelain, ostrich eggs and even stoneware from the Rhineland were also mounted to make cups, jugs, tankards and salts. They have often survived simply because it was not worth recovering the metal used to mount them. In France, indeed, so little survived the depredations of war and tax-gatherers that one often has to rely on the style of surviving mounted pieces and on drawings to sense the true magnificence of silversmiths' work there in the mid-16th century. But since so much goldsmithing was international, with craftsmen as well as their designs travelling from city to city and court to court, it is possible to build up a picture of the whole of Europe from the remaining treasures of Italy, Germany, the Low Countries, England, the Iberian Peninsula and Scandinavia.

Standing salts, nefs and standing cups, often of immense proportions, provided the chief ceremonial silver of the nobles dining in the great halls of castles and palaces throughout Europe, and for the members of important City Councils and flourishing trade guilds. Most of this silver would be gilded, both for show and for obvious practical reasons, since elaborate chasing was much in favour and over-cleaning would be detrimental as well as difficult. Incidentally, very little gold plate was ever made: the term 'gold' generally meant gilded, while silver was sometimes referred to as 'white'.

The chief casualty of the new Renaissance styles was the shallow

font-shaped cup, though it could be said to have survived in the shallow standing dishes and bowls usually called *tazze*. As a rule, the standing cup was tall, with a domed cover terminating in a many-tiered architectural finial, sometimes surmounted by a human or animal figure. The stem was generally knopped, sometimes further enhanced with cast scroll brackets below the bowl, which might be repeated on the cover. The body of some early cups was tapered in the manner of Venetian glass goblets, but more often it was a tapering cylinder with perhaps a bulbous base. However, variations, especially with the advent of Mannerism, were legion.

In Germany one variant was the double-cup, a standing goblet with a narrow band at the lip which closely fitted that of its pair so that the second formed a cover in mirror-image of the lower one. Some cups were supported on figure stems, others had tree-trunk-like stems, with the bodies shaped like gourds. The late medieval passion for cups shaped as animals and birds was unabated, though of course details were now in the Renaissance manner. Globe cups, engraved with maps of the earth and the heavens, were a speciality from Nuremberg, while a host of natural themes—columbines, bunches of grapes, pineapples and pumpkins—suggested new shapes to the ever-inventive craftsmen, and the designs and variations quickly spread throughout Europe.

Closely related to the standing cups in design, the shallow footed dishes of the 16th century were made both with and without covers. Those left uncovered often made the interior as elaborate a feature as the foot and stem, with applied plaques, often illustrating Classical or Biblical scenes, or even with central figures, such as the famous set of the Twelve Caesars once owned by Cardinal Aldobrandini and now scattered in museums in London, New York and elsewhere, and the amusing swan *tazza* made in London in 1599. More often, however, a portrait medallion centred the shallow bowl. Covered *tazze* are rarer, the domed cover with a tall and elaborate finial echoing the elaborate stem of the dish.

Still a central feature of the ceremonial at table, the Renaissance period standing salt was primarily architectural in design—a tall covered receptacle, often square or a cylindrical drum with a small well for the salt in the top, usually covered, and supported on a stepped base or cast feet. Some of the most spectacular 16th-century salts have survived in English collections, such as the pillared Gibbon Salt of 1576 belonging to the London Goldsmiths' Company,

410 The tall and elegant wine cup of the turn of the century was a style later to be adopted by the glassmakers of the 17th century. This example is clearly marked at the rim, 'TF, London, 1604'.

with its central column of rock crystal enclosing a gilt figure of Neptune. A very large salt of 1592, the Vyvyan, in the Victoria and Albert Museum, has the sides applied with enamelled glass panels and with portrait medallions on the cover, surmounted by a figure of Justice. A wholly English style of salt was the bell salt formed of three tiers, with skirt-like base and domed top terminating in a small caster. Decoration on these salts, which date from the 1580s to about 1620, was usually flat-chasing of strapwork on a matted ground, though a few are engraved.

In France and elsewhere on the Continent, the standing salt was usually replaced by the nef, or ship centrepiece. It is interesting that in his great gold salt for Francis I, Cellini located the precious mineral within a ship. Nefs of the 16th century—including the **386** superb Burghley nef—incorporate Renaissance imagery in the decoration.

For personal use at table, small trencher salts, of circular, square **292** or, more often, triangular outline, were the forerunners of the ubiquitous small salts of later centuries. Ornament usually consisted of running scrollwork of stamped, chased, or engraved arabesques, and with stamped ovolo or egg-and-dart mounts. A variation found as far apart as Spain and Denmark was the triangular spice-plate, with three wells for salt and spices instead of a single cellar.

The oldest form of small drinking vessel, the tapered beaker, remained a firm favourite throughout the Renaissance period and well into the 18th century. It is said that in 16th-century Denmark, everyone of any pretensions to wealth or position had a silver **408** beaker and a silver spoon. They were made in all sizes, but the most popular ones were tall, at least 6 inches (15 centimetres) high; in northern countries, especially in Norway and Holland, one or two applied bands were usual round the body, which was often supported on three or four cast feet—claw and ball, and lion couchant being popular variations of the usual spreading or stamped foot. In England, engraved strapwork borders with pendant details were popular, though occasionally plain ones were applied with medallion heads. Similar styles were made in Holland, but in Germany many beakers were much smaller—their bowls the size of those used for goblets (and Communion cups) in England during the 1570s and 1580s. Many German beakers were made in sets of four or six fitting into one another—the 'nests' mentioned by the much-travelled William Harrison as being common throughout England also.

Among the most attractive are the beakers with cylindrical bowls and short stems with spreading bases. Below the lips are moulded girdles, and the cups are decorated, usually with engraving, showing hunting scenes or representations of the months. Another kind **401** of beaker, though not strictly one, was the *Jungfrauenbecher*, in the form of a young woman, whose skirt formed a wine cup when inverted, and who held aloft, on a swivel, a smaller 'tumbler' cup which would, like her skirt, be filled. These cups were much used at weddings, when the groom would be expected to drink from the skirt-cup and present the piece, without spilling a drop, for his bride to drink from the smaller upper cup. Between weddings, such cups soon became used for wagers.

Capacious covered pots for beer-drinking were among the most important products of the Scandinavian and German workshops. The drum-shaped bodies provided a wonderful setting for the rich repoussé chasing, strapwork and scenes, both sacred and profane, that demonstrated the skill and virtuosity of the silversmith. The scroll thumbpiece, the cast thumbpiece and the cover all received their share of Mannerist ornament. A few beer-pots were of baluster shape, but by far the greater number were cylindrical, the taller examples usually with a moulded rib applied near the base.

Both the straight-sided and the baluster form were used for jugs and flagons for serving beer, wine or water, and the design and decoration of these was similar to the tankards. It may be that the smaller silver-mounted stoneware pots, usually nowadays called jugs, but never spouted, were in fact tankards.

The more imposing jugs of the 16th century are usually termed ewers, and were accompanied by large oval or circular dishes. They **391** were used for handing rosewater at table in an era before forks

were introduced. Usually supported on a high domed foot, the bodies might be globular, pear-shaped, vase-shaped, cylindrical or thistle-shaped. It is generally considered that the globular styles were of southern origin, from Italy, and tapered vase shapes to northern taste. However, most types were prevalent everywhere that these ewers and dishes were in fashion—a fashion that did not spread, for instance, to the far north. In Spain, ewers were almost always cylindrical, the body intersected by applied moulded bands, the handle angular and the lip pronounced and usually extending about two-thirds of the way down the body. Since rosewater was clear, there was no reason to limit decoration of the interior, and besides engraving and repoussé chasing, usually covering every inch of the basin, an enamelled central boss might bear the owner's arms and also serve as a support for the ewer when not in use. The bulbous-bodied style of ewer with a long spout may have been inspired by imports of Turkish pottery or perhaps by Chinese wine-pots which, as mentioned above, were frequently mounted in gold or silver. Portuguese dishes (of which more survive than their companion ewers) are usually richly chased—the true Renaissance **403** styles surviving in an almost pure form, with only hints of Mannerism in the inclusion of strutting birds, dragons and animals among the scrolling foliage.

Though contemporary inventories tantalisingly list many other items of plate, such pieces as candlesticks, sconces, toilet silver, strainers, saucepans and other domestic silver are so rare that any survey of their style is impossible. Spoons changed little from the **396** late medieval type, with fig-shaped bowl, hexagonal tapered stem and decorative finial—a subject that itself is deserving of fuller study than can be briefly outlined here.

410

17th-CENTURY SILVER

Judith Banister

For a few years at the beginning of the 17th century there was relative peace in Europe. It heralded, however, two distinct and different paths for the arts: the aim in the south to restate the position of the Catholic Church and restore its glory ran parallel with the chillier taste for Protestantism in England, Switzerland, provincial areas in France, Germany and northwards into Scandinavia.

Spain's hold on the Low Countries was weakened, leaving Holland to concentrate, as England could also, on her maritime ventures and colonial conquests. Trade with America and the East Indies, and southwards to Africa, flourished. Spain still ruled most of Italy, however, and her argosies still brought back vast plunder from the Americas, and with Spanish money, the Catholics were set to battle against the Calvinists and Lutherans who seemed to shrink into the north. The seemingly endless wealth of Brazil, her gold and gems, and Mexico's silver, kept the workshops of Antwerp and Augsburg, Paris, Prague and a dozen other established centres of the craft busy for 100 years to come.

At first, the chief cultural influence flowed from Holland, though it was in Prague that the eminent Paul van Vianen was able to create and disseminate the rich Baroque style with which he and his brother and nephew were always to be associated. Paul van Vianen had been born in Utrecht, but most of his work·was produced in 418 Munich, Salzburg and Prague. His brother Adam, on the other hand, made Utrecht a byword for spectacular silversmithing, and in turn Adam's son spread the style of the lobed grotesque to England where he was appointed goldsmith to Charles I. These styles were perpetuated and developed by Jan Lutma and his son, also Jan, working in Amsterdam, and by Thomas Bogaert, a pupil of the van Vianens, who also worked in Amsterdam.

The van Vianens produced highly accomplished silver in an extension of the Mannerist style, using grotesques, scrolls and lobed ornament to set off sculptural scenes in low relief decorating the centres of standing dishes, bowls, ewers and standing open salts. Most of their silver was intended for display rather than use, and every corner was filled with ornament, even on the underside. Paul seemed to have been the chief innovator of the lobed, muscle-like ornament, but after his death in 1613 it was adopted and interpreted by Adam in Utrecht, who also designed bowls, dishes and so on himself—designs that his son Christian seems to have used rather than troubling to create his own. The work of the van Vianens and their followers, many of them highly skilled at casting and chasing, was esteemed throughout Europe, an esteem demonstrated by Dutch paintings of the time, several of which included pieces of their work. One of the most outstanding, a 10-inch 418 (25.5-centimetre) high ewer made in 1614, appeared in no fewer than 20 paintings. This piece, on show at the Royal Scottish Museum from 1954 until it was sold in 1976, has now returned to Holland, to the Rijksmuseum in Amsterdam.

Not all Dutch silver of the early 17th century was on such a magnificent scale. The well-to-do merchants appear to have had a much more practical, even bourgeois, taste in silver, and wanted neat beakers, tankards, dishes and plaquettes rather than immense standing cups. Domestic silver as we know it was now gradually beginning to appear, made for mercantile rather than royal patrons.

In Spain, in contrast, the style was richer than ever, and the Catholic centres of power—Italy, Austria, Belgium and France, followed suit. Germany was divided against itself, and when the Bohemians resisted, the Thirty Years' War (1618 to 1648) began its devastation of the old Europe. Silver, as usual, went into the melting-pot to pay for arms and men.

England, too, was destroying its treasures under its wise and foolish King Charles, and the Civil War that culminated in the King's death in January 1649 meant untold losses of plate from supporters of both sides. The Commonwealth, with its Puritan denigration of all that smacked of monarchy and majesty, meant a death-knell for all but a few stalwart silversmiths, who were hard put to it to find enough silver to work even if patrons felt the un-Cromwellian desire to own plate.

The end of the Thirty Years' War had left many countries—Denmark, Germany, Holland, and France—denuded of their silver. During the years to come, the silversmiths once more set out to turn arms into arts, most of all in Holland, the United Provinces, struggling with self-government for the first time and growing wealthier through the efforts of their merchant-venturers overseas. And there the exiled Stuart court found new inspiration for its Restoration, and learnt anew the arts and crafts of peace.

By the late 1630s, despite the war, a new style was sweeping the low-lying lands we call Holland. Tulipmania had made Holland the Garden of Europe, and it became a famous garden indeed in the pattern books of the goldsmiths. It was almost a provincial taste, with boldly repoussé chased ornament, tulips and other spring flowers casually arranged and sometimes interspersed with animals of the chase, but it appealed to the burghers of Amsterdam and Rotterdam, and to their guests from England and Ireland, who in 1660 took the style back with them. It spread eastwards and northwards, and by the 1680s the naturalistic motifs of this Dutch Baroque was established throughout Scandinavia, Holland and England.

Meanwhile,. there was a growing taste throughout northern Europe for finely engraved detail. Sometimes this was based on the 415. flower-abundant designs, sometimes it was an extension of 16th-century foliate and strapwork ornament, sometimes it was scenic, with portraits and events depicted in consummate detail—a skill especially associated with the Dutch engravers.

Though silversmiths unhesitatingly borrowed shapes, styles and decorative detail from one another, there was still a very 'nationalist' tendency in what was made. In France, for instance, there are shallow one-eared wine tasters, while the Hollanders liked their spirits in small two-handled bowls and had a taste for windmill and 417 other elaborate cups that could not be set down until empty. Marriage caskets and holders for glasses were also typically Dutch. English silver of the first half of the century is almost as scarce as French. At first there was little change from late Tudor styles, and tall wine cups and standing cups and salts with steeple finials were 413 distinctively English. The shallow two-handled porringer on a spreading foot, the ring-handled ox-eye cup and the plain tankard on a skirt foot were essentially English styles; the three-legged saucepan or skillet and the shell-shaped spice or sugar box also appear to be only of English origin, just as the bulbous *bratina* continued to be virtually exclusive to Russia alongside the boat-shaped *kovsh*. In Spain and Portugal, caskets and dishes retained an 429 ecclesiastical appearance, and the same could be said of much Italian and south German work. Nuremberg silversmiths still excelled at mounting rare objects such as ostrich eggs—often converted into exotic bird shapes—mother-of-pearl, coral, nautilus shells (seahorses were a favourite conceit of Leipzig masters), coconuts and carved ivory.

The standing cup continued to be an important piece of display 413. plate throughout the first half of the 17th century, especially in England and in Germany. Traditional Renaissance and Mannerist

411 Still in the Mannerist tradition, silver-gilt squirrel of about 1630 made in Augsburg, holding a 'memento mori' shield dated 1682.

412 Cagework cup and cover, c. 1670, with pierced and chased silver sleeve over plain gilt interior, a fashion perhaps brought to England from Holland.

413 Silver-gilt standing cup and cover, with London marks for 1611, but perhaps the work of a Flemish craftsman.

414 Tall standing cups and covers, often of fanciful design, such as this bunch-of-grapes cup, sometimes called a pineapple cup, remained dominant in Germany. This example was made in Nuremberg c. 1620-30.

411

412

413

414

styles were hardly developed at all in the silversmithing of specially high quality still being done in the traditional centre of Nuremberg. In England, the so-called steeple cup, with its pyramidal finial, usually on a relatively simple chased wine goblet with a domed cover, was an unusual pattern between 1599 and 1646, and a few cups and covers with what is really applied filigree bands are recorded about 1610. Dutch and Flemish cups were nearly always silver-mounted nautilus shells, coconuts and the like.

In the hands of the van Vianens and the Lutmas, the standing dish became a sculptural tour-de-force, combining the mobile, cartilaginous ornament with plaques chased in high relief. In Germany, however, strapwork, flower and foliate motifs, demi-figures and masks perpetuated earlier inspiration, though none the less extravagant in design and showiness.

The importance of the great standing salt gradually dwindled during the first quarter of the century. In England, a few architectural salts were made at the turn of the century, and the bell salt remained fashionable until about 1620, when it was replaced, chiefly for college or civic use, by the spool-shaped or capstan salt, a plain design usually with three or four brackets around the central well, generally supposed to have supported a napkin or

flat cover. In Holland and Belgium, similar spool-shaped salts, though usually decorated with naturalistic chasing, were made—and there were, of course, those extravaganzas by the van Vianens and the Lutmas formed as shells supported by figures and garnished with the scrolling 'kwabornament'. The small trencher salt, how- 432 ever, was becoming more general, and though still very rare, occasionally oval, octagonal and circular examples are recorded— styles that in England were to remain popular well into the 18th century.

In Germany and in Scandinavia, the covered tankard reigned 416,423,426 supreme, made in every size from about half a pint to half a gallon, and in every style from a simple drum with the minimum of applied detail to grandiose examples enriched with chased or inset plaques and medallions. In Norway especially the tankard was sometimes tall and slender, with one or two applied ribs around the cylindrical 424 body, though many conformed to the more usual Scandinavian type—a drum shape on spreading foot or on four cast supports, usually with pegs soldered inside, a custom used at drinking parties for wagering (the origin of 'taking down a peg'). In England, the tall drum tankard on a spreading foot, usually decorated with chased strapwork and applied medallion heads, was going out of

135

415 Delicately engraved dish with incurved sides, formerly at St Monica's Priory, Louvain. Made in Antwerp in 1616.

416 Large tankards were mostly of northern origin–German, Scandinavian, Baltic and English. This example of about 1620, chased with fruit, foliage and strapwork on a matted ground, was made in Augsburg.

417 Dutch windmill cup with blowpipe behind, chased in 16th-century style but made in Amsterdam in 1635.

418 This highly original ewer, 10 in. (25.5 cm.) high, by Adam van Vianen, Utrecht, 1614, is represented in some 20 well-known pictures and portraits painted between about 1615 and 1660.

419 One of a pair of Italian ewers and basins made in Genoa *c.* 1619, superbly chased with Classical legends with gods, *putti* and warriors in the Mannerist stile.

415

416

417

418

419

fashion, and by the second quarter of the century the plain, slightly tapering tankard with scroll handle and thumbpiece to a flat cover was introduced. Smaller tankards were almost globular, chased with matted panels and floral strapwork, but both these types shortly gave way to the plain drum on a skirt foot, with a slightly raised cap cover, scroll handle and twin thumbpiece.

Of all 17th-century silver for drinking, the beaker was undoubtedly the most widespread, and appeared in almost every country of Europe. Most were tall and elegant, the sides slightly tapering to the rim, and supported on a simple stamped or rim foot. Some were quite plain, others engraved with arabesques and strapwork below the rim. In England, the taller style gradually dwindled into a squat flared cup, only $3\frac{1}{2}$ or 4 inches (8.8 or 10 centimetres) high, with little or no decoration. In northern Germany, Scandinavia and Holland, however, the tall beaker was everywhere evident, each country or district seemingly favouring its own style. In Sweden, Norway and in Friesland, for instance, there was a taste for an applied band, or sometimes, two bands of ornament around the body–Friesland beakers nearly always have a thorn-like girdle, while interlacing ribbon-like detail, cherub heads and rings were sometimes featured in Sweden and Norway. Danish beakers, often matted overall except for an oval for initials,

are usually rather shorter and sometimes covered; many were buried during the Thirty Years War and so have survived in fair numbers. Overall engraving, repoussé chasing and simulated staving–the latter especially popular for interlocking double beakers–all appeared on German examples, but it was in Holland that some of the most beautiful beakers of all were made. The Dutch brought the standard of engraving to a very high order during the first half of the century, and besides fine designs of flowers, foliage and scrollwork, they adorned beakers with birds, animals, hunting scenes, ships and men. Sometimes views of towns or battles were engraved with great precision, while many of the figures show a lurking sense of humour.

The high standard of Dutch engraving was also evident on other silver, notably on dishes and salvers which were often engraved with religious, household or hunting scenes and with borders of elaborately intertwining foliage and scrollwork. It was a much gentler style than the boldly cast and chased plaques which were fashionable in almost all the central European countries–not excluding, of course, Holland. During the first half of the century, a few exceptional rosewater ewers and dishes were made. The superb virtuosity of even the van Vianens, however, pales beside the work of an unidentified Genoese silversmith who between 1619 and 1622

422

415,42

420 Even after the Restoration of Charles II, silver bullion was in short supply, and this small wine cup of 1662, 3¾ in. (9.5 cm.) high, follows Commonwealth style in its simple flower-chased motifs on a matted ground.

421 Much of the silver that survived the Civil War in England consisted of spoons, simple mounted cups, a few wine cups and shallow saucer-dishes, such as this typical embossed and beaded example of 1634 by William Maundy.

422 In Holland, fine engraving was lavished on commemorative beakers, such as this example made in Enkhuisen in 1656. The medallions contain Biblical scenes between scrolling foliage and strapwork, while below, van Tromp and other Dutch admirals are shown battling in the Anglo-Dutch war of 1652-54.

423 Typical of the intricate casting and chasing achieved in north Germany, a pair of Baroque tankards made in Hamburg *c.* 1680 illustrating the Rape of the Sabine women.

420 · 421

422 · 423

419 created the magnificent Lomellini ewers and dishes chased in relief with scenes from the Battle of the Po in 1431.

In the early years of the century, silver baskets made an appearance in small numbers; the earliest known appears to be the English circular basket, probably a dessert dish, now in the Victoria and Albert Museum. A few others are recorded both in England and on the Continent, forerunners of the bread and cake baskets of the 18th century.

Covered cylindrical or six-sided boxes with screw-on covers and hinged handles were typical Augsburg products first introduced in the early Baroque period.

The ascendancy of France

In 1661, Louis XIV, now aged 22, took the reins of government into his own hands. It was the beginning of a new era of monarchy and of magnificence. The previous year, Charles II had been restored to the throne of England. Four years later, the death of Philip IV of Spain gave Louis the opening to invade the Spanish Netherlands and despite the efforts of England and Sweden, set out to destroy the United Provinces of Holland. William of Orange was given tremendous powers by his countrymen in an effort to stem Louis's invasion. Protestant though he was, he gained the help of Spain, the

Emperor Leopold and many of the German rulers. Peace was dictated by Louis in 1678/9, but he had another trump card to play against the Protestants. In 1685 he revoked the Edict of Nantes, the act tolerating the Huguenots, and a flood of French Protestants, many of them the country's finest craftsmen, fled to Holland, Germany, Switzerland, England, Ireland and America. Thus, ironically, the cruelty of war gave the rest of Europe the skills to interpret the undoubted supremacy of French design, and these influences spread rapidly throughout Europe to the fens of the north where a young Prince, Peter, was fighting for power that was to create him Emperor and founder of St Petersburg, and to the new Europe across the Atlantic.

Louis XIV was as skilled in the arts of peace as of war, and at Versailles he laid the foundations of the French cultural influence that was to last for more than a century. Sumptuousness and the Sun King were virtually synonymous. Already French silversmiths had proved their ability at fine chasing, and it was a craft that was to be in great demand for the next half century. Meticulous, intricate Baroque ornament such as had been introduced about 1645 under the auspices of Anne of Austria was applied to thrones, tables, gueridons, sconces, mirrors, toilet services, caskets and display silver of every kind. The taste for such splendour spread

137

424 In Scandinavia, the cylindrical tankard of conventional form remained popular well into the 17th century. This fine Renaissance-style flagon with its contrasting relief-chased and finely engraved decoration is by Lucas Steen of Bergen, and dates from the first half of the 17th century.

425 The cylindrical tankard with three cast

supports was popular in England, first being made in York about 1650, then in London 12 years later. This fine large example of 1673 was the work of the recently identified Thomas Jenkins.

426 The first half of the 17th century in England saw a taste for plain, functional silver, such as this small tankard of 1638, unadorned

except for the cast demi-figure thumbpiece and the plumed cartouche for the owner's armorials.

427 In Sweden and Holland, filigree work was a specialised craft. On this covered parcel-gilt beaker of 1696, made in Stockholm by Rudolf Wittkopf, it is given a Baroque look, with insets of naturalistic flower forms.

424   425   426

427   428   429

through Europe as fast as the silversmiths could acquire the pattern-books. Of course, not all patrons could afford the higher flights of fancy or, perhaps, cared for them overmuch. But all over Europe there was a leaning towards this new Baroque, and a renewed demand for silverwares, especially in England, Holland, and Scandinavia where so much earlier silver had been lost during the strife of the first half of the century. There was, too, the increasingly wealthy mercantile class to cater for, householders who wanted more than a silver spoon and bowl and emulated the 'silver cupboards' of the aristocracy.

Quantities of silver still arrived in Europe from the Americas, but so extensive was the demand for the metal that many governments were seriously concerned about the conversion of coinage into domestic plate. In England this came to a head in 1696, with the Act appealingly entitled 'for encouraging the bringing in of wrought plate to be coined' which imposed a new higher standard of 95·8 per cent, compulsorily replacing the long-established 92·5 per cent sterling standard. Called the Britannia Standard because it was marked with 'the figure of a woman commonly called Britannia', it in fact brought the English silver up to approximately the same standard as that in France. It remained obligatory from 1697 to 1720, but because of the export trade with the Continent, it was retained as an alternative when sterling was once more permitted.

Though the names of a few of the most renowned French silversmiths, such as Claud Ballin the Elder, are known, hardly anything of their work survives: a decree of 1689–and another equally destructive in 1709–consigned to the melting-pot every piece of silver on which the King could lay his hands. It was of no avail that it was said the moulds remained. The treasures were never re-made.

Happily, some very fine 17th-century French silver had already found its way abroad, to England, Holland, Sweden and Germany. This was assiduously copied and imitated, as were the designs put about by Jean Bérain, Daniel Marot, and by the hundreds of refugee Huguenots who fled Louis' oppressive laws.

Since many of the emigrés were of provincial origin, the high style of Paris and Versailles was less often 'exported'. Instead, the

Huguenots introduced the sturdy simplicity of the early Louis XIV period, the cut-card ornament, gadrooned mounts and more formal details that had been occasionally used in England and elsewhere about the middle of the century but which, until the late 1680s, had generally been subjugated to the more florid tastes of the Baroque. By the 1690s, they had revolutionised silver design. The simple cylinder and the fluted column of tankards, coffee-pots, candlesticks and casters became the baluster; caryatid and scroll handles became harp-shaped, formal flat flutes became applied cut-card detail, and husks, trelliswork and chased detail in the Régence manner superseded the naturalistic flowers, running hounds and free-style ornament of the past 20 years.

Though French styles were almost everywhere acclaimed, not all the aspects of French silver were accepted. The shallow two-handled covered bowl, or écuelle, traditionally given to nursing mothers, was seldom made outside France, any more than tankards were made in France, or in any of the Latin countries. With the exception of those made for vintners, few wine tasters were made in the beer-drinking countries, where tankards and mugs were scarcely affected by French styles, at least until the early 18th century. There was still a taste in Germany for standing cups, figures of men and beasts, tazze and mounted wares. In England and Ireland, the two-handled porringer only gradually gave way to the taller two-handled cup and cover, and in country districts lingered on well into the 18th century, while in Scotland, thistle cups and quaichs remained traditional items.

Perhaps of all the silver made for use as well as display during the second half of the 17th century, the traditional bridal toilet service best typified the grand Baroque. Made up of as many as **437** 20 or more pieces–table mirror, candlesticks, caskets, perfume flasks, boxes, porringers, brushes and so on–they were often the work of several silversmiths, and, since they were usually made to special order, many are wholly or partly unmarked. In recent years, those coming on to the market are often split up, as it is considered individual items will sell more readily. Besides the intricately chased Baroque style with cupids, birds and so on in bowers of

428 By the end of the 17th century, the baluster-shaped mug had been introduced from France, but was often given a local style, as in this swirl-fluted example of 1693 made by Benjamin Pyne of London.

429 Russian *kovsh* of typical boat shape, embossed with the Imperial Russian eagle and with a presentation inscription, dating from the late 17th century. By this date the vessel had become almost wholly ceremonial. Its form was based on the ancient dipper or ladle.

430 Naturalistic flowers typical of the late 17th-century Baroque for a triple spice plate made by Simon Mathieson of Odense, Denmark, *c.* 1680-90.

431 The medieval bottle or 'pilgrim flask' was revived for large silver wine bottles during the Baroque period, here engraved with drinking scenes in the manner of Adrian van Ostade. Made in Augsburg by J. C. Treffler, *c.* 1690.

432 Practical, unpretentious trencher salts, with incurved octagonal sides, marked in the circular wells 'London 1684'.

430

431

432

leaves and flowers, two other distinctive styles of toilet service were popular. In England, many were flat chased, or occasionally engraved, with exotic birds and plants in the Chinese manner, a style that seems to have been exclusive to England. Towards the end of the century, there was also a taste for simpler octagonal forms, sometimes decorated with Chinoiseries, sometimes with finely engraved armorials or monograms, setting off boldly gadrooned mounts. In Augsburg, where many of the finest German toilet services were made, and in The Hague, these simpler patterns were also made and, in Augsburg especially, the new Régence motifs were engraved on oval boxes, which were sometimes applied with small medallions as well. These, like tankards, were also inset with chased plaques in the manner of J. A. Thélot.

While most ewers and dishes were included in smaller versions in toilet services, a few were made for display and use in the dining room. The mid-century style of cylindrical jug on a high foot, with harp-shaped handle and short spout gradually gave way to the ewer of helmet-shape, with high-flying scroll handle and curved lip integral with the body, which was usually divided by a moulded rib and applied with cut-card work or applied strapwork. The dish, oval or circular, with a broad flange, was often finely decorated in the Régence manner, in a style similar to the few sideboard dishes or chargers made for display.

Wooden furniture – tables, chairs, thrones, candlestands and wall mirrors – was covered with chased silver sheet to splendid effect during the second half of the century. Several suites, mostly London or Augsburg work, have survived. Silver was also used to decorate andirons, pokers, tongs and other hearth furniture.

Often associated with wealthy patrons for whom silver furniture was made were the tall beakers, vases, flasks and 'ginger jars' used to decorate mantelpieces and side-tables. Again, the high Baroque style with its massed flowers and foliage, *amorini* and birds was the most fashionable. In Germany, embossed and chased plaques by J. A. Thélot (1654-1734) and his school were often framed for display, as well as being set in the sides and tops of caskets and other toilet boxes. This was a fashion that remained popular in many parts of Europe until the 1730s.

Apart from ecclesiastical figures made in Italy, South Germany, Spain and Portugal, the Germans retained their taste for secular silver figures of birds, animals and, now more frequently, representations of human beings, sometimes portrait busts, sometimes fantasies, or showing Classical figures, craftsmen or even groups, very much in the manner of porcelain models. Nefs in the traditional manner continued to be made, though few were to be found outside Germany. By the later 17th century they had lost their place as salts, but were made as table centres, along with elaborate table fountains, gem-set extravaganza, and occasional *tazze*.

Though silver candlesticks were recorded in the 16th century, few secular examples survive until the second half of the 17th century. The most prevalent style was the fluted cluster column on a square base, with a flange at the base and matching border to the socket, a style that in France was often beautifully chased with *amorini*, masks and scrollwork, though generally plain elsewhere, except for those included in toilet services. Variations included candlesticks with octagonal, lobed and circular bases. About 1680 the new baluster styles were introduced from France by the Huguenot refugee silversmiths, and these were soon adopted in England by most candlestick-makers, although the column pattern, by now usually with a gadrooned stepped foot, continued to be made until the early 1700s. Early candles needed frequent trimming, or snuffing, and special scissors, of which the earliest date back to the 16th century, were made in silver and held in a stand, the upper part of open box form and usually with a loop handle. Occasionally surviving English examples also include a conical extinguisher and even a small chamber-candlestick. These were broad-panned shallow candle-holders for bedroom use, the bases large and steady to reduce the danger of fire. Other snuffers were simply laid in shallow trays approximating to the outline of the scissor-like implement.

A few rare silver chandeliers are recorded, but more numerous were sconces, or branched candleholders with an oval or shaped backplate fixed to the wall. Most were richly chased in the Baroque

433 A curiously English taste for toilet services, porringers and so on, flat-chased with exotic Oriental scenes, lasted from about 1665 to 1690. This footed salver of 1685 is typical of the style.

434 Oval dish, repoussé-chased with birds among fruit, the centre chased with a seated cupid. Stockholm, c. 1695.

435 This unusual inkstand of 1639, with panels

emblematic of the arts and sciences, bears a London mark, probably for Alexander Jackson.

436 Shallow silver-gilt bowl with two cast scroll handles made in Paris in 1686 by Claude Payne.

437 This Paris-made toilet service of c. 1685 is almost identical to the Lennoxlove service now in the Royal Scottish Museum.

438 Covered cups, usually known as porringers, dominate English silver during the second half of the 17th century. This superb example, chased with formal acanthus foliage, has cast foliate and caryatid handles. The arms are later.

439 Tapering cylindrical coffee pot by Anthony Nelme, 1701. Applied scrollwork, foliage and other cut-cardwork round the bases

433

434

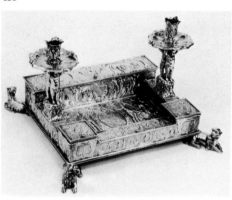

435

436

style, but later examples were usually simpler, with engraved detail within a gadrooned mount or, in England, with flat-chased Chinoiseries.

The long-established standing cup did not entirely disappear during the later Baroque period, but was generally given a more elongated bowl and shorter stem, the bowl becoming the chief vehicle for chased or applied ornament. Many cups were still massive and tall, surmounted by modelled figure finials, sometimes appropriate to the civic or guild patron for whom they were made. **438** More often, however, especially in England, the two-handled cup, based on the covered porringer or caudle cup, with shallower tapering cylindrical or bombé bowl on a low foot, was preferred. Hundreds of such cups were made by English silversmiths in all shapes and sizes, some showing French influence with cut-card ornament and even the favourite French coiled snake handles, others still echoing Dutch tulipmania. The arrival of the Huguenots tidied up the designs, and spindly cast caryatid handles and even the bolder scroll handles gave way to elegant harp-shapes, the bowl was elongated to an inverted bell, usually with a rib around it, and balanced by a domed cover topped with a baluster or urn finial. In Germany, Switzerland and Scandinavia, silversmiths were slow to discard the old standing cup styles. Their version of the English and American porringer was the two-handled bowl – in Scandinavia called drinking bowls, in Holland brandy bowls – which, along **417** with individual country cups, like Dutch windmills, German wager cups and nesting beakers, Scottish quaichs and thistle cups, and each country's style in tankards, all tended to follow national rather than international styles from now on.

There remained a huge demand in all northern countries for the covered tankard and its smaller companion, the mug. In England the mid-century style was basically plain, a cylinder on a narrow moulded foot, with scroll handle, decorative thumbpiece and low

domed cap cover. Decoration took the form of chased formal acanthus foliage round the base, occasionally a band of cut-card work or, between about 1675 and 1690, the whole would be engraved or chased with Chinoiseries. More often, however, the only decoration was the engraved arms of the owner in a plumed mantling. A few, often fine quality, tankards made in the north of England and in London a little later followed the Scandinavian **425** style, supported on cast feet formed as lions couchant or other animals or birds, with a matching thumbpiece, while a few others featured intricate grotesque handles. Nearly all Scandinavian tankards were straight and drum-shaped, on cast supports, most **424** usually claw-and-ball, and with applied foliate detail at the junction of feet and body. Covers were generally slightly rounded, and often featured a medallion or other decorative disc in the centre. On some, especially those made in Norway, decoration extended over the body as well. In Sweden, it appears that cast tops for the covers were possibly imported from Hamburg and other north German centres. There was also some filigree work done there, as also in northern Holland. Certainly, the north German style of tankard, and to a lesser degree those made in Augsburg and other towns, nearly always had ornament cast and chased in high relief, a far cry from the more restrained influence from France, which had virtually no effect there, though in England, Scotland and Ireland there was a slow change from the cylindrical to the baluster form for both tankards and mugs, starting about 1695.

Beakers, too, were generally in the typical northern style in Scandinavia, and in Holland fine engraving on tapered tall beakers also followed the old tradition. In England, small tapering beakers, plain, chased with acanthus foliage or flat chased with Chinoiseries were not often made after about 1700 except for travelling canteens. Some of the late 17th-century examples were very finely engraved in the Dutch manner with overall scrollwork, matching the spice of bowls, tankards and cups was a French fashion quickly adopted in England.

440 One of a pair of single-light sconces made in Paris *c.* 1680, applied with chased acanthus foliage around a figure of Victory.

441 Set of four cluster column candlesticks on square bases finely cast and chased with masks and demi-cupids among foliage. Made between

1678 and 1680 by Pierre Massé of Paris.

442 Less elaborate column candlesticks were made in large numbers in England, concurrently with the new baluster shapes. This pair on gadrooned and fluted octagonal bases are late examples, made in 1701 by Thomas Ash.

443 Silver was lavishly and extravagantly used everywhere during the late 17th century. This

pair of English firedogs, chased with cupids, acanthus foliage and flowers, on heavy paw feet, was made *c.* 1670.

444 French designs began to dominate all Europe. This heavy wine cistern, 44½ in. (113 cm.) long, shows chased and matted ornament, fine casting, and bold gadrooning, now formalised. Made in Brussels, *c.* 1690.

438

437

439

440

441

442

443

444

445 A candlestick of 1717 in the Régence style by Nicolas Besnier of Paris, featuring formal foliate and guilloche ornament and cameo busts on the baluster stems.

446 A pair of octagonal baluster candlesticks of 1717 with octagonal faceted bases, made by the specialist candlestick-maker Thomas Merry of London.

box, knife, fork and spoon and other pieces that fitted together for the huntsman's or soldier's canteen. For strong spirits, the tumbler cup was a delightful English fashion – small, heavy-bottomed cups that rolled when placed on the table. They were made in the provinces as well as in London. On the continent, these little cups were usually made with a kick-in base, so that they stood flat.

The standing wine cup, with bell-shaped bowl and baluster stem, was virtually banished by the new flint glass, made in the same design, in the London glassworks of George Ravenscroft (see p. 200), though in Germany short-stemmed beaker-cups – both engraved and chased – were still produced.

Entertaining on a grand scale required large serving vessels. 431 Flasks, shaped like the medieval bottles carried by pilgrims, were made in all sizes, some of them massive and hung with great chains. 444 Equally massive were the wine cisterns, often weighing 64 pounds (29 kilograms) or more, used for cooling wine, and wine fountains with spigots and taps like urns. Smaller ewers both covered and lidless were used for serving wine and beer respectively. In Germany there was a fashion for silver-mounted coloured glass bottles, forerunners of the 18th-century decanter. In England large bowls, usually with notched rims which were removable, were used for the spiced drink, punch, which was exceedingly popular from about 1660 onwards. In association with punch bowls are found capacious ladles, orange strainers and nutmeg graters.

The most important beverages to arrive in Europe in the middle of the 17th century were, however, tea, coffee and chocolate. All were immediately acclaimed in England, France and Holland, though they took rather longer to reach Scandinavia and Germany. In England silversmiths at first tended to adapt the tankard for coffee and chocolate pots – indeed, they did so for the first recorded 439 teapot, but soon they developed a tall tapering pot, with the spout at right angles to the handle, and a high domed cover for coffee and chocolate, and a small squat pot, based on the Chinese wine-pot, for tea. By the end of the century, however, the baluster shape from France helped to produce the pear-shaped teapot and then eventually the baluster coffee and chocolate pot, though in fact the French style on three legs was only very rarely made in England. Even cups for drinking tea were made in silver, rare survivals generally having handles, unlike porcelain teacups of the period, since the metal held the heat so effectively. The new drinks also brought new smaller spoons, shallow trays for spoons and small bowls and tongs for sugar.

The *tazza*-like footed salver remained in fashion throughout the period, circular, octagonal or lobed in outline, but a newcomer in the late 17th century was the sugar caster, a cylinder, often with a moulded rib about it, with a slip-lock pierced domed cover. Again, under French influence, the curved baluster shape was adopted by most silversmiths by the end of the century. Salts, now only rarely of great size, were usually simple, round, oblong or octagonal in outline with a shallow well for the salt. A few were spool-shaped, miniatures of the larger salts of the early part of the century, or of compressed circular form. In Scandinavia, triple dishes were still fashionable for salts and spices. Shallow fluted dishes were used for serving dessert or sweetmeats, and a few baskets were made, but most more familiar table silver did not come into general use until the 18th century.

The end of the 17th century saw some of the most striking changes in the pattern of spoons, which had flattened stems and oval bowls by the middle of the century. Two types of terminal became popular – the 'three-toed' trefid and the shield-ended 'dog-nose' – while a long rat-tail along the back of the bowl added both strength and attraction. A newcomer to the table firmly established by 1700 was the fork, at first two-pronged, later three-pronged. Spoons and forks are chiefly 'table' size, dessert spoons and forks being much rarer. Knives, too, became more 'domesticated', with silver cannon-shaped or pistol-grip ends. Very large spoons, with either flattened or tubular handles, were used for basting and serving.

18th-CENTURY SILVER

Judith Banister

Régence and Rococo

France continued to dominate the applied arts. Indeed, during the 18th century her craftsmen extended their influence far afield, to Russia and Sweden, Italy, Spain, Portugal and, of course, to the now United Kingdom. At first the French style was disseminated by the Huguenot refugees who had settled in Protestant countries and wherever else they were free of religious persecution. Among them were both silversmiths and engravers, such as Daniel Marot, and Simon Gribelin who published books or ornaments, and their designs were supplemented by the published designs of other French engravers such as Jean Lepautre, Jean Bérain and Paul Ducerceau.

The French style of the early years of the century combined a neat formality with a richness interpreted by applied detail and a high standard of both chasing and engraving. Usually called Régence, since it chiefly flourished during the minority of Louis XV, this style featured cut-card ornament of a more intricate design than ever before, chased flowerheads, trelliswork, masks, shells and husks. For the silversmith it required an ability at chasing, piercing and casting and, above all, most meticulous soldering, to create in metal what the carvers of wood and the makers of gesso achieved with more tractible materials.

It must not be forgotten that the exchange of gifts between monarchs throughout Europe also helped to spread the new fashions, and certainly throughout the 18th century the royal houses all tended to favour the French taste for splendour, even if some of their native craftsmen were unable to capture its highest refinements. Some, such as the King of Sweden, employed French craftsmen such as J.-F. Cousinet and the architect Nicodemus Tessin, whose correspondence reveals so clearly how the French styles spread through Europe.

In Augsburg and Amsterdam, Copenhagen and Christiana, London and Lisbon, Turin and, indeed, in every town where silversmiths had patrons with taste and money, French designs and, in some instances, French-type vessels, were being made. The German/Dutch Baroque disappeared, even in places such as Hamburg and Riga – though in the latter the inspiration may have been by way of England, for it was in Riga that 'The English Factory' was established. But by the early 18th century, English silver design was wholly under French influence: second- and third-generation Huguenot silversmiths and native-born English craftsmen were producing similar work, though in fact the best was most often the work of those of French origin, such as Paul de Lamerie, Paul 449 Crespin, Simon Pantin, the Courtaulds, the Tanquerays, David Willaume and Peter Archambo. 453

The formality of the Régence and the huge demand for silver, especially domestic silver for the dining-table, the tea-table and for lighting and writing, introduced plainer designs that could be made at less expense for practical use in the home. Often these were made by silversmiths tending to specialise in one type of object, notably candlesticks, which were cast, and salts, casters and the like. Some silversmiths tended to concentrate on making the ubiquitous

447 Kettle, stand and lamp made in 1723 by Abraham Buteux, one of the many Huguenot craftsmen in London. Heavy-gauge silver and plain surfaces enriched with fine engraving, flat-chased ornament and applied cut-card work were keynotes of much London-made silver of the early 1700s.

448 This coffee urn with three taps made in Amsterdam in 1734 by Dirk Westrik hints at the coming Rococo style. The coffee urn was a lasting style in Holland.

449 Small oblong salver of 1726 by Paul de Lamerie, the most famous of all the Huguenot silversmiths. Most of his work is instantly recognisable, with fine engraved detail and use

of shells and latticework in the Hogarthian manner.

450 By the 1740s taste in decoration had become more lavish, and silver was enhanced by shells, scrolls and other asymmetrical details, as in these superb candlesticks made in Paris in 1740.

445

446

447

448

449

450

waiters and salvers which were produced in every size, from stands for tea- and coffee-pots, *écuelles* and kettles, up to the large trays, called tea-tables, which held all the accoutrements for the fashionable tea-drinking ceremony. Other specialist makers were concerned with flatware—spoons and forks and other serving pieces. It is also likely that most engraving and some chasing was sent out to specialists, and there seems to have been in some silver towns a common source of castings, such as spouts, finials, tureen handles and the like.

The inevitable desire for change, the striving for newness and the incredible wealth of the French King and his royal compeers introduced a new and yet more sumptuous style during the 1730s. It was a style that in some ways owed its origins to Mannerism, for its primary themes were those of the grotto and the grotesque. In France its chief exponents were the Italian-born J.-A. Meissonnier, who entered as a goldsmith in 1725, but was also an architect, and the incomparable Paris silversmith, Thomas Germain, master in 1720. Rococo, or *rocaille*, was swiftly acclaimed by the leading silversmiths of Europe, who at this time seem to have been in advance of other craftsmen in their promotion of the style. In London, Paul de Lamerie, Paul Crespin, Nicholas Sprimont (later to found the Chelsea porcelain factory), George Wickes, Frederick Kandler and a dozen others at once embraced the style, creating some of the most splendid silver ever made in England without falling into the trap of asymmetry for its own sake. In Augsburg, J. N. Spickermann, Emmanuel Drentwett, and J. L. Biller produced their own versions of the Rococo, and the patrons of Europe commissioned the leading master silversmiths to create silver for use and display in the intriguing and joyous new taste.

The chief characteristic of the Rococo was asymmetry. At its simplest, scrolls and fluting were curved and recurved. At its most complex, it was a confection of scrolls, shells, wave ornament, rockwork, grotesque masks, and figures—nymphs and satyrs, birds

and beasts, butterflies, sea serpents, dolphins, lizards and insects. Underlying the richness of the ornament, which was nearly always cast and chased, usually in high relief and with superb craftsmanship, was the basic baluster form. Even when the whole appeared asymmetrical, the sturdy curve was still important and obvious, so that the most extravagant piece of Rococo silver remained, as a rule, a functional object.

The most important silver ornament throughout the 18th century was the two-handled cup and cover. Basically of vase shape, on a moulded foot, with two handles and a domed cover with architectural finial, it proved a superb basis for every changing style of decoration. There was still a taste for massive sideboard dishes for display, and occasionally ewers and basins were still made. Silver furniture was another extravagant rarity, but it was chiefly for lighting and for wining and dining that the most important silver was made.

The basic form of candlestick remained the French-inspired baluster on an octagonal, circular or square-cut-cornered base. In France the elongated vase-shaped stem was often richly chased with husks, trelliswork and other Régence motifs, but in England most candlesticks were quite plain, although David Willaume did produce a few with applied lion masks at the shoulders of gadrooned baluster 'sticks. By 1715, the faceted octagonal, the hexagonal and occasionally umbrella-like variations were being made, but until about 1730 basic simplicity was almost universal outside France, where the full splendour of the Rococo was already making itself evident. Soon other countries followed suit, and all but the most practical styles were everywhere being enhanced with the shells, scrolls and other Rococo ornament. By the 1740s, fluted and twisted stems suggested asymmetry, and there was a growing tendency to turn simple candlesticks into two- or three-branched candelabra. The height of the 'stick itself was gradually increased from about 6 or 7 inches (15 to 18 centimetres) in the early part of the century

451 Even practical silver was decorated during the Rococo period. These circular-bellied salts, made in 1744 by Edward Wood of London, are applied with swags of flowers between the lion mask and paw feet.

452 In Germany and Italy, stepped fluting was a favourite Rococo theme, as in this soup tureen made in Naples *c.* 1720. The style was followed up to as late as 1760.

453 Magnificent wine fountain of *c.* 1728 by Peter Archambo, a leading Huguenot craftsman. In England, duty on silver was a heavy burden, and several large and important pieces were not sent for proper assay; this was one such.

454 Teapot by Elizabeth Godfrey, 1741, and sugar bowl by Edward Gibbon, 1730. The bullet-shaped teapot made in England was practical and usually plain, though spouts were often scroll-fluted at the base. Sugar bowls were usually covered, the cover being reversible to form a spoon tray—common before the advent of the saucer.

451

452

453

454

455

to as much as 8 or 10 inches (20 to 26 centimetres) by the 1760s. A few chandeliers were made—there are two beautiful examples of 1734 and 1735 by Paul de Lamerie in the Kremlin in Moscow—but wall sconces are unexpectedly rare. For the bedroom, the chamber candlestick remained a generally plain and functional piece of silver with a short candleholder and broad pan, often the only hint of the decorative being the leaf-capped handle. Snuffers trays were usually shaped oblongs, the rims enriched with shells and scroll mouldings.

Several notable toilet services are recorded from this period, though they were less often made than during the late 17th century. A few very fine services made in Augsburg were of gold, but more usually silver-gilt was sufficiently showy and practical. As Régence styles waned, so swirl-fluting, elaborate cast feet and chased detail in the Rococo style came in. The only plain toilet silver, used in fact in the dining saloon and, on the Continent, in smaller patterns, in church, was the chamber pot or *bourdaloue*. In Holland an oblong chased and pierced basket was customary for holding a baby's layette, while the shallow covered *écuelle* presented to nursing mothers remained an almost wholly French custom. Occasionally small vases with pierced covers, used for pot pourri, made their appearance, successors to the 17th-century 'perfuming pot'.

In the dining room there were new refinements in serving and eating. The new century saw the first of the great soup tureens which were to remain the most important single piece of dining-table silver until the middle of the 19th century. Either alone, on a massive stand, or with matching sauce tureens, it even at times formed a great centrepiece for the table, complete with stands for casters, salts, side dishes and so on. Some of the most magnificent were the work of Thomas Germain of Paris, whose work was sought after notably by the Empress Catherine of Russia, but there

were fine examples made in England, too, such as the great Rococo tureen and stand by Paul Crespin now at Minneapolis. Complementary to the soup tureen were the first sauceboats. At first these were double-lipped, with handles on either side, but later a single lip and scroll or flying scroll handle opposite became general. Towards the middle of the century, there was, however, a return to the shallow boat-like sauce dish, generally considered to be a French style. For serving there were fish and meat dishes in sizes, usually with gadrooned, or shell and scroll rims. Fish dishes were fitted with pierced oval or circular strainers known as mazarines, while there was a host of different shaped shallow dishes, with and without covers, for serving entrées, vegetables and desserts. Cast trencher salts, usually octagonal, were soon followed by more decorative examples of spool shape, on a high circular foot chased with stiff foliage and with chased or applied detail round the bowl. Soon, however, the Rococo was to breed more fanciful designs, notably shells and scallops, decorated with mermaids or tritons, rocks, seaweed and other marine motifs. Spice and sugar casters, often made in sets of three, were at first of simple baluster shape, flat-chased with Régence-style panelwork, but soon they too were overlaid with all the confections of the Rococo. In England, sets of casters and silver-mounted bottles for oil and vinegar were sometimes mounted in stepped frames, called Warwick cruets—an idea that on the Continent was to be used for serving chocolate as well, with a salver-like *présentoir* with cups, sugar bowl and the like fitting into ring frames on the supporting tray.

One of the most successful and beautiful of the crafts was that of piercing, and baskets both large and small were made, for bread, cakes and sweetmeats. Dessert centrepieces, known as *épergnes*, brought a series of baskets and dessert dishes together, fitted on to branches around the central large basket for fruit or, when lined, for flowers. Formal wickerwork-style piercing of the early part of

455 High Rococo for a candlestick from a set of four by London silversmith, Thomas Gilpin, 1744.

456 Candlestick by Duvivier after a design by Meissonnier, the essence of the asymmetrical Rococo style.

457 Chocolate was more popular on the Continent than in England. This elegant baluster pot on three shell-knuckle feet is flat-chased with Rococo strapwork. Made in Basle, mid-18th century.

458 Fine cup and cover by Frederick Kandler, London, 1740. Silver for display, such as this

piece, generally followed the latest fashions, often with great virtuosity.

459 Decoration is confined to the shaped foot and the 'grotesque' handles in this pair of practical shell-shaped sauce boats by Pezé Pilleau, London, 1752.

456

457

458

459

the century gave way to elaborate scroll and diaper piercing in the Rococo period, with impressive highly decorative mounts on the rim, swing handles springing from demi-figures and other motifs, and cast and pierced apron supports. A few Rococo baskets were made in the form of pierced scallop shells. In Holland, baskets were often finely pierced, and occasionally were fitted with condiment bottles.

453   The wine fountain, the great ewer and the wine cistern represented the most grandiose silver during the first part of the 18th century and, since such great vessels were always special commissions, surviving examples generally show all the latest design trends. On a smaller scale were beer and wine jugs, and punch bowls. The simple baluster form, used in miniature for cream jugs, became the basis for beer jugs, usually uncovered, and for the more elegant wine jugs which were soon to be decorated in *rocaille*. Huge wine cisterns were made in France, Germany and England, and exported to other countries—in the Hermitage in Leningrad, for instance, there are several English cisterns dating from between 1699 and 1735, while almost every major stately home can boast one, sometimes with an accompanying fountain. How many superb French and other European examples have been lost can only be guessed. While glass gradually overtook silver for wine, beer mugs and tankards continued to be made in Germany and England. In Scandinavia, Holland and Russia, beakers remained popular, especially in the country districts—where traditional local styles continued to be made. In Sweden, for example, tall beakers with wide mouths were usual.

   As the production of tea, coffee and chocolate increased and prices fell, all three became of great importance, spreading throughout Europe, so that by the end of the century, as writers everywhere recorded, they were drunk by almost everyone. Coffee was perhaps the most common of all, followed by tea, though in France and

Germany chocolate—a rich thick drink, quite unlike cocoa—never lost its popularity. Coffee and chocolate pots were virtually identi- 457 cal, except that in France and Germany a rather shorter-lipped jug, rather like a hot-water jug, was used, and in England, at least until the 1740s, chocolate pots generally had a small aperture in the cover through which the stirring rod could be inserted. By the time English silversmiths began to adopt the continental style of chocolate jug, the taste for the drink had dwindled in the face of tea. Tea was very expensive in the first part of the century, and pots were consequently small. The pear shape, sometimes with its own small burner, remained in favour until about 1730, followed by the globular or bullet shape. In Scotland, teapots of globular shape 454 were mounted on a circular stepped foot, but the low-footed style remained the fashion not only in England but in Scandinavia—always much influenced by England in tea-table silver—in France, Germany, Switzerland and so on. Small baluster jugs for cream, egg-shaped or globular covered pots for warmed milk or cream, covered sugar bowls, and large hot-water kettles with spirit-lamp stands completed the tea-table equipage.

Neo-classicism

Though it could be said that it was the Italian Piranesi and the German Joachim Winckelmann whose drawings and studies gave the impetus to Europe's new Classical revival, the style was a logical reaction to the more exuberant and unrestrained shapes and motifs of the Rococo. All over Europe, intellectuals were striving to create some sort of order. Science and industrialisation together with the recent discoveries of the ancient world in excavations in Italy and Asia Minor reawakened an admiration of reasoning and a search for man's highest achievements.

   Because later examples of Neo-classical silver were often relatively plain, there is a tendency to think of it as an ascetic style. It

460 Oval toilet box chased with *rocailles,* made in Augsburg, 1753-55, by Gottlieb Satzger. Similar but smaller boxes were made for sugar.

461 Superb mastery of Rococo detail for a French *écuelle* made in Orléans *c.* 1770.

462 Pair of wine-bottle or decanter coasters pierced with formal pales and applied with laurel festoons and *paterae* between beaded borders. By Robert Hennell, 1772.

463 Chinoiserie's second appearance in English silver was during the Rococo period, here used for a fine centrepiece or *épergne* with a bell-hung canopy, made by the specialist basket-maker Thomas Pitts in 1762.

464 Very much influenced by France, a Viennese soup tureen of 1781 from a pair by Johann Sebastian Wurth.

465 Rococo basket pierced and engraved with flowers, foliage and butterflies. Made in The Hague by Cornelis de Haan in 1777.

466 This Greek-style coffee pot by Martin-Guillaume Biennais, Paris, *c.* 1795, was part of the service given by Napoleon to his sister Princess Borghese.

460

461

463

462

464

465

was, in fact, far from that. Early work was sumptuous, and yet was a reaction to the confections of the Rococo. The skills of the caster and chaser and the modeller were no less important than they had been during the Rococo—or any earlier age. But the shells and scrolls, the foliage and figures, were now orderly, formally presented. Stiff leafage and laurel festoons, applied medallions enclosing Classical scenes in low relief, classical busts and masks, flat fluting and beaded borders interpreted in silver the marbles and bronzes that were being found at Spoleti and Herculaneum and which so enthralled the artists and architects such as Robert Adam and E.-L. Boullée, Charles Cameron and Freidrich Ermannsdorff.

For the silversmith, the most dominant shape of Neo-classicism was the urn and the vase. In essence, the objects made changed little. Only the outward form and the decorative style changed, as they did in every field of applied art. There was still a very close relationship between the forms of silver, pottery, glass, furniture and architectural details—which at this period was hardly surprising as everyone was studying the same source—antiquity. Not that Matthew Boulton or Josiah Wedgwood, Scott & Smith or Henri Auguste, Biennais, Roentgen or Kohlheim slavishly copied the ancients. They adopted and adapted the forms, details and ideas of Classicism and applied them to their own uses, so that each artist, each country continues to reveal native characteristics within the Neo-classical framework, just as they had appeared during each previous 'design period'.

The 18th-century Neo-classicism was, however, subject to forces that had been much less evident in earlier times. Europe was becoming progressively more industrialised. Small wonder, then, that the *haute couture* of the early style was soon watered down into less extravagant and hence less expensive silverwares and, exactly coincident with the arrival of Neo-classicism, silver-plated wares for a wider middle-class market. The applied ornament of the first flowering of Neo-classicism was soon interpreted by chasing and then by stamping. The gauge of the metal became thinner, to keep the price down—a trait that was extended in England after the reimposition of duty in 1784, at first 6d. an ounce, but gradually

467 The factory-workshops of Sheffield largely specialised in candlesticks such as this set, incorporating the new Neo-classical idioms. Made by Winter & Co. in 1780.

468 Pair of Rococo tea caddies and a sugar basket with blue glass liner, a popular innovation in the 1760s. By William Vincent, London, 1769.

469 Shape as well as decoration changed, and the straight-sided oval and the drum became popular in England for tea-table silver. This teapot on its stand and the matching caddy are superbly decorated with bright-cut engraving. By Charles Aldridge, 1787.

470 An early Neo-classical cup and cover to a design by Robert Adam made for Richmond

Races by Smith and Sharp of London in 1764.

471 Fine Neo-classical tureen and stand from the Orloff service made for the Russian Court by Nicolas Roettiers of Paris in 1770.

472 Oval swing-handled cake basket pierced in formal geometric pattern and with beaded borders, made in 1779 by Hester Bateman.

466

467

468

469

470

471

472

increasing during the wars with France until it reached a peak of 1s.6d. an ounce in 1804. Even the exquisite bright-cut engraving that added such brilliance and appealed, like so much English Neo-classicism, to the Scandinavians, was often reduced to a narrow border or a few lines of wrigglework. By the end of the century the arbiters of taste, in England at any rate, and in Revolution-torn France, knew that something grander was needed to reinstate their importance and to counter these 'sippets of embroidery'.

Almost all the objects made during the earlier part of the century were converted to Neo-classicism—from tea- and coffee-pots to soup tureens and display vases. There was a revival of taste for great sideboard dishes, two-handled trays assumed massive proportions, made even more massive after the end of the 'oval' period of the 1780s by the addition of heavily cast and chased borders. Dishes, baskets and bowls all acquired a Graeco-Roman air.

Two important additions to the range of silver for dining and wining, which had been introduced about the middle of the century, were now made in large numbers: the wine cooler, one of the most

happily vase-shaped of all grand silver, and the decanter coaster or wine slide, for holding a single glass decanter. A revival, especially in England, was the wine goblet. The tankard virtually disappeared, though a few baluster examples with high domed covers, and some straight-sided examples with bands of reeding and flat covers were made, though not by the more fashionable silversmiths such as Scott & Smith, Paul Storr, or Wakelin and Taylor.

At the tea-table the kettle was banished and replaced by the urn—at first an elegant tall urn with high loop handles, but later to be Romanised and made squat and self-important with its matching teapot, hot water jug, cream jug and large sugar basin.

More and more often, wealthy patrons were ordering silver in suites or services both for the dining room and the tea-table. Complete tea services, first found about 1750 (with rare earlier exceptions) were now almost the rule, while not only plates and serving dishes, but every item for the table was available in distinctive patterns—forerunners of the standard designs soon to be made in the factories, and still made today in both hollow-ware and flatware.

147

473 Casting and chasing in the Classical manner on a covered vase 8 in. (20.3 cm.) high from a set of four by Digby Scott and Benjamin Smith, 1805. This was a favourite pattern in the stock of the royal goldsmiths, Rundell, Bridge & Rundell.

474 French wine fountain in the international Empire/Regency style by the leading Paris silversmith J. B. C. Odiot, c. 1810.

475 The marble vase at Warwick Castle was frequently interpreted in silver for vases and wine coolers. This version of 1814 is one of a pair made for Rundell's by Paul Storr.

19th-CENTURY SILVER

Judith Banister

The ferment in Europe at the beginning of the century might be said to have been the instigator for the multiplicity of silver styles that appeared during the next 100 years or so. New manufacturing techniques were mastered, bringing all the variety, good and bad alike, that contributed to large-scale production. Silver was relatively inexpensive, and demand was enormous, as some of the vast centrepieces that were created testify. For those who wanted at least some of the glitter, there was the slowly dying Sheffield Plate industry to serve them and, soon to come, the quickly growing electro-plating trade.

In the early years of the century, France still chiefly dominated design in Germany, Italy and the Iberian Peninsula, and even in Scandinavia and Russia. England, too, still owed something to French influence, but designs inclined more towards ancient Rome than to the cold severity of Greek Classicism as preferred in France, where the huge workshops of Biennais and Odiot poured out vases and urns enriched with Classical masks, festoons and figures of which the laurel wreaths seemed to suggest an eternal obeisance to the laurel-garlanded Napoleon I.

Napoleon's exploits in Egypt added a new and extraneous style to the purer earlier Classicism, and the silversmiths of Regency London followed suit with occasional sallies into the Egyptian, so that sphinxes and papyrus columns, and lotus and lily settled down beside Greek anthemion and Roman scrollwork. It was, perhaps, the first intrusion of the multifarious themes and motifs that made 19th-century design an amalgam of so many different and oddly assorted styles.

The first hint of this came in the first decade of the century in London, when one or two silversmiths, notably Robert Garrard, began to look back to the mid-18th-century Rococo. Successive firms and individuals in every country also began this emulation of the past: Gothic and other medieval designs were revived, the Renaissance was born anew, there was a taste for naturalism that smacked of tulipmania, while Neo-classicism still held sway in many European cities, especially Berlin, Vienna and Amsterdam.

The end of the Napoleonic Wars saw Europe exhausted, physically, mentally and culturally. The old order was changing rapidly. Nationalism was rearing its head in Germany and Italy. The already self-governing nations tended to look outwards to their colonies and to trade rather than to their European neighbours for inspira-

tion. Cities grew overnight, crammed with country people seeking work in the reeking factories. What had been an industrial expansion of craftsmanship in the 18th century became a revolution that brought smoke and grime and overcrowding to the cities, and money to the owners of those satanic mills.

Some of those factories were engaged in making silver, Sheffield-plated and silver-plated goods for anyone and everyone who had money in his pocket. Of course, in some countries the changeover to the age of the common man took a little longer–in Russia, for example, and other princely states where the old order survived in large estates peopled by serfs (the craftsmen) and peasants. But the long-established idea of personal patronage seems to have vanished on the plains of Waterloo.

Noble efforts were made to reinstate craftsmanship. Among the leading protagonists was the Prince Consort, who made art and industry his personal business. The disappearance of the wealthy patron was, however, an insurmountable problem. True, there was wealth abounding, but the style of the patron changed. Never before had there been so much talk of 'taste' and so little of it.

The attempt to recapture the greatness of the past was stimulated by the series of great exhibitions that were held in London, Paris, Dublin, Vienna, Glasgow, New York and Philadelphia. Every workshop and factory proud of its products submitted work for display 'indicating the wealth and resources of the manufacturers'. There was little need to try to stimulate exports. The world, and most of all the world of the British Empire and the German, Dutch, French, Portuguese and Spanish colonies, was at the feet of Europe. In return, Europe was ready to assimilate the styles, techniques and ideas of every far-flung corner of empire or wherever trade led the way.

In the silver manufactories of Europe–for most were now on a large scale–there was a tendency to turn out superlative examples of craftsmanship, though mostly rather self-consciously designed, alongside the everyday tea-table and dinner-table silver that every self-respecting household required to outdo the neighbours. If the tea and coffee service became a standard wedding present, much as the toilet service had been in the more opulent days of the late Baroque, so a grand centrepiece became the mark of a man who had made his way in business and the symbol of a country landowner whose horses had made their place in racing history or whose sons

473

474

475

476 One of a pair of silver-gilt sideboard or display dishes by Edward Farrell, London 1824, the everted borders richly chased in relief.

477 The century ended with the Art Nouveau – once again of French origin, but here interpreted in London on a vase made in 1900 by William Comyns.

478 About 1820 London silversmiths often imitated the Rococo designs of the past – sometimes fairly faithfully, sometimes freely, as with this four-piece tea and coffee service by Paul Storr made in 1827.

479 Revival of another kind – a 'Gothic' bottle stand, one of a pair of 1841 made in London by Reily & Storer.

476

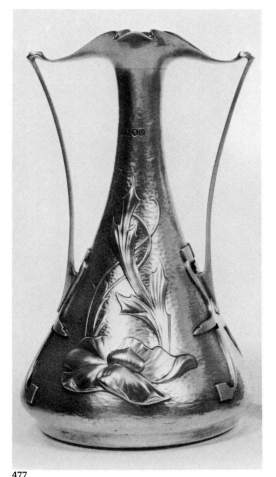

477

478

479

had achieved prowess in war or government.

In this welter of production, where the spout of a pot and the body of another were quite likely to be unnaturally wed to create the 'newest pattern', there did remain a nucleus of craftsmen still skilled in handwork. In England in the 1840s, Henry Cole and his circle had attempted to create a naturalistic style. Perhaps their failure was that they tried too hard. The direct descent of design since the Renaissance had been broken. Any design, old, new, from any part of the world, was gathered together and made the subject of the historical study of design.

The first source of inspiration was the Renaissance – or the 19th-century idea of it – followed by the Gothic, the Rococo, the Baroque and Louis XV styles. Though emulating the decorative motifs and forms, manufacturers were not afraid to apply them to all sorts of objects that would not or could not have been made by their originators. There were Renaissance and Gothic tea services, for instance, while the so-called Cellini ewer and basin was a firm and much reproduced favourite – this was rather more accurate. The Louis XV style was especially popular for a variety of tea and

coffee services, inkstands and flatware and cutlery – designs that have continued to be factory-made even today.

Much the same adulation for the past inspired the craftsmen, who, it seems, imagined that all the finest silver was of immense proportions. A piece that would in the hands of Hans Holbein have been a gem-set figure jewel, perhaps 3 or 4 inches (7.6 or 10 centimetres) long, became a massive centrepiece perhaps 3 feet (91.4 centimetres) long, with allegorical figures and mixed design metaphors that marred the sense of the superb modelling and craftsmanship of it all.

Many of the firms established at the turn of the century flourished with such productions. The severe Neo-classicism of the Odiot workshops, for instance, was replaced by excursions into Neo-rococo, Neo-renaissance, and even Moorish. Even in Malta, where simplicity had been the keynote for so long, and in Italy, so recently liberated, silver was made a slave to the ornament piled upon ornament that was mistaken for taste.

One of the curious results of this passion for over-ornamentation was a fashion for humorous silver: animals, birds, and figure

149

480 Tea service known as the Aesop's Fables Tea Service from its animal decorations based on the stories. Joseph Angell, 1850.

481 Probably the most usual theme for revival silver was 'after Cellini', and richly cast and chased ewers and goblets in so-called Renaissance style were made from the time of the Great Exhibition onwards. This set by

Charles Boyton dates from 1884.

482 Presentation and testimonal silver produced many large-scale centrepieces such as this trophy designed by Raphael Monti and made by Hancocks & Co. in 1869 as the Brighton Race Cup. The subject shows the Britons led by Druids resisting Caesar's invasion.

483 The aesthetic movement fostered a taste for Japanalia, with engraved themes of birds, bamboos and fans predominating, as on this tray made in 1879. It bears the mark of F. Elkington of the great Birmingham firm.

480

481

482

483

484 Standing Communion cup, with the lower part of the bowl fluted, a baluster stem and a gadrooned foot. Jeremiah Dummer, 1700. Museum of Fine arts, Boston.

485 Hartt tea set with oval teapot, helmet creamer and urn-shaped sugar engraved with with bright-cut bands. Paul Revere, late 18th century.

groups of all kinds were turned into claret jugs and coffee pots, condiment sets and candlesticks. It was as though they were laughing at the pretensions of mid-century 'taste'.

A more important digression for the future was the work of the various craft guilds and sponsors of new styles that owed as little as possible to current production. In the 1860s a lecturer called Christopher Dresser began to design extremely ascetic silver, often combined with glass, for some of the large manufacturers in Birmingham and Sheffield. In 1887, C. R. Ashbee founded the School and Guild of Handicraft, which was followed by Arthur Dixon's similar establishment in Birmingham. In Paris, the Hamburg firm of S. Bing, René Lalique and others also broke away from the

straitjacket of ornamentation for its own sake and Art Nouveau was born (see p. 295). Once again, design became international, and the style—in Germany called *jugenstil*, in Italy *stile Liberty* from the London exporter/importer, and elsewhere Art Nouveau or the **474** Crafts Movement—penetrated and was adopted or shunned according to taste. But it took firm root in many countries—in Norway and Sweden, Denmark and Germany, France and Austria and Belgium, and by the First World War had created the dichotomy between crafts workshops and mass-production factories from which we still suffer today. This is only slowly being broken down as manufacturers come to understand the importance of good design, whether made by man or machine.

AMERICAN SILVER

Katharine Morrison McClinton

The craft of the silversmith prospered in Colonial America as early as 1650. The styles were fundamentally English, as the silver brought to America by the early colonists afforded the models, and the first American silversmiths were trained in London. But although to understand the sequence of American silver one must look to Europe, especially England and Holland, early American silver has a definite character of its own. It reflects the tastes and life style of the people, and does not imitate the elaborate baronial silver made in England.

Each section of the country had its own characteristic style. The New Englanders, for instance, who were opposed to the English court and nobility, found ornamental silver distasteful, and produced silver which was chiefly utilitarian and undecorated. The Southern colonists, on the other hand, were not opposed to worldly things, and their more luxurious tastes were reflected in their silver. In New York and Pennsylvania life was in between these two extremes.

The earliest American silver was made in New England in Boston, and the first silversmiths whose work has survived were Robert Sanderson (1608-93) and John Hull (1624-83), both of whom had been trained in England. The first native-born silversmith was **484** Jeremiah Dummer (1645-1718), who served an apprenticeship with Hull. The skill of the Colonial silversmith was based on careful training: the English apprenticeship system had been brought to Massachusetts, and the seven-year apprenticeship period was adopted in Boston in 1660. The custom was closely followed in Rhode Island, Connecticut, New York and Pennsylvania.

487 Another apprentice of Hull was John Coney (1656-1722), who

made, not only the usual tankards, standing cups and caudle cups, but also punch bowls and elaborate sugar boxes. Equal in importance to Coney were Jacob Hurd (1703-58) and Edward Winslow (1669-1753), while other well-known New England contemporaries included Thomas Savage (1664-1749) and Benjamin Burt (1729-1805). American silver at this time was influenced by the conservative plain English styles of the late Stuart and William and Mary periods, and there was little difference between English and American plate. Caudle cups were decorated with flat chasing of flowers and leaves, and two-handled cups and standing cups had borders of fluting.

The earliest silversmiths of New York (originally New Amsterdam) were Dutch, and the shapes of the silver were those of their native land, the heavily wrought beaker illustrated being a very characteristic piece. Silversmiths such as Gerrit Onckelbag (1670-1732), Jesse Kip (1660-1722), Cornelius Kierstede (1675-1757), **486** Jacob Boelin (1657-1729) and Myer Myers (1723-95), produced beakers decorated with strapwork, pendant flower sprays and engraved figures of Faith, Hope and Charity in medallions; and also baptismal basins; tankards; bowls; mugs; wine-cups; porringers and teapots. The pieces were ornamented with engraving, repoussé, flat-chasing and cast ornaments.

New York later turned to English styles, and Philadelphia, where silversmithing developed in the 18th century, also followed English fashions. Important silversmiths were Philip Syng, Jr. (1703-89), Joseph Richardson (1711-84), Nathaniel Richardson (1754-1827) and Richard Humphreys, who made camp cups for George Washington.

484

485

486 Two-handled bowl made as a racing trophy, with shaped panelled sides and scroll handles with terminal female busts. Jesse Kip, New York, 1699.

487 Sugar box with hinged lid and snake finial, embossed and chased with large lobes on scroll feet. John Coney, 18th century.

488 Water jug and tray. Renaissance design with hand-chased dolphin-head spout, and dolphins, squirrels, a faun's head and leaf-work on the body. Samuel Kirk, 1879.

486

487

488

In England, the reigns of William and Mary and Queen Anne ushered in a quiet period, when the silver was simple in style. An important influence at this time was a law which required English silver to be of a particular higher standard (see p. 138), and it came to be fashioned in heavier forms, relying largely on shape, with fluting and gadrooning as decoration. Candlesticks and standing cups had baluster forms, and bodies of mugs and teapots were bulbous. American silver reflected these changes in style and decoration, although there was no requirement for a change in the quality of the silver. Articles made at this time included the punch bowl, chocolate pot, teapot, creamer and bowl-shaped sugar dish and the *tazza*, a circular plate with trumpet-shaped foot. Teapots of the Queen Anne style had a simple globular shape, and trays had a molded incurved rim and were engraved with a characteristic shell border.

The Georgian Rococo style, which dominated English silver between 1730 and 1765, had been brought to England by the French Huguenots, and reached America about a decade later. Shapes were built up by curved lines, and bodies of pieces were of inverted pear shapes. Handles were in the form of double scrolls, spouts were curved and scrolled and feet were in the form of scrolls, shells, or moulded as animals' hooves, lions' paws or claw-and-ball. The ornamentation was embossed, engraved or cast. The straight-sided beaker became a bulbous bell-shape, and the tankard had a tapering body and a high domed lid with a finial of an acorn, flame or pineapple. Mugs and cans also had bulbous shapes, and two-handled cups had covers and were ornamented. The inverted pear-shaped teapot was embossed and chased with flowers.

In the Federal Period (1790-1810), the elaborate asymmetrical Rococo forms gave way to refined symmetrical Classicism of the Adam style which, in America, reflected influence from France as well as from England. The Federal period produced much silver in the form of tea and coffee services. The pieces were elegant and formal with upright structural lines, in forms inspired by Classical columns, urns and vases. Fluting and a type of engraving known as bright-cutting brightened the surfaces.

Little silver was produced during the War of Independence, and after the war silver production was no longer centred in New York, Boston and Philadelphia. There were now silversmiths working in such cities as Albany, New York; Providence, Rhode Island; New

Haven, Connecticut; Baltimore, Maryland; and Charleston, South Carolina as well as many smaller cities.

The most notable silversmith in Boston in the period just before and just after the War of Independence was Paul Revere (1735-1818), who provided a bridge between the Rococo and the Classical, working in both styles. His inverted pear-shaped coffee-pots with cast gadrooned mouldings and pine-cone finials, together with the famous Sons of Liberty punch bowl, were made in the late 1760s. Another of his pieces, a teapot of oval shape with elliptical sides and straight spout engraved with bands of bright-cut ornament, was in the Federal style, and towards the end of the century he made ovoid-shaped tea urns and elliptical fluted tea-sets engraved with bright-cut bands and garlands in this same style. Such a set was recorded in Revere's day-book in 1792.

Other silversmiths who made silver of Classical design that straddled the century were Hugh Wisart, John and Joel Sayre and William G. Forbes of New York; Joseph and Nathaniel Richardson, Joseph Lownes and Christian Wiltberger of Philadelphia; and Thomas Warner and Charles Louis Boehme of Baltimore.

The delicate Adam-style Federal was followed by the robust Empire which was inspired by the French Empire styles. American Empire silver had a national style of ornament which included cast and chased sheaves of wheat, leafage, and garlands of fruit. Bands of cast ornament, gadrooning, laurel motifs, grape and acanthus borders and animal feet, caryatid figures and sphinxes ornamented the monumental presentation pieces made for the heroes of the War of 1812 and for important citizens like De Witt Clinton. The majority of these massive pieces, often copied from antique vases, were produced by the important silversmiths Fletcher & Gardiner; Simeon Chaudron and Anthony Rash of Philadelphia and John W. Forbes of New York. Domestic hollow-ware was also heavy and large in scale. The bodies of tea-sets were melon-reeded with applied bands of Greek frets, and handles and spouts of tea- and coffee-pots were moulded in eagle and animal-head motifs. The bases were turned on square plinths supported by winged paw feet. These Empire elements continued into the early 1840s.

From the mid-1840s through the next few decades American silver was influenced by European revivalism. Silver was now factory produced, but the designers in the best American manufactories such as Tiffany & Company and Gorham Manufacturing

485

489

489

489 Coffee pot in the high cylindrical French style, with an animal-head spout and bands of beading and leaves. Simeon Chaudron, c. 1810.

490 Teapot with melon-reeded body, dolphin handle, head spout and berry finial. Charles A. Burnett (1785-1849).

491 Silver tea-set owned by President James K. Polk. Ball, Tompkins and Black, c. 1845-50.

489

490

491

Company were men trained abroad. Although Tiffany and Gorham were the most important, there were many others. In New York, there were William Gale & Sons; Cooper and Fisher; Wood and Hughes and Ball; and Tompkins and Black (who became Black, Starr and Frost in 1876). In Boston the manufacturers were Jones, Ball and Poor, and the Laforme Brothers; in Philadelphia there were Bailey and Kitchen and J. E. Caldwell; in Baltimore Andrew E. Warner and Samuel Kirk & Son; and in San Francisco, W. K. Vanderslice, and Shreve & Company. The discovery of silver deposits in the West provided ample supply to meet the demands of the many makers and the increased buying power of the people.

The Rococo was the first important stylistic influence in American Victorian silver, and it lasted for many years, mingling with Gothic and Elizabethan strapwork. The forms of the hollow-ware had exaggerated shapes with heavy bulging bodies, and were over-loaded with acanthus leaves, grapevines, C and S scrolls and Oriental landscapes enclosed in Rococo cartouches. Repoussé, which had been introduced by Samuel Kirk & Son in 1824, now became one of the chief methods of decoration.

The Renaissance Revival with its straight-line architectural forms was introduced in the great expositions of the 1850s, and soon Classical vase forms began to replace Rococo shapes. Objects were described as Greek, Etruscan or Pompeiian, and motifs of ornamentation included the anthemion and palmette, while borders of beading and Greek key were used on tea-sets, and elaborate pieces were decorated with symbolic motifs. The Renaissance influence continued into the 1870s, when the famous William Cullen Bryant vase was made by Tiffany.

Between 1870 and 1900 the styles included revivals of every known decorative period including Baroque, medieval, Oriental, Queen Anne and Louis XVI. In the 1890s Gorham exhibited East Indian designs and pieces with sculptured scenes from mythology, while Tiffany exhibited a tea-set with a design of repoussé American flowers. Tiffany also produced designs with American Indian motifs. All these motifs were reflected in the design of domestic hollow-ware and flat-ware.

In about 1895 the Art Nouveau influence (see p. 295) began to be felt in American silver, the Martelé silver of Gorham Manufacturing Company with its flowing hand-wrought forms being the most important silver produced at this time.

LOCKS AND KEYS

Anne Somers Cocks

A visitor to any museum will see that nearly all the European decorative locks exhibited date from between the 15th and probably the middle of the 18th centuries, and that by far the greatest number of these are from the 16th and 17th centuries. If many decorative locks were made earlier than 15th century, then their fatality rate must have been very high, while technical innovation in the second half of the 18th century enabled locks to be made which were small enough to be inserted in the door itself, thus dispensing with the need for decorated rim locks.

For the whole of the period under discussion, in all European countries the locksmith formed a branch of the blacksmiths' guild, since early locks had to be made by the smiths' techniques of forging, embossing and chiselling. Indeed in France, a pair of park gates would, for example, be made by a *serrurier*, in other words a locksmith, and a glance at a pattern book such as Lamour's *Recueil des ouvrages en sérrurier* shows wrought iron gates (which King Stanislas had erected in the Place Royale Nancy), stair balustrades and irons as well as locks and lock plates.

Technically, locks did not change fundamentally throughout the whole period, the simple tumbler lock being used. This depended

492 Decorative lock of wrought iron, the tracery combined with finely wrought statues of the Virgin and Child with saints. Cologne, late 15th century.

493 German lock and key of chiselled and etched iron, dated 1610. Two soldiers stand guard on either side of the keyhole, which is decorated with an imperial eagle.

494 French lock and key of chiselled and engraved steel, mid-17th century. The T-shaped keyhole is characteristic of many French locks.

495 Lock of pierced brass and blued steel, English. This is signed by Richard Bickford of London, and was probably made for Grand-Duke Cosimo de' Medici, whose arms it bears, when he visited London in 1669. The little dials indicate how often the key has been turned in the lock.

496 Design for five alternative key escutcheons, *c.* 1666, from Pierretz le Jeune's *Livre Nouveau de Sérrurier.*

492

493

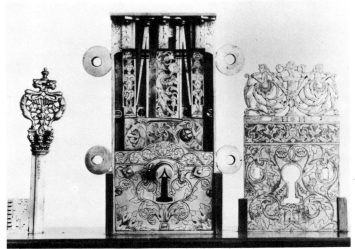

494

495

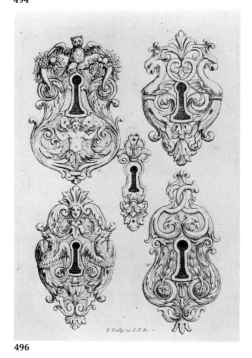

496

497

498

497 Anonymous portrait of a court locksmith (*c.* 1780) holding the design of a lock mechanism for a money chest. A Rococo key lies on the table.

498 Designs for door locks by A. W. N. Pugin, published by Ackerman and Co. (London, 1836). These are in a revival of the late 15th-century style, though the 19th century locks

would have been made in fine cast rather than wrought and chiselled iron.

499 Lock of gilt-brass and steel, Munich, 1750-60. Engraved with the arms of Bavaria and cast with a portrait of Maximilian III, Joseph of Bavaria.

500 Brass key, chiselled with a lion rampant beneath a German Elector's bonnet. German, 18th century.

501 Chest with 12 bolts operated by a single lock mechanism with details of the various parts. From the *Encyclopédie*, Vol. IX.

499

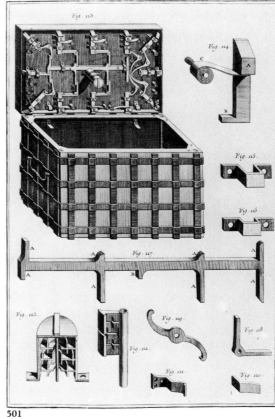

501

500

on a spring-operated tumbler which, so long as it was lifted high enough for the talon of the bolt to pass underneath, allowed the bolt to be moved back and forth. The system was obviously highly insecure, because any instrument which could reach inside could easily raise the tumbler, and many ingenious devices were thought of to prevent access to it. A common one was to conceal the keyhole behind some part of the decoration, as on the lock by Richard

495 Bickford, where it is obscured by the angel's head; another was to chisel fantastic and complicated 'wards' inside the approach to the tumbler so that only the correspondingly complicated key could turn in the lock. This, as well as a desire for maximum decorative effect, explains the very fine work on many old keys. Another attempt to improve security involved increasing the number of bolts operated by the lock, as shown in the chest illustrated, but although this increased the strength of the fastening, every one of those twelve bolts could still be thrown by raising the one tumbler in the lock.

The decoration on locks and keys generally shows the same ornamental development as in the other crafts. The grandest locks

492 of the 15th century displayed the same tracery, crockets, pinnacles, and miniature statuettes found on silver monstrances or tomb canopies of the same period. All this detail had to be painstakingly forged and chiselled, because the technical developments which enabled iron to be cast finely did not take place until the second half of the 18th century. Sometimes the iron was gilded, as in the case of the Beddington lock at the Victoria and Albert Museum, which belonged to Henry VIII.

A grand lock was a highly prized possession, and would often be moved with the owner, together with the hangings and furniture of a house. Indeed, an indication of how much such a lock continued to be appreciated long after it seemed to be any use, and even when it was made in an outdated fashion, is given by a careful engraving in Lamour's book of a Gothic lock which belonged to him.

All over Europe, the 16th century brought with it, by gradual degrees, a new Classical vocabulary of ornament—acanthus leaves, *putti*, masks and scrolls. Many locks make use of very flat chiselled scrolling patterns and engraving, incorporating these Classical motifs. The 17th century saw the first publication of engraved

496 designs specifically for the use of locksmiths, such as Mathurin Jousse de la Flêche's *La Fidelle, Overture de l'art du Sérrurier* (1627) and Jean Rembeur and Nicholas Seigneurie's *Livre nouveau pour*

l'art du Sérrurier (1668). Many of these early engravings, however, are relatively crude, obviously done by the locksmiths themselves, and little more than 'pulls' of the engraved decoration on a lock-plate. The first mentioned treatise includes the interesting statement that, although the author greatly admired the fine locks which he had seen, such work was rare nowadays and only made by apprentices presenting their masterpieces. But certainly many locks which seem fine by modern standards and were obviously intended for everyday use continued to be made. For example, there are at least three surviving brass locks by John Wilkes of Birmingham with the amusing figure of a man of fashion on the front. His leg covers the keyhole and can only be removed by pressing on a secret lever, and the locks have indicator dials to show how often the key has been turned.

Brass began to be used a great deal in the 17th century, often in conjunction with steel: a large and fine lock in the Victoria and **495,499** Albert Museum is engraved on the surface with the luxuriant flowers fashionable during the second third of the 17th century, and further ornamented by a red composition which has been rubbed into the lines. On the grand locks iron was more frequently chiselled than wrought, and then tempered and sometimes blued.

From the technical point of view, the crucial development in locksmithing was the invention of the double-acting tumbler lock by Robert Barron around 1778. This could only be opened by lifting both the tumblers to precisely the same height, which then permitted the talon of the bolt to pass under it. Most modern domestic locks are still made on this principle. By this time, however, and independently of him, locks had already become small enough to be fitted into the door, for rooms being completed at the great houses of Kedleston and Osterley in the 1760s have dispensed with the rim lock and display nothing on the doors but the gilt-bronze handles and key escutcheons designed by Robert Adam.

Rim locks, as opposed to door furniture, which continues to be more or less decorative to the present day, were revived from the second third of the 19th century onwards, among all the details of the historicist trend of architecture. This revival was principally of the Gothic style, and the great Gothic Revival architect and polemicist, Augustus Welby Pugin, among others, applied himself to the design of Gothic locks, many of which were made by the firm of **498** J. Hardman & Co of Birmingham, who styled themselves 'Medieval Metalworkers'.

502 Spanish iron coffer, 16th century, superbly decorated, and showing the locksmith's technique at its most brilliant. Even the mechanism is ornamented.

503 Four cast-iron firedogs, showing the variety of design applied to these artefacts. Firedogs are among the earliest examples of cast-iron work made in England.

DOMESTIC METALWORK

Raymond Lister

502 The metal most commonly used for domestic artefacts is iron, of which there are two forms, wrought and cast. Wrought iron is
506 usually reduced to shape by being hammered or forged while it is red hot, but sometimes it is shaped by chisels, saws and drills without being heated, a technique called locksmithery from the fact that its most extensive use was for producing locks and keys (see above). Cast iron is melted and poured into moulds, normally made by ramming sand in a box around a wooden pattern, which is then withdrawn, leaving a cavity to receive the molten metal.

In medieval times, especially in France, many beautiful objects
502 were made by locksmithery, some as elaborately carved as architectural stonework, and they varied from handbag frames, *bonbonnières* and perfume bottles to waffle irons and caskets. Decorative techniques used were often adapted from the armourer's craft, and included chasing, perforating, engraving and damascening (gold wire hammered into dovetailed slots arranged in a pattern on the iron's surface).

From the 15th century, and especially during the 16th and 17th centuries, locksmithery was often combined with forging to make fittings for oak furniture, such as key escutcheons, latches and hinges. Generally speaking, the more elaborate the fittings, the later their date.

After the 16th century, the use of locksmithery waned and most wrought iron domestic equipment was made by forging. The variety was enormous, ranging from elaborately wrought chan-
506 delier-hangers and chimney-cranes (adjustable hangers for suspending cauldrons over a fire) to toasting forks, trivets, simple candlesticks and rushlight holders (upright tong-like holders for burning rushlights, set in a base, usually of wood).

Kitchen appliances form an interesting group of wrought ironwork. Sometimes forging and locksmithery are combined in objects such as pastry-jiggers (small revolving wheels set in a handle for cutting pastry) and sugar-nippers (hinged shear-cutters for breaking sugar-loaves), which were extensively used in the 18th and 19th centuries. Forged work of the same period includes the salamander (a wrought iron disc which was heated and held over food to brown it) and fire-irons – tongs, shovels, log-forks and pokers.

Cast iron was first used domestically in the 15th and 16th
503 centuries for firebacks and firedogs, and for cauldrons and other hollow ware. Firedogs, or andirons, supported the logs in the fireplace. They consisted of a stauke, the upright decorated part which prevented the logs from falling forward out of the fire, and a billet bar, the undecorated horizontal bar which supported the logs, which was usually made of wrought iron. Early firedogs were very rugged and simple, but also beautiful. Examples made after the 16th century began to show more elaboration, and in time became merely decorations; they were by this time made of other materials, including brass, wrought iron, and even silver.

504

Cast-iron hollow ware, such as mortars, pots and cisterns, was being made by the 16th century. Much of it was imported from Holland, but in 1704 Abraham Darby of Bristol visited Holland, returning with Dutch craftsmen, who joined his staff, and before long, with their help, he had made the manufacture of hollow ware into a flourishing English trade.

From the closing years of the 18th to the end of the 19th centuries, everything from coffins to tobacco pipes, chessmen to fireplaces, mirror frames and door-knockers to teapots and beakers, was being cast in iron. Not only did the forms proliferate, the styles, too, varied infinitely.

The most collectable cast-iron objects include door porters, first made about 1830, on which appear all kinds of motifs – dogs, advertisements, horses, national heroes and comic characters. They are usually made with a flat back to stand against the door and sometimes have a small lip to go under the door to prevent them from toppling forward. Closely related to these are chimney ornaments, made on the Continent, and especially in Germany, which often depicted biblical scenes.

A further technique used in making many domestic artefacts is that of the whitesmith or sheet-metal worker. This is sometimes used for wrought iron, but more often for pewter (an alloy of tin and lead), brass (an alloy of copper and zinc), copper and tinplate (sheet steel dipped in molten tin). The last-mentioned is often misnamed tin, but pure tin is almost unworkable except by casting. Even here its use is, in the present context, extremely rare except for tiny objects like toy soldiers and dolls' house furniture.

Briefly, whitesmithery is the shaping of sheet metal by cutting, hammering, rolling, and otherwise shaping or 'raising' it. It was developed partly from the craft of the leadworker or plumber, partly from that of the bronzeworker and partly from that of the armourer. Considered in this way, it is a craft with very old connections, but the collector is unlikely to come across any work made

502

503

504 Pair of brass andirons by Paul Revere, the American silversmith. Late 18th century.

505 English ½-pint and 1-pint baluster or bellied measure, pewter, *c.* 1770-1800.

506 Wrought-iron chimney cranes such as these were used in kitchens to suspend cauldrons and kettles over the fire.

507 English copper bed-warming pan, made *c.* 1780. The lid was originally engraved with designs, but these are now virtually indistinguishable.

508 Butter cooler in electroplated nickel silver with a glass lining. Made by William Gough & Co., Birmingham, *c.* 1851.

509 Art Noùveau metalware: two jugs, two crumb trays and a small pewter pot.

504

505

506

507

508

509

much before the 17th century. Sheet-metal is easily damaged, and the survival rate of tinplate is especially low.

Generally speaking, the largest use of tinplate was for functional objects such as funnels, nutmeg graters, milk cans, sieves, boxes for spice and for candles, and bins. Yet among these there are some very attractive items, like the decorative tea canisters which were once used extensively in grocers' shops and which may, indeed, still be seen in some high-class establishments in London, Paris and Vienna. Toys were often made of tinplate, particularly in Bavaria during the 19th century, and so was theatrical armour, including, in Sicily, that of puppets. Decorative boxes for biscuits, chocolates, sweets, tobacco, cakes and other supplies were also made of it, and these are now popular collectors' items. An attractive example is the Lewis Carroll Biscuit Tin, made by Hudson of Carlisle and issued by the Irish biscuit makers, Jacob and Co., in 1892. It is decorated in colour with characters from the *Alice* books. Some indication of the ephemeral nature of such items will be gained from the fact that although 50,000 were made it is now of the greatest rarity.

Japanned tinplate coal-vases, trays, tea- and coffee-pots, plate-warmers, candlesticks and Dutch ovens were made in the 17th, 18th and 19th centuries, and are usually beautifully decorated with 512 Chinoiserie and other elaborate scenes and patterns. Japanning was first practised in England in the reign of Charles II, at first at Bilston, the trade later spreading elsewhere to include Wolverhampton and particularly Pontypool. Copper or pewter was sometimes used instead of tinplate.

Undecorated tinplate candlesticks were also made, especially in the 19th century, but more striking specimens were made in brass and pewter during the 17th and 18th centuries. They were sometimes made by whitesmithery, but more usually by casting.

5,510 Other artefacts, too, were made in brass and pewter, including ladles, plates, dishes and spoons, but if they were of brass they were tinned before use, as untreated brass can sometimes poison the user. A kitchen utensil commonly made of sheet brass was the skimmer, a slightly concave round plate perforated all over with holes, fitted with a handle, and used, as its name implies, for skimming milk, cream or cheese. There was also the brass or copper *couvre feu* (from which the word curfew is derived), used for placing over the embers of a fire before retiring for the night. Roughly speaking, it was in the form of a quarter sphere, open at the back so that it could be stood against the back of the fireplace, and with a

handle at the top. Sometimes it was decorated with repoussé work (decoration raised by hammering and punching the metal from the underside).

Brass, and more often copper, were used for making warming 507 pans both in England and on the Continent, from the 16th century onwards. Early specimens were sometimes fitted with elaborate wrought-iron handles, but wood handles were usual later. As a rule decoration was reserved for the lid, which was either perforated or stamped or raised by repoussé. Closely related in shape to warming pans, but smaller, are chestnut roasters, which are almost invariably made of sheet brass.

So far as small brass artefacts are concerned, one of the most interesting is the horse brass, which possibly originated centuries ago in the form of an amulet to protect the horse and its driver from witchcraft. Horse brasses were made from about 1750 to 1920. Most early examples were made from heavy sheet metal in the same technique as that used for cold-worked wrought iron, but later most of them were cast. There are hundreds of different shapes and sizes and an even greater number of decorative motifs; in their place on leather harness they did much to enliven the appearance of farmers' and traders' equipages.

Sheet copper, and cast pewter and Britannia metal (an alloy of tin, copper and antimony) were all used for making jelly moulds from about 1820, although pewter, due to its lead content, was unsuitable, and such moulds are therefore rare, Britannia-metal moulds being sometimes misdescribed as pewter. Copper, like brass, develops poisons in contact with certain foods and was tinned before use. Some metal jelly-moulds are very attractive, varying from abstract shapes to representations of animals, flowers or fruit.

The finest manifestations of pewter include some really splendid examples of church flagons, comparable with fine silver, and much domestic equipment is equal in quality to them. Tankards and plates are the commonest pewter ware, but salt cellars, spoons, boxes and measures also occur. Pewter made in England between 505 about 1580 and 1760 is often stamped with guild- or hall-marks.

Little high-quality pewter ware was made after 1800, its place being taken largely by Britannia metal, and indeed it is one of the 511 pleasures of that alloy that objects made in it, while still retaining some of the austerity of pewter, frequently show prettier aspects of Victorian design – sugar bowls like little Classical scuttles, salt

510 Miniature pewter 'pigeon-breasted' teapots, American, early 19th century.

511 Coffee-pot of electroplated Britannia metal by James Dixon & Sons, Sheffield, from a design registered in 1850.

512 Japanned tinned-steel tray. In this technique, the lacquer decoration was stoved at a low temperature for as long as three weeks.

510   511   512

cellars with wreaths of roses cast on their sides and so on.

Sheffield plate is in a grander class than most of the other metals and alloys discussed above. It is made from a special laminated plate, a sheet of copper being fused and rolled between two sheets of silver foil. The technique by which these sheets were made was the invention of a Sheffield cutler, Thomas Bolsover, who first made it in 1743. With his partner, Joseph Wilson, he first used it for making buttons, but before long all kinds of things were being made – in fact everything that was made in silver was in time also made in this less expensive material. The manufacture of Sheffield plate prospered for over a century before it began to decline, although some ten tons a year were still being made in Birmingham in the 1860s.

508 The decline of Sheffield plate was largely attributable to the invention of electroplating (the depositing of silver or gold on the surface of another metal by electrolysis), which was introduced about 1840 by the Birmingham gilt-toy and spectacle manufacturer,

George Richards Elkington, who based his method on a discovery by a surgeon, John Wright, that the best liquids for electroplating are cyanides of gold and silver in cyanide of potassium. Using this and other processes Elkington, in partnership with his cousin Henry, and Josiah Mason, soon made a commercial success of the process.

Despite this success, electroplate is not to be compared in quality with Sheffield plate. However, some beautiful work has been produced by the process, as is shown by the plain yet rich and heavily plated tableware used until recently in railway dining saloons and buffets, emblazoned with railway-company insignia. This is to some extent still used in hotels and restaurants, with the name and device of the establishment deeply engraved on the surface. As with Sheffield plate, everything made in silver has also been made in electroplate, including cutlery, *épergnes*, candelabra, entrée dishes, condiment sets, tea services, rose bowls, presentation cups and hosts of other objects.

ORNAMENTAL BRONZE AND ORMOLU

Edward Saunders

Ormolu, in other words gilded ornamental bronze, is synonymous with the exquisite refinement and splendour of the French aristocracy during the 18th century. The very term *or moulu*, referring to the ground or powdered gold used to gild the metal, conjures up an image of luxurious objects, such as a porcelain vase delicately encircled with ormolu commissioned by Madame de Pompadour or a jewel-like mount on a piece of furniture made for Marie-Antoinette.

The fashion for ormolu in France began in the 1660s with the centralisation of the arts under Louis XIV – from this period all art and decoration became directed towards the glorification of the monarch and thereby the country. Gilded bronze mounts were initially applied as an opulent protection to the fragile tortoiseshell and brass veneers of the furniture created by André-Charles 513 Boulle (1642-1732), but rapidly the mounts began to take on an ornamental life and decorative character of their own, establishing for ormolu a predominant position as the epitome of formal magnificence. The demand increased for a range of luxury items made from finely finished and gilded metal, and apart from mounts on furniture and porcelain, ormolu was soon being used for objects as varied as are candelabra, wall sconces, clock cases, firedogs, inkstands and table centres.

The great period is the 18th century, particularly the latter half extending into the Napoleonic era. A series of skilful and lengthy processes are required to create ormolu, the most vital being the final process, the decoration of the bronze with an enduring covering of gold. It is this covering that distinguishes ormolu proper from objects dipped in acid and lacquered to simulate gold (*mis en*

couleur d'or). The gold was applied in an amalgam of mercury which, on heating, evaporated, leaving the gold permanently fixed to the surface. The major drawback to this method is that the mercury fumes are extremely poisonous; today gilding is performed by electrolysis.

Before being gilded, the actual object was cast in a foundry from a model, either of wood or wax. Emerging from the hands of the caster (French *fondeur*), the metal then passed to the chaser (*ciseleur*), who was responsible for the excellence of the finished product. Working mainly by hand, the chaser would not only smooth the roughly cast surface but, in creating textural differences between matt and highly polished areas, could produce work that is sometimes hardly less refined than jewellery.

In the early 18th century, ormolu mounts had a certain bulky vigour, reflecting the late Baroque spirit of the grand and stately works of Boulle, the cabinet maker to Louis XIV. Being protected by royal patronage, Boulle was responsible for the design and 513 manufacture of a number of his mounts, as was Charles Cressent 516 (1685-1768), the cabinet maker to the Regent and his family from 1719. The dazzling embellishments on Cressent's furniture, where gilded dragons, monkeys and cherubs take on a life of their own against the veneers of light woods, must be considered in relation to the growing fashion for carved wall-panelling picked out in gold leaf, against which such furniture decoration should be imagined. It is worth noting, however, that Cressent was brought to court on several occasions by the Guild of *fondeurs-ciseleurs*, as their regulations forbade the furniture maker, unprotected by the crown, to cast his own mounts. This division of labour, which prevented

513 Ormolu handle on a French commode, early 18th century, in the manner of the designs of André-Charles Boulle. The geometric veneer shows the move in the early 18th century towards lighter woods, providing a suitable background for the increasingly magnificent furniture mounts.

514 The 'Avignon' clock, case by Pierre Gouthière, after a design by L. S. Boizot, movement by N. P. Delunésy, signed and dated 1771. This outstanding example of bronze-work by its greatest exponent contains the symbolic figures of Avignon and the two rivers, Rhône and Durance, supported on a plinth of marble. It was presented to the Governor of Avignon by the City Council in 1771.

515 Ewer of Meissen porcelain, one of a pair, decorated with ormolu mounts attributed to Jacques Caffieri, late 1740s. The mounts are stamped with a crowned 'C', an excise stamp used from March 1745 to February 1749.

516 Chest-of-drawers by Charles Crossent, c. 1730, decorated with exotic, finely rendered ormolu.

513

514

515

516

159

517 Candelabrum of Derbyshire 'blue john' and ormolu made by Boulton and Fothergill at their Soho factory outside Birmingham, England.

518 Cradle of the King of Rome, woodwork by Jacob-Desmalter, ormolu decoration by Pierre-Philippe Thomire, after a design by Prud'hon, 1811.

519 Engraving by Martin Schongauer (c. 1445-91) of Gothic foliage and birds, one of the earliest engraved designs intended primarily for goldsmiths.

520 This German silver belt buckle of the late 15th century demonstrates the vivid naturalism of the Gothic period.

517

518

collaboration between the two crafts, is most clearly seen in the way mounts are normally applied in a rough and ready way, with the screws clearly evident even in the most sophisticated pieces. It is only in the 1760s that an attempt began to be made to conceal the screws, associated with the workshop of J. F. Oeben and his famous assistant and follower J. H. Riesener (1734-1806).

With Cressent's bulbous curves and splendid mounts one can see the stirrings of the full riot of movement and love of exotic decoration that is the Rococo. The most outstanding of the creators of ormolu whose mid-century works epitomise the scrolling, entwined natural forms of Rococo decoration is Jacques Caffieri (1678-1755). Working towards the end of his life with his son Philippe, his most famous creation is the case of the astronomical clock presented to Louis XV in 1753, today in Versailles.

We have considerable knowledge of the works of the Caffieri family because, unlike most bronze-workers, they sometimes signed their work. The mark of a crowned 'C' on some mid-century ormolu has until quite recently been interpreted as a maker's mark, but is now established as being an excise mark used between 1745 and 1749 to signify that the requisite duty on goods containing copper had been paid. Thus it is a useful piece of information for dating purposes.

Possibly the greatest name in the history of French ormolu is Pierre Gouthière (1732-1813/14), a master of the Guild from 1758. He worked principally in the delicate, symmetrical idiom of early Neo-classicism and, although few pieces can be attributed to him with any certainty (an exception being the example illustrated), his name is associated with some of the most superb ornamental metalwork ever created. He seems to have perfected the technique of contrasting finely chiselled areas with plain surfaces, as well as producing a type of gilding that left a matt surface. The range of ormolu in general during the final decades leading up to the Revolution is of a standard that has never again been equalled, and such perfection obviously inspired attempts in other countries to emulate the French example.

Outside France bronze founders who produced ormolu remain largely anonymous except for the English firm of Boulton and Fothergill. Ormolu manufacture was started at their Soho factory outside Birmingham around 1768, and during the next decade the firm produced some of the best examples of non-French work. Boulton's most inspired idea was to combine his ormolu with the veined crystalline stone from Derbyshire, known as 'blue john', thereby creating a range of elaborate candelabra and vases. Unfortunately costs of production were high, and not being able to generate sufficient markets for his work, Boulton turned his attention in the 1770s to the promotion of the newly invented steam-engine.

The French tradition of superb metalwork continued through the Revolution, and the quality of design and execution were maintained during the Empire period, particularly by Pierre Philippe Thomire (1751-1843). He developed the most important bronze-casting firm of the early 19th century and received many important commissions from the imperial family, including the decoration for the two cradles made for the King of Rome in 1811 (one in the Hofburg, Vienna; the other in the Louvre).

Although the firm of Thomire et Cie continued after its creator's death into the second half of the century, standards of ornamental metalwork were radically affected in France and elsewhere by the onslaught of machine techniques and mass production. In pre-Revolutionary France standards had been maintained at the highest level by the stringent, indeed oppressive and exclusive, guild regulations. These were abolished in 1791, so that individual excellence thereafter had to compete increasingly with cheap reproductions of earlier styles.

Craftsmanship is therefore the first test in differentiating between 18th-century ormolu and later work. Early work is also distinguished by the use of mercurial gilding, a process which creates a resonance, depth and patination not easily achieved by electrolysis. In the case of mounts, only the exposed parts would have been gilded in, whereas today they will be gilded front and back.

ART IN MINIATURE

JEWELLERY
FROM THE 16th TO THE 18th CENTURIES

Anne Somers Cocks

Jewellery is designed to complement dress, and thus its history is bound up with changing styles in costume. It is also, like the other arts, influenced by the economic fluctuations within a society, and to some extent reflects society's preoccupations and aspirations–although not always as directly as the miniature guillotines worn as earrings by ladies during the French Revolution.

Throughout the 16th century jewellery, of all the applied arts, was closest to the large-scale arts, such as sculpture and painting. By training and the structure of guilds, jewellers and goldsmiths were one and the same thing, and during the early part of the 16th century the goldsmith was regarded as being pre-eminent among craftsmen, a training in his art being seen as the best basis for work in the other crafts, whether it be painting, sculpture or engraving. Albrecht Dürer was the pupil of his goldsmith father, while the artists Antonio Pollaiuolo, Domenico Ghirlandaio, Sandro Botticelli, Benvenuto Cellini, and many others were all goldsmiths as well. It is not surprising, therefore, that Gothic and Renaissance jewellers made use of the same forms used, for instance, in the design of a luxuriantly naturalistic tomb-canopy or of a great Classical fireplace at the Palace of Fontainebleu. There is a description of a collar given by Isabella of Castile to Maria of Portugal in 1500, which is an example of the first type. This had 50 burnished and stippled gold branch-elements with vermilion enamel tips, joined by green links with gold shoots and buds, and topped with vermilion and white flowers. The 'A' monogram pendant with its two elegant elongated reclining ladies in enamel and gold is a perfect example of the second type, recalling Francesco Primaticcio's designs for the arcade figures of the Gallerie Basse at Fontainebleau. At the base it incorporates the masks and strapwork which were also an essential part of those and many later decorative schemes.

The Classical vocabulary of the Renaissance was quick to catch on and, by the second decade of the 16th century, had supplanted the Gothic nearly everywhere. In the earlier part of the century, jewellery had tended to be relatively simple, with the stones predominating in rather chaste unfigurative settings, but under Italian influence, towards the middle of the century, the pendant grew in importance, the settings becoming miniature works of sculpture. The techniques used were cast and chased or chiselled gold with extensive use of *champlevé, basse-taille* and cold enamelling, the gems tending to be used merely as decoration. A whole group of designers produced engravings for work of this sort–the Frenchman Pierre Woeriot in 1560, Erasmus Hornick of Nuremberg in 1562 and Hans Collaert the Fleming in 1581, all helped to propagate the style, which soon became an international fashion worn and made in all the major European centres.

The second half of the 16th century was a period of Spanish influence in court fashion. Clothes grew stiffer and richer, dresses were studded with gems, and *parures* often of matching jewellery, were popular. A portrait of the Queen of Spain, painted in the 1560s by Alonso Sanchez Coello, shows her wearing a short jewelled collar (*carcan*), a chain with a pendant (*cotière*), a belt, and a head-dress (*bordure*), all matching. Such pieces were obviously very vulnerable to changes in fashion, and tended to be broken up and re-made to suit the new style. *Carcans*, for example, disappeared towards the end of the century when ruffs grew bigger, leaving no more room for them. During the first half of the century men wore more jewellery than women, but from the 1550s onwards, they tended to confine themselves to a heavy collar, the odd *aigrette*, or

519

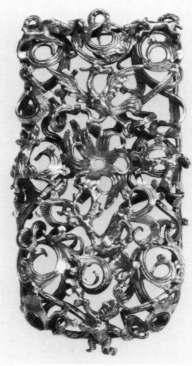

520

521 Enamelled gold pendant set with 12 table-cut diamonds, made about 1560. The initial 'A' stands either for the Elector Augustus of Saxony or for his wife Anna.

522 Model for a pendant jewel, a 'lost wax' casting in gilt-bronze, set with garnets. Flemish, second half of the 16th century.

523 Enamelled gold chains in the Cheapside

Hoard, found in London beneath the floor of a cellar near St Paul's, and almost certainly part of a jeweller's stock from around 1610.

524 Portrait of Queen Elizabeth, c. 1574, possibly by Hilliard. This illustrates some of the contemporary fashions in jewellery; the queen wears a head-dress (*bordure*), a collar (*carcan*) and a large table-cut breast ornament with,

hanging from it, an enamelled pendant of the Pelican in her Piety.

525 Miniature case of enamelled gold, possibly French, and resembling the designs of the Frenchman Jean Toutin, which were published in 1619.

526 Miniature case, gold decorated with enamel, probably French, c. 1670.

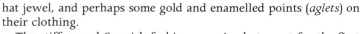

524

525   526

hat jewel, and perhaps some gold and enamelled points (*aglets*) on their clothing.

The stiff, grand Spanish fashions survived at court for the first two decades of the 17th century, but then, under Dutch influence, there came a reaction, and black became all the rage. Fabrics softened, and the emphasis was on exquisite linen and lace rather than on the brilliance of jewels. Men almost gave up jewellery, except for the occasional chain, often worn with military allusion, diagonally, as though supporting a sword. It is no coincidence that this was a time of warfare and economic stress all over Europe. Spain was in rapid economic decline, and repeated sumptuary laws appeared, for once, to be making their impact. England was going through, first the Civil War, and then the Commonwealth; Germany was fighting the Thirty Years War. In Spain and Italy it was the age of the Counter-Reformation, and men wore their orthodoxy on their sleeves – almost literally, for a great deal of jewellery was made which showed that the wearer belonged to a particular faction or sect. Allusive jewellery was, of course, no innovation: posy rings, which conveyed love messages; heraldic jewellery with emblems such as the white hart of Richard II, which showed that the wearer was a certain lord's liegeman; memento mori jewellery

to remind one of death, had all existed for a long time, but now the quantity and variety of such jewels became telling. For example, Spaniards, anxious to show their support of the Inquisition, wore jewelled and enamelled badges which incorporated its emblem; others, who were lobbying for the promulgation of the dogma of the Immaculate Conception, wore pendants which included the symbol of the dogma, the Virgin in an aureola on the sickle moon. Cavaliers, and later, supporters of the Restoration in England, had slides, buttons and pendants made with the portrait of Charles I.

Champlevé and *basse-taille* enamel were still used extensively in the first third of the 17th century. Usually, however, the designs, from being very structured and representational, had become abstract, stylised floral or arabesque. The Dutch love of flower-painting and the botanical enthusiasm spreading around Europe meant, however, that from the 1630s onwards designs showed a more closely observed naturalism than ever before. True enamel was often replaced by painted enamel, so backs of lockets, covers for watches (which had only just become common), slides and so on were often floral studies in miniature.

From the 1640s a fashionable emphasis shifted again, this time from Holland to the French court. Dresses became even more loose-

527, 529 Two designs from Gilles Legaré's *Livre des ouvrages d'orfèvrerie*, 1663. A watch cover with naturalistic flowers, a *girandole* earring; and a bow.

528 Flower-shaped brooch in pink topazes and diamonds, *c.* 1780.

530 Three pieces of political and religious jewellery. Badge of a supporter of the Inquisition, Spanish, 17th century; pendant with painted miniatures of Charles I and Charles II, English, *c.* 1650; locket for devotees of the Holy Shroud.

531 Rococo jewellery design by I. C. Mallia, 1757.

532 A *demi-parure* consisting of breast ornament and earrings. Gold and silver set with diamonds and almandines.

533 A selection of 18th-century silver shoe buckles bearing well-known makers' labels.

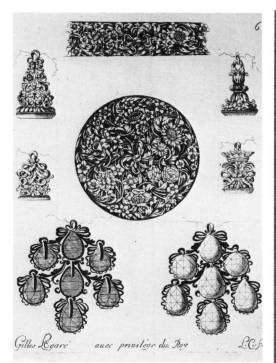

527

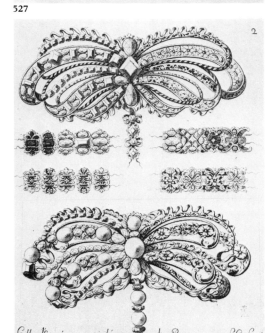

529

531

528

530

532

533

flowing, often deliberately *negligé*. The paintings of the period show fine fabrics, usually of pale colours, such as yellow, light blue or oyster, with bows decorating the bosom and sleeves, and pearls sometimes worn in long strands or tight around the throat. The fashion was to be painted in semi-undress, but ladies certainly did

532 own grander jewellery. Earrings and breast ornaments were the most popular. Enamel retreated in importance – literally – from decorating the front of the jewel to adorning the back, or perhaps the sides of the settings. Now the gemstones themselves became pre-eminent. The mines of Brazil and of Golconda in India were being exploited, and for the first time in history, large quantities of stones were arriving in Europe. Furthermore, the technique of cutting stones was being continually improved, to liberate their brilliance and fire.

The simplest and the most common type of cut in the 16th century and earlier was the table cut, although around 1500, gem-cutters had mastered the more complex art of rose-cutting, that is, of giving a stone a flat round base and numerous triangular facets, usually 16 or 24. This technique was relatively little exploited until

527,529 the 17th-century French designer, Gilles Legaré, who worked for the Parisian court and had quarters in the Louvre, produced designs in which almost every millimetre was closely set with stones. His shapes, echoing fashion, were nearly all based on the bow, often with three oval pendant jewels. These were probably the most successful designs in the history of jewellery, and their basic shapes were copied with variants in their proportions throughout the whole of the 17th and 18th centuries.

An invention at the end of the 17th century made gemstones so attractive that their use in jewellery became supreme throughout the 18th. This was the brilliant cut with its 58 facets, which exploits the optical properties of the diamond to their fullest extent, perfected by the Venetian lapidary Vincenzo Peruzzi. From this time onwards the jeweller became a gem-setter rather than a goldsmith; enamelled jewellery had virtually disappeared by 1800, and even the backs of jewels were plain metal.

However, in the mid-18th century, from the 1730s to the 1760s,

531 the Rococo style had made some impact on jewellery design. This was one of those phases which occur from time to time in the history of art when symmetry is put aside, and natural sinuous forms are allowed to predominate – the Art Nouveau style is another example. Rococo makes much use of a stylised naturalism, such as shells, or water flowing over a stump of wood, but it is always incorporated with a design which, although asymmetrical, is pleasingly balanced. One of the greatest masters of this difficult feat was the goldsmith,

sculptor, painter, architect and furniture designer J.-A. Meissonier. The effect of the Rococo style on jewellery was liberating, dissolving some of the more rigid forms, and adding to its repertoire of designs the floral spray, still a favourite with designers.

The predominance of precious stones lasted until the end of the 18th century, when daytime jewellery began to make an appearance. This more ephemeral and less valuable jewellery was very much influenced by the growing knowledge and awareness of the past, and became even more so during the 19th century, when the discovery of a new archaeological site, such as Sir Henry Layard's much publicised excavations at Nineveh, could result in the production of the 'Assyrian' jewellery shown at the Great Exhibition of 1851. Winckelmann's methodical studies of Classical sculpture indirectly stimulated Josiah Wedgwood's production of imitation Classical cameos and intaglios, advertised in his 1773 catalogue to be set in bracelets and rings. His imitations were precise and quite intentional, indeed he even stated in writing that he was prepared to come and take casts of Classical gems in private collections.

The popularity of daytime jewellery led to the development of a vast industry in the field of imitation gems, which continued through the 19th century. Now, with so many cheaper jewels of excellent quality available, the really expensive pieces could be saved for evening entertainments. The paste industry had already been given a strong impetus by the invention of lead-glass by Ravenscroft about 1675. Lead glass had all the characteristics suitable for the cutting of imitation gemstones: a high refractive index, heaviness, lustre, and the capacity for taking a high polish. Paste jewellery became increasingly popular, while the technique for making the paste itself was further improved. The large shoe buckles worn by men were sometimes made of paste, though cut 533 steel, an invention of Matthew Boulton of Birmingham, was a more common medium. This metal, cut and polished to resemble a diamond, also became much used for jewellery of all kinds, both in England and in France.

As well as imitation stones, there was imitation gold, the best of which was that known as pinchbeck after its inventor Christopher Pinchbeck. This was widely used for shoe buckles, watch cases, buttons, and sometimes for another characteristic day ornament of the period, the chatelaine, a broad decorated hook from which were hung various objects such as keys and scissors. Chatelaines, however, were usually made of gold, often elaborately enamelled or with fine *repoussé* work, and such objects, in which gemstones were infrequently used, became one of the finest expressions of the art of the goldsmith.

19th-CENTURY JEWELLERY

Joan Bamford

The richness and variety of much 19th-century jewellery reflects the life style of this long period of peace and development, when prosperity was within reach of a far larger section of the population than had hitherto been the case. The 18th century had seen the beginning of production of good but relatively inexpensive jewellery, which stimulated a demand for adornments of all kinds, and the 19th century, aided by the technological advances of the Industrial Revolution, continued this trend.

One of the outstanding facts which emerges from a study of 19th-century jewellery is the exceptional quality of much of it, although this does not apply to the somewhat tawdry factory-produced imitation pieces purchased in large quantities by the masses during the second half of the century. The rising wealth of the middle classes produced a growing demand for handsome and valuable jewellery of the kind which had previously been the province only of the noble families, and a large quantity of fine pieces

was made to meet this expanding market. Thus there is fortunately a plentiful supply of good individual pieces remaining today, although sadly, many of the *parures*, or matching suites, have been broken up or the stones reset in more modern settings.

The period was a long and varied one, and naturally public taste changed with the times, indeed the 19th century is characterised by an almost bewildering variety of styles. Many of these were the direct result of world events, for instance, the opening of gold mines in Australia and California and the discovery of diamonds in South Africa had a great impact on jewellery designs in Europe and America, giving added scope to designers, who could use these 524 new-found materials more lavishly as they became more plentiful. The new awareness of the past also played a major part in 19th-century jewellery design, as it did in the other arts. The 18th-century excavations in Italy and Greece, together with the increasing ease of travel abroad, had done much to encourage interest in

534 19th-century cameos: sardonyx cut-stone brooch and earrings depicting Terpsichore, the Greek muse of dancing, c. 1820; and a cameo of a Roman emperor's head, in jasper ware with a blue and white enamel setting, c. 1840. The latter is part of a set of brooch and earrings.

535 Necklace, brooch and earrings of seed pearls. *Parures* of seed-pearl jewellery were much worn during the early part of the century.

534

535

Classical design, and Classical Revival styles, which began during the 18th century, continually reappear in the 19th. We also see copies of Gothic, Renaissance and Romantic designs, while Napoleon's Egyptian campaign brought in a craze for sphinxes and scarabs.

Fine mosaic work was also the result of Italian influence, and was used extensively in jewellery for a time. During the early years of the 19th century, seed pearls were much worn, as were cameos of all kinds–these were to prove an enduring fashion, and were extremely popular with Queen Victoria herself.

Cameo cutting is an ancient craft, first practised in Imperial Rome and later in Byzantium, where cameos and intaglios (incised carvings) were cut in hard stones such as onyx and agate, ingeniously using the natural layers of colour in the stones to form designs. These had become popular again in the 18th century–they had been imitated by Josiah Wedgwood–and cameos of many kinds, particularly portraits, were included in the jewellery fashionable at the court of Napoleon I, indeed they were one of the favourite ornaments of the Empress Josephine. Fashions from Paris had a considerable influence in Britain and elsewhere, and thus a demand for cameos of all kinds soon arose in Britain. Many of the 19th-century examples were carved in gemstones such as amethyst or turquoise, but shell cameos also became fashionable about 1835, when some Italians began carving them in Paris, and they continued to be in vogue throughout the century. These small pieces of skilful relief sculpture, with their natural layers of contrasting coloured stone or shell, were made into brooches, earrings or necklaces for daytime wear, or set with gold or precious stones for more formal evening wear. Lava cameos from Italy, especially Pompeii, were also greatly favoured, in a variety of colours from dove grey to rich burnished brown, and the author has recently seen a fine example carved in bright green malachite.

Another factor that led to such a wide variety of jewellery being made and worn in the 19th century was the part it played in social

etiquette, an important aspect of middle-class life. All moderately well-to-do households had one or more domestic servants, and elegant clothes with appropriate jewellery could be worn all day by the mistress of the house, who enjoyed a busy social life. Home entertaining, with large family parties, was *de rigeur*, as were afternoon tea-parties, social calls and exchanges of dinner parties, all of which naturally made women fashion and jewellery conscious. Early in the century, many head and hair ornaments were worn, set in elaborate coiffures, and for day wear there was informal jewellery, known as secondary jewellery, usually made from silver or gold and semi-precious stones, such as coral, amber, ivory, cornelian, malachite, jet and so on.

Coral was particularly popular: this natural substance, varying in shade from white through palest pink to vivid red, was thought to have talismanic qualities to ward off evil. When the Italian coral industry was at its height, it was the custom for children to be given necklaces of coral beads or other small pieces of coral by their godparents at their baptism, to protect them through life. From about the 1840s to about 1870, coral jewellery, much of it set with diamonds, pearls, turquoise and other stones, became very fashionable throughout Europe; there is a great demand for these fine pieces today.

Formal jewellery, known as primary jewellery, made with precious gemstones, was always worn on important social occasions or at evening engagements. Such pieces were frequently made into handsome *parures* of matching jewellery, for instance, a necklace, earrings, a bracelet and a brooch would be made by one designer to be worn together. It was also the custom in the early part of the century for a bridegroom to present his bride with a *corbeille*, or bridal casket of jewels, on their marriage. These usually included a number of pieces made with a profusion of coloured stones in valuable and elaborate settings. Coloured stones were apparently considered suitable for young girls, while diamonds were the prerogative of married women. Young girls also wore elaborate

536 A selection of gold and coral jewellery of the Romantic period, about 1840 to 1860.

537 Three fire-gilt tiaras, *c.* 1840. The example at the top has finely moulded leaves and flowers with centres of black enamel; the centre piece is composed of formalised leaves; while the tiara at the bottom is formed of a delicate tracery of leaves in a fire-gilt setting, carved in the semblance of Greek heads.

538 Unique mid-Victorian brooch of a carved coral ram's head set in gold.

539 A typical early Victorian garnet suite.

540 Victorian set of carved ivory brooch and earrings in the form of a rose spray.

541 Cross, earrings and medallion of Whitby jet, mid-Victorian.

536

537

538

539

540

541

542 Early 19th-century emerald and diamond bracelet on silver and yellow gold.

543 Jewellery designed for Liberty's by Archibald Knox. Silver buckles, and a pendant and chain set with chrysoprase, 1900-04.

544 Citrine and gold fob brooch of the mid-Victorian period.

542

543

544

jewellery at balls—bracelets, necklaces, earrings, brooches and head ornaments—but they were made from pearls or coloured gems rather than diamonds.

The Victorians, in spite of their formality, were not afraid to show romantic sentimentality in celebration of life's happy occasions, such as marriages and births, and they indulged in a positive orgy of mourning and morbidity to commemorate death. Mourning jewellery of all kinds was much worn by the general public throughout the era. This was not a new fashion: in the 16th and 17th centuries a large quantity of such jewellery had been made, for instance, memorial jewels and remembrance rings had commemorated the 'martyrdom' of Charles I. The Crimean War and the Indian Mutiny were two causes for the revival of this fashion in 19th-century Britain, as was the long widowhood of Queen Victoria after the death of her husband in 1861, which encouraged the British public to mourn in sympathy. Much Victorian commemorative jewellery included ingeniously executed designs made from, or incorporating, the hair of the departed. This hair-work jewellery now belongs exclusively to the past, as the secret of the skills used in making it died out with the craftsmen who used hair in so many intricate ways.

Jewellery made of jet became very fashionable about 1820, and reached its height of popularity during the period of the Queen's mourning. She introduced jet into court circles, and the fashion spread rapidly across the Channel. The result of this was that a prosperous industry was built up in Whitby, Yorkshire, where a quantity of jet was found in seams in the cliff and on the beaches round about. In 1870 some 1,400 men and boys were employed in this local industry, producing jewellery of a high standard of

workmanship. By 1856 the estimated value of jet articles sent out from Whitby to other parts of England and the Continent was about £20,000.

Jet articles were also made in Spain, but the quality of the jet did not equal that found in the Whitby area. In Paris a quantity of so-called French jet jewellery was made but, although very attractive, it was actually a form of cut black glass, unlike Whitby jet, which is a natural substance.

Another popular type of jewellery was piqué, composed of fine gold or silver inlay on tortoiseshell, requiring considerable skill to make. It was fashionable in the early part of the 19th century, and much of it was made in France, but the craft was revived in Britain at the end of the century.

Jewellery to mark happy occasions was abundant, with love tokens forming the largest part of this category. Hearts, flowers, named brooches and brooches carrying messages such as MIZPAH (which means loosely 'good fortune' or 'the Lord watch over Thee') were frequently presented to the betrothed. Rings of all kinds were given and received, love rings being a particularly popular fashion. These were set with coloured stones of which the first letter of each were combined to spell a message, for example, a ring set with diamonds, emeralds, amethysts, rubies, emeralds, sapphires and topaz spells 'dearest'. Lockets of all kinds were worn, often containing a precious portrait and sometimes a lock of hair.

This fashion extended to men, who often carried a gold locket in a waistcoat pocket, attached with their watches to a watch-chain. Victorian gentlemen had their own jewellery fashions too—gold or silver curb watch-chains with a bar, known as Alberts, were generally worn, waistcoats having a special buttonhole for the

167

545 A group of mourning jewellery, mainly of the mid-Victorian era, including examples of hair-work, enamel, miniature paintings and a cameo.

546 A wide silver bangle of the late Victorian period, engraved and with applied decoration.

547 A group of typical Victorian diamond jewellery.

548 Snakes were considered lucky in the 19th century, and much jewellery was made in this form. The gold necklace on the left has a head set with rubies and pearls; the other necklace is gold and pavé set with turquoises, and eyebrows of diamonds. The rings are also gold, and two are set with precious stones.

545

546

547

chains, and a pocket to hold the watch on one end. In those days, when gold was still part of the legal currency, a sovereign purse was also a necessity. These were made of gold, silver or pinchbeck, and had a sliding action with an adjustable shutter inside to hold the gold sovereigns and half sovereigns. Men also wore ornamental cuff-links, finger rings, tie pins or tie rings, often of attractive designs or containing precious stones, while jewelled or pearl studs were worn with evening dress.

Towards the middle of the century, the work of a talented
553 Italian family called Castellani became the rage in Europe; and their gold jewellery decorated with granulation in the Etruscan style, shown at the International Exhibition in London in 1862, created a sensation. The Castellanis had discovered the secrets that lay behind techniques used by Greek and Renaissance jewellers but,

as often happens, their copies of the older jewels were even finer work than the originals. As the fashion grew, jewellers outside Italy began making similar pieces. John Brogden and Robert Phillips, both first-class London jewellers, became famous for this type of work, and the archaeological style was also widely imitated in America and France.

The mid-19th century was marked by the re-appearance of naturalism, and magnificent diamond jewellery based on natural forms was produced. Sprays of diamond flowers composed the necklaces, tiaras, earrings and brooches worn by the ladies of the era, many being set 'tremblant', so that the flowers and leaves moved with the movement of the body to make them more realistic. Countless bees, butterflies, dragonflies and birds made of diamonds were worn, as were stars, crescent moons, etc. Snake and serpent 548

549 A selection of gold and silver piqué jewellery.

550 Scottish circular brooch in a gold frame set with agates, and with an agate star in the centre.

551 Two mid-Victorian love rings, set with semi-precious stones. The first letter of each stone is combined to spell a word.

552 American sapphire cameo on an enamel pendant, with a chain of silver and pearls.

553 Gold necklace and pendant by Castellani, c. 1860. The sliding pendant is set with diamonds, and the centre is a cameo carving of the head of Christ in pale sapphire.

554 Black enamelled gold brooch set with seed pearls, 1870-90.

548

549

550

551

552

553

554

bracelets and necklaces, diamond and emerald lizards, spiders' webs in gold and so on, were also typical of the period. It was not until the Boer War, which stopped the supply of South African diamonds, that coloured stones returned to general fashion.

At about the same time, at the other end of the social scale, mass produced jewellery, with the settings stamped out of metal, began to be popular. These pieces, which enabled those who could not afford 'real' jewellery to follow the fashions, were set with coloured paste in imitation of gemstones.

After the death of Prince Albert, jewellery quietened down, and a somewhat sombre period followed. The queen's prolonged stays in the Highlands, at Balmoral, started a vogue for Scottish jewellery, such as engraved silver brooches, similar in form to those worn on the shoulders of Highlanders to fasten their plaids. These usually contained cairngorms or amethysts found in Scotland, and pebble jewellery in traditional Scottish designs became fashionable. Sad little brooches made from a grouse's foot, or a miniature jewelled dirk, all went with the contemporary fashion for wearing tartan.

Gold was plentiful, and in the 1870s and '80s, gold hunting motifs, such as brooches in the form of foxes or foxes' heads, whips, horses, etc., were much worn. Other sporting emblems, such as tennis rackets, golf clubs and bicycles, were also considered 'smart' as the taste for these pastimes became more general.

During the late 1870s and for the following ten years a quantity of silver jewellery was produced – lockets, heavy bangles, necklaces, brooches, earrings, chains, etc. The workmanship of such pieces was often very fine, and most of them were engraved. Silver was also used for many other personal ornaments such as clasps for

550

546

555 An early Victorian cut-steel butterfly brooch.

556 Dragonfly corsage ornament in gold, enamel and chrysoprase, by René Lalique, c. 1898.

557 Brooch designed by C. R. Ashbee and made by the Guild of Handicrafts, c. 1900.

558, 559 Gold and enamelled jewellery designed by A. W. N. Pugin, 1850.

555

556

557

558   559

belts and collars, chatelaines, hat-pins, buckles, buttons, muff chains and vinaigrettes. The last-mentioned are intriguing little pieces which have made a recent fashionable come-back; they were actually of 18th-century origin, but continued to be produced and used throughout the 19th. Containing a tiny sponge soaked in aromatic liquid to sniff in order to avoid an attack of the 'vapours', some were worn on a chain around the neck like a pendant; others were attached to a finger ring by a short piece of chain, or they were carried in the pocket or handbag.

The decorative shoe buckles worn in the 18th century continued to be fashionable, and many jewellers and silversmiths stated on their trade cards that they also 'specialised in buckle making'. A wide variety of materials was used for this fashion, such as silver, gold, cut steel, pinchbeck, brass and mother-of-pearl, and for special occasions they were set with precious stones or paste. These buckles had a strong, detachable fastening, so did not have to be kept attached to one pair of shoes.

Religious emblems were generally favoured throughout the century, and the cross in some form was an almost essential part of every jewel case. Crosses made in a great variety of stones and materials were worn by women of every Christian denomination as emblems of piety and devotion. It will indeed be seen that most 19th-century jewellery was closely allied to representational symbols of some kind, and that abstract or imaginative designs had little or no place during this comparatively secure period in history.

Early in the 20th century there was a revulsion in Britain against Victorian products of all kinds, indeed it was not until about the 1950s that this attitude began to change. However, as the Victorian era recedes, art historians and collectors have come to appreciate fully the fine craftsmanship of the period, and to admire what was once derided—the lavish use of precious gems and metals and the

typical generosity of design. The quality of Victorian jewellery is now seen in its true perspective, and the demand for it is growing—it is eagerly sought by museums, private collectors and the general public.

This dislike of all things Victorian had its beginnings within the Victorian age itself. At the end of the century drastic changes came about in public taste. The social scene was changing fast, particularly for women, who were beginning to pursue their own careers, and make every effort to secure their right to vote. Revolt against the immediate past was in the air, and artists such as the pre-Raphaelites, William Morris and Walter Crane were becoming increasingly influential.

Decoration and ornament in all the arts became less lavish, and the contemporary jewellery fashions were smaller and more delicate. Typical of this period were ornaments made from pale-coloured or unostentatious stones such as moonstones, opals, turquoise and half pearls. Another development was for inconspicuous settings, the introduction of platinum and the use of pewter greatly emphasising the beauty and importance of diamonds and other gemstones.

In contrast to the work of professional jewellers using precious stones and metals, the Arts and Crafts Movement in the middle 1880s produced a style which, although appealing to a limited public, had a strong influence and led on to Art Nouveau style (see 543,5 p. 295). The Arts and Crafts jewellery was of superb workmanship, but some of the pieces were inclined to be heavily designed with massive scrolls and flowing lines, and somewhat too fussily ornamented to seem attractive today. The Movement was, however, an important influence in every sphere of art and design, and C. R. Ashbee and others created some jewellery which is certainly **557** striking, and attracts many modern collectors.

560 Lilies of the Valley egg by Fabergé. It is signed by Michael Perchin, a craftsman in Fabergé's employ, and was presented to the Dowagor Empress Marie Feodorovna by Nicholas II. Dated April, 1898.

OBJETS DE VERTU

Anne Somers Cocks

During the second half of the 17th century, when the more complex goldsmiths' techniques in ordinary jewellery were less in demand – the fashion was for brilliantly cut gems in relatively unobtrusive settings – the habit of snuff-taking became common, giving a new impetus to goldsmithing. Snuff boxes and small gold boxes in general survive in very small numbers from the late 17th and early 18th centuries, but they became quite common by the 1720s, when the *marchands-merciers*, who were entrepreneurs, suppliers of *de luxe* objects, and designers, began to play an important part in creating a demand and in harnessing the skills of craftsmen to the production of such objects. The skills involved were chasing, embossing, all kinds of enamelling and gem setting, combined with the high-precision goldsmithing necessary to produce a box with a tightly fitting lid. These boxes often served as a delicate way of showing gratitude, or of making payment for a service rendered, indeed, a goldsmith would often buy back a box from the recipient at a price close to the cost of manufacture, and then sell it again, often to the original donor, who would give it away yet again . . .

French boxes are generally considered to be the finest ever produced, but they were rapidly imitated in England, Germany and Switzerland, and even as far afield as Russia and Portugal. In the first half of the 18th century, minute chasing and embossing were a favourite form of decoration, as on the fine English box illustrated. This piece, which is embossed with a scene of Ariadne consoled by Bacchus, has a very finely textured background, as though it had been sand blasted (the finish called appropriately enough *sablé*), and equally fine matting on some of the details. Not only does this box show that English work could be just as good as French, it also provides an excellent example of a characteristic preoccupation of 18th-century goldsmiths – to explore to the full the potential effects which could be achieved with gold, both by varying the texture and the colour. The latter was achieved by altering the alloys added to the gold – silver producing a greenish tinge, copper a reddish one and so on. Up to four different shades of gold might be used on one box, as with the Swiss example dated around 1770. This, like many of the gold boxes produced by the prolific Swiss makers, bears imitation French marks, a practice which can partly be explained by the prestige enjoyed by French boxes.

From the middle of the 18th century onwards, enamelling replaced chasing as a favourite method of decorating boxes. Often it was translucent *basse-taille* enamel, most commonly dark blue and dark green; sometimes the whole surface was covered with translucent enamel on an engine-turned pattern. It is known that this technique was invented at least as early as the mid-18th century. Another, particularly difficult technique, known as *en plein*, became very popular in the Louis XIV period, when subjects were often taken bodily from Boucher and other painters: the enamel was fired on the actual surface of the gold, usually in a pictorial design, with each successive colour laid on separately and re-fired. Painted enamel of the type so popular in the 17th century was also used, an example being the watch and chatelaine made by Adamson and Millenet in Paris 1775-6. This is decorated with painted enamel showing scenes of Dutch peasant life after Teniers, known in 18th-century France as '*à figures Flamands*'.

The techniques used for gold boxes were of course the same as those applied to the *nécessaires*, spectacle cases, watch cases and chatelaines which were also made in large numbers during the 18th century. A group of craftsmen specialising in one or all of these various types of enamel work would often have the ready-made boxes sent to them as piece work, and after decoration they were returned to the goldsmith to be sold. Innovation in the materials and techniques used in the production of boxes and related goldsmiths' work was often due to the *marchands-merciers* who, from the 1740s onwards, encouraged the use of hardstone and lacquer panels set *en cage*, and of miniature paintings on vellum by artists such as Van Blarenberghe.

In England James Cox the 'toy maker', who between 1766 and 1782 specialised in the designing and making of objects which incorporated clocks and mechanical devices, adopted the German fashion for setting hardstone panels in gold mounts.

During the 19th century the tradition of small *objets de luxe* in gold and enamel continued, and a particularly active centre of production was Switzerland. This was because Swiss craftsmen had, by close imitation of French boxes, mastered the French styles and techniques, but they produced cheaper work because their differ-

560

171

561 Enamelled watch and chatelaine with watch key and seal by Adamson and Millenet, with a Rococo gold frame. The painted enamel shows scenes of Dutch peasant life. Made in Paris, 1775-76.

562 Sealing-wax case of enamelled gold. French, made in Paris c. 1773-74.

563 Back and front cover to an engagements notebook, made of tortoiseshell with gold mounts in a revival of the Régence style, and set with enamel portraits of King Louis Philippe and Queen Marie-Amélie. It is signed 'Bury Frères, Genève', and was made 1830-40.

564 Hardstone vanity case made c. 1925 by an unidentified maker for Lacloche Frères, Paris. The stones include jadeite, black onyx, rose-cut diamonds, lapis lazuli, turquoise, malachite, rhodochrosite, smoky quartz and mother-of-pearl.

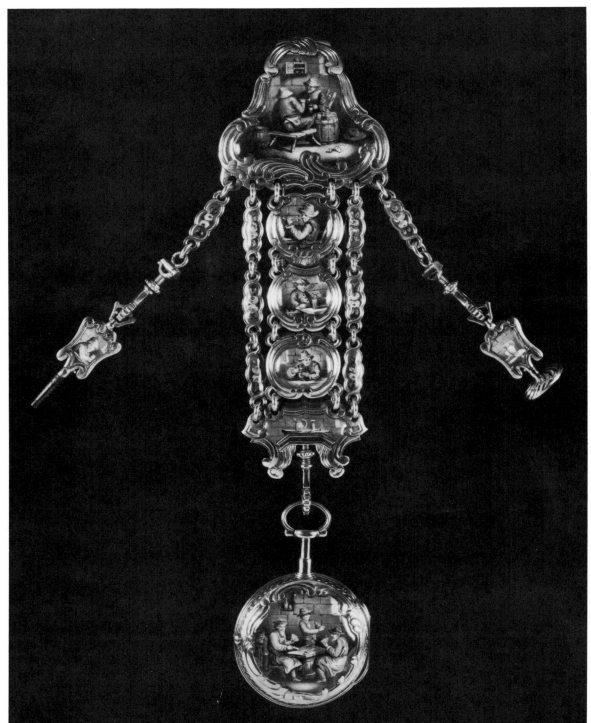

561

562

563

564

565 English *nécessaire* with watch, made around 1770 in the form of a writing-desk. Gold cagework and pink agate.

566 Gold box, the bottom chased with the arms of Carmichael, and a scene showing Bacchus consoling Ariadne on the front. English, *c.* 1730.

567 Swiss box in three-colour gold, set with splinter diamonds and emeralds. Stamped with imitation French marks, and made *c.* 1760-70.

568 One of Fabergé's extravaganzas: an engraved rock crystal pot on a gold and enamelled stand, filled with strawberry flowers in chalcedony with nephrite leaves. The strawberries themselves are purpurine seeded with gold.

566

567

565

568

ent guild regulations specified that they must work in lower carat gold than the French. The special Swiss characteristic was the use of brightly coloured painted enamel, often to create picture-postcard scenes such as the Swiss Alps or peasant girls in local dress.

Around the 1850s to '60s in the Austro-Hungarian Empire, particularly Vienna, there was a conscious attempt to revive the 570 16th-century *kunstkammer* style with its enamelling, crystal and wrought gold, but now the patrons were not princes, but the large and expanding bourgeoisie. It is interesting to see how the economics of increasing mass production led to the cutting of corners, making the product of such a workshop immediately recognisable even where stylistic features do not give the object away. Silver, for instance, is frequently used instead of gold or silver-gilt; the enamelling tends to be thick and unevenly applied; and many 19th-century pieces which in the 16th century would have been embossed and chased are cast.

The greatest exception to this general trend was Peter Carl 560,568 Fabergé (1846-1920), who owes at least part of his enormous fame

to the fact that he had a princely patron of the old style and thus did not need to stint on the quality of his work. At the height of his success in the 1890s Fabergé had branches in Moscow, St Petersburg, Odessa, Kiev and London, and more than 500 craftsmen working for him to produce the bibelots favoured by the members of the doomed Romanov family. The most famous of these were the Easter eggs made for the Tzar to give to his many relations every 560 Easter, in the tradition of ritual present-giving of earlier times. In technique and style Fabergé consciously owed a great deal to the French goldsmiths of the 18th century, the Louis XV period in particular. Like the products of the Englishman James Cox which, 100 years earlier had been exported to Russia and China, many of Fabergé's creations contained mechanical surprises. His workshops also produced miniature hardstone sculptures of animals and some charming imitations of flowers in gemstones, crystal, enamel and 568 gold.

In France during the last two decades of the 19th century, there was an attempt by the jewellers to break away from the pervading influences of the century before, and inspiration began to be drawn

569 *Pliqué à jour* enamel and silver plate, made in Paris around 1905 by Eugène Feuillâtre.

570 Footed salver of engraved rock crystal mounted in silver-gilt, decorated with multicoloured enamel. Austro-Hungarian, made *c.* 1875 but unmarked.

571 Box of lapis, set with a Roman mosaic of the Colosseum. Italian, early 19th century.

569

570

571

from Japanese styles and techniques. Metals both precious and base were combined to form textures and colours never before seen; cabochon was used instead of brilliant-cut gems; sometimes even glass in various textures was used, as by Lalique; and the forms and structures of nature were imitated – also under the influence of the Japanese. One of the leading craftsmen to exploit the new trends was Eugène Feuillâtre (1870-1916), known principally for his fine enamel jewellery. His tour de force was the salver illustrated, enamelled in the very difficult technique called *pliqué à jour*, which involves firing the enamel without any backing, so that it is translucent, being held in place only by the cells of silver. This too is a technique which, although known earlier in the West, was in this case copied from the Japanese, and the pale green turquoise colours used were also of Eastern inspiration.

New customs in the 20th century gave rise to new bibelots: the last jewelled objects to be produced were the cigarette cases and vanity cases which any person of fashion in the 1920s and 30s would have carried about with them. Distinguished Art Deco designers in Paris, such as the painter and cinema director Gerard Sandoz (born 1902) and the jeweller Raymond Templier (1891-1968) were responsible for some outstanding examples in the avant-garde styles, and even the more commercial firms, such as Cartier and Lacloche Frères, showed that they could cut the ties with the traditional decorative vocabulary and produce work which was not only of very fine quality, but in tune with these advanced designs.

ITALIAN AND GERMAN MEDALLISTS

Anne Somers Cocks

This section is confined to the 15th and 16th centuries, because it was during this period that the medal enjoyed its greatest importance as a work of art, and that the major technical innovations in its production were made. The medal may be said to have been 'born' in Italy of the painter Andrea Pisano da Verona, originally in imitation of the coins of Classical antiquity. There was, as far as is known, only one earlier attempt at producing medals, at the highly sophisticated court of the Duc de Berry in late 14th-century Bourges.

Here, the Duc's goldsmith made medallions representing the Roman emperors who had been important in the history of Christianity; those of Heraclius and Constantine have survived in the form of after-casts. This experiment had no sequel, and the true origin of these medals was so totally forgotten that in 15th-century northern Italy they were copied in the belief that they were antique coins.

Andrea Pisano's medals, however, were enthusiastically imitated, owing their popularity partly to his close dependence on Classical

572, 573 Medal by Andrea Pisano, Verona, *c.* 1445. The obverse is a portrait of Domenico Novello Malatesta, lord of Cesena, and the reverse shows him kneeling before a crucifix.

574, 575 Italian bronze medal of the late 15th century. The obverse

is the head of Christ, and the reverse the head of St Paul.

576, 577 Bronze medal by Annibale Fontana, Milan, second half of the 16th century. Obverse: portrait of Giovanni Paolo Lomazzo; reverse: Lomazzo being presented to Fortune by Mercury.

578, 579 Bronze medal by Giovanni del Carino, Padua, mid-16th century. Obverse: Marcus Aurelius; reverse: Victory seated on a pile of armour.

580 Lead medal by Pastorino da Pastorini, Siena, 1561.

581 Bronze medal by Hans

Schwartz, dated 1518, with a portrait of Urban Labenwolf.

582, 583 Bronze medal by Matthias Gebel, Nuremberg, 1528. The obverse is a portrait of Albrecht Dürer at the age of 56, and the reverse bears arms and inscription.

572   573

576   577

580   581

574   475

578   579

582   583

art, which was in accord with the taste of the age, and partly to his subject, portraiture. This appealed to the princes, noblemen, scholars and clerics who, since the early 15th century, had been having their portraits painted in ever-increasing numbers. The pure profile portrait then in vogue was also the type most suited to the medal, which had the advantage over the painted portrait of being durable, portable and two-sided, enabling a man to send his likeness on long journeys as a present to friends and allies and combine it with his personal device or *impresa* on the reverse. Every Italian of any standing had such a device, which encapsulated his hopes, tastes, ambitions or superstitions in a visual image, sometimes combined with a motto. Medals also served the function of encapsulating a piece of history for later centuries: a letter to Sigismondo Malatesta, dated 1453 says, 'The many medals of gold, silver and bronze which transmit this prince's appearance to posterity are to be buried in the foundations and walls of his buildings and sent to foreign princes'.

Andrea Pisano's techniques consisted, slightly unusually, of taking a 'negative', probably in clay or sand, from a wax model, and then casting the bronze in that; other medallists cast directly from the wax model by the lost wax process so that the number of examples of any given medal was necessarily limited. These early medallists in Italy were artists who normally worked on a larger scale, for example, Pisano was a painter, while another medallist, Sperandio, was a sculptor.

In the 1530s there was an important technical development which made it possible for far larger quantities of any one medal to be produced: the perfection of the die-stamping process. In the third quarter of the 15th century the Parmesan medallist Gianfrancesco Enzola had experimented in engraving dies for striking medals, but these had been nothing more than slightly larger-than-

average coins. The new system, however, in which a medal was engraved in intaglio with graver and wheel on a square block of steel, was capable of making true medals, as described by Benvenuto Cellini. Cellini himself improved on this by carving punches in relief for the head and the details, which were driven into the die, the various parts of the design then being connected up by graver. This process was repeated on another steel block for the reverse of the medal, and the two dies, with a blank in between, were then forced together by a large screw worked on a capstan arrangement. The die engraving was executed from a wax model, which was still made of the subject, and these models, since they were not destroyed in the medal-making process, tended to become works of art in themselves, leading eventually to the wax portraits and wax figurative sculpture so popular in the 17th century.

The first Germans to adopt the Italian fashion were the Fuggers of Augsburg, the Habsburg bankers, and the greatest merchant family in Germany. With their network of agents and connections all over Europe, they were *au fait* with art styles abroad, and were in a good position to introduce foreign modes into Germany. Portrait medals immediately became popular, particularly in Augsburg and Nuremberg, but there were certain important differences between the Italian and the German styles. While in Italy it was princes, noblemen and people of great standing who patronised the medallists, in Germany the patrons were the rich mercantile families of Nuremberg and Augsburg, the principal trading cities of Southern Germany—members of the Welser, Imhoff, Pfinzing, Tetzel, and other families. This gave rise to less idealisation of those portrayed—sometimes husband and wife together are depicted in a solidly realistic way without the least attempt to flatter.

Also unlike the Italians, the German medallist was not usually a

581, 582, 583

584, 585 Silver medal by Hans Reinhardt the Elder, Leipzig, 1569. The obverse shows the Trinity, and the reverse bears the text of the Athanasian Creed. Reinhardt was born in Breslau, and had become master of the goldsmiths' guild there by 1561. His main

period of activity was between about 1560 and 1600, during which time he made numerous portraits of Duke Maurice of Saxony, and also of ordinary citizens, such as Balthasar Dietrich, pastor at Gorlitz. Works by him in silver, boxwood, lead and bronze survive.

586 Unfinished model for a medal in Solnhofen stone, by Tobias Wolf. German, c. 1580.

584

585

586

fine art craftsman, but one used to small-scale work in wood or precious metals (though there were exceptions, such as Lukas Cranach the Younger and possibly Albrecht Dürer). Furthermore, he did not work from a wax model; the Augsburg medallists most frequently used boxwood models, while the Nurembergers preferred Solnhofen stone. These materials could be carved in minuter detail than wax, with greater finesse of inscription, narrow elegant borders and dotted circles. Since personal devices were uncommon in Northern Europe, the reverse was usually taken up with a finely worked coat-of-arms.

The most important Augsburg medallist was Hans Schwarz, born about 1492, who was to Germany what Pisano was to Italy. He trained in Augsburg as a sculptor, and in 1517 executed his first medal, the portrait of the humanist Konrad Peutinger. The 1518 Reichstag in Augsburg gave Schwarz his great opportunity, and he executed portrait medals of many of the great princes who attended it: George the Bearded of Saxony, Frederick II of Pfalz, Cardinal Albrecht of Saxony, and Jakob Fugger. During the rest of his career Schwarz travelled widely: he made frequent visits to Nuremberg; in 1522 he was in Poland and probably also visited the Danish Court; and in 1532 he was in Paris, where he made a medal of Jean Clouet, court painter to Francis I. It is not known where and when he died. Before beginning each medal, Schwarz would always

make a quick sketch of the sitter; there are 136 surviving examples of these drawings.

The leading Nuremberg medallist was Matthias Gebel, born around 1500. He was very prolific, producing some 350 medals between about 1525 and 1554, some of which are signed 'MG'. Gebel portrayed people from an even wider section of society than Schwarz, including some quite humble burghers of the town and many artist-craftsmen, such as Hans Sebald Beham, the goldsmith, Kaspar Ulrich and the card-painter Johann Erber. He also attended the 1520 Augsburg Reichstag, where he made medals of the Emperor Charles V and Isabella.

By the second half of the 16th century, medals had become popular all over Germany, but the function of this art form was gradually changing. Medals were being put to the service of politico-religious quarrels, for instance a series of medals executed by Hans Reinhardt for the Dukes of Saxony have the text of the whole Athanasian Creed on the reverse—a public affirmation of their faith. The increasing use of political allusions combined with the technical improvements in die-stamping led medals to assume more and more the political and military commemorative role for which they are now used almost exclusively, while the role of glorifying and perpetuating the individual—as opposed to the head of state—declined.

ENGLISH MINIATURE PAINTING, 1558-1830

Elizabeth Drury

The first English-born miniaturist of distinction was Nicholas Hilliard (1547-1619). The son of an Exeter goldsmith, he was apprenticed in London to Robert Brandon, a goldsmith and jeweller and his future father-in-law. He was accustomed from the beginning, therefore, to working with precision and delicacy and on a small scale. The connections between the goldsmith's trade and the art of miniature painting were to remain close for many generations. By 1572 Hilliard had found favour at court, and in 1584 he was granted the monopoly of the Queen's portraits in miniature. He was also commissioned to design and execute her second Great Seal.

In his *A Treatise Concerning the Arte of Limning*, Hilliard acknowledged his admiration for the limnings (or portrait paintings in miniature) of Hans Holbein, who had worked for a time at the court of Henry VIII. In 1539 the King had sent Holbein to Düren to make a portrait of Anne of Cleves, whom he was considering making his fourth wife. The miniature of her was painted on his return, and illustrates his ability as a painter of the small, formalised image.

Hilliard's style, in comparison with the earlier master's, is freer

both in technique and composition: his sitters are less constricted in their pose and they have livelier facial expressions. In general Hilliard continued the practice of setting the figure against a blue background, but after 1580 he relinquished Holbein's circular format in favour of the oval, which he found more satisfactory for head-and-shoulders portraits. It was the most consistently popular shape from this time onwards.

Hilliard's miniatures, like those of his Elizabethan contemporaries, were executed in opaque and translucent watercolour on vellum, gummed on to card. Technically and stylistically they relate to manuscript illuminations. Indeed, the term miniature derives from *minium* (red lead), the red pigment used for the initials on manuscripts. His limnings are as detailed and as brilliant in colour as the elaborate clothes and jewellery they depict. In them are expressed the languor, the melancholy and poetry of this romantic age.

When James I acceded to the throne in 1603, Hilliard's services were retained at court. He was by then in constant financial difficulty, and in 1617 he was committed to prison for debt. The most

587 Hans Holbein: *Anne of Cleves*, *c.* 1540.

588 Nicholas Hilliard: *Queen Elizabeth I*, *c.* 1588-90. The mount is 17th century.

589 Nicholas Hilliard: *Unknown Young Man among Roses*, *c.* 1590.

590 Isaac Oliver: *A Lady, called Frances, Countess of Somerset*, *c.* 1600.

587

588

589

590

590 talented of his pupils, the French Huguenot Isaac Oliver (d. 1617) was also patronised by the King and his courtiers, soon rivalling Hilliard in popularity.

Oliver was familiar with contemporary Flemish and Italian painting, and the mature style of his Jacobean miniatures has affinities with that of the painters of large-scale works in oils–painters such as Marcus Gheeraerts, to whom he was related by marriage. In particular, he gave depth and texture to the images of his sitters, modelling their faces, hands, dress and ornamental accessories in light and shade. Hilliard had declared that the only appropriately delicate method of shading was by hatching with minute brush-strokes in the manner of an engraver such as Dürer, and that surface detail in an object of small dimensions surpassed in importance the illusion of substance and space. While Hilliard's training had given him the eye of a goldsmith, Oliver worked with the instincts of a painter.

Peter Oliver (1594?-1647) and Lawrence Hilliard (1581/2-1640) 592
followed their fathers as limners, though neither of them achieved comparable stature in the profession. There was a demand for pictures of royal and other eminent persons, and they often found employment making replicas of existing miniatures. Peter Oliver was also commissioned to make miniature copies of large-scale

591 Nicholas Hilliard: *Portrait of Sir Christopher Hatton.*   **592** Peter Oliver: *Edward, Prince of Wales,* after Holbein.

591

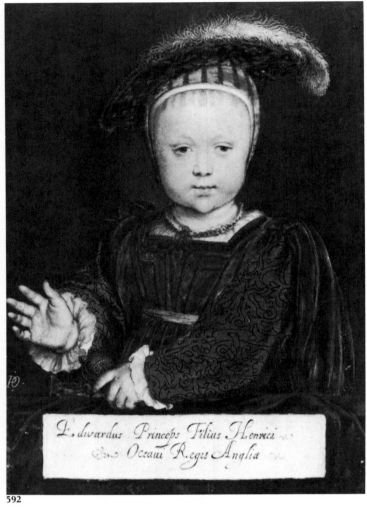

592

paintings. For Charles I he copied Titian's painting, once in the royal collection but now lost, of the Flight into Egypt. Holbein's portrait of Edward, Prince of Wales, was a painting more suited to copying in miniature, being the representation of a static figure isolated against a plain background.

593   John Hoskins the elder (d. 1664) probably worked as a painter in oils before turning his hand to miniatures in watercolour. From simple images in the manner of the Elizabethan and Jacobean limners, he progressed to an altogether grander and less intimate style. Together with several of his contemporaries, he fell under the influence of Van Dyck, who was working in England after 1632.

594   Hoskins was the uncle and teacher of Samuel Cooper (1609-72), the most admired and copied limner of the 17th century and the friend of such distinguished men as Pepys, John Aubrey and Samuel Butler. With Cooper the miniature became not simply a likeness, but a study of personality. In abandoning the attention to surface detail of the earlier masters and achieving delicate variations of tone in his colouring, he created a quieter, more sensitive style of portraiture. Some of the surviving examples of Cooper's work are unfinished, and they show how he built up his paint from an opaque white ground. His miniatures were generally mounted in simple wooden or metal frames and were sometimes signed with the initials S.C.

The portraiture of Samuel Cooper dominated miniature painting in the second half of the 17th century. None of his imitators possessed such insight into character; none had his instinct for composition and tonal delicacy. Among his followers were Thomas

596 Flatman (1635-88), lawyer and poet as well as painter, and Susan
597 Penelope Rosse (1642?-1700). She was the daughter of Richard Gibson, a dwarf who became a page at the court of Charles I and was himself a limner of some competence. Both her copies of Cooper's work and her own original miniatures are in some instances technically and stylistically so similar to his that they have often

595 been mistakenly attributed. Samuel Cooper's elder brother Alexander (d. 1660), also brought up and taught by Hoskins, became a

miniaturist. He worked principally on the Continent, in Holland and Sweden, the country where he died.

Following Samuel Cooper's death in 1673, Nicholas Dixon (active 598 1667-1708) was appointed limner to Charles II. When, during his lifetime, a collection of 70 of his miniatures was mortgaged to cover his debts, it was recorded that they were copies of Old Master paintings. At this period it became fashionable to have cabinet furniture specially made for the display of miniatures, and particularly popular were the small-scale reproductions of Italian and Flemish masterpieces of art. Dixon was, in fact, Keeper of the King's Picture Closet in which were included the miniature copies of paintings made by Peter Oliver for Charles I.

In the later years of the 17th century there were two miniaturists at work with the name of Cross. It is now generally assumed that P. Cross was the father of Lawrence Cross (or Crosse), who died in 599 1724. Still using the traditional materials—vellum and watercolour— they adopted a new technique. Instead of applying the paint in parallel brushstrokes or following the contours, as practised formerly, they painted in minute dots of colour. During the reigns of the later Stuarts and up until the middle of the 18th century, there was a vogue for miniatures in plumbago (graphite) on vellum or paper—there had already been various, not very successful, attempts to paint miniatures in oils on vellum, notably by Cornelius 600 Johnson. Pale washes of grey or sepia were sometimes used to strengthen the shading; the miniature painter David Loggan (1635-92) used a variant of this, a beige or slightly orange wash. Preliminary drawings for portrait engravings were occasionally executed in plumbago, as exceptionally fine detailing could be achieved in this medium.

Enamel miniatures were introduced by Jean Pettitot (1607-91). Born in Geneva, he spent the middle years of his life in England in the company of Jacques Bordier (1616-84), to whom he had originally been apprenticed as a goldsmith. He was employed by Charles I as a jeweller and was commissioned by him to execute portraits in enamels, an art that he had learned while working at

593 John Hoskins: *Queen Henrietta Maria.*

594 Samuel Cooper: *Anthony Ashley, 2nd Earl of Shaftesbury, c.* 1665.

595 Alexander Cooper: *Prince Rupert.*

596 Thomas Flatman: *Charles II*, after Lely.

597 Susan Penelope Rosse: *Mrs Priestman, c.* 1690-95.

598 Nicholas Dixon: *General Charles Churchill.*

599 Lawrence Cross: *Portrait of a Lady.*

600 David Loggan: *Dr Thomas Willis.* Plumbago (graphite).

601 Christian Friedrich Zincke: *King's Serjeant Sir Giles Eyre.* Enamel.

593

594

595

596

597

598

599

600

601

602 Gervase Spencer: *Portrait of a Young Woman* (thought to be Lady Mary Wortley Montagu in Turkish costume), signed and dated 1758. Enamel.

603 Bernard Lens: *Colonel Kellet.*

604 Nathaniel Hone, RA: *Harry Earle, junior, at the age of fifteen,* signed and dated 1758.

605 Richard Cosway, RA: *George IV as Prince Regent.*

606 Jeremiah Meyer, RA: *A Young Officer* (thought to be John Smith Budgen).

602

603

604

605

606

the court of Louis XIV. Surviving examples of Pettitot's work in England, often done in collaboration with Bordier, are mainly copies of large paintings by, among others, Van Dyck.

The process of enamelling miniatures involved the application of powdered enamel paint to a white ground that had already been fired; the whole was then refired. Artistic ability had to be combined with the technical skill required to fire so fragile an object. Although enamels are liable to cracking and chipping, the colours cannot fade, a tendency that has spoilt and distorted so many watercolour miniatures exposed for too long to the light. Enamel miniatures are recognisable by the creamy brilliance of their colour, as if they are coated with a layer of varnish. The painted surface is often convex in form.

The art of enamel portraiture lapsed with the departure of Pettitot from England, but was revived by the Swedish-born Charles Boit (c. 1662-1727). He arrived five years after his compatriot Michael Dahl, of whose full-size portraits he made a number
601 of miniature copies. He was followed by Christian Friedrich Zincke (1683/4-1767).

Born in Dresden, Zincke came to England in the early years of the 18th century at the invitation of Boit, by whom he was trained in the technique of enamelling. Boit had obtained a commission to execute a large enamel picture of the Battle of Blenheim and employed Zincke as one of his assistants; but the ambitious project was never completed.

Zincke enjoyed considerable success at the English court until failing eyesight, the blight of several other miniature painters, brought his career to an end. His technical skill as an enameller perhaps exceeded his talent for painting, and his portraits are sometimes wanting in sensitivity. A concern with imitating Kneller's portrait style may have affected his ability to make his own observations of character.

An innovation of the early 18th century was the use of ivory as a ground for watercolour miniatures. The practice is thought to have been invented in the 1690s by the Venetian, Rosalba Carriera. The earliest English miniatures on ivory are by Bernard Lens (1682- 603 1740) and are dated 1708. Although Lens' use of transparent, rather than opaque, watercolour was sparing, the soft colouring of his paintings was much admired by contemporary artists, who found it a refreshing contrast to the rich tones of miniatures in enamel and the sombreness of some contemporary paintings on canvas. The mannerisms of Baroque portraiture did not adapt well to the small dimensions of the miniature, and some of his least successful paintings are those in which he tried to introduce elements of Kneller's style.

Lens' limnings are often in the shape of an elongated oval, and framed in pearwood. He also made copies of earlier miniatures and reductions of mythological paintings, as well as accomplished topographical drawings. The son and grandson of artists, he was himself the father of two miniaturists, Andrew Benjamin (b. 1713?) and Peter Paul (1714?-1750?), the latter noted for his charming paintings of children. Besides instructing them, he had a number of aristocratic pupils including the Duke of Cumberland, Princess Mary, Princess Louisa and Horace Walpole.

Between 1740 and 1770 a distinct change of mood became apparent in English miniature painting. Graham Reynolds has given to the artists active at this period the name 'The Modest School of Miniaturists'. He refers to a quality of unpretentiousness that succeeded the stylisation of the earlier Baroque manner and preceded the elaborate sophistication of Rococo portraiture. The naturalness that pervades the paintings of Hoskins and Samuel Cooper in the previous century made a brief and unexpected reappearance.

Because the period was not dominated by any one artist or, indeed, group of artists with a shared intention or technique, it is easier to judge a miniature of this date on its individual merit. That

607 John Smart: *The Hon. Harriet Hervey Ashton*, signed and dated 1781.

608 John Smart: *Portrait of a Lady with the initials L.V.W.*, painted in India and signed and dated 1795.

609 Ozias Humphry, RA: *Lady Henrietta Cavendish Bentinck, Countess of Stamford*, signed and dated 1772.

607

608

609

is to say, there is no artist to whom it is irresistible to look for comparison.

602 Gervase Spencer (died 1763) executed portraits in enamel as well as in watercolour. His style varies considerably in response to the character of the sitter, and the quality is uneven. In common with most of his contemporaries, he worked on a particularly small scale, his miniatures not generally exceeding $1\frac{1}{2}$ inches (38 millimetres) in height.

604 Nathaniel Hone (1718-84) worked in enamel and watercolour, and as a portrait painter in oils. It was as the latter that he was elected a founder-member of the Royal Academy. This institution, from its inauguration in 1768, was to play a considerable part in putting annually before the public eye a selection of works of art in all media. It helped to establish a reputation for the arts, and did much to mould the artistic taste of the nation. Several miniature painters were trained in the Royal Academy Schools, and a few were elected Royal Academicians.

Besides Hone, whose miniatures were often set into bracelets, the notable mid-18th-century miniaturists were Thomas Day (1732-1807), Luke Sullivan (1705-71), and Samuel Collins (d. 1768) and Samuel Cotes (1734-1818), who signed their work with the same initials, S.C. Recognisable in all their work is a certain appealing naivety, a quality not infrequently encountered in English art, and it was modest in size as well as in manner. The subjects, often with small features and prim expressions, tend to fit awkwardly into their frames because of their stiff postures.

605 Simplicity could not be said to characterise the mature artistic style or the way of life of Richard Cosway (1742?-1821). Born in Devon, the son of the headmaster of Blundell's School, his talent was recognised early and, at the expense of relations and friends, he was sent to London to be trained. First, he was apprenticed to Thomas Hudson, who had been Reynolds' master, and then to William Shipley. He entered and won various competitions and in the 1760s exhibited paintings at the Society of Arts and the Free Society of Artists. There, in 1762, he exhibited an enamel miniature. In 1769 he entered the newly founded Royal Academy Schools, becoming an Associate of the Royal Academy in 1770 and a full Academician in the following year.

Having established his reputation as an artist, he soon achieved a position in society. His fashionably foppish appearance earned him the sobriquet, the 'Macaroni' Miniature Painter. In 1784, after his marriage to Maria Hadfield, a protegée of Angelica Kauffmann, he moved to apartments in Schomberg House, Pall Mall, where Gainsborough was also living. His *salons* and entertainments, reputedly of rather dubious propriety, were as extravagant and flamboyant as his taste in interior decoration.

The friendship and patronage of the Prince of Wales was probably the result of a miniature he painted of Mrs Fitzherbert. The Prince is supposed to have worn it close to his heart for the rest of

his life, and gave instructions that it was to be buried with him. Cosway's royal commissions included the decoration of the ceiling of the Grand Salon at Carlton House for the Prince of Wales. It was at this period that he began to inscribe in Latin on the back of his miniatures R^{dus} *Cosway RA Primarius Pictor Sereniissimi Walliae Principis Pinxit*.

His early ambition had been to succeed as a portrait painter in oils, but it was as a miniaturist that Cosway excelled. Although ivory had been used as the ground for miniatures since the beginning of the 18th century, Cosway was the first to realise that the natural cream colour of the material could be used as an integral part of the colouring. By applying only a transparent veil of watercolour, he allowed the luminous tone of the ivory to remain visible, and even in his earliest surviving works a light and dexterous touch is apparent. Gradually, as his miniatures increased in dimensions, he developed a confidence that led him to exaggerate certain features—the length of the neck and the size of the pupils of the eyes—for fashionable effect. The studied elegance of the period was exquisitely captured by Cosway in his miniatures, as it was by Reynolds and Gainsborough in their canvases.

Towards the end of the century Cosway was affected by the current interest in the occult, and he became something of a religious fanatic. When the Prince of Wales became regent in 1811, Cosway ceased to enjoy his patronage. The miniatures of his last years are less delicate in handling and tone, but the character of his sitters is, perhaps, more intensely observed.

In employing transparent, rather than opaque, watercolour, Cosway may have been following the lead of the slightly older miniaturist, Jeremiah Meyer (1735-89). Born in Germany, Meyer **606** came to England at the age of 14 and studied the enamelling technique with his compatriot Zincke. He enjoyed a considerable reputation at court, where he obtained official appointments from both the King and Queen, and in artistic circles. He was the only painter to be elected a founder-member of the Royal Academy as a miniaturist.

By the 1770s his miniatures painted in watercolour on a sliver of ivory had acquired a luminosity and delicacy that was to be a characteristic of the finest late 18th-century work in the medium. His own technique was to render density in a series of vertical and intersecting lines, heightened with touches of opaque white. Distinctive of Meyer's style is a particularly angular treatment of the facial features.

Richard Crosse (1742-1810) was a prolific miniaturist between **611** the years 1777 and 1780, and is known to have worked in enamel as well as in watercolour on ivory. His portraiture can often be recognised by the greenish-blue he used in the shading, attributed to the influence of Reynolds. His meticulous touch was well suited to the complicated hair-styles and dress of the period.

At the first competition held by the Society of Arts in 1753 the

610 Richard Cosway, RA: *Maria, daughter of W. Smythe* (afterwards Mrs Fitzherbert).

611 Richard Crosse: *Mrs Siddons, née Sarah Kemble*, 1783.

612 George Engleheart: *Princess Charlotte Augusta* (daughter of George III), after Cosway.

613 Covered goblet with 'jewel' enamelling, c. 1480. The glass has a bluish tinge, and bowl, pedestal and cover are ribbed.

614 Jug with Renaissance ornament in coloured enamels on blue glass, 15th century.

615 Standing beaker with an enamelled bowl, ornamented with small protuberances in coloured enamel. Late 15th century.

611

610

612

607,608 second prize, to Cosway's first, was awarded to John Smart (1742/3-1811). Three years later the positions were reversed, Smart gaining first prize. In 1785 Smart left England for Madras in the knowledge that his services would be much in demand by both the English residents and the Indian princes. He was, in fact, retained throughout the 10 years he spent there by the Nawab of Arcot.

Smart's style developed little in the course of his life, though his miniatures increased slightly in size in accordance with the prevailing fashion. Compared with some of his contemporaries it is distinguished by an unusual directness. His backgrounds are generally plain, the colouring clear and strong, the modelling firm. He was, perhaps, less intent than some upon an impression of prettiness: he depicted the idiosyncracies of his sitters as well as their finest features. While in India he often signed and dated his work, adding the letter 'I' beneath the year.

609 Like Smart, Ozias Humphry (1742-1810) went to India in search of his fortune, working in Calcutta, Benares and Lucknow between the years 1784 and 1787. Although other English artists prospered there, the climate was damaging to Humphry's health, and in particular his eyesight deteriorated, and he had difficulty in exacting the fees due to him. He returned disappointed. In 1791 he became a Royal Academician and thereafter concentrated on making larger and less detailed portrait drawings in crayon.

His circle of acquaintances included the three portrait painters of the day, Gainsborough, Reynolds and Romney. It was Reynolds who, in 1764, persuaded Humphry to move from Bath to London, and with Romney he went on a tour of Italy. Some authorities recognise an affinity with Reynolds' paintings in the air of distinction that he gave to his sitters and in their elusive, faintly smiling expressions. The feathery technique that he employed in the latter part of his career has similarities with Cosway's mature style.

George Engleheart (1750-1829) was a pupil of Reynolds, and 612 although he made miniature copies of Reynolds' paintings, he did not apparently attempt to imitate the style of his master. His early miniatures are not particularly accomplished, tending to be awkwardly composed and painted with diffidence. In the 1780s and early '90s, a high point in the art of miniature painting, Engleheart achieved a charming style of portraiture, in which he overlaid the watery colour of Cosway with meticulous detailing that seems drawn rather than painted. Most of his female sitters at this period were portrayed beneath a large straw hat set at a fashionable tilt.

The miniature was a form of portrait painting particularly well suited to the Late Georgian period. Cosway, Meyer, Smart, Engleheart and their contemporaries overcame the naivety of their predecessors, and evolved a fragile, sophisticated manner that expressed perfectly the graceful affectations of their patrons and the exaggerated fashions. Aristocratic faces look contentedly from the luminous ivories. In them English society is portrayed at a moment of great self-confidence.

GLASS

VENICE

Douglas Ash

Glassmaking was an Oriental art which originated in Egypt, Syria or Iraq before 2000 BC, and was introduced to Europe by craftsmen of the Eastern Mediterranean after the establishment of the Roman Empire under Augustus Caesar in 27 BC.

The chief ingredient of fused glass is silica, one of the most widely distributed elements in the world; but as pure silica melts at a temperature above 1,720 degrees Centigrade, it was necessary to make use of an alkaline flux, which had the effect of lowering the melting-point. In the Mediterranean basin this flux consisted of sodium carbonate, which occurred native in Egypt in the form of a substance known as natron. This was obtained elsewhere by burning certain plants, such as *salicornia*, which grew on coasts and in salt-marshes. This soda of vegetable origin was also accompanied by lime, which was essential to stabilise the chemical structure of the glass.

The term 'Roman glass' is almost invariably used to mean artefacts from the Eastern provinces of the Empire and not from Rome itself, where glassmaking was of little account, and the earliest European centre on Italian soil where a significant industry became established was Venice. Another was founded at Altare near Genoa, but proved less durable in the face of Venetian competition and politico-commercial spite.

When the Huns under Attila sacked Aquileia on the north-eastern Italian mainland in AD 452, at a time when the Roman Empire was in decay, refugees retreated across the shallow lagoon, where they helped to expand the future city of Venice on piles driven into the sea-bed.

It is possible that they took existing glassmaking skills with them, for Syria had been a Roman province since 64 BC, and Aquileia had been at an important cross-roads of international trade. However, evidence is virtually non-existent until the 12th century, by the end of which a flourishing industry was undoubtedly already in being. Its growing importance was recognised in 1224 when the glass-manufacturing confraternity was accorded the official status of a guild.

Their activities, which appear to have been pursued in the heart of Venice near and upon the island of Rialto, evidently underwent a steady expansion, with the chimneys of an increasing number of wood-burning glasshouses sending an increasing quantity of sparks into the air. The authorities became so exercised by the fear that the glassmakers might set fire to the city that, in 1291, the entire industry was banished to the island of Murano in the lagoon, where it remains to this day.

Shortly after this change in location, an initially modest export-

613

614

615

616 Dish with enamelled armorials, *c.* 1500. At this date coats-of-arms began to be commonly applied to glass.

617 16th-century dish with milk-glass in a net pattern, known as *vetro a reticelli.*

616

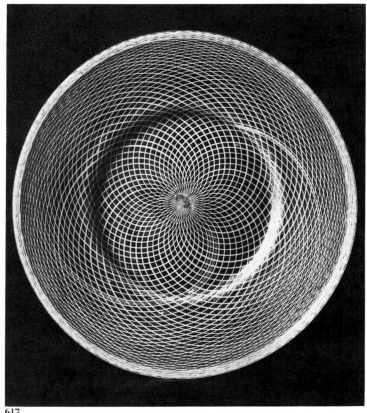

617

trade began to develop. But Venetian artefacts of the period, if they have survived at all, were doubtless of an Alexandrian or Syrian character and are thus unfortunately not identifiable, and we have to wait until the second half of the 15th century for glass objects of an easily recognisable character to appear in any quantity.

By this time, Venice occupied an almost monopolistic position in the craft, for Syrian competition had been virtually destroyed in 1402 when the Mongoloid conqueror Timur Lenk, better known as Tamerlaine, took Damascus and deported most of the artist-craftsmen to Samarkand.

It was accordingly at this period that Venice began to attain the status of a fountainhead of inspiration for most later sophisticated European glassmaking, though the rulers of the Republic endeavoured, with the authoritarian blackguardism of a modern Communist or Fascist state, to prevent Venetian craftsmen from carrying their skills elsewhere. They prescribed fearful penalties for any who attempted to do so, and are known, on occasion, to have sent professional bravos to murder some who had left. But these draconian measures were not to fulfil their purpose for long.

From the middle of the 15th century the Venetian 'metal' – a name given to the substance of glass – reached a standard which was not equalled on a significant scale anywhere else in Europe, and its makers were so gratified by its quality that they began to call it *cristallo*. Although to modern eyes it might seem excessively flattering to describe the glass in question as 'crystal', it must have seemed apt enough against the background of what had gone before, and of other European glass. Most other glass of the late medieval period was heavy, crude, and in various gloomy tones of green, while the Venetian metal, for all its lingering greyish or brownish tint, appeared comparatively clear by contrast. It was not only basically purer, but was made to appear even more so by being thinly blown.

Naturally enough, as in the case of silver objects, the largest surviving category consists of drinking vessels, and some of these are important-looking goblets whose outstanding quality has ensured for them a better chance of preservation.

They were treated in various ways. Some were entirely in colourless metal (the term colourless being used comparatively); some were in coloured glass throughout; some represented a combination of both, with a bowl, often of large size, mounted on a darker, coloured stem and foot. With these last, the tonal contrast between

the parts served to enhance the apparent purity of the *cristallo*.

Many drinking vessels had a trumpet-shaped stem broadening out into the circular foot, the mouth of the trumpet forming the base. A popular type of English silver standing cup was of similar form, and it is quite possible that the design of these glasses was actually inspired by contemporary silver.

Despite their period, there was little Gothic influence in the surface-treatment of these or other objects. The Renaissance movement, or *Rinascimento*, meaning the rebirth of the Classical spirit, had begun in Italy shortly after the middle of the 15th century, having been stimulated by the arrival of Byzantine scholars with their manuscripts and traditions after the capture of Constantinople by the Turks in 1453. The Gothic style was a Northern importation, and its influence was quickly dispersed by the new enthusiasm. It is not surprising, therefore, to find the stems of glass drinking vessels embellished with gadroons, which were of Classical origin, and the bowls sometimes bearing the same kind of gadroon-like 613 ribs which had frequently occurred on a common and widely distributed type of Roman domestic bowl.

The foot was almost invariably folded over upward, giving an extra thickness of glass all around the circumference with a small air-space between. This device protected the vulnerable part against chipping, as it imparted a certain shock-absorbent resilience to an otherwise fragile and brittle material.

Another important type of surface decoration was enamelling. 613,61 This had been practised in the Roman Empire, but attained special distinction in Syria in the 13th and 14th centuries, notably in connection with mosque-lamps. The enamel consisted of metallic oxides, which varied according to the colours required, melted with glass. After it had set, the material was pulverised to form a frit, and after being mixed with an alkaline flux and a liquid medium, could be applied with a brush like paint, fine detail being incised with a needle-like tool. After being fired in a kiln, the enamel, which melted at a lower temperature than the glass, was vitrified and fused into the surface.

There is probably little doubt that the glass-workers of the maritime Republic of Venice, which traded extensively in the Aegean and the Eastern Mediterranean, learned the art of enamelling from the craftsmen of Damascus, and by the end of the 15th century they had developed a high degree of technical skill.

The decoration occurred in two main forms, the one incidental,

618 Bowl with the coloured or streaked markings known as *calcedonio*, c. 1500.

619 Ewer of *c.* 1550, in lace glass, or *vetro di trina*, which came into use in the second quarter of the 16th century.

620 The purpose of this 17th-century stemmed vessel is not clear; it would have been almost impossible to drink out of. Such glasses may have been purely decorative.

621 Glass with a flamboyant stem of clear and blue glass, 17th century.

622 Another example of the Venetian glassmakers' delight in their skill is this glass with a wreath stem.

618

619

620

621

622

the other pictorial. The first apparently set out to achieve an effect of jewelling, with separate, shaped blobs of coloured enamel applied in a manner suggestive of small gem-stones set into the surface of the fabric.

In addition to the 'jewelling', Classical scrollwork was often used, **614** but this was sometimes employed together with Renaissance ornament of a more ambitious kind which demanded a high degree of artistic ability, with nereids, tritons, or other mythological figures appearing among motifs of a floral or foliate character.

Apart from the above forms of decoration, which were integrated into the designs of the vessels which they embellished rather than competing with them for the attention of the observer, portrait busts sometimes occurred. It is probable that these set out to depict the owners, for they displayed details of contemporary costume without any elements of Classicism. Although they had some slight affinity with the wreathed medallions containing heads or busts of the Graeco-Roman era, the surrounding cartouches were seldom of Classical type and the heads tended to be too large, no doubt to gratify the clients who had commissioned the work. This was partly, of course, an experimental phase, and surface-ornament became less exuberant with the passage of time.

At the end of the 15th century we begin to notice the standing **615** beaker, that is, a flat-based cylindrical receptacle mounted on a stem and foot. In the specimen illustrated the main stem-feature is a compressed ball knop between two collars, marking the inception of a tendency towards elaboration of the stem which increased through the 16th and 17th centuries. The treatment of the bowl should be noted. It will be seen that, in addition to the circuit of 'jewelling' immediately below the rim, the ornament consists chiefly of small protuberances in coloured enamel, enclosed in trailed and pinched reserves of reticulated form, somewhat reminiscent of chicken-wire. This net-like pattern had occurred with some frequency in the Roman imperial era, and was destined to attain popularity in England in the 17th century.

616 In about 1500, coats-of-arms first began to be applied on a significant scale to appropriate glass objects, including dishes, with consummate skill, the heraldic tinctures being accurately rendered in coloured enamel.

At the same time, a number of decorative techniques either made their first appearance or attained a noticeably higher incidence, to gain further ground as the 16th century advanced. Among these

may be mentioned a metal which imitated certain valuable hard-stones such as agate, jasper, onyx and chalcedony. The colours or streaked markings which characterised this type of glass were not merely on the external surface, but went right through its substance. It was known in Venice as *calcedonio*, and occurred slightly **618** later in the Habsburg Empire. Drinking glasses as well as bowls, such as the example illustrated, were sometimes made in this substance. Though such glasses were decorative enough as *objets d'art*, the substance had a serious defect as a material for drinking vessels compared with *cristallo*, for its opacity deprived the user of the pleasure of enjoying the play of light in the wine through the walls of the bowl. Perhaps it was for this reason that *calcedonio* never became as popular as clear glass, though it looked well enough in vessels such as vases which were not intended for drinking purposes.

A style of glass which was also developed in Venice at the beginning of the 16th century is known as *millefiori* (a thousand flowers), familiar three centuries later in certain glass paperweights. *Millefiori* was made in the Roman period, and the Venetians improved it, though the technique cannot be said to have been perfected by them. It was made by arranging thin canes of coloured vitreous enamel together in various forms and combinations, then cutting them transversely into thin composite slices. These were placed in a mould into which molten, clear glass was then introduced so that it fused to the slices. The whole mass was then removed, and after re-heating, could be subjected to the normal processes of rolling, blowing and so forth, with the coloured sections forming an integral part of any object so fashioned. However, *millefiori* of the 16th century is not encountered with any great frequency. The technical processes were troublesome and expensive, while the ultimate effect was liable to be almost vulgar.

It is not certain when another type called 'ice-glass' or 'crackle-glass' first appeared, but it was certainly well established by the early 16th century. This was produced by one of two methods. The hot vessel might be plunged into cold water which made thousands of minute cracks all over the surface, and it was then re-heated to ensure the sealing of any through-fissures. Alternatively, it could be rolled, while still in a plastic state, on a bed of small glass fragments which became embodied in the surface. The result was an icy, translucent roughness which doubtless looked attractive while the object was fairly new, but which naturally tended, with the

185

623 Two graceful, if hardly practical, wine glasses of the 17th century.

624 Emerald green glass goblet, second half of the 15th century.

625 Tazza in purple-blue glass decorated with gilding and green and white enamel. 16th century.

623

625

624

passage of time, to harbour dirt, acids and other airborne matter, producing eventually an effect of dinginess which was almost impossible to amend if the texturing was anything but shallow and comparatively smooth. The style soon spread to other European centres and was used for vases as well as practical vessels, but its incidence was always low in comparison with that of more orthodox forms of treatment.

Perhaps one of the most successful of the 'Roman' decorative techniques developed by the Venetians in the first half of the 16th century was that which involved the use of *lattimo*, or milk-glass. This opaque white material was welded into the hot clear glass, the finished artefact displaying straight, undulating, or spiralling bands of white, alternating with clear *cristallo*. It was exported to various countries and used in objects of all kinds. The body of a glass tankard in the British Museum, with English silver mounts bearing the London hall marks for 1548, is a pleasing Venetian example of the style.

The many differing effects achieved by this method have come to be described by the generic term *latticino* or *latticinio*, but the original Italian words for some of the later, more complex variations are more specific. First among these may be mentioned *vetro di trina*, or lace-glass, which came into use in the second quarter of the 16th century and was described in a technical treatise published in 1540. The small ewer in the illustration was 619 probably made about 10 years after this. Colour was occasionally introduced, but was not used extensively.

A related style comprised comparatively fine, criss-crossing lines of milk-glass forming small lozenge-shaped compartments, which might sometimes have a minute air-bubble in each. This was known as *vetro a reticelli*, or net-glass. It appeared in all kinds of 617 glassware including dishes, but as its appeal persisted for a good two centuries, it is sometimes no easy matter to assign a date to any specimen encountered.

Apart from the foregoing ornamental complexities in the actual substance of the metal, surface decoration was sometimes applied in the form of gilding, often in a scale-pattern, and diamond-point engraving, though the latter is so rarely seen that we may probably assume that it was not widely used.

As the 16th century wore on, the Renaissance exerted an increasing influence on form, particularly in the stems of wine glasses. One of the most important details to be introduced in this connection was a bold, hollow knop or protuberance suggestive of a late Classical urn, often with the sides moulded into shallow masks. The urn was sometimes capped with radial gadroons in a manner somewhat reminiscent of the bulbous legs of an English Elizabethan table. A protuberance of similar basic character but differing in detail appeared soon after and flourished concurrently. It was of an urn-like nature, but less precise and more attenuated, so that it approached the shape of an inverted architectural baluster, but still with a moulded surface.

By the end of the 16th century *cristallo* had greatly improved in quality, partly owing to an increasingly competent use of manganese dioxide as a decolorising agent. As this coincided with a more interesting and elaborate type of manipulation, the effect was often delightful. After 1600, the skill of the glass-workers attained unprecedented heights, and they often gave full rein to their dexterity in a fanciful and even fantastic manner, though graceful, well-proportioned glasses were also made in a simple style.

The so-called *aventurine* glass seems to have appeared in the early 17th century, but was never as popular as *cristallo*. It consisted of ordinary glass containing numerous small particles of copper which, being imprisoned in the metal and accordingly protected from the air, preserved the appearance of gold spangles. As the technique was revived in the 19th century, inexperienced enthusiasts should approach *aventurine* with some caution. The objects concerned often consist of over-elaborate goblets, standing dishes with shallow bowls, and oil-flasks in the form of dolphins with their tails in the air and standing on their chins. They are sometimes attractive, but display a certain coarseness in comparison with early Venetian glass.

Certain Muranese stemmed vessels of the 17th century seem distinctly impractical for drinking, and it is possible that they were intended either to contain trinkets or dry sweetmeats or to be purely decorative. The one illustrated could have held only a minute quantity of liquid, and could have been used for drinking only if the greatest care had been exercised. There seems little justification, however, for the modern tendency to call such objects *bouquetiers*, for any normal flower placed in such a shallow receptacle would instantly fall out.

The glass industry of Venice had begun seriously to decline by the end of the 17th century. Chandeliers were made for the home and export markets together with mirrors, and some at least of the glassmakers executed orders for foreign importers. But the situation was entirely different from that of the previous century. Many European countries had or were developing efficient glass industries of their own, often with the assistance of runaway Venetian craftsmen, and the requirements of the Italian market were insufficient to maintain the industry in its erstwhile flourishing state.

Some activity continued throughout most of the 18th century, but ceased entirely in 1797 when the Republic was dissolved and its territory ceded to Austria. The industry was revived in 1838 and has continued to the present day.

THE NETHERLANDS

In 1477, Charles the Bold, Duke of Burgundy, was killed by a Swiss halberdier in battle outside Nancy, capital of Lorraine. By this time, the duchy consisted only of what we now call Holland and Belgium, for the rebellious dukes had forfeited their French possessions to their overlords, the Kings of France. The remaining portion was, however, one of the wealthiest and most cultured parts of Europe, and when Charles the Bold's heiress, his daughter Mary, married the future Emperor Maximilian I after her father's death, the duchy became an appanage of the Habsburg Empire.

Three years before the abdication of the Emperor Charles V, Maximilian's grandson, in 1558, the Netherlands had been ceded to Charles's son Philip, who had become King of Spain in 1556. Already, under Charles V, the domestic Inquisition had done to death over 30,000 people for heresy; but after the introduction of the Spanish Inquisition by Philip II of Spain, the hangings, drownings, beheadings and burnings reached almost unbelievable proportions. The miseries of the Protestant Dutch provinces in the north remained unalleviated until 1609, when they finally gained their independence from Spain.

These brief historical facts should be remembered if we are to appreciate the background against which glassmaking was carried out in the Netherlands in the 16th and 17th centuries. It seems remarkable that any significant glass industries should have existed at all, especially during the governorship of the third Duke of Alba, but in fact, Netherlandish glass manufactories of the period were the most renowned outside Italy.

Despite the savage edicts of the Venetian Senate, many glass-workers were lured away to other parts of Europe where, together with other craftsmen from Altare, near Genoa, they assisted in the establishment of local industries, which naturally produced work of a strongly Italian character. These immigrants had settled in Antwerp in the second quarter of the 16th century and in Liège before 1570, while Venetian-style glass was being turned out slightly later at Amsterdam, Middelburg, Maastricht, The Hague and Rotterdam.

Glass produced in these and other places during the formative years is often described as *à la façon de Venise*, a phrase used at the time in the Netherlands, and much of it is hardly distinguishable from actual Venetian work. The goblet shown in the illustration has a bowl the lower part of which is in ice-glass exactly like that of Venice, while the stem is in the form of a hollow, moulded urn capped with radial gadroons. It dates from the second half of the 16th century and was almost certainly made at Liège, the bosses applied to the bowl being considered a characteristic feature.

Drinking vessels naturally accounted for the largest volume of production, as they were made in sets, although some important looking goblets were made singly. All the current varieties were made including beakers, which formed one of the most ancient categories of vessels in the world, whether in precious metal, ceramics or glass, and were the forbears of modern tumblers. They were particularly prevalent in Northern Europe, Netherlandish examples being sometimes decorated with integral stripes of milk-glass, the Venetian *lattimo*.

The beaker of the second half of the 16th century, made at Antwerp or Liège, is not without a certain refinement despite its uncomplicated shape. It will be observed that there is a widely spaced girdle of applied glass blobs running round the middle. These were destined to become an important form of decoration later, on another type of vessel. They are known in English as 'prunts', and were either plain or moulded with minute hemispheres which gave them the appearance of raspberries. They were not only decorative but also had the functional advantage of ensuring a firm grip, though which of these considerations provided the dominant motive for their application it would be difficult to say, for they had been known since the 15th century and might have been purely traditional.

At the turn of the century, we note the fairly extensive manufacture in the Netherlands of tall glass tankards or flagons, with silver or pewter lids hinged to the top of the handles. The larger versions were used either for drinking or for serving liquor into smaller receptacles. Vertical or spiral bands of opaque milk-glass were frequently present, presumably to enhance the interest of a plain, cylindrical vessel. It is not known what degree of competition they offered to similar objects in silver or pewter, but enough have survived to suggest that they were not rarities in their own day.

It is occasionally possible to attribute various items to distinct manufacturing centres with some degree of probability because documentary evidence exists, but in general, the lack of certainty

187

626 Glass with straight-funnel bowl and stem comprising headed balusters, *c.* 1650.

627 Glass with bracketed stem, 17th century. The brackets are rather similar to those on English steeple cups of the period.

628 Glass with inverted baluster stem, *c.* 1600. The only decoration here is the shallow ribbing of the bowl and the moulded gadroon at the top of the stem.

629 Glass with multi-knopped stem and a simple round-funnel bowl, *c.* 1650.

630 16th-century goblet with a bowl of ice-glass, and the stem in the form of hollow, moulded gadroons.

631 The increasing simplicity of Netherlandish glasses is demonstrated by this early 17th-century example with a rudimentary handle.

626

627

628

629

630

631

632

633

632 Beaker with lines of milk-glass, made *c.* 1570 at Antwerp or Liège. The applied glass blobs later came to be known as prunts.

633 Goblet with a serpent stem, 17th century. This cannot be positively attributed to a glassmaking centre, though a Venetian is known to have made 'cups with serpents' at Amsterdam.

634 Flagon with milk-glass spirals, *c.* 1600. These vessels, with silver or pewter lids hinged to the top of the handle, were popular in the Netherlands.

635 A *Kuttrolf* in pale green glass decorated with knobs of green, purple and blue. Early 17th century.

636 Dutch engraved *Roemer*, with raspberry prunts, *c.* 1650.

637 Shaft-and-globe decanter in green glass, 1674.

634

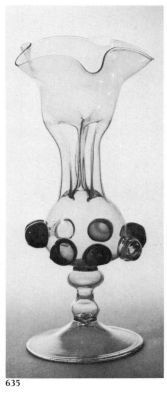
635

636

637

633 renders the descriptive phrase 'Netherlandish' safer as a generic term. The serpent-stemmed goblet of the 17th century is a case in point. A record of the 1660s informs us that a Venetian made 'cups with serpents' at Amsterdam, but it would hardly be sound to assume from this that they were never made anywhere else and had not been familiar for many years.

Not all Netherlandish glass displayed the Venetian-inspired, over-elaborate exuberance of the serpent stem. Many others, perhaps the majority, had a graceful, well-proportioned sobriety from the later years of the 16th century and were often fashioned from stronger metal than their Venetian counterparts. Costly fragility may not have troubled wealthy, noble clients, but most harder-headed Northerners were no doubt anxious that their glassware should not be reduced to fragments by the end of a meal or drinking-bout.

631 The growing simplicity of treatment exemplified by glasses of a normal, non-ostentatious character was by no means a disadvantage in the aesthetic sense, for it involved a greater emphasis on form and proportions as opposed to embellishment. Any lingering tendency towards extraneous attachments, such as ostensible handles on the bowls or brackets on the stems, was sober and disciplined.

7,631 The glasses depicted illustrate both the features mentioned, the brackets on the second being reminiscent of a similar detail which occurred on the stems of English silver steeple-cups of the same period.

The next glass is wholly innocent of even the most rudimentary **628** applied ornament, the only decoration being a shallow, spiral ribbing of the bowl and slight moulded gadroons on the surface of the small knop beneath the *merese*, or thin collar, at its base. The main feature of the stem is an inverted architectural baluster, surely one of the most pleasing devices ever to be used on a stemmed vessel of either glass or silver. The fine proportions and simple treatment, which prevent the eye of the observer from becoming lost among irrelevancies, confer greater dignity on this glass than is often found on expensive objects of a more elaborate nature.

Towards the middle of the 17th century, styles in the Northern provinces of the Netherlands became bolder, especially in relation to the stems of drinking glasses, with greater emphasis on knops, **629** which often occurred in multiple form. The illustration shows a glass with a simple round-funnel bowl, mounted on a tall stem consisting of three identical robust knops which increase the importance of its aspect without detracting from its comeliness. The other tall-stemmed glass with the straight-funnel bowl makes use of **626** headed architectural balusters, divided from each other by *mereses*, and is reminiscent of turnery designs in certain contemporary oak furniture both in the Netherlands and in England.

While such bolder forms were gaining in popularity in the seven independent United Provinces of the north, Liège continued to maintain an attachment to more fanciful conceptions, including, in particular, stems with wing-like excrescences on each side of the central support. They seem to have been manufactured in some quantity, but it is possible that the type was introduced immediately from Germany, and did not originate in what we now call Belgium. These glasses were made to appear excessively squat by the elaboration of the stems.

But another kind of vessel of immediate German origin achieved great distinction in the glasshouses of the northern Netherlands. This was a modified beaker known in Germany as a *Roemer*. The **636** word is an adjective meaning 'Roman', but was used also as a noun to denote the kind of glass under discussion. It existed in two related versions. The first, which appeared in the Netherlands at the beginning of the 17th century, differed from an orthodox beaker only in the profile and the treatment of the surface. Instead of expanding upward from the base in a more or less regular manner, it usually consisted, in the lower part, of a true cylinder which suddenly spread outward to the rim, above a trailed-on, horizontal stringing. The cylindrical portion was commonly embellished with numerous prunts, which might either be smooth or tooled to look like raspberries.

This variety remained current for a while alongside another which, although it appears to have been first made in the Netherlands slightly later, nevertheless displayed a form which must have been known in Europe for several centuries. The lower part of the body was cylindrical, as in the case of its simpler relative, and was covered with raspberry prunts; but instead of a flat base with a narrow moulding round the edge, it had a definite foot, made of spiral threads of glass, which spread outward in a hollow curve. Above the cylinder, the upper part of the bowl had the appearance of a sphere with a slice cut off the top.

A vessel of this general type, in an unknown material which might have been silver or pewter, has been noted in an English illuminated manuscript of the 11th century.

These glasses enjoyed immense prestige in Holland, where their owners either used them as they were, or had them mounted on a tall silver stand with a stem and foot, called a *Bekerschroef*. This was

638 Dutch *Roemer* with coiled foot, in green glass, supported by a gilded stand of a cavalier. Mid-17th century.

639 Flute glass with cover, made of milk-glass with the threads arranged in a net pattern. Early 17th century.

640 Glass with drawn stem, late 17th century. Such vessels, made in only two pieces, were the everyday glasses of the period, relatively cheap to make and to replace.

641 Flute glasses, *c.* 1675, with the engraved decoration that became popular in the mid-17th century.

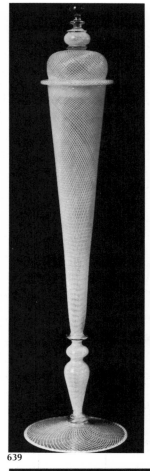

639

640

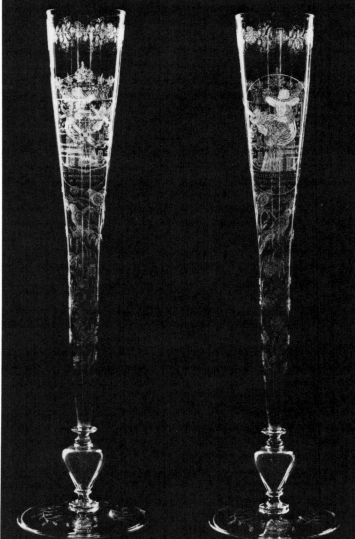

638

641

642 This engraved goblet with a bucket-shaped bowl, *c.* 1660, shows a more painterly approach to the decoration than some earlier examples.

643 English glass stipple-engraved in the Netherlands in 1728 by Frans Greenwood of Rotterdam. The man holds a *Roemer* of the type illustrated in plate 636.

644 Glass from Newcastle, wheel-engraved in the Netherlands *c.* 1670 with a representation of the 'Flying Dutchman'.

642

643

644

equipped with brackets at the top which gripped the foot of the glass, but from which the latter could be detached to facilitate cleaning. The bowls were sometimes decorated with engraving, as 636 in the example illustrated.

Despite the comparatively high quality of the colourless Dutch equivalent of Venetian *cristallo*, these glasses were, for some reason, almost invariably in green glass. It is quite certain that they did not owe this tint to the careless preparation of the ingredients charged into the melting-pots, but to the fact that it was preferred. It should be remembered, of course, that an extensive glass industry, using green metal, had flourished in the region between the Seine and the Rhine from the 2nd to the 8th centuries, and the *Roemer*, which was simply a modified beaker, may have been linked by its Dutch makers with an ancient tradition.

Some other contemporary objects were often in green glass as 637 well, an example being afforded by the fine shaft-and-globe decanter in the illustration.

Apart from the *Roemer*, one of the most striking glasses which developed in Holland from humbler originals was the flute, a type often to be seen in contemporary *doelen* pictures. It may well have developed from the footless cone-beaker of the Roman period, which was extensively manufactured in the Seine-Rhine region in the 6th and 7th centuries after the Romans had departed, but in the hands of the Netherlandish craftsmen it attained great distinction. The factor which distinguishes the flute from other kinds of drinking glass is the noticeable tallness of the bowl in relation to its width. Some of them were immensely high–as much as 15 inches (38 centimetres), but were redeemed from clumsiness by their elegant proportions. The bowl was in the form of an attenuated straight funnel, resting on a *merese* at the base. Beneath this, the stem consisted of a small subsidiary knop above an inverted baluster, which developed, in the second half of the 17th century, something of the proportions of an urn.

Like any other kind of important glass or silver cup, flutes were 639 sometimes equipped with covers, as in the illustration, which shows an example of the early 17th century made of milk-glass with the threads arranged in a net-pattern–the Italian *vetro a reticelli*.

Not only was this inherently decorative material expensive and difficult to make, but it also had the disadvantage, for a functional wine vessel, of obscuring the contents. As time passed, therefore, flute glasses were more frequently fashioned from clear glass, sometimes decorated with engraving, which scarcely impaired the 641 transparency of the bowl.

The engraving of glass became of increasing importance in Holland from about 1600 onward. It was executed in diamond-point, often by talented amateurs of both sexes, and mostly consisted, in the first half of the century, of small motifs such as flowers and fruits together with the sort of swashed calligraphy which we have already seen on the bowl of the *Roemer*. The handling gradually became bolder and more solid; this was achieved by cross-hatching and by massing the minute incisions closely together. The change was probably inspired by wheel-engraving which was beginning to be introduced from Germany and which produced broader effects. The latter technique was hardly practised in Holland until the 18th century.

The goblet with bucket-shaped bowl illustrated here, which 642 probably derived its form from that of contemporary silver standing cups, demonstrates the contrast between the later, more painterly style, and the rather scratchy, linear effects of the earlier engraving. The decoration in question was naturally not applied to the ordinary drinking glasses which existed in large numbers in all households of any but the least prosperous kind. It added notably to the cost and accordingly tended to be found mostly on objects which were deemed especially worthy of preservation.

Common glasses were regarded as expendable, and were normally of a kind which could be replaced at little cost, a consideration which undoubtedly applies to the specimen illustrated. This glass, 640 which dates from the late 17th century, was made in only two pieces, with the stem drawn from the base of the bowl and welded to the foot, a minimising of manufacturing processes which naturally reduced the expense. While adding to the risk of breakage, the thinness of the stem imparts great delicacy in an aesthetic as well as a physical sense and, although made at low cost, the glass is undoubtedly attractive.

From the beginning of the 18th century, the industry in both

191

645 Pair of covered English glasses, wheel-engraved in the Netherlands, 1762. These were given in commemoration of a birth.

646 Newcastle glass stipple-engraved by David Wolff, c. 1780.

645

646

parts of the Netherlands went into a progressive decline. Activity did not cease altogether, but was no longer of any great significance in the context of European glassmaking. The position of Holland became even worse after the end of the War of the Spanish Succession in 1713, when she became unable to stand up to the competition offered by the German and British glass industries.

The Dutch, however, have always been an industrious and resourceful people. From the 16th century they had been distinguished engravers on silver and on copper plates for printing, and had developed their skill in the engraved decoration of glass. This now became an artistic and commercial activity of great importance, for, if they could no longer compete successfully in the field of manufacture, they could use good-quality glasses from elsewhere as a profitable basis for ornamental enhancement.

An extension of the diamond-point technique emerged in the form of stipple engraving. This was done with a diamond or a sharp-pointed steel tool, with which minute chips were made in the surface of the vessel. They were massed closely together to make the highlights, and diminished through the sub-tones down to the untouched glass which formed the shadows. The effects achieved by skilled exponents of the art seem almost magical, with designs, often of an ambitious pictorial character, appearing and disappearing as the point of view is changed and giving the impression of having been blown on to the glass.

One of the most accomplished artists in this field was Frans Greenwood of Rotterdam (1680-1761) who was probably of English extraction. Signed and dated examples of his work have survived from 1722 to 1755, and include many kinds of subject, often of a Classical, amatory or bibulous nature taken from paintings. The glass illustrated belongs to this category and shows a man holding a 643 *Roemer* of the simpler type mentioned earlier. It seems remarkable that the strong, three-dimensional modelling could be achieved by such a technique. It is signed and dated 1728.

Like many other Dutch engravers throughout much of the 18th century, Greenwood chiefly used glasses made in England, especially at Newcastle-upon-Tyne. They were unusually handsome objects and had the additional advantage that the metal from which they were fashioned was softer than the soda-glass in general use on the

Continental mainland, so that they were easier to engrave in line, stipple, or with the wheel.

Wheel-engraving in Holland in the early 18th century was German in style, and the technique made but slow headway against diamond-point and stipple until after 1750, when it began to achieve a wider popularity in the work of a certain Jacob Sang, though it never ousted stipple altogether. The subjects were mostly heraldic, pictorial, or with emblems and sentiments appropriate to personal gifts. The pair of covered glasses in the illustration, with 645 rudimentary stems, were given in commemoration of a birth. The baby is shown on one, and its mother is depicted in bed on the other. The glasses themselves, which are signed and dated 1762, are of a well-known English type which appears in some of the engravings of William Hogarth.

Also English and from Newcastle-upon-Tyne is the taller glass with elegant, knopped stem, with the bowl skilfully engraved with a representation of the Flying Dutchman. Stemmed English glasses 644 of this kind were particularly popular with the Hollanders because of their excellent proportions. After enhancing their appearance — and their value — by their painstaking artistry, they sold them to Continental buyers or even exported them back to Britain.

There were many competent but anonymous practitioners of wheel-engraving in Holland in the second half of the 18th century, but, as stated earlier, stipple was never wholly supplanted by it. One well-known engraver named David Wolff, who was born in the 646 province of North Brabant in 1732, remained devoted to the technique until his death in 1798. While his work cannot be considered as superior to that of his predecessor Frans Greenwood, he undoubtedly achieved remarkable effects of *chiaroscuro*. The typical Newcastle wine glass shown in the illustration was engraved by Wolff in the last quarter of the 18th century with two men in contemporary costume shaking hands under a scroll bearing the legend *Vriendschap* (Friendship).

It is sometimes supposed that many of the English glasses engraved with various emblems relating to the Jacobite cause after 1745 were decorated in Holland, but this seems unlikely in view of the simplicity of the designs which were probably well within the capacity of British engravers at Newcastle or Edinburgh.

647 This strangely shaped bottle is one of the few remaining pieces of early glass from the region. German, *c.* 1430.

648 Beaker with a high internal 'kick', a common feature of the type. German, *c.* 1470.

649 Beaker of globular form with applied prunts, German, *c.* 1500.

GERMANY AND BOHEMIA

Douglas Ash

Despite the destruction by Hermann of the Roman army under Quintilius Varus in the Teutoburger Wald in the early 1st century, there was enough Roman influence East of the Rhine and on the Mosel to ensure the survival of glassmaking traditions. For many centuries these modified traditions found expression in a greenish or brownish material called *Waldglas* (forest-glass), in which the soda used as an alkaline flux in the Mediterranean region was replaced by potash obtained from the ashes of burnt wood.

647 Little remains from before the 15th century, and the majority of surviving German objects of this century and later consist, as elsewhere, of drinking vessels, often in the form of various kinds of

648 beaker. The short, wide beaker illustrated displays the tall internal 'kick' rising from the base which was a common feature of the type,

649 while the second beaker of more globular form is embellished with applied glass blobs known as prunts. A later variant of cylindrical shape was so covered with prunts that it was known as a cabbage-stalk (*Krautstrunk*).

These excrescences commonly occurred also on a larger cylindrical beaker which was so tall in relation to its diameter that it was called a *Stangenglas*, or pole-glass. Prunts were also a normal detail on the *Roemer* of the 17th century. But beakers of more orthodox proportions were more numerous and, in the 16th century, were often made of clear glass, which began to be produced on an increasing scale under the stimulus of imported Venetian *cristallo*. The

651 example illustrated is decorated with horizontal trails; beakers with this form of decoration, which might be separate or in a continuous spiral, form a sub-species known as *Passglas*.

German beakers and other vessels sometimes embodied the

652 threads of milk-glass known in Venice as *lattimo*, and in many instances were probably made by Venetian escapees who had chosen the shortest route into the Habsburg Empire over the Brenner Pass.

It is generally considered that these roving Italian glass-workers were largely responsible for the establishment of industries at Villach and Vienna in the second half of the 15th century, at Halle, Innsbrück and Nuremberg in the first half of the century following, and later in Upper Bavaria, Silesia and Bohemia. But it was not long before the decorative enamelling of glassware in colour, introduced from the same source, took on a characteristically German flavour,

and continued in general esteem throughout the 17th century and after.

Many types of vessel were subjected to the process, but one of the most popular was the *Humpen*, possibly because its uncompli- 657 cated cylindrical shape provided a large and convenient surface for the application of the enamel. It had been known in the 16th century as a *Willkomm*, or welcome-glass, from which we may probably assume that it was customarily offered to a guest on his arrival. The ornament occurred in many forms including personal armorials, religious subjects, imperial eagles, portraits of notables and scenes from daily life, frequently of an occupational character. The last may be seen on the uncovered vessel illustrated, dating from the 657 mid-17th century.

The fact that a surviving *Humpen* is not equipped with a cover does not, of course, mean that it never had one. The presence of the expensive enamelled decoration indicates a high degree of esteem on the part of an owner, and the importance of such a vessel's aspect was greatly increased by a cover—a consideration which applied to a far less extent to the earlier kind of beaker with sides expanding upward. The latter type was, however, sometimes enamelled with coats-of-arms, as ornament of this kind did not 653 require a great deal of space.

Although the colours in this enamelling were strong and bright and the execution of a vigorous nature, a general absence of subtle refinement and the occasional presence of somewhat lewd inscriptions has led some critics to classify it all as 'peasant art'. However, it seems unlikely either that the work was executed by peasants or that its acquisition was within the financial resources of persons far down the social scale, while the draughtsmanship was often of such competence as to make it inappropriate to dismiss this dynamic ornament so lightly.

In the middle of the 17th century, a Hamburg painter named Johann Schaper (1621-70), working in Nuremberg and Regens- 654 burg, began to apply to the decoration of glass vessels a method which had already been used to a minor extent in connection with windows. He was what is known as a *Hausmaler*, that is, an artist who worked independently in his own home embellishing plain objects which he bought from the makers. He worked chiefly in *Schwarzlot*, or black enamel, sometimes with a little red and gold,

647

648

649

650 Jug in Lithyalin glass, Bohemian, *c*. 1835.

651 Clear glass beaker, or *Passglas*, decorated with horizontal trails. German, 16th century.

652 German beaker with the milk-glass threads known in Venice as *lattimo*, 16th century.

653 This type of beaker, with sides expanding upwards, was frequently enamelled with coats-of-arms. German, 1623.

654 Beaker on three ball feet, enamelled in black by the *Hausmaler* Johann Schaper, *c*. 1660.

655 Square bottle, enamelled with figures of Bacchanalian infants, *c*. 1680, probably by Benckertt in Frankfurt-am-Main.

656 Covered goblet enamelled in black, probably by Abraham Helmhach, 1690.

650

651

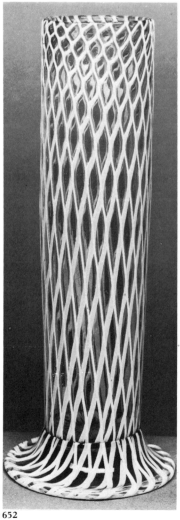

652

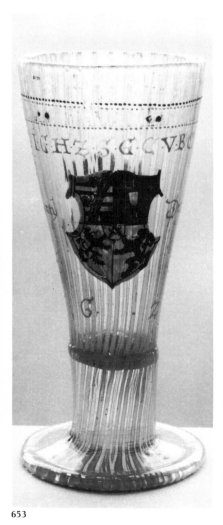

653

654

655

656

657 Enamelled *Humpen* showing the Emperor and Electors of the Holy Roman Empire, with scenes of paper making below. German, 1656.

658 Vase cut and engraved on the wheel, with yellow and pink stains and silvering. Bohemian, c. 1830-40.

657

658

and although the results lacked the coarse chromatic brilliance of the earlier style, they displayed undoubted sensitivity and a feeling for atmospheric perspective which was sometimes expressed in 654 landscapes. The cylindrical beaker on three ball feet is a specimen of his work. Beakers of this form were typical productions of Nuremberg, though the shape and the ball feet also occurred with contemporary German and Scandinavian silver tankards.

Other practitioners, known and unknown, soon followed 656 Schaper's example. The covered goblet, with the main part of the stem in the form of an inverted baluster, was probably painted by 655 Abraham Helmhack in 1690, while the square bottle with canted corners and figures of Bacchanalian infants is thought to have been painted by an artist named Benckertt in Frankfurt-am-Main in about 1680. Whatever the identity of the enameller, the modelling of the figures is masterly.

Opaque white glass looking like porcelain had been made in Venice in the 17th century and in Germany before 1700, after which its popularity increased. The earlier enamellers of this material, in the form of cups, saucers, tankards, cans, vases and so forth, were probably artists who also decorated ceramics. The large can or mug 659 illustrated, which has the appearance of china, is painted with Oriental figures above Rococo scrollwork, the latter detail suggesting that it dates from shortly after the middle of the 18th century.

Such objects might be enamelled in black, colour, or a combination of both and, together with clear-glass vessels decorated by the same method, remained fashionable well into the 19th century. The 668 beaker with the strongly modelled landscape was painted by Anton Kothgasser of Vienna in about 1815, while the other, bearing an 661 oval medallion with a contemporary adaptation of a Classical composition, was decorated a few years earlier in Dresden.

In the Roman period, glass had been engraved and cut by lapidaries with small, abrasive wheels used otherwise for the cutting of gems, but a long gap of uncertain duration in the application of the process was first closed in a significant manner by Caspar Lehmann who, from 1588, at about the age of 18, occupied

the post of official cutter of gems at the court of Kaiser Rudolf II in Prague.

It was inevitable that the technique should eventually have been extended to glass, and the windowpane, engraved by Lehmann in 662 the early years of the 17th century, representing the legend of Perseus and Andromeda, is remarkable for the three-dimensional effect achieved simply by grinding incisions and depressions in the surface.

A younger successor to the above artist was Georg Schwanhardt, who worked in Prague until Lehmann's death in 1622 and then returned to Nuremberg, where he had been born, to found an important school of glass-engravers. Heinrich, one of his sons, is believed to have discovered the art of etching glass with hydrofluoric acid, but this dangerous technique remained virtually unpractised until the 19th century.

Georg Schwanhardt, his family, and other Nuremberg artists who followed in his footsteps, often used diamond-point in addition to the wheel, a method frequently employed in the decoration of glass goblets.

German glass-engravers attained the highest point of technical and artistic accomplishment in the late 17th and early 18th centuries, a development which was facilitated by a growing improvement in the material on which they worked, though there were still occasional defects in its chemical composition. Important drinking glasses and related vessels received most of their attention in various parts of the Habsburg Empire, and were converted from objects of use to objects of art as well. The covered beaker, which 664 has the proportions of an English silver Magdalen cup of the 16th century, was superbly engraved with an elaborate figure composition at Berlin in about 1695, while the more shapely stemmed goblet 660 was also decorated in North Germany at about the same time. The flask or decanter, which bears a medallion containing ornament of an Oriental character surrounded by what is known as *Laub-und-Bandelwerk* (foliage-and-strapwork) was engraved in Nuremberg 663 in 1719.

659 Can of white glass enamelled with Oriental figures and Rococo scrollwork, *c.* 1760.

660 Covered goblet engraved with a mythological scene. North Germany, *c.* 1695.

661 Enamelled beaker painted by Gottlob Samuel Mohn of Dresden, *c.* 1812.

662 Windowpane engraved by Casper Lehmann with the legend of Perseus and Andromeda, *c.* 1605.

663 Engraved flask with a central medallion bearing an Oriental scene, surrounded by foliage and strapwork. Nuremberg, 1719.

659

660

661

662

663

664 Covered beaker engraved in Berlin with an exquisite figure composition, *c.* 1695.

665 Ruby-glass goblet, facet-cut. Potsdam, *c.* 1725.

666 Bohemian vase, case and engraved through red, *c.* 1730.

667 Covered goblet, engraved through ruby flashing. Bohemian, *c.* 1850.

668 Enamelled landscape beaker, painted by Anton Kothgasser of Vienna, *c.* 1815.

669 Tumbler decorated in the *Zwischengoldglas* technique. Bohemian, *c.* 1730.

670 Beaker in Lithyalin glass, an opaque marbled glass patented under this name by Friedrich Egerman. Bohemian, *c.* 1840.

664

665

666

667

668

669

670

Meanwhile, in about 1679, the celebrated chemist Johann Kunckel had discovered how to make glass of a ruby-red colour. It was particularly fashionable in Berlin and nearby Potsdam, where he worked, but was used in all the German-speaking regions, especially in the 18th and 19th centuries.

Facet-cutting, an extension of engraving but involving the use of larger wheels, was also increasing in incidence, and the ruby-glass goblet illustrated, which is Potsdam work of about 1725, has been treated in this manner, though cutting was undoubtedly more effective with colourless glass which offered less impediment to the refraction of light.

In the last quarter of the 18th century glass-engraving, which was more consistent with the Baroque and Rococo styles than with the Neo-classical style then coming strongly into vogue, was beginning to die out in Germany, and was replaced by brilliant cutting, influenced by English work of the same period. This influence persisted into the 19th century.

A rare but important type of glass which began to appear in Bohemia in about 1725 was almost certainly inspired by a technique displayed by certain fragmentary glass vessels found in the catacombs of Rome and dating up to the early 5th century. This is known as *Zwischengoldglas* and consisted, as the name suggests, of gold ornament sandwiched between two layers of glass. Cut and engraved gold leaf was applied to the outer surface of the vessel, which was then enclosed in a glass sleeve through which the ornament was visible but entirely protected.

In the period of comparative prosperity and stability which followed the Napoleonic wars, a reaction gradually began to develop against colourless crystal. The latter was never wholly discarded, especially for functional vessels, but far more use was made of colour, and there was widespread technical research which extended the spectrum. These developments brought about a resurgence of artistic glassmaking in Bohemia, where an extensive range of effects was now available. In addition to the blues, amethyst, yellow and ruby-red already in use, lime-green was derived from uranium, and topaz and amber resulted from mixing oxides of this metal with antimony.

All these colours and white tin-oxide enamel found a new appli-

197

671 Goblet by Verzelini, decorated with diamond-point engraving. The hollow ball knop impressed with vertical gadroons. Dated 1581.

672 *Roemer* with ribbed bowl, stem and foot by George Ravenscroft, *c.* 1680. The lowest of the applied prunts on the stem is impressed with his trade mark, a raven's head.

673 Glass with inverted baluster stem, typical of the plain but well-proportioned glasses of the late 17th century.

666,667 cation in the form of casing or flashing, processes by which glass of a different colour could be laid over another then cut through to the lower surface in formal patterns, giving a sharply contrasting effect. Once introduced, glass of this kind became increasingly elaborate with the passage of time and even greater opulence resulted from the addition of gold. Later examples were often somewhat overwhelming and showed a preoccupation with ornament at the expense of shape.

A glasshouse in southern Bohemia owned by Graf von Buquoy was responsible for the introduction of a metal which was either a rich sealing-wax red or a dense, opaque black; these fabrics were called Hyalith. At another factory at Blottendorf, Friedrich Egermann, a distinguished maker of coloured glass, patented a virtually opaque marbled glass under the name of Lithyalin, though it was **650,6** probably inspired at some distance by Venetian *calcedonio*.

Much Bohemian and German glass of this phase was lumpy and inelegant, despite the vitality of ornament and colour, but in the latter part of the 19th century a rather pedantic sobriety supervened, with shapes and decoration deriving from earlier periods. This in turn gave way to the naturalistic style inaugurated by the French designer Emile Gallé, a tribute to its youthful freshness being the German name *Jugendstil* which was used to denote it.

BRITAIN
Douglas Ash

In Britain, as in many other parts of Europe, glassmaking traditions were established under the Roman Empire. Although it is probable that most requirements of the Romans and Romanised Britons were satisfied by imports from the region between the Seine and the Rhine, where a flourishing industry had been founded in the 2nd century, there is no doubt that glassmaking was conducted on a small scale in Britain itself.

After the departure of the legions in the 5th century, native manufacture and traffic with the mainland came to a virtual standstill. But it seems likely that the import trade was resumed about 100 years later, and glassmaking was undoubtedly carried out in north-east and south-west England in the late Anglo-Saxon period.

Evidence, however, remains scanty and of a literally fragmentary kind throughout the Middle Ages and up to the last quarter of the 16th century, by which time, sophisticated glassware was already being imported from Venice and the Netherlands. Native manufacture continued, however, and William Harrison, in his *Description of England* (1586), referred to glasses 'such as are made at home of ferne and burned stone'. We may deduce from this that the material concerned contained potash as an alkaline flux, obtained by burning ferns, bracken, and doubtless wood, and that one of the sources of the silica was calcined flints. In other words, it was a product similar to the French and Burgundian *verre de fougére* and the German *Waldglas,* and appeared in the form of murky looking objects in various tones of green and brown.

The expensive Venetian *cristallo* naturally enjoyed greater prestige and eventually established a criterion. But as its cost placed it beyond the reach of a large, untapped market, and the Republic of Venice was cordially disliked throughout Europe, any attempt at providing a worthy substitute was as welcome in England as it had been elsewhere.

The history of British vessel-glass of high quality accordingly

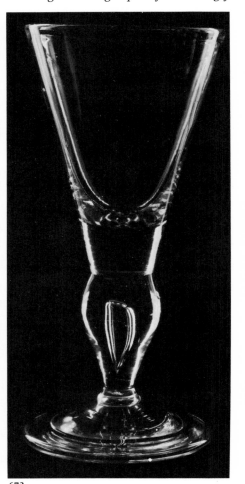

671

672

673

674, 675, 676, 677 Four late 17th-century glasses showing the different features of stems. From left to right: drop knop, ball knop, angular knop and acorn knop.

678 A fine example of another early 18th-century innovation, the cylinder-knopped stem.

679 Glass with a 'Silesian' stem, *c.* 1715. This was introduced after the accession of George I, probably from Lauenstein, and was made in a mould.

680 Two mid-18th-century glasses with airtwist stems, one knopped and the other plain.

674   675   676   677

678   679   680

begins with the arrival in England of the Antwerp glassmaker Jean Carré, who was granted a licence by Queen Elizabeth I in 1567 to make, *inter alia*, all sorts of crystal drinking glasses like those of Venice. He set up a glasshouse in London which was staffed chiefly by expatriate Venetians, and another at Alfold in Sussex where window-glass was made with the aid of workers from Lorraine. The latter side of the business did not survive Carré's death. Among the Venetian craftsmen whom he brought in for the London operations was Jacopo or Giacomo Verzelini (1522-1606).

Carré died in 1572, whereupon Verzelini decided to continue on his own account. In 1575 he was granted a patent by Elizabeth 'for the makyne of drynkynge glasses such as be accustomablie made in the towne of Murano', with the proviso that he should teach the art to the Queen's 'naturall Subjectes'.

Several of his more important glasses are fortunately still in existence, and probably owe their survival to the fact that they were not ordinary domestic drinking vessels made in sets, but individual goblets of monumental aspect, decorated with diamond-point engraving and of special significance to their owners, their heirs and assigns. The example illustrated, which is dated 1581, has a hollow ball knop on the stem impressed with vertical gadroons. No doubt some of his more common productions have survived as well, but are assumed to be either Italian or Netherlandish.

Although, owing to the predilections of the English market, there is a slightly non-Venetian character about some extant specimens of Verzelini's work, they must be broadly considered as Venetian glass made in England. But he must receive credit for founding a tradition which enabled his successors to lay the foundations of a national industry.

He was followed by Sir Jerome Bowes, erstwhile Ambassador to Russia, Sir Edward Zouche, and the retired Admiral Sir Robert Mansell. Mansell started new glasshouses or took over existing ones

681 Decanter by Ravenscroft ornamented with what he described as 'nipt diamond waies'. Late 17th century.

682 Decanter in the shape of a stoppered jug, late 17th century.

683 One of the new features introduced in the 18th century was the annulated, or ringed, knop, as shown in this early 18th-century glass.

684 Glass with a true baluster stem, as used in architecture, as opposed to the earlier inverted baluster. Early 18th century.

685 Two typical flute glasses of the Regency period.

686 Regency decanters cut with strawberry diamonds and prismatic cutting, c. 1830.

681

682

683

684

685

686

all over the country including, and most important, Stourbridge, Newcastle-upon-Tyne and Wemyss in Fifeshire (though the last proved unsuccessful), his monopolistic activities spreading the craft of glassmaking over a wide field.

The Duke of Buckingham entered the industry early in the reign of Charles II and, according to contemporary accounts, eventually produced, among other things, excellent looking-glasses at Vauxhall.

Meanwhile, the Glass Sellers' Company of London, which had received an unratified Charter from Charles I in 1635, was granted a new Charter by his successor in 1664. Correspondence between the Company and one of its suppliers, Allesio Morelli of Venice between 1667 and 1673 is still in existence, and includes English designs for glasses which were sent to Morelli for his guidance. Among these is a drawing of a short, conical flute with narrow bowl, which is clearly inscribed 'for sack', a fact which disproves

the commonly held view that short flutes were dedicated exclusively to strong ale.

Commercial relations between Morelli and the Glass Sellers' Company at last became so unsatisfactory that the latter began to look about for an alternative source of supply. They soon fixed their sights on the retired shipowner George Ravenscroft, an educated man with a taste for experiment in glass technology, and in September 1674 he was appointed official glassmaker to the Company. Late in 1675 he added lead oxide to the other ingredients of his glass, which proved a momentous step, for it led to the birth of English lead crystal, which was perfected by Ravenscroft's successors.

The new metal had different properties from Continental soda glass. As it contained about a third by weight of lead it was heavier and resisted the glassblower's breath. It also took longer to set, but it was very ductile and had a refractive brilliance only slightly less

687 Jacobite glass engraved with a portrait of Prince Charles Edward, and an elaborate knopped airtwist stem, c. 1750.

688 Mid-18th-century glass with an opaque-twist stem, an adaptation of the Venetian *lattimo*.

689 Shouldered decanter with cut decoration, c. 1760. Cut glass began to be produced on a

large scale in the mid-18th century, and after 1777, when a tax was imposed on the enamel used for opaque twists, it became the main form of luxury glass.

690 Rummer engraved c. 1800 in commemoration of the opening of the Sunderland Bridge in 1796.

691 Crystallo-Ceramic paperweight containing a cameo head of the young Queen Victoria, c. 1840.

692 Wheel-engraved water jug showing a cottage scene, dated 1860.

693 Decorative glass fountain including a ship, a a speciality of the fancy glass trade in Victorian times. Made c. 1860.

687

688

689

690

691

692

693

694 Cameo vase by Thomas Webb & Sons, late 19th century. The white overlay is cut away in patterns of chrysanthemums.

695 Water jug and goblets with intaglio cut decoration. Probably Stourbridge, 1850-53.

696 Striped jug of the Nailsea type, c. 1800. The glass made at the Nailsea factory became so popular that it was widely imitated, making it virtually impossible to identify the place of manufacture.

695

694

696

than that of the diamond. This, combined with its softness, made it especially suitable for cutting later. English glass-workers accordingly had to develop a new technique, which resulted in the emergence of a robust national style.

672   A few *Roemers* were produced, such as the one by Ravenscroft himself, but these were exceptional pieces, as were large goblets. Most glasses of the late 17th century were plain but of satisfying proportions, with stems embodying as their main features an in-
673,674,675 verted baluster, a drop knop or truncated cone, a ball knop, an
676,677 angular knop with a rounded triangular profile, or an acorn knop.

    Objects other than drinking glasses also made at this time include bowls, standing dishes, salvers on stems and decanters, the last being either of shaft-and-globe form, with or without a handle, or in the shape of a stoppered jug. The Ravenscroft decanter of the first type, illustrated here, is covered with a net-pattern which
681 Ravenscroft called 'nipt diamond waies'. This pattern, of Roman origin, was used on Venetian beakers, and sometimes occurred on English drinking glasses.

    In the 18th century, the same robustness of treatment was evident for a time, but new stem-features were introduced including the
683,684 annulated or ringed knop, the true baluster as used in architecture,

the cylinder knop, the mushroom knop, and a rarer type called an 678 ovoid knop which was shaped like an elongated egg.

    In about 1714, after the accession of George I, the so-called Silesian stem appeared, having probably been introduced from the 679 Hanoverian glasshouse at Lauenstein. It was made in a mould, originally in the form of a four-sided pedestal, but soon the sides were increased to six and then eight, and finally the stem was reeded and twisted. The type persisted on drinking glasses until about 1730, but lasted longer with glass candlesticks and dessert utensils and was found on stemmed salvers throughout the Georgian period.

    Soon, glasses of lighter construction began to appear, as did glasses with plain, cylindrical stems. These were made in two pieces, the shank being drawn from the base of the bowl and welded to the foot.

    Just before 1730 there was an important innovation in glass-making: the air-twist stem, an English invention in which spiralling 680 threads of air, varying in number, ran down to the bottom of the stem, giving such a glass a brilliant and lively appearance. Many had plain surfaces but others were knopped – the knop was intro- 687 duced in about 1740. These glasses continued in production for

697 Pair of vases in 'Queen's Burmese' ware by Thomas Webb & Sons, *c.* 1807.

697

another two decades. Very occasionally, they were of double-series type, that is, with one set of twists spiralling round another in the centre.

In 1745 two events occurred which were to have important effects on glass. The first was the passing of the Glass Excise Act, which discouraged the use of the folded foot, as this involved the use of extra glass and added to the tax. The other was the rebellion in favour of Prince Charles Edward Stuart. The second event stimulated the engraving of glasses with portraits of the Prince and **687** various arcane Jacobite symbols, one of the most popular being a rose with one or two buds, sometimes springing from the same stem as an oak or a thistle. As these glasses have always been favoured by collectors, there are a great many modern forgeries, with fairly recent engraving applied to genuine 18th-century glasses.

At about the same time, we note the first appearance of opaque-twist stems and the beginning of a large-scale production of cut **688** glass. The opaque-twists, mostly in double-series form, consisted of spiralling threads of tin-oxide enamel, thus constituting an adaptation of Venetian *lattimo,* though colour was sometimes introduced later. These lasted only until about 1780, because an Act of 1777 doubled the existing impost and imposed a tax on the enamel

which was the raw material for the twists. Thereafter, cut glass had the luxury end of the trade entirely to itself.

Cutting was first confined to the stems, which were sometimes knopped, and consisted chiefly of shallow diamond or hexagonal facets, but might later be extended to the bowls. Other contemporary objects such as jugs, bowls and decanters were often cut as well, **689** mostly in a restrained manner, and there was a marked increase in the manufacture of cut-glass chandeliers, or lustres, as they were originally called.

A new type of drinking vessel appeared in the late 18th century in the form of the Neo-classical rummer, which owed its stylistic **690** inspiration to the art movement of which the architect Robert Adam was the main exponent. The name had nothing to do with rum, but was a corruption of the German word *Roemer* which we have encountered earlier. These glasses were of various sizes, though the most popular held something under half a pint. The stem was rudimentary and the ovoid bowl dominated the design, which derived with some fidelity from originals discovered in the excavation of the Roman cities of Herculaneum and Pompeii. These early rummers looked, in fact, like gigantic glass egg-cups, and their bowls were frequently embellished with fluting. Sometimes

698 Nailsea-type bottle with enamel flecks and applied vertical ribs, dated 1827.

699 Heavy cut crystal, of which this decanter made *c.* 1850 is an example, began to be manufactured in large quantities in the mid-19th century.

700 Waterford decanter showing arch-and-rectangle design, *c.* 1800.

701 Decanter with double neck-rings made by the Cork Glass Company, *c.* 1790.

698

699

700

701

the flutes were cut but moulding was more common.

Other bowls which became fashionable in about 1800 included one shaped like a bucket, which was especially popular in the Regency period. These bowls were often cut with vertical fluting, which had begun to supersede diamond and hexagonal facets three decades earlier, while others might be decorated with wheel-engraving. This type of adornment had been used increasingly from the 1730s, and often took the form of small flowers and foliage, fruiting vines, and hops and barley, indicating that the glass concerned was intended primarily for strong ale or beer. Other engraving showed such subjects as popular heroes—Lord Nelson was a favourite, especially after the battle of Trafalgar in 1805—ships including privateers, political themes, Masonic emblems and important local events. The rummer illustrated was engraved in celebration of the opening of Sunderland Bridge in 1796, doubtless several years after the event.

All this was pleasing enough, but the quality of the engraving never approached the work of the German and Dutch engravers of the 17th and 18th centuries.

During the Regency, a new taste for massiveness, advocated by such professional designers as Charles Heathcote Tatham, gave rise to more ponderous styles in several of the applied arts. But it was not a period which lacked its elegances, and certain flute glasses of the early 19th century, in lustrous English lead-crystal, did not compare unfavourably with what had gone before. Though of more modest capacity than the towering Netherlandish flutes of the 17th century, they were superbly suited for the sparkling champagne for which they were chiefly used.

The so-called Bristol Blue glass, which had in fact been produced in every important glassmaking centre in the country, also became more widely used at this time, especially after the end of the Napoleonic Wars. It was, however, never more than a very small proportion of the national glass production and sales.

During the same period, the cut decoration of glass became commoner and more abundant than ever before, a process which was facilitated by the use of steam power to drive the machinery. In the second half of the 18th century, cutting had been subordinated to form, and the designs employed, consisting of shallow facets and fluting, did not impair the transparency of the metal. After 1800, however, new designs came into vogue which often presented large numbers of small reflecting surfaces which sometimes gave the glass an unquiet, bristling appearance.

The most popular of these designs was relief diamonds, comprising small, sharp pyramids formed by making deep opposed incisions with a triangular-edged cutting wheel. This was followed by cross-

cut diamonds which were produced by making two incisions at right-angles across the very apex of each pyramid. As this was difficult and hazardous, this design is found less often.

Three other patterns involved the embellishment of larger, flat-topped diamonds created by making the cuts further apart so that a plain zone was left between them. In the Georgian period this lozenge-shaped zone was never left unadorned. Strawberry diamonds were produced by making numerous incisions at right-angles across the plateau and forming a field of smaller diamonds, often 16 in number. In a simpler variant, known as chequered diamonds, the top was divided into four by the same method. The hobnail pattern, which appeared in about 1820, existed in two main versions. In the less complicated form, the flat-topped diamond had only two diagonal incisions running into the corners. In the other, two further incisions were made at right-angles to the sides, thus producing an eight-pointed star in intaglio. The name of this design is often misapplied to some of those already mentioned.

Large objects such as jugs and decanters often bore several different kinds of cutting, which were separated from each other by continuous channels of V-section, making between them sharp ridges which constituted prisms. These prisms were later multiplied until they formed a design in their own right which was known as prismatic cutting. On the shoulders of decanters it looked somewhat like steps, which has caused this technique sometimes to be mis-named 'step-cutting'. Glass cut with these and further patterns remained in demand up to the middle of the 19th century.

Meanwhile, in 1788, a bottle and crown-glass factory had been opened at Nailsea Heath, about eight miles from Bristol, by a bottle-manufacturer named John Lucas. Four or five years later he met an expert on vitreous enamel named Edward Homer, and from this contact emerged the idea of making all kinds of glassware, decorated with enamel, from bottle-glass, which was taxed at a lower rate than the clear glass of better quality generally used for normal domestic utensils in polite surroundings.

Manufacture commenced in 1793 and met with such immediate success that glassmakers in Stourbridge, Warrington, Newcastle-upon-Tyne, Sunderland, Bristol and other places at once began to make similar products. As it is generally impossible to identify the place of manufacture, the generic term 'Nailsea' is applied to it all. The actual Nailsea factory continued in operation until the last quarter of the 19th century, and most surviving specimens are Victorian. Dating is usually a matter of guesswork. Early Nailsea objects were of a greenish-brown metal, splashed and spotted with white or coloured enamel, but similar treatment has been noted on occasional dated examples made long after 1800. Some, such as jugs

690

685

689

702 Cut-glass bowl with high foot, probably Irish, late 18th century.

and flasks, were actually or ostensibly functional, but others, like tobacco-pipes, walking-sticks, swords, bellows and decorated rolling-pins were mostly of an ornamental nature.

696 Many were trifling and crude, but a high aesthetic standard was sometimes attained, as in the striped jug illustrated. The enamel-
698 flecked bottle with applied vertical ribs impressed with notches is also undoubtedly attractive and leans heavily on ancient traditions, though it seems improbable that it would have been used in place of a crystal decanter, since the dark tone, combined with the enamel decoration, would have made it almost impossible to see the contents.

In 1819, Apsley Pellatt (1791-1863), a distinguished London glassmaker, took out a 14-year patent for a process which involved the enclosing of ceramic bas-relief plaques or cameos within clear glass. The general method was communicated to him by a Frenchman, but Pellatt devised his own means of preventing the distortion of the cameos. This distortion had been caused initially by the differing rates of contraction of the ceramic substance and its glass covering while cooling, and in earlier Bohemian counterparts, had often resulted in defects. Pellatt described his productions as
691 'Crystallo-Ceramie' or 'Cameo Incrustation', and their subjects included cupids, Classical heads and figures, and portraits of celebrities. They appeared in many sizes and as parts of many objects from decanters to earrings, and were sometimes cut in broad facets through a coloured casing which enhanced the appeal of the fine crystal and the enclosed cameo.

Crystallo-Ceramie began to suffer a decline in popularity in about 1830, but in common with the whole range of British glass production, took on a new lease of life after 1845, when the Glass Excise Acts, which had placed increasing burdens upon the industry from 1745, were at last repealed.

699 Heavy cut crystal began to be manufactured more extensively, and vast quantities were displayed–together with coloured and other glass showing foreign influences–at the Great Exhibition of 1851, where one of the most striking exhibits was a cut-crystal fountain 27 feet (8·2 metres) high, weighing four tons. Decorative fountains of more modest proportions were made for home decora-
693 tion, the one illustrated including a ship of doubtful relevancy. Glass ships were themselves a speciality of the fancy trade at the same period, so that the irrational nature of the juxtaposition doubtless attracted no criticism.

Many types of decorative glass fabrics were current at this time, including Amberina, Opaline, Cranberry and Satin glass, while a Bohemian form of treatment involving the painting of figures of children in white enamel on a blue, green, ruby or other coloured background was quickly copied in Britain and the United States. For some unknown reason, it has come to be known as 'Mary Gregory' glass, after an American lady who practised the technique.

Of undoubted American origin was a greenish-yellow metal which its inventor called 'Burmese' in 1855. Examples were sent as a present to Queen Victoria, who at once ordered a tea service and vases decorated with enamel flowers and gold. Soon after this, it began to be manufactured under licence in Britain under the name of 'Queen's Burmese' but, owing to its high cost, it never became
697 a common article of commerce. The vases illustrated, which display some contemporary French influence, were made in England at about the time of Queen Victoria's jubilee.

In 1842 the Registration Mark was introduced to discourage the copying of designs; this is seen with some frequency on the bases of objects made by press-moulding, an American process which came into use in Britain in the 1830s. The mark was shaped like a lozenge surmounted by a circle, and the latter contained a Roman numeral which related to the class of manufacture: I for metal, II for wood, III for glass, and IV for pottery. The lozenge was divided into five compartments, the central one containing an abbreviated form of 'Registered'.

From 1842 to 1867, the compartment below the circle enclosed a letter which indicated the year, a figure in the right-hand corner of the lozenge the day, and a letter in the left-hand corner the month. A figure at the base identified the manufacturer, indicated

702

by the abbreviation 'Mfr' in the examples shown.

The disposition of letters and figures in the lozenge then underwent a change which remained in force from 1868 to 1883. The figure below the circle containing the class-mark gave the day, the letter at the base the month, the letter in the right-hand corner the year, and a figure in the left-hand corner indicated the manufacturer. Although some of the year-letters occur in both cycles, they cannot be confused, as they occupy different positions in the lozenge. The following tables give the letters for the years and months.

YEARS

1842	X	1855	E
1843	H	1856	L
1844	C	1857	K
1845	A	1858	B
1846	I	1859	M
1847	F	1860	Z
1848	U	1861	R
1849	S	1862	O
1850	V	1863	G
1851	P	1864	N
1852	D	1865	W
1853	Y	1866	Q
1854	J	1867	T
1868	X	1876	V
1869	H	1877	P
1870	C	1878	D
1871	A	1879	Y
1872	I	1880	J
1873	F	1881	E
1874	U	1882	L
1875	S	1883	K

MONTHS

January	C	July	I
February	G	August	R
March	W	September	D
April	H	October	B
May	E	November	K
June	M	December	A

Ireland

Although the British Glass Excise Act of 1745 imposed no taxes on Irish glass, it specified that only British glass could be imported, and the export of any glass whatsoever was banned.

Profiting by the immunity from taxation, Benjamin Edwards of Bristol started a small glasshouse at Drunrea in 1771. Five years later, he transferred his operations to Belfast, where, with the aid of an English cutter, he supplied local markets. In 1780, the ban on export was lifted, and Edwards began to manufacture on a larger scale and then to advertise.

His only identifiable productions are decanters which, being mould-blown, bore underneath them the moulded legend 'B Edwards Belfast'. They were generally similar to the contemporary British tapering decanter and had two neck-rings of triangular section which were also popular in Bristol. The glasshouse ceased operations in the second quarter of the 19th century.

A short-lived glasshouse existed near Waterford in the first half of the 18th century, but its productions are unrecognisable. In 1783, two Irish promotors named William and George Penrose, realising the advantages conferred by immunity from taxation and the raising of the export ban, established a glasshouse in the city itself. They induced a Stourbridge glassmaker named John Hill to pioneer the venture, and Hill took with him 'the best set of workmen he could get in the county of Worcester'.

Unusual trouble was taken to ensure that the glass was pure and crystalline, and the myth started by a late 19th-century writer that Waterford glass was always blue is insulting to this very worthy Anglo-Irish venture. Most of its productions cannot be distinguished from glassware made in England and Scotland, but some mould-blown jugs and decanters were marked underneath 'Penrose Waterford'—a legend which continued in use long after the Penrose brothers disposed of their interest in 1799. Free-blown objects were not marked at all.

The decanters were of the Prussian shape, that is, their bodies were in the form of a cask, below a wide, upward-tapering neck, embellished with three triple neck-rings, and surmounted by a mushroom-stopper with a small ball knop in the shank.

Similar decanters were made in Britain and in Cork, so that a plain, unmarked specimen cannot be attributed to any particular glasshouse. Assistance is sometimes provided, however, by a cut pattern known as the arch-and-rectangle design, which seems to **700** have been confined to Waterford. This consisted of round-headed arches filled with fine diamonds, springing from rectangles embellished in the same manner.

Some of the best productions of Waterford were large standing bowls, one type being shaped like a boat, the other being circular and with a turned-over edge. The cut decoration was never excessive and some of these are very handsome objects indeed.

In Cork, a glasshouse operated from 1783 to 1818, and was staffed for many years by Englishmen. This factory took far less trouble than Waterford over the colour of its glass, which often displayed a bluish tint, due to the use of impure lead oxide. It was called the Cork Glass Company and some of its jugs and decanters **701** were marked underneath with this name. Cut or engraved decoration tended to be slight, the most typical design being the vesica pattern, consisting of a circuit of linked horizontal ovals, pointed at the ends. Another glasshouse, the Waterloo Company, Cork, lasted from 1815 to 1836, while a less important factory at Dublin was started by Charles Mulvaney in 1785. All the survivors, however, were ruined by the extension of the Excise Act to Ireland in 1825, and after a gallant struggle, Waterford too closed down in 1851.

FRANCE AND SPAIN
Douglas Ash

It seems anomalous that France, to which the rest of Europe owes so much in the cultural and artistic fields, should have so little to show for itself in the way of noteworthy glass, at least until the second quarter of the 19th century. In the Middle Ages and later, the Roman tradition persisted in the making of vessels in the common green glass, analogous to German *Waldglas* (forest-glass). This is known as *verre de fougère* because the alkaline flux used in its manufacture was potash obtained by burning ferns or bracken. But the later periods, when the production of sophisticated glass vessels was burgeoning in Germany, the Netherlands and England, have little to offer.

It is known that glassmaking was established in various French centres in the 16th century by immigrant Italian craftsmen from **705** Venice and Altare. The variegated vase illustrated is an example of **706** their work. Other artefacts which have survived from this time and later are also of a Venetian character, but with glasses of this kind **703** one can seldom be quite certain that they were made in France and not imported. The beaker with enamelled figures in the costume of about 1560 is, however, more likely to be of French origin.

To the 16th century also belongs the foundation of an industry at Nevers on the Loire, which was of sufficient local fame for a visitor in 1708 to call it 'little Murano'. But this description was excessively flattering, for its main production consisted, not of vessels, but of small glass figurines which although sometimes having a simple charm, were of a comparatively trifling nature.

In attempting the frustrating task of studying French glass of the historic periods, the student or amateur is constantly brought to a standstill by the fact that so much was imported from England, Germany and the Netherlands. Furthermore, a glasshouse estab- lished at Petit Quevilly in 1784, with a later branch at Rouen, had the stated intention of making 'clear crystal wares of the style and quality of England', so that any vessels from these sources would be mostly quite impossible to distinguish from contemporary English work. The same considerations apply to the celebrated glasshouse established in 1765 at Baccarat. Again, its productions were in the English style.

Certain cut-glass decanters of the second half of the 18th century have found their way from France to England. They are English in style, and if made of lead-glass, as opposed to the noticeably lighter soda-glass popular on the European mainland, are very possibly of English origin. Those in soda-glass are more likely to be French, especially if they show traces of gilt decoration. They are sometimes very poorly finished, with bubbles in the metal cut through with facets or flutes, leaving small but unsightly craters in the surface.

It will be seen from the foregoing that French glass of the latter part of the 18th century was almost entirely imitative, a situation which is understandable enough when we recall that the Revolution broke out in 1789 and was followed by almost continuous warfare until after the battle of Waterloo in 1815. But various movements were in train which eventually produced artistic ferments, enabling the French native genius to assert itself on an increasing scale from the second quarter of the 19th century. Glassmaking began to be actively encouraged in the Directoire, Consulate and Empire periods, and a fashionable glass establishment in Paris called A l'Escalier de Cristal achieved an international reputation as a result of being visited by allied magnates during the short peace of 1814 before Napoleon's escape from Elba.

Although the quality of workmanship showed a marked distinc-

703 Beaker with enamelled figures, *c.* 1650. This is more likely to have been produced in France than the wine glass (plate 706).

704 Vase made in the Syrian style by Emile Gallé.

705 Variegated vase made by immigrant Venetian craftsmen in France, *c.* 1560.

706 Wine glass, possibly made in France, 17th century.

703

704

705

706

707 Paperweight with 'mushroom' design and star-cut base. Baccarat, mid-19th century.

708 *Millefiori* paperweight, Baccarat, 1846.

709 Vase by Emile Gallé, who inspired a new artistic movement in glassmaking in France. Late 19th century.

710 Baccarat vase engraved in the Japanese style, late 19th century.

711 Andalusian vase, 16th century, with the rather excessive ornamentation typical of the region.

707

708

709

710

711

tion, styles in general still remained unoriginal, but an important manufacturer named D'Artigues was already experimenting with coloured opaline glass, and popularised a new technique which involved the embodying of ceramic cameos within the substance of various glass objects. It is not quite certain whether this technique was invented in France or Bohemia, where it had been practised rather unsatisfactorily before 1800. But the fact that the celebrated British glassmaker Apsley Pellatt, who took out a patent for the process in 1819, admitted that it had been communicated to him by 'a French gentleman', may well be significant, and Boudon de Saint-Amans had already been granted a patent in France in 1818.

These ceramic cameos and medallions were sometimes enclosed in paperweights as an alternative to the more popular multicoloured *millefiori*. The main factories where these paperweights were produced were at Baccarat near Lunéville, which, as already mentioned, had been founded in 1765, at Saint-Louis, which commenced operations two years later, and at Clichy, production in these and other centres showing a marked expansion after 1845.

Many of the Baccarat examples bear the initial B and a date, 1848 being, for some reason, one of the most frequently encountered. Certain rare specimens are encased in glass of contrasting colour, which is cut through to the underlying clear metal to reveal the *millefiori* or other type of enclosed ornament. These are especially attractive since they provide two different kinds of pleasure for the eye of the observer. Sometimes, the composite floral motif expands upwards in the form of a mushroom, but the normal **707** *millefiori*, consisting of crowded flower-heads, evidently exerted a **708, 7** wider and more durable appeal.

The paperweights produced by the Cristallerie de Saint-Louis are sometimes of a less brightly coloured appearance, but those in which the main motif is some kind of bouquet, or in which *millefiori* decoration is ancillary to boldly represented fruits, are often of extremely high quality and correspondingly attractive.

An agreeable Saint-Louis mannerism was to base the motif on a cabled ring, somewhat reminiscent of an heraldic torse. The initials **713** SL are sometimes found among the decoration.

712 French *millefiori* paperweight, Baccarat, 1853.

713 Faceted 'bouquet' paperweight, Saint-Louis, mid-19th century.

714 Two-handled Andalusian vase, 17th century.

715 Andalusian vase with winged handles, 17th century.

716 Catalonian vase with characteristic ornament, 18th century.

712

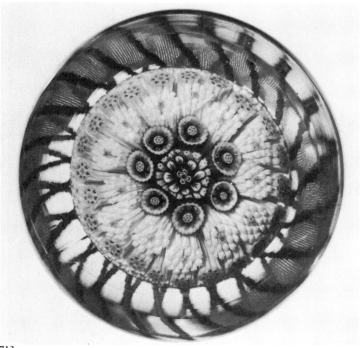

713

714   715

716

At Clichy, brightness of effect was achieved by enclosing the ornamental detail, whether it was the characteristic rose motif or ordinary *millefiori*, within glass of exceptional clarity; but although Clichy paperweights attain occasional excellence, the standard of execution was often somewhat lower than that of Baccarat or Saint-Louis. Apart from other more subtle factors, within the grasp of those who have made a special study of the subject, the presence of the initial C is generally accepted as evidence of a Clichy origin.

Although French and other paperweights of the 19th century occupy a fascinating and important field of connoisseurship, their beauty is wholly internal, and they cannot be said to display either artistic freedom or any great distinction of form, which is usually that of a bun-shaped glass blob. Vessel-glass of many kinds was, however, extensively manufactured; but whether it was coloured, cased, or in clear crystal and decorated by cutting or engraving, it partook of the general characteristics displayed by the fashionable types of glassware in north-western Europe as a whole. As these characteristics were largely dictated by Germany and Britain, the imitative phase of French glassmaking may be considered as persisting into the second half of the 19th century. But great changes were at hand which were to make France pre-eminent in Europe.

Emile Gallé of Nancy (1846-1904) and Eugène Rousseau (1827-91) began to inspire a new decorative artistic movement in glassmaking. This derived certain elements from the arts of Japan and China and abandoned symmetry and mechanical perfection as primary *desiderata*, but made use of objects of a satisfying if unfamiliar shape. By a complicated technique involving tonal gradations in coloured glass of varying degrees of opacity, the deliberate and controlled use of air-bubbles and *craquelures*, and treatment of the surface by wheel-engraving and etching with hydrofluoric acid, Gallé achieved naturalistic floral and foliate ornament distinguished by a curious feeling of poetic mystery. This had never been seen in Europe before, and conferred upon his vases a strange quality which owed nothing to the influence of German or British prototypes.

In addition to coloured glass, a normal crystalline fabric was also

704,709

709

717 Covered jar made at the 18th-century glasshouse of La Granja de San Ildefonso, *c.* 1770.

718 Catalonian *porrón* in clear glass, *c.* 1800.

717

718

extensively employed as a field for decoration, and was sometimes embellished with highly skilled engraving with an Eastern flavour, somewhat reminiscent of ancient work on rock crystal and Chinese glass-carving of the previous century.

This was the great revolutionary age of French artistic glass-making. Apart from Gallé and Rousseau, an associate of the latter named Léveillé, together with other craftsmen, carried the movement forward until it conquered the Western world. It was from such beginnings that Art Nouveau emerged as a derivative at the end of the century (see p. 295), worthy at first, but displaying an increasing decadence when subjected later to the processes of mass-production.

Spain

It is probable that glassmaking in Spain, having been introduced under the Roman Empire, continued after the Empire disintegrated. But most surviving specimens are lacking in distinction, and it is frequently impossible to determine whether surviving specimens are native or brought in from abroad. This is especially true of 16th-century glass made in Catalonia and Castile, where Venetian influence was strong. But in the Southern province of Andalusia a distinct national style developed, though it is seldom possible to date any example with accuracy in the absence of a known history and provenance, because forms remained stylised over a very long period.

The glass-workers of this region were much addicted to extraneous hyaloplastic ornament, that is, ornament created by manipulation rather than blowing. This had a strong element of fantasy which sometimes reduced the practicability of the glass, even though the results may be attractive in a slightly barbaric fashion.

Most of this glass was of a greenish or amber tint, but later vessels made in Catalonia, which had thrown off much of the Venetian influence of earlier periods, were often in a relatively colourless metal and in characteristic local forms, though threads of milk-glass, deriving from the *lattimo* of Venice, were sometimes present even in this.

An example is furnished by the *porrón*, dating from about 1800, shown in the illustration. This vessel was designed to be passed round among the company, a jet of wine squirting out of the long, tapering spout from the elevated *porrón* into the drinker's mouth without coming into contact with it. This strange utensil is still extremely popular in Spain, but later examples have the neck bent backward to prevent the contents pouring out of it over the user's head.

Other Catalonian vessels were the *almorrata*, a long-necked sprinkler for rose-water, perhaps of Islamic origin, and the *cantaro*, or water pitcher.

Even in the most famous of all 18th-century Spanish glasshouses, that of La Granja de San Ildefonso in the province of Segovia, which was founded in 1728, the fact that it was staffed by foreign workers prevented any markedly Spanish characteristics from emerging. Some of its productions were pleasing but are hardly distinguishable from similar objects made in other parts of Europe in the second half of the 18th century.

Certain small, stemmed dessert glasses dating from the same period often had a touch of the old fantasy in the florid treatment of the handles, and this is sometimes considered as typically Spanish. It was, however, undoubtedly of Venetian origin, so that its use in 18th-century Spain was a mere stylistic anachronism.

AMERICA

Douglas Ash

The earliest glasshouse in North America of which we have any knowledge was a small venture which commenced operations at Jamestown, Virginia, in 1608, to make bottles for the settlers and beads for trade with the native population. Judging by the long time which elapsed before anything in the way of colourless flint glass appeared elsewhere in America (not until the 18th century), the Jamestown fabric was almost certainly akin to *verre de fougère* or *Waldglas*. Although drinking vessels and other domestic glass were probably produced on a small scale in addition to bottles and beads, there are no facts available, and the last reference to the glasshouse occurred in 1625. But the mere fact that it existed at all so early in the life of the colonies, when times were difficult and dangerous and the settlers were fighting for survival, provides evidence that there was a demand for glass at the time. Glassmaking was destined to be pursued further when circumstances were more favourable.

It is known that there was some glassmaking activity in the 17th century in Pennsylvania, Massachusetts and New Amsterdam (later New York), but we have to wait until 1739 for the establishment of a manufactory of any real significance. In that year, a German or Dutchman named Caspar Wistar (1695-1752), who had arrived in America in 1717, opened a factory at a place in Salem County, New Jersey, which came to be known as Wistarberg, and established a thriving business which was continued somewhat inefficiently after his death by his son Richard until 1780.

The Wistars were difficult men to get on with, and some of their European craftsmen found certain of their characteristics, which included, apparently, a disinclination to pay wages, so insufferable that they left and started industries elsewhere. Among others, the Whitney glasshouse at Glassboro, New Jersey, began in this manner in 1775. The main commercial products of these places were bottles and window-glass, but there is little doubt that much domestic ware, blown and manipulated in a naive but attractive form similar to that found in British country markets, was made as well. Most of the objects concerned were in green metal and survivors are of some rarity, but these were still early days and glassmaking was spreading all the time.

The next important figure in the history of American glass was Heinrich Wilhelm Stiegel (1739-85) from Cologne, who anglicised his forenames to Henry William shortly after arriving in America from the Rhineland in about 1750. Stiegel was a great opportunist, and founded his temporary fortune by marrying the daughter of a wealthy iron-manufacturer in Lancaster County, Pennsylvania, in 1752. It was this convenient source of capital which enabled him to begin his glassmaking, first at Elizabeth Furnace in 1763, and at Manheim two years later.

719 Vases and bottle in Tiffany Favrile Glass, 19th and 20th centuries.

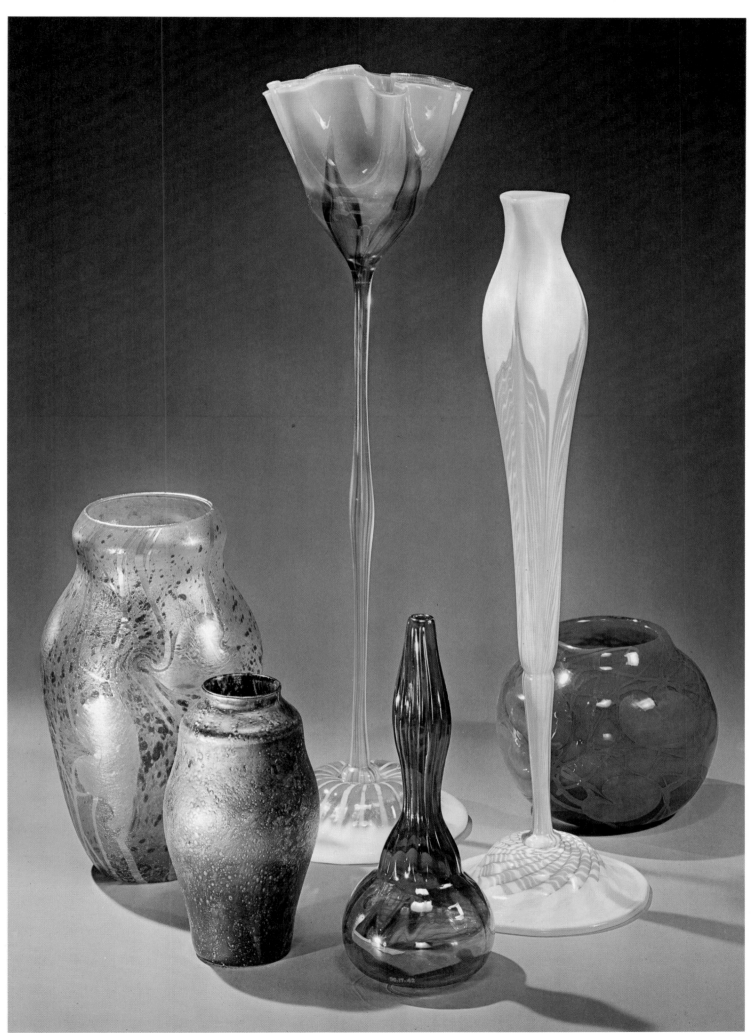

719

720 Jug, from the New Bremen manufactory of John Frederick Amelung, *c.* 1820.

721 Press-moulded salt, *c.* 1835.

722 Sugar bowl, *c.* 1825, possibly made by Bakewell and Company of Pittsburgh.

723 Mould-blown decanter with pseudo-cut decoration, *c.* 1830

724 Engraved tumbler from the Manheim manufactory of Henry William Stiegel, *c.* 1765.

725 Pressed glass tray commemorating the warship *Constitution*.

720

721

722

723

724

725

Unfortunately, he suffered from delusions of grandeur which impelled him to assume the title of Baron and to attempt to maintain a state which was beyond his financial resources, and he spent vast sums in the construction of a larger factory at Manheim in 1768. Although his natural propensities ruined him and brought about the closure of the new glasshouse in 1774, his significance lies in the **724** fact that he turned out an increasing quantity of colourless tableware, which indicates that pre-independence America was gradually beginning to reach upward to the more sophisticated standards of Europe. Extant lists relating to the years 1769 and 1770 mention every conceivable kind of domestic glassware, and although most of it was in lime-soda metal, and we need not take too seriously the statement in an advertisement that it was 'allowed by complete judges to be equal to most imported from England', there is no doubt that quality and demand were slowly increasing.

As might be expected, most of this glass was derivative in style and tended to display British, Bohemian and Netherlandish influences, but one mould-blown design appears to have been exclusively American. This was the diamond-daisy pattern, in which lozenge-shaped compartments were filled by a conventionalised flower-head like that of a daisy.

Also derivative were the productions of the New Bremen Manufactory which was established in Frederick County, Maryland by John Frederick Amelung in 1784. He made use of lead crystal as well as lime-soda glass, and manufactured a wide range of domestic ware which was mostly indistinguishable in appearance from that of Great Britain. Much of it was decorated by cutting and engraving, and it is very possible that some such objects attributed to Amelung's factory had been, in fact, imported from Britain or the Anglo-Irish glasshouse at Waterford. Unlike Stiegel, Amelung was an efficient manager, but it appears that through no fault of his own, he over-estimated the potential demand for sophisticated glassware in the new Republic, and his works ceased operations in 1795. He had helped, nevertheless, to establish criteria from which other glassmakers were to benefit later, though simple, traditional **720** utensils continued to be made.

Among the most distinguished of the 19th-century glasshouses were the New England Glass Company of Massachusetts and **729** Bakewell and Company of Pittsburgh. Of the latter, a traveller in 1817 said, 'His cut glass equals the best I have seen in England', but another commentator stated a year later that the inhabitants of Eastern America were still importers from 'the Old Country'. The

726 Pair of vases, decorated with coloured stripes, New England Glass Company, c. 1840.

727 Green glass decanter encased in silver, c. 1880.

728 Vase in Pomona glass, patented by Joseph Locke in 1885, and made by the New England Glass Company until 1885.

729 Opal decorated vases and pitcher. From left to right: Boston and Sandwich Glass Company, c. 1870; New England Glass Company, c. 1870; Mt. Washington Glass Works, 1870-80.

726

727

728

729

truth probably lies somewhere between these two positions.

Glassmakers were constantly endeavouring to find ways of shortening manufacturing processes to render their wares both attractive and competitive, but the results were not always 723 successful, as may be seen from the mould-blown decanter in the illustration, which represents an over-ambitious and vain attempt to reproduce cut relief diamonds. But the same restless desire for innovation resulted in America's most important contribution to 19th-century glass technology – mechanical press-moulding.

Bakewell and Company of Pittsburgh and Deming Jarves of the Sandwich glasshouse took out patents from 1825 when the method was still experimental, but later advances enabled almost any kind of glass object to be made cheaply and quickly. By 1830 the use of the technique was widespread and was soon introduced to Great Britain. The simplest objects to produce were, of course, those which could be made in one operation, and vast numbers of dishes, trays, plates, commemorative plaques and cup-plates began to be 2,725 turned out with a kind of elaborate lace-like decoration which could scarcely have been achieved by any other means. (A cup-plate was used to stand the cup on while the tea was drunk from the saucer.)

Trade began to show a marked improvement in the 1840s, with a notable increase in the manufacture of useful and fancy wares in an idiom akin to the British Victorian style. The illustration shows a pair of vases decorated with coloured stripes and surmounted by 726 hollow glass balls in the same fabric. In this instance, the balls are purely decorative, but they were used earlier and later as stoppers for jugs. Bohemian and other foreign techniques such as casing or overlaying and enamel decoration became popular after the middle of the 19th century, together with the enclosing of vessels in pierced and engraved silver for wealthy customers, but an inven- 727 tion which owed nothing to extraneous sources was a greenish-yellow metal known as 'Burmese'. This attractive material was patented by F. Shirley of the Mount Washington Glass Company of Massachusetts in 1855, and after some specimens had been tactfully sent as a present to Queen Victoria, it began to be made under licence in England, where it was called 'Queen's Burmese'.

This brief account of the development of the American glass industry, through striving, floundering, and striving again, demonstrates how the stage was being set for the future, and forms an essential preamble to its full flowering when the 19th century was passing into history.

THE PANOPLY OF WAR

ARMOUR

A. R. E. North

The history of arms and armour is the story of two competing technologies: that of the armourer striving–in the motto of the Armourers and Braziers Company of London–'to make all sure', and that of the cutler and others, endeavouring to penetrate the armourer's defences with a multiplicity of weapons. For the early history of armour, historians must rely on the evidence of representations found in brasses, effigies and manuscript illuminations, for very few fragments of armour have survived from before the late 14th century. Sources such as the Bayeux Tapestry show the armoured warrior wearing a long mail shirt made up of closely linked flat circular rings riveted together, divided in the middle to facilitate riding, and tailored to fit the body. Under this mail shirt, or hauberk, was worn a padded undergarment to protect the wearer from the rough surface of the mail. In addition a conical helmet was worn, sometimes beaten from a single piece of iron, but more usually made up of segments or bands of metal, with a separate protective guard for the nose. Because of the dangers of mail being driven into a wound, especially by arrows, and because it did not protect the wearer against heavy bruising, by the early 14th century it was reinforced in places by the addition of small plates of leather, and later of iron at the elbows and knee. These can be seen on a brass in Westley Waterless Church, Cambridgeshire, dating from 730 about 1325-30, which depicts a knight with a coat of plates, a garment of leather or cloth lined with metal plates to protect the body, and defences for the arms and legs. By the close of the 14th century, the mail was almost entirely covered by plates. An armour in the Metropolitan Museum, although composed from associated 731 pieces, demonstrates the appearance of a harness of about 1390, showing a pointed helmet with separate vizor, a textile-covered breastplate and gauntlets with flaring cuffs.

The great period of the armourer's art is always considered to be from the early 15th century to its close; it was during this period that the fully developed harness emerged. Several armours survive from this period, including a celebrated Italian one preserved in the castle of Churburg in the Tyrol. This, the earliest complete suit known to survive, can be dated to about 1420. It has a rounded breastplate, cut off at waist level, with a smaller plate known as a plackart overlapping it, a backplate also made from two plates, defences for arms and legs, and a form of helmet known as an armet. In this case, the armet lacks its vizor and mail tippet–a curtain of mail which hung from the lower edge of the helmet to protect the neck. The cheek-pieces of the helmet are hinged at the side, and are secured at the chin by a raised stud.

In the mid-15th century, the German 'high Gothic' style of armour was beginning to emerge, a fine example of this style at its apogee being the armour made for the Archduke Sigmund of Tyrol 732 by the armourer Lorenz Helmschmied in about 1480. By this time, the tournament, which had originated as a practice battle, had

730   731   732   733

730 Brass of Sir John de Creke, *c.* 1325-30.

731 Italian armour of *c.* 1400.

732 Armour of the Archduke Sigmund of Tyrol, made by Lorenz Helmschmied of Augsburg, *c.* 1480.

733 Armour of George Clifford, Earl of Cumberland, made by Jacob Holder at Greenwich, *c.* 1590.

734 Armour for the German joust known as the *Gestech*, by Valentin Siebenburger of Nuremburg, *c.* 1530.

735 Steel gorget, French, *c.* 1610.

736 Pavise of wood covered with canvas, painted with St George and the Dragon.

737 Shield with breech-loading matchlock

pistol, almost certainly made in England for the bodyguard of Henry VIII by Giavan Battista of Ravenna, *c.* 1544.

738 Parade of armour of Henry II of France, Milanese, made *c.* 1540 in the Negroli family workshop.

739 Harquebus armour of James II, made by Richard Hoden of London in 1686.

734   735   736   737

turned into what was virtually a stage performance, and elaborate allegories of romantic love, with each competing knight bearing a legendary title, were carefully staged. Special armours were developed for the different courses run in these events, and a few have survived which were designed for the German *Gestech*, a kind of joust in which the object was either to unhorse the opponent or splinter a lance against him. There is a fine example made by the 734 Nuremberg armourer Valentin Siebenburger in about 1530, and preserved in Nuremberg, in which the helm is screwed to the cuirass, while the breastplate is short and very thick and has a lance-rest and a curved bar to support the lance at the back.

The 16th century saw the full development of armour designed more for parade than for war, and using every refinement of 738 decoration. The black and silver parade armour of Henry II of France made by the workshop of the Negroli brothers between 1537 and 1547 is covered with silver damascening in a pattern of symbols and scrolls, and the helmet is suitably adorned with the laurel leaf of a victor. The armoury workshop started by Henry VIII of England in about 1514 produced a number of fine harnesses, distinguished by their compact construction, fine form and work- 733 manship. The armour made for the Earl of Cumberland by Jacob Halder at Greenwich in 1590 is a fine example of the work of this school, as well as being one of the best-preserved suits to survive.

The development and improvement in firearms and gunpowder throughout the 16th century had important effects on armour, one of the results being that mobility became more important than defence. By the 17th century, the soldier's defence often consisted only of a breastplate and backplate, with a light open-faced helmet, while officers often wore only a gorget or collar over a buff-coat. 735 These gorgets were frequently elaborately chased and embossed, and were sometimes made from silver.

By the end of the 17th century armour had ceased to be worn, but even as late as the last quarter of the century, armourers were 739 still capable of fine work, as is shown by the 'harquebus' armour made in 1686 for James II by Richard Hoden of the Armourers Company of London.

Since ancient times, the warrior has given himself extra protection by carrying a shield, as well as wearing armour. Those shown in the Bayeux Tapestry are shaped like a kite, with straps for the arm and a loop at the top so that they can be suspended from the neck; they were generally made of wood covered with leather. The triangular shield always associated with the medieval warrior had evolved by about 1200, and was simply the old kite-shaped shield with a flat top and smaller dimensions.

The shield, as well as giving protection, was also a vehicle for the display of personal heraldry. Some of those in the Bayeux Tapestry show individual devices, but it was not until the early 13th century that shields were first blazoned with the owners' 736 coats-of-arms. Because of their fragile nature, examples from before the 15th century are rare, but the shield of Edward the Black Prince, which was suspended with other arms over his tomb in Canterbury Cathedral in 1376, shows that the surface decoration was usually

738   739

executed in gesso and leather on a wood backing. Civilians at this time often carried a small circular parrying shield known as a buckler, used in association with the sword, and often worn adjacent to it.

Shields generally began to be discarded by the mid-15th century, but the late 16th-century soldier William Garrard advocated the use of the 'old Romaine [Roman] shield'. This warrior had served for many years in the Spanish service, whose troops favoured the use of the *adarga*, a shield in the form of two shells, and these troops armed with swords and shields were one of the dominant forces in Europe at this time. For the protection of archers and crossbowmen, a large rectangular shield was employed, fitted with a piece of wood at the back to support it, and sometimes with small grilles at the top to enable the sheltering man to see his opponents. An interesting group of shields in the Tower of London, probably made for the bodyguard of Henry VIII by a certain Giovan Battista 737 of Ravenna *c.* 1545, have breech-loading matchlock pistols in their centres. These shields are of wood covered with iron plates, some bearing traces of engraved ornament.

In the 16th century, the shield was no longer used in warfare, except in Spain, but it was retained for the joust, and a number of steel parade shields were also produced. These were usually circular with embossed and inlaid decoration, often based on Classical themes, and decorated *en suite* with the owner's armour. In Scotland, a kind of shield called a *targe* was retained until the mid-18th century. These were made of two thicknesses of oak or fir boards covered on the back with cowhide, while the front was covered with embossed leather, adorned with brass and occasionally with silver, bearing ornament in the late Celtic style.

740 Steel mace, weighing 51 lbs (23 kilograms), with flanges terminating in points. The haft of octagonal section is decorated with punched dots. Western European, probably German, early 16th century.

741 War hammer, steel damascened with gold and silver with foliage, strapwork and figures. The head fits over a bolt on top of the shaft and is held by a faceted nut. A long hook for securing it to the belt is fitted to the top.

742 Sporting crossbow with etched steel bow, the carved stock overlaid with plaques of engraved staghorn. The bow is decorated with a design incorporating foliage and masks. German, late 16th century.

EARLY WEAPONS

A. R. E. North

Apart from the sword and gun, the warrior has over the centuries armed himself with a variety of offensive weapons. One which enjoyed a wide popularity in the Middle Ages, and to a limited extent in later periods, was the mace. Those depicted on the Bayeux Tapestry appear to have plain heads, although it is not clear from what material they were made. However, some extant examples which probably date from the 12th century have heads of cast bronze, and are in the form of closely grouped pyramidal spikes attached to a short socket in which the handle could be fitted. Some of the sockets are adorned with cast foliage or animal decoration.

By the early 14th century, the head of the mace was made of iron, and consisted of a tube to which was attached a radiating series of long angular flanges, sometimes with a short spike at the top. Some very fine examples of maces dating from the late 15th and early 16th centuries survive, the flanges lending themselves particularly well to the elaborate piercing and tracery so fashionable at the time. Several examples are overlaid with laton bands, often inscribed. Some south German maces have heads consisting of a man's hand grasping a spike, the head being of bronze and the spike of steel.

In addition to the mace, the axe and war-hammer were also used. Apart from a stout blade, these axes usually had a beak-like projection on the opposite side for piercing armour. The war-hammer, which continued in use until the 17th century, and was particularly popular in Eastern Europe, had a flat hammer head and, like the axe, a steel beak on the opposite side.

The chief missile weapons of the Middle Ages were the bow and

crossbow. Bows for war were usually about six feet (1·82 metres) long and made from a variety of woods, including basil, wych elm, hazel and yew. In the 14th and 15th centuries composite bows were common, consisting of laminations of horn or sinew, glued to a back of wood, horn or whalebone and covered with parchment. Much shorter than the longbow, they were more resilient and could be drawn much further back, giving extra power.

The main reason for the longbow's success in battles such as Crécy and Agincourt was that it could be discharged a great deal faster than its rival the crossbow–moreover, the long sharp bodkin points of the arrows had great powers of penetration. Its range was about 340 yards (310 metres). The crossbow in its earliest form was constructed of wood, but by the early 14th century steel bows were being used, which shot a short heavy bolt, with leather or wooden flights. The advantage of the crossbow lay in its considerable power, but this decreased its speed, because a mechanical device had to be used to draw the bow-string until it was held by the trigger. Early examples had simply a stirrup attached to the end of the bow and a hook on the belt for the cord, but with the more powerful steel bows, a windlass was employed.

Crossbows were particularly popular for sport–unlike firearms, they were silent, and thus did not frighten off the game–and the wooden stocks were often elaborately inlaid with hunting scenes and mother-of-pearl. A form of bow with a pouch in the centre of the cord to take a pellet or stone was still being used in Lincolnshire and Lancashire in the latter part of the 19th century.

740

741

742

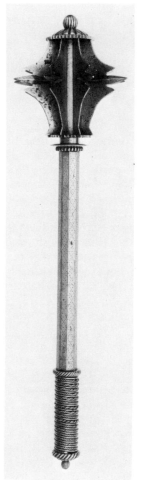
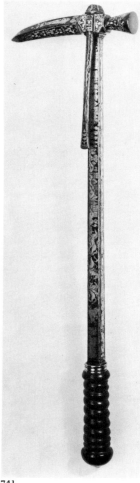
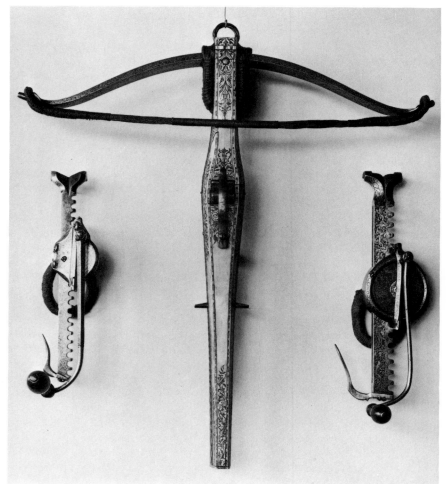

740

741

742

743 Sword, dagger and by-knife with hilts of blued and chiselled steel, part of the equipment of the guard of the Elector of Saxony. On the blade of the sword is a version of the Milan town mark. Saxon, *c.* 1590, from the armoury of the Elector of Saxony.

744 Dagger and sheath, the horn hilt carved with diamond-shaped bosses and mounted with brass. The blade is etched, and was formerly gilt. The sheath of embossed leather is fitted with an iron ferule. Italian, early 16th century.

745 Stiletto and scabbard, Italian *c.* 1620. Chiselled iron.

746 Plug bayonet for hunting, made in Madrid *c.* 1770-80. The grip and mounts are of gilt and chiselled steel, and are probably by the engraver and seal-cutter Jacques Lavau.

743

744

745

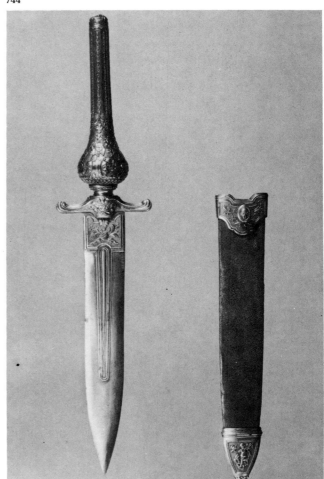

746

747 Plug bayonet with ivory handle decorated with silver piqué, the blade engraved with a portrait of William III. The cutler's mark of a rose and crown was granted to William Hay in 1686. English, late 17th century.

748 Left: German pole-axe, early 16th century. Right: halberd with the axe-blade pierced with a cross. On the halberd's blade is stamped a maker's mark, a fleur-de-lys. Swiss, early 15th century.

749 Pole-axe, the axe pierced with trefoil, the blade inlaid with vertical bands of laton. Inscribed on a laton strip inlaid into the hammer is the motto 'De Bon' (good heart). The staff, and the disc which protects the hand are restorations. English, c. 1470.

747   748   749

744   Daggers were carried almost universally during the Middle Ages, being used principally for cutting up food. It is not until the 13th century that the dagger appears as a weapon of war, and from then until the mid-17th century they were carried as part of the knight's usual costume. From the 16th century they were usually made *en*

743 *suite* with the sword, and were an essential part of the art of fencing. Daggers show an infinite variety in their construction, some of the most important forms including the ballock-knife, with plain wooden haft and guard in the form of two lobes; the 'rondel' dagger, the guard and pommel of which are formed as two discs;

745 and the stiletto, a dagger of Italian origin. This last type, which has a stiff blade of triangular or square section, and was used almost exclusively as a stabbing weapon, was particularly popular in the 17th century.

The word bayonet originally described a form of knife made in Bayonne, the precise form of which is not known. The earliest record of the bayonet being used with guns is in an account by a French commander dated 1642, which tells of troops armed with bayonets in case they were attacked after they had fired their guns.

747 The early form of bayonet is the 'plug bayonet', a short, broad dagger with a tapering grip which could be pushed into the muzzle of a gun. This, of course, prevented the gun from being fired, a disadvantage which was overcome in the early 18th century by attaching the blade at an angle to a tube which would fit over the muzzle. This was the form which with variations and improvements was in use until the 19th century. Although the bayonets made for purely military use were usually plain, some very elegant silver mounted examples were made in London at the end of the 17th century, and in Spain during the 18th century fine chiselled steel

746 bayonets were produced, designed to be used with sporting guns.

During the Middle Ages the poorer levies armed themselves with a variety of staff weapons, which originated from the implements used for agriculture, such as the bill-hook. They were adapted for war by being attached to long wooden shafts, which often had metal plates running down them from the head to prevent the heads being cut off by the opponent's sword or axe. The bill, perhaps the most common of all staff weapons, is first shown in mid-13th-century manuscript illustrations, and was particularly favoured in England. Its basic shape remained the same until it was abandoned in the 17th century.

There is evidence to suggest that the halberd originated in **748** Switzerland during the 13th century; certainly the Swiss were skilled in its use, and employed it to great effect in battles such as Morgarten (1315) and Sempach (1386). By the early 16th century, this weapon was widely used in Europe, and although it ceased to be a military weapon after the late 16th century, elaborately decorated halberds were carried as symbols of rank or office until the 19th century.

A weapon very popular in England during the 15th century was the pole-axe, the chief weapon for the foot-combat in tournaments. **748,7** Several elaborately decorated examples survive, with finely worked heads of bronze set with iron spikes and blades. A very elaborate pole-axe said to have belonged to Edward IV of England (1442-83) is preserved in Paris.

The pike, employed principally to repel cavalry, was used from the end of the 15th century until about 1650. It had a small diamond-sectioned head with straps extending down the long shaft. From 16–22 foot (4·87–6·7 metres) long, pikes were used *en masse* to present a hedge of points to approaching cavalry, and gave protection to the musketeers. William Garrard, writing in 1591, suggested 'to a tall man a pike, to a mean stature a halberd and to a little nimble person a peece [a gun]'.

750 The Conyers falchion, a sword of tenure for the Conyers family of Sockburn, Co. Durham, who held their lands by presenting it to each new bishop entering the diocese.

751 English sword, about 1300, found in Wittelsea Mere. On the blade is an inscription inlaid in laton which was thought to have magical and protective properties.

752 Sword with a hilt of chiselled iron. Extra guards spring from the crossguard, or quillon, to protect the hands and forefinger. German, *c.* 1500.

753 Sword with an iron hilt damascened with gold and encrusted with silver. It has the large pommel and single fore-quillon (guard) characteristic of English swords of the period. English, *c.* 1600.

754 Cup-hilt rapier with a guard of pierced and chiselled steel, signed by the Neapolitan artist Antonio Cilenta. Naples, *c.* 1640.

SWORDS AND GUNS

A. R. E. North

The sword has always had a place of honour in the field of weapons, indeed its symbolic significance has often outweighed its importance as a weapon. The sword of the 11th century consisted of a long double-edged blade designed primarily for cutting, fitted with a simple crossbar as a guard – the quillons – and a heavy wheel-shaped pommel, with a grip of wood bound with cord or other material. In the 13th century, perhaps because of the introduction of plates to cover suits of mail, the proportions of the blade changed. More emphasis was placed on the thrust, and thus a long, sharp-pointed, stiff blade was developed, which retained something of the weight and edge of the earlier type, and could still be used to deliver a cutting stroke. By the 15th century, hilts began to be fitted with additional rings on top of the guard, curving upwards towards the blade to protect the finger, which was often placed around the base of the blade near the guard. By the middle of the century a corresponding ring was added to the other side of the guard, and in about 1480, hilts began to be given extra bars, linking the guard to the pommel, with a solid shell and sometimes side-rings. But not all swords followed this particular line of development: some early 15th-century swords from Germany have quillons which are horizontally recurved.

A type of sword illustrated in a number of manuscripts is the falchion, one of the very few extant examples of which is the celebrated Conyers falchion, preserved in Durham Cathedral Library. On the pommel are the arms of England and the Holy Roman Empire, and the sword is probably connected with Henry III's younger brother, Richard of Cornwall (1209–72). It formerly belonged to the Conyers family of Sockburn, County Durham, who

held their lands from the Bishop of Durham, and renewed their tenure by handing their falchion to the new bishop when he entered his diocese.

By the first quarter of the 16th century, the hilts of swords had become increasingly complex, as more and more bars were added to protect the hand. This change was in part due to the ending of the judicial procedure of trial by organised battle in favour of the private duel, after which gentlemen began to wear swords as an essential part of everyday dress.

By the 1550s the rapier, which took its name from the Spanish *espada de ropera* (sword of costume) had appeared, with its complicated ring-guards and long narrow blade designed principally for thrusting. Often the hilts were lavishly decorated with applied silver and gold, and for the first time distinctive local styles in both form and decoration can be perceived. Fine examples in virtually pristine condition have been preserved in armouries, such as that of the Electors of Saxony in Dresden. During the 17th century several exclusively English forms of hilt were in vogue; English swords often have large, rather ungainly, hollow spherical pommels with stout and compact hilts. A form of basket-hilt known at the time as an 'Irish hilt' was fashionable in England in the first half of the century. This form was also popular in Scotland, a country which developed its own traditional weapons, including the two-handed claymore and, from the 16th century, the basket-hilted broadsword. The basket-hilts produced in the first half of the 18th century by such makers as Walter Allan of Stirling and John Simpson of Glasgow are much admired for their decorative qualities. A form of hilt which came into prominence in the late 16th century, particu-

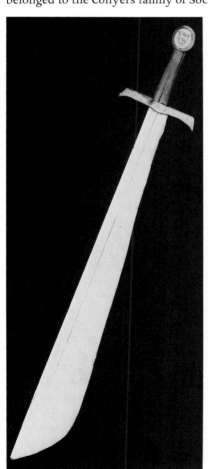

750

752

751

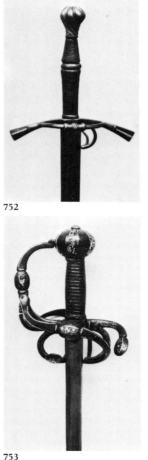

753

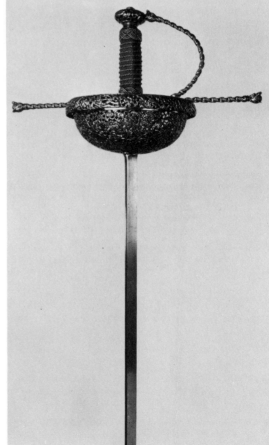

754

755 Rapier, German, c. 1550, with a hilt of chiselled iron with extra ring guards and back guards. The blade is inscribed Sebastian Hernandez – German swordsmiths often used the names of Spanish smiths on their blades.

756 Broadsword, the hilt of chiselled iron, with the original lining of canvas covered with velvet. Scottish, c. 1740.

757 Small-sword, the hilt of blued steel heavily encrusted with gold, and the grip bound with silver wire. French, c. 1730.

758 Small-sword, the steel hilt blued and damascened with floral ornament in gold. Made in India for the Western European market c. 1770.

759 Small-sword, the hilt of cut and polished steel set with studs and Wedgwood plaques. Made c. 1780 by Matthew Boulton at his Soho Manufactory near Birmingham, established in the last quarter of the 18th century.

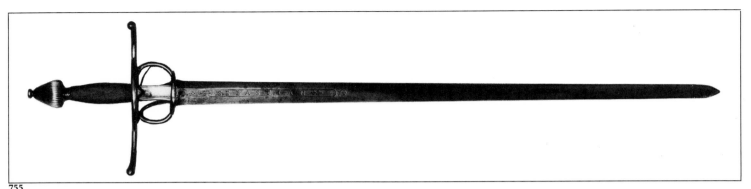

755

756

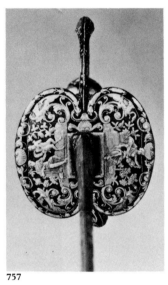

757

758

759

larly in Spain and in those territories under Spanish rule, such as the Kingdom of Naples, was the cup-hilt rapier. The large bow-shaped guard not only gave increased protection to the hand, its greater surface area also provided an ideal medium for chiselled **754** decoration. Makers such as Antonio de Cilenta, a Neapolitan crafts-man, produced some beautifully chiselled and pierced guards for swords of this type, which continued to be fashionable until the end of the 18th century.

757 In about 1640 a light form of rapier, known as a small-sword, was developed, possibly first in France. These light swords were designed almost exclusively for thrusting, and were fitted with long, narrow, triangular-sectioned blades, with a guard in the form of two shells and a special device to protect the knuckles. Although in general shape the small-sword did not change radically from 1670 until about 1800, the current changes in fashion were quickly reflected in the form of decoration employed on these hilts; during **756,757** the 18th century, jewellers and gold-box makers produced elabor-**758** ate sword hilts. But the same century was marked by the wider use of standard regulation hilts for armies and navies, and by the early 19th century, hilts had lost much of their individuality. However, some of the factory-made hilts, particularly those made by **759** Matthew Boulton, are fine examples of the Neo-classical style, the polished steel contrasting with the Wedgwood plaques with which they were sometimes set.

Firearms

The origin of firearms is still obscure, although it seems clear that the Chinese were using gunpowder for fireworks and rockets by the 11th century AD. It was possibly brought to Europe by the Arabs in the mid-12th century; the main principles were clearly under-stood in Western Europe by the first quarter of the 14th century, for an English manuscript dated 1326 has an illustration of a knight somewhat diffidently firing an arrow from a large vase-shaped gun. **761** What is thought to be the earliest surviving gun, excavated at Loshult, Sweden, in 1851, confirms that this manuscript illustrates guns that really existed. The Swedish gun is bronze, quite small, some 11¾ inches (30 centimetres) long, and has a touch-hole drilled at right-angles to the chamber. Its small size suggests that it

was used as a hand cannon. The few surviving guns which almost certainly date from before 1400 are made of bronze, have barrels of polygonal shape and are fitted with a hollow socket to which a wooden handle could be fixed. Some have a lug projecting under-neath so that they may be hooked over a parapet; guns of this type are called 'harquebus', which derives from the German word *hackenbüchse*, 'hook gun'.

By the early 15th century there was a new development: the lighted match held to the powder in the touch-hole to fire the gun was attached to the end of a pivoted arm fixed to the stock, instead of being held in the hand. This, as well as an improved stock, enabled the gunner to aim, and firearms became increasingly important in warfare from this time on. This form of gun, called a matchlock, underwent several improvements and became the **762** standard form of military weapon until the late 17th century, its mechanical simplicity and low cost ensuring continuous popularity.

An important technological improvement in the history of fire-arms was the invention of the wheel-lock. A drawing of a wheel-lock in Leonardo da Vinci's 'Codex Atlanticus', which dates from about 1500, appears to be a design rather than a drawing of a lock which already existed. It thus seems likely that Leonardo was in fact the inventor of this type of mechanism – certainly by the 1530s this form of lock was in wide use in Europe. However, it had dis-advantages, being expensive to make and easily broken, and with the limited technology of the period, could not be easily repaired. But it nevertheless had one major effect on warfare, as for the first time fire could be 'held' until the right moment, which led to the development of a whole new system of battle tactics.

The disadvantages of the wheel-lock soon led gunsmiths to seek alternative systems of ignition, one of which was the snaphance **760** lock, first recorded in a Florentine ordinance dated 1547. The snaphance was based on the principle of the tinderlighter – a flint and a piece of steel striking together and producing a spark. The flint was held in a short arm pivoting on the side of the lock-plate, the steel was held on another arm directly opposite, over the powder. The arm holding the flint, known as the cock, was pulled back against a powerful spring until locked. On pressing the trigger this came forward, striking spark from the steel and thus igniting

760 Carbine with snaphance lock, the walnut stock inlaid with engraved and pierced steel. The barrel is signed Lazarino Cominazzo. Brescia, c. 1650.

761 Bronze gun with counter-sunk touch-hole to form a pan, found at Loshult, Sweden in 1861, and believed by some to be the earliest known gun. Its small size, about one foot

(30.4 centimetres) indicates that it was designed for hand use. Probably Swedish, early 14th century.

762 Matchlock gun with walnut stock, inlaid with scenes showing monkeys, and Hercules overcoming the Nemean lion, the ground filled with scrolls in engraved staghorn. French, second half of the 16th century (the attribution

to a French gunsmith is based on comparisons with French wheel-lock pistols).

763 Pair of double-barrelled flint-lock pocket pistols. The stocks are of walnut, the octagonal barrels are blued, and the signature 'J EGG London' is inlaid in gold. English, with the London hallmark for 1823-4.

760

761

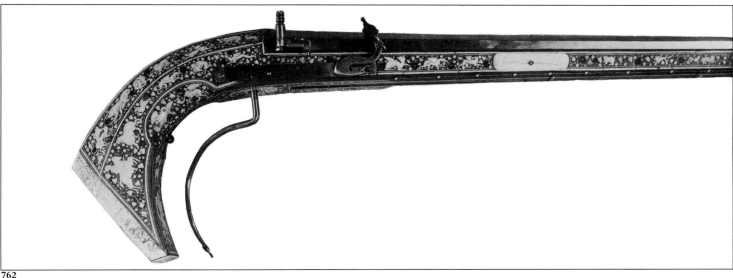
762

763

the powder contained in the pan. This system was particularly popular in England and Scotland. Some very beautiful chiselled locks of this type were made by the gunsmiths of Brescia in Italy in the 17th century.

The flintlock is really an improvement on the snaphance system. the steel and pan-cover were made as one unit, and a vertical catch engaging in two notches enabled the arms holding the flint to be put on half-cock, as well as full-cock for firing. A current theory suggests that the flintlock was invented by a member of the Bourgeoys family of Lisieux of France, in about 1610; Marin le Bourgeoys worked for Louis XIII, who was fascinated by guns himself and formed a large collection, much of which still survives.

Also in the 17th century, various attempts were made to develop a gun which would fire several shots without having to be reloaded each time. Successful magazine-repeaters, which would fire several shots, were made by Peter Kalthoff in 1641, and by the Italian Michael Lorenzoni in about 1675. The English gunsmith, John Cookson, working in London at the end of the 17th century, made some very fine repeaters based on the Lorenzoni system.

After 1650 the flintlock became the standard system of ignition for firearms, and remained so until it was replaced by the percussion lock, patented by the Rev. Alexander Forsyth in 1807.

The Forsyth lock was mechanically similar to the flintlock, but this system, in which a flat hammer struck a detonating powder, or fulminate, proved more reliable than the previous flint and steel system. The percussion lock was much improved with the invention in about 1820 of a cap to contain the fulminate, which fitted over a small tube attached to the breech and connected by a small hole to the main charge. By 1830 this system was generally adopted for most muzzle-loading firearms. Various centres in Germany were renowned for gun-making, the towns of Augsburg, Nuremberg and Suhl being particularly famous, especially in the 16th and 17th centuries. In Italy and France, fine guns were made in Brescia and Paris during the 17th and 18th centuries, while the sober decorations and impeccable workmanship of English guns of the 18th and 19th centuries made them much sought after.

The soldier's equipment

A glance at any of the military treatises written during the late 16th and early 17th centuries reveals that the soldier was obliged to bring a considerable amount of military paraphernalia to the battlefield. Musketeers, in particular, had a substantial number of special tools and accoutrements to assist them with the discharge of their muskets. Contemporary writers recommended that the musketeer should wear a short rapier and small poignard in addition to his gun. The great weight and length of the military musket of the 16th and 17th centuries also necessitated the use of a rest. This was a short pole, usually of wood with a V-shaped metal fork at the top to hold the stock of the gun, and a spike at the other end to stick into the ground.

221

764 Duelling pistols with steel mounts and twist barrels with London proof marks, signed 'Riviere, London'. The percussion lock is Isaac Riviere's closed pattern, patented in 1825.

765 Pair of duelling or officer's pistols made by Clark of London, c. 1790.

766 Powder flask of staghorn, the steel mounts engraved with hunting scenes. On the horn is carved the conversion of St Hubert. The spring-catch which closes the top of the horn is chiselled in the form of a hunting dog. South German, 16th century.

767 Cartridge box of gilt bronze cast and chased with the Judgment of Paris, the base

decorated with an etched design of strapwork. The box is fitted with a hinged lid. South German, 16th century.

768 Wheel-lock key of pierced and engraved steel. The end opposite the spanner is chiselled to form a screwdriver, and a ring is provided to attach it to the vest. Italian, c. 1640.

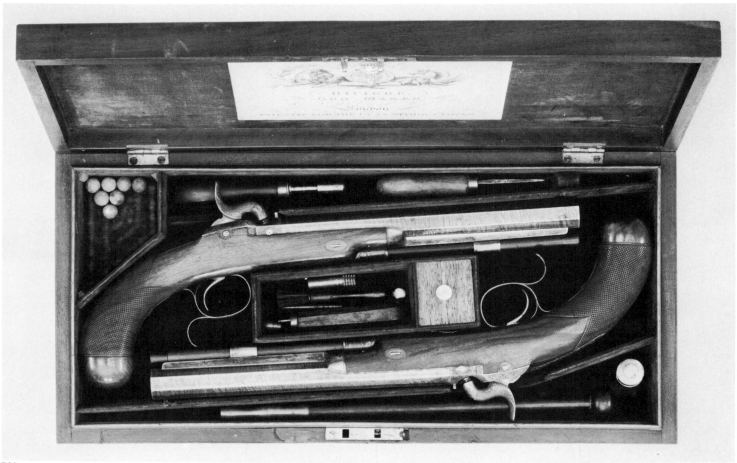
764

765

766

767 768

Powder for charging the gun was carried in a flask suspended at the belt. Flasks were made from a variety of materials, including silver, but more usually from brass, leather, wood or horn. Special small flasks were made to carry the finer-grained priming powder. In the 17th and 18th centuries, it was found more convenient to have powder already made up into a paper container or cartridge, and portable boxes fitted with tubular openings were designed to carry them. Powder charges were often carried in a bandolier—a strap or baldric from which hung tubes, each containing sufficient powder for one shot. They were usually made from wood or pewter, and were fitted with caps to protect the powder from the damp. Their principal disadvantage was the possibility of the

separate tubes of powder—usually about a dozen—being ignited by the discharging of the musket, and by the end of the 17th century, bandoliers had been discarded by most Western European armies.

Another necessary piece of equipment was a special spanner, which was needed to wind up the mechanism of the wheel-lock. It was often combined with a screwdriver, used to tighten the jaws holding the pyrites and for dismantling the lock. These wheel-lock spanners were often elaborately pierced and chiselled, and contrasted with the sober but workmanlike finish of the accessories that accompany English cased duelling pistols of the early 19th century.

769, 770 Matchlock revolver with three barrels
and a plain wooden stock. The barrels are
rotated by hand. Italian, *c.* 1480, probably the
weapon described in an inventory of 1548.

RIFLES AND REVOLVERS

A. R. E. North

A rifle is a gun with the inside surface of the barrel cut with spiral grooves to impart a spinning motion to the bullet. The principle that spinning projectiles were more stable in flight was already well known by the 15th century – flights on arrows were often deliberately off-set in order to make them spin. Although the early history of the rifle remains obscure, it seems likely that the invention was made, perhaps in Germany, at the end of the 15th century, and the credit has been given to various craftsmen including August Kotter, an armourer of Nuremberg; Gaspard Koller, a gunsmith of Vienna; and an unknown gunmaker of Leipzig. Some authorities believe that the earliest dateable rifle is a matchlock gun, though this is not now generally accepted, made about 1500. This is a hand-gun of the so-called *Lanzknecht* type, with a bronze barrel. Inside the muzzle can be detected faint traces of what may be rifled grooves. This gun, which unfortunately has no lock, is painted on the stock with an eagle, of a design used by Maximilian I between 1497 and 1508.

By the middle of the 16th century, rifles were apparently well established. At least two dated examples of this period survive, a German wheel-lock rifle dated 1542 in the Tøjhusmuseet, Copenhagen, and a detached barrel dated 1547. Rifles were principally used for sport and target practice, but as early as 1611 Danish forces were using them as military weapons, and it is recorded that in 1631 the Landgrave of Hesse had a troop of riflemen. The weapons were used in England to a limited extent during the Civil War, but always enjoyed more popularity in Germany and France, for instance, in the early part of the 18th century, Louis XIV had some carabiniers armed with rifled carbines.

A turning point in the history of the rifle as a military weapon was the American War of Independence, in which three main types were used. On one side was the skilled American hunter armed with the Kentucky rifle, and opposing him were German and Danish levies, armed with the short Jaeger rifle and the breech-loading Ferguson. The Kentucky rifle was first made in Pennsylvania by 733 German immigrants who brought their knowledge of rifle manufacture with them. These guns, at their best period of production, from about 1825-30, had long octagonal barrels, a calibre of about ·50 and a curly maple stock, often carved with scrolls and geometric patterns. Two types of lock were employed: a plain lock with simple engraved lines imported from Germany, and an ornate type with fine engraved decoration which came from England. The Jaeger rifle, a development of the heavy German sporting wheel-lock gun, and originally a hunting rifle, also had a long octagonal barrel, seven-groove rifling and a curious indented trigger guard.

The Ferguson, designed in 1774 by Patrick Ferguson, was the 722 first English breech-loading rifle intended specifically for military use. A threaded plug passed vertically through the breech, made so that with a single turn of the trigger guard it could be lowered, allowing powder and ball to be placed in the aperture thus revealed in the breech. Ferguson arranged for the manufacture of 100 of these rifles, and armed a detachment of men with them to fight in the American War.

The rifle was developed further in 1826 by a French captain, Gaspard Delvigne, whose gun had a powder chamber with a bore which was smaller than that of the barrel. By hammering the ball into this chamber with an iron mallet, it was forced into the rifled grooves. A number of important rifles were manufactured in the 19th century, including the Brunswick rifle of 1839, which had

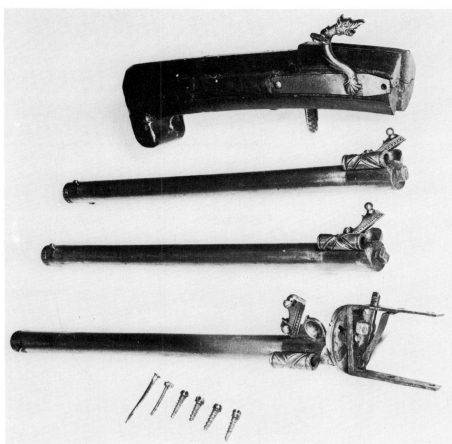

769

770

771 Snaphance revolving rifle with eight chambers, the stock inlaid with staghorn. Dated 1597, probably by Hans Stopler of Nuremberg.

772 Ferguson breech-loading rifle, the barrel signed D. Egg, London. On the lock plate is the royal cipher of George III and the maker's name. This rifle is said to have been presented by

Ferguson to his second-in-command. Made by D. Egg, London, about 1776.

773 'Kentucky' rifle made in Pennsylvania, the lock signed S. Moore, and the barrel signed N. Kile and dated 1817. The mounts on the curly maple stock are of engraved brass, and inlaid into the patch box is the figure of a lady.

774 Snaphance revolver with six chambers and single action, with brass and steel mounts. English, c. 1680, possibly by John Dafte of London.

775 Colt Paterson revolver, 1836 model, steel, ivory and silver.

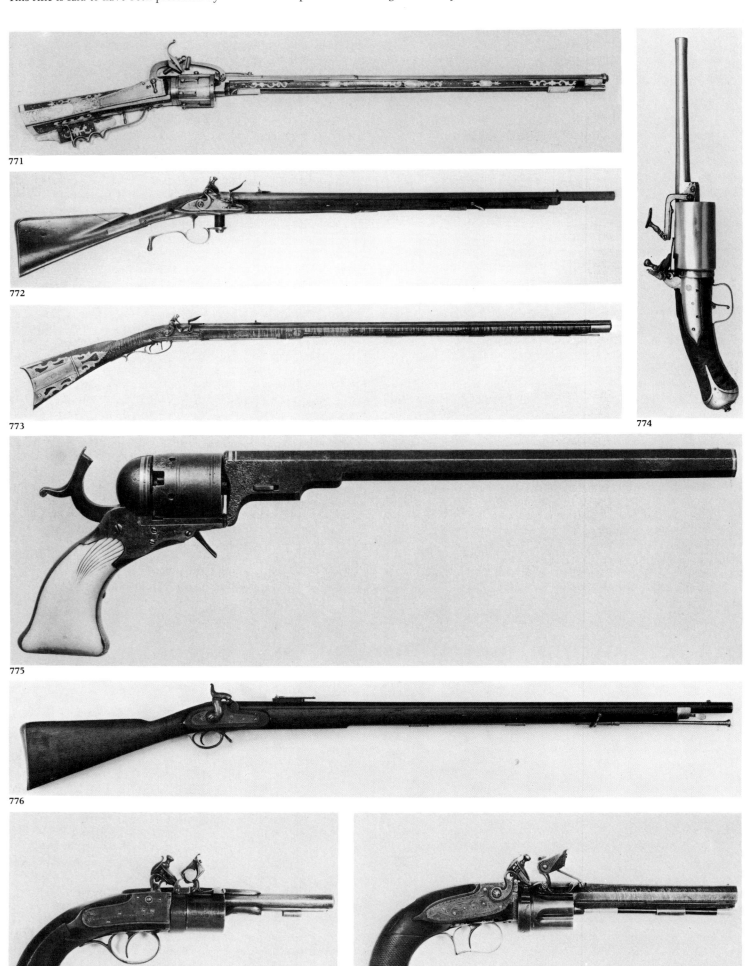

771

772

773

774

775

776

777

778

776 Minié rifle, pattern of 1851. The explosion of the charge drove an iron cup into the hollow base of the bullet, which thus expanded into the rifled grooves.

777 Flintlock revolver with mounts of engraved steel, patented by Elisha Collier in 1818. This is the first model with ratchet-operated priming magazine, internal cock and plain cylinder.

778 Flintlock revolver, the improved model of the Collier revolver. This has a silver escutcheon plate in the stock, and the steel mounts are engraved with foliage and trophies.

776 only two rifled grooves into which a raised band on the bullet fitted on loading, and the Minié rifle of 1849, which had a bullet which was expanded by the explosion into the rifled grooves. The Brunswick rifle continued in favour until the Crimean War, although most European countries equipped their troops with smooth-bore guns. But in the latter part of the 19th century, the rifle was almost universally adopted, as the invention of the Von Dreyse needle-gun sufficiently demonstrated its advantages for military use.

Revolvers can be divided into two basic forms, those with revolving cylinders and those with revolving barrels. The first type consists of several chambers each loaded with a charge, which are rotated on a central spindle to bring them in line with a single fixed barrel. The other system consists of a number of loaded barrels which are rotated, usually by hand, to bring them in line with a fixed chamber, for firing. One of the earliest examples of a gun with a revolving cylinder is a matchlock dating from the mid-16th century, described in a German treatise on firearms published in the 19th century. A group of late 16th-century German wheel-locks with revolving cylinders are also known. In the Tøjhusmuseet, 771 Copenhagen, there is a snaphance revolver dated 1597, made by Hans Stopler of Nuremberg, which works on this principle.

The difficulties of preventing all the charges from igniting at one time, as well as getting a proper alignment between chamber and barrel, led to various experiments during the 17th century. A Swiss gunsmith working in London at the end of the century, Jacques Gorgo, made some pistols and guns, which superficially resemble the 'turn-off' forms of the period. In fact they have two chambers converging on a single barrel, and are fired by separate 774 locks. John Dafte of London, working in about 1680, produced a snaphance revolver in which the cylinder was automatically turned when the pistol was cocked. A small lever pressed against a ratchet on the cylinder, pushing it round one turn. This was the system 775 adopted much later by Samuel Colt for his celebrated revolvers. In 1718 James Puckle of London patented a gun which worked on the revolver principle, with a manually rotating system of cylinders each with a conical projection, which could be cranked into the countersunk breech, thus ensuring a tight and well-aligned joint between the two sections. An article in the *London Journal* for 1722 describes a successful demonstration of the gun when it was fired 63 times in seven minutes. In 1818 a Captain Wheeler of Concord,

Massachusetts, patented a 'gun to fire seven or more times without re-loading', and later that year, one of his associates, Elisha Haydon Collier, patented an improved version of this revolver in London. 777,778 Although Collier's patent was obviously only an improvement of Wheeler's invention, the London patent was the one that was officially recognised, and a number of so-called Collier revolvers were manufactured in London. The cylinder was turned by a spring and escapement when the lock was cocked. In the second model, the mechanical system of rotating the barrel was later replaced by a manual system. An important feature of the Collier was that the chamber was held in position against the barrel by a wedge, which was automatically pushed forward when the cock fell. This ensured a gas-tight seal between chamber and barrel. The invention of the percussion system by Forsyth in 1807, a system which did not require priming powder, enabled further improvements to be made to revolvers, and a large number of patents were taken out for different mechanisms both in Europe and America.

Guns with revolving barrels, the alternative system, were already in use by the early 16th century. The celebrated 'holy-water sprinkler' reputedly belonging to Henry VIII, now in the Tower of London, works on this principle. A matchlock with three barrels 769,770 now in the Palazzo Ducale in Venice is recorded in an inventory of 1548, but is possibly slightly earlier. About 1630, revolving guns working on the so-called *wender*, or 'turning', system became popular. Usually fitted with two barrels which could be revolved by depressing the trigger guard which acted as a catch, these revolvers were very popular in the latter part of the 17th century. Firearms with revolving barrels again became popular after the invention of the percussion system. Called 'pepper-boxes' because of their resemblance to pepper-pots, the earliest examples had hand-rotated barrels. A patent for a single-action pepper-box was taken out by the Darling brothers in 1836. In the same year Samuel Colt took out the patent for a revolver with a percussion-lock, the 775 cylinder rotating automatically by means of a lever and ratchet. Initially Colt was unsuccessful, and his Patent Arms Manufacturing Company, set up in Paterson, New Jersey, failed in 1841. However, the Mexican War of 1847 brought Colt the contracts for his revolver, which eventually enabled him to open a factory at Hartford, Connecticut. This became extremely successful, and brought the Colt revolver the international fame it still enjoys.

ORDERS, MEDALS AND DECORATIONS

Frederick Wilkinson

Most civilisations have recognised the need to reward acts of devotion, heroism or public service, for instance the pharaohs of Ancient Egypt made gifts of small gold flies to those who had shown bravery in battle, the number indicating the degree of bravery. The Romans, with their numerous campaigns and great military organisation, had a wide range of awards. One such was the *corona* (crown), which was sometimes made from natural leaves but also from gold or silver, while another type was the *phalerae*, circular medallions suspended from the shoulders on leather straps. Another medal, which is shown on some contemporary monuments, was suspended by a chain from the neck in much the same fashion as present-day awards.

In more recent times special services have frequently been recognised by the admission of a person to select military, civil or religious societies in which membership was graded and the various ranks indicated by some form of badge. Such societies usually took rather grand-sounding titles and were known as orders, while their badges and insignia are described as decorations. Amongst the earliest of such orders, which has continued to the present day, is the British Most Noble Order of the Garter, founded in 1348 by

King Edward III, and another long established one is the Most Ancient and Noble Order of the Thistle, which goes back to 1687. Membership of such orders is restricted and the various grades are indicated by the difference of ribbons attached to the badge, as well as the size and complexity of the badge itself.

The number of European orders increased rapidly from the 18th century onwards, and reached a peak after the Second World War when so many régimes changed and so many new, independent countries were created. Admission to membership also became more widespread so that, from a collector's point of view, the more recent and widely granted orders are of less value than earlier examples. Some orders, especially in Britain, also utilise a most elaborate collar, a kind of necklace from which a badge hangs, the links often having a symbolic significance. Many of the more exclusive orders demand the return of the insignia on the death of a holder and consequently such items are extremely rare.

These orders are usually very ornate both in style and naming – Japan has an Order of the Sacred Treasure, Sweden has the Royal 780 Order of the Sword, Finland has the Order of the Holy Lamb and France has the Legion of Honour. Gold, silver, enamels and jewels

779 The Most Distinguished Order of St Michael and St George, created by King George III in August, 1818. It has three classes, and is generally only granted to British subjects for services to the Commonwealth.

780 The Japanese Order of the Sacred Treasure or the Order of the Mirror (Zuihosho), founded in 1818.

781 East India Company medal for the Battle of Seringapatam, 1799.

782 Medal awarded by the Bengal Presidency Rifle Association to the winner of the Long Distance Shoot. Struck 1895.

783 German medal struck to commemorate a Zeppelin raid on London during the First World War.

779

780

781

782

783

are used in the construction of many orders and consequently most are expensive items. Few such pieces of insignia ever carry the owner's name which means that it is difficult, if not impossible, to ascribe an order to any particular person. They are usually collected simply as objects of aesthetic pleasure.

Medals for the recognition of specific acts of bravery did not become common in Europe until comparatively recently. Like the civil orders some of these gallantry decorations are graded in terms of merit, for instance only really outstanding acts of bravery are **785** recognised by the award of the British Victoria Cross—only just over 1,350 have been issued. This medal was first granted in 1856 and is fashioned from the metal of Russian guns captured in the Crimean War (1854-56). Britain also has, among many others, the Military Medal (begun in 1916) and the Distinguished Conduct Medal (begun in 1854). Examples of these do appear on the antique market, but the chances of acquiring a Victoria Cross are minimal.

In Germany probably the best known gallantry decoration is the **786** Iron Cross, which was founded in 1813. Originally there were only two classes of the Iron Cross, but in 1939 two more degrees were created. Practically speaking the rarest and highest grade is the

Knight's Cross with Golden Oak Leaves, Swords and Diamonds; in fact there was an even higher grade, the Grand Cross, but this decoration has only ever been awarded twice. America's highest award is the Medal of Honour (started in 1861) which has its origins in the American Civil War of 1861-65, whilst the Purple Heart was first awarded during the Revolutionary War of 1776-81. The Medaille Militaire of France was introduced in 1852, and has now been awarded over one million times.

Campaign medals were issued to all troops who served during **781** some particular war, although there are usually certain conditions which the recipient had to meet. These are a constantly expanding field for medal collectors. There are isolated examples of early campaign medals, such as the award by Queen Elizabeth I in honour of the defeat of the Armada, and there were some British issues for various battles during the English Civil War of 1642-9 and later, but the first to be made as a general issue to troops taking part was the Waterloo Medal. This was issued on the orders of the Prince Regent, later to become George IV of England, in honour of the great victory in 1815. Britain was not alone in issuing a medal for this battle and the event was also marked by Hanover, Brunswick, **787**

784 Collingwood's Trafalgar Flag officer's medal, gold, made by Pingo.

785 The British Victoria Cross, awarded for acts of outstanding bravery. First granted in 1856.

786 German Iron Cross, 2nd Class, with original blue envelope and red, white and blue ribbon.

787 Obverse of the Brunswick Waterloo medal.

788 American Purple Heart, with citation and ribbon. The medal bears the portrait of George Washington on a purple ground.

784

785

786

787

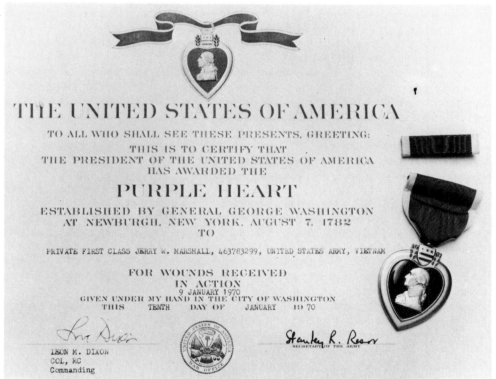

788

Belgium, Saxe Gotha and Nassau. Early campaign medals were also issued by the East India Company for battles in which their troops took part. In 1847 Britain decided that there should be a general issue of a medal to all surviving soldiers who had served in the British Army during the Napoleonic Wars–this was the Military General Service Medal. In 1848 a Naval General Service Medal was given to all who saw service in the naval wars of the same period. With the continuing involvement of British troops throughout the world during the 19th century a wide range of campaign medals was issued for China, Africa, India, Canada and New Zealand. The vast majority of these British campaign medals bear the name of the recipient–some other countries also named their medals–and this enables the collector, albeit sometimes with difficulty, to trace the history of the owner provided that it is possible to get access to the official records.

Another group of growing importance is that of commemorative medals. These were not issued but were struck in honour of a particular event and were available for purchase. Most date from the 17th and 18th centuries onwards. The majority of them should, strictly speaking, be described as medallions, for they are usually not intended to be worn and have no means of suspension.

Many countries also issue long service and good conduct medals and there are also, of course, many different prize medals awarded for discoveries, scientific achievements and sporting prowess.

For the collector of medals and decorations condition and authenticity should be the two prime considerations. However, condition naturally has a direct bearing on the price, and thus it is sometimes necessary to make do with examples of slightly poorer quality to fill a gap in a collection. The naming of medals is important and should always be checked to ensure that it is correct. Most carry the recipient's name and regiment, but sometimes the recipient lost his medal and then acquired a duplicate from which he removed the original name and had his own substituted. This greatly reduces the value of a medal. Campaign medals were often used to cover wars that lasted several years and the participation in specific battles is indicated by attaching to the fitting of the medal a small bar bearing the name of this battle. Again details of the bar and the regiment marked on the medal should be checked.

Unfortunately the increase in demand and the corresponding rise in price of all medals and decorations has led to an increase of altering and reproductions. The collector is well advised to check each specimen very carefully looking for any indication of renaming, the addition of extra bars and repairs. Except for the commemorative issues, most medals hang from a ribbon, and there are numerous reference books which will tell the collector the correct colour and style for any issue.

TEXTILES AND COSTUME

EUROPEAN TAPESTRIES

Susan Mayor and Christopher Lennox-Boyd

Tapestry work, that is, the weaving of an overall design or picture into the cloth, is one of the oldest methods of decorating fabric. Tapestries are made by weaving coloured weft threads through plain warp threads (those running lengthwise in the loom) to form a design. Each coloured thread is woven only as far as it is needed, and another one then takes up the line. Normally the weaver leaves the back rough, and a mass of small threads can be seen.

The centre of medieval tapestry production was France, but in the 15th century, it moved slowly to Flanders as a result of war: in 1418 the English occupied Paris, driving the weavers to Arras, and when the French occupied Arras in 1477, the weavers scattered to 789 other towns, notably Tournai, Bruges and Brussels. The Flemish weavers of the late Middle Ages made exquisite tapestries, either crowded with figures, or with small scenes against a background of *millefleurs* (thousand flowers). In Tournai, slightly later, these busy jewel-like tapestries developed to more spacious scenes in bright colours, while in Brussels the colours became softer, with a silvery sheen.

The cultural expansion of the Renaissance led to a great demand for tapestries, although castles and palaces were still cold, and the walls often bare and colourless. The need for show and splendour became greater than it had been in the Middle Ages, when rich noblemen had carried their tapestries from castle to castle.

A Renaissance style made its appearance quite suddenly, revolutionising Brussels tapestry design, when in 1514 Pope Leo X commissioned a vast suite of tapestries of the Acts of the Apostles from cartoons by Raphael, with a limited number of figures against a bare landscape or formal architectural background.

Soon after this, a series of administrative reforms began, one of which required the weavers to sign their work, usually with initials, and place a town mark on it—Brussels weavers used a 'B' with a shield, and those of Tournai a tower. This enables us to know the sources of many Renaissance and post-Renaissance tapestries.

The cities of Oudenarde, whose mark was a pair of spectacles, and Enghein, which used a shield Gyrony (rather like a pair of windmill sails), developed the *millefleurs* style into *verdures*, 790 characterised by leafy foliage with birds and beasts, as well as producing heraldic designs.

As the 16th century progressed, other countries began to set up their own tapestry industries. The Este at Ferrara, the Gonzagas at Mantua and the Medicis in Florence, all employed Flemish weavers, while religious persecution drove other weavers to Holland, Denmark and Sweden, and also to England. Here a Worcestershire squire, William Sheldon, started a tapestry works producing vast woven maps and small cushions and book covers.

The Danish and Swedish factories were originally set up as acts of patronage of the expatriate Flemish craftsmen, but King Gustavus Vasa of Sweden encouraged native apprentices, and when the Royal Stockholm factory closed at the end of the 16th century, these weavers dispersed through the country. In 17th-century Sweden, tapestry weaving became a folk art, as it did in neighbouring Norway, both countries making charming cushion covers filled 791 with naively represented figures, the subjects often taken from the Bible. This craft continued well into the 19th century.

By 1600, the interference of the State in the Flemish weaving industry began to take its toll, indeed it might have suffered seriously had it not been for the splendid designs of Rubens and his followers. Such artists as Jacob Jordaens, and Teniers, who pro- 797 duced scenes of peasant celebration (much repeated in later times) gave new impetus to tapestry design, which had tended to copy earlier successes. To be free from the State restrictions, many of the more enterprising craftsmen went abroad: some to Spain, some to Holland; others to Nancy in France, where the Duke of Lorraine started a factory in 1610; and yet others to parts of Germany, where ambitious princes dreamed of setting up their own tapestry works.

As other countries redoubled their efforts to produce tapestries, the French crown financed vast workshops in Paris, and in the mid-17th century, Fouquet and Colbert respectively established huge factories at Maincy (1658) and the Gobelins in Paris (1663) to fill the royal palaces and to provide a visual sign of cultural suprem-

789

790

789 Flemish tapestry, made in Tournai about 1540, when Flanders had become the main centre of tapestry production.

790 The city of Oudenarde developed the earlier *millefleurs* style into *verdures*, characterised by leafy foliage, sometimes with birds and beasts.

791 In Scandinavia tapestry weaving became a folk art, and cushion covers such as this example were produced well into the 19th century.

792 One of a set of hunting tapestries made in Brussels in the second half of the 17th century.

793 'The Triumph of Venus', one of a set of Louis XIV Gobelins tapestries with themes from Classical mythology.

794 One of a set of tapestries by Thomas Poyntz commemorating the Battle of Solebay.

791

792

793

794

acy. The Gobelins factory employed the leading decorative painters of the time to produce cartoons and, under the direction of Charles Le Brun, produced work of unsurpassed quality and colour. The subjects favoured were historical ones, such as 'The History of the King' (Louis XIV) and 'The History of Alexander'.

James I of England, inspired by the French example, set up a factory at Mortlake in 1620 under the direction of Sir Francis Crane. It was Crane who acquired the Raphael cartoons from Genoa; these have remained in England ever since, and are now on loan to the Victoria and Albert Museum from the Royal Collection. The Mortlake tapestry works, under the patronage of James I, Charles I and then Oliver Cromwell, produced work as fine as any in Europe; their Acts of the Apostles in particular rival any tapestry produced in Brussels or France. However, all these 17th-century prestige tapestry works lacked staying power. The Civil War in England weakened Mortlake, while financial hardship closed even the Gobelins temporarily in 1694.

In the 18th century, the need for tapestries declined; great historical compositions with propaganda overtones ceased to be made and the subjects became frivolous. At Beauvais in France, a small factory established in 1664 heralded the Rococo with a delightful series of grotesques designed by Jean Baptiste Mannoyer after Jean Bérain. At the Gobelins, which was re-opened in 1699, tapestry themes also became less serious. Such subjects as children gardening were typical of this period, and Oriental scenes were produced until 1733, when the animal painter J. B. Oudry became artistic director. Oudry introduced hunting scenes into the repertoire until he in turn was succeeded by François Boucher, who created such designs as the 'Loves of the Gods' – treated with frivolity – scenes from plays and other light-hearted subjects.

Another new departure at this time was to weave scenes with elaborate borders, also woven, in imitation of carved and gilt frames, such as those by Charles Coypel illustrating *Don Quixote*. The weavers of Aubusson and Felletin, two provincial French factories, went even further, adding an outer border to give the appearance of coloured drapes.

In England, the Mortlake factory, which had been beset with financial difficulties for years, shedding weavers to numerous small workshops, finally collapsed in 1703. The best of the independent weavers was Thomas Poyntz, famed for his tapestries of the Battle of Solebay (1672). Other small firms followed, such as that of John Vanderbanks, who succeeded Poyntz as the king's tapestry weaver from 1689 to 1727. He specialised in Chinoiserie scenes with groups of figures, reminiscent of lacquer work of the period, while another small firm, Joshua Morris's workshop in Soho, produced cushions and seat covers, arabesques with vases of flowers and parrots, and copies of fashionable French and Flemish designs.

In Spain, the Flemish family of Van der Goten started a factory in 1730, producing traditional Flemish tapestries and romantic subjects of everyday life. This family commissioned the painter Goya to design for them, and between 1776 and 1791 he supplied 45 cartoons which, unlike his better-known later paintings, are filled with sunlight and happiness. The factory remained in the hands of the same family for over 200 years, and during the 19th century took to carpet making, with tapestry as a second string.

Brussels continued to produce for all markets, using the old designs by Teniers and his contemporaries, with a few contemporary subjects such as the Battle of Marlborough as an occasional change. However, as the industry began to decline everywhere, Brussels, which was the biggest if not always the best, suffered the

229

795 A delightful Rococo tapestry of *c.* 1700 by Philippe Behagle, with a scene from the Italian Comedy and typical 'grotesque' ornament in the borders.

796 An arabesque by Joshua Morris of Soho, *c.* 1725. This firm also produced cushions and seat covers.

797 A Lille tapestry after Teniers woven by Guillaume Warniers in the early 18th century.

798 A Brussels tapestry from the 'Art of War' series after Lambert de Hondt. Second quarter of the 18th century.

799 Crimson silk velvet with an elaborately woven cut and uncut pile on a silk ground.

Italian, early 16th century. These luxurious furnishing materials were produced at Genoa, Venice and other centres, and exported all over Europe for use as wall-coverings, bed-hangings and window curtains during the 16th and 17th centuries.

795

796

797

798

worst, and the last tapestry weaver died in 1794.

For most of the 19th century, tapestry was a neglected art form. The French Revolution damaged Gobelins and Beauvais; many cartoons were burnt, and their main productions thereafter were small hangings for private houses, with the occasional suite for a large public building, such as those in the high court at Rennes in Brittany. Many hideous substitutes were made by machine, uniformly yellow in tone in an attempt to imitate the delicate fading of vegetable dyes. The designs were often badly copied from Teniers, or poorly drawn in imitation medieval scenes.

In 1881, when tapestry weaving had reached its nadir, William Morris began his factory at Merton Abbey, with the aim of recovering the splendour of the craft in medieval times. Surprisingly he succeeded – The Quest of the Holy Grail, after Burne-Jones, ranks with the finest products of Mortlake and Gobelins as a worthy successor to the great medieval weavers.

EUROPEAN FURNISHING FABRICS

Lisa Clinton

Apart from tapestries and carpets, the history of European furnishing fabrics embraces a wide variety of textiles used to cover windows and walls, beds, chairs, stools, loose cushions and covers. They can be divided into three main types: first, fine patterned woven silks, which from the 15th to the 18th centuries were mainly of Italian manufacture, and thereafter of French, and their imitations in wools and cottons; second, embroidered textiles which were produced both professionally and by amateurs and are therefore of varying quality; and third, printed cottons and linens, which from the middle of the 18th century began to play a major role in interior decoration. Beside these elaborate textiles there were equally varied plainer cottons and woollens, and mixtures of these, which were used for more economical day-to-day furnishing. However, little of this type of fabric has survived, and its history is far from fully researched.

In the 15th and 16th centuries the most luxurious and expensive furnishing materials were the finely woven silk damasks and velvets manufactured and exported from Italy, and generally referred to as 'Genoa', although they were made in other Italian centres (such as Venice) and later in France. They were woven in

799

800 Silk damask, Italian, mid-17th century. This furnishing silk has a formal pattern that became almost traditional in interior decoration in the 17th and early 18th centuries and was used in large quantities for wall-hangings, curtains, bed and chair covers designed and furnished *en suite*.

801 Crewelwork bed curtain, English, 1696. Cotton and linen twill embroidered with coloured worsteds in stem, long-and-short, chain, buttonhole, satin, Roumania, coral and detached chain stitches with French knots and speckling.

802 Bed valance, embroidered in coloured wools and silks on canvas, with the story of

Cyrus after Herodotus. Probably French or Flemish, late 16th century.

803 Bed curtain, English, late 17th century. One of a complete set of curtains and valances made and signed by Abigail Pett, embroidered in crewelwork (in coloured worsteds) and linen and cotton.

799

800

801

802

803

large, formal patterns, usually with symmetrical diamond shapes composed of or enclosing stylised leaf-forms, flowers or pomegranates. These patterns remained comparatively few in number and only changed slowly, and thus it is difficult to date them very exactly. With velvets, rich effects were achieved by cutting the pile in two or sometimes three different lengths or by leaving uncut areas of pile, or by incorporating gold thread in the flat-woven ground and in loops in the pile. Strong colours were favoured, such as crimson, inky blue, leaf green and gold, particularly in the earlier period, although greater variety in colours occurred during the later 16th and 17th centuries, with paler greens, blues, yellows and mauves. In the early 17th century some more naturalistic patterns also appeared, such as those incorporating small birds among sprigs of leaves. Many of these velvets, especially those with smaller patterns, were also used for costume, but the furnishing velvets became wall hangings and state beds in the grandest rooms.

Plain silk velvets, also woven in Italy, were used in great quantities in the 16th and 17th centuries for upholstery on chairs and stools; in some cases, the material covered the entire wooden frame, legs as well as back and seat, and was embellished with elaborate fringes and gilt nails. Plain velvets were also used for bed hangings, as for instance on the simple type of 'French' bed where they obscured the wooden frame completely. Bed curtains were sometimes 'paned', that is, arranged in panels with a border of a contrasting colour, and also with elaborate silk fringes. Large numbers of cushions, covered in the same material, completed both seat and bed furniture for additional comfort.

Italian silk damasks were made in the same patterns and colours

as the velvets, and although some gold- and silver-brocaded damasks were used for very luxurious furnishing (royal or grand state beds), the poor wearing qualities of such material, especially for upholstery, made its use rare and its survival almost impossible. However, multicoloured brocaded damasks were used for the covers of best chairs, which were made, during the late 17th and early 18th centuries, to slip over plainer coverings for everyday use. Less ornate monochrome damasks were used in very large quantities for all types of furnishing, and were particularly favoured as window and bed curtains when these did not need lining.

By the end of the 17th century Genoa damasks and velvets dominated the European market for luxury furnishing fabrics, and continued to hold that reputation well into the 18th century, although other centres, such as Lyon, and for a time London (Spitalfields) also produced some high-quality furnishing silks. This dominance was strengthened by the development in Paris from the 1620s of the concept of unified schemes for the decoration of rooms or suites of rooms: the large, formal, Baroque patterns of the Italian damasks and velvets combined well with grand gilt furniture of the period and remained an essential part of formal fashionable decoration all over Europe for the first half of the 18th century. Even at the height of Rococo decoration, these furnishing silks deviated little from their traditional patterns apart from admitting slightly more naturalistic ornament from about 1740-60. This was in marked contrast to the dramatic changes in patterns for dress silks at the same time.

These elaborate Italian silks were soon imitated in Northern

799

800

799,800

804 Seat cover for a settee, English, mid-18th century. One of a set with six chair-seat covers, embroidered in silks and wool on canvas to designs after Kent and Wooton's illustrations to John Gay's *Fables*. The settee cover depicts the story of 'The Painter and The Jugglers'.

805 Bed valance, French, late 18th century, embroidered in coloured silks and chenille on white satin.

806 Printed cotton and linen, English (Old Ford), dated 1769, plate-printed in purple and over-printed with woodblocks in red, blue, yellow and brown. This bears the inscription of Robert Jones, proprietor of the Old Ford

manufactory from 1761-80.

807 Printed cotton, French (Jouy), *c.* 1790, plate-printed with rustic scenes. The design for this print, by Jean-Baptiste Huet, one of the most famous produced at the Jouy manufactory under the direction of Christophe-Philippe Oberkampf, is in the Musée des Arts Décoratifs, Paris.

804

805

806

807

Europe in a variety of cheaper woollen, silk and cotton fabrics for less extravagant furnishing. Among such English fabrics were Harrateen, a figured worsted, Moreen, a watered worsted (both used for window and bed curtains) and Calimancoes, which were glazed worsted damasks. Italian velvets were imitated in England, the Netherlands, Germany and France in varieties of woollen pile fabrics (Utrecht and Manchester velvets, plush and moquette). Another fabric widely used in England in the 17th and early 18th centuries for standard hard-wearing upholstery was 'Turkey-work', a cut-pile textile made with a carpet-knotting technique. Finally, from about 1730, plain woven, checked or striped woollens, and cotton and wool mixtures were used for loose covers for chairs (thus preserving the expensive fitted damask covers) and for the simplest types of bed and window curtains.

From about 1775 to 1820 fashionable furnishers rejected the traditional grand patterns of the previous periods in favour of plain woven silks and velvets. But these were arranged in elaborate styles, for instance, wall-hangings were pleated or draped, bed curtains were hung from domes and tied up with sashes, window curtains were looped on either side of windows beneath lavish pelmets of material wound and draped over the curtain poles. All these plain fabrics were edged with expensive silk or silk and wool braids and fringes. Some of them were woven locally (for instance **809** in England at Spitalfields and Macclesfield), but by the early 19th century French silk manufactures began to dominate the European market and continued to do so for woven silk fabrics throughout the century. During the 1830s the increased use of the Jacquard loom, which enabled complex patterns to be produced quickly and more economically, coincided with a revival of taste for elaborate designs, whether in the Gothic, Renaissance or any of the 'Louis' styles, which were woven in silk damasks and many mixtures of **811** silk and wool damasks and brocades, and in increasingly sombre colours during the late 1840s and 1850s. In the second half of the 19th century French and English materials dominated the European market in woven furnishings, using many of the same revival

patterns, and introducing more Neo-classical revival patterns in the 1880s and 1890s, and Renaissance and medieval patterns and colours (for instance in the woven furnishing fabrics designed and produced by William Morris), and some of the leading firms established at this time survived well into the present century.

Embroidered textiles form the second major group of furnishing fabrics. In the 16th and 17th centuries embroidery of the highest quality, some professional and some amateur, was used for bed **801,8(** hangings, chair covers, cushions and coverlets, and even for large **804,8(** wall-hangings. Especially popular in this period was appliqué-work, made up either of plain material or *petit-point* panels, cut out and laid on plain velvet or silk grounds, and forming strap-work and arabesque patterns with ornamental spangles and gold and silver thread and fringes. Another type of exceptional quality in the later 16th and early 17th centuries was English flower-scale embroidery, in which scrolling patterns of flowers on stems, worked in silks on silk, or silk on linen, were made into seat cushions, pillow covers, bed coverlets and tablecloths. A further group consisted of full pictorial scenes, embroidered in *gros-* and *petit-point* in silks and wools for table covers and bed valances, for which designs were selected from contemporary pattern-sheets, illustrated stories, **802** bestiaries and books of heraldry. During the later 17th and early 18th centuries, bed hangings and window curtains were made in crewel-work (in coloured worsteds on a linen ground) with floral **801** patterns, and in later years with tree patterns in imitation of the expensive Indian printed and embroidered hangings that were appearing on the European market. Amateur work of this sort continued to use the same patterns until about 1750.

From about 1600-60 professional and domestic needlework was used extensively as covers for upholstered chairs, settees and stools, usually in combinations of silks and wools on a linen ground in *gros-* and *petit-point* stitches. Floral patterns were most common, especially those with a vase or bunch of flowers – such designs were often taken from contemporary tapestry. These adapted well into colourful asymmetrical panels for elaborately carved and gilded

808 Chair seat cover, English, early 19th century, block-printed in madder colour in a floral pattern. Made at the Bannister Hall manufactory near Preston, Lancashire, for the furnishing supplier Richard Ovey of London.

809 Furnishing damask, English, mid-19th century. Woven by Messrs Baily and Jackson of Spitalfields, this represents a type of damask woven either in silks or silks and cottons and used throughout the second half of the 19th century for drawing-room walls, curtains and chair covers.

810 Printed cotton, English, 1883. Designed by William Morris, this print, 'Strawberry Thief', was produced at his Merton Abbey works, and is still being used as a furnishing fabric.

811 Furnishing damask, English, c. 1850. This cotton and worsted mixture, woven on a power loom, was possibly shown at the Great Exhibition of 1851.

808

809

810

811

furniture in the Rococo style. Other sets of chair seats and backs were embroidered with pictorial scenes, for instance from Aesop's Fables, or rustic scenes, with floral borders. Later in the 18th century, however, the Neo-classical taste for plain furnishing fabrics severely restricted the use of embroidery in furnishing except for use in border patterns, of honeysuckle, Greek key or acanthus scrolls, or in flat stitches of naturalistic ornament on plain satins and velvets. Seat covers were either of plain woven horsehair, or, more decoratively, painted satin panels. This exclusion of embroidery continued through the early 19th century, and although there was a considerable revival of amateur embroidery, first in the craze for 'Berlin woolwork' from about 1830-60, and at the end of the 19th century in 'art needlework' with medieval patterns and colours, embroidery for furnishing never regained the prominent position it had held in the period 1500-1760.

The third main group of furnishing fabrics used in Europe were printed cottons and linens. In the middle of the 18th century these began to replace the laboriously worked embroidered hangings in bedrooms and dressing rooms, and gradually spread throughout the house as summer furnishings for drawing rooms and parlours. The first furnishing prints produced in Europe in the late 17th and early 18th centuries imitated either the formal velvet and damask patterns from Italy, or native embroideries, or the Indian chintzes whose import was quickly forbidden but never entirely prevented. After about 1750, when the restrictions on cotton printing began to be lifted and the industry expanded rapidly all over Europe, patterns in great varieties appeared for furnishings as well as for costume. Outstanding among the English furnishing prints in the 18th century were those produced by Robert Jones at the Old Ford manufactory (1761-80), which used copper plates and woodblocks to depict rustic scenes in shades of red, purple, blue and brown. By 1800 numerous printworks in Lancashire (e.g. at Peel, Church, Burnley and Foxhillbank) and linen printworks in Ireland produced fine furnishing prints in floral, striped and pictorial patterns for wall and bed hangings and chair covers. In France the

finest printed cottons were the famous *Toiles de Jouy*, produced from 1749-1843 at the factory founded by Christophe Philippe Oberkampf at Jouy near Versailles. The productions included Eastern-inspired designs with exotic fruit, flowers and birds; fairly straightforward 'furniture prints' with alternating stripes and bands of flowers, or small flowers scattered over plain grounds; and most important of all, copper-plate prints. These were pictorial scenes designed by such artists as Jean Baptiste Huet, sometimes taken from Fontaine's *Fables* or *Don Quixote*, with a variety of rustic, hunting, fishing and commemorative illustrations, usually printed in a single colour on a white ground. From 1800 to 1815 the factory also produced superb prints in the Neo-classical style, with Classical and mythological subjects framed in medallions on diapered grounds. Other workshops of high quality in France were those at Nantes, Rouen and Marseilles. In Alsace the Mulhouse workshop of the 'Cour de Lorraine' established in 1746 by Kochlin, Schmaltzer and Co. started a reputation for fine furnishing cottons that lasted far into the 19th century, and dominated the French market after the Jouy workshops closed in 1843. Other factories all over Europe produced good roller-printed furnishing cottons, in Switzerland, Germany (centred on Augsburg with the Schüle and Schöppler and Hartmann factories, as well as Berlin, Cologne and Hamburg), and in Austria and North Italy.

In England control of the numerous print works in the 19th century lay largely with the main linen-drapers and furnishing suppliers in London, who chose designs, colours and amounts for cottons produced in Lancashire—as did Richard Ovey and later Thomas Clarkson, 'Furniture Printer' to Queen Victoria, as managers of the Bannister Hall factory. Other important firms were Abraham Allen, who supplied the Prince Regent at Carlton House, Duddings, Jackson and Graham (established 1836) and Miles and Edwards. In general, patterns for these prints included a vast number of floral designs, of all shapes and sizes, and occasionally some with specific birds, botanical specimens, animals, or architectural, rustic or commemorative scenes. Striped chintzes were used extensively from about 1825 for loose chair covers, wall hangings and bed furniture, and cotton roller blinds became popular, with printed designs of Gothic windows. The printed cottons produced in Europe between 1800 and 1850 were generally of good quality and imaginative design, though after this date there was some decline in printing standards and experiments with new chemical dyes produced some harsher colours.

The return to the use of natural dyes, wood blocks and elements of traditional patterns in the 1880s by William Morris at Merton Abbey was in direct reaction to the highly industrialised manufactures of the 1850s and 1860s, and his work was of the greatest importance as it re-established high standards in design and technique, as well as re-creating an individual type of manufacture alongside mass production, which has remained an essential part of the furnishing trade in the present century.

233

812 Spanish carpet, possibly from Murcia, 15th century.

813 Savonnerie carpet, a Louis XIV design, but made in the second half of the 18th century.

814 Savonnerie carpet, late 17th or early 18th century, with richly coloured baskets of flowers on a dark brown ground.

EUROPEAN CARPETS

Bertram Jacobs

The Worshipful Company of Weavers, the oldest livery company or craft guild in Britain, was already prospering when its charter was granted by Henry II in 1130, for British cloth, wool and weavers were famous even at that date. But, strangely, although the art of carpet making has flourished in the East for over 2,000 years, no carpets were woven in Britain until after 1520, and rushes and bracken, scented with aromatic herbs, sufficed to conceal the filth on the floors.

The Muslim conquest of North Africa carried the craft westwards, through the great carpet centre in the holy city of Qairouan. From there the Berbers and the Moors brought it farther west, until it was established by the latter in southern Spain: factories were working 812 in Cuenca and Alcaraz in the 12th to 13th centuries and in Murcia and Ronda in the 14th to 15th. Elinor of Castile, when she came to England to marry Edward I in 1255, brought carpets from Spain as part of her dowry, while crusaders and other travellers returned with Eastern carpets for use as hangings and furniture coverings. Carpets were rarely used for the floor, though the inventory of Westminster Abbey for 1388 mentions 'foot carpets', one of which is described as 'A grete carpet to lay under ye Kyngs fete' – presumably Richard II.

It was the cupidity of Cardinal Wolsey that accidentally laid the foundation for what was to become the British supremacy in carpet production. He had imposed a ruinous tariff on the Venetian traders' imports of wines and spices, so they persuaded their ambassador, Guistinian, to bribe him with 'seven fine Damascene Carpets'. Typically, he demanded 100 for his new palace, Hampton Court, but the traders, by emptying their exchequer, managed to satisfy him with 60. Thus Hampton Court became the first house in Britain to be actually furnished with carpets on its floors.

This set a fashion among the nobility, and demand soon began to exceed imports. Upright looms were erected wherever wool was available, and according to Richard Hakluyt, teachers were brought

from Turkey, as the method was foreign to the British weavers, who had previously used the horizontal cloth-loom. They soon mastered the skill, however, and developed their own styles and colourings. These early carpets reflect a love of gardens and of heraldry, as is 818 shown by the Verulam carpet made for Elizabeth I in 1570 as well as other fragments of the period.

The Spanish and Portuguese, particularly the latter, produced 812 carpets with fine designs and colourings, but they were not of such good quality as the British, and production generally declined (though it is still alive in the national factories of Madrid and Barcelona). By far the finest in the early 17th century were the elegant productions of Pierre Dupont who, in 1608, began in the Louvre in Paris what later became the Savonnerie carpet workshop, set up by his partner Simon Lourdet at Chaillot in 1627. This was the first of the French royal factories, soon to be followed by the tapestry manufactories of Gobelins and Beauvais and the other great carpet factory, Aubusson.

The Bourbon kings ushered in an era of artistic excellence, cul- minating in the exquisite Louis XV style, and throughout this 813 period, the carpets of Savonnerie and Aubusson inspired the whole 814,8 of Europe – as indeed they still do. Even the East was affected: the import of Eastern carpets was forbidden in France, to encourage the native industry, but Eastern craftsmen working in France took back French designs when they returned to their homelands.

Although the carpets made in the royal factories were destined mainly for the great palaces rather than for private homes, their designs reflected contemporary tastes and they, in turn, exerted a considerable influence on the furnishings and decoration of the buildings for which they were made, especially the ceilings. Carpets were the dominant feature of the room, and the designs for them were executed by leading painters, so that they were always in the vanguard of the period styles that developed, while other furnish- ings followed their lead.

812

813

814

815 Carpet designed by Robert Adam for the Red Drawing Room at Syon House, and still *in situ*.

816 Aubusson carpet, Louis XVI period, bought by Baron Ferdinand de Rothschild.

817 English Wilton carpet made 1740-50 and exported to America. Now restored, and *in situ* at Tryon Palace, North Carolina.

815

816

817

235

818 Panel from an English heraldic carpet, dated 1600, with the arms of Queen Elizabeth I.

819 Aubusson carpet, early 19th century. The central medallion, with its acanthus frame, is set off by ribboned bouquets round the border.

820 Exeter carpet, made 1757.

821 English carpet, probably Axminster. Thomas Whitty, c. 1780-90.

818

819

820

821

In England during the same period there was a different but equally vital development. Hand-knotted carpets were very expensive, as they are now, too much so for the emerging middle classes who wished to emulate the style of the nobility. In response to demand, the British cloth weavers evolved a new floor covering, woven on the native horizontal cloth-looms in yard widths from coarse wool unsuitable for clothing. This, known as fotecloth, was sewn together for carpets, and is first recorded in the 1619 inventory of Naworth Castle as 'seven carpets of Kitterminster stuff'. Kidderminster appears to have stolen a march on its mother cloth-weaving centre, Wilton, but both were at the time famous for broadcloth. It was from these horizontal cloth-looms, not the upright knotting looms, that the modern power looms descended.

During the Civil War the weaving of the luxurious hand-made carpets languished, but the production of fotecloth continued, and the present Wilton factory was started in 1655. Stuff for apparel was the main product, with the fotecloth as a sideline. However, demand for this increased, and the influx of Huguenot refugees after 1685 brought new techniques, so that fotecloths began to achieve design and colour. This was done by the addition to the loom of extra heddles carrying varicoloured warps, and the use of different coloured wefts, the actual design being produced by the skill of the weaver. In 1735 Pearsall and Broom opened the first factory in Kidderminster for the weaving of multicoloured ingrain (fotecloth), which they called Kidderminster carpet.

At much the same time a parallel development took place on the Continent, resulting in the birth of the Brussels loop pile carpet at

Tournai. This was adopted by Savonnerie, and so much impressed the 9th Earl of Pembroke when he visited Chaillot that he defied the law and persuaded two royal master weavers, Antoine Duffossee and Pierre Jemaule, to break their indentures and come with him to Wilton. There they set up their Brussels loom and taught the weavers to make loop pile carpet by the insertion of wires into the warp. In 1740 'Anthony' Duffossee invented the Wilton pile carpet by cutting the loop with a knife. He was possibly inspired by the *tranche-fil* used by the hand-knotters at Savonnerie – a small rod on which the knots were wound, with a sharp knife edge at one end and a hook at the other. The width of Wilton pile was not the British yard but the French ell, 68 centimetres (27 inches).

Wilton prospered, supplying both royal palaces and great houses. The oldest piece, made in about 1740, is still *in situ* in the Tryon Palace Foundation, North Carolina. Pearsall and Broom, not to be outdone, stole two weavers in 1749, and a Brussels loom was set up in Kidderminster. By the end of the century there were 1,000 looms there – Kidderminster had become, and was to remain, the centre of the British carpet industry.

In 1749 two other royal weavers escaped from Savonnerie, hand-knotters who fled to London and set up their upright loom in the lodging of a fellow emigré, Peter Parisot, who was a friend of the Duke of Cumberland. The latter bought their first carpet for Princess Charlotte and established them in a small factory in Paddington, managed by Parisot. Their carpets were beautiful and orders abounded, other Frenchmen joined them and they took apprentices, all of which soon necessitated a move to larger

817

822 The Redcar pattern carpet, designed by William Morris, late 19th century.

823 Axminster carpet designed by Thomas Leverton for Woodhall Park. Late 18th—early 19th century.

822

823

premises. Those chosen were near the Golden Lion in Fulham.

Again, French influence was to have a dramatic effect on the 821 British carpet industry. In 1754 Thomas Whitty, cloth weaver of Axminster, was seeking to augment his income. He had seen a large Turkey carpet, but could not work out how to make it in one piece, so he wove an 8-inch (20-centimetre) square on a 54-inch (137-centimetre) cloth loom and took it to London, where friends assured him of demand, if it could be made in the right width. Hearing of Parisot's factory, he went to take coffee with the father of one of Parisot's apprentices who, pretending he was a relative, took him round the factory.

As soon as Whitty saw the great wide upright looms, the problem was solved. He promptly built one himself, taught his five daughters to tie the Ghiordes knot on warps, and on Midsummer Day, 1755, 1,823 the weaving of the first Axminster carpet was begun. This was bought by the Countess of Shaftesbury, whose friends were quick to put in their orders, and Whitty's fame spread. He was not only a fine weaver and spinner, but a keen botanist, skilled in the use of vegetable dyes, and his carpets glow with colourful bouquets.

Other factories followed: Jesser set up at Frome and Thomas Moore at Moorfields, while the Swiss Ulrich Passavent moved Parisot's factory to Exeter to give employment to fellow refugees, but Whitty, using female labour, maintained the lowest prices. From 1757 to 1759 they all competed for prizes from the Royal Society of Arts, Whitty sharing the first with Moore and the second with Passavent, and finally winning.

Frome failed, and Exeter went bankrupt in 1760, but Axminster and Moorfields prospered, the latter through the prestige of Robert Adam, for whom Moore made glorious carpets, such as those 815 at Osterley and Syon House. Moorfields died with its founder in 1795, but Axminster became world famous, and flourished under Whitty's sons, grandsons and great grandsons. Many of the carpets 821 made by Whitty can still be seen, for Axminster exported widely—to Russia, Naples and Turkey, but mainly to America. In 1778 Whitty sent his cousin and apprentice, Peter Sprague, to open an Axminster factory in Philadelphia, and in 1790, a carpet was made there for Congress. The original Axminster factory was moved to Wilton after a disastrous fire in 1835, and continued there until 1957.

At the beginning of the 19th century, carpet making was revolutionised by the Frenchman Joseph Marie Jacquard's invention of the loom which bears his name. This, the first 'computer', was exhibited in Paris in 1801, and by 1825 it was in general use for Brussels, Wilton and Ingrain carpet. Its permanent punch-card system took the initiative in design from the weaver at his treadle to the artist in his studio.

The subsequent history of the British carpet is bound up with Anglo-American relations. In 1831 John Humphries loaded the SS Sarum with looms and Kidderminster weavers and their families and set up a carpet factory in Massachusetts—he also took the Jacquard loom. In 1839 his colleague Erasmus Bigelow responded by sending his ingrain power loom to Britain, and the two-way traffic had begun.

Because the Jacquard limited the number of colours available, efforts were made to emulate the multicoloured Axminster in machine-made. This was started by Richard Whytock of Edinburgh who, inspired by a printed silk cravat, invented the 'tapestry' method by printing colours direct on yarn wound on drums each carrying a warp thread. These were then wound on beams in the pattern order, and woven on a simple loom with loop or velvet pile, a method popular also in America and Europe. Whytock shared his invention with Crossleys of Halifax, who developed it, and when in 1851 they bought Bigelow's Brussels power loom they embodied the principle and sent their tapestry power loom to America.

In 1832 another Scot, James Templeton, invented the machinery for making chenille carpets, having produced reversible shawls made with a straight chenille. When one of the weavers in his Paisley factory accidentally pressed a length of this into a V-shape, producing one-sided pile, Templeton realised the potential of the method for carpet making. In 1839 he opened his famous factory in Glasgow, which was soon exporting carpets and looms to Europe and America. At the Great Exhibition of 1851, the carpet exhibits were dominated by Templetons, Crossleys, Brintons (the oldest Kidderminster firm) and Wilton; Templetons made the carpet for the Queen there and Wilton exhibited five great carpets for Windsor Castle.

The continued popularity of the knotted Axminsters in America had a dramatic effect on trade. In 1855 Alexander Smith of Yonkers asked his foreman, Halcyon Skinner, to work out a method for making knotted Axminsters on a power loom, and a model was patented a year later. All the colours in each row of pile were wound on spools, placed on an endless chain, and as this moved into place, tufts were taken off by nippers and wound round the warp. Soon a small plant was in operation, and Smith exhibited a loom in London in 1862. It was acclaimed by the press, but did not impress the trade, so Smith sold it to a Belgian and took home some Whytock's tapestry looms. These proved very successful, and in 1870 Smith asked Skinner to rethink the Axminster process, which resulted in the principle being changed to the present efficient method of inserting tufts round wefts.

This was even further improved when Michael Tomkinson of Kidderminster, whose Scots partner Adam had invented the

824 The Syon Cope, linen embroidered with gold and silver thread and coloured silks in underside couching, stem, cross and long-armed cross stitches, laid and couched work. English, 1300-20.

825 Sampler, linen embroidered with coloured silks in back, satin and long-armed cross stitches. Italian, 16th century.

826 Cover, detail with the Coronation of the Virgin, linen embroidered with linen thread in chain and braid stitches, North Germany, Westphalia, late 14th century.

827 Altar dossal, detail of central panel with the Holy Trinity, designed by an artist of the school of the Master of Flémalle. This, part of the vestments of the Order of the Golden

Fleece, is linen embroidered in gold thread, coloured silks, pearls, topazes and sapphires in *or nué*, split and satin stitches and couched work. Netherlands, Brussels (?), second quarter of the 15th century.

828 Three bed valances in the French style with the story of Solomon and the Queen of Sheba. Linen canvas embroidered with coloured

chenille power loom, heard about Skinner's miracle from his New York customers. He promptly secured the rights, and Adam refined the process, eliminating the nippers by leading the yarn ends through the spools through a row of attached tubes, so that the whole was lifted off by arms and plunged into the warps, secured by wefts, set free and replaced. Tomkinson and Adam made their first piece of Royal Axminster in 1878 and gave the rights to Templetons and other British firms, as well as to a factory in Holland. Wide looms came in in 1890, the same year that Brintons adapted another Skinner invention, the Gripper, to their Wilton looms, to produce the Brinton Jacquard Gripper Axminster, popular all over Europe.

Although these innovations, the fruits of the Industrial Revolution, brought Britain to the fore in the manufacture of carpets, the Victorians tended to exploit mechanisation by excessive ornamentation. In the 1870s William Morris arose, like an Old Testament prophet, to preach against all this ostentation, and opened a factory in Hammersmith (later moved to Merton Abbey) making carpets, 822 tapestries and printed fabrics. He and his disciples simplified drawing and restored clean lines and plain areas: his designs, though well-covered, prove that superb effects can be produced by economy in colour and ornament. Morris had many followers, men such as Charles Voysey, who kept his ideals alive, and his designs, which still bear his name, exert a considerable influence today.

EUROPEAN EMBROIDERY

Patricia Wardle

Embroidery is the ornamenting of an already existing fabric with a needle and thread. All kinds of materials—wool, silk, linen, metal threads, cord, hair, beads, sequins, precious stones—may be used, while the embroidery itself may lie on the surface of the ground material or be raised above it by padding. It may also involve removing threads from the ground, pulling them together to change its texture, or applying to it material of another type or colour.

824,826,827 Most surviving medieval embroidery owes its preservation to having been made or adapted for ecclesiastical use. Much of this is the work of professional embroiderers, who were known as 'painters with the needle' (*acu pictores*), and worked in close collaboration with contemporary painters, usually in the principal cities. The embroidery they produced often represented a considerable capital investment, involving the use of large quantities of gold and silver thread, seed pearls and even precious stones.

In the 13th and 14th centuries England took the lead in embroidery, *opus anglicanum* being much sought after and finding its way all over Europe. It exhibits a lively yet refined pictorial style akin to the East Anglian school of manuscript illumination, and an extreme fineness and delicacy of execution in the skilled tech-

nique of underside couching, along with split stitch and laid and couched work. Copes and other vestments were adorned with 824 scenes from the Bible or the *Golden Legend* in architectural settings, with additional ornament such as birds, naturalistic foliage or angel musicians. With the Black Death and the wars of the second half of the 14th century, *opus anglicanum* declined in quality, and a cheaper method of ornamenting vestments was invented, in which standardised embroidered motifs were applied to silk or velvet grounds. Such work, featuring winged cherubim, exotic flowers, fleur-de-lys, bells and so on, still retained a typically English flavour.

In the 15th century the Franco-Flemish school of embroiderers came to the fore, thanks to the patronage of the wealthy Dukes of Burgundy. Their work is mainly characterised by the use of the *or nué* technique, whereby pictorial scenes were embroidered in coloured silks over lines of gold thread. The most famous 15th-century pieces are the vestments of the Order of the Golden Fleece, 827 the making of which occupied a large part of the century. They exhibit the styles of successive artists—the Master of Flémalle, Rogier van der Weyden and Hugo van der Goes. Fine work of the

824

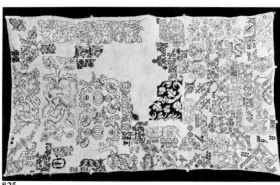

825

826

827

wools and silks mainly in tent stitch. English, late 16th century.

829 Crewelwork bed hanging, cotton and linen twill embroidered with green wools in stem, braid, satin, long and short and link stitches. English, second half of the 17th century.

830 Coverlet, part of a set of bed furniture in the French taste bearing an earl's coronet and the initials G.M. of George Melville (1636-1707), who was created 1st Earl of Melville in 1690, white Chinese silk damask with couched crimson braid. Probably English, *c.* 1700.

831 Coverlet, silk embroidered with metal thread and coloured silks in long and short, stem and satin stitches, French knots and couched work, English, early 18th century.

832 Coverlet, designed by William Morris and worked by Mrs Catherine Holiday for Morris, Marshall, Faulkner & Co. Linen embroidered with coloured silks in long and short stitches and couched work. English, *c.* 1876.

833 Berlin woolwork chair back, linen canvas embroidered with coloured wools and silks in cross stitch. English, *c.* 1850.

828

829

830

831

832

833

same type was also produced in Italy and Spain at this period.

Another important medieval tradition was the white linen embroidery of Germany, of which many pictorial church hangings survive. Much armorial work was also done for ecclesiastical use, and enormous quantities for secular purposes, though little has survived. The most famous secular embroidery of the Middle Ages, the Bayeux Tapestry, is totally different in character. Its technique of couching in wool on a linen ground is found again in Icelandic hangings of a much later period.

The Reformation put an end to the tradition of ecclesiastical embroidery in countries that went over to Protestantism, but it was maintained elsewhere. In the Southern Netherlands, for example, much fine work in the *or nué* technique was produced in the 16th century in a Renaissance style, while the 17th century favoured pictorial medallions in heavy raised gold embroidery of Baroque design.

The Renaissance brought with it a great growth in amateur embroidery, the lead being taken in the highest circles. Catherine de' Medici and Mary, Queen of Scots, were among the first royal ladies to establish the tradition kept up in later centuries by other queens and princesses. The movement may have owed something to Near Eastern influence. Certainly some types of linen embroidery seem to derive from the Arab countries, notably the linear geometric designs that became so widespread early in the 16th century. Linen samplers now became important as a means of storing designs, as well as training girls in needlework, while pattern books also began to be published. Some of the earliest pattern books, like that published by Peter Quentel in Cologne in 1527, contain numerous geometric patterns and coiling stem designs of the type familiar from portraits by Holbein and his contemporaries, where they appear at the necks and cuffs of shirts and shifts. From this beginning developed a whole repertoire of linen embroidery, jackets, caps, covers and pillow covers with flower sprigs in rows or compartments or coiling stems with flowers, birds and animals worked in metal thread and coloured silks or monochrome black in a wide variety of stitches. Cutwork and drawn-thread work in white also became notable at this time.

Another important branch of 16th-century embroidery was canvas work, which was widely used for cushion covers, table carpets, bed valances and hangings, often with pictorial as well as floral designs. Motifs in canvas work were also applied to velvet for cushions and hangings, while another type of applied work with finely drawn plant motifs done in woollen cloth was also popular.

All these types of embroidery were done by professionals as well as amateurs, but the professionals also produced more sophisticated work in rich silks, including elaborate and often bejewelled court costume. In fact the finest metal thread and silk embroidery, along with armorial work, always remained the province of the professional.

Fashions in embroidery were slow to change in the 17th century, though more subdued patterns in couched cords gradually came in for costume, while upholstered furniture, often in flame patterns in Florentine stitch, made cushions less necessary. In England a craze arose for embroidered pictures on canvas or satin grounds, and for cabinets, mirror-frames and pictures in a fanciful type of raised work now known as stumpwork. These were mostly the work of little girls. An important new mode was crewelwork embroidery **829**

834 Band of *lacis* and cutwork embroidery with birds and animals after designs in *Les singuliers et nouveaux pourtraicts* by Frederico Vinciolo. Italian, end of the 16th century.

835 Standing collar, *reticella* and *punto in aria*, Italian, late 16th or early 17th century.

on a ground of cotton and linen twill in stitchery derived from linen embroidery. Designs varied from monochrome coiling stems of rows of motifs in relatively simple stitchery to branches bearing elaborate Baroque leaves and flowers featuring an extensive range of filling patterns.

Indian embroidery began reaching Europe soon after the Portuguese voyages of discovery, and eventually embroidery began being made in India specially for the European market. By the early 17th century numbers of Oriental embroideries are found in the inventories of great houses, but it was not until later that they made their real impact. At the court of Louis XIV there was a veritable craze for Chinese textiles, and much work in a Chinoiserie style was also commissioned from, for example, the Convent of St Joseph, patronised by Madame de Montespan. The bright colours and the flat and chain stitch techniques of Chinese embroidery profoundly influenced crewelwork, already affected by the interplay of European, Indian and Chinese influences resulting from the ordering of work in India for the European market. The old sombre colours were now abandoned in favour of brilliant multicoloured work, while designs became more exotic or naturalistic with trailing flower stems, Chinoiserie birds and figures, sprigs or bunches of flowers in flat or chain stitches. Similar changes are detectable in silk embroidery.

In the late 17th and 18th centuries French influence was all-pervading, whether in the canvas work with floral or pictorial designs produced in quantity for upholstery, hangings and carpets, 830,831 or the rich shaded silk and metal thread embroidery in designs of bold naturalistic flowers with cornucopiae, vases, shells, baskets, strapwork and Rococo ornament, which was used both for sets of quilts and pillows and for court dresses and waistcoats. Quilting also enjoyed immense popularity, often as a background to richer work, or in silk for coverlets and petticoats or in monochrome white or yellow on linen, while whitework developed a new sophistication with drawn-fabric work on linen and the newly introduced

muslin. A leading centre here was Saxony, which produced ruffles and kerchiefs rivalling the finest lace of the period.

Around the middle of the 18th century, more delicate sprigs and trails of flowers came in, often worked in chain stitch with the tambour hook introduced from China around 1760. Towards the end of the century there was a general decline, with more emphasis on minor fancy-work, pictorial embroidery and applied work and patchwork of printed cottons. At the same time forms such as linen embroidery, quilting and whitework became standardised in peasant work, establishing traditions that persisted for a century or more.

In the 19th century a type of canvas work known as Berlin woolwork—the first patterns appeared in Berlin around 1804—took 833 Europe by storm. Quantities of blowsy flower patterns and sentimental pictures were copied in wool or beads for practical or ornamental purposes. Some fine whitework was still produced at this time, notably in Scotland, but general standards were low, and the invention of the embroidery machine by Josué Heilmann of Mulhouse in 1828 threatened worse to come.

Clearly the time was ripe for a revival, and this was initiated in England around 1850 by architects such as A. W. N. Pugin, who wanted good furnishings, including embroideries, for their Neo-Gothic churches. They studied and resuscitated medieval designs and techniques, and their work was continued and taken further by William Morris, who drew much inspiration from crewelwork. 832 The movement rapidly gathered momentum, and embroidery in the later decades of the century was dominated by 'Art Needlework', which again stressed the importance of studying old techniques and applying them to modern designs for practical use. These leads were taken up in various ways elsewhere in Europe, with results ranging from the revival of pictorial embroidery for church use in Belgium to the upsurge of interest in peasant techniques in the Scandinavian countries, all of which laid the foundation for the striking developments of our own day.

EUROPEAN LACE

Patricia Wardle

Lace is a decorative openwork textile made of threads looped, twisted or plaited together independently of any supporting fabric. It falls into two main categories: needlepoint lace, made with a single thread by means of a needle, which has a texture composed of small loops of varying densities, and bobbin lace, consisting of a number of threads woven or twisted together by means of bobbins and pins attached to a pillow, which may have a woven, twisted or

plaited texture. In both types parchment patterns are used. A further branch of lacemaking is embroidered net, while related techniques are macramé, a variety of knotting, and crochet and tatting, looped or knotted textiles made with a hook and a shuttle respectively.

Both needlepoint and bobbin lace go back to around the beginning of the 16th century. Needlepoint lace developed out of the

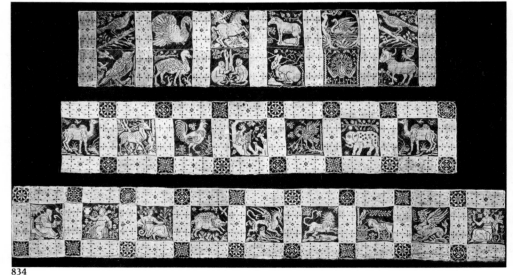

834

835

836 Circumcision cloth with insertion and scalloped border of bobbin lace. Flemish, *c.* 1640.

837 Jabot (detail) *gros point de Venise, c.* 1675-95 quarter of the 17th century.

838 Border of an alb, *point de France*, early 18th century.

839 Four borders, Valenciennes bobbin lace, mid-18th century.

840 Enlarged detail of a cap crown, Brussels bobbin lace, mid-18th century.

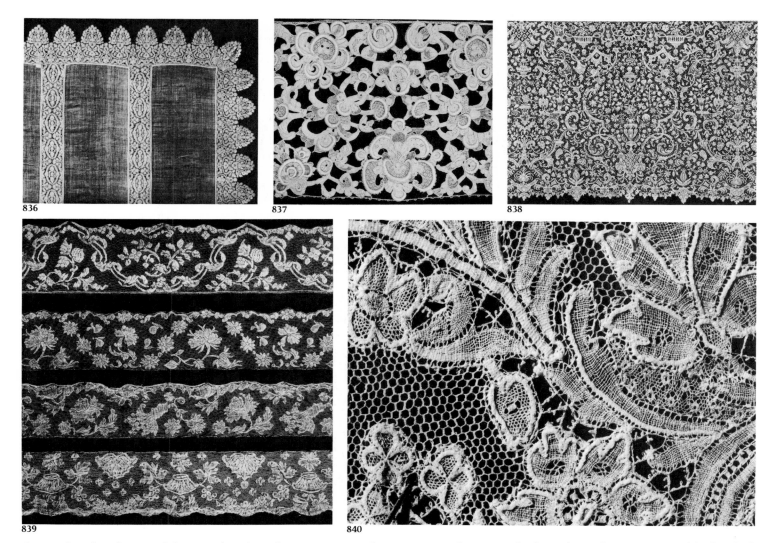

836

837

838

839

840

drawn-thread and cutwork linen embroidery that came into wide use at the time of the Renaissance. The earliest type, *reticella*, still retained a basic square framework of threads from a linen ground, but it soon came to be edged with small pointed or scalloped motifs which eventually developed on their own away from any ground (*punto in aria*). Bobbin lace was an offshoot of the practice of making fast and ornamenting the ends of the warp threads of linen by knotting or plaiting them into a pattern. Pattern books for both types appeared in great numbers in the second half of the 16th century and were disseminated throughout Europe. The most influential were those of Cesare Vecellio and Frederico Vinciolo. Vinciolo's *Singulier et nouveaux pourtraicts* of 1587 was dedicated to Catherine de' Medici, and contains a large number of designs for the *lacis*, or darned netting, of which she seems to have been particularly fond. *Lacis*, which has a longer history than needlepoint or bobbin lace, going back into the Middle Ages, was widely used in the 16th century for ecclesiastical purposes as well as for hangings and covers for domestic use.

The patterns of needlepoint and bobbin lace used for costume in the 16th and early 17th centuries were mainly geometric, though figurative designs often appear in covers composed of squares of lace sewn together. When ruffs and standing collars were replaced by falling collars in the second quarter of the 17th century, elaborate scalloped patterns came in, often with beautiful formal floral motifs. The most important centres of lacemaking at this period were undoubtedly Italy and Flanders, with Italy taking the lead in design, and Flanders in fineness of thread and workmanship. Lace was made in black linen thread as well as white, though very little black lace survives from before the 19th century. Lace of gold and/or silver thread was also widely used from the 16th to the 18th century. It is usually much coarser in execution, but makes a very showy effect.

The most notable development during the 17th century was probably the creation of the remarkable sculptural lace known as *gros point de Venise* which, with its close texture and high relief, often looks almost like carved ivory. In its earliest form the flowing symmetrical designs of scrolling stems with Baroque flowers and leaves show almost no joining bars, or *brides*, the rather stark effect of the holes between the motifs being an important part of the design. Similar designs are found in flat Venetian needlepoint and in contemporary Italian (Milanese) and Flemish bobbin lace. More solid types of bobbin lace with close-packed flower scrolls were also made in Flanders and seem to have been particularly popular in Holland.

Towards the end of the century lighter types of design began to appear in which an airy mesh background begins to play a more prominent role. Frothy rose point with its little flowers on long trailing stems now replaced *gros point de Venise*, and a similar tendency is noticeable in bobbin lace. An important development of this period was the introduction of needlepoint lacemaking into France by Colbert in 1665 in an effort to break the overwhelming monopoly of Venetian needlepoint. At first Italian modes were imitated at Alençon, where the industry was established, but *point de France* soon took on a life of its own and began to exhibit elegant designs with motifs such as figures under canopies, acanthus scrolls, vases, shells and exotic flowers characteristic of the style of Jean Bérain. From now on France was to be the undisputed leader in lace design.

Two distinct types of needlepoint lace developed in France in the 18th century, *point d'Alençon*, with a delicate ground of looped meshes, and *point d'Argentan*, with a more solid ground of hexagonal meshes. These laces are much finer in texture and lighter in appearance than their 17th-century predecessors, and the same is true of bobbin lace, in which France and Flanders now took the lead. Both types further exhibit the development of a great variety of decorative filling patterns used to vary the texture of both the ground and the solid parts of the lace. Several distinct types of bobbin lace also emerged in the 18th century, which can be grouped

241

841 Bonnet veil, silk blonde lace, French, c. 1830-40.

842 Shawl (detail) Chantilly silk bobbin lace, French or Belgian, 1860-70.

843 Enlarged detail of lace made on the Leavers lace machine, English or French, mid-19th century.

841

842

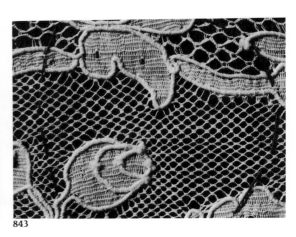
843

according to whether they are made in a solid piece with the same number of bobbins on the pillow throughout, like Valenciennes, Binche or Mechlin, or whether, as in Brussels lace, the motifs are made separately first and the ground worked round them afterwards. A further distinguishing feature is the ground, the strong **839** diamond-shaped mesh of Valenciennes contrasting with the lighter **840** hexagonal meshes of Brussels and Mechlin or the even airier grounds of Lille and Chantilly. Brussels was also noted for fine needlepoint and a mixed lace with bobbin-made motifs and a needle-made ground.

All types of 18th-century lace largely followed the fashions of silk design, with solid patterns of large naturalistic flowers and Rococo motifs giving way around the middle of the century to wavy bands and smaller flower sprigs. In the latter decades of the century lace design became more open and also more rigid with rows of tiny sprigs and edges of serried flowers. Mechlin and Lille laces with such designs were extensively imitated in England and Denmark, countries with lace industries going back to the 16th century.

In the second half of the 18th century, attempts began to be made in Nottingham to produce lace on the stocking-frame, and by 1800 various types of net were being manufactured and embroidered in imitation of lace in both England and France. In 1808 John Heathcoat patented his bobbin-net machine, which produced a close imitation of the Lille variety of mesh. This marks the beginning of **843** machine-made lace proper. It gave a tremendous filip to the embroidered net industry, and numerous variants of the bobbin-net machine were produced in attempts to perfect and improve plain and patterned nets.

The early years of the 19th century, following the French Revolution and its aftermath, were a difficult period for hand-made lace, and a revival during the First Empire was again followed by depression as a result of the Napoleonic wars. In the 1830s, how-**841** ever, things began to improve again. Silk blonde lace, which had

begun to be made in Normandy in the mid-18th century, enjoyed a great vogue, especially for bonnet veils and bertha collars edged with large flower motifs. In the following decades the Normandy industry showed a great revival, with Alençon needlepoint and black Chantilly lace being produced on a large scale in character- **842** istic mid-19th-century designs of exuberant flowers and ferns and boldly patterned strapwork. These modes were followed in Belgium too in familiar types of lace, as well as in new varieties (which might now be made in cotton): application lace with bobbin-made motifs applied to a machine-made net, Duchesse lace, a heavier bobbin lace with motifs joined by *brides*, and fine *point de gaze*. Quantities of black silk lace were also made in Belgium. In England Honiton lace developed its distinctive style with rose-like flowers and characteristic fillings, while in the East Midlands the staple laces of Lille and Mechlin type were joined by heavier torchon laces and silk Maltese lace. Embroidered net became a flourishing industry at Limerick, while Ireland also saw the rise of Carrickmacross work, muslin motifs joined by *brides* or sewn on net, and crochet lace, often featuring rose patterns.

Meanwhile machine-made lace had also been branching out, and by 1860 there were not many types of bobbin lace that the machines in Nottingham and Calais could not imitate. The economic decline consequent on the fall of the Second Empire in France dealt the hand-made lace industry a blow from which it never really recovered. In both France and Belgium it moved from the towns to country areas where labour was cheaper, and largely went over to *guipures* and *torchons*, which were quicker and easier to make. There was a certain recovery around 1880 with the return to favour of *gros point de Venise*, and a lace industry was even started up again at Burano, but in spite of various efforts made around the turn of the century, the machines had clearly won the day, especially after the invention in Switzerland in 1883 of a method of making imitation needlepoint on the embroidery machine.

AMERICAN NEEDLEWORK

Mary Gostelow

Although weaving was a long-established tradition among the Navaho and other Indian tribal groups, American textile arts in general developed from styles introduced to the eastern seaboard by European settlers from the 17th century on. The first group of 120 which arrived in Plymouth, Massachusetts, in 1620, included a fustian worker and a silk dyer. Immigrants brought with them clothing, bedding and materials, but they were soon encouraged to produce their own threads and fabrics, and as early as 1640 Massachusetts families were required to grow flax and farm wool and spin the thread.

Fabrics, woven on four-poster or other looms, included linsey-woolsey, a loosely woven coarse fabric with a linen warp and wool

weft, which was used for clothing and household items. Weaving was either done in the kitchen or attic at home, or by professional weavers, often itinerant craftsmen who carried their looms from house to house and produced such items as bed covers, usually about 82 inches (208 centimetres) square, to order.

Lengths of fabric were sometimes embroidered with designs taken from satin damasks and taffetas. Unlike weaving, American embroidery at this time was exclusively an amateur and distaff skill. Women used crimp floss silk thread brought from the Orient, other silks and wools imported from Europe and, increasingly, local woollen yarns, some of which they dyed themselves with madder, butternut bark, pokeberry juice and other natural dyestuffs.

844 Sampler signed and dated thus: 'Mary Ann Crafts work finished in the 10th year of her age Baltimore October the 15th 1822'. The picture, worked in floss silk cross and straight stitches on a linen ground fabric, portrays St Patrick's Church, Baltimore.

845 'Tumbling block' quilt, with multicoloured silk diamonds pieced, or patched, to make one large star surrounded by grey silk and subsequently quilted with small running stitches. Made in 1852.

846 Appliqué design, green oak leaves with a red inner circle. After the motifs were applied to the white cotton ground, the whole item was quilted with small running stitches. Pennsylvania, 1830-50.

844

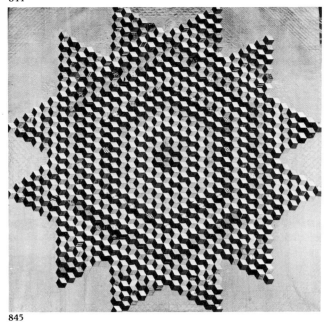

845

846

847 *Broderie perse*, small cut-outs of chintz applied on an American quilt, *c*. 1800.

848 Detail from a coverlet, with pieces of printed cotton fabric applied to white cotton.

849 One of the chair seats worked by Martha Washington shortly before her death in 1802.

850 Coverlet, woven *c*. 1850, summer-and-winter design.

851 'Fishing lady' picture, mid-18th century. Linen canvas embroidered with wools, silks, metal threads and beads.

852 Kaleidoscope or crazy quilt.

847

848

849

850

851

852

Economy was always necessary, and yarn was sometimes unravelled from old gowns and rewoven or used for needlework. Similarly, small scraps of fabric were made into hooked rugs or rag carpets.

One of the oldest items of needlework thought to be American is a raised-work picture finished by Rebekah Wheeler in 'ye month of May 1644'. Most early American embroideries, however, were essentially practical, embellishing costumes, curtains, bed hangings and covers and tablecloths. Stitches and patterns were often at first copied from examples brought from overseas, but by the end of the 17th century some distinctive styles had already evolved.

American crewel needlework, done mainly in New England but also in Pennsylvania and New York, is characterised by flowing naturalistic designs which are often lighter in effect than their European counterparts. Embroiderers left more of the ground unworked, both to save time and to make their thread go further. The scarcity of threads also led to the use of one-sided satin stitch, known locally as New England economy stitch.

Crewel embroidery was used to decorate husifs, pocket aprons, and curtains and other bed hangings. Sometimes the most costly items of household furniture, beds and their textiles, reflected the owners' wealth and aspirations. One famous set of bed hangings was worked by a lady from York, Maine, Mary Bulman, after her husband's death at the Battle of Louisburg. As well as typical crewel flowers she embroidered verses from Isaac Watts' 'Meditations in a Grove' on the upper testers.

Bed rugs, especially popular in the Connecticut Valley, were loosely woven wool or linen covers embroidered with woollen running stitches which, when cut, gave the effect of a sheared carpet with shaggy pile. Some of the floral designs on surviving examples indicate that they could have been copied from imported Indian palampores.

Alternatively, fine woollen calamanco coverlets were made, with the wool ground set above a padding of wool or cotton wadding, itself above a final backing fabric, the three layers held together with quilting, small running stitches worked in spiral or trellis patterns. Because of their size, many coverlets were quilted while the layers of material were supported between two rollers set on a horizontal frame so that several women could work together.

Scraps of left-over or new fabric were used for patchwork. The material was temporarily stitched over a template in a geometric shape and pieced, sewn to another 'patch' in such a way that the designs and colours of the patches formed the desired pattern. Popular patchwork formations included the 'log cabin', which had a ground fabric built up with lengths of differently coloured materials joined at right angles and worked outwards from a central point, and the 'tumbling block' design. Such lengths of patchwork could be used for aprons, but large coverlets were more usual.

Coverlets could also be formed from fabric decorated with appliqué, pieces of another coloured fabric sewn to the material to form a pattern. Especially attractive were *broderie perse* quilts such as the 'Westover-Berkeley coverlet', made by two Virginia families *c*. 1770. The Byrds and the Harrisons met together regularly to apply small floral and other motifs carefully cut from printed chintz on to unbleached calico, holding the motifs with buttonhole or blanket stitch. Appliqué, like quilting, was often a communal affair, and 'marriage' and 'friendship' items are two examples of quilts made for a lucky recipient.

By the 18th century canvas work, generally known in America as 'needlepoint', was practised by many eminent ladies including Martha Washington, who worked a set of chair seats in a distinctive shell design. Some patterns were copied many times, and there are 58 known versions of the 'Boston Common' or 'fishing lady' picture, some originally intended as ornamental 'chimney pieces'. The series, the earliest of which was worked by Priscilla Allen of Boston in 1746, is named after a lady in 18th-century dress who is shown fishing with a male companion. They are often flanked by two other couples and the foreground is filled with birds, ducks, deer and flowers. Behind the people are tree-covered hills with buildings, one of which may be the magnificent Boston mansion built by Thomas Hancock in 1737. This and other houses can be recognised from a contemporary watercolour *A Prospective View of Part of the Commons* by Christian Remick.

The Boston Common pictures were mostly worked in silk and wool tent, or half cross, stitch, but some canvas works of this time were executed partly in rococo, then generally known as queen's stitch. Florentine or Bargello stitch, also called Irish stitch, was also popular. Different shades of silks and wools were executed in

845
845
846
847
849
851

parallel rows of vertical stitches in formations, often stepped in carnation or flame-shaped motifs, decorating chair seats and such smaller items as drinking-cup holders and handy pocket books carried both by men and women.

Girls' schools, especially in Pennsylvania and Massachusetts, played an important role in the development of American needlework styles. In the 1740s nuns of the Protestant Moravian church in Bethlehem, Pa, taught their students distinctive floral patterns worked in silks and ribbons. A few years later Bridget Suckling was one Boston teacher who advertised 'plain Work, Dresden, Point (or Lace) Work for Child Bed Linnen, Crosstitch, Tentstitch, and all other kinds of Needlework'.

844 Westtown School, opened in 1799, was typical in that for two weeks out of every six girl students worked on samplers. A beginner perfected practical sewing with darning samplers, often with her name and the date. After mastering other stitch samplers and practising embroidered alphabets and numbers, she progressed to more complicated samplers with maps and pictures, including architectural scenes.

Memorial samplers, worked generally to commemorate the death of parents and siblings, were executed primarily in New England and the Middle Atlantic States as well as in Pennsylvania and New York. Some of the first items were worked in a school run by Mary Balch in Providence, and 'Rhode Island' memorial samplers are typified by urns, tombstones and other memorabilia set upon hillocks with graceful trees around, another illustration of designs copied from imported palampores.

The colonial textile industry was hampered by restrictive mercantile laws, but immediately before the Revolution the Daughters of Liberty boycotted British textiles, and in 1768 the members of the graduating class at Harvard all wore homespun suits.

Once independence was gained, American textile production was boosted by cotton. By 1793 Samuel Slater, who had worked for Arkwright and Strutt, had established a mill in Pawtucket, Rhode Island, that mechanically spun cotton, and in that year Eli Whitney's sawtooth gin, which removed the seeds from cotton, revolutionised the cotton economy of the South.

The Jacquard attachment, which reached the continent in 1820, enabled more complicated weaves such as intricate chequered and floral patterns to be produced. As lands in the West opened up and there was a gradual migration in that direction, American consumers increasingly placed reliance on commercially manufactured fabrics, made-up costume and other items. Correspondingly less time was devoted to fine needlework, although in the first decade of the 19th century Berlin woolwork was introduced. Known in America as Zephyrs, Berlin wools were executed in patterns more or less similar to those in Europe. Designs became cruder and colours more garish after the discovery of artificial dyes in 1856.

About this time, too, obtrusive styles were evident in patchwork. Coverlets and small scatter rugs were formed from kaleidoscope 852 or crazy quilting, with small scraps of velvet and other brightly coloured patches joined haphazardly, the seams covered with multicoloured herringbone or other big stitches.

The decline of decorative needlework which set in during the Civil War was to some extent reversed through the example of the Philadelphia Centennial Exhibition, and a principal activist, Mrs Candace Wheeler, a New York decorator. Despite designs by Tiffany, Art Nouveau had less effect on American needlework designs than in Europe and there was a return to traditional styles, including crewel. In 1896 the Society of Deerfield Blue and White Needlework was formed by Ellen Miller and Margaret Whiting, and outworkers produced mats and other small cloths with blue floral crewel designs.

Uninterrupted by wars in her own lands, America was in the vanguard of textile development throughout the early part of the 20th century. With increased mechanisation, the cotton industry was able to benefit from the Great War and consequent dislocation in Europe. Artificial silk, later known as rayon, was also put into production; indeed it was the advent of artificial fibres, and later the popularity of crease-resistant knitted fabrics, that eventually led to a decline in the relative importance of cotton.

In needlework, the Needle and Bobbin Club, started in 1916, initiated a study of the heritage of American needlework, and in 1938 Georgiana Brown Harbeson published an influential book on the subject. Continuing waves of immigration, especially from Eastern Europe, meant that a steady supply of expatriate embroiderers amplified the variety of needlework techniques practised across America.

EUROPEAN COSTUME

Susan Mayor and Christopher Lennox-Boyd

At the beginning of the 16th century female dress consisted of a kirtle–a skirt and bodice sewn together–and a shift or chemise, over which was usually worn a gown which fell from the shoulder to the ground in deep folds. The sleeves were large with deep cuffs and were sometimes trimmed with fur, and the necklines were square and low, showing the chemise tops above them (men at this time wore a similar neckline). The shirts and chemises were delicately trimmed with an embroidered frill, threaded with a string and drawn tight; it was from this frill that the ruff developed later in the century.

Men wore doublets with wide sleeves which were often deliberately slashed to reveal another sleeve in a contrasting colour below, while the doublet was partly open at the waist in front to show the codpiece. Over the doublet a jerkin was sometimes worn, and on top of that a full-length gown. The legs were covered with breeches and stockings, which could be sewn together and attached to the doublet by means of points. Hats were always worn. All these clothes were made of rich velvets, usually red, and often heavily embroidered and trimmed with jewels, or cloth of gold.

But in the middle of the 16th century the bright colours vanished. There was a dramatic change of fashion, partly due to the growing power of Spain, and black became the norm. Men now wore doublets and hose stuffed with bombast (consisting of rags, or horsehair) to eliminate all folds and creases and to emphasise tiny waists and show an expanse of leg covered with the new knitted stockings. In the 1570s, to add to this already stiff and formal dress, the ruff came into fashion.

The ruff was also worn by women, although it was often open in the front to allow for décolletage, and thus to look more alluring. Women's clothes grew more rigid in other ways too, with stomachers over stiffened bodices, sometimes held in place by unbending wooden busks, corsets and a farthingale, or a hooped underskirt of wire, flexible willow or whalebone.

This Spanish influence survived into the 17th century, and the ruff was retained for a time, although the stuffing of doublets was abandoned, and women's clothes became softer, dispensing with the farthingale. Towards the middle of the century, ruffs began to disappear, and the deep falling collar came into fashion for both sexes. These were trimmed with expensive lace, as were the 'funnel' boots with wide turnovers worn by men. Some historians claim that costume was widely influenced by the Puritan movement, but most fashions seem to have remained more or less un-

853 A young man's shirt embroidered in blue cross stitch at the collar, cuffs and seams. 16th century.

854 Linen nightcap, made c. 1600 and embroidered in red and green silk, silver-gilt thread and sequins.

855 A pair of kid gloves of the 17th century. The scalloped linen cuffs are embroidered in coloured silks.

856 The closed robe of green silk brocaded with bunches of flowers (left) was made c. 1750, though the silk itself is of an earlier date, c. 1730. The dress of challis (right) dates from c. 1835.

857 The open robe of white silk brocaded with flowers and a sack back (right) is English, made c. 1763. The model on the left shows a French open robe of brown shot taffeta brocaded with flowers, also with a sack back, of c. 1770.

853

854

855

856

857

858

changed during this period, though perhaps simpler in colour and form.

At the time of the Restoration there was a fashion called 'petticoat breeches'—very wide loose breeches, like divided skirts, trimmed with numerous ribbons—and in about 1665 a vest 'after the Persian mode' first appeared at the English court, resembling a long slim-sleeved waistcoat. The falling collar disappeared, to be replaced by a lace cravat; King James II paid £30.10s.0d. for the one which he wore at his Coronation. Women at this time wore gowns with pointed stiff bodices and full skirts, the low décolletages covered or trimmed with lace-embroidered collars. Later in the century women wore more lace—deep flounces on their skirts and a high lace frill and *fontange* as a head-dress to balance the men's wigs.

853 Few actual garments survive from the 16th and 17th centuries; our knowledge comes mainly from pictures. A handful of 17th-century suits, an Elizabethan doublet or two and one early Tudor 853 shirt are the only major items remaining, although a number of 854,855 informal embroidered coifs, nightcaps, gloves and stockings and lace accessories survive in slightly larger quantities, particularly after 1600.

18th-century costume, however, survives in some quantity. 857,858 Most women's dresses comprised an open robe worn over a matching petticoat (sadly many robes survive without their petticoats, which were cut up and used for children's clothes and furnishing materials). In the first half of the century it was fashionable to wear short decorative embroidered aprons which, because they were small and of little use for cutting up, were often later framed and kept as decoration. Men's waistcoats also survive in some quantity for similar reasons, but there are very few of the sumptuous men's suits of cut-velvets and figured silks complete with coats, waistcoats and breeches. It is usually the breeches that have been lost over the years.

856 Women sometimes wore closed robes, that is, a dress without a

front opening, and a separate petticoat. Lace or embroidered muslin flounces were always worn at the cuffs and lace 'dress robings' at the neckline. This finishing touch continued well into the 19th century. As the illustration demonstrates, dresses were often re-used, either because the colour or pattern came partly back into fashion at a later date, or because of thrift—these 18th-century silks were very expensive.

On the whole, fashion did not change a great deal in the 18th century, except for details such as the width of sleeves and skirts, though in the 1740s very wide hoops were worn briefly (and later retained only at court). By the 1780s, however, the standard of dressmaking had improved considerably, and dresses became much slimmer, as were men's coats. Fashions tended to change according to the materials used, rather than reflecting any deliberate attempt to introduce new styles, for instance, the Huguenot silk mercers in Spitalfields produced two collections a year which the really fashion-conscious at court had to try to keep up with. Silk was still produced only in narrow widths of 18–21 inches (45·7–53 centimetres), and silk garments were never made with wide seams, but joined by the selvages, so as to waste nothing. Dressmakers rarely matched patterns when joining two pieces of material, indeed considerable ingenuity would have been required to match up the often large-scale patterns.

Dresses were either made with 'English' backs, neatly fitted, or with 'sack backs', a trained back flowing from the shoulders. The 857 dresses are dated more often from the pattern of the silk than from the cut of the garments themselves, as one often comes across sack-backed dresses which have been remade as English-backed ones, there having been so much material to play around with.

There are a number of surviving 18th-century accessories, such as a pierced vellum hat, embroidered garters, shoes, pattens (or clogs), capes and muffs. Early in the 18th century, shoe heels were rather high, becoming lower and wider by the 1740s, while the

858 Left to right: French open robe, *c.* 1775; little girl's cape of blue satin, *c.* 1775; yellow lustring polonaise, *c.* 1785, and hat of *c.* 1780.

859 Left to right: dress of printed challis, *c.* 1836; boy's dress of *c.* 1860, and a Regency dress of maroon and pink striped silk of *c.* 1815.

860 Ball dress of lilac watered silk, *c.* 1868, and a black lace mantlette by Worth, *c.* 1885.

859

860

uppers were often covered in brocades to match the dresses, or embroidered in a similar style. By the 1780s shoes were very pointed with neat little heels, and at the turn of the century these heels became low wedges. At this time shoes were usually made of coloured kid or plain coloured satins, like modern dancing pumps, and shoemakers' trade labels are often found inside them, although most other costume and accessories remain anonymous.

By the end of the 18th century fashion plates had arrived. Changes in fashion no longer had to be passed around by letter, word of mouth or dressed dolls, and thus fashions and the cut of clothes altered much more rapidly. From the 1790s onwards, waists rose, and at the turn of the century, dresses became much simpler, exemplified by the Directoire style of clinging white muslin worn with Kashmir shawls.

In the 19th century, trimmings became very elaborate, with padded *rouleaux*, etc. at the puffed sleeves and hems, and towards the end of the 1820s 'gigot' or 'bishop' sleeves became popular. The

1840s, however, were much more demure, with natural waists and slim sleeves. In the 1850s the skirts grew enormous, until the number of petticoats worn underneath required a crinoline to support them. By the end of the 1860s the width of the skirt had passed to the back, and soon after this extra width was raised, developing into the bustle of the mid-1870s, which by 1878-80 had lowered and flattened. In 1885 a second bustle emerged, only to disappear again by 1890, and in 1895 there was a short-lived fashion for huge sleeves, which vanished before the turn of the century.

The invention of the sewing machine in the 1850s made it easier for dresses with elaborate trimmings to be made, and by the 1870s we begin to find dressmakers' labels in the waistbands of dresses. Examples of most 19th-century costume survive in considerable quantity, particularly from the second half of the century, as many families have kept such garments as wedding dresses and Christening robes. These and other Victorian items such as fans and shawls are finding their way to the sale rooms in great numbers.

EUROPEAN AND AMERICAN WALLPAPERS
Brenda Greysmith

Wallpaper, being one of the more recent developments in mural decoration, has been strongly influenced by its predecessors in that field, especially since it has often been thought of as a substitute for something more luxurious. Thus the silks, damasks and tapestries of the past (and particularly leather hangings and black-work embroidery) are reflected in the designs of early wallpapers. Although the technique of paper-making was known in the East in very early times, it was not until the Middle Ages that its production spread to Europe, and hand-painted paper wall hangings began to make their appearance, especially in Sweden.

Marbling was also used as a decoration, mostly for the endpapers of books, but doubtless also for walls. The first known printed wallpaper, which dates from approximately 1509, utilises the reverse side of paper bearing text relating to the first year of the reign of Henry VIII (waste paper was often used in this way). Many decorated papers at this time were produced to line deed boxes of

guilds and so on, and have an armorial character; they cannot be differentiated from those designed specifically for walls, since all paper was produced in small pieces.

At first, papers were printed in monochrome only, but within 100 years additional colours were being stencilled on to the block-printed outlines. During the 17th century textiles began to be imported from India, and papers from China and Japan, and these encouraged European manufacturers to print with colours and to use more naturalistic designs. In China, paper had been used for lining walls, and was sometimes decorated with freehand drawings, but the Chinese papers which were sold in Europe at this time appear to have been produced especially for export to the West. These original and spacious wallpapers, delicately hand painted with long-lasting colours, and usually showing scenes from domestic life, landscapes and, most popular of all, birds, plants and insects, became extremely fashionable. The patterns were non-repeating

861

861 A photographic reconstruction of a block-printed paper by Hugo Goes, active in the early 16th century. This was discovered in 1911 in the Master's Lodge, Christ's College, Cambridge.

862 Panel of early 18th-century English flock wallpaper from Hurlcote Manor, Towcester.

863 Block-printed paper in black, white and grey on a blue background, produced by Ebenezer Clough in Boston in 1800 in commemoration of George Washington.

864 Chinese wallpaper given by Queen Victoria in 1856, but probably older. It closely resembles the original paper used in the first

decoration scheme in the salon of Brighton Pavilion.

865 Two panels from the series illustrating the story of Cupid and Psyche, first produced by Dufour in Paris in 1816. The paper is block printed in distemper *grisaille*.

861

862

863

864

865

866 English paper of *c.* 1870, with chrysanthemums on an embossed ground.

867 'Compton', designed by William Morris in 1896, and printed by the firm of Jeffrey & Co.

866

867

and, as the sets were expensive and fragile, there was a ready market for European imitations, however grotesque – these tended to be far more cluttered in feeling. Chinese papers enjoyed another great vogue towards the end of the 18th century, and have always remained a strong influence on Western productions.

European papers were usually printed from carved wood blocks, although engraved plates were sometimes used. The technique of block printing also allowed the production of 'flock' papers: the paper was printed with glue instead of colour, and powdered wool or silk was shaken over it, the excess being brushed off when the glue had dried. From the late 17th century onwards flock wallpaper was a favourite in England, but rather less popular in France. It apparently found little favour in America, where European Chinoiserie was being imported during the 18th century, their own wallpaper industry being still in its infancy.

Two other particularly English phenomena were the use of papier mâché, imitating plaster work, for wall- and ceiling-motifs, and 'print rooms', where fine art prints of excellent quality were arranged in orderly profusion and surrounded by paper borders.

During the 18th century many fine papers were designed, often rather restrained, though frequently making use of silver or gold or other techniques for adding lustre. But in France at the beginning of the 19th century, hand printing reached a magnificent and rather flamboyant peak with the production of 'scenic' papers, sets of non-repeating *trompe l'oeil* designs. They often depicted views or historical scenes, although folded curtains, or statues in niches, were also popular. Scenic papers usually necessitated the use of thousands of printing blocks, and the organisation and financial commitment were so enormous that production had to be kept up for many years to recoup the outlay.

Although England did attempt to compete with the French in the production of quality papers, much of her energy seemed to go into, firstly, the production of 'endless' paper, which did not necessitate the joining of small sheets, and secondly, into the industrialisation of the printing process itself. This was achieved by Potters of Darwen in 1839 with a method similar to that of calico printing. The

quality of design in England at this time was generally poor, but there are some interesting examples of commemorative papers. This journalistic aspect of wallpaper can be seen in the designs produced for the French Revolutionaries, and also in some American papers, but the chauvinism of 19th-century England particularly encouraged such treatment. One such paper depicts the Great Exhibition of 1851.

It was partly the wallpaper and other exhibits shown there that precipitated the reaction of the English artist-designers in the last half of the 19th century against commercial production and over-elaboration. The architect and writer A. W. N. Pugin had already advocated that wallpaper should be entirely honest about itself, pretending neither to be something else, nor to be three-dimensional. This idea was taken up by a whole group of artists, the best-known and most influential being William Morris. Although Morris wanted to produce all his artefacts himself, he never mastered the technique of wallpaper production, and his designs were hand printed by the firm of Jeffrey & Co. They commissioned, among others, many members of the Arts and Crafts Movement, some of whom were greatly impressed by Japanese design (this influence can be seen particularly in American papers of the late 19th century). Nursery papers also became very popular at about this time.

Much of the wallpaper of the late 19th century is in the formula of 'dado-filling frieze', the wall being divided into three with a deep frieze at the top, a strip of about 3 feet (91 centimetres) at the bottom, of heavy duty, sometimes embossed, paper to take the wear and tear of the household, and a filling in between. This scheme was part of a long tradition of breaking the surface of a wall with borders, panels, over-door designs etc., which culminated at the turn of the century in elaborate and imaginative friezes set off against plain papers. But the most far-reaching effect of the British design renaissance was the birth of the Art Nouveau movement (see p. 295), which swept across Europe and America, and inspired many fine wallpapers. This, however, was eventually superseded by the Modernist movement (see p. 308), which had no time for wallpaper at all.

249

TIME, SPACE AND CLIMATE

CLOCKS AND WATCHES, *c.* 1500 TO *c.* 1700

Nigel Raffety and Richard Garnier

It is difficult to say when the mechanical weight-driven clock was invented, since in Latin manuscripts the sundial, water-clock and mechanical clock are all referred to as *horologium*. There is, however, some evidence that the mechanical clock was in existence in the late 13th century, and timepieces are thought to have been well established by the middle of the 14th century – it is probable that London had its first public striking clock at about this time.

Throughout Western Europe bell towers began to rise, synchronising the daily lives of people in their work, rest and prayer. The construction of these early clocks was extremely expensive, requiring the employment of highly skilled blacksmiths and itinerant workmen, and so at first it was only the churches and town halls that could afford them. They were large iron-framed clocks viewable at ground level; they possessed neither hands nor dials, and simply acted as an alarum to the clock-keeper to sound the hours on a bell situated within the bell-tower. The appearance of exterior dials came later: examination of late 15th-century illuminated manuscripts and panels shows that a number of church towers possessed these dials by that time. They are usually painted and gilt, and quite small, which explains why they are invariably positioned fairly low down on relatively low buildings. Further dials may be seen slightly later in panoramas of towns, notably Amsterdam (1544) and Innsbruck (1557).

Some clocks struck divisions of the hour, the earliest example being that at Rouen, dated 1389, which strikes the quarters, and as a further complication the carillon was introduced. This device,

868

869

868 German iron chamber clock; 16th century.

869 Iron lantern clock with two-balance foliot escapement.

870 Clock movement showing fusee.

871 German striking book clock, late 16th century. The movement has a dumb-bell foliot and stackfreed.

872 German tabernacle clock, probably made *c.* 1600, and signed 'S.A.H.A.'

870

871

872

which probably originated in the Low Countries, allowed a tune, 'pinned' on a rotating barrel, to be played at the hour, while increasing segments of this tune were played at divisions of that hour.

There are few preserved examples of these early clocks in Europe. In England the earliest surviving clock is thought to be that at Salisbury Cathedral which is dated 1386 and has been recently converted to its original state. The clock at Wells, dated 1392, shows similarities to the Salisbury example, but is somewhat more advanced; the movement sounds the quarters in addition to the hours and incorporates 'warning' into the striking.

There are existing records of several other 14th-century clocks in England—those at Glastonbury, Exeter, Norwich, St Albans, Ottery St Mary, Wells and Wimbourne. Some of these incorporated automaton figures, or 'jacks' as they are called, to strike the hours, and others were designed with automata. The Glastonbury clock,

erected in 1325, was described as 'a great clock distinguished by processions and spectacles'. John Leland, the 16th-century antiquary, described it as 'Horologium Petrus Lightfote Monachus fecit opus', and thus it is known as the work of Peter Lightfoot, a monk of Glastonbury. At one time it was thought that all the four West of England Clocks, Wells, Wimbourne, Ottery St Mary and Exeter, might have been made by this monk, but the theory has now been largely discredited.

Early chamber clocks

By the 15th century, town and church clocks had become commonplace, and a demand arose among wealthy individuals and noblemen for clocks of a similar kind but smaller and more suitable for use in the chambers of their castles. These 'chamber' clocks were constructed on ecclesiastical lines, having four iron corner-posts **868**

873 Gilt-metal clock watch, *c.* 1600, by Vibrandi of Leonardiae, Holland, the case pierced and engraved with floral designs.

874 Left: German verge clock watch, unsigned, with stackfreed; steel wheels with metal gilt front and back plates. Right: oval verge alarum watch by Nicklaus Rugendas, Augsburg (d. 1658).

875 Rare example of a gold skull watch, 3½ in. (8.89 cm.) high, the movement signed Jan Heyder, Amsterdam.

876, 877 Front and movement of an astronomical crucifix watch 2½ in. (6.35 cm.) long by J. Tryon, Poitiers, *c.* 1620. Case and movement are entirely of silver.

878, 879 Rare early French striking globe watch, *c.* 1650, the gilt-metal case engraved with a map of the world. The contemporary case (879) is of tooled leather with a velvet lining.

873

874

875

876

877

878

879

with buttresses. They were decorated with crochets and motifs of Gothic ornament and surmounted by a bell, housed within a rudimentary spire, for striking or alarum. This style of clock was mainly produced in Northern Italy, Germany and France and to a lesser extent in Switzerland. The Liechti family from Winterthur are known to have produced this type of clock for several generations. Although few examples by this family remain today, the main London museums have three examples dating from between 1579 and 1599.

All clocks mentioned so far have relied upon a weight to provide the power or 'motive force' to drive the mechanism. The principle of a series of wheels and pinions in conjunction with a weight had been known for several centuries before being incorporated into a clock; the difficulty had been controlling the rapid running down of the weight. This problem was eventually solved by the introduction of the 'escapement', which checked in an orderly manner the running down of a train of geared wheels. It consisted of an escape or 'crown' wheel, so termed because its triangular teeth give it the resemblance to a crown, and the verge with integral pallets that runs across this wheel. The verge swings, allowing one tooth at a time to pass whilst the other pallet restricts further movement. The rate of escape is varied by a cross-bar or 'foliot' which is formed at the top part of the verge. This has two weights which can be moved out from its centre, causing the clock to go more slowly. Early chamber clocks sometimes had a foliot, but this was largely replaced by the balance wheel which, in more elaborate forms, has continued to be used in watches until the present day.

With few exceptions, medieval clocks were designed so that the wheelwork was fitted into a four-posted frame and the separate 'trains' of wheels were placed one in front of the other or side by side. If the clock was additionally quarter-striking and alarum, two additional trains of wheels and two extra weights would be incorporated in the movement. The spindles on which the wheels were mounted were held between narrow uprights slotted into the frame and securely wedged. The sides of the clock were open and the wheelwork exposed.

These clocks would have been hung on the wall in the great hall so that the large bell would sound throughout the house – since

they were very expensive it is unlikely that even a wealthy man would have owned more than one. Their weights made them awkward to move, and it was not until the introduction of the mainspring that clocks became truly portable. The springiness of a flat blade of iron or steel had long been used in locks and crossbows, but it took considerable skill and ingenuity to fashion a ribbon of steel into a coiled spring for use in clocks. It is uncertain when the mainspring was first introduced, but its origins could well have been in Flanders or Burgundy or even Northern Italy. No Italian timepiece of the late 15th century appears to have survived, but documentary research indicates that portable timepieces were made as early as 1488.

The introduction of the mainspring prompted two further inventions. When the mainspring is fully wound it exerts a much greater force than when nearly run down and, to equalise the pull of the spring, the fusee was introduced. This consists of a truncated cone 870 on which is cut a spiral groove. The mainspring is contained within a drum and a gut line is wound around the outside of the drum and connected to the greater diameter of the fusee; the spring is wound by drawing the gut on to the fusee. Theoretically the increased leverage exerted by the fusee compensates the decreased tension within the spring. In Germany the 'stackfreed' had been 871 introduced for the same purpose but met with little favour elsewhere, and died out in the early 17th century. In early watches the verge escapement was used, consisting of a scaled-down version of the escapement used in clocks.

The art of the watchmaker

The first centre of watchmaking was almost certainly established in Nuremberg in the early 16th century. It was not until this time that watchmakers and clockmakers settled in communities; in earlier times accomplished craftsmen had travelled the lands to wherever their skill was rewarded, often journeying from court to court. In this way the resplendent court of Philip the Good of Burgundy attracted many artisans skilled in metalworking. Shortly afterwards centres became established in Rouen, Lyon, Blois and Paris, the latter two cities no doubt encouraged by the patronage of the king of France. For some while after clock- and watchmaking

880 Oval verge alarum watch, the lid with an engraved sundial. Early 17th century, signed 'J. Chesneau à Orleans'.

881 Small square verge watch in gold and enamel with protecting case, by Baroneau, Paris, *c.* 1650.

882 Gold and enamel verge watch, the case signed 'Huaud le puisné fecit', *c.* 1680.

883 From left to right: German table clock with detachable alarum, unsigned. German hexagonal table clock signed 'Wilhalm Köberle, Eichstätt'. Circular table clock signed 'Leonard Macaire'.

884 Iron domestic clock by Vallin, 1598.

885 English brass carillon lantern clock with automaton figures in the gallery, signed 'Davis Mell, Londini', *c.* 1660.

886 German gilt-metal table clock with alarum, *c.* 1600.

880

881

882

883

884

885

886

had become distinct crafts, the makers belonged only to allied Guilds—it was not until 1543 that the Annaberg Guild specifically included clockmakers as distinct from locksmiths. In the same year the Nuremberg Corporation was petititioned to specify the masterpiece for the *kleinuhrmaker* ('small clock maker'), indicating the distinction between the makers of large and small clocks, in which latter category watches were included. An apprentice in any guild was required to supply a 'masterpiece' specified by the guild in order to qualify as a trained craftsman, known as becoming Free of the Company. The requisites of the different guilds were very varied, for instance the masterpiece in Geneva was an alarum clock, while in Nuremberg two items were requested: firstly, a clock standing 6 inches (15.24 centimetres) high, striking hours and quarters with an alarum and showing minutes, the length of the day and the date; and secondly, a neck watch which struck the hours and had an alarum.

In 1631 the Worshipful Company of Clockmakers was incorpor-

ated in London, largely as a result of the influx and competition from foreign craftsmen or 'straingers', many of whom were political refugees who had settled in the city. The Charter granted by the King to the Clockmakers' Company enabled its officers to enter any premises or workshops within a 10-mile (16-kilometre) radius from the centre of the city, and seize or destroy any bad work or any work made by a person who had not served a seven-year apprenticeship.

The earliest watches were really small portable clocks, drum-shaped, and worn on a cord around the neck. The cases were of engraved gilded brass and the front cover was pierced to reveal the hour chapters beneath. The dial was often set with subsidiary indications showing the phases of the moon, date, and signs of the Zociac in addition to the striking and alarum work. Some watches also had a sundial by which they could be accurately set, for mechanical timepieces of this period were abysmal timekeepers. There were also spherical watches being made at this time: a

887 Silver-gilt enamelled table clock, only 3¼ in. (8.25 cm.) high, with both striking and alarum facilities. Probably made in Augsburg, c. 1600.

888, 889 Two views, open and closed, of a square gilt-metal table clock by Jeremias Büch of Graz.

887

888

889

Nuremberg chronicler records a Peter Henlein, who died about 1540, as a locksmith artist who made watches 'in the form of musk balls at that time in use'. These musk balls were the scent bottle of the period, and were also worn on a cord around the neck. The earliest French watches were also spherical; some of these were 878,879 made in the Blois region in about 1550. The interesting 'globe' watch illustrated, probably by Jacques de la Garde, has a gilt-metal case engraved with a map of the world, the dial positioned at the north pole. Later in the century, the drum-shaped case gave way to the circular case with domed back and front covers, and then 874,880 oval and octagonal cases began to appear. The end of the century saw the emergence of the 'form' watch, the case taking the form of 876,877 birds, flowers, books and crosses. A favourite style was in the form 875 of a skull, an example of which, in the Worshipful Company of Clockmakers, is thought to have been presented to Mary, Queen of Scots.

The beginning of the 17th century was the richest period of all for decorated watches. The form watches were made in silver and brass and combinations of these; others were shaped out of rock crystal, agate and garnet and finely faceted. The cross watch 876,877 illustrated is extremely rare, since not only the case but the entire movement is of silver. The covers and sides display the finest engraving of the period, depicting the Resurrection.

The use of opaque and translucent enamels had begun in the last 881,882 years of the 16th century, but now enamel was being used more extensively. Few plain gold cases have survived, as they were

254

890 Oval watch engraved with Venus and Cupid in the centre of the dial. Early 17th century, signed 'Edm. Bull in Fleetstreet Fecit'.

891 Rectangular table clock with subsidiary calendar dials, by Georg Shulz, Königsberg.

892 Cast silver case for a form watch, mid-17th century. One of the petals forms the cover over the dial of the watch, which is by Henry Grendon.

893, 894 Two views of a German striking and astronomical hexagonal table clock, signed 'Michael Schultz, Dantzigg', early 17th century.

895, 896 Front and rear view of a 17th-century South German tabernacle clock with astrolabe by Peter Schegs of Nuremberg.

891

890

892

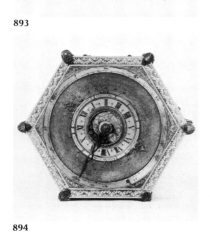

893

894

895

896

897 German crucifix clock on ebonised base by Jacobus Mayr of Augsburg, 17th century.

898 German crucifix clock on gilt-metal base by Pauli Den Zug, early 17th century.

899 Detail of a backplate showing the cycloidal cheeks and silk suspension used in Holland. Dutch, *c.* 1670.

897

898

899

usually melted down for their gold content when times were hard.

The Blois region of France became established about 1630 as a centre of enamelling, and the goldsmith Jean Toutin introduced the art of painting scenes and figures in enamel with the utmost delicacy. No signed work by Jean Toutin is known, but some examples by his sons Henri and Jean are recorded. In Geneva a little later, Jean Petitot founded a school of enamellers and became particularly well known for his portraits in enamel. From then on, Geneva became established as the centre of enamelling, and has continued to flourish in this work until the present day.

The Huaud family of enamellers produced a number of fine enamel watch cases in the second half of the century, the cases being always signed, but differently so according to the period in which they were produced. The example illustrated is signed 882 'Huaud le puisne', and dates from about 1680. The work of this family is distinguishable from the earlier Blois work by the harsher and more garish colours. These delicate enamel watches required an outer protective case, the earliest of which were made of stiffened leather. Few of these cases have survived, but the idea of a double case paved the way for the introduction of the pair-case, in which the inner case, containing the movement, was usually left plain, whilst the outer received the decoration. Later an additional third case was sometimes added to protect the outer pair-case.

A comparison of the cases containing movements of French manufacture with those movements bearing an English signature suggest a common origin; certainly English makers imported French cases, and possibly the engraving was taken from French pattern books or even executed by French workmen in England.

Chamber and table clocks

Weight-driven chamber clocks continued to be produced until the 17th century, and in England they enjoyed renewed popularity, although on the continent they became less common. The English 869 clocks, which came to be known as 'lantern' clocks, were modelled on their foreign predecessors, though the cases became squatter and were decorated with ornamental side-frets, while turned pillars were substituted for the Gothic columns of earlier times. There are some transitional examples, but the fully developed lantern clock appeared about 1620. An example by one of the earliest members of the Clockmaker's Company, William Bowyer, now in the British Museum, has balance-wheel control, which in its original state is extremely rare. Usually these early lantern clocks with balance wheels were converted to later, more accurate forms

of time control as they were invented. However, a lantern clock with original balance wheel escapement can be dated prior to 1660. A particularly rare and interesting carillon lantern clock by N. Vallin, also in the British Museum, is made entirely of steel with 884 brass outside plates which are pinned to the framework. Apart from the trains for the time and for striking, the clock has a mechanism which plays a tune on 13 bells at each quarter by means of a pinned drum. This is the earliest known surviving musical clock, dated 1598.

Another rare carillon lantern clock of this period has a matted dial, signed 'Davis Mell, Londoni', while the base bears the name of 885 Thomas Crawley. Although these craftsmen are not recorded as being in partnership, they are both known to have worked in about 1660. This clock is weight-driven, has three trains of wheels and is quarter striking on three bells. Every three hours the carillon plays a tune on ten bells with twenty hammers and the upper gallery displays revolving musician figures.

The earliest type of spring-driven table clock had a horizontal 883 dial and was in the form of a circular drum which was often provided with an additional alarum. This alarum could be detached from the clock proper, and when required was positioned above the dial, being set off by a detent triggered by the single hour hand. The cases are usually gilt with silver chapter-rings and secured 886 within their cases by latches. These drum-shaped cases were superseded by square and hexagonal shapes with turned or cast claw feet, often in silver. The two photographs of the square table clock by the 17th-century maker, Jeremias Büch of Graz, show the 888,8 florally engraved surround to the chapter-ring and the hinged base containing the bell which reveals, in particular, the decorative balance-cock and hammer head on the signed backplate. Another table clock of the same period but of unusual rectangular form, signed 'Georg Shulz, Königsberg', has a profusely engraved dial 891 plate set with subsidiary calendar dials, the central chapter-ring centred with an engraved scene. Clocks of this type became popular in a hexagonal form; an outstanding example with astronomical indication, signed 'Michael Schultz Dantzigk', also has subsidiary 893,8 indications showing the time of the rising and the setting of the sun, signs of the zodiac, the date and the month. There is another hexagonal table clock by this maker in the British Museum. Such table clocks continued to be made, principally in Germany, well into the 18th century. The majority are striking, but some just tell the time and have a separate alarum train; additionally, others have a quarter-repeating train, a device which allows the hours and quarters to be struck on pressing a lever.

A number of small spring-driven table clocks in the form of a tower were produced in the 16th and 17th centuries. These **872** 'tabernacle clocks', as they are called, were also mainly made in Germany, especially in the regions of Augsburg and Nuremberg. Tabernacle clocks, which usually have two or more vertical dials, giving many indications other than the time, were extremely finely made, displaying the height of craftsmanship and ingenuity of the period.

5,896 The fine example illustrated is signed by Peter Antoni Schegs of Nuremberg, and has numerous dials on all four faces. In addition to the main time-indicating dial which has a 'twice twelve hour' chapter-ring with outer perpetual calendar showing the saints days, the rear dial is set with an astrolabe and has subsidiary dials to differentiate between the 12- or 24-hour striking systems (left), the Dominical letter (right), the two lower dials for regulation and hour/alarum indication. The 12- or 24-hour striking had its origins in Italy where the 24-hour day was used, beginning at sunset. This striking system was most frequently incorporated into German tabernacle clocks in addition to the ordinary 12-hour striking system. Another clock of similar design was made by Johannes Benner, who is recorded working in Augsburg in the mid-17th century. This clock is surmounted by an elaborate cupola and has some nine dials arranged on its four sides. It is quite common for these clocks to be unsigned though a number bear the town stamp, 'AG' (Agustae).

The variation in design of the Augsburg clocks is inexhaustible, many taking the form of animals or monstrances and usually standing on wood bases. However, one of the commonest forms is the **7,898** 'crucifix clock', the crucifixion being a popular theme of this period, and a number of these clocks survive. They are similar in construction, the hour being indicated by a band encircling the globe at the top of the cross, whilst the going and the striking trains are housed within the base beneath. In the fine example illustrated, **897** by the maker Jacobus Mayr of Augsburg, the movement is contained within the moulded ebonised base and is viewable through the pierced side-frets. Although the silver figures of the Virgin Mary and St John are not in themselves unusual, the latter figure is interesting because it is additionally articulated, and raises a chalice when the hour is struck.

Technical advances

The second half of the 17th century heralded two inventions in horology which radically improved the time-keeping of both clocks and watches: the pendulum and the balance spring. A clock of 1650 might keep time to within a few minutes a day, but 20 years later the error had been reduced to some few seconds, while after 1675 watches, previously extremely erratic, would show the time up to within a few minutes. Several valiant attempts were made to improve the performance of time-keeping, the most successful being those of Jost Burgi and his pupil Hans Buschmann, who together perfected the cross-beat escapement. The high performance of their clock was largely due to the extreme precision of the wheels and pivots and overall workmanship combined with the

symmetrical functioning of the 'cross-beat'. These clocks require a degree of skill which was beyond the average clockmaker of the period, and other forms were experimented with, especially devices employing a rolling ball.

It was the famous astronomer Galileo Galilei who discovered the isochronism of the swinging pendulum, and when he became blind towards the end of his life he dictated to his son Vincenzio a description of a timekeeper with a pendulum. Vincenzio only started construction of this clock in 1649 and died before he completed it, but his widow on her death some years later records in an inventory of her belongings 'an iron clock, unfinished with pendulum, the first invention of Galileo'. Christiaan Huygens, the great Dutch physicist, is generally associated with the practical application of a pendulum to a clock, and he made his experimental model in 1656, patenting it the following year.

Salomon Coster, a fine clockmaker working in The Hague, was commissioned by Huygens to produce clocks incorporating the pendulum. As soon as news of the invention reached England, John Fromanteel was sent from London to learn the construction of the clocks. On John's return the Fromanteels were able to advertise clocks that 'go exact and keep equaler time than any now made without this Regulater . . . Made by Ahasuerus Fromanteel who made the first that were in England.' The Dutch makers at this period originally suspended the pendulum by a silk thread held between 'cycloidal cheeks', but the English makers quickly altered **899** this arrangement and attached the pendulum directly to the verge.

In about 1670 England's growing reputation was further established by the invention of the anchor escapement. There is some doubt about the inventor of this escapement, but probably it was either the scientist Robert Hooke or the clockmaker, William Clement. Hooke was a great genius and inventor of the day, and he made several extremely important contributions to horology. The combination of the anchor escapement with the seconds pendulum brought about the introduction of the longcase or 'grandfather' clock. It should be noted that there are very few genuine examples of transitional longcase clocks utilising a short bob pendulum and the older verge escapement.

The dramatic improvement in timekeeping resulting from the advent of the pendulum was followed in about 1675 by the introduction of the balance spring to watches. As with the other significant inventions already discussed there is considerable uncertainty as to the inventor. There is little doubt that as early as 1658 Hooke has conceived the idea of controlling the timekeeping of a watch by means of a spring. In his Cutlerian lectures of 1664 and later to the newly created Royal Society in 1668, he dealt with 'the application of springs to the balance of a watch'. By 1674 Huygens appears to have successfully experimented with the balance spring in collaboration with the French maker, Isaac Thuret. It was only when Huygens attempted to patent 'his' invention that Hooke stirred himself and enlisted the help of the master, Thomas Tompion, to construct a watch to his specification. Watches incorporating the Huygens-Thuret and Hooke-Tompion springs were presented to the King, but after a considerable dispute the coveted patent was refused – much to the advantage of English horology.

THE BRITISH SUPREMACY IN CLOCKMAKING

Nigel Raffety and Richard Garnier

The Restoration of the Monarchy in 1660 brought an end to a period of austerity, and gave a filip to the clock and watchmaking professions. This, in conjunction with the recently introduced pendulum, resulted in the introduction of the 'bracket' clock. Although some of these bracket clocks did originally have a bracket for mounting the clock on a wall, the term has come to mean a

wood-cased clock of a particular type that could stand on a piece of furniture or a shelf. The early bracket clock illustrated, by **900,901** Ahasuerus Fromanteel, shows the architectural form of these clocks at this period; the cases were usually ebony-veneered with restrained fire-gilt mounts. The dial has corner mounts or 'spandrels' which were also fire-gilt, a slender chapter ring and a finely matted

900, 901 Front and movement of an ebony timepiece bracket clock by Ahasuerus Fromanteel, London, *c.* 1680.

902 Ebony striking bracket clock by Joseph Knibb, London.

900

901

902

centre. The movement of this clock displays the elegantly engraved signature but lacks the additional engraving typical of a clock made later in the century. This style of bracket clock was made by the most eminent makers of the time, including Edward East, watchmaker to Charles I, and his apprentice Henry Jones, William Clement, and Robert Seignior.

The verge escapement in conjunction with the short pendulum continued to be used in bracket clocks from this period until the early 19th century in preference to the newly invented and somewhat more accurate anchor escapement. Since the verge escapement was easier to 'set up' and did not depend on the clock being level, it was more suitable for bracket clocks which were carried from room to room.

Clocks at this period were still very expensive, and even a wealthy household would probably own only one bracket clock. As a result portability was important, and the clocks became increasingly more compact, with some having the additional advantage of repeating-work. The provision of this work was particularly useful when the clock was positioned by the bedside at night for, simply by pulling a cord at the side of the case, the hour and last quarter passed could be struck.

902 The Knibb family are particularly noted for their production of fine bracket and longcase clocks. Joseph Knibb established himself as a clockmaker in Oxford, setting up his business outside the City limits. In 1667 he applied for the Freedom but he was opposed by other local tradesmen. The following year he did gain his Freedom but he did not stay long in Oxford, moving to London and becoming Free of the London Clockmakers in 1670. Knibb incorporated repeating work into many of his bracket clocks and, in contrast to the Fromanteel clock described earlier, the backplates were usually florally engraved, the Dutch tulip being a popular motif. He was also an inventor, and made a number of clocks that had a duration of a month or more. Obviously considerable power is required to drive a clock of this type, and for this reason Knibb invented and introduced 'Roman Striking'. The longcase clock

903 illustrated uses this unusual and economical striking system, which employs two bells of varying pitch, one to strike a blow for the Roman numeral 'I' and another bell to strike 'V'. For instance, eight o'clock would sound one blow for the V and three blows on another bell for the three Is.

905 The clock by John Miller is interesting in that it is strongly Knibb in style, and documentary evidence reveals that Miller was apprenticed to Joseph Knibb, having been 'turned-over' from his cousin, Samuel. Clockmakers in London were in close association with each other, and occasionally when a client ordered a certain clock that was not in stock at the time, a maker would 'buy in' an unsigned clock and engrave it with his own name. Hence some

clocks which are obviously in the style of one particular workshop may bear a different signature. It is evident from the volume of work that all the clocks bearing the name Joseph Knibb could not have been made by his own hand alone; the manufacture of clocks was becoming much more commercial and large workshops were being established in the City.

One of the finest craftsmen in the history of British horology, Thomas Tompion, is known to have been in London by 1671 when he was elected a 'Brother', by Redemption, of the Clockmakers Company in London. Tompion, an ingenious designer of complicated clocks, was principally responsible for raising the standards of English clockmaking to a position of pre-eminence in Europe. His finest clocks include two made for the Greenwich Observatory and an astronomical longcase clock that is now in the Fitzwilliam Museum, Cambridge. The illustration shows the engraved backplate **906** of a timepiece bracket clock by Tompion and in particular the bar that actuates the repeating mechanism. Tompion's repeating work is, like the rest of his work, extremely finely executed and precise. A somewhat later bracket clock signed 'Tho. Tompion, Londini, Fecit', has two additional upper dials, one of which regulates the timekeeping, the other silencing the striking work.

Evidence of the size of Tompion's output is provided by the fact that he was soon seen circumventing the regulations of the Clockmakers' Company in order to increase the number of workmen in his employment. According to a rule of the Company, a workmaster could take only a single apprentice at a time and could not take another before the first had served two of his seven years. Apprentices provided cheaper labour than qualified journeymen, and by 1695 Tompion had seven, many of them 'turned over' from the workmaster under whom they had started their apprenticeships. Furthermore, Edward Banger, as one of Tompion's journeymen, took an apprentice within a year and a half of obtaining his own Freedom.

Around 1701, Tompion's increasing age and declining health (he spent more and more time at Bath taking the waters) made it necessary for him to make Banger, his best journeyman and pupil, a fellow workmaster, and their joint productions are signed with both names: 'Thos. Tompion and Edw. Banger'. Banger had married **907** a niece of Tompion's, but evidently quarrelled with him, and by 1708 the partnership had broken up. From then on George Graham became Tompion's principal assistant. Having served his apprenticeship under a different maker, Graham joined Tompion's workshop in 1696 and proved, unlike Banger who, although a fine and hard-working craftsman, was no genius, to be a brilliant inventor. His experiments resulted in some very significant advances in horology. He too married a niece of Tompion's and from about 1710 until Tompion's death in 1713 their work is signed jointly.

903 Ebony three-month-going Roman striking longcase clock by Joseph Knibb, London, c. 1690.

904 Late 17th-century longcase clock by John Barnet, London, the plinth and trunk door inlaid with panels of floral marquetry on an 'oyster' walnut ground.

905 Ebony striking bracket clock by John Miller, London.

906 Detail of an engraved backplate of a timepiece bracket clock by Tompion, showing the repeating-work bar and floral engraving.

905

903 904 906

Graham carried on the business after Tompion's death, working in the same style and continuing his system of numbering clocks and watches: there were different series for ordinary watches, repeating watches, special watches and a further series for clocks, both weight- and spring-driven. There had been also a series prefixed with 'O' for Tompion's early experimental watches when he began to employ balance springs.

Tompion's method of making clocks in batches and only finishing the wheel-work and executing the engraving once a clock was sold has caused some oddities over the actual numbering. For instance, bracket clock No. 92 is signed by Tompion and Banger, although it is in a style dating from before their partnership, about 1689, and

must have been finished about 1702, just after they became partners. Most Tompion and Banger clocks are numbered in the 300 and 400s. No. 272 is signed by Graham only and could have been sold and completed after Tompion's death, as numbers up to about 540 are jointly signed. Clock No. 292, a month-going longcase, was presumably finished just after Banger's parting, since the dial plate bears both their signatures, over which Tompion fixed a plaque with his name only.

The efforts of the equally pioneering contemporary clockmakers such as Quare and the Knibb family, together with Tompion's method of work (an embryonic form of mass production) and his standard of craftsmanship all contributed to the superiority of

907 Ebony chiming bracket clock, the dial signed 'Tompion and Banger, London', with subsidiary chime/silent and regulation rings. No. 92, c. 1710.

908 Ebony timepiece bracket clock with double repoussé basket-top and verge escapement, by Ledgard, London.

909 Ebony timepiece bracket clock by Daniel Quare, London.

910 George III mahogany ormolu-mounted musical bracket clock, which plays four tunes on eight bells. By Eardley Norton, London, c. 1790.

911 George III mahogany striking bracket clock by John Richard Junior, Exeter.

912 George III tortoiseshell and ormolu-mounted bracket clock on matching base made for the Turkish market by John Drury, London.

913 Louis XV boulle tortoiseshell bracket clock by Boisebelland, Paris.

907

908

909

910

911

912

913

English clockmaking. The Tompion-Graham style spread outwards through 'followers' and apprentices who set up on their own.

Leaving aside for the moment the question of advances in precision timekeeping, the history of domestic clocks in the 18th century is really one of changing fashions of cases and dials. Spring clock movements settled down into a number of standard types: timepiece or striking, either with or without repeating work; later in the century quarter-striking and musical clocks became more common; whilst the longcase clock movement with rack striking became very stereotyped.

At first longcase dials had been 10 inches (25·4 centimetres) square or smaller, with narrow chapter-rings with small Arabic minutes, sometimes with every minute numbered, plain 'spade' hands and spandrels that were at first engraved and then with simple applied castings of winged cherub heads. Gradually dials were made 11 inches (27·9 centimetres) square, with wider chapter-rings on which the Arabic five-minute numerals on the outer rim and the half-hour markings became more obtrusive. By about 1700 the size of dials had increased to 12 inches (30 centimetres), and a fashion arose for embellishing them with engraving, especially round the edge of the dial plate, between the spandrels and around the calendar aperture, which was often shaped rather than square.

As bolt and shutter maintaining power was phased out, so by 1710 the winding apertures on most dials were ringed, a practice which probably originated to prevent scratching the dial with the winding key. Around 1720 the arched dial came into vogue, with a narrower arch above the familiar square dial. The dial plates of these clocks are continuous, but examples abound of arched dials formed from 12-inch (30-centimetre) dials with separate arches tacked on. There are two possible explanations for this: the first, and probably most obvious being that clockmakers were unwilling to dispense with their stocks of square dials and merely altered them to suit the fashion; while the second suggests that this modification may have been a result of later (and often unscrupulous) marrying of earlier movements to arched-dial cases and the consequent need to add to the dial. One rarely finds a bracket clock dial with an added arch, though they underwent a similar evolution (although of smaller sizes than longcase dials) from square to arched, also becoming larger and more elaborated.

The arch was at first used as a place for the maker to sign the clock, or the strike/silent lever was positioned there, by which the striking work could be disconnected and silenced. Later, especially in north country clocks, it often showed the phases of the moon enclosed by a motto or the maker's signature. North country makers

914 George II walnut longcase clock by
Edward Herbert, London.

915 George II blue lacquered longcase clock by
Nicholas Lambert, London.

916 George III mahogany longcase clock by
Thomas Cook, London.

917 George III musical mahogany longcase clock
by Thomas Ashton, Macclesfield.

914   915   916   917

particularly liked to have astronomical indications on their long-case clocks; William Barker of Wigan, who produced a number of complicated clocks, is an extreme example.

Arched dials soon settled down into less elaborated forms with a silvered chapter-ring enclosing the matted dial centre with sub-sidiary seconds and calendar rings, and spandrels that had passed through a number of scrolled cherub or mask designs to plain Rococo scrollwork. From 1760 or so painted dials were used on cheaper provincial clocks, especially those of 30-hour duration, which had continued to be made throughout the century. London clockmakers by this stage were beginning to use plain silvered dials engraved with chapter-rings, or dials with enamelled chapter-rings, both of which are very attractive and easily legible.

The cases of longcase clocks naturally changed as their dials did. The early architectural ebony-veneered case gave way to less severe styles. Walnut was soon employed, while ebony was used into the 18th century and throughout it for bracket clocks. Marquetry came into fashion in the 1680s, at first in panels on the trunk door and eventually spreading over the whole front face of the case. Once longcases were made taller and with 12-inch (30-centimetre) dials, the hood covering the movement was con-structed with a hinged door to pull forwards rather than rise up the

backboard of the clockcase. Arched trunk doors followed soon after arched dials, about 1730.

As marquetry decreased, so lacquered cases increased in favour. The first examples date from the late 17th century, and they are found up to the mid-18th century, most commonly black, dark green or blue, and more rarely red, white or yellow. Painted dial and 30-hour clocks are normally associated with oak cases. North country makers developed an elaborate style of case, while London makers favoured elegant proportions and finely figured veneers. After the first quarter of the 19th century the demand for longcases began to die out, although there was a revival in the late Victorian and Edwardian eras.

Examples of marquetry and lacquer are not as numerous in bracket clocks as they are with longcases: just as the verge escape-ment continued to be employed in bracket clocks, so throughout the 18th century their cases were very often ebonised with con-trasting fire-gilt mounts. In the evolution of case styles, the most notable alteration occurred in top of the case. From the shallow wooden basket or caddy top of the 17th century developed the gilt-metal *repoussé* basket top of 1700-20. During the reigns of George I and II the inverted bell-top was the current style, the lines of which changed into the bell top in the early part of George III's

918 Ebony striking 'balloon' clock by Johnson of Gray's Inn Passage, c. 1780.

919 Louis XIV *pendule religieuse* with velvet dial.

920 Louis XV ormolu and Meissen porcelain-mounted clock signed 'Jn Baptiste, Baillon'.

921 Louis XV ormolu striking cartel clock by Denis Masson, Paris.

922 Louis XV ormolu and bronze elephant mantel clock.

923 Dutch Friesland clock with 30-hour striking movement and verge escapement. Late 18th century.

918

919

920

921

922

923

reign. In the second half of the 18th century some clock cases became more ornate, especially quarter-striking and musical clocks with tortoiseshell veneered and ormolu-mounted cases, many of which were made for the Turkish market. Much of this ornamentation followed French models and the balloon-cased English clocks of the turn of the century trace their origins from French bracket clocks.

The standard French bracket clock of scrolling form, its ormolu-mounted case of boulle, lacquer, *vernis martin* or tortoiseshell, had developed from much more severe clocks in the Dutch taste. The *pendule religieuse* of the late 17th and early 18th centuries was so called because its comparatively stark case was equated with religious simplicity. However, the trend towards standard movements with all concentration focused on the appearance and decoration of the case was already apparent: in contrast to the highly engraved backplates of contemporary English bracket clocks, the rectangular movements of *pendules religieuses* have plain backplates simply signed at the base. The French preference for 'decorative' clocks is typified by the lion, elephant and bull mantel clocks and the porcelain-mounted confections that were produced in such large numbers in the 18th and 19th centuries. It can be seen from the illustrations that the movements of these clocks, circular with enamel dials, have dispensed with the fusee, employing going barrels toothed directly into the going and striking trains.

Dutch clockmaking, after its pioneering sprint in the mid-17th century, steered during the 18th a midway course between French profusion of decoration and English solidity. Though there were some makers working completely in the French style, Dutch bracket clocks tended to have severer cases. Equally their movements were generally simpler and less substantial than contemporary English ones. Longcase clocks were popular in Holland, as in England, though their cases were normally larger and more ornate, and their dials showed more calendar complications. 'Friesland' clocks, as shown in the illustration, represent a regional form of Dutch clock which was constructed on similar lines to a lantern clock.

924, 925 Two views (top plate and side view of movement) of a watch movement with cylinder escapement by George Graham. London, No. 5717.

926 Detail of the bob of Ellicott's compensation pendulum.

PRECISION TIMEKEEPING

Nigel Raffety and Richard Garnier

The history of ordinary domestic clockmaking through the 18th century was interwoven with a continuing struggle to perfect a precision timekeeper. As early as 1530 a Dutch astronomer, Gemma Frisius, had pronounced that a timekeeper could be employed to calculate longitude at sea by the comparison of local time with the time of a known longitude as shown on the timekeeper. By an Act of Parliament of 1714 The British Government offered a £20,000 prize for a timekeeper that was sufficiently accurate to calculate longitude within half a degree after a voyage to the West Indies and back. There were smaller prizes for lesser accuracy. In 1720 The French Academy of Science offered a reward, and Spain too held out financial inducement for the perfection of a marine timepiece.

The problem concerned both stationary weight-driven clocks for use in astronomical observations to determine longitude more exactly on land and spring-driven portable timepieces for use particularly at sea. In both weight- and spring-driven clocks and watches the two greatest obstacles to better timekeeping were fluctuations due to temperature changes and the difficulty of freeing the regulator (either pendulum or balance) from interference by the train. The 'Royal Pendulum', 61·1 inches (155 centimetres) long, beating 1¼ seconds, was an attempt in the late 17th century to improve on the 39·1 inch standard pendulum in conjunction with the anchor escapement, which in itself had been a marked improvement on the verge. The one major drawback of the anchor escapement was its recoil: in an ordinary longcase clock with anchor escapement the seconds hand after each jump forward is seen to draw back slightly, and this indicates that for an instant the pendulum is pushing against the train and trying to raise the driving weight. The idea behind the 'Royal Pendulum' was that in beating more slowly its swing would be affected fewer times in a given period by interference from the train. Graham succeeded in eliminating recoil in his dead-beat escapement, a modified form of

924

925

926

927 George III mahogany regulator signed on the silvered dial 'Spencer and Perkins, London'. Late 18th century.

928 French wall-mounted month-going regulator clock with dead-beat escapement and gridiron pendulum, signed on the backplate 'Breguet No. 3300'.

929 English 19th-century mahogany regulator with mercurial pendulum, signed 'Evans, Shrewsbury'.

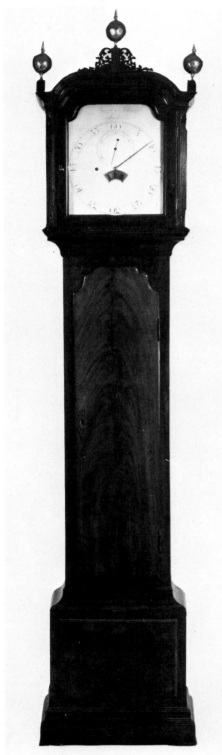

927

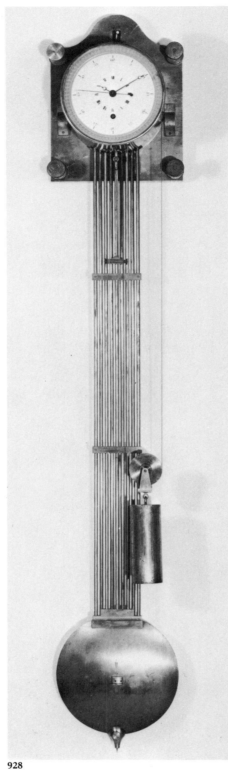

928

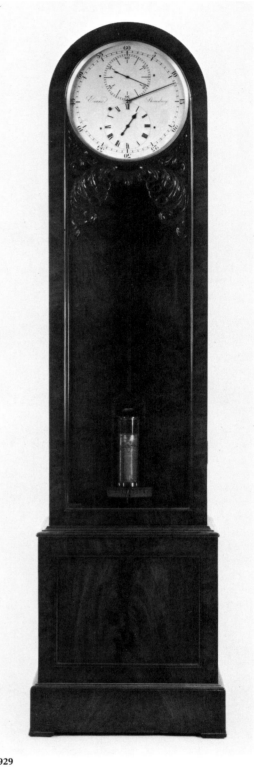

929

the anchor invented in 1715, in which the pallets of the escapement represent segments of a circle with the pallet arbour as its axis. Thus the pallets merely lock the escape wheel as they in turn engage its teeth (instead of driving it backwards as in the plain anchor escapement with its straight-sided pallets) as the pendulum swings to its full extent.

In addition to being free from interference from the driving force, a pendulum depends on constant length to beat at a constant rate. Around 1721 Graham devised the mercurial pendulum, in which the changing length of the pendulum rod due to temperature fluctuation is compensated by the changing level of mercury in the jar acting as the bob. Graham's own trials of his compensated pendulum over the period June 1722 to October 1725 showed its maximum error to be one-sixth of that of an ordinary good time-keeper with dead-beat escapement. Other makers followed Graham's lead in employing the differing coefficients of expansion of two metals. Harrison's pendulum is known as the gridiron

pendulum because of its appearance, whereas John Ellicott, after some experimental examples, developed a pendulum with a single **926** rod formed from brass and steel. The greater expansion of the brass side of the rod depressed a spring lever which in turn raised the bob. But Ellicott's pendulum was expensive and difficult to make and tended to move in jerks. It never became widely used, unlike the mercurial pendulum, which was extensively used in England, **929** and the gridiron pendulum, which was very popular in France, especially for month-going regulators in fine ormolu-mounted **928** cases of the Empire period. English longcase regulators are char- **929** acterised by plain silvered dials, at first shaped and then circular, with separate arbors for the hands recording seconds, minutes, and hours, though sometimes the hour is indicated in a sector. 18th-century longcase regulators normally have finely veneered cases of good proportions. By the turn of the century the case often has a glazed door to reveal the pendulum, and with Victorian regulators the sides of the case are often glazed as well.

930 John Harrison's marine timekeeper No. 1.

931 John Harrison's second marine timekeeper, completed in 1739.

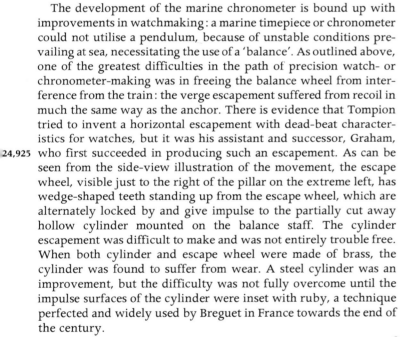

930 John Harrison's marine timekeeper No. 1.

931 John Harrison's second marine timekeeper, completed in 1739.

930

931

24,925

The development of the marine chronometer is bound up with improvements in watchmaking: a marine timepiece or chronometer could not utilise a pendulum, because of unstable conditions prevailing at sea, necessitating the use of a 'balance'. As outlined above, one of the greatest difficulties in the path of precision watch- or chronometer-making was in freeing the balance wheel from interference from the train: the verge escapement suffered from recoil in much the same way as the anchor. There is evidence that Tompion tried to invent a horizontal escapement with dead-beat characteristics for watches, but it was his assistant and successor, Graham, who first succeeded in producing such an escapement. As can be seen from the side-view illustration of the movement, the escape wheel, visible just to the right of the pillar on the extreme left, has wedge-shaped teeth standing up from the escape wheel, which are alternately locked by and give impulse to the partially cut away hollow cylinder mounted on the balance staff. The cylinder escapement was difficult to make and was not entirely trouble free. When both cylinder and escape wheel were made of brass, the cylinder was found to suffer from wear. A steel cylinder was an improvement, but the difficulty was not fully overcome until the impulse surfaces of the cylinder were inset with ruby, a technique perfected and widely used by Breguet in France towards the end of the century.

Friction and its concomitant, wear, were a constant source of difficulty to watchmaking, but in 1704 a patent was granted for a method of using jewels for pivot bearings, thus reducing friction. The secret of jewelling was preserved in England for some way through the century, despite attempts by foreign makers to learn it, and continental makers had to be content with using a hardened steel plate instead. However, even in England jewelled bearings were not used until about 1750 throughout the train, as distinct from the use of a diamond endstone in the centre of the balance cock for the upper pivot of the balance staff, as seen in the movement by Graham. Early on in the century, Sully, an English maker who set up a manufactory at Versailles, developed an alternative system of oil sinks (reservoirs of oil) for pivot bearings.

The properties of springs were not fully understood in the early part of the 18th century. All springs had been assumed to be isochronous until Pierre Le Roy in 1759 declared that they were not, and showed that each spring has a certain length at which it is so. Any increase over that optimum length will make the spring

describe small arcs quicker than longer ones, and vice versa. It had long been realised that temperature changes affected the performance of balance springs. Indeed Hooke records 'At Whitehall saw the King in the Gallery he spoke to me in the park that weather had altered watch.' This was the watch mentioned above, made by Tompion and employing Hooke's balance spring. To begin with the only way to correct a watch for temperature variation was to alter the length of the balance spring by manual setting, and to combat this problem Harrison invented the bimetallic compensation curb using the principle of differing coefficients of expansion of two metals. He formed a strip of brass and steel fused together, which bent or straightened in response to temperature fluctuations (because of the greater expansion and contraction of brass over steel) and drew two curb pins along the balance spring, thus lengthening or shortening the effective length of the spring. Later makers were to make the balance itself of two metals fused together.

Harrison will always be remembered chiefly for his work on marine chronometers, culminating in his winning the prize offered under the 1714 Act of Parliament, but in the long run his work proved to be on the wrong track. However, his bimetallic compensation curb was of great value considering the extremes of temperature to which a timekeeper would be subjected on a voyage to the West Indies and back. In addition Harrison worked on a form of dead-beat verge in an attempt to find an escapement that allowed the balance spring to operate freely while also compensating for any inequality in driving force from the main spring. In all he constructed five machines, some of which were subjected to rigorous testing by the Board of Longitude set up under the Act. His first 930,931 marine clock, since known as H I, could have won the longitude prize had the question of 'rate' been fully understood at this stage. If a clock maintains a constant or perfect rate and thus gains/loses exactly the same amount a day, then calculations can be made in compensation: H I would have been correct to within approximately three seconds a day, an accuracy within the most stringent provisions of the Act. H I was tested at sea in 1736, but it was not until three models later, after a prolonged struggle to convince the Board of Longitude and in face of financial difficulties, that H 4 was recognised by Parliament in 1773 as accurate enough to win the prize.

Thomas Mudge, who had been appointed by the Board of Longitude as one of the judges to examine Harrison's clocks,

932

932 The marine timekeeper by Thomas Mudge, known as 'Green', 1777. The brass case has a polished green shagreen band, and the dial has separate chapter and seconds rings surrounded by silver scroll spandrels.

932 determined to improve on Harrison and win one of the remaining prizes offered under the Act. Accordingly he abandoned his flourishing watch and clock business in London to his partner William Dutton and left for Exeter in 1770 to devote his entire energies to the problem. Apart from the fact that his 'Blue' and 'Green' failed on test to be accurate enough, his constant force escapement (a form of modified verge), like Harrison's escapement, was too complicated to be produced economically in large numbers. H 4 had taken 15 years to complete; Mudge's Blue and Green still took four years to build.

Magnificent as his three marine timepieces are, Mudge's work on them proved to be of no lasting significance. His escapement was not only difficult to construct, it also failed to allow the balance to swing freely. It seems that work on detached chronometer escapements came to a head at much the same time in both France and England. Pierre Le Roy may have been the first to devise a detent escapement. The detent serves to lock the train which is unlocked only on every alternate swing of the balance which then receives impulse but is otherwise detached from the train. Berthoud, another Frenchman, also arrived at a form of detent escapement after much experiment, but it was John Arnold and Thomas Earnshaw in England who were the first to produce marine chronometers commercially. They both invented detent escapements independently and at much the same time around 1770. There was intense rivalry between Arnold and Earnshaw, and they both emphatically signed their chronometers 'Invt. & Fecit'. It was Earnshaw's form of escapement and compensated balance that was generally adopted by subsequent chronometer makers. At first individual captains were responsible for providing their own chronometers, but in 1818 the Admiralty made a general issue of them to ships of the line.

Despite his wholehearted devotion after 1770 to marine timekeeping Mudge's most significant contribution to horology was his invention of the lever escapement shortly before 1769. In some ways analagous to the anchor escapement for pendulum clocks, it is a simple and practical way of detaching the balance, and the principle of it is still employed in the majority of mechanical watches

today. But Mudge used it only a few times before he departed for Exeter. 'Queen Charlotte's Watch', made by Mudge and with the London hallmark for 1769, has long been thought to employ the first example of the lever escapement, but there is also a small 'travelling' clock by Mudge which may well have been the prototype for the lever escapement on which Mudge worked out his ideas before making the Queen's watch.

CLOCKS AND WATCHES FROM THE 18th CENTURY

Nigel Raffety and Richard Garnier

Once the balance spring had passed the experimental stage and became established by about 1690, the pair-cased verge watch led a useful, if unadventurous, life throughout the 18th and first half of the 19th centuries. Because the verge watch was comparatively simple to construct and trouble free it continued to be made in large numbers during this period. It did benefit from the inventions and improvements outlined above in the quest for precision timekeeping, and thus the pre-eminent position achieved for English watchmaking by Tompion, Quare and the like was maintained through the first half of the 18th century and longer.

A London-made watch was considered superior, and several watches falsely signed by 'London' makers have survived: a typical signature is 'Tarts, London'. The intention presumably was to provide a better market for these watches, which are characterised by generally inferior movements with continental-style bridgecocks for the balance and enamel dials with arcaded minutes in the Dutch style. Until recently these watches were assumed to be of Dutch origin, but this has now been challenged. Many of the movements may have been made in Geneva, but the charge has stuck, and they are known as Dutch forgeries.

Some of the improvements in watchmaking were incorporated in verge movements, for instance the use of diamond endstones, but

the principal changes in 18th-century verge watches were in decorative 'externals'. The table and feet of balance clocks, instead of being pierced right to their edges as in the early 17th century, had by 1680 developed a firm outlined border, and by 1730 the foot was increasingly left solid and not pierced, their upper surface merely engraved. In response to the cylinder escapement, by 1750 balance cocks were generally made smaller on verge watches too. The pillars holding the plates of the movement together followed a succession of styles, and by 1750 were generally of simple cylindrical design instead of the square baluster form or the tulip design of the late 17th century.

Watch dials from the earlier 17th century had normally been profusely engraved and with an applied narrow chapter ring, but in the last quarter of the century this form was generally superseded by the champlevé dial in gold or silver. French watches at this date 933 tended to be even fatter and larger than English examples and thus became known as 'oignons', and by 1720 English watches began to 935 be fitted with one-piece enamel dials that had developed from multipart oignon dials. Initially the layout of these early full enamel dials closely followed that of the champlevé dial, but later in the century only the hour chapters were shown, and at the turn of the century there was a fashion in France and Switzerland for Arabic

933 Silver pair-cased verge watch with silver champlevé dial and beetle and poker hands. By Godfrey Poy, London, c. 1710.

934 Silver sun-and-moon verge watch by Clarke and Dunster, c. 1710.

935 Large gilt-metal 'oignon' verge watch by Jean Hubert, Rouen, c. 1690.

936 Gold quarter-repeating verge watch with elaborately pierced balance cock and engraved dust ring, by James Renou, London.

937 Gold and enamel verge watch made and signed by William Story, London.

938 Gold and enamel verge watch by Windmills, London, the case with an enamel of a shepherdess, signed 'W. Craft fecit', 1782.

939 Gold and enamel pair-cased cylinder watch and chatelaine depicting the story of Alexander and Darius.

933

934

935

936

937

938

939

hour chapters. Because of their clear legibility, enamel dials became highly popular and many earlier watches were adapted to fit them, just as early 17th-century watches had been converted to balance springs. This has meant that champlevé dials are comparatively rare and sought after.

In 18th-century England, beetle and poker hands were commonly used in conjunction with enamel dials, whereas continental makers preferred scrolling forms. Breguet in France towards the end of the century set a fashion for 'moon' hands that was to last throughout much of the succeeding century in France and Switzer-

land, while English 19th-century makers often employed 'spade' hands.

Around 1688 both the Reverend Edward Barlow and Daniel Quare devised repeating mechanisms for watches, and the King was asked to judge whose method was the better. He decided on Quare's since it required only one lever to be depressed to strike a full quarter-repeat, whereas Barlow's system required separate levers for the hours and quarters. By 1700 half-quarter repeating had been developed, in which a further blow is struck once $7\frac{1}{2}$ minutes after the quarter has been passed, and by the late 18th

940 Gold and enamel watch case and chatelaine, the case with enamel *en grisaille*, and the chatelaine enamelled with a sacrificial scene, *c.* 1780.

941, 942 Two repoussé watch cases. Left: reverse with pierced band and symmetrical border; right: reverse with asymmetrical border enclosing mythological scene.

943 Gold *montre à tact* ruby cylinder witch by Breguet, No. 683. The case, with revolving back, is enamelled in blue with an arrow, and hallmarked for the period 1798-1809.

944 Quarter-repeating jacquemart watch, the dial with jacks on a blue *guilloché* enamel ground.

941   942

940

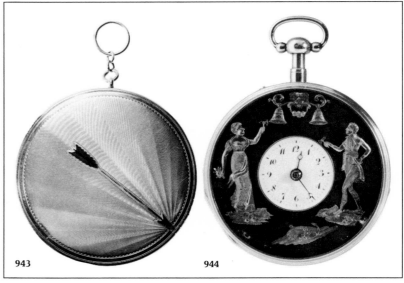
943   944

century, five-minute repeaters were fairly common. It was not until about 1800 that minute repeaters were widely made, though Mudge had won fame for making, about 1750, a minute repeating clock watch mounted in a cane head for Ferdinand VI of Spain. Early repeating watches are characterised by a loud ringing which could have become embarrassing to the user. To solve this problem, pulse-pieces were often fitted which protruded from the inner case and when depressed silenced the bell but allowed the blows to be felt in the hand. The dumb repeater, a later development, dispensed with a bell altogether and the blows were struck against a steel block, giving a clicking sound.

Some 17th-century watch cases had had shutters for the winding hole to keep out dirt, but the need to hinge out the movement in order to regulate the balance spring and also the pierced cases that were necessary for repeating watches, meant that further protec-**936** tion was needed. The watch by Renou illustrated here shows the first solution, a removable band which fits round the plates of the movement while allowing access to the top plate for winding and regulating. The dust band was introduced about 1700 and was used on occasions by Tompion, but was superseded in about 1715 by the dust cap (possibly devised by Graham), which fitted over the whole movement, protecting the balance as well but with apertures for the winding square and the regulation disc.

As mentioned above, with a pair-cased watch it was usually the outer of the two cases which was decorated. The inner was left plain except for repeating or alarm watches where it was often elaborately pierced and engraved. The square hinge on the typical outer case of about 1700 gradually developed rounded shoulders and later was merged into the outline of the case. Pendants evolved through the century, becoming more prominent.

Enamelling continued to be employed in the 18th century, but the work does not have the charm of either the Blois or Huaud Schools. Generally subject painting was reduced to a circular or oval panel enclosed by translucent enamel overlaying an engraved ground (called *guilloché* enamel) and simulated seed pearls. But there were more elaborate pieces, such as the fine watch and chatelaine illustrated, fully enamelled *en suite* with the story of **939** Alexander and Darius.

In the 1720s a fashion arose for repoussé outer cases, normally **941,94** depicting Classical or mythological subjects, and for over 50 years this was the most common form of decoration. The illustration shows a repoussé case dated 1723, in which the scene is enclosed by **941** a symmetrical border, but within a very few years the frame was more commonly asymmetrical. By no means all repoussé cases are of such a high standard; fine-quality ones in pristine condition are now something of a rarity. There are numerous examples that are ill defined and poor, the nature of repoussé leading to badly rubbed highlights and sometimes cases which have worn through in places. Because of the care needed when wearing watches with enamelled or repoussé cases, they were often provided with alternative 'every-day' cases covered in leather or shagreen. The leather-covered outer case of the Renou watch is probably the working case—the watch would originally have had a fine outer case for formal occasions. Shagreen, leather or tortoiseshell were used as standard decorative treatments for the outer cases of more ordinary watches, these materials being affixed to the case by brass, silver or gold pins which were often worked up into patterns, known as piqué decoration. Translucent horn was an even cheaper form of decoration, and was often underpainted with military or other subjects. Many watches, however, were furnished with plain cases of gold, silver or gilt-metal, without any of the decoration described above, especially in the latter part of the 18th century.

It was symptomatic of the state of French watchmaking in the face of English pre-eminence that the manufactory set up early in the 18th century by Sully at Versailles floundered before long. The great revival of French watchmaking was principally due to the efforts of the Le Roy family. Julien (1686-1759) praised Graham's cylinder escapement and used it widely himself. He was probably the first to use gongs of coiled steel wire in place of bells for repeating watches, and he invented the system of dumb repeating, while his son Pierre, who has already been mentioned, was noted for his work on the properties of springs and the detent escapement. In the second half of the 18th century there was a demand for slimmer watches because of the closer-fitting clothes of the day and, while English makers continued as before, the French seized on the new fashion and built up a flourishing trade on it. In about 1770 J. A. Lepine devised a system of replacing the top plate of a movement with bars or bridges, a layout generally known as 'Lepine calibre'.

The Lepine calibre and gong repeating represent perhaps the two greatest steps towards the development of the thinner watch that was raised by A.-L. Breguet (1747-1823) to such heights of elegance and technical perfection. Born in Switzerland, Breguet had arrived in Paris by 1768. His early success was based on his self-winding watches or *montres perpetuelles*, which were wound by the swinging action of a pivoted platinum weight. The idea did not originate with Breguet, but he perfected it by making the weight responsive to very slight movements of the watch. Seeking to produce a high-quality inexpensive watch, Breguet devised his *souscription* series which, after a short evolutionary period, always employed Breguet's perfected ruby cylinder escapement. Simplicity is the keynote of the *souscription* watches: they have only a single hand, since Breguet realised this was sufficiently precise for everyday use.

943 His *montres à tact*, produced for more fashion-conscious patrons, enable the time to be 'read' from touch pieces on the side of the case by how far an arrow on the revolvable back of the case can be rotated.

Breguet's more standard watches were made in three grades: the lowest with movements merely finished in his workshops, the second wholly made in the workshops, and the best grade made to the highest standards with fully jewelled movements employing lever escapements with compensated balances. His watch cases were of gold or silver with engine-turned engraving, and the dials were either enamelled and with Arabic chapters or engine-turned gold or silver with Roman chapters. He invented the ratchet key to prevent his watches being damaged by being wound in the wrong direction, and devised a form of shockproofing for the balance known as a 'parachute'. In 1795 he invented the *tourbillon* to compensate for the alteration of rate that occurs when a watch is held in different positions. These differences are cancelled out by mounting the escapement on a rotating carriage. Breguet's first *tourbillons* revolved every minute, but some of his later examples complete a revolution in four, five or six minutes.

Carriage clocks and later watches

As well as making a number of fine domestic clocks and a longcase regulator with double pendulum in the Royal Collection at Buckingham Palace, the watch- and clockmaker A.-L. Breguet seems to have been the first to have made carriage clocks. The earliest travelling clocks had been in the form of large watches and are known as coach or carriage watches. The carriage clock was **945** probably developed from the *pendule d'officier* (officers' campaign- **946** ing clock) and the *capucine* clock. *Capucine* clocks often had cylinder escapements with the balance let into the backplate, an arrangement to be seen in the earliest carriage clocks by Breguet. He made three sorts of carriage clocks: first the architectural cased examples, secondly wooden cased ones with gilt-metal mounts, and lastly the hump-backed form. All three styles, though first produced in that order, continued to be made concurrently. It was typical of Breguet to be the first to take advantage of the ready market for travelling clocks by producing the first really practical examples,

and that his work should not have been surpassed since. Beautifully made, his carriage clocks always have *grande sonnerie* striking and **947** often incorporate complicated calendar work.

Following Breguet's lead the French carriage clock industry expanded rapidly and developed an enormous export market. Their manufacture became organised and standardised. In place of the slightly individual movements with particular escapements by early makers such as Paul Garnier, standard movements evolved of varying quality. Timepiece movements with cylinder platform escapements represent the lowest quality, the standard rising to *grande sonnerie* movements with alarm and platform lever escapements with compensated balances. Refinements such as chrono- **948** meter escapements, minute repeating and centre-seconds are less common. The first cases had been cast largely in one piece, but as the industry expanded a number of set case styles evolved. These standard cases were assembled from a number of cast components which were sometimes finished to higher standards by means of fine engraving or mounted with porcelain or enamel panels instead of the usual glass. The standard corniche case is familiar enough, and commonly contains a standard timepiece or striking and repeating movement with lever escapement. Higher quality movements are normally in better cases, such as the oval, gorge or enamelled types, although these styles are found in conjunction with ordinary striking movements.

Because of the highly organised nature of the industry, many French carriage clocks have the names of English traders on their dials. These clocks must not be confused with true English carriage clocks which are characterised by larger proportions and are of more individual workmanship, employing fusee and chain drive rather than going barrels toothed directly into the train as in French examples. Arnold, Vulliamy, McCabe, Frodsham and Dent are names particularly associated with English carriage clocks. Illustrated here is a clock by Robert Roskell with a style of case **948** often used by McCabe, and a silver hump-back cased clock with tourbillon by Nicole Nielson. Both J. F. Cole in the 1840s and Jump **949,950** at the turn of the century made clocks with cases and dials very similar to Breguet's hump-backed carriage clocks.

Breguet was adept at surrounding himself with brilliant pupils, many of whom later set up in business on their own, often signing their productions 'élève de Breguet'. During the Reign of Terror in France Breguet left Paris, first for London and then Switzerland. He returned as soon as conditions permitted, since opportunities were greater in France, but retained links with his native country. In addition to his own high-class watches, he and his pupils after him imported Swiss *ébauches* (movements in the rough) to be sold once they had been finished and cased up. Soon after 1800 Swiss watchmakers began to challenge the French lead, both through this trade in *ébauches* and because of their concentration on 'fashion' watches. The illustration shows a typical Swiss quarter-repeating jacquemart watch of the period in which the automated jacks seem **944** to strike out the quarters which are in fact sounded on gongs. The skeletonised dial and Arabic chapters are characteristic. The late 18th century also saw the revival of the form watch in France and **951,952** Switzerland, though in contrast to the religious symbolism of the 17th century, 19th-century form watches are totally secular in feeling, commonly taking the form of musical instruments. They normally contain cylinder or verge movements of average quality.

The Swiss built on their success with such fashionable watches by the introduction of mechanisation. In the late 18th century the Japy family began to use machinery for making *ébauches*, and very early in the 19th, Swiss makers were making finished watch parts by machine. But it was the Americans who were to develop this trend even further. At first the lack of a watchmaking tradition in America, and hence the absence of any division of watchmaking craft skills amongst specialists, was an advantage. It meant the Americans fully established the mechanised production of cheap, quality watches on a large scale through the concept of interchangeable watch parts made by one company. But this very lack of traditional division of skills told against the American companies once methods of mechanical manufacture became more technically

269

945 French gilt-metal *pendule d'officier* with alarum and pull repeat, by Robert of Courvoiser, *c.* 1800.

946 French brass striking *capucine* clock with separate pull-wind alarum, *c.* 1820, signed 'Bois de Chesne au Pont St Esprit'.

947 Silver-cased *grande sonnerie* carriage clock with calendar, by Breguet, No. 4529.

948 English striking chronometer carriage clock with subsidiary month, day and date dials, the sides inset with a thermometer and barometer. By Robert Roskell, London, 19th century.

949, 950 Front and backplate of an English *grande sonnerie* striking carriage clock by Nicole Nielson & Co., London.

951 Swiss gold and enamel automaton butterfly snuff box by Piquet of Meylan, containing a watch and musical box, *c.* 1810.

945

946

947

948

949

950

951

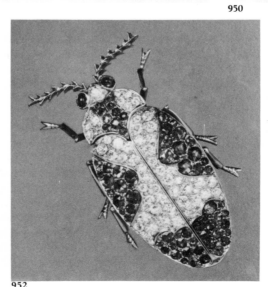
952

953

952 Swiss gold and emerald form watch designed as a beetle, 20th century.

953 Gold consular-cased pocket chronometer, No. 1956, by John Arnold, London, with Arnold's spring detent escapement.

954 'Acorn' clock, American, made *c.* 1850 by the Forestville Manufacturing Company.

advanced. A single company could not compete against the Swiss makers who, through organisation and integration, used mechanisation to the benefit of their traditional skills. Thus they manufactured well-regarded lever watches and less good cylinder watches, both selling at comparable prices with the generally less sophisticated American products.

Whilst the American watch industry survived by means of cutting production costs, English watchmaking was in definite decline by mid-century in the face of such competition. English watches continued to be principally hand produced, and makers clung tenaciously to the fusee. Thus English watches were comparatively expensive and out of date because of the difficulty of incorporating keyless winding in a fusee watch. It was principally due to the popularity of keyless winding that the fusee was generally abandoned around the 1880s in England. However, the continued use of the fusee is another indication of the high standard of English watch- and clockmaking in the second half of the 19th century, which has already been demonstrated by the superior nature of English carriage clocks. Indeed there was a late flowering of precision timekeeping in England at this period. Large numbers of marine chronometers and pocket chronometers were produced and, in addition to the carriage clock mentioned above, Nicole Neilson made a number of fine tourbillon watches. In 1892 a modified form of tourbillon, the karrusel, in which the carriage rotates every $52\frac{1}{2}$ minutes was invented by a Coventry maker. Simpler in construction and cheaper to produce, the karrusel is just as effective as the more fragile tourbillon.

Fine English watches continued to be made into the 20th century, though English domestic clockmaking had already succumbed to competition from cheap mass-produced German and Austrian clocks made of thin rolled brass and punched-out parts. In face of such strong Swiss and American competition English watchmaking did not survive the upheaval of the First World War. Today, in view of recent developments in horology, the table has turned full circle and it remains to be seen how the Swiss mechanical watch industry will respond to competition from electronic watches.

953

954

ENGLISH BAROMETERS

Nicholas Goodison

The mercurial barometer is an instrument for the measurement of the weight of the air. Most people think of it as a weather-glass because its only domestic application is to give guidance about the weather, but this application is in fact a secondary use of the instrument. The basic principle of the barometer was discovered in 1644. Later in the 17th century it was noticed that a connection existed between the alterations of the weight of the air and the alterations of the weather.

The simple barometer consists of a glass tube of circular section, sealed at its upper end, which stands in a cistern of mercury in such a way that its lower end is well immersed. The top of the tube contains a vacuum, so that the weight of the air on the surface of the mercury in the cistern balances the mercury in the tube. In England the mean pressure of the atmosphere is balanced by a column of mercury of about 29·5 inches (74·9 centimetres). At sea level the column seldom drops below 28·5 inches (72·3 centimetres) or exceeds 30·5 inches (77·4 centimetres). A barometer assesses the weight of the atmosphere by measuring the height of the mercury column above the surface in the cistern. Most domestic barometers are fitted with scales measuring 28–31 inches, but very few are equipped with any method of adjusting for the inaccuracy of measurement caused by the fact that as the mercury rises against the scale it falls in the cistern. The scales are usually marked with

weather indications but these are not, as is popularly supposed, reliable guides to the weather. It is the movement of the mercury, not its absolute height, which presages changes in the weather. From about 1760 scales were often fitted with a vernier scale which gives readings to an accuracy of ·01 inches.

Various devices were used in the early days to make the cistern barometer portable, the most successful being a screw which bears on a plate which in turn presses on the leather bottom of the improved cistern and pushes the mercury into the space normally occupied by the vacuum. This device, and improvements of it, has been used commonly since about 1702-3.

There have been many variations of the traditional cistern. Robert Hooke, writing in 1665, proposed a bent tube for his wheel barometer in which the movement of the mercury took place in the short open limb of the tube because the cistern was placed at the top of the closed limb. Several remarkable barometers which use this principle survive from the late 17th century and later. Of other ideas by far the commonest was the fitting of a bulb-shaped cistern in the short limb of a bent tube. Called a *baromètre à bouteille* on 961 the Continent, this tube, with all its inaccuracy, was the common type used in 'stick' barometers in the late 18th and 19th centuries.

Also popularised during the same period was the wheel baro- 959 meter, in which the movement of the mercury in the short open

955 Cistern barometer by George Adams, a leading instrument maker of the 18th century.

956 Open cistern barometer of *c.* 1740 by an anonymous maker.

957 18th-century angle barometer by Finney, a Liverpool clockmaker.

958 Angle barometer of *c.* 1800 by Balthazar Knie of Edinburgh.

955

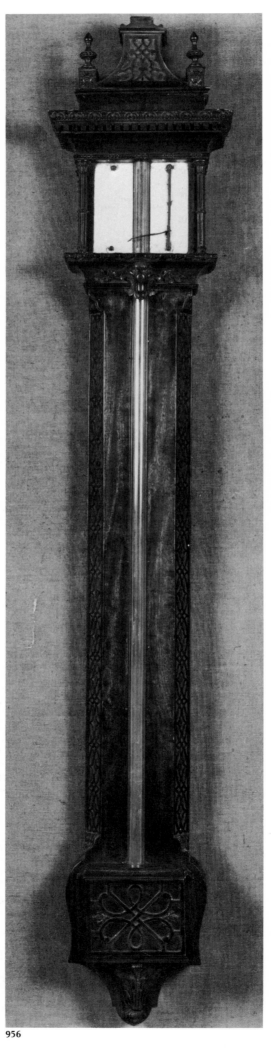

956

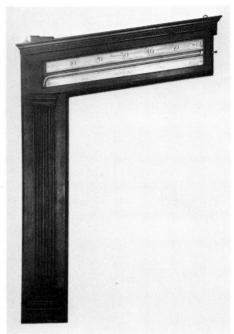

957

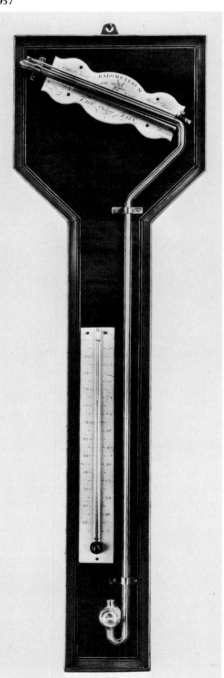

958

limb of a bent tube is transmitted to an index on a dial by means of a floating weight, cord and pulley wheel. Vast numbers of barometers of these two types survive from the 19th century, a period of material prosperity in which demand for furniture of all kinds increased very substantially and industrial methods of manufacture rapidly advanced.

Barometers first became fashionable as pieces of furniture among rich patrons and natural philosophers at the end of the 17th century, and many fine examples survive from this period, particularly in the royal collections. Illustrated here is one of the least grand of **962** these, a cistern barometer mounted in a frame attractively veneered with walnut. This probably dates from about 1700-10, as does the **960** splendid ivory portable 'pillar' barometer by the clockmaker Daniel Quare, also illustrated. The finely engraved hood of this example has weather indications in English on one side and in French on the reverse. There appear to have been very few specialist barometer makers in the 18th century. John Patrick, who died in about 1720, was a notable and rare maker to the trade—examples of his signed barometers survive in the British Museum, the National Maritime Museum and the Metropolitan Museum, New York—but throughout the first three-quarters of the century barometers were largely retailed by clockmakers, instrument-makers and opticians. Clearly they subcontracted much of their work.

In spite of the constraints imposed by the simple shape of the barometer, 18th-century cases display great variety, often reflecting the changing tastes in furniture and clock case design through **956** the century. The illustrations show: an open cistern barometer of about 1750 by an anonymous maker, set in a mahogany frame in the **957** Chinese taste with enamelled register plates; and an 'angle' barometer with an open glass cistern by Finney, a Liverpool clockmaker, whose mahogany case displays a not very successful grasp of Classical idiom. The angle barometer was devised in the 17th century in an attempt to magnify the movement of the mercury. The tube is bent at about 27·5 inches (69·8 centimetres) above the cistern level, the extent of the movement depending on the obtuseness of the angle. It was never a successful device, because of capillary action and the angle of the meniscus, but many notable examples survive from the 18th century. Charles Orme, who worked at Ashby-de-la-Zouch, produced in the 1740s angle barometers in fine walnut-veneered cases with one, two or even three tubes. **958** Balthazar Knie, probably a German by birth, who settled in Edinburgh, probably in 1776, made many of a distinctive type, one of which is illustrated. Also shown is a fine example of a cistern **955** barometer in a mahogany frame by George Adams, one of the leading instrument makers of the second half of the 18th century. An oatbeard hygrometer is mounted at the top.

Towards the end of the century demand increased sharply. Many retailers besides opticians, instrument-makers and clockmakers took to stocking barometers—sellers of looking-glasses, picture frames, prints, hardware and so on—and certain specialist makers began to supply barometers to retailers in large quantities. These developments coincide with the immigration of large numbers of Italian glass-blowers and barometer-makers from the continent from about 1780 onwards. They brought with them several designs of barometer. The two most prevalent of these were those already **961** mentioned—the straight-tube baromètre à bouteille, of which an example with herring-bone mahogany veneers is illustrated, and the wheel barometer. A typical example of the latter type, of c. 1790-1820 with mahogany veneers and shell inlays, is also shown **959** here. Enormous numbers of these two types were produced in the early years of the 19th century and retailed in towns throughout the country. The wheel barometer, examples of which are often mounted with thermometer, hygrometer and level, admitted a great variety of decoration. Both these types, along with the cistern barometer, continued in ample production, their casework reflecting changing tastes, until towards the end of the century demand tended to concentrate more on the smaller and more portable aneroid barometers.

959

960 'Pillar' barometer by Daniel Quare, probably dating from *c.* 1700-11.

961 *Baromètre à bouteille* by Gatty of London.

962 Cistern barometer probably dating from *c.* 1700-10, by an anonymous maker.

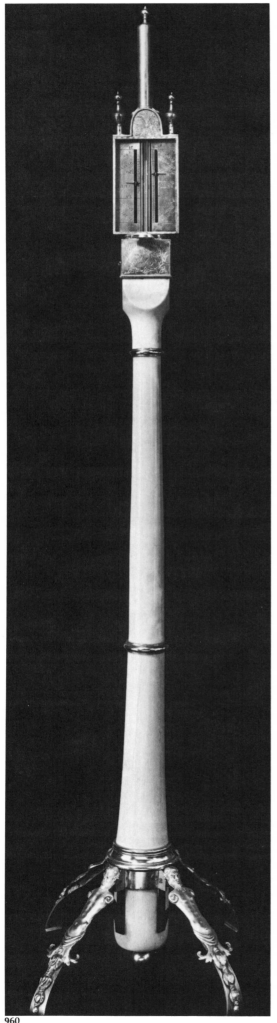

960

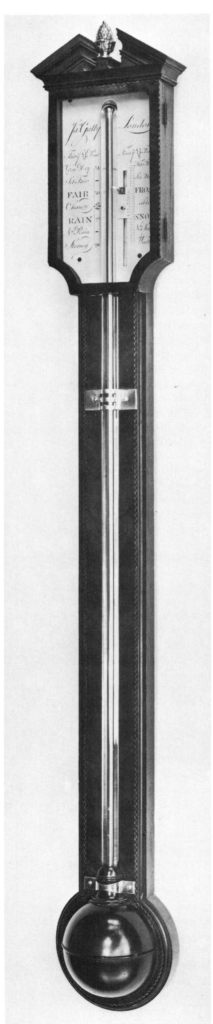

961

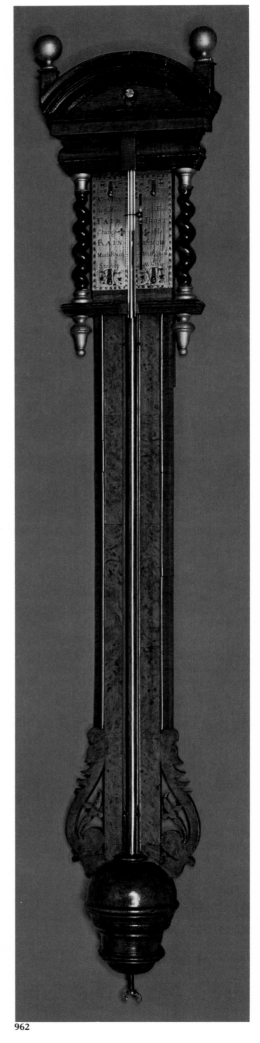

962

SCIENTIFIC INSTRUMENTS

Harriet Bridgeman

Scientific instruments represent a relatively new collecting area, and hence the purpose of this chapter is to describe the scientific instruments most likely to be of interest to and available to the collector and also, briefly to trace the development of the main types of instruments employed in astronomy, navigation, surveying and optics.

Astronomy is not only the oldest of the sciences but the most important since its principles are the basis of the rest, so it is only proper that astronomical instruments should be dealt with first. They fall into two main groups; astronomical instruments used in observation and measurement, such as quadrants, telescopes, sundials and astrolabes; and objects illustrating the results of observation and the theories and hypotheses about the heavenly bodies such as globes, armillary spheres and orreries.

The original idea of a quadrant, which in its earliest form was used by astronomers to measure the altitudes of the stars and the planets, is attributed to Ptolemy. He advocated the use of a quarter-circle arc rather than a full circle because he logically maintained that the arc could be marked out in more legible divisions. A plumb-line was suspended from the angle and two sights were fitted to one of the radii so that the observer could look through the sights at the object whose altitude was to be observed while the plumb-line indicated the altitude on the arc. Variations of the quadrant were introduced, notably by Edmund Gunter (1581-1626), who in 1618 designed a small pocket-size quadrant by means of which the sun's ascension and declination could be found, and from it, the time of day.

Monumental quadrants were used by astronomers until the end of the 18th century – it having been rightly assumed that the larger the instrument, the more accurate its result. It was also realised that the chances of accuracy were increased if an instrument remained fixed in position. Mural quadrants were made by John Bird (1709-76) and Jeremiah Sisson (fl. 1736-88) for both English and foreign observatories, both instrument-makers being highly skilled and setting a new standard of technical excellence throughout the industry. Few of these monumental mural quadrants have survived, but smaller instruments, based on the same scientific principles and with a radius of 10 to 20 inches (25·4 to 50·8 centimetres), can occasionally be found. The commonest form of observational quadrant is, however, the portable quadrant developed specifically for navigational and geodetic use.

The invention of the telescope and the introduction of telescopic sights after 1670 led to increased accuracy in the use of the quadrant and also to the production of new types. The telescope was discovered by accident in 1608 and it is generally accepted that the man responsible was the spectacle maker Hans Lippershey of Middelburg. He found, by chance, that if he were to view the church spire from his window with two convex lenses held apart, it appeared much larger. He started work on the construction of an instrument, based on his discovery, consisting of two similar lenses which he mounted on a tube and presented to the Dutch Estates General, Prince Maurice.

The news of this telescope soon spread throughout Europe, reaching Galileo in Venice in 1609. After only a day's study of the optics involved he designed the now well-known *Galilean* telescope, which consisted of a plano-convex object-glass and a plano-convex eyepiece mounted on a lead tube. It produced an upright and reasonably bright image in a well-illuminated field, and for this reason was particularly well suited to the military and naval needs of contemporary society. A disadvantage was that only a very small area of vision could be achieved, even when a low magnifying power was used.

The images seen through telescopes in those days were limited in their quality for three main reasons; the quality of the glass, spherical aberration and chromatic aberration. Spherical aberration is caused by light passing through different parts of the lens and focusing at varying distances from the lens. Chromatic aberration is produced by light of the different spectral colours being refracted in varying proportions on passing through the lens. Astronomers and telescope makers found that by reducing the curvature of the object-glass and thereby increasing its focal length, the effects of both spherical and chromatic aberration were reduced. This resulted in a phase during the middle of the 17th century when unwieldy telescopes were progressively lengthened, culminating in the 150-foot (45·7 metre) telescope of Herelius of Danzig and the aerial telescope by Christian Huygens which was devised as a means of using a long focal length without having to manipulate a heavy and cumbersome tube.

Isaac Newton, aware that the lengthening of the telescope would not provide the complete answer, since it was impossible to obtain a lens which was free from chromatic aberration, turned his attention to the magnifying properties of mirrors and a series of experiments which were to result finally in the reflecting telescope.

The history of the reflecting telescope is complex, dating back to at least the mid-17th century, when several suggestions were proposed, the most notable being that of the Scotsman James Gregory (1638-75), who published a design in his *Optica Promota* (1603). However, he failed to find an optician capable of figuring his mirrors to the correct curvature, and so he abandoned his theories and left it to Isaac Newton to produce the first reflecting telescope in 1668, a small instrument only 6 inches (15·3 centimetres) in length but in quality comparable to a 4-foot (122-centimetre) retractor. The mirror was made of an alloy known as bell-metal which consisted of six parts copper to two parts tin. Although initially it gave a high polish, it failed to retain it, and was later succeeded by speculum metal, an alloy of similar components but different proportions, better suited to the retention of a high polish and the skills of the grinder.

George Hearne, together with Edward Scarlett, established the techniques of speculum metal mirror-making in the London optical trade with the publication in 1738 of Robert Smith's *A Compleat System of Opticks*, while John Hadley and Samuel Molyneux brought the reflecting telescope into general production.

Between 1737 and 1768, James Short (1710-68) was the outstanding telescope-maker, producing 1,370 telescopes mainly based on the design of James Gregory.

In the second half of the 18th century, largely owing to the work of John Dollond (1706-61), the refracting telescope came back into favour. The new version consisted of two lenses, a concave one of flint glass and a convex one of crown glass, a combination which greatly reduced chromatic aberration. Chester Moor Hall, a barrister, first proposed this method in 1729 but it was patented by John Dollond in 1758, who manufactured it in partnership with his son Peter Dollond (1730-1820).

In 1773, William Herschel (1738-1822), who was a professional musician, started to take an interest in astronomy and in making his own telescopes. These were Newtonian reflectors which he cast and polished himself. He was soon making the best astronomical telescopes in Europe, for which there was an enormous demand despite their high price – £200 for the standard 7-foot (213-

963 Armillary sphere by Caspar Vopel, brass, 1542, Cologne.

964 Portugese mariner's astrolabe, brass, signed 1555.

965 English theodolite, brass, signed 'H. Cole', 1586. One of the earliest known theodolites, the compass needle and glass and three sights for the horizontal circle are missing.

966 Portable brass sundial by Christopher Köhler of Dresden, 1677.

967 German diptych dial, ivory and gilt brass, signed 'Hans Troschel Noriberga Faciebat', 1618.

963

964

965

967

966

centimetre) model. Comparatively few of them were bought by private individuals and today they are rare outside scientific institutions.

971 Spy-glasses and telescopes for terrestrial use with generally from one to eight draw-tubes were produced throughout the 18th century. Their paste-board tubes which were initially covered in paper, vellum or leather were increasingly, throughout the 19th century, displaced by telescopes with brass-bound mahogany bodies and brass draw-tubes. On the other hand, the familiar leather-bound brass telescopes made their appearance towards the end of the 18th century. The size of this type of telescope varies considerably when fully extended, from just over 12 inches (30·4 centimetres) to rather more than 4 feet (121·9 centimetres) in length, the larger types sometimes being made with a stand to which the tubes could be attached.

974 The manufacture of the microscope – which facilitates the detailed viewing of minute objects – was slow, and it lagged behind the telescope in popularity. However, the second half of the 17th century saw a great increase in demand, and in the 18th century several different forms of mounting were introduced, including the Wilson screw-barrel type which enabled the microscope to convert into a compound instrument. The botanical microscope was also well received in the late 18th and early 19th centuries, while

increasing attention was paid to precisely balanced compound lenses for eye-pieces and object pieces.

Like the telescope, the sundial with its ancient origins was another object which contrived to be made and used for the popular understanding of astronomy, and also as the only accurate means of checking the performance of clocks and watches. For this purpose, small, portable dials were made in large quantities in the 16th, 17th and 18th centuries, and it is these examples which are most readily available to the collector today.

The ring dial was perhaps the commonest and certainly the **969** simplest of the pocket sundials; when held vertically and in the plane of the sun by means of a small ring at the top, the ray of sunlight passed through a small hole in the side of the ring and indicated the time on a scale of hours engraved on the interior of the ring. Since in this form the dial was correct for only one value of the sun's declineation, the hole was usually placed in a sliding collar at the centre of the ring which could be adjusted for declineation against a calendar scale.

One of the most attractive dials to be made in the great age of dialling, as this period was called, was the horizontal plate dial. Large dials of this kind, made of heavy bronze, brass or slate for outdoor use in a fixed position can still be found quite easily. Small portable dials of this type, which also incorporate a compass for

968 French string-gnomon dial, *lignum vitae* and ivory with silver clasps, unsigned, *c*. 1600.

969 Ring dial by Edmund Culpeper, 17th century.

970 Early French mariner's compass by Joseph Roux, *c*. 1775. Wooden bowl.

971 Folding pocket spyglass by Watkins and Hill, *c*. 1830. Ivory body and six gilt-brass draw tubes.

972 Replica of the reflecting telescope of Sir Isaac Newton, made in 1668. Wood and brass.

973 Ship's quadrant, 1769. National Maritime Museum, Greenwich.

974 Hooke's microscope, unsigned, possibly by Christopher Cock, *c*. 1675. Wooden case with steel column; tubes of cardboard covered in vellum and leather. Eye and field lenses mounted in *lignum vitae* holders, objective lenses mounted in brass (not original). Other fittings in brass.

968

969

970

971

972

973

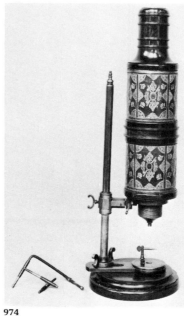
974

orientation and are intended for use in only one latitude, can also be found. An adaptation of the horizontal dial, known as the Butterfield dial and attributed to an Englishman called Michael Butterfield, was extremely popular throughout the 18th century, and was sold as an attractive package in a fish-skin box.

Another pocket dial which was produced in great quantities throughout Europe was the equinoctial dial. It was generally made in gilt and silvered brass and so constructed that all parts of the dial could be folded flat and fitted into a thin case. Although it basically consisted of a compass set into a base plate, usually on feet, with an hour-ring hinged to the north point of the compass and bearing the gnomon, or indicator, its design differed in varying ways according to its place of origin.

Perhaps the commonest form of multiple dial is the diptych dial which, in its simplest form, consists of two leaves made of wood, ivory or, more rarely metal, hinged to open at right angles to each other. The inner face of the lid incorporates a vertical dial and the lower face incorporates a horizontal dial with an inset compass. The dials share a string gnomon.

Often very similar to the diptych dial, and among the finest of all, are the gilt-brass dials which were produced in the 16th and early 17th centuries, and which often include a number of other instruments such as a miniature astrolabe, an alidade or a geographical map. Extremely expensive, even in their own day, they seem mainly to derive from the workshop of a German instrument-maker, Christoph Schisler.

The astrolabe, without which no collection of astronomical instruments is complete, is becoming increasingly difficult to find and correspondingly expensive; a number of convincing fakes make this a particularly difficult area for the buyer. An astrolabe is a two-dimensional map of the three-dimensional heavens and was used for a number of purposes, including determining the time, judging altitude and ascertaining the position of celestial bodies at any particular moment. Three types were developed in the 16th and 17th centuries, the Gemma Frisius universal; the Rojas projection astrolabe; and the universal, developed by Philippe de la Hire at the end of the 17th century.

Turning away from the group of astronomical instruments used in observation and measurement to those illustrating the result of these observations, we have a category including such objects as globes, armillary spheres and orreries.

Although we know that globes were probably constructed as early as *c*. 400 BC, the earliest globe to have survived is the marble Atlante Farnese globe in the Museum in Naples made *c*. 200 BC. Celestial globes were made in Islam throughout the Middle Ages and up to the 18th century, but mainly of brass and by the *cire perdu* method. In the late 15th century a new method was adopted in the West whereby the printing of the map was done on pieces of paper of a special shape called gores. These were cut so that they were pointed at the two ends and wide in the middle and designed so that a set of twelve, when pasted over the sphere with their points at the two poles, would completely cover it. At first they were hand-drawn on parchment, but later they were printed on paper. From about 1500 onwards, terrestrial and celestial globes were made in pairs and mounted on ornately carved wooden supports for use in a library or study.

Large globes have always been sufficiently popular to demand their continued production, but while many of the earlier examples have deteriorated through age and being maintained in poor conditions, later examples, although accurate and clear, show none of the fastidious craftsmanship of their illustrious antecedents.

When it was realised that it was not always necessary to have a

975 Twelve-inch (30.48 cm.) terrestial globe by John Senex, 1738.

976 Equatorially mounted reflecting telescope by James Short with a 9-in. (22.86 cm.) aperture. Wooden mount, brass telescope.

977 *The Chess Players* by Lucas van der Leyden (1494?-1533).

978 Ivory chessmen and board, a present given to Samuel Pepys by Charles II.

975

976

map of the stars to demonstrate the use of the lines drawn on a
963 celestial globe, armillary spheres were constructed. They consisted
of a skeletal globe made up of imaginary circles including the
Equator, the Tropics, the Arctic and the Antarctic circles. A small
sphere in the centre of this annular grid represented the earth, with
radial arms representing the moon, the sun and sometimes the
planets around it. The whole skeletal frame was lodged in a ring
mounted on an imposing stand formed of four quadrants with a
baluster support.

It was in 1713 that the word 'orrery' was first used as the name
for models of the solar system, although models to demonstrate and
explain the motions of the heavenly bodies, sometimes under the
name planetarium and sometimes under the name globe, are recorded from early times. Many English instrument-makers constructed them to satisfy the interest in astronomy which had been
stimulated by Isaac Newton's new theories. In the earliest orreries,
the moving bodies, whether they were the earth, the moon or the
planets, were carried around on a thin plate turning in one piece at
the top of a cylindrical box, or on a set of overlapping annular
plates. In later models, following a design of Benjamin Martin, the
planets were carried on radial arms. The designers took great pride
in devising a train of gears which would give an accurate representation of the relative periods of the planets in their journey round the
sun, but little attention was paid to the linear scale of the model.
They were used for teaching in university or bought by people
with an interest in astronomy.

Surveying is another area which has provided the collector with
a number of interesting scientific instruments – of these, one of the
965 most important is the theodolite, an angle-measuring instrument

which gradually ousted the less accurate circumferentors and
graphometers in the early 18th century. Another important invention for surveyors was the vernier, an indispensable device on the
scale of a sighting instrument, while for the 19th-century surveyor,
the sextant was a useful instrument which he could use for a quick
meridian bearing. A series of serviceable compasses suitable for the
surveyor and the mining surveyor were used from the 16th century
onwards, and examples of these can still be found.

Navigational instruments provide a clear area of interest for a
collector. They include the compass, the marine chronometer, the 970
sea quadrant, one of the first elevation-finding instruments, the
mariner's astrolabe and the cross-staff, which was an instrument
for measuring distances between two stars or the angular elevation
of a heavenly body above the horizon. On a more picturesque level,
they include the sandglass which was used by mariners for relating
distance to time, and consisted of two hand-blown bulbs with
flanged ends containing either sand, marble dust, alum, iron filings
or powdered eggshells.

Generally speaking, in the 18th century, art and science were
complementary to each other – art embellished science with beautiful details, engraved cartouches and the best of her natural materials
such as ivory and mother-of-pearl. In the 19th century, scientific
instruments tended to be made of more functional materials – brass
was particularly popular – and the manufacturers were for the most
part more concerned that they should function efficiently than that
they should look beautiful. For the collector there is always the
challenge of finding an instrument which is not only technically
perfect but also embellished with such aesthetic qualities that it has
become a work of art in its own right.

COLLECTOR'S CORNER

CHESS SETS

Harriet Bridgeman

The ancestry of chess is older than recorded history, dating back some 5,000 years to when Neolithic peoples played a game of chance on a surface delineated by squares in which the moves were determined by a drop of sticks or a roll of dice.

The exact date of the development of chess has not been determined, but it is agreed that it was known in its more sophisticated form in north-west India as a game of war. The simple playing pieces on the traditional board were replaced by miniature symbols representing the different sections of the Indian army. Chariot, horse, elephant, king, counsellor, elephant, horse, chariot, each side behind its rank of foot soldiers, were lined up in the same order as modern chess pieces on a board of 64 equal squares.

Persia learned chess from India during the reign of King Khusrau I (AD 531-578) where it soon became established as highly popular and a game of some intellectual merit. After the Muslim conquest of Persia (AD 638-651), the game spread rapidly; within 100 years, Arabs were playing on their roll-up 'boards' of cloth or leather throughout their enormous empire which extended from the north-west corner of Spain to the south-east corner of the Indus Valley.

While the Arabs were extending the practice of the game, they were also developing the design of chess sets. The designs they inherited from Persia and India in the 7th century were figurative, with naturalistic figures representing the names of the pieces. The new Muslim religion, however, prohibited iconography, and so in order to retain the game, the Muslims designed non-representational sets in which the shapes were so abstract that Occidentals often have difficulty in distinguishing one piece from another. It is interesting that this quasi-abstract style has had a remarkably durable design tradition, reappearing after a time-lapse of 10 centuries in such primitive societies as those of Africa and Alaska.

When the Muslim armies conquered Spain in the first quarter of the 8th century, it is likely that they brought with them the game of chess. Sometime later, Western Europeans took up the game, initially using Arabic nomenclature, rules, problem books and even Arabic chess sets. At the same time, they began to fashion the game to connect more closely with the tastes of Western civilisation, gradually changing the rules, the names of the pieces and their design. The abstract designs, prompted by the remote God of Islam, were succeeded by the representational designs of the Western Church. The abstract head of a horse, for example, acquired two eyes; the two abstract tusks of the elephant—perhaps partly because Europeans did not know what an elephant looked like—developed into two representational heads.

By the 13th century, European craftsmen had transformed the Arabic chess set into an image of their own culture. The Oriental game of war, played with a miniature army, had been developed into a game of life, played with a miniature state. The shah had become a king. The vizier, his companion and adviser, had become a queen, and in partnership they ruled the state and ran the wars. The bishops, who stood beside them, gave spiritual as well as political and military counsel backed up by the knights, who represented the army, and pawns, who were the foot-soldiers of war.

As the game began to spread beyond the confines of the nobility in the late 12th and early 13th centuries, the need for inexpensive chess sets developed. This resulted in a highly abstract European design which was influenced by the Arabic lathe-turning tradition and which, during the 15th and 16th centuries, blended with the parallel traditions of naturalism to produce the basic characteristics of modern design.

By the end of the Renaissance period, the multiplicity of possible shapes had been reduced to a fairly standard design. The king and queen had become distinctly taller than the other pieces and usually incorporated some symbolic reference to a crown. For the bishop, knight and castle, a standard set of symbols drawn from the entire European tradition of chess design slowly emerged. The head of a horse, which had been used spasmodically for several centuries, was recalled to service, to be joined by the tower of a castle. Both of

977

978

980

979 Chess pieces of walrus ivory from the Isle of Lewis, 12th century, Scandinavian.

980 The Charlemagne King, Indian (left), and an early French chess piece (right).

981 Ivory chess set from Bengal, 1790, depicting the officials of the East India Company.

982 Rare set of Russian chess pieces cast in bronze, 19th century.

983 Chess set in silver-plated copper, designed by Man Ray, 1927.

984 Chessman in blue and white stoneware, 18th century, designed by John Flaxman for Josiah Wedgwood.

979

980

981

982

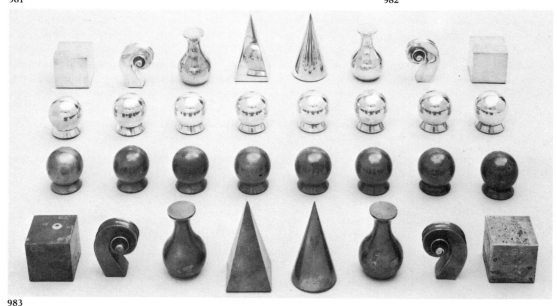
983

984

these were an immediate success, and became standard pieces.

During the 17th and 18th centuries, partly because of the increase in the popularity of playing-cards, there was a sharp decline in the quality of chess set design. The Rococo movement had a predictably deleterious effect, producing an abundance of plump porcelain cherubs dancing on castle turrets, and shell-laden queens.

In the late 18th and early 19th centuries, there was a return to sobriety in design, caused by the discipline imposed by the **984** Classical Revival, and also by the renewed interest in serious chess

among the secure upper-middle class. This also produced the Directoire style in chess design, where the role of the pieces was differentiated mainly by height—often leading to confusion.

In the early 19th century, the energies of serious designers turned yet again towards finding a satisfactory and consistent standard for chessmen, and success was achieved in 1839 by an unknown artist, whose design was registered at the British patent office in 1849 by Howard Staunton, the English chess master. It is generally felt that the Staunton design has never been surpassed. The pieces are indi-

985 Dolls' house made in Dorset in 1760,
modelled on an 18th-century English country
house.

986 A Victorian version of the ever popular
card game, Snap.

vidually well proportioned and formally inter-related by means of classical balusters, crowning balls and grooves that, in elevation, are either the same height or at proportionate intervals. The pieces are graduated in height, and the abstract crowns that cap the king and queen are clear, as is the difference between the bishop and the castle.

The history of modern chess sets begins with the Dadaist movement in general and with Marcel Duchamp (b. 1891) in particular, who gave up painting for chess in the early 1920s. His first executed chess set, exhibited in 1944, is based on a standard chess wallet which he subtly altered to suit his own peculiar talents. Alexander Calder and Richard Kamholtz are other members of the Dadaist movement who, in the design of chess sets, exemplified their principle that everyday objects should be used to represent some-thing other than themselves. In the case of Kamholtz, he used a highly successful combination of painted nuts, bolts and screws.

Like the Dadaists, the Surrealists were also interested in chess, and one of their most successful sets was designed by Man Ray in 983 1926. He worked in silver to an average height of four inches (10·1 centimetres) and to an overall geometric design.

The reversion to abstract design in the 20th century away from the traditional Staunton design, with its naturalistic images of medieval armies, suggests a game between contestants who enjoy the process of thinking. Designers are now producing technically brilliant essays on the concept that the pieces are the tools in a purely intellectual game, whereas in the past their technical brilliance largely depended on their success and conviction as tools of Army or State.

TOYS AND PASTIMES

Harriet Bridgeman

Life in the earliest days was largely a question of survival, leaving little time for the amusement of children and the carving of toys. As communities became established, however, life became more leisurely, and early civilisations are known to have produced such basic toys as balls, hoops, skittles and dolls.

The growth of the merchant classes in the 15th and 16th centuries led to the education of a greater number of children, and an awareness that a literate child could improve family business. Contemporary prints show children playing with cup-and-ball games, kites, windmills, toy cradles, soldiers and dolls. Craftsmen were now organising themselves into guilds, and restrictive practices existed even in the toy world, so that a doll's head, for example, could not be painted by the man who had turned it. Most of the toys were made in Germany and the Netherlands, but some were obviously made in England since the industry was protected by an import duty.

Very few toys of this period exist outside museums, although comparatively recently, a stump doll was burnt as it had 'so little shape left, and woodworm'. Fake model soldiers of the period have been made and primitive dolls of recent origin sometimes parade under the name of stump dolls.

The 18th century was the great age for the dolls' house and the 985 'baby house', a miniature house made from about 1700-90 purely for the amusement of adults. It flourished with the importation of the first commercial toy furniture from Holland, which included items such as tilting-tables, chairs, fenders and chandeliers, all made in brass. No detail was too difficult for the craftsmen to imitate: balustrades, porticos and steps were faithfully reproduced in miniature, as were metal grates, door furniture and fire-places.

Early 19th-century dolls' houses were usually made on a larger scale, about four and a half by four feet (121 × 137 centimetres), which enabled a small child to play inside them, but by the end of the century, standards had declined, and they were often factory made, with thin walls and cramped rooms.

To populate the houses, and as the continuation of a long tradition, dolls were made in large quantities. When Queen Victoria was 987 a child, most European dolls were made of carved or turned wood, varying in size and quality according to price, but with the Industrial Revolution new methods were introduced. Papier mâché was used as a popular material for dolls' heads; china arms and legs as well as the head-and-shoulders china bust were stuck or sewn on to a leather body or even a jointed wooden body, while delightful

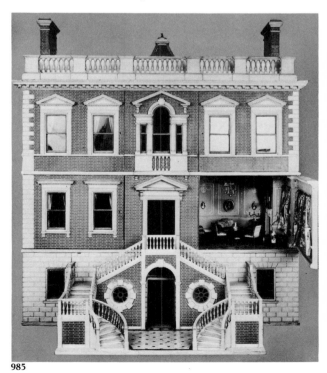

985

986

987 Doll, English, made in the late 19th century and dressed in Victorian clothes.

988 Rocking horse, English, 1840, natural pine.

989 Prince Albert jigsaw puzzle, English, *c.* 1839. Issued shortly before Queen Victoria's wedding on 10th February, 1840, this is a very early jigsaw puzzle.

990 Penny toys made in Germany for the English market, *c.* 1890. Painted tin, maximum height 3½ in. (8.89 cm.).

991 Polyphon with metal discs, *c.* 1880. This came before the phonograph and after the musical automaton.

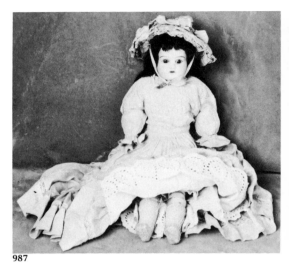

987

988

989

990

991

families of parian portrait dolls and miniature dolls were also produced. Among French and American makers, there was a strong predilection for novelty mechanical dolls, and as early as 1845, Nicholas Théroude produced a clockwork doll which moved its arms and looked from side to side as it rolled along on a three-wheeled platform.

The increase in technical knowledge in the 19th century, coupled with the expansion of the middle classes, made it a golden age for toys. The rich bought them in the bazaars and fashionable arcades; the poor at fairs and street-markets, where they were sold from **990** barrows. Many of these cheap toys were imported from Germany while others were made in the back streets of English towns; they included all the traditional toys such as trumpets and drums, buckets and spades, hoops and tops and kites with faces.

Another group of toy-makers who were very active in the early years of the century were the print-sellers. They produced jigsaw **986,989** puzzles, cards, table-games and toy theatres. Jigsaws, known as 'dissected puzzles' were first introduced towards the end of the 18th century, but it was not until the beginning of the 19th century, with the advent of such makers as Edward Wallis and William Darton, that they were made in quantity. Early jigsaws consist almost entirely of maps and political histories, although Darton also issued a series of moral poems with the titles *My Mother, My Grandmother, My Bible*, each illustrated by six hand-coloured engravings. William Spooner and John Betts followed Wallis and Darton as superior jigsaw-makers. While Spooner concentrated on

the production of everyday subjects with titles such as *The Sugar Plantation* and *A Loaf of Bread*, John Betts mainly produced maps and bible stories, and included a key picture and a book with his puzzles. There were also many unknown publishers who produced puzzles, often of poor workmanship, which appealed to popular taste, featuring such subjects as the Lord Mayor's Show, the coronation and wedding of Queen Victoria, and the seaside.

The toy theatre provided another absorbing interest for children at this time. The characters and scenery were reproduced from current productions and sold in the stationers' shops for 'a penny plain and twopence coloured'. The first sheets were published in 1811, and the first toy theatre was made in 1813 by William West. His theatre was designed with small tin footlights to contain wicks burning colza-oil. The characters were pasted on card, cut out and pushed on and off the stage on wire slides. The toy theatre had its heyday in the 1830s and '40s, and about 100 publishers issued between them 300 different plays. From 1875 Benjamin Pollock was selling toy theatres in his shop in Hoxton Street, one of the poorer quarters of London, indicating that the fashion had even spread to the humblest nurseries.

Toy soldiers have always been popular with militant young boys. In the early days, they were made of painted wood or cardboard, mounted on small blocks, so that they could be arranged in serried ranks or imposing armies. German firms such as Haffner and Heyde also produced flat and solid lead soldiers, but these were inevitably heavy. It was left to the English manufacturer, Britain, **992**

992 Group of toy soldiers made by Britain, English, 1893-99. Hollow-cast and painted alloy of tin and lead. These early models, much smaller than those produced after the Boer War, represent a wounded soldier with nurses and a medical officer, three Guards' bandsmen and a Rifle Brigade soldier.

993 Collection of Victorian games and toys including American alphabet blocks, pegs, humming tops, a scripture cube game entitled 'The Genteel Boy and his Doings' and a clown from an American toy circus.

994 Clockwork dancing figures made by a member of the Crandall family, 1860-70, American.

995 Victorian building-blocks which double up as a puzzle, each face featuring a part of a different picture.

992

993

994

995

who had first set up business in 1850, to market the first hollow-cast toy soldier. This was made of an alloy which was not only light but also easy to produce and to paint. Britain's first line was the Life Guards, shortly followed by the Grenadier Guards and a kilted Highland regiment; although initially viewed with suspicion, these models eventually swept the market and replaced their heavy German counterparts.

Toys often reflect the events of the age in which they are made, and the advent of the steam age produced a number of crudely made painted, wooden trains which were sold with a length of wooden track and every indication that the maker had never actually seen a train.

During the 1870s, well-made wooden engines were produced alongside metal models which were made mainly in Germany for the export market, although the Americans produced excellent cast-iron trains together with trackless tin pull-alongs. Toy catalogues also offered a variety of accessories: gas lamps, stations in both the Gothic and the Classical styles, bridges and station staff, so that a complete railway complex could be devised by an ingenious child.

During the 19th century, scale remained completely unimportant, and was not rationalised even to the extent of a standard gauge until after the turn of the century. All the toy trains made before the 1890s appear to have been made of coarse scale.

One of the major manufacturers of early model railways was the German firm of Marklin, while possibly the most sought-after of

English models are the products of the firm of Bassett-Lowke, which were collectors' pieces even in their own day. The Ives locomotives, which were made in America, are also keenly sought as collectors' pieces as so few have survived.

The mass production of clockwork toys began in about 1850. Apart from its use in trains, clockwork was deployed to reproduce the characteristic movement of professional people or animals. A trick cyclist, for example, was made to ride around in erratic circles; a bear to walk and turn its head from side to side, a couple of negro dancers to jig about on a box.

Pictorial toys were another feature of the 19th century. The magic lantern had been known for centuries, but now simple devices were used to give the pictures movement. Hand-painted glass slides were set in wooden frames, and by sliding one piece of glass behind another, a staring tiger slowly rolled his eyes from side to side; by pushing a lever up and down a clown skipped; by winding a handle, a volcano erupted. Toy lanterns with miniature slides which operated on the same basis enabled children to give their own magic lantern shows.

In 1825, a new invention appeared in the shops, a box labelled 'Thaumatropical Amusement'. The thaumatrope was a small paper disc with different objects drawn on each side of it and thin cords attached. When the cords, held one in each hand between finger and thumb, were twirled, the figures presented separately on either side gave the illusion of being united.

In 1832, the Plenakistiscope appeared on the market. This was a

283

996 Gauge 1 clockwork train and a section of a bridge made by Bing of Nuremburg, *c.* 1905.

996

a figure in various stages of movement so that when the spindle was spun, the images seen through the apertures gave the illusion of movement. Further scientific experiments produced more realistic and sophisticated optical toys, leading in time to such inventions as the Kinetoscope, from which the cinema film of today was developed.

Throughout the 19th century, American toys were modelled closely on European imports, but from about 1860 onwards, the toy industry began to make a bid for overseas markets. The Tower Toy Company was one of four American companies to show examples of their products at the Paris International Exhibition of 1878, while for resource in the American toy industry, no firm could rival the products of the Crandall family. One of their best-known inventions was for nursery nesting-blocks in the form of five-sided boxes, graduated in size and painted with pictures or letters.

Although the Civil War curtailed the supply of metal, it stimulated its use for making all kinds of articles when firms returned to peacetime production. When George W. Brown and Company, specialists in tinware, and J. & E. Stevens joined forces to form the American Toy Company, their catalogue showed more than 200 metal toys. They also produced a number of typically American cast-iron mechanical banks.

Antique toys have now become collectors' pieces, but they provide a happy precedent for contemporary toy-makers against which to ally or match their technical skills, and many of the original designs are still in production.

large cardboard disc cut around the edge with deep notches with figures placed between the notches in different stages of movement. The disc was spun on a spindle in front of a mirror.

The disadvantage of the Plenakistiscope was that only one person at a time could view the picture so it was soon succeeded by the Zoetrope, a metal drum pierced with a number of slits which was revolved on a metal spindle in a wooden stand. A paper strip the length of the circumference and half the depth of the drum showed

BOXES AND CASES

Therle Hughes

A box may be as imposing as a Victorian carriage basket or tiny as a thimble case, but whatever the size or shape, for centuries men have valued and found uses for containers of all kinds—as guardians of treasure, bearers of gifts, mementoes of loved ones or souvenirs of places and events. Many of them are now collected: either they appeal because of the pleasing rituals they once served, or they show the skill with which an attractive material could be handled by a specialist craftsman.

Fitted caskets, superb displays of craftsmanship, have always been popular. Queen Elizabeth I accepted from Sir John Alee a coffer in oak, carved, painted and gilded, set out with such luxuries as combs, steel mirrors and silver perfume pomanders. The little cabinet-compendiums made in the 17th century offered the new delight of tiny drawers and perhaps a looking-glass in the lid, and 1007 by Victorian times such a mirror was taken for granted—perfectly angled to reflect the jewelled fingers. By then the fine wood veneers were sometimes enriched with porcelain plaques or 'medieval' mounts in silver or bronze; or a case in ivory or alabaster might be fitted with its own small musical box which played when the lid was opened.

997 Equally interesting to many modern collectors is the knife box. This was illustrated by Randle Holme as early as the 1680s, already with characteristic forward-sloping lid.

Around the 1770s such boxes were sometimes urn shaped, with the lid supported on a central shaft, decorative but rather less practical than the late Georgian sarcophagus shape on brassy paw feet or the Victorians' vast cutlery canteen.

Ever since China tea was brought to Holland in the early 17th century, tea caddies have formed a major category of purpose-made boxes. Since then they have attracted imaginative design, 1004 using a score of materials—ceramics, metals, glass, ivory and tortoiseshell, papier mâché and inlaid, veneered and painted wood. Although the tea equipage served a ritual especially dear to the English, the pleasure of tea-drinking is universal, expressed alike

in delicate European china, Chinese porcelain and Russian glass.

Through the last three centuries fashionable ladies and gentlemen have carried innumerable little boxes in hand, pocket and reticule. Boxes for snuff can be collected in almost every material, and yet 999,100 more served the cigar and cigarette smoker. Victorians, for instance, had cigar 'magazines' and dispensers, while some early cigarette boxes were fitted for matches and tinder. The etiquette of calling and 'leaving cards' made it necessary for ladies to carry visiting- 1001 card cases, slender little boxes covered in materials as varied as 'gem painted' glass and porcupine quills.

Toys and games had their own containers, one of the most sought after types being the bone-work games boxes that Napoleonic conscripts (including Dieppe ivory carvers) were uniquely privileged to sell while prisoners of war in England. Noah's arks are perhaps the shrewdest form of toybox ever devised, but through the 19th century boxes in general became ever more appealing to the young at heart. There were comic German china-fairing pin boxes, and money boxes in a great variety of forms. Piggy money boxes were the traditional type, and continued to be used, but there were also fish, hen-and-chicks, cottages, dog kennels, and the painted cast-iron figures that seemed to put drama into the swallowing of pennies. And about 1880 a whole new world of imitative shapes, from toy caravans to piles of books, opened for the biscuit makers, with improved lithographic colour printing applied to easily shaped tinwares.

If the field is wide, so is the range of materials employed by specialist box makers. Wood, naturally, is most often the basis, for dressing case, lace box, tea-caddy chest and all the workaday boxes for candles, spices and so on, usually known as treen. Wood carving and staining were, in fact, popular amateur hobbies around 1900, and white-wood boxes were sold for the purpose, so collectors should be warned that not all such objects are the work of professional box makers.

Designs in contrasting inlays let into solid wood were augmented

997 Knife box, one of a pair, veneered in yew wood with silver mounts, and made *c.* 1770. This characteristic design enabled the owner to see at once if any cutlery were missing.

998 Unusual compendium in tooled leather, made *c.* 1865. The fittings of the lid are of steel mounted with mother-of-pearl.

999 A very early table snuff box in Sheffield plate, possibly made *c.* 1750 by Thomas Bolsover, the inventor of the metal. The pull-off cover is tortoiseshell.

1000 Ivory table snuff box with a lift-off cover carved with a portrait of George IV.

998

997

999

1000

from the 17th century by more difficult marquetry, in which the whole surface was covered with thin, joint-masking veneers cut into intricate patterns of contrasting woods.

Early English marquetry work adopted bird and flower designs from Holland and developed delicate 'seaweed' scrolling, but in the late 18th century even marquetry had to include Neo-classical motifs of urn and swag.

Health resorts in Britain and abroad sold many souvenir boxes in decorated wood, some naturally stained to slaty tones by iron-rich water, as at Spa in Belgium. Sorrento, in Italy, became noted for marquetry mosaics in artificially coloured woods, but the most renowned English 'wood pictures', known as Tunbridge ware, made a feature of natural coloured woods from around Tonbridge and Tunbridge Wells. Here traditional styles of marquetry culminated in Victorian mosaic, a 'mass production' technique in which small strips of the contrasting woods were cut and glued together and cut and glued again. From the resultant solid block slices were sawn, each carrying the same pattern, such as a local view, formed of tiny edge-glued squares of end-grain wood, to be applied as veneers to shawl boxes, papeteries and so on. At the Great Exhibition Edmund Nye showed a workbox bearing a view of Bayham Abbey containing 15,000 pieces of naturally coloured woods. Obviously this method was considerably cheaper than traditional marquetry.

Sometimes marquetry work, always laborious, was replaced by varnished painting. Some of the most effective, known as pen work, was described by Thomas Sheraton and taught to Victorian young ladies as substitute ebony and ivory inlay. Usually the background was black, and the design painted in white (now yellowed under the varnish) and the effect depended on final deft pen lines in indian ink executed by such experts as the period's many writing masters.

Scotland is noted for fine souvenir boxes, though such attractive details as the so-called Scottish invisible hinge also appear in small wooden boxes from many parts of Northern Europe. This perfectly fitting hinge is cut as an integral part of both box and lid. It was

improved rather than invented by Charles Stiven of Laurencekirk, Kincardineshire, snuff box maker from 1783, whose firm continued to 1868. Name-stamped Stiven boxes date from about 1819, when competition came both locally and from Mauchline and Cumnock in Ayrshire; Edward Pinto noted some 50 specialist box makers in Scotland in the 1820s to '30s. The Smiths of Mauchline, beginning about 1820, continued into this century.

Many of these boxes relied for ornament on the attractive grain of sycamore wood, which was varnished and polished. Some were hand painted and others patterned with pen-work in meander lines, from which evolved chequer patterns, and then vividly colourful tartan wares. The Smith firm at Mauchline devised multiple pens and rollers used with varnish colours (patented 1853 and 1856) for the clan tartan lines, often surrounding painted views.

In the 1840s the Smiths' Scoto-Russian ware imitated scroll patterns in Russian niello and silver inlay. The boxes were covered with paint over metal foil so that engraved lines showed a pattern in glinting foil, preserved by varnish. These won a gold medal in 1851. Scoto-Damascene ware, made by the same firm, was a variant, but is now quite rare.

Tartans painted directly on the boxes were soon replaced by painted papers carefully pasted to the wood. And in another attempt to cut prices, in the 1840s, early pen-work was augmented by transfer-printed views supplied to tourist centres far beyond the British Isles. Transfer work in turn prompted some firms to paste their boxes with photographs under varnish.

Boxes shaped as wooden shoes have been popular in many parts of Europe. Others are to be found in simple turnery, their circular lids often having impressed, rather than carved, ornament. Another time-old style for hardwood boxes was patterning with hot irons, imitating sepia drawings. This technique, popular again among late Victorian craft-minded amateurs, is known to experts as pyrography, and better-known to laymen as pokerwork.

Some glossy little boxes, looking like mottled burr wood, were in fact carved from the coquilla nuts which had been brought to Europe from South America since the Tudor period, and others,

01,1008

1006

1001 A selection of card cases, all more unusual than the common mother-of-pearl style. Upper row, left to right: papier mâché painted to harmonise with the owner's Paisley shawl; Oriental lacquer; red leather impressed and brilliantly coloured in blue, green and gold. Centre: carved sandalwood with ivory mosaic border. Lower row: clan tartan painting;

tortoiseshell framing a painted glass panel; Tunbridge ware wood mosaic.

1002 The granular texture of the animal-skin shagreen shows clearly on this tea chest of the 1760s to '80s. This, which has a silver lock and mounts, would have contained tea caddies.

1003 Writing box in South Staffordshire painted enamel, the pastoral scene surrounded by gilded raised Rococo scrolls, with a raised diaper pattern over the coloured ground.

1001

1002

1003

bearing moulded medallions of famous personages in sharp and precise relief, were made from *bois durci*, an early plastic (sawdust and albumen), invented by Parisian Charles Lepage and patented in France and England in 1855. Birmingham Museum's Pinto Collection of Wooden Bygones includes such items as book-shaped cases for daguerreotypes.

Wood, of course, was the basis for many more boxes faced with exotic materials such as the mother-of-pearl applied in diamond shapes to visiting-card cases – there were as many as 730 pieces in one exhibit at the Great Exhibition. But some of the richest surface
1005 effects appear in straw and paper. Straw-work had a long history before becoming associated with prisoner-of-war work; the craft originated in the East, and imports can be confusing to the collector. The straws were split and glued to paper before being applied to the box surfaces. By laying them in different directions, the artist could achieve a sense of radiating light behind, for instance, a figure motif or landscape. There was also mosaic work in minute straw squares, which looks rather similar to Tunbridge ware.

Rolled paper work is an attractive and simple form of decoration. Very narrow strips of paper or vellum were rolled and edge-glued to silk-covered wooden boxes in elaborate spirals, loops and scrolls. Frequently the resemblance to mosaic or to gold filigree was heightened by colouring or gilding the outer edges of the paper. The craft was popular in England around the 1660s to 1710, and again about a century later. Princess Elizabeth in 1791 ordered 16 ounces of filigree papers and a box and teacaddy with suitable slightly sunken panels rimmed with ebony mouldings.

Exotic shells delighted many other 18th- and 19th-century amateurs – one tea caddy shown at the 1851 Exhibition was covered with 100,000 shells. Sometimes a hinged wooden box and the inside of the lid would be filled with careful shell arrangements on tinted silk, offered as a 'shell album'.
1002 In the 18th century shagreen was much used for light, waterproof coverings to cases of rust-vulnerable instruments, cutlery, spectacles and so on. This type of leather has a long history: originally it came from the backs of Persian and Turkish wild asses, but when more easily available, horse or camel skin was substituted. This was given a similar rough granular appearance by trampling plant seeds into the back of the soaked skin. In the 18th century a more decor-

ative substitute was found in lightly tanned shark-skin ('nurse' or 'fish-skin'), suitably smoothed to a mosaic pattern of spine-roots.

Boxes and cases of tortoiseshell shimmering with gold piqué are strictly speaking classed as jewellers' work, and scarcely less opulent looking was the intricate surface ornament combining tortoiseshell or ebony with metal such as brass, known as *intarsia-tura* in Italy and as boulle or buhl in England where it was made from about 1815, in imitation of French imports. Turtle shell proved an ideal material for plainer boxes, too, as heat rendered it plastic so that it could be moulded, pressed, even welded. Substitutes included horn, equally malleable. The Huguenot craftsman John Obrisset (d. 1731) from Dieppe made steel dies for impressing portraits on tortoiseshell and horn snuff box lids.

From the mid-18th century, even boiled up horn shavings were moulded into somewhat fragile snuff boxes, but more interesting is the snuff mull made from a ram's horn, the exterior polished, the interior cut with sharp ridges for grinding snuff from a plug of tobacco. Far into Victorian days, Highland cattle horns were used for huge table snuff mulls, and a later alternative was a box made from a ram's skull.

The obvious substitute for costly ivory was bone, and whalebone carvings, known as scrimshaw work, were produced by sailors all over the world (see p. 293). The teeth ('whale ivory') provided the best basis, bone being coarser, with fibrous black bone (baleen) sometimes used for contrast.

Boxes in ceramics range from tea caddies in Chinese porcelain and European delft to workaday Victorian pots with their tops printed in full colour – these are now assiduously collected as picture pot-lids. Strong little boxes suggesting the delicate porcelain made through much of the 18th century are now collected as English painted enamels (occasionally confused by 19th-century 1004 French imitations). Opaque glassy enamel was fused over a thin core of copper and decorated with enamel colours fixed by heat. This technique was widely applied to boxes for snuff, patches and comfits, along with *étui* sets, tiny writing equipment and eventually larger tea chests, tobacco boxes (with inner press-lids) and even knife cases. Battersea was briefly (1753-56) a source of monochrome transfer-printed ornament, while Birmingham and South Staffordshire applied colourful painting set within gaily gilded Rococo

1004 Delightful little tea caddies in English painted enamels, showing the fine finish of the best Birmingham and South Staffordshire work. The decorations, painted by hand in heat-fixed enamel colours, are framed in raised-gilt scrolling.

1005 Cabinet covered on all surfaces with straw-work, including the sham drawers on the front. The straws have been coloured green, red and blue to give the maximum sheen and lustre. Attributed to French prisoners-of-war in the early 19th century.

1006 Presentation box of tartanware (McDuff), sycamore, with the lid lined with velvet. Second half of 19th century.

1007 Rosewood compendium inlaid with mother-of-pearl. The extensive leather-work is red, stamped in gold, and the fittings are of cut steel. Second quarter of the 19th century.

1008 Tunbridge ware boxes, paperknife and thermometer.

1004

1005

1006

1007

1008

287

1009 Mirror case of papier mâché, lacquered and gilded. Persian, c. 1770-80.

1010 King tray with Chinoiserie ornament and a floral design on the edge of the rim.

scrolls. Late work of this kind, however, was often poor.

Tôle peinte is a name often given to magnificent boxes in tin plate (iron soaked in molten tin) known to their first makers as Pontypool japanning. From late in the 17th century iron snuff boxes were sometimes japanned, that is, painted with colours and layers of clear varnish fixed by prolonged stove heating as a basis for ornament imitating newly fashionable Oriental lacquer. Thomas Allgood (d. 1716) was a pioneer in this craft, which was further developed by his family when early 18th-century inventions produced smooth-surfaced mill-rolled tin-plate. This gave a subtle radiance and gloss to rich colours smoothly hand polished. The work was continued until 1810 by the Allgood family at Pontypool, Monmouthshire, and then at Usk until 1860. As 'Welsh lacquer' it was widely exported – though always challenged by cheap Midlands wares – until largely forgotten in the enthusiasm for lighter papier mâché (see below).

The starry figurings natural to this tinned iron plate were exploited successfully by the Birmingham manufacturer Edward Thomason for tea canisters and similar items, and patented in 1816 as moiré metal – clear hard varnish preserved the silvery radiance.

In the 1830s some was colour-stained and painted by china decorators, selling as crystallised ware.

Other metal boxes for snuff, tobacco, tinder, spices, balls of string (from the 1820s) and the rest may be found in copper and brass, pewter and the 19th-century's hard pewter, known as Britannia metal. Some Georgian and Victorian tobacco boxes cast in lead now look extraordinarily old, as does Edwardian pewter.

Brass and copper 'Lancashire snuff boxes', with keyless lock mechanisms, were especially ingenious. These locks were a late Georgian and Victorian speciality of Prescot craftsmen, in which combination controls were devised using pointers on a case lid roughly numbered like a watch face. Setting the pointers at a pre-arranged 'time' released the box's catch fastener, often shaped as a half moon.

Occasionally even the boxes for early friction matches were given secret opening devices, but match boxes are appealing even without such a device. Most modern collectors find pleasure enough in the imaginative shapes – from owls to old boots – of the late Victorian tiny vesta case that joined seals and cigar-cutter on the gentleman's Albert watch chain.

VICTORIAN PAPIER MÂCHÉ

Shirley de Voe

Papier mâché objects, the outgrowth of the invention of paper making in China, have been produced since ancient times; some existing examples can be attributed to the Han dynasty, about AD 206, and there are also examples of thick pasteboard made in Tibet at a remote period. Making paper by hand was a slow and costly process, so creating objects of pulped paper and pasteboard was a thrifty way of utilising the waste. Both these basic materials are classed as papier mâché.

The knowledge of the craft spread from the Far East to the Middle East, and in the 17th and 18th centuries, to Europe and England. Typical Middle Eastern products were mirror cases, caskets and pen boxes; Germany and France produced tobacco and snuff boxes, while England made small architectural ornaments and gilded wall brackets as well as the snuff box made in every available material during this period. Towards the end of the 18th century, England took the lead in papier mâché production when in 1772 Henry Clay of Birmingham patented a laminated paper board that was an improvement over any earlier type of board – it was heat resistant and could be steam moulded or worked like wood. When Clay's patent ended other japanneries began mass producing papier mâché wares of all kinds, varying in size from a button to a piano.

Mrs Papendiek noted in her journal in 1783, that when she was married she was the recipient of a 'Clay tea-board, a waiter, bread basket, snuffer tray and four little [bottle] stands, all alike; a black background with a silver pattern.' Fifty years later she wrote: 'The tea-board is only just now worn out.'

Due to the popularity of tea, the tea-tray was the most widely produced of the many papier mâché wares, and the demand inspired many new forms, although the rectangular and oval gallery-edged types remained in favour. The popular Gothic tray was edged with cyma curves; those with a shallow curve were known as the king's while those with deeper curves as the queen's. A variation of this type was the parlour-maid's tray, which had an inward curve on one side that fitted the waistline and helped to support the weight of a heavily laden tray. In 1837, George Wallis designed a round tray with bold scallops around the edge which he named Victoria in honour of the young queen. Quantities of smaller trays were also produced such as card, snuffer and knife trays, waiters and bread baskets.

Small attractive papier mâché trays 4 inches (10 centimetres) or less in length were made to hold the counters used for the card game of Pam or Loo, which, like poker chips, were used to represent coins. They were made of mother-of-pearl and were round, oval or fish-shaped, the latter derived from the French word *fiche* (counter). Many boxes in a variety of shapes were created to hold jewellery, gloves, handkerchiefs, fans and sewing equipment. A

1009

1010

1011 Red 'bottle stand' or wine coaster, probably c. 1830.

1012 Small trays made by the firm of Clay & Co. to hold the counters used for the card game of Pam or Loo.

1013 Parlour-maid's tray, with exceptionally fine pearl work.

1014 A group of papier mâché objects: letter-holder, album, snuffbox, sewing box and hand screen.

1011

1012

1013

1014

1015 handsome one called a 'dressing box' or the Ladies Companion, was lined with crushed velvet and was equipped with crystal and silver fittings. All these boxes had a lock with an escutcheon of white metal, ivory, pearl shell or silver. The firm of Jennens & Bettridge, which had Queen Victoria's royal warrant, marked the silver escutcheons on important boxes with V.R. and a crown.

Papier mâché was also used for tea caddies, which had either one or two compartments, and were sometimes lined with lead paper. These are now rather scarce; perhaps many are worn out from constant use, the hinges on papier mâché boxes being their most vulnerable point.

Lady Leicester, a character in Charles Dickens' *Bleak House*, is described as sitting on a sofa by the fire shading her face with a hand-screen. These, sold in pairs suggesting a twosome by the fire, were roughly square, oval or helmet-shaped and were mounted on intricately turned handles of ebony, ivory or gilt-wood. But Dickens evidently considered this Victorian conceit impractical,

for he observed: 'It happens that the fire is hot where my lady sat and . . . the hand-screen is more beautiful than useful being priceless but small.'

In days when all communication was by letter, the accoutrements of correspondence were much in demand, and papier mâché ink-stands, lap desks, blotters, desk folios and letter holders were produced in large numbers. The lap desks had a slanted lid under which was a tooled velvet writing board, a slot for pens, a crystal ink bottle and a small box for wafers. The letter holders were of the proper size to hold the folded and sealed notes that were used before envelopes.

Cases for calling cards were made as early as 1826, and continued to be in favour throughout the 19th century. They were lined with silk or plush and were available in the folio style or with a hinged lid. Rather pretentious instructions were suggested for their use, for instance, a lady was advised when making a visit to hold the case in full view while extracting her card. It was also suggested

289

1015 Lady's companion, opened to show the fittings of crystal and silver and the crushed velvet lining of the lid.

1016 Papier mâché vase, hand painted with flowers, c. 1890.

1015

1016

that a fancy handkerchief be carried to form an appropriate backdrop to the handsome case. To hold the calling cards in the home there were round trays, some with scalloped or curved edges. The majority had heavy gilt metal handles, much too heavy for the lightweight trays.

All these objects were richly ornamented: paint, metal leaf, pearl shell and bronze powders were used to depict realistic flowers, landscapes, castles, ruins, and bridges within borders of fine gold pen work, C and S scrolls or pearl shell. Although coloured grounds were sometimes used, black was the standard background on which the metal leaf and pearl shell showed to the best advantage. After the death of Prince Albert in 1861, ceremonial ware was produced on which subdued grey and mauve paint was combined with mother-of-pearl. Shell had been used early in the trade, but the mid-Victorian period is particularly noted for lavish shell ornament.

Of all the uses to which pulp and pasteboard have been put over the centuries, none has equalled the japanned and ornamented papier mâché products of the English Midlands where, in the 19th century, its manufacture reached the greatest heights in both quantity and quality. Many of the products made at that time are now only curiosities, but they are still much admired by collectors for their well executed ornamentation.

VICTORIAN PICTORIAL IMAGES

June Field

Although a certain amount of craftwork produced by the Victorians originated a century or so earlier, mid-19th-century women, and occasionally men, carried the whole process several stages further. This was the age of embellishment, and there appeared no end to the imaginative items, sometimes useful, but more often purely ornamental, to which the inventive and industrious could turn their hands. Not all of this work was artistically noteworthy, but many

of the decorative fancies and pictorial images produced are evocative of the age, endearing mementoes of the patience and skill of a more leisured existence.

The Victorians did not take long to discover the delights of beachcombing, particularly after the seaside was given the royal seal of approval when the young Queen bought Osborne House, Isle of Wight, as a holiday home. They were soon emulating that

1017 A 19th-century composition of shell, coral and seaweed.

1018 A 19th-century picture of a wicker basket containing flowers of various dried seaweeds mounted on paper.

1019 Skeleton leaves, dried seaweed and flowers were used for this delicate picture, made *c.* 1840.

1020 Sand picture of Osborne House, Isle of Wight, holiday home of Queen Victoria. This was probably done after 1848, when the second tower was completed.

1021 Cut paper flowers, mid-19th century.

1017

1018

1019

1020

1021

indefatigable 18th-century craftworker Mrs Delany, by collecting shells and seaweeds. While the more common varieties such as the periwinkle, (the natural greyish outer scaling was removed with acetic acid to reveal the pearly iridescence beneath), mussel, cockle, cowrie and pink tellin could all be gathered on local shores, boxes of shells could also be bought commercially, ready-cleaned and sorted. Rare species came from traders from the East and West who offered them for sale on City wharves, or they were sought from naval relations returning from travels in far-away places.

1017   Exquisitely modelled shell floral pictures and nosegays were designed, each petal and leaf composed of tiny delicate shells, sometimes as many as twenty for a single bloom. Minute opalescent
1024 rice shells were used for baskets and card trays. Particularly attractive objects were figurines, small wooden dolls complete

with shell gowns, bonnets and baskets. Popular items made later in the century, such as glove, trinket and money boxes, mirror and picture frames all heavily encrusted with shells, were more in the souvenir or gift class.

Shell boxes, which became known as 'sailor's Valentines', because men took them home to their sweethearts and wives, were attractive groupings of shells in octagonal wood frames hinged together to form a box. Because most of the boxes that have survived are similar in design, with little clusters centring around a heart or a loving platitude such as 'Forget Me Not', it is thought that they were made commercially in the West Indies rather than by the seamen themselves.

Pressed and preserved seaweeds were also used to complement 1017
shell work, or interspersed with skeleton leaves as well as forming 1019

1022 Cut silhouette work with pin-pricking and embossing. This was done *c.* 1870 by Jane E. Cook, wife of the headmaster of King Alfred's Grammar School, Wantage.

1023 19th century tinsel picture of Madame Vestris as Don Giovanni.

1024 Flower basket made of the tiny opalescent rice shells so popular in the 19th century for work of this kind.

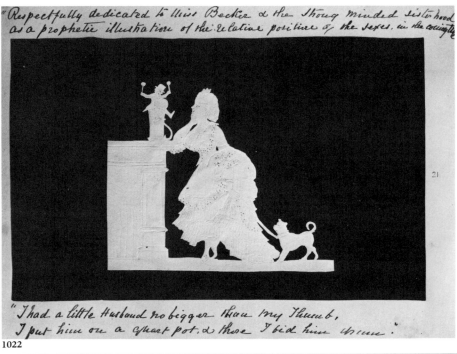

"Respectfully dedicated to Miss Becker & the strong minded sisterhood as a prophetic illustration of the relative positions of the sexes, in the coming..."

"I had a little Husband no bigger than my Thumb, I put him on a quart pot, & there I bid him drum."

1022

MADAME VESTRIS as DON GIOVANNI

1023

1024

1025 Two mid-19th-century pieces of scrimshaw work. That on the left, from America, is a whale's tooth, inscribed 'Ship Metacom, New Bedford'. The whale's tusk, on the right, is incised with a long-boat flying the Royal Ensign.

1026 19th-century cork picture, with castles, houses, bridges, trees and foliage all cut from cork.

1027 Victorian ribbon picture, with walls, window frames and thatched roof made of ribbon, while flowers, foliage and trees are of a silk gauze called aerophane.

1025

1026

1027

a picture display of their own. A seaweed album was made of two large scallop shells joined together with ribbon, into which leaves of paper were fitted to take the strands of weed.

Artistry in sand was a strange and attractive art which developed in this country in the late 18th and early 19th centuries through the work of some talented immigrant confectioners employed at the court of George III. These men were 'table deckers', whose job was to make decorative arrangements of coloured sugar, powdered glass, marble dust and eventually, coloured sands for the festive table. All these were laid out in a design on a cloth, tray or board, and after the party was over, were swept away.

One of the best-known table deckers was Benjamin Zobel, who was born in Memmingen, Germany, in 1762, and who, although trained as a confectioner, also studied portrait painting in Amsterdam before going to London at the age of 21. Installed at the Court of Windsor, he eventually discovered an adhesive whereby he could make the art of *marmotinto*, as the craft was called, permanent, and proceeded to produce faithful copies of paintings by George Morland, Stubbs and others.

Sand painting became commercialised in the 1840s, when some Isle of Wight artists, principally Edwin Doré and J. Neat, followed much later by R. J. Snow in 1910, produced local views worked in the coloured sands of Alum Bay which range from pale yellow through to pink and olive green.

Another speciality of the Island was sand bells, where bell-shaped glasses of varying sizes were filled with layers of the different coloured sands, representing a local beauty spot. In America around 1889, Andrew Clemens of Mississippi built up incredibly detailed scenes of figures and landscapes in large round-top bottles.

Scrimshaw, the pictorial art of sailors, is, at its most basic, the etching or incising of designs into a hard surface such as bone, ivory, wood, shell or horn. The word has been credited as deriving from a Dutch expression meaning lazy person; and it was during the comparatively lazy spell on board ship, known as the dog watch, that sailors on whaling ships in the 19th century evolved what came to be known variously as scrimshaw, scrimshanting, or scrimshonting—according to the spelling used in the ship's log.

The art has come to be associated with whaling, particularly during the golden era from 1825-1865, for whalemen obviously had access to the basic raw material such as whale's teeth and whalebone. The supply of scrimshaw has been mainly attributed to the American whalemen, because they had the biggest fleet, did the longest voyages (sometimes two to three years), and were usually hunting the sperm-whale whose teeth were ideal for scrimshaw. But the British also made their contribution, their shorter-voyage catch being the Greenland whale, which has fibrous strands instead of teeth. The art was of course, practised by sailors of all nationalities, Indians, Eskimos, Japanese and Norsemen being the earliest recorded.

There was said to be an unwritten law that the teeth-filled lower jaw of a sperm whale belonged to the crew, the teeth being doled out by the second or third mate. A good-sized sperm whale would have about 50 teeth from 4 to 10 inches (10 to 25·4 centimetres) long, all in the lower jaw. When taken out from the jawbone, the teeth are rough and ridged, but soft, although they harden with age. After a tooth was removed, the first step was to file down the surface to a smooth finish, polishing it off with a pumice or ashes and rubbing with the palm of the hand to give it a sheen.

The tools used for the etching and carving were of the simplest kind, such as sail needles, jack-knives, and gimlets made from nails to use as a drill. Designs were carefully scratched and pricked on the tooth, for a slip of the hand might spoil the whole thing. The incised lines were rubbed over with Indian ink, lamp-black mixed with a little varnish or a red pigment. Excess colour was wiped off leaving the picture sharp and defined.

Flat pieces of bone were shaped to the size of a corset busk, and decorated with romantic scenes and sayings, intended as a token for a loved one. Jagging-wheels or pie crimpers used for marking the rims of pies were another popular item, while portions of bone and cut teeth were fashioned into handles for tools, canes and umbrellas. Such items as pierced work baskets, wool winders, note pads and watch stands were often very intricately carved. Other objects which come under the heading of scrimshaw are those made from coconut shells and walrus tusks.

The art of cutting paper was in its heyday in the mid-1700s. The only tools needed in addition to fine scissors were razor-sharp and

1028 'Oriental' or 'Pearl' painting of about 1850. Flowers were painted on the back of glass, and crushed foil smoothed out and placed behind the blooms to give a tinselled effect.

1029 19th-century feather picture. The pheasant, made up from original plumage, perches on a painted bough.

1028

1029

pointed quill knives in various sizes, plus a hone and oil for continual sharpening.

Princess Elizabeth, George III's third daughter, was an ardent paper-cutter in pictures, shadow perforations and pin-pricking, and could well have been taught by Mary Delany who invented paper mosaics. These were cut in paper and then mounted on a thick piece of drawing paper which was washed over in Indian ink to 1021 make it a dull black, a perfect foil for the colourful subjects, usually flowers in bloom.

Cut-paper work was also given the additional refinement of 1022 piercing with a pin, to produce pin-prick pictures. The fashion for this work also started in the 1700s, but continued through the 19th century. The face, hands and feet were first drawn and coloured, and the outline and folds of the drapery marked with a tracing needle. The paper was laid on a piece of smooth cloth or some sheets of blotting paper, and the punctures inserted in the folds of the dress from the front to the back of the paper. The drawing was then laid with its surface downwards, and the interior of the various outlines filled up with punctures made with a very fine needle, from the back to the front of the paper. Folds and creases were reproduced by wide bands pierced with a large pin from the front at regular intervals. The fabric of a dress or texture of feathers could be suggested by closely grouped minute piercing from the back done in such a way as to cause a slightly embossed effect accentuated by unpierced portions.

The cutting of portrait silhouettes started as far back as the Ancient Greeks, who learnt the trick of drawing the outline of someone's shadow cast on a wall. It was not given its popular name until around 1759: so stringent were the economies of Louis XV's Minister of Finance, Etienne de Silhouette (1709-67), that *silhouette* became a popular word for something reduced to its most basic form – cheap with no trimmings.

The original shaded profiles popular in the early 18th century were believed to have been traced from the shadow cast by a candle, hence another popular term, 'shades'. From the early 19th century a mechanical device called a physiognotrace was used to produce a profile or silhouette.

Although the golden age of portrait silhouettes was roughly between 1770 and 1840, the cutting of silhouettes continued as a popular pastime well into Victorian times. With the advent of photography, scissor-cutting lost its appeal, although some artists still worked in the fashionable watering places, such as Brighton, particularly on the pier, advertising 'portraits finished in one minute'. This attraction continues today in some places, particularly at fairs and exhibitions.

In the mid 1800s there was a craze for buying theatrical prints, usually of famous actors and actresses in exaggerated stance. The pictures were bought ready-coloured, or with packets of tiny fabric scraps and tinsel and bead trim to stick on as ornamentation. Mr Elton as Richard Coeur de Lion would be given realistic armour and jewelled sword, while Madame Vestris as Don Giovanni would 1023 have a lavishly decorated blue tunic, red-fringed sash, jewelled sleeves, head-dress and anklets.

Another form of tinsel picture, made on glass, with a montage of coloured tin-foil and silver paper pressed on to the back, was known as Oriental or Pearl painting, and was particularly popular in 1028 America. Flower studies were painted on the glass in transparent oil stains, the background filled in with light tints or lamp-black, and then crushed foil was smoothed out and put behind the painted flowers so that the petals glittered.

Later in the century complete pictures were built up of left-overs of ribbon and pieces of coloured silk gauze known as aerophane. A 1027 cottage scene would have its walls, window frames and thatched roof made of ribbon, with flowers, foliage and trees and a chicken on a painted path, made from the gauze.

Particularly striking were pictures made principally of sheets of cork, cork raspings and old bottle corks. The tools used were a 1026 sharp penknife, bradawls, hammer, chisel, scissors, paint and varnish brushes and a pencil. To create a three-dimensional effect for architectural scenes, the cork was cut in layers.

Other materials used to make pictorial images were the scales of fir-cones, straw, wax, moss, fern, bird-feathers – even the iridescent wings of butterflies all contributed to the numerous pictures without paint so beloved of the Victorians.

TWENTIETH-CENTURY STYLES

FROM ART NOUVEAU TO c.1960

Philippe Garner

The 20th century has been a century of quite extraordinary achievement, especially in the world of science, which has in turn engendered a remarkable evolution of ideas in the fine and applied arts. The pace has been rapid, one idea, one style overtaking another at an unprecedented rate. The century opened at the very height of the fashion for the convoluted excesses of Art Nouveau which, as expressed in the exotic creations of the top French designers, was the last of the great decadent romantic styles and has been described by art critic Mario Amaya as '. . . one of the most imaginative innovations in the history of design.' Within a period of 30 years design had evolved to the other extreme. From the rarified aestheticism of Art Nouveau, a style most suited to literary dandies, fashion evolved towards the clinical coldness of the Modernist style, the hallmarks of which were angles or geometrically controlled curves, glass, tubular chromed metal and cold steel, a style conceived for functional living and the practicalities of the machine age.

If the 20th century has been the age of rapid change, it has also been the age of diversity and contrast, and the paths of design evolution have never been clear-cut. There is a paradox in the fact 1030 that whilst Hector Guimard was conceiving the lush curves of his 1046 famous Paris *métro* entrances in 1900, Charles Rennie Mackintosh in Glasgow was designing furniture in a style in which the straight line reigned supreme, or in the fact that some 30 years later, whilst 1078 such designers as Mies Van der Rohe or Le Corbusier were creating modern classics of seat furniture in chromed metal, the Surrealist 1080 imagination of Salvador Dali brought forth a red-upholstered sofa in the shape of Mae West's lips.

The 20th century presents one with a diversity which makes classification difficult. For the purposes of this survey the history of the 20th-century objects has been broadly divided into the following categories: Art Nouveau, which must, of necessity, backtrack a few years into the 19th century to present a complete picture; Art Deco, which term has been used in its true sense to designate the styles that followed Art Nouveau and reached their zenith in 1925 and the Paris International Exhibition of that year; Modernism, which incorporates all those schools and manifestations of the late 1920s and the '30s concerned with functionalism and the evolution of 'modern' design; Surrealism, a limited category but, nonetheless, amongst the most intriguing facets of 20th-century design; and 'post-war styles', which covers the search for new identities after the hiatus of the war years.

While every attempt has been made to be comprehensive and to adopt as international a perspective as possible, history has dictated certain biases. Each period threw certain media into prominence. 1050 Just as the delicacy of Rozenberg eggshell earthenware perfectly expressed the subtle refinement of Art Nouveau, so the brashness of the Custom Car reflected the raw excitement of youth, the new dictators of style in the late 1950s and the '60s. Thus those media have been highlighted which best reflect their era.

If French artists earn more attention than any other it is because France, at least for the first quarter of this century, was the undisputed centre of the decorative arts. If the coverage of other countries seems haphazard it is because they enjoyed less uninterrupted success than did the French. Various countries have excelled at different times and in different media, and credit has been distributed as justly as possible, to the United States, for example, at the turn of the century for Louis Comfort Tiffany's extraordinary 1047 glass, to Great Britain in the first years of this century for silver, to Sweden in the 1930s for exciting innovations in glass and to post-war Italy for furniture.

Art Nouveau

Art Nouveau is not a style but a series of styles having in common the desire for novelty, for an escape route from the 19th century's depressing tendency to ressurect earlier styles rather than create new idioms of design. Many Art Nouveau designers returned to nature as a source of inspiration, following the doctrines of John Ruskin; others in Glasgow and in Vienna exploited the more subtle interplays of straight lines and geometric forms. The Art Nouveau movement, at its height between about 1895 and 1905, was spontaneously international and remarkably inventive. However, its sheer exuberance was its downfall, for so total and demanding a concept in design could only hold a fashionable and fickle public for a limited number of years. Nowhere was Art Nouveau more developed nor more successful than in France.

The most curious feature of French Art Nouveau was that it developed in two distinct forms in two different centres. Paris brought forth many artists of exceptional talent, but at the same time the genius and vision of one man, Emile Gallé, inspired a whole 1036,1039 generation of craftsmen and artists in his home town of Nancy in Lorraine, establishing the reputation of this town as a rival to Paris as a centre for the decorative arts. Whilst all French Art Nouveau is characterised by a return to nature for inspiration, an essential difference can be drawn between the creations of these two rival centres. The Nancy style was more naturalistic whilst the Paris style showed a greater tendency to stylise the lines of nature.

The Paris style of Art Nouveau might be said to have had its origin in a shop at number 22 Rue de Provence. When in December 1895 Samuel Bing sent invitations to the opening of his Galeries de l'Art Nouveau at the above address he unwittingly christened the movement. This Hamburg-born entrepreneur became one of the most inspired patrons of Art Nouveau, promoting the work of hitherto little-known artists whose reputations were ultimately to eclipse his own. During the last quarter of the 19th century Bing was steeped in the study of Japanese art, an enthusiasm which is evident in the refined lines and colours of the work of his protégés. The most gifted and versatile artist to emerge under the auspices of Bing's Maison de L'Art Nouveau was Georges de Feure.

Of Dutch-Belgian origin, de Feure arrived in Paris in 1890. It was not long before the sophistication of his draughtsmanship was appreciated. De Feure's work has been described as a 'hymn to the beauty of woman'. His palette was of a feminine delicacy, favouring 1034 subtle muted tones, greys, watery lilacs or pinks, and there was a lightness, a preciousness to his use of line. De Feure designed furniture and furnishings of every kind, wallpaper, fabrics, hangings, and stained glass, decorative porcelain, metalwork and graphics, including posters and the most exquisite decorative prints. He created an artificial world of fine gilt-wood or blonde-wood furniture, embroidered silk panelling and drapery inhabited

1030 Cast-iron decorative panel from a Paris *métro* entrance, designed by Hector Guimard, *c.* 1900.

1031 Pectoral jewel in gold, enamel and emeralds, incorporating a watercolour on ivory. Designed by Alphonse Mucha and executed in the workshop of Georges Fouquet. 1900.

1032 Enamelled vase by Eugène Feuillâtre, *c.* 1900.

1033 Printed velvet designed by Alphonse Mucha, *c.* 1900.

1034 'Le Retour'. Lithographic print by Georges de Feure, *c.* 1900.

1030

1031

1032

1033

1034

by strangely distant, highly refined women, greyhounds and exotic, slightly sinister flowers.

Bing's two other most important protégés were Eugène Gaillard and Edward Colonna, both of whom showed particular talent in the designing of furniture and triumphed with their masterful contributions to Bing's Pavillon de L'Art Nouveau at the Paris Exposition Universelle of 1900. Their styles had much in common with that of de Feure but without his added quality of mystery and symbolism. The room settings created by these three artists for the Paris 1900 exhibition are amongst the greatest achievements of Art Nouveau.

The most extraordinary and the most fully developed Paris Art Nouveau furniture was that designed by the architect Hector Guimard, who felt that it was a part of the architect's duties to create not just the outer shell of a building but every detail of furniture and furnishings–the complete environment. He was the most plastic of French Art Nouveau designers, and his furniture has a freedom of form that contradicts the grain of the wood from which it is made. Cabinets, vitrines or couches sweep over doorways or fireplaces, embrace the unusual curves of walls in a tense interplay of whip-

lashing lines. Guimard's most dynamic furniture dates from about 1895-1900; after this date his style mellowed until around 1905-10, during which period he designed his most refined furniture, usually executed in steamed pearwood. Guimard designed for various media including ceramics and bronze, though one of his most successful ventures was in creating a series of architectural fittings in cast iron, a medium which allowed him complete freedom, manufactured as *Fontes Artistiques* from 1907 to 1937. 1030

René Lalique, celebrated above all during the Art Nouveau period for his superb jewellery, was an artist of remarkable versatility, capable of designing on every scale, from the most precious small jewel to his entire home and studios. His greatest innovation was in his fresh attitude to materials–for Lalique the commercial value of materials was of secondary importance to their appropriateness within the context of his designs. He showed daring in his novel incorporation of carved horn and ivory into his jewellery; he would juxtapose glass and diamonds, or base and so-called precious metals to achieve his desired effects; his use of enamelling was quite extraordinary, as indeed was every aspect of his craftsmanship. Lalique's most exceptional talent, however, was his imagina- 1038

1035 Glass vase by René Lalique, a rare piece made by the *cire perdue* process *c*. 1910 in the transitional phase before Lalique's commercialisation.

1036 Glass vase with elaborate internal, *marqueterie* and carved decoration, by Emile Gallé, dated 1900.

1037 *Pâte de verre* dish, modelled by Amalric Walter in the Daum workshops, *c*. 1905-10.

1038 Hair ornament in carved horn and diamonds, designed by René Lalique and executed in his workshop, *c*. 1900.

1039 *Canapé* on the theme of the wheat sheaf, designed by Emile Gallé for the Paris Exhibition of 1900.

1040 Figure of Loïe Fuller, case in bronze from the original model by Raoul Larche, *c*. 1900.

1035

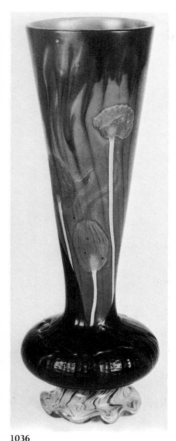

1036

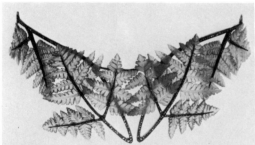

1038

1039

1040

tion, his ability to conceive endless variations on the Art Nouveau themes of symbolist women, grotesque insects and animals, exotic flowers and plants, and to render his ideas with a sustained piquancy and a taut graphic elegance.

1032 Eugène Feuillâtre, having learnt his craft under René Lalique, emerged around 1900 as an enameller of remarkable technical virtuosity. Henri Véver, Lucien Gaillard and Georges Fouquet were three other creators of jewellery and *objets de vertu* to achieve great

1031 success in the Art Nouveau period. Georges Fouquet is perhaps best known for the extraordinary creations that resulted from his collaboration with Alphonse Mucha, the Czech artist who settled in Paris and evolved his own delicious and highly popular style of Art Nouveau.

1033 Alphonse Mucha created the archetypal Art Nouveau woman, ethereal, surrounded by the stylised arabesques of her hair within highly wrought settings of formalised flowers, her drapes, her jewels all combining to weave flat patterns of great delicacy in an infinite variety of pastel hues. His first success was as a poster designer for Sarah Bernhardt; he established his popularity with his series of decorative lithographic panels on such themes as 'The Four Seasons', 'The Times of Day', 'The Four Stars' or 'The Four Flowers', and it is for his graphic work that he is best known. Mucha was also the creator of a number of objects, bronzes and jewels which are amongst the greatest works of art produced around 1900. Commissioned to design an interior for Georges Fouquet's new

1031 showrooms, Mucha and the jeweller worked together around 1900 on a series of quite extraordinary jewels, Mucha providing the ideas, Fouquet transforming the drawings into three-dimensional

objects of meticulous quality. Mucha created elaborate *parures de corsage* incorporating his typical dream maidens, carved in ivory or cast in gold within enamelled, be-jewelled halos, incorporating exquisite watercolour on ivory panels set in gold heightened with *pliqué-à-jour* enamel, hung with Baroque pearls or curious misshapen semi-precious stones. Mucha's rare ventures into sculpture produced equally remarkable results.

Many French artists of around 1900 turned their skills to the manufacture of decorative sculptures, conceived as dishes, lamps, inkwells or paper knives. The typical themes were draped female figures, usually with heavy-lidded eyes and long liquid curves of hair, and flowers, usually poppies or lilies. Maurice Bouval was amongst the best of these artists, and his sculptures have a quality of tenderness and mystery. The dancer Loïe Fuller inspired many artists with her magical Play of Light and Movement, and the bronze lamp sculptures of her by Raoul Larche are perfect examples 1040 of the decorative French style of Art Nouveau. The poster artist Jules Chéret captured the fluid, transient magic of the dancer in his poster of 1893 for her first season at the Folies Bergère.

The Nancy school of Art Nouveau owed its momentum to Emile Gallé, whose personality dictated the essential character of the 1036,1039,1048 work of the 'Ecole de Nancy'. The Nancy style was more naturalistic and less contorted than that fashionable in Paris. Gallé, indeed, criticised in his writings the excesses of which he felt certain Parisian artists were guilty. Emile Gallé's driving force was his passion for nature, and throughout his working career he sought to convey his love in his poetical evocations of plant and animal life. He would evoke the mysteries of the ocean within the body of a

1041 Art Nouveau bronze lamp, designed by Gustav Gurschner, the light fitting concealed in a nautilus shell, *c.* 1900.

1042 Pair of silver candlesticks, designed for Liberty & Co. by Rex Silver, 1905.

1043 Bronze and glass lamp, the bronze by Gustav Gurschner, the glass from the Loetz factory, *c.* 1900.

1044 Austrian blue iridescent glass vase with silver overlay, possibly from the Loetz factory, *c.* 1900.

1041

1042

1043   1044

glass vase or create a buffet that was a hymn to the seasons and the cycle of life. He would apply the logic of natural growth to the construction of his furniture, and he worked ceaselessly at researches into the chemistry of glass to recreate a universe of symbols and textures within his *tours de force* of glass production. It is important to realise that Emile Gallé, as well as being a sensitive artist whose personal creations are of considerable interest, was also a good businessman who built up a very large factory where he applied production-line methods to the manufacture of the comparatively unexciting glassware for which he is so well known.

Louis Majorelle proved to be the most exciting of the Nancy cabinet makers to be inspired by Gallé. Abandoning his work as a manufacturer of reproduction period pieces, he applied the principle of truth to nature, which he had learnt from Gallé. Whilst Gallé favoured elaboration of detail and rich fruitwood marquetry, Majorelle preferred undecorated woods, usually rich red mahogany, and strong plastic forms enhanced with gilt-bronze appliqués. His finest achievements were his suites of furniture *aux nénuphars* (water lilies) or *aux orchidées* (orchids), in which the sensual lines of the stylised ormolu flowers drape themselves decadently along the limbs or over the elegant curves of the wood.

Eugène Vallin designed furniture using wood as if it were poured concrete. The results showed a sculptural freedom, but at the same time a tendency to be ponderous. It is not surprising that he turned to architecture and was among the pioneers in the use of poured concrete. Jacques Gruber was another of Gallé's protégés, best known for elegant furniture designs, often incorporating cameo glass panels using techniques introduced by Gallé.

The brothers Auguste and Antonin Daum followed very closely **1063** in Gallé's footsteps, building up the success of their Nancy glassworks by imitating the master's work. Essentially a commercial enterprise, the Duam brothers' workshops were nevertheless capable of producing prestige pieces of great quality, using Gallé's innovations in internal decoration, cameo or applied decoration, though even their best pieces lack the poetry of Gallé's work. Their only notable innovation was a process of making glassware from a paste, *pâte de verre*. The process was exploited most successfully by their collaborator Amalric Walter, for whom they set up an inde- **1037** pendent workshop in 1906. Walter made dishes, coupes, vases or pots and covers in this curious opaque, rough-surfaced glass. He drew from a decorative repertoire of bizarre animals or insects, and favoured shades of green and blue and a dull yellow. The Daum

1045 Pilkington 'Lancastrian' lustre glazed pottery charger, decorated by Charles Cundall from a design by Walter Crane, 1907.

1046 High-backed oak chair designed by Charles Rennie Mackintosh, *c.* 1897.

1047 Flower-form iridescent glass vase, from the Tiffany workshops, New York, *c.* 1900.

1048 Symbolist hand emerging from the sea, sculpted by Emile Gallé, typical of the greater freedom of form in Gallé work in the last few years before his death in 1904.

1045

1046   1047

1048

brothers made lamps in collaboration with Louis Majorelle, the latter designing metal plant-form bases to which the brothers added glass flower-form shades.

The British version of Art Nouveau was far more restrained than the voluptuous styles fashionable on the continent. Evolving as it did through the pseudo-socialism of the Arts and Crafts Movement which preached a return to the lost ages of domestic craft and truth to materials and function, the British style shunned the luxury and decadence of Paris. There are, however, two curious parallels that can be drawn between Britain and France, for in Britain also there developed a rival centre to the capital with Charles Rennie Mackintosh and his Glasgow group, and in Britain also there was an inspired entrepreneur who, like Bing in Paris, popularised Art Nouveau and gave the style one of its names. In Italy Art Nouveau is known as Stile Liberty after Arthur Lazenby Liberty and the store that bears his name. Liberty was amongst the first to appreciate Japanese art, opening his Oriental Warehouse in 1862 to cater for a clientèle that included Wilde, Whistler and Rossetti. He was subsequently the first to commercialise the avant-garde taste for Art Nouveau and, indeed, helped shape the ideas of many designers, giving their work a distinctive corporate identity.

Liberty's greatest success was won when he launched his Cymric silver range in 1898/9. The Cymric range was characterised by Celtic-influenced *entrelac* decorations, cabochons of semi-precious stones, often turquoise, chrysoprase or opals, and areas of brilliant blue-green enamel. The most prolific and the best of Liberty's silver designers was Archibald Knox and, though the designers received no specific acknowledgement, Knox's style is quite distinctive. The silver proved so popular that within a few years Liberty's brought out their Tudric range, manufacturing similar designs in pewter for a wider market. Liberty's two other most successful areas were furniture and fabrics. Such celebrated artists as Walter Crane and Charles Annesley Voysey were commissioned to design charming fabrics using restrained motifs of formalised flowers. Liberty's furniture was of two types, more elegant designs, cabinets, desks or tables in mahogany of restrained outline and enlived with stylised floral marquetry decoration, or more gutsy pieces in oak, often with beaten copper or pewter decoration.

Of all Britain's Arts and Crafts Movement designers, perhaps the most notable was Charles Robert Ashbee, founder of the Guild of Handicraft. His most interesting designs were for silverware, and his elegant loop-handled porringers or green glass decanters with

1042

1061

299

1049 Bronze and leaded glass lamp from the Handel workshops following the style of the Tiffany Studios, c. 1910.

1051 'L'Oasis', a magnificent five-fold screen in various wrought metals, designed by Edgar Brandt for the Paris Exhibition of 1925.

1052 Cabinet with fine veneer of walnut inlaid in ivory, designed by Emile-Jacques Ruhlmann for the Paris Exhibition of 1925.

1050 Hand-painted glazed eggshell earthenware vase, from the Rozenberg workshops, c. 1900.

1049

1050

1051

1052

inventive silver wirework mounts are amongst the best examples of English design in the period around 1900-05.

1045   The most exciting English ceramics included the lustre wares produced by Pilkington under the trade name of Lancastrian. These were richly decorated, often with medieval images of galleons, knights in armour and royal flowers, thistles or roses. Of great interest also were the rich high-fired glazes produced between 1900 and 1933 by William Howson-Taylor at West Smethwik under the trade name of Ruskin. There is a kind of Abstract Expressionism in the remarkable controlled accidents of the kiln exploited by Howson-Taylor, who has been described as 'the greatest of all English art potters'.

The most important designer in Britain active at the turn of the century was Charles Rennie Mackintosh. Although little appreciated by his contemporaries, indeed he and his misunderstood colleagues were labelled 'The Spook School', historical perspective has confirmed Mackintosh as one of the major pioneers of modern design and a figure of international importance. The Glasgow group comprised Mackintosh himself, his friend Herbert MacNair and the sisters Margaret and Frances MacDonald, who eventually married their male partners. The group had come together around 1893 and came into prominence around 1900. Other Glasgow artists came under their influence, such as the illustrator Jessie M. King, though without being admitted to their tight-knit circle.

Mackintosh's training was as an architect and, like Guimard in France, he was concerned with every detail of environment. All the furniture and furnishings which he or his colleagues designed were 1046 conceived to fulfil specific requirements within commissioned interiors. Their designs were never commercially available out of context. Mackintosh was an artist who combined the practicality and good sense of a fine architect with the imagination and brilliance of the most refined decorator. He appreciated the value of clean lines and disciplined volumes, and his purist's eye knew unfailingly when restraint and elimination could provide more than any decor-

1053 Lacquer screen by Jean Dunand, c. 1925.

1054 Bench seat in oak, ebony and gold lacquer, by Pierre Legrain, created for Jacques Doucet, c. 1920.

1055 Lacquer bracelets and earrings, by Jean Dunand, modelled by Josephine Baker and photographed by d'Ora of Paris, c. 1925-30.

1056 Theatrical design by Erté, 1920s.

1057 Head-dress and earrings by Raymond Templier, designed to be worn by Brigitte Helm in the film *L'argent* of 1928.

1053

1054

1055

1056

1057

ative detail. Mackintosh created the first all-white rooms, he designed table silver 25 years ahead of its time, and raised the designing of chairs to the level of sculpture.

The artists of Vienna were amongst the few to appreciate the qualities of Mackintosh's work, and he was a great influence on them in the early years of the 20th century. In Vienna the straight line reigned supreme under the influence of architect-designer Josef Hoffmann, whilst the painter Gustav Klimt suggested new ideas in patternmaking and decoration. Hoffmann was Austria's guiding light. In conjunction with designers Joseph Olbrich and Koloman Moser, he founded the Vienna Secession in 1897 and between 1905 and 1911 designed almost every detail of the Palais Stoclet, which, although – ironically – constructed in Brussels, is the finest monument to the Vienna style. The rigidly disciplined lines of Hoffmann's silver anticipate the tastes of the late 1920s, and he adapted the same distinctive style to decorative glassware and other media.

The curvilinear style of Art Nouveau enjoyed a certain success in Austria, most notably in the decorative bronzes of Gustav Gurschner and in the glass produced by the Loetz factory. Gurschner modelled flowing Art Nouveau maidens into hand mirrors or lamp bases and sometimes used Loetz glass for the shades. **1041,1043**

The Loetz factory produced highly decorative vases in iridescent glass, their undulating silhouettes enlivened with fine feathered or splashed decoration, usually in shades of peacock blue or pale greens and golds, and more rarely, red and black. Amongst the most attractive Loetz vases are those with applied Art Nouveau motifs in silver. **1044**

Germany was particularly strong in the manufacture of metalwork during the early years of this century. The Wurttembergische Metallwaren Fabrik (WMF) was the largest producing company, and the proliferation of their debased versions of French Art Nouveau maidens or Viennese geometry, stamped or moulded in base white metals, have served to give Art Nouveau a bad name.

1058 Furniture designed for Jacques Doucet, by Pierre Legrain, in a setting designed by Pierre Chareau *c.* 1924-5.

1059 'Pleyela' glass and metal piano, designed by Pierre Legrain for Pleyel, late 1920s.

1060 Silver tea service, designed by Jean Puiforcat, late 1920s.

1061 Twin-handled silver dish, executed by the Guild of Handicraft Ltd from a design by Charles Robert Ashbee, London, 1901.

1058

1059

1060

1061

Of greater interest was the pewter-ware manufactured under the trade name Kayser zinn, the organic forms of which appealed to Arthur Lazenby Liberty, who retailed it in his London store.

The delicate eggshell earthenwares produced at The Hague are probably the finest creations in this medium in the decorative Art Nouveau style. Wafer-thin and with the fragility and translucence of porcelain, the white-glazed Rozenberg bodies were decorated with consummate linear grace with a wealth of fantastic flowers and birds of paradise in colour schemes reminiscent of Georges de Feure.

1050

Perhaps the most extraordinary Dutch artist at the turn of the century was Jan Toorop, whose drawing *The Three Brides* (1893) is considered to be one of the earliest developed examples of Art Nouveau graphics. Toorop designed unusual posters in which the spaghetti-like scrolls of women's hair formed mazes of intricate pattern filling every available area.

In Belgium, the talents of two particular architects won international praise and established a distinctive national style. Henry Van de Velde and Victor Horta were, like Guimard, Mackintosh or Hoffmann, architects concerned with every detail of an environ-

ment. The Belgian style which they inspired was curvilinear, though more virile than the French style. Horta was more of a decorator, introducing his first profusions of Art Nouveau tendrils into an architectural scheme as early as 1893. His greatest surveying works are the Hotel Solvay and the building that is now the Musée Horta, both in Brussels. Van de Velde was imbued with a desire for functionalism in his designs, and matured from the decorative idioms of Art Nouveau to become an important contributor to the development of 'modern' design.

In the United States, Tiffany has become a household name, largely as a result of the extraordinary range of leaded glass and bronze lamps created by him in the early years of this century. 1049 Louis Comfort Tiffany experimented in the late 19th century in an effort to recreate lustres found on ancient glassware. He evolved new techniques and marketed his gold and peacock iridescent glass with considerable success. His team of glassblowers created internally decorated, so-called 'paperweight' vases, *millefiori* and intarsia vases of great complexity. Of particular beauty were Tiffany's giant, surreal flower-form vases. Tiffany inspired many 1047 imitators.

1062 Lacquer screen, designed and made by Eileen Grey for the couturier/art patron Jacques Doucet, 1913.

1062

The United States had their own equivalent of the English Arts and Crafts Movement. The most significant artist of this school was Gustav Stickley, who designed good plain oak furniture, the austere lines of which anticipated the simplicity of form that was to become more generally accepted by subsequent generations.

The most innovative American architect-designer of the early 20th century was Frank Lloyd Wright. His forte was domestic architecture, and his specialities were open-planning, exposed structure, including bared beams, and bare stone or brick inner walls. Wright's spacious interior schemes were characterised by a sense of informality. He designed the furniture to complement these interiors in a sturdy, simple style and with the emphasis on straight lines.

Art Deco
Certain commentators have attempted to label all styles of the inter-wars period under the Deco banner, but this is quite misleading. Art Deco embraces several quite different decorative styles, as did its predecessor Art Nouveau, but these are distinct from the development of the functional 'Modernist' style that was to become

so influential after the mid '20s. Art Deco is more easily understood if appreciated as a decorative manifestation, in some cases evolving out of Art Nouveau, in other cases developing as a reaction to Art Nouveau. The characteristics of Art Deco first came into evidence as early as about 1910, and the phase reached its peak in 1925. The Paris International Exhibition of that year served as a showcase for the achievements of some of the most important craftsmen of the day. France was the most influential country during these years, and produced the finest craftsmen and the most inventive designers.

Wealthy patronage has always provided the spur to great craftsmanship, and it is one of the most interesting features of the Art Deco period that a new breed of patrons emerged who were to oust the aristocracy as arbiters of taste. Dress designers had, until the late 19th century, been treated as tradesmen; it was the advent of the flamboyant Charles Worth, an Englishman operating in Paris, that revolutionised the social role of the couturier, who was henceforth to be respected as a creative artist. During the first quarter of the 20th century several highly imaginative couturiers were to emerge who became significant influences in the decorative arts, either by opening design studios or by taking an initiative in

1063 Etched glass vase from the Daum workshops, 1920s.

1064 Glass vase by Maurice Marinot, c. 1925.

1065 *Pâte de cristal* bowl, by François Décorchemont, c. 1925.

1066 Commemorative bronze medallion, by P. Turin, for the Paris Exhibition of 1925.

1067 Tufted rug, designed by Marion Dorn, c. 1930.

1063

1064

1065

1066

1067

patronising new artists and popularising new tastes. The best known of this first generation of couturier patrons were Jacques Doucet, Jeanne Lanvin and Paul Poiret.

Paul Poiret was a quite exceptional personality, brimming with schemes and ideas, providing inspiration to the artists around him. His career took him to extremes of fortune – at one stage one of the most extravagant hosts in Paris, he died penniless. Poiret made his name after the first startling impact of Diaghilev's Ballets Russes on the Parisian public in 1910. He adapted Leon Bakst's costume designs for *Schéhérézade* into wearable fashions, and his decorating company, L'Atelier Martine, could create an interior to match the clothes, in the opulent style of Bakst's sets and littered with heavy harem cushions. Poiret commissioned Paul Iribe and Georges Lepape to illustrate his fashions, and their published drawings helped consolidate Poiret's reputation as well as establishing their own. Lepape was to become one of the foremost fashion illustrators of the Art Deco period, designing countless charming covers for *Vogue*. Iribe designed furniture in a pretty Neo-classical style that was becoming very popular, incorporating stylised swags and garlands and a distinctive stylised rose, drawn as a scalloped spiral, that became a favourite motif for artists in various media.

Other designers to emerge from the Poiret stables included José de Zamora, who became leading costume designer at the Casino de Paris, and Erté, whose meticulous theatrical and fashion drawings have the perfectionist fascination of Persian miniatures.

The pretty Neo-classical style of Art Deco was a natural successor to the sophisticated feminine style of Art Nouveau as exemplified by Georges de Feure. Amongst its great exponents were the decorators Louis Süe and André Mare whose Compagnie des Arts

Français was founded in 1919. This Neo-classicism was also favoured by two designers who had been active in the Art Nouveau period but who, as heads of design studios in leading department stores, were to help popularise the new style. Maurice Dufrêne founded the atelier La Maitrise at the Galeries Lafayette in 1921, whilst Paul Follot became director of the atelier Pomone at the Bon Marché in 1923.

One of the most unusual Neo-classical interiors was that designed for the couturier, Jeanne Lanvin, by Armand Rateau in 1920-22. Rateau's furniture designs, including low tables, floor lamps and chairs, were cast in bronze and embellished with ivory in a hybrid style evocative of Minoan or Graeco-Roman originals. The room settings were decorated with Classical friezes, most delightful of which was the gold and white frieze of bouquets and swags against the strong blue silk of the bedroom walls.

Wrought iron enjoyed a revival during the Art Deco period. The greatest craftsman in this medium was Edgar Brandt, who established his reputation around 1920 and triumphed with his extensive contribution to the Paris 1925 exhibition. Brandt designed on every scale from table lamps to massive screens. His decorative motifs were typical of the Neo-classical taste, and included bouquets, fountains and the ubiquitous scalloped spiral.

The greatest exponent of the Neo-classical taste, and the foremost cabinet maker of the period, was Emile Jacques Ruhlmann. His taste was for a blend of monumentality and simplicity, and he was at his best when designing on a grand scale, as can be seen from his designs for 'Le Pavillon d'un Ambassadeur' and 'Le Pavillon d'un Collectionneur' at the Paris Exhibition of 1925. Ruhlmann set his artisans very exacting standards, and the apparent simplicity of his

1056

1051

furniture is deceptive, for his attention to detail was prodigious, and he was fortunate in establishing a wealthy clientèle for which perfection was more important than cost. He brought dark, heavy-veined woods, such as macassar ebony, back into fashion and also
1052 used lighter woods, amboyna or burr walnut, with great success. The hallmarks of his style included fine legs tapering almost to a point, inlaid Neo-classical motifs such as bouquets or female figures in ivory, and ivory details of every sort, sabots, drawer or cabinet handles or fine inlaid lines.

The craft of lacquer was brought into fashion in France in the
3,1055 1920s, and its greatest exponent was the Swiss-born Jean Dunand. Dunand started his career as a *dinandier*, or worker in non-precious metals, making painstakingly hand-hammered gourd-form vases in the Art Nouveau period. He became fascinated with lacquer after first using it to give patina to his metalwork. After the First World War he set up workshops for lacquer and gradually abandoned his preoccupation with metalwork. Dunand achieved a total mastery of his new-found medium: he was capable of covering large areas
1053 in faultless undecorated lacquer, and would cover entire screens or table-tops in minute particles of crushed eggshell set into the lacquer. He employed the talents of several designers, but was at his best when working in a cubistic style or on pieces with little decoration in which the natural qualities of the lacquer could best be appreciated. He collaborated with various cabinet makers and designers, including Ruhlmann and Eugène Printz, enhancing their ideas with the slick sophistication of his lacquer surfaces. Dunand triumphed at the Paris 1925 Exhibition with his superb design for a smoking room, though in a quite different vein from the Neo-classicism of Brandt or Ruhlmann. The smoking room had severe lacquered walls relieved with decorative panels in red and silver lacquer, whilst the ceiling was lacquered in silver and stepped to conceal light fittings. This represented Dunand at his very best, working in an uncompromising, aggressive and highly sophisticated style the origins of which were to be found in primitive African art and Cubist painting.

The Neo-classical and feminine styles of Art Deco grew naturally out of French Art Nouveau; the aggressive, Cubist style, however, represented a complete volte-face. It was in 1904 that Maurice de Vlaminck bought his first African sculptures. Within a few years he had infected André Dérain, Georges Braque, Henri Matisse and Pablo Picasso with his enthusiasm for the forcefulness of African art, its bold disregard for realism. African masks were the influence behind the first Cubist portraits. Within a decade the character-istics of African and of Cubist art entered the decorative vernacular of a number of designers, whilst a more polished version of Cubism became the favoured style of a whole generation of designers.

The most fascinating character to emerge in the context of the influence of African and Cubist art on the decorative arts was the couturier Jacques Doucet. After years spent acquiring the finest 18th-century French works of art, he sold his entire collection at auction in 1912 and set out to buy or commission the very best contemporary work. Doucet had a remarkable eye, patronising artists who were considered avant-garde and little understood by their own generation but whom posterity has recognised as the masters of 20th-century art. Doucet collected works by Modigliani, Braque and Picasso, Douanier Rousseau, Csaky, Chirico, Ernst and Miro; he bought African works of art, and the furniture and fur-nishings he commissioned to complement his art collection are amongst the most fascinating achievements of their era. The designers to whom he turned and whose talents found expression
1058 under his patronage included Eileen Gray, Pierre Legrain, Marcel Coard and Pierre Chareau.

Eileen Gray, an Irish woman who had studied at the Slade before settling in Paris, was possibly the first to revive the craft of lacquer, pre-dating Dunand's interest but never attempting to commercial-
1062 ise her ideas. She made a remarkable lacquer screen for Doucet before the First World War, decorated on one side with curious Neo-classical figures, and on the other with a remarkable bold abstract design. She also designed lacquer tables for Doucet, one with legs modelled as giant lilies in white lacquer.

Miss Gray evolved a more exciting personal style in her interior schemes of 1924 for Mme Mathieu Levy, proprietor of a Paris fashion house. Here she used flat rectangular bricks of lacquer to line walls or in free-standing screens, glass floors, lacquer furniture of remarkable invention including a futuristic standard lamp in two shades of brown lacquer in the form of a streamlined rocket, and a sublimely elegant daybed in the form of a canoe. Ashanti stools, Egyptian antiquities and wild-animal skins completed the schemes. Eileen Gray's output of such luxury furniture was very limited and, abandoning lacquer around 1926, she turned her interests to architecture and functionalist furniture.

Pierre Legrain started his career working under Paul Iribe. This close association lasted until 1914, when the latter emigrated to America. It was in 1917 that Legrain came to the attention of Doucet and the couturier took Legrain into his employ to design bindings for his library. Legrain designed over 300 bindings for Doucet, sumptuous creations in a strong abstract style. Over the following few years he also designed many items of furniture and furnishings 1058 for him, culminating in his collaboration with Pierre Chareau in 1926 on the creation of interior settings for the new villa at Neuilly in which Doucet planned to house his collection of contemporary art.

Legrain's debt to African art is particularly evident in many of the pieces designed for Doucet. He designed a bench seat in ebony, 1054 dark-stained limed oak and gold lacquer that shows a strong parallel with Mangbetu marriage stools, a series of stools in various material including ebony and mother-of-pearl or lacquer and sharkskin that were copied directly from the form of Ashanti stools, and he designed a curious tall clock-case that incorporated an attenuated highly stylised mask reminiscent at once of Marka tribal masks or the sculptures of Modigliani. Legrain showed considerable inven-tion, and was daring in his use of unusual materials. He would contrast the smoothness of lacquer with the warmth of vellum or hides, the sleek polish of chromed metal with the coarse open grain of palm wood, and would line walls in unusual textures such as cork, rough papers or oil-cloth. Doucet in turn found other patrons for Legrain, among them the milliner Mme Jeanne Tachard, for whom he designed exceptional pieces of furniture whose only link to the past was their rigid adherence to French traditions of fine quality. Legrain was gradually turning his energies from decoration and furniture design back to the design of bindings when an early death ended his career in 1929.

Marcel Coard created a breathtaking canapé for Doucet, vast, boat-shaped, fully carved in wood imitating basket work, the con-tours emphasised with lines of ivory. Coard was, like Legrain and to a lesser extent Eileen Gray, influenced by African originals. He made a tall cabinet, its corners carved like ceremonial spears, and a chest of drawers, part of a superb bedroom suite, its front an aggressive zig-zag decorated with panels of lapis lazuli and mother-of-pearl.

The sculptors Gustav Miklos and Joseph Csaky designed objects and decorative details for Doucet including a pair of fire-irons by Miklos in enamelled gilt-bronze in the form of cubistic lions, and carved panels after designs by Csaky on the furniture of Legrain or Coard.

The strong forms of Cubist art provided the ingredients of a style that enjoyed great popularity in the mid and late 1920s, and found expression in every medium. Silver and jewellery were particularly well adapted to the demands of this new style in the hands of such outstanding designers as Jean Puiforcat, Jean Fouquet, Raymond Templier, Paul Brandt and Gérard Sandoz. Puiforcat designed 1057 silverware adorned only with handles or finials of rock crystal or darkwood, and having the appearance of the most sophisticated pieces of machinery. Fouquet, Templier, Brandt and Sandoz created jewels in cold materials, platinum, silver, black lacquer, rock crystal and diamonds that were like miniature Cubist sculptures, or wafer-thin cigarette cases in plain eggshell lacquers that were miniature decorative interpretations of Cubist painting.

Maurice Marinot was the most important creative artist working in glass. Abandoning his original interest, painting, he transferred

1068 Glass and mirror glass in a fashionable 1930s interior. Baba Beaton, photographed by Cecil Beaton.

1069 Extravagant bronze and ivory figure by Demetre Chiparus, *c.* 1925.

1070 'The Flame Leaper', bronze and ivory figure by Frederick Preiss, 1930s.

1071 Glazed pottery group of Diana and a hind, modelled by David Evans, typical of English Neo-classical sculpture of this period, 1928.

1068

1069

1070

1071

1072 Detail of furnishing designed by
Jean-Michel Frank in discreetly luxurious
materials, fine woods, rock crystal and lacquer.
Late 1920s.

1073 Silver and eggshell lacquer cigarette case,
a strong 'Modernist' design typical of the late
1920s. French.

1074 Decorative bronze panel in the Chanin
Building, designed by Jacques Delamarre, 1928.

1075 White-painted metal vases, executed by
the Wiener Werkstatte from designs by Josef
Hoffmann, *c.* 1910.

1072

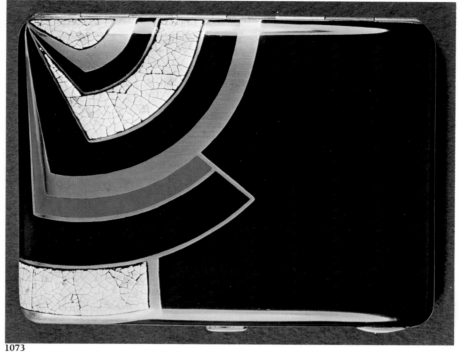

1073

1074

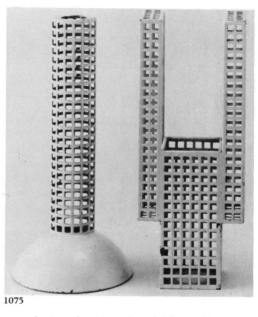

1075

1064 his artistic energy to the creation of a series of some 2,000 pieces of glass, largely vases or flacons. All blown and worked by him alone, these pieces are amongst the most exciting works of art of their period. Marinot blew massive vases with flights of air bubbles trapped within the body of the glass; he would etch barbaric abstract motifs deep into the glass, leaving textures like broken ice, or would blow flacons with decoration of chemical reactions frozen within the glass. Marinot inspired imitators, notably André Thuret and Henri Navarre, but his talent as a sculptor in glass was unequalled. The Daum factories made a series of decorative imitations of Marinot's deep-etched glass.

1035 René Lalique demands attention in any survey of French Art Deco glass, though less for the quality of his glass than for his skills as a graphic designer and a salesman. Lalique was certainly the most prominent manufacturer of decorative glassware in the 1920s and '30s, playing an important role at the Paris 1925 Exhibition, and being the inevitable choice as the creator of glass panelling and fittings for prestige commissions such as the salons of luxury liners or the *de luxe* compartments of the Wagon-lits. His style was a mixture of fashionable motifs and his own lingering taste for the subtle graphics and symbols of Art Nouveau.

François Décorchemont, working in the *pâte de verre* process launched commercially by the Daum factory, evolved from his Art Nouveau phase towards a more simple style, making superb monu-

mental dishes and vases during the 1920s in a high-quality paste known as *pâte de cristal*, mostly in mottled blues, greens or amber. 1065

Emile Decoeur made the most refined ceramics. Subtle matt glazes in subdued tones on bodies of very simple form, his creations have a simplicity that belies his mastery of technique and his artistic refinement.

In comparison with the creativity of French design between the wars, Great Britain seems very much the poor relative. Revival styles enjoyed more popularity than new ideas, and the majority of decorating firms were happier to satisfy the uninspired but safe market in Sheraton- or Hepplewhite-style or neo-Tudor pieces than to risk launching new designs that might prove unsaleable. English furniture designers such as Gordon Russell still seemed preoccupied with the ideals of the Arts and Crafts Movement, more concerned with 19th-century than with 20th-century problems, and their creations look decidedly dreary beside the work of French designers. The firm of Waring and Gillow showed exceptional courage when in the late 1920s they employed the combined talents of Paul Follot and Serge Chermayeff to design furniture and interiors in the French style. Chermayeff designed charming cabinets with carved graphic decorations and finished in silver leaf, or monumental pieces, undecorated and veneered in strong-patterned woods, and rugs or carpets of Cubist inspiration. Follot designed lacquer panelling with elaborate jungle scenes.

1076 Red, yellow, blue and black armchair, designed by Gerrit Rietveld. Painted wood, 1917.

1077 Wassily chair, designed by Marcel Breuer for Wassily Kandinsky, 1925.

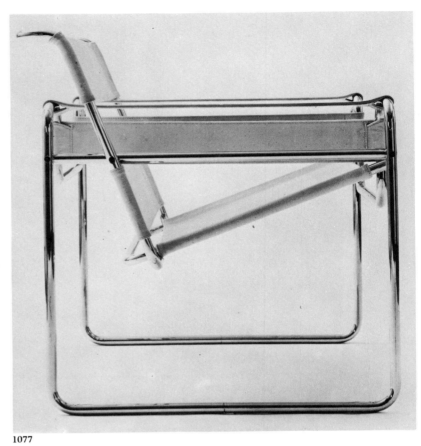

1076

1077

A notable exception to the relatively unexciting standard of English furnishings were the carpet designs of two particular artists, Edward McKnight Kauffer and Marion Dorn. Decorative rugs were the perfect vehicles for the flat geometrical style of decoration that became so popular after about 1925. Kauffer and Dorn were both masterful in adapting abstract motifs to the demands of rug and carpet design. Dorn showed mastery in incorporating into her designs strong motifs of parallel spiralling or undulating lines. Her more interesting commissions included the new carpets for Claridges Hotel when it was re-decorated in 1930.

Mirror-glass became very fashionable and was used for every purpose. The decorator Syrie Maugham used slender verticals of mirror-glass at varying angles to give depth and light to her cream sitting room of 1933, whilst at Claridges mirror-glass was used to disguise old mouldings and create a more fashionable atmosphere. Mirror-glass furniture enjoyed considerable popularity, but in many homes the only concession that was made to 'modern' design was the ubiquitous cocktail cabinet.

One of the more bizarre fashions to enjoy considerable popularity in Great Britain between the wars was for small decorative sculptures of half-naked females, sometimes highly stylised but often disturbingly life-like, with the skin meticulously carved in ivory and the clothing in painted bronze. The two great exponents of this genre were Frederick Preiss and Demetre Chiparus, neither artist of British origin, but both finding their largest market in Great Britain. Each had a distinctive style. Chiparus carved exotic dancing girls in elaborate but often highly revealing costumes inspired from the Ballets Russes or from the chorus lines of the Casino de Paris, the Ziegfeld Follies or George White's Scandals. Chiparus' creations were more extravagant and certainly less sinister than those of Preiss, who seemed obsessed with dynamic sporting figures with more than an undertone of fascist idealism.

Americans certainly had more spending power than the British, at least until the Wall Street Crash in 1929. In most cases, however, they looked enviously towards French achievement, and either imitated the French styles or, if they could afford to, imported leading French craftsmen and designers to decorate their homes. American *Vogue* of August 1929 describes one such home as '. . . one of the most beautiful apartments in the world'. It was the San Francisco apartment of Mr Templeton Crocker, created by leading French decorator Jean-Michel Frank, whose highly personal style is characterised by the *Vogue* description of Frank's taste in colours— 'ranging from ivory to brown, through the gamut of oyster-white, golden-grey, soft yellows and tans, dull gold' and in materials— 'translucent glass or crystal, gilt-bronze and other metals . . . walls and furniture of parchment and straw, tables of sharkskin, andirons of rock-crystal, curtains of lacy woven steel like fairy coats of mail . . .' The scheme included three rooms by Jean Dunand, a dressing room by Mme Lipska and a guest bathroom by Pierre Legrain.

Art Deco found its most exciting expression in the United States in architecture during the late 1920s and, despite the Depression, into the 1930s. The skyscraper was, in itself, a unique contribution to the history of architecture, but of special fascination is the vigorous decorative style that evolved to decorate the new monoliths. The favourite motifs were those that implied energy—sunbursts, the hard zig-zags of thunder-bolts, athletic human figures, machinery or bird forms, 'the speed of wheels and wings powered by machinery, automobiles, trains and airplanes'. Amongst the most exciting new buildings in New York in this dynamic style were the McGraw-Hill building of 1931; the Chrysler building of 1930, with its celebrated eagle gargoyles; the Rockefeller Center, incorporating the spectacular Radio City Music Hall; and the Chanin building of 1928, whose decorative bronze details exemplify the energy of this characteristically American style.

Modernism

It is not always possible to establish hard rules in categorising the styles of the 1920s and '30s, for there were constant overlaps, and many designers fluctuated between styles, and could be in turn self-indulgent in luxury or conscientiously austere. It would, nonetheless, be true to say that certain tastes became increasingly influential during the '20s and created the ingredients of a distinct style. The Modernist style was founded on Functionalist ideals, and its exponents aimed at a stylishness that avoided the purely decorative. The Modernist style had a long history; indeed, Christopher Dresser's designs for silverware from the late 1870s are probably the earliest identifiable precursors. Modernism evolved more specifically from the teachings of Austrian, German and Dutch schools of design.

1076
1069
1068
1069
1070
1072
1074

1078 *Chaise-longue*, designed by Le Corbusier. Painted and chromed metal, hide, 1928.

1079 Table and chairs designed by Eero Saarinen, 1956.

1080 Lip sofa, designed by Salvador Dali, 1936-37.

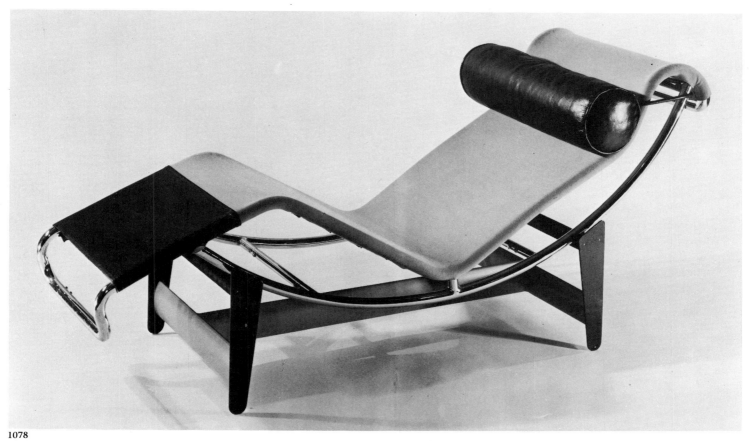

1078

1079

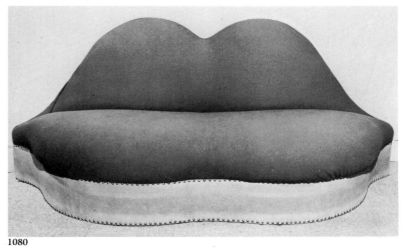

1080

The rectilinear Austrian style of Art Nouveau as exemplified by Hoffman and his colleagues of the Vienna Secession was a natural stepping stone towards Functionalism. In 1903 Hoffmann and Kolo Moser established the Weiner Werkstatte and extended the scope of Viennese production in a prophetic new style.

In Holland the name of a magazine, *De Stijl*, founded in 1917 by the artist-writer Theo van Doesburg and edited by him until his death in 1931, was adopted as a group label by a number of artists and designers with strong new ideas who were highly influential in shaping the Modernist style. The De Stijl group characteristics were the use of pure colour, that is to say the primaries, plus black, white and grey, the absence of decorative detail, the pursuit of rectangularity, of the man-made as opposed to the natural. Piet Mondrian's paintings are the purest examples of the principles of De Stijl, whilst Gerrit Rietveld's red-blue armchair of 1917-18 has been described as '. . . the most compact visual statement of the principles of De Stijl'. The chair is built up on an undisguised structure of black wood, always of square or rectangular section, and the exposed ends painted yellow, the seat and back are plain rectangles of blue and red painted plywood.

It was at the end of 1914 that the German architect Walter Gropius began his plans for the re-organisation of the Weimar Art School, of which he had been elected principal. In 1919, Gropius opened

the new school called Staatliches Bauhaus, which combined an academy of art and a school of arts and crafts. The Bauhaus was to become one of the major sources of design ideas of the 20th century, encouraging such important artists as Wassily Kandinsky, Paul Klee, Oskar Schlemmer and Laszlo Moholy-Nagy, and architects and designers such as Marcel Breuer and Ludwig Mies van der Rohe. The significance of these new schools of design was in their willingness to design for the machine age, in their search for forms and materials that would lend themselves to mass-production.

The most valuable and lasting contribution made by the Bauhaus to the progress of 20th-century design was in the elegant application of tubular steel to the creation of chairs. The Wassily chair of 1925, designed by Marcel Breuer for the painter Wassily Kandinsky, is an important landmark. Of quite complex construction, it is reminiscent of Rietveld's red-blue chair in its sculptural interplay of rectangular planes and angular members. The materials, however, are quite different – this was the first chair ever designed with a framework of chromed tubular steel; the seat, back and arms are of heavy hide. The following year Mies van der Rohe designed his MR chair, a revolutionary application of the cantilever principle to tubular metal furniture.

The progressive, Modernist English firm of Isokon, founded in 1931, manufactured furniture by Bauhaus designers including an

1081 Rooftop solarium of the Carlos de Beistigui apartment, a Baroque/Surrealist décor imposed on an architectural scheme by Le Corbusier.

1082 Post-war Italian Modernism: chair designed by Carlo Mollino, early 1950s.

1083 The 670/1 lounge chair and ottoman, designed by Charles Eames, 1956. Hide, plywood and steel/aluminium base.

1081

1082

1083

elegant chaise-longue of 1936 by Marcel Breuer in laminated birch, and various tables and fittings by Walter Gropius, as well as manufacturing the designs of English artists including Wells Coates and Gerald Summer, the latter being one of the most inventive designers of plywood furniture. The possibilities of plywood as a material well-suited to commercial production were appreciated by the Finnish architect Alvar Aalto, whose first success was a cantilever armchair of 1930 with a plywood seat on a metal frame. He experimented with the cantilever possibilities of laminated wood and produced various designs after the early '30s, manufactured under the trade name Finmar.

In France the Modernist movement took the official guise of the Union des Artistes Modernes. Founded in 1930, this association of designers sought to revitalise design in France, forging a simple new style appropriate to the techniques and the new materials of the 20th century. The first committee of 1930 included architects René Herbst and Robert Mallet-Stevens and the jeweller Raymond Templier. The UAM was to include among its members many designers who had become celebrated in the 1920s in a more luxurious, more decorative vein, designers such as Lambert-Rucki, who had furnished designs for Jean Dunand; Rose Adler, who had created superb objects for Doucet; Paul Colin, famous for his wild posters for Josephine Baker; Eileen Gray, turning her attentions from the luxury of lacquer to the practicalities of designing furniture in chromed metal; and the sculptors Miklos and Csaky. All of these artists were still active members in the 1950s when the move-

310

1084 Neon signs, Fremont Street, Las Vegas, Nevada.

1084

ment was still the most influential force in French design.

1078   Amongst the most exciting innovators in France was Le Corbusier, who created three superb chairs in tubular chromed steel in 1928, and became one of the most controversial designers of the UAM. His most seductive design was his 1928 chaise longue, the adjustable chromed frame following the shape of the body and sleekly upholstered in pony skin. Pierre Chareau is also worthy of special mention for his clever use of plain wrought iron in cabinets, stools, dressing tables or desks with swing work surfaces, for his effective solutions to the problem of designing simple, attractive light fittings and for his ability to give a sense of stylishness to designs that were also supremely practical.

In the United States Modernism was best expressed in the work of a designer such as Eliel Saarinen, whose aim was to '. . . begin with simple forms looking for truth and logic in regard both to construction and material'. At its most extreme, American Modernism expressed itself in an almost demented obsession with streamlining, with the symbol rather than with the essence of modern design.

Surrealism

It was not until the mid-1930s that Surrealism showed its influence on fashion and decoration. The British public's first major encounter with Surrealist objects was at the Surrealist Exposition of 1936 organised at the New Burlington Galleries by Roland Penrose. The confrontation with such bizarre objects as Meret Oppenheim's fur teacup, saucer and spoon caused a considerable cultural shock. This exhibition and comparable exhibitions in New York and Paris encouraged the short-lived yet unbridled enthusiasm amongst the fashionable for outlandish objects and settings of Surrealist inspiration. There was a craze for Baroque objects and furnishings, such as the blackamoors and Italian gilt-wood oyster-shell furniture used by Helena Rubinstein to decorate her Paris home in 1938. The fore-

1081 most decorator of this Baroque-Surreal style was Carlos de Beistigui, whose Paris apartment has been described by Cecil Beaton as 'a dazzling hodgepodge of Napoleon III, Le Corbusier modernism,

mechanism and surrealism'. The extraordinary feature of this apartment was the roof garden, '. . . an open-air room carpeted with a daisy-strewn lawn, a real fireplace with a clock, candlesticks surmounted by a circular picture which was actually a view of the Arc de Triomphe and a marble "commode" supporting a birdcage with a mechanical songster.' Here was Man Ray's 'chance encounter' applied to domestic decoration.

The most adventurous patron of Surrealism in England was Edward James, who created an exaggerated image of himself as obsessive collector in the hero of his novel, *The Gardener who saw God*, published in 1937. James bought works from Salvador Dali, whose fantastic designs included telephone receivers disguised as lobsters and a voluptuous red sofa in the shape of Mae West's lips. 1080

Dali's fertile and extraordinary imagination was a great inspiration to the couturier Elsa Schiaparelli and they worked together to create a succession of amusing Surrealist fashions. Schiaparelli was the first of the Paris couturiers to open a boutique for ready-to-wear fashions and accessories. This venture of 1935 proved a great success, thanks in part, no doubt, to the collaboration of such creative minds as those of Dali. The boutique was designed by Jean-Michel Frank as a gilded bamboo birdcage and included a giant stuffed bear given by Edward James to Salvador Dali who dyed it shocking pink and put drawers in it. 'Shocking' was the name given to the scent launched by Schiaparelli in bottles designed by Leonor Fini in the shape of a Victorian dummy. Amongst the clothes designed by Schiaparelli in collaboration with Dali were a hat in the form of a lamb cutlet with a white frill on the bone and another in the shape of a shoe, black with the heel picked out in shocking pink velvet.

The Surrealist drawings of Jean Cocteau found their way on to such diverse items as Schiaparelli's dresses and porcelain plates produced by Christofle. For a few, brief years Surrealism was the height of fashion and found many forms of expression from such objects as Dali's lip sofa to a revival of the *trompe l'oeil* mural and the exploitation of Surrealist motifs and ideas in the fashion photography of such artists as Cecil Beaton.

1085 'Arco' lamp, designed by Achille and Piergiancomo Castiglioni. Marble and steel.

1086 'Chantal Meteor 200' Juke Box, designed by David Fry, 1952. An exceptional design, and unusual in being of British manufacture–for this has always been a market dominated by American companies.

1087 Plastic wedding dress designed by Paco Rabanne, the model escorted by Paco Rabanne, 1966.

1088 The Oldsmobile Dynamic 88 Holiday Coupé, designed in 1958.

1089 Leather upholstered chair, designed by Allen Jones, 1969, with fibreglass sculpture (edition of six).

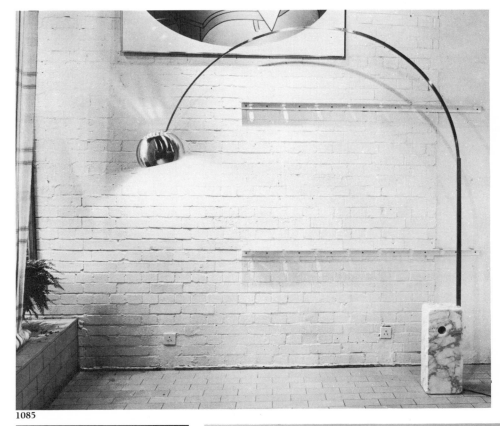

1085

1086

1087

1088

Post-war styles

After the hiatus of the Second World War, Europe and the United States experienced an initial phase of austerity, a phase characterised by the drabness of utility furniture and by the grim determination of the 'Britain Can Make it' exhibition of 1946. Slowly, however, a new style emerged to celebrate the gradual lifting of austerity measures and the growing sense of optimism. In Great Britain the new style was crystallised at an early stage in the context of the Festival of Britain South Bank Exhibition of 1951, which confirmed many features of the new style and inspired many others.

Perhaps the most obvious characteristic of the new style was a passion for soft-contoured shapes. Typical were kidney-shape tables and objects in the shape of artists' palettes. Slender tapering legs, often terminating in small spheres or dome feet, became very fashionable, evoking in their shape the graceful lines of the Festival's celebrated Skylon. The Dome of Discovery inspired many objects in the form of flying saucers. The molecular structure motif of small spheres connected by straight lines became a hallmark of the new style, epitomising the excitement of the quest for knowledge and new ideas, and was used on every scale, from small domestic objects to the Brussels Atomium or Edward Mills' Abacus Screen to Waterloo Road in the setting of the Festival of Britain.

The new post-war style emerged in various countries, each bestowing its particular national characteristics. The most exciting designs came from Italy and Scandinavia, whilst the most brazen expression of the new style came from the United States. England had a few good designers, including Robin Day, Clive Latimer and Ernest Race, but the Italians were the undisputed sophisticates of the era.

Italian furniture designers subjugated the new decorative motifs in creating pieces of great sculptural quality with new, relaxed contours that have been described as a marriage between streamlining and Surrealism. The foremost designer was Carlo Mollino, 1082 whose creations were made up by the firms of Cellerino of Milan and Apelli e Varesio of Turin. Other designers of talent were Enrico Rava and Osvaldo Borsani.

The lasting supremacy of Italian post-war design is evidenced by a *Sunday Times* Supplement feature of 1965 discussing certain Italian designs of the late '50s and early '60s that had just become available in Great Britain. The feature presented a red low table, 'a mixture of Italian *brio* and Japanese austerity', by Vico Magistretti, superb seat furniture, hide-upholstered in a lacquered wood frame, by Tobia Scarpa, and the celebrated Arco parabolic lamp by Achille 1085 and Piergiancomo Castiglioni, with the claim that '. . . there is no furniture in London to touch them.'

Scandinavian furniture set its own standards of quality and restrained design, characterised by the use of pale, waxed woods, teak being a particular favourite, and by soft edges and uncluttered

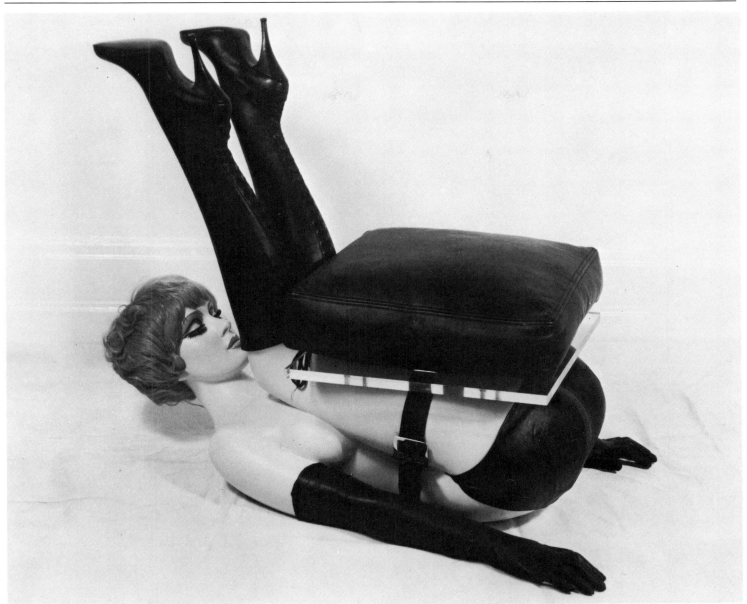

1089

surfaces with recessed handles and minimal detail. The Swedish glass works of Orrefors and Kosta consolidated a reputation they had earned during the 1930s, though the new tendency was towards sculptural forms and minimal decoration in preference to the fine engraving of intaglio figures that such artists as Simon Gate and Vicke Lindstrand had perfected before the war.

1083 The United States produced designers of great merit, designers of the calibre of Charles Eames, whose lounge chair 670 of 1956 is amongst the most outstanding designs of its decade. The chair, developed from a model first conceived in 1944, consists of a metal base supporting softly curved laminated rosewood forms which in turn cradle the soft leather upholstered seating. The most fascinating features of American design, however, were the twin cults of youth and what essayist Tom Wolfe has cynically described as '. . . a prole vision of style'. The great symbol of this 'prole vision' is Las Vegas, described by Wolfe as the Versailles of America, a city whose sky-

1084 line is made up of '. . . neon sculpture . . . fantastic fifteen-storey-high display signs, parabolas, boomerangs, rhomboids, trapezoids . . . the landmarks of America'. These dynamic free forms he establishes as the significant common denominator of the new style, which he dubbs Baroque or Boomerang Modern. He finds a fascinating parallel between the unconscious desert sculpture of Vegas' neon and the intellectual parabolas of Eero Saarinen's 1961 design of the TWA Terminal at Kennedy Airport.

1088 The motor car emerged as a vigorous and revered symbol of affluence, and American car styling of the 1950s, with emphasised chromed fenders, tail fins and bullet-shaped lights, became a virtual art form when carried to extremes in the craze for 'customising'.

The 1960s are still so close that it is not easy to distinguish the most significant aspects of design and fashion during the decade. It seems likely, however, that the '60s will be remembered as the decade in which Pop Art enjoyed an influence on the design of furniture, clothes and objects; also as a decade that turned from one revival style to another with unprecedented fickleness. Perhaps most significantly, it will be remembered for its new materials—fibreglass, stretch fabrics, cast foam and, in particular, plastics.

The first single-form plastic chair was designed in 1960 by the Swiss, Verner Panton; the Spanish-born Paris couturier Paco Rabanne created remarkable fashions in the mid and late '60s, 1087 making clothes and jewellery from articulated pieces of metal or plastic; smoked perspex acquired a ubiquitous chic for any object from cigarette box to dining table, and inflatable plastic furniture enjoyed a certain popularity.

The Pop movement generated artefacts of all kinds. In certain instances leading artists of the Pop school turned to the creation of objects. Roy Lichenstein designed enamelled jewellery, decorated ceramics and decorative sculptures in his easily identified blown-up strip-cartoon style. In England, Allen Jones made a limited edition of furniture in 1969 as three-dimensional versions of his graphic 1089 work, life-size and life-like voluptuous fetishistic women in painted fibreglass, contorted into appropriate positions, one on all fours supporting a glass table top, another on her back, legs in the air supporting a leather seat. The Mr Freedom shop in Kensington Church Street retailed some of the most exciting Pop designs, very much inspired by Claes Oldenburg. Typical of these were the seat designed by Jon Wealleans as a giant, open set of false teeth, and pouffes in the form of giant liquorice allsorts, in self-consciously garish colours.

The accelerated pursuit of styles that characterised the 1960s is very well expressed in Francis Wyndham's impression of his visit to the Paris apartment of Yves Saint-Laurent in 1969, published in the *Sunday Times* Supplement. 'St Laurent's house in the Place Vauban . . . is an interior decorator's dream which, through sheer excess, has turned out to be a nightmare of *chic*. Egyptian art, Chinese art, Japanese art, African art, minimal art and Art Nouveau—the visitor feels like a drowning dilettante as every recent "good taste" fad swims before his indiscriminate gaze. The only really ugly room, a sentimental shrine to Bernard Buffet, comes almost as a relief: here at least one can smugly identify the *démodé*. Stumbling out into the garden, one finds an artificial lake on which a gigantic navy-blue plastic turd is pointlessly afloat. "It's by César, you know," says a public relations man in reverent tones.'

INDEX

ACKNOWLEDGMENTS

Illustrations 166, 595 and 962 are reproduced by Gracious Permission of Her Majesty the Queen. The other items illustrated in this book are reproduced by courtesy of their owners and are in the following collections:
Accademia de Belle Arti, Venice 151; American Museum in Britain, Bath 32, 195, 357, 364, 510, 845, 846, 848; Anne of Cleves House, Lewes 506; Ashmolean Museum, Oxford 289, 291, 600; Bassett-Lowke Ltd., London 996; Collections Baur, Geneva 37; Bayerisches National-museum, Munich 131, 136, 192, 499; Bethnal Green Museum, London 985, 993, 998, 1005, 1007, 1024; Bibliothèque Nationale, Paris 162, 371, 980; Birmingham Museums and Art Gallery 1006; Bristol City Art Gallery 704; British Museum, London 6, 8, 61, 65, 66, 75, 76, 77, 78, 624, 681, 682, 872, 887, 954, 979, 984, 1021, 1022; The Brooklyn Museum, New York 250; Burnley Borough Council, Towneley Hall Art Gallery and Museums 22; Castle Museum, Nottingham 330; Cathedral Treasury, Aachen 372; Centraal Museum, Utrecht 145; Trustees of the Chatsworth Settlement 592; Christ's College, Cambridge 413; City Art Gallery, Manchester 321, 390; City Museum, Stoke-on-Trent 328; City of Gloucester Museum 958, 960, 961; Clare College, Cambridge 400; Colonial Williamsburg, Virginia 197; Conran Interiors, London 1085; Corning Museum of Glass, New York 657, 728, 729; Master and Fellows of Corpus Christi College, Cambridge 391; Daughters of the American Revolution Museum, Washington D.C. 844; The Dean and Chapter of Durham 750; Deutsches Schloss und Beschlägemuseum, Velbert 497; Shirley de Voe, New York 1011; Dundee Museums and Art Galleries 964; Evenepoel Collection, Brussels 287; Fitzwilliam Museum, Cambridge 69, 70, 72, 324, 416, 593; Frick Collection, New York 138, 139; Fundacion Tavera-Lerma, Toledo 149; Galleria Dell'Accademia, Venice 7; Galleria Spada, Rome 152; Geffrye Museum, London 205; Gemäldegalerie, Berlin 977; Gemeentemuseum, The Hague 252, 286; Germanisches Nationalmuseum, Nuremburg 135, 734; Grand Rapids Public Museum 248; Grünes Gewölbe, Dresden 377, 383, 521; Phillip H. Hammerslough 490; Harris Museum, Preston 1001; A. Henning Ltd. 685; The Henry Ford Museum, Dearborn, Michigan 244, 247, 486, 491; Henry Francis du Pont Winterthur Museum, Delaware 176, 217, 220, 221, 359; Hessisches Landesmuseum, Darmstadt 347; Honourable Society of the Inner Temple, London 395; Hôtel de Lauzun, Paris 178; Ickworth House, Bury St Edmunds 607; Imperial War Museum, London 785; Iveagh Bequest, Kenwood, London 533; Edward James Foundation, Brighton 1080; Allen Jones 1089; Knoll International (U.S.A.) and Marcel Breuer, New York 1077; Kunsthistorisches Museum, Vienna 376, 732, 827; Kunstmuseum, Düsseldorf 267, 268; Landesmuseum, Münster 148, 150; Landgrafliche Kunstkammer, Kassel 292, 378, 381, 382; Lehmann Collection, New York 64; Liverpool City Museum 290; Mrs Sherwood Martin 1015; Metropolitan Museum of Art, New York 396, 504, 719, 725, 726, 731, 733, 775, 821; Metropolitan Museum of Art—Gift of Mrs R. W. Hyde 243; Metropolitan Museum of Art—Gift of Paul Martini 249; Metropolitan Museum of Art—Gift of Mrs Frank W. McCabe 251; Metropolitan Museum of Art—Rogers Fund 35; The Mount Vernon Ladies' Association of the Union 849; Munson-Williams-Procter Institute, Utica, New York 242; Musée de l'Armée, Paris 738; Musée des Arts Décoratifs, Paris 56, 253, 353, 456; Musée du Louvre, Paris 54, 263, 293, 369, 518: Musée de Strasbourg 159, 160, 296; Musée des Tapisseries, Angers 3; Musée National de Céramique, Sèvres 265, 295, 309; Musées Royaux d'Art et d'Histoire, Brussels 834, 836, 839, 842; Museo degli Argenti, Florence 373, 380; Museo Arqueologico, Madrid 146, 502; Museo de Artes Decorativas, Barcelona 141; Museo des Artes Decorativas, Madrid 215; Museo Internazionale delle Ceramiche, Faenza 261; Museo Nazionale, Florence 140; Museo dell'Opera del Duomo, Florence 284; Museo dell'Opificio delle Pietre-Dure, Florence 153, 161; Museu Escola de Artes Decorativas, Lisbon 216; Museu Nacional de Arte, Antiga, Lisbon 127, 196; Museum of the City of New York 246; The Museum of Fine Arts, Boston, Massachusetts 219, 484, 485, 487, 851; Museum of the History of Science, Oxford University 965, 967; Museum für Islamische Kunst, Berlin 53; Museum für Kunsthandwerk, Frankfurt am Main 187, 259; Museum für Kunst und Gewerbe, Hamburg 288, 350; The Museum of London 523, 535, 679, 978, 986, 990; The Museum of Modern Art, New York 1078; The Museum of Modern Art—Abbey Aldrich Rockefeller Fund 983; The Museum of Modern Art—Gift of Philip Johnson 1076; Museum Roseliushaus, Bremen 264; National Gallery, London 2, 5, 13, 16; National Maritime Museum, London 784, 930, 931, 973; Nationalmuseet, Copenhagen 198, 222, 430; Nationalmuseum, Stockholm 14, 297, 427, 761; Neues Schloss, Bayreuth 181; New Hampshire Historical Society, Concord 175; New Jersey State Museum Collection, Trenton 368; New York State Historical Society, Cooperstown, New York 173; Österreichisches Museum für Angewandte Kunst, Vienna title page, 492; Palacio Nacional, Madrid 194, 213; Palazzo Ducale, Venice 769, 770; Palazzo Bargello, Florence 280; Palazzo della Farnesina, Rome 129; Palazzo Reale, Turin 191; Pepysian Library, Magdalene College, Cambridge 165; Percival David Foundation of Chinese Art, London 43; Petworth House 168; Philadelphia Museum of Art, Pennsylvania 83, 143, 363, 552; Pilkington Glass Museum, St Helens 692; Residenzmuseum, Munich 189; Rhode Island Historical Society, Providence 199; Rijksmuseum, Amsterdam 128, 133, 137, 155, 156, 548, 835, 837, 838, 840, 843; Royal Palace, Stockholm 218; Royal Pavilion, Brighton 512, 864; Salisbury and South Wiltshire Museum 270; Sanssouci, Potsdam 185; Schatzkammer, Residenz, Munich 374, 375, 379; The Schenectady Museum Collection, New York 852; Science Museum, London 868, 869, 870, 884, 957, 963, 966, 969, 970, 971, 972, 974, 975, 976; Scotney Castle 224; Courtesy of the Smithsonian Institution, Washington D.C. 554, 772, 773; The Smithsonian Institution—Cooper Hewitt Museum of Design 863; The Smithsonian Institution—Freer Gallery of Art 48, 49, 57; Lord Spencer, Althorp 455; Spode Factory Museum, Stoke-on-Trent 334; Staatliche Kunst-sammlungen, Kassel 292, 378, 381, 382; Staatliche Museen zu Berlin 59, 132, 147, 269; Sterling and Francine Clark Art Institute, Williamstown, Massachusetts 439; Stourbridge Glass Museum 694; Syon House, London 20, 815; Taylor and Dull Inc., New York 358; Temple Newsam House, Leeds 206, 332; Tøjhusmuseet, Copenhagen 771; Tower of London 736, 739, 740, 764, 774, 776; Treasury, Altötting 370; Tryon Palace, New Bern, Carolina 817; Vestlandske Kunstindustrimuseum, Bergen 258; Victoria and Albert Museum, London endpapers, 9, 10, 18, 23, 24, 25, 26, 28, 29, 33, 36, 38, 39, 40, 41, 42, 44, 46, 47, 50, 51, 55, 58, 60, 62, 67, 71, 88, 95, 96, 102, 105, 106, 107, 109, 118, 142, 154, 163, 164, 167, 169, 170, 171, 172, 174, 179, 182, 183, 184, 190, 202, 203, 207, 209, 212, 214, 223, 226, 227, 229, 230, 231, 232, 233, 234, 235, 236, 237, 238, 239, 240, 241, 255, 256, 257, 260, 262, 266, 271, 272, 273, 274, 275, 276, 277, 278, 279, 281, 282, 283, 285, 297, 298, 299, 300, 301, 302, 303, 304, 305, 306, 307, 308, 310, 311, 312, 313, 314, 316, 317, 318, 319, 320, 323, 325, 326, 327, 329, 331, 333, 335, 336, 337, 338, 339, 340, 342, 343, 344, 345, 346, 348, 349, 351, 352, 354, 355, 384, 386, 407, 410, 464, 466, 493, 494, 495, 496, 498, 500, 501, 503, 508, 513, 517, 519, 520, 522, 525, 526, 527, 529, 530, 531, 532, 557, 558, 559, 561, 562, 563, 564, 566, 567, 569, 570, 571, 572, 573, 574, 575, 576, 577, 578, 579, 580, 581, 582, 583, 584, 585, 586, 587, 588, 589, 590, 591, 594, 597, 598, 601, 602, 603, 604, 606, 608, 609, 611, 613, 614, 615, 616, 617, 618, 619, 620, 621, 622, 623, 625, 626, 627, 628, 629, 630, 631, 632, 633, 634, 636, 637, 639, 640, 641, 642, 643, 644, 645, 646, 647, 648, 649, 650, 651, 652, 653, 654, 655, 656, 658, 659, 660, 661, 662, 663, 664, 665, 666, 667, 668, 669, 670, 671, 672, 673, 677, 680, 684, 688, 690, 691, 693, 695, 696, 698, 699, 700, 701, 702, 703, 705, 706, 707, 708, 709, 710, 711, 713, 714, 715, 716, 717, 718, 720, 721, 722, 723, 724, 730, 735, 737, 741, 742, 743, 744, 745, 746, 747, 751, 752, 753, 754, 755, 756, 757, 758, 759, 760, 762, 763, 766, 767, 768, 777, 778, 783, 799, 800, 801, 802, 803, 804, 805, 806, 807, 808, 809, 810, 811, 812, 818, 820, 822, 824, 825, 826, 829, 830, 832, 833, 834, 841, 862, 866, ʼ890, 892, 956, 981, 997, 1000, 1002, 1003, 1004, 1009, 1010, 1013, 1014; Waddesdon Manor 516, 565, 816; Wallace Collection, London 157, 177, 180, 186, 188, 193, 200, 201, 204, 211, 514, 515, 596, 599, 610, 612, 677, 684, 748, 749; Walker Art Gallery, Liverpool 524; Walters Art Gallery, Baltimore 52, 605; Messrs Wartski, London 560; Josiah Wedgwood and Son, Barleston 322; Whitworth Art Gallery, University of Manchester 861, 865, 867; William Morris Gallery, Walthamstow 228; William Rockhill Nelson Gallery of Art, Kansas City 84, 85, 86; Woodhall Park 823; Worshipful Company of Goldsmiths, London 387, 388, 389, 392, 393, 453, 480, 556.
Those not listed are in private collections.

Photographs

A.C.L., Brussels 834, 836, 839, 842; Alinari, Florence 140, 151, 152, 153, 191; Antique Dealers (Exhibitors and Organisers) Ltd. 537; Architectural Review Library, London 1081; Asprey and Co., London 451; Cecil Beaton 1068; John Bethell, St Albans 34; Bildarchiv Preussischer Kulturbesitz, Berlin 53, 977; N. Bloom and Son, London 536; Bluett and Sons Ltd., London 73; Foto Borchi, Faenza 261; Robert Braunmüller, Munich 370; Brighton Corporation 864; Cameo Corner Ltd., London 538, 540, 544, 545, 546, 548, 550, 555; Christies, Geneva 398; Christies, London 4, 119, 120, 121, 122, 123, 124, 442, 452, 457, 458, 459, 461, 463, 471, 474, 475, 476, 568, 789, 790, 791, 792, 793, 794, 795, 796, 797, 798, 828, 831, 853, 854, 855, 856, 857, 858, 859, 860, 871, 873, 874, 875, 876, 877, 878, 879, 880, 881, 882, 883, 885, 886, 888, 889, 891, 893, 894, 895, 896, 897, 898, 899, 900, 901, 902, 903, 904, 905, 906, 907, 908, 909, 910, 911, 912, 913, 914, 915, 916, 917, 918, 919, 920, 921, 922, 923, 924, 925, 926, 927, 928, 929, 932, 933, 934, 935, 936, 937, 938, 939, 940, 941, 942, 943, 944, 945, 946, 947, 948, 949, 950, 951, 952, 953; Maurice Chuzeville, Paris 56; P. and D. Colnaghi and Co., London 11, 19; Cooper-Bridgeman Library, London 32, 217, 219, 357, 364, 399, 528, 542, 543, 694, 704, 728, 729, 985, 987, 988, 989, 990, 992, 993, 994, 995, 996, 1016; Country Life, London 224; Yolande Crowe, London 63; Peter Dale Ltd. 765; Delmosne and Son, London 678, 683, 686, 687; Department of the Environment—Crown copyright 736, 739, 740, 763, 774, 776; Eskenazi Ltd., London 79, 80, 81, 82; Form International 1079; John Freeman Group, London 177, 188, 211, 515; Gabinetto Fotografico Nazionale, Rome 210; Garrard and Co., London 447; Mrs Cora Ginsburg, New York 847; Photographie Giraudon, Paris 3, 159, 160, 456, 518, 980; Josephine Grahame-Ballin, St Albans 549; Gunshots, London 781, 782, 786, 787, 788; Hamlyn Group Picture Library title page, 13, 16, 17, 21, 90, 126, 130, 134, 142, 144, 162, 195, 208, 214, 225, 254, 265, 275, 278, 295, 313, 319, 323, 325, 326, 327, 335, 337, 343, 344, 345, 348, 349, 351, 352, 505, 507, 508, 511, 512, 624, 697, 727, 785, 890, 892, 986, 991, 1008; Hamlyn Group—Martin Bladon 234, 235, 236, 238, 240, 241, 564, 569; Hamlyn Group—Sally Chapell 766; Hamlyn Group—A. C. Cooper 480, 500, 520, 526, 530, 562, 567, 570, 571, 735, 743, 768, 777, 778, 815; Hamlyn Group—John Gates 580, 582, 583; Hamlyn Group—Kenneth Jackson 1007; Hamlyn Group—Graham Portlock 18, 496, 498, 501, 519, 531, 1085; Hamlyn Group—John Webb 15; Harvey and Gore, London 553; R. Hatfield Ellsworth, New York 87, 89; David Hodges, London 1088; Angelo Hornak, London 1074; The Director of the National Geological Survey—Crown copyright 541; John Jesse, London 361, 1035; A. F. Kersting, London 1, 27; Landesbildstelle Rheinland, Düsseldorf 267, 268; Edward Leigh, Cambridge 165; Mallet and Son, London 1017, 1018, 1019; Foto Mas, Barcelona 141, 146, 194, 502; Herman Miller 1083; Ann Munchow, Aachen 372; Musées Nationaux, Paris 54, 263, 293, 369; The National Trust, London 168, 607; John Ogden Ltd., London 547, 551; Perez, London 814; Howard Phillips, London 635, 638; Phillips, London 412, 423; Photo Lefevre, London 91, 92, 93, 94, 97, 98, 99, 100, 101, 103, 104, 108, 111, 112, 113, 114, 115; Popperfoto, London 1084; Premier Photographic Services Ltd. 228; Stanley Reed, Middleton-on-Sea 813, 819; Foto Rodriguez, Toledo 149; Scala, Antella 7, 129, 161, 284; Science Museum, London 931; Sotheby Parke Bernet and Co., London 30, 31, 45, 362, 403, 404, 414, 417, 422, 429, 431, 434, 436, 438, 443, 444, 450, 454, 467, 470, 477, 478, 482, 483, 675, 968, 1025, 1031, 1036, 1040, 1042, 1044, 1045, 1046, 1047, 1049, 1065, 1068; Spink and Son Ltd., London 779, 780; Staatliche Kunstsammlungen, Dresden 377, 383, 521; State Department of Archives and History, North Carolina 817; Hildegard Steinmetz, Munich 15; Sussex Archaeological Society, Lewes 506; Foto Stickelmann, Bremen 264; Verlag Gundermane, Würzburg 181; Vestlandske Kunstindustrimuseum, Bergen 258; Victoria and Albert Museum, London 455, 523, 998, 1005, 1024; Waddington and Tooth Galleries Ltd./A. C. Cooper, London 1089; Christopher Warner, Harrogate 539; Weidenfeld and Nicolson Archives, London 982; Jeremy Whitaker, London 20; Worshipful Company of Goldsmiths, London 391, 395; Messrs D. J. K. Wright, London 74; Z.E.F.A., London 12.

In all other cases photographs were supplied by owners of the objects illustrated.